Volozhin; the Book of the City and of the Etz Chaim Yeshiva

(Valozhyn, Belarus)

Translation of
Wolozyn; sefer shel ha-ir-shel yeshivat "Etz Chaim"

Original Book Edited by: E. Leoni

Originally published in Tel Aviv 1970

Volume I

A Publication of JewishGen
Edmond J. Safra Plaza, 36 Battery Place, New York, NY 10280
646.494.2972 | info@JewishGen.org | www.jewishgen.org

Volozhin; the Book of the City and of the Etz Chaim Yeshiva Volume I

Translation of *Wolozyn; sefer shel ha-ir-shel yeshivat "Etz Chaim"*

Copyright © 2024 by JewishGen. All rights reserved.
First Printing: November 2024, Cheshvan, 5785
Editor of Original Yizkor Book: E. Leoni
Project Coordinator: Anita Frishman-Gabbay
Emeritus Coordinator: Moshe Porat (Perlman) z"l
Cover Design: Rachel Kolokoff Hopper
Translator: Jerrold Landau
Layout and Formatting: Jonathan Wind
Name Indexing: Stefanie Holzman

JewishGen Press is not responsible for inaccuracies or omissions in the original work and makes no representations regarding the accuracy of this translation. Digital images of the original book's contents can be seen online at the New York Public Library website or the Yiddish Book Center website.

Library of Congress Control Number (LCCN): 2022948329

ISBN: 978-1-954176-64-5 (hard cover: 590 pages, alk. paper)

About JewishGen.org

JewishGen, is a Genealogical Research Division of the Museum of Jewish Heritage - A Living Memorial to the Holocaust, serves as the global home for Jewish genealogy.

Featuring unparalleled access to 30+ million records, it offers unique search tools, along with opportunities for researchers to connect with others who share similar interests. Award winning resources such as the Family Finder, Discussion Groups, and ViewMate, are relied upon by thousands each day.

In addition, JewishGen's extensive informational, educational and historical offerings, such as the Jewish Communities Database, Yizkor Book translations, InfoFiles, Family Tree of the Jewish People, and KehilaLinks, provide critical insights, first-hand accounts, and context about Jewish communal and familial life throughout the world.

Offered as a free resource, JewishGen.org has facilitated thousands of family connections and success stories, and is currently engaged in an intensive expansion effort that will bring many more records, tools, and resources to its collections.

Please visit https://www.jewishgen.org/ to learn more.

Vice President for JewishGen: Avraham Groll

About the JewishGen Yizkor Book Project

Yizkor Books (Memorial Books) were traditionally written to memorialize the names of departed family and martyrs during holiday services in the synagogue (a practice that still exists in many synagogues today).

Over the centuries, as a result of countless persecutions and horrific atrocities committed against the Jews, Yizkor Books (Sefer Zikaron in Hebrew) were expanded to include more historical information, such as biographical sketches of famous personalities and descriptions of daily town life.

Following the Holocaust, the idea of remembrance and learning took on an urgent and crucial importance. Survivors of the Holocaust sought out other surviving residents of their former towns to memorialize and document the names and way of life of those who were ruthlessly murdered by the Nazis. These remembrances were documented in Yizkor Books, hundreds of which were published in the first decades after the Holocaust.

Most of these books were published privately, or through *Landsmanshaftn* (social organizations comprised of members originating from the same European town or region) that still existed, and were often distributed free of charge. The languages used to document these crucial histories and links to our past were mostly Yiddish and Hebrew. JewishGen has undertaken the sacred responsibility of translating these books into English so that the culture and way of life of these communities will be preserved and transmitted to future generations.

In 1986, a group of farsighted JewishGenners started a project to pool their efforts together in groups based upon their ancestors' towns and donate funds to translate the Yizkor books of their ancestral towns into English. As the translated material became available, it was made accessible for free at https://www.JewishGen.org/Yizkor . Hardcover copies can be purchased by visiting https://www.jewishgen.org/Yizkor/ybip.html (see below).

It is our hope that the translation of these books into English (and other languages) will assist the countless Jewish family researchers who are so desperately seeking to forge a connection with their heritage.

Director of JewishGen Yizkor Book Project: Lance Ackerfeld

About JewishGen Press

JewishGen Press (formerly the Yizkor Books-in-Print Project) is the publishing division of JewishGen.org, and provides a venue for the publication of non-fiction books pertaining to Jewish genealogy, history, culture, and heritage.

In addition to the Yizkor Book category, publications in the Other Non-Fiction category include Shoah memoirs and research, genealogical research, collections of genealogical and historical materials, biographies, diaries and letters, studies of Jewish experience and cultural life in the past, academic theses, and other books of interest to the Jewish community.

Please visit https://www.jewishgen.org/Yizkor/ybip.html to learn more.

Director of JewishGen Press: Joel Alpert
Managing Editor - Jessica Feinstein
Publications Manager - Susan Rosin

Notes to the Reader

The original book can be seen online at the Yiddish Book Center website:

https://www.yiddishbookcenter.org/collections/yizkor-books/yzk-nybc314103/leoni-eliezer-voloz-in-sifrah-shel-ha-ir-ve-shel-yeshivat-ets-hayim

OR

at the New York Public Library Digital Collections website:

https://digitalcollections.nypl.org/items/ade5e2b0-2ff3-0133-6e56-58d385a7b928

To obtain a list of Shoah victims from **Volozhin (Valozhyn, Belarus),** the reader should access the Yad Vashem web site listed below; one can also search for specific family names using family name option. These lists are continually updated by Yad Vashem, so it is worthwhile to periodically search them.

There is more valuable information (including the Pages of Testimony, etc.) available on this website: https://yvng.yadvashem.org/

A list of all books available from JewishGen Press along with prices is available at: https://www.jewishgen.org/Yizkor/ybip.html

Additional Resources:

https://kehilalinks.jewishgen.org/Valozhyn/Volozhin.html

Cover Photo Credits

Cover Design by: Rachel Kolokoff Hopper

Front Cover:

Center: Volozhin yeshiva, Valozhyn, Belarus. Wikipedia.

This work is in the public domain in Russia according to article 1281 of the Civil Code of the Russian Federation, articles 5 and 6 of Law No. 231-FZ of the Russian Federation of December 18, 2006 (the Implementation Act for Book IV of the Civil Code of the Russian Federation).

This work is in the public domain in the United States, because it was in the public domain in its home country (Russia) on the URAA date (January 1, 1996), and it wasn't re-published for 30 days following initial publications in the U.S.

Bottom Right: Rabbi Chaim ben Yitzchok of Volozhin. Wikipedia.

Photo is in the public domain in its country of origin and other countries and areas where the copyright term is the author's life plus 70 years or fewer.

This media file is in the public domain in the United States. This applies to U.S. works where the copyright has expired, often because its first publication occurred prior to January 1, 1929, and if not then due to lack of notice or renewal.

Front and Back Cover Background Photo: *Dried Winter Grass*, Rachel Kolokoff Hopper.

Back Cover

Top Right: *Rabbi Yehoshua Heschel Levin. Sitting (right to left): Menachem Fridland, Menachem Mendl Nahumovski, Rabbi Moshe, Mordechai Epstein, Yaakov Mordechai Alperin. Standing (right to left): Rabbi Avraham Yaakov Flakser, , Yaakov Mordechai Zingman, Chaim Lerman. (The photo was received from the Russian Zionist Archives, founded by Aryeh Rafael-Tzenzifer).* [Page 121].

Middle Right: *Rabbi Avraham Droshkovitz.* [Page 4].

Bottom Left: *Rabbi Meir-Noach HaLevi Levin.* [Page 147].

Bottom Right: *The Tarbut School Mandolin Orchestra. Standing right to left: the teacher Shlomo Bar-Shira (Beikalski), Gershon Lunin, Feigel Berman, Golda Rubinstein, Itka -- , Chaya Rudnitzki, Velka Brodna. Seated from right to left: Sonia Perski, Fruma Podborski, Etel Rogovin, Fruma Golobenchich, Fruma Alperovitch, Miriam Levin.* [Page 436].

Poem on Back Cover: *There is no Beis Midrash*, Leib Yaffe. [Page 289].

Geopolitical Information

Map of Belarus showing the location of **Valozhyn**

Volozhin

Valozhyn, Belarus is located at 54°05' N 26°32' E and 44 miles WNW of Minsk

	Town	District	Province	Country
Before WWI (c. 1900):	Volozhin	Oshmyany	Vilna	Russian Empire
Between the wars (c. 1930):	Wołożyn	Wołożyn	Nowogródek	Poland
After WWII (c. 1950):	Volozhin			Soviet Union
Today (c. 2000):	Valozhyn			Belarus

Alternate Names for the Town:

Valozhyn [Bel], Volozhin [Rus, Yid], Wołożyn [Pol], Volozhyn, Vałožyn, Volozin

Nearby Jewish Communities:

Vishneva 13 miles WNW

Kamen' 16 miles SSE

Haradok 16 miles ENE

Ivyanets 16 miles SSE

Liebiedzieva 17 miles NNE

Bakshty 18 miles SW

Krevo 19 miles NNW

Maladzyechna 21 miles NE

Zaskevichi 22 miles N

Rakov 22 miles ESE

Naliboki 23 miles S

Halshany 24 miles WNW

Krasnae 25 miles ENE

Traby 25 miles W

Derevna 27 miles S

Smarhon 28 miles NNW

Radashkovichy 29 miles E

Lyubcha 30 miles SW

Jewish Population (1897): 2,452

INTRODUCTION TO TRANSLATION OF THE VOLOZHIN YIZKOR BOOK

As one of several translators who contributed to the English translation of the Volozhin Yizkor Book, it is an honor to have been asked by the current coordinator, Anita Gabbay, to write a few words of introduction.

Volozhin – for those familiar with the world of Eastern European Torah learning, the name implies far more than a remote city somewhere in Belarus. The term 'Volozhin' is sanctified in the Torah world as the location and namesake of the flagship Yeshiva of the Lithuanian style, *Misnagdic* houses of Torah learning that used to dot the landscape of Eastern Europe, and continue on to this day in Israel and North America. The rabbinic dynasty of Volozhin, known as 'Beit Harav' [The household of the rabbi], with names such as Berlin, Bar-Ilan, Soloveitchik, continues to be prominent in the Yeshiva world of today. Many of the leaders of what is today known as religious Zionism, as exemplified by the Mizrachi movement, went through the Volozhin Yeshiva, including Rav Kook, Rabbi Mohilever, and Rabbi Reines. Rabbi Isser Zalman Meltzer, whose son-in-law Rabbi Aaron Kotler, founded the prominent Lakewood Yeshiva of New Jersey, is a product of Volozhin. The Soloveitchik family of Yeshiva University fame, are direct descendants of the Volozhin dynasty. It is no understatement to say that Volozhin, its Yeshiva, and the students who were educated there have shaped the landscape of Jewish Orthodoxy, and guaranteed the continuation of serious Torah study in the world today and into the future. The famous Yiddish writer Chaim Nachman Bialik, the renowned businessman and tea-magnate Wissotzky, as well as many other influential people in the general Jewish world were also alumnae of the Volozhin Yeshiva.

This book has two sections. The first section deals with the Yeshiva and rabbinic personalities. The second section deals with Volozhin as any other city in Eastern Europe, with its culture, factions, education. Like any other Eastern European city, the Shoah did not skip over Volozhin. Everything that once was, the Jewish community and the communal infrastructure, was destroyed during the Holocaust period. Whatever small remnants might have remained were then subject to the brutal rule of the former U.S.S.R.

Several translators have been involved in this translation and each had their own style. Therefore, the reader will find that some names and terms are spelled differently in different chapters. Out of deference to the late coordinator and translator of large parts of this book, Moshe Porat of blessed memory his stylistic form and modes of spelling have often been preserved. Most of Mr. Porat's translations were written in summary form. I personally edited and enhanced many of his translations, ensuring that all quoted sources and original detailed footnotes were included. On the other hand, Mr. Porat, himself a scion of Beit Harav, often enhanced his translations with his own original material and personal photos. In order to remain true to the integrity of the original text, while simultaneously showing respect for Mr. Porat's legacy, I moved such enhancements to the footnotes, unusually in an unedited fashion.

The translation effort, and subsequent editing and reorganization of prior translations, was a momentous task that took far longer than originally anticipated. The translation coordinator for this project, Anita Frishman Gabbay, deserves a hearty Yasher Koach for persevering, dealing with unanticipated delays, and ultimately seeing this project to conclusion. We owe a debt of gratitude to Lance Ackerfeld and his team of volunteers from JewishGen tireless work and sage advice in order to bring this project to completion.

It has truly been an honor to participate in the task of translating the Volozhin Yizkor Book. I hope that my translations, and those of my colleagues, do justice to the city and its significant legacy within the Jewish world. May the Yizkor Book and its translation serve as a memorial to the victims of the Shoah, and as a testament to the ongoing vitality of the Jewish people and its Torah.

Jerrold Landau
Toronto Canada
July 15, 2024, 9 Tammuz, 5754

Table of Contents

Volozhin	Isser Yehuda Unterman, Chief Rabbi of Israel	2
The Power of Volozhin	Rabbi Moshe Zvi Neriya	6
The Story of Volozhin	Eliezer Leoni (Ben David)	9
History of the Community of Volozhin	Eliezer Leoni	15
Sources Regarding the History of the Jews in Volozhin	Eliezer Leoni	61
The History of the Etz Chaim Yeshiva of Volozhin, and its Heads	Eliezer Leoni	69
The Volozhiner Family Tree [Beit Harav]	Eliezer Leoni	146
Among the Great "Etz Chaim" Yeshiva disciples	Eliezer Leoni	155
Sources for the History of the Etz Chaim Yeshiva of Volozhin	Eliezer Leoni	172
The Great Etz Chaim School of Volozhin	Rabbi Shimon Langbort	189
The Yeshiva of Volozhin During the Period of the Gaon Rabbi Rafael Shapira	Dr. Hirsh-Leib Gordon	198
About Rabbi Rafael Shapira		202
The Volozhin Scholars		
Three Torah Pillars in Volozhin	Eliezer Leoni	205
The Gaon Rabbi Chaim Hillel Fried	Chaikel Lunsky of blessed memory	221
The Rabbi and Gaon Rabbi Rafael Shapira	Yitzchak Rivkind	224
Rabbi Moshe Shmuel Shapiro	Shimon Zak	230
Rabbi Meir Bar-Ilan (Berlin)	Shimon Zak	233
The Home of Rabbi Shmuel Avigdor Derechinski (Memories and Impression)	Yona Ben-Sasson	239
Conversations of the Sages	Eliezer Leoni	248
Of Those Who Continued the Tradition of Volozhin		
Of Those Who Continued the Tradition of Volozhin	Eliezer Leoni	281
Mordechai Eliasberg	Eliezer Leoni	281
Zalman Epstein	Eliezer Leoni	283
Moshe Mordechai Epstein	Eliezer Leoni	284
Yehuda Leib Don-Yechia	Eliezer Leoni	287
Alter Droyanow	Eliezer Leoni	288
Kalonymus Zeev Wissotzky	Eliezer Leoni	290
Leib Yaffe	Eliezer Leoni	291
Mordechai Gimpel Yaffe	Eliezer Leoni	294
Shmuel Mohilewer	Eliezer Leoni	296
Isser Zalman Meltzer ("Zunia Mirer")	Eliezer Leoni	299
Mordechai Nachmani	Eliezer Leoni	301
Yitzchak Nissenbaum	Eliezer Leoni	302

Yosef Zundel Salant	Eliezer Leoni	303
Shmuel Salant	Eliezer Leoni	304
Avraham Itskhok Hakohen Kook (the Raaya'h)	Eliezer Leoni	307
Yitzchak Rivkind	Eliezer Leoni	310
Yitzchak Yaakov Reines	Eliezer Leoni	312
Sources	Eliezer Leoni	314

Memories

A Bundle of Memories - Prior to the First World War	Osher Malkin	320
Inside Volozhin	Avraham Halevy	330
The Volozhin Yeshiva and Town During the Time of Rabbi Raphael Schapiro	Aharon Zvi Dudman-Dudayi	332
Looking Back (Memories From the Time of First World War)	Yehuda Chaim Kotler	334
The Flour Mill, Electricity and the First Movie House in Volozhin	Michael Vand-Polack	337
Estate Owners in Volozhin	Meir Shiff	338
Flour and Torah in Volozhin	Chaim Zvi Potashnik	341
Market Days in Volozhin	Israel Levinson	343
Volozhin During and After the First World War	Reuven Rogovin	344
The Economic Situation in Volozhin Before the First World War	Reuven Rogovin	346
Volozhin Memories	Shoshana Nishri-Berkovich	361
I Shall Remember You, Volozhin	Pesach Berman	365
The Volozhinka River	Yaakov Kagan	376
Zabrezhe	Moshe Eliyaswhkevitsh	379
Mijeyki (village)	Barukh Tsivony (Farberman)	383
The Jozefpol Estate	Benyamin Kutshevitski	384
Volozhin Stories	Benyamin Shafir (Shishko)	386

The Zionist movement

Tzeirei Zion (Zion's Youth) in Volozhin	Shlomo Bunimovich and Tzvi Rogovin	390
Hechalutz in Volozhin and its Activities	Group of pioneers	392
Pioneering Hachshara in Yuzefpol	Leah Nachshon-Shiff	402
The Hachshara Group of Hechalutz Hamizrachi in Volozhin	Ariye Charutz	403
Beitar in Volozhin	Beitar members	409
On Hachshara in Volozhin	Rachel Kna'any (Berman)	421
Keren Kayemet L' Israel (JNF) in Volozhin	Binyamin Shapir (Shishko)	424
The Outlook of Rabbi Chaim Volozhin Regarding the Exile and the Redemption		428

Education and the Arts

The Tarbut School	Group of graduates	431
Culture war in Volozhin	Binyamin Shapir–Shishko	442
The Volozhin Kindergarten	Miriam Levitan (Rosenberg)	445

The Library	Fruma Guzman (Yuzefovitz)	447
Religious Education During the Thirties	Menachem Mendel Potashnik	449
Polish Schools in Volozhin	Miryam Levitan (Rosbberg)	454
"The Sale of Joseph" Show	Reuven Rogovin	460
Plays that I Recall	Fruma Twebner (Kivilevitch)	462
The Maccabee Basketball Team	Reuven Rogovin	466

Figures & Types

Emissaries, Rabbis and Slaughterers	Eliezer Leoni	470
Rabbi Zvi Yehuda Namiot (aka "Der Shaliver")	Benyamin Shafir (Shishko)	474
Rabbi Shmuel Fried	Benyamin Shafir (Shishko)	476
My father, Rabbi Yehoshua Hacohen Kaplan z"l	Rabbi Meir Hacohen Kaplan	477
The Slaughterers of Valozhyn (Before the Second World War)	Moshe Elishkevitsh	479
Rebbetzin Feyga Unterman	Rabbi Israel Shapiro	480
Rayne Batya Berlin, (A Granddaughter of Rabbi Chaim of Volozhin)	Rabbi Bharuch Halevy Epstein z"l	481
Batiya Miryam Berlin (nee Epstein)	By Meyir Berlin	482
My Grandmother Miryam	Tova Berlin-Papish	485
The Cheder of Rabbi Betzalel the Melamed	Rachel Rogovin (Rubinstein)	488
Our Melamdim	Reuven Rogovin	489
Reb Kalev the Melamed	Reuven Rogovin	484
The Melamed and Teacher Reb Avraham Gorelik	Reuven Rogovin	490
My Father, the Melamed Rabbi Moshe Shlomo Volkovitz	Mendl Volkovitz	491
Yaakov Lifshits	Benyamin Shapir (Shishko)	493
Noach Perski	Benyamin Shafir (Shishko)	495
Reb Eliyahu Yitzchak Shwarzberg	One of his students	496
Abraham Berkovich	Fruma Zitrin (Rogovin)	498
Yaakov (Yani) Garber	Lea Baksht (Faygenboym)	501
Rabbi Yisroel Lunin	Shulamit Golovenchitz-Berger	506
My Grandfather Reb Menahem Mendl Potashnik	Chaim Ashlagi	508
Doctor Avrum Zart	Shoshana Nishri (Berkovitz)	510
Shneur Kivilevitsh	Reuven Rogovin	512
Grandfather Rabbi Aharon Rapoport	Miryam Levitan (Rosenberg)	516
Rabbi Avraham "Asher Yatzar"	Yaakov Kagan	517
Rabbi Moshe Eliyahu Bunimovitz	Rabbi Dov-Natan Brinker (z"l)	518
Reb Shlomo Chasid (Reb Shlomo Shepsnvol)	David Kohen	521
Figures I Knew	Reuven Rogovin	523
R' Avraham Chaim Marshak	Israel Ben Nahum (Goloventtsitz)	527
Grandmother Roche Reize	Israel Ben Nahum (Goloventtsitz)	529
Patcholke - The Famous Hostel Owner	A. Litvin	530
Dov Ber Kaplan	Yehuda Chaim Kotler	532
A "Luft Gesheft" Story	Benyamin Shafir (Shishko)	533
Mera Schnyder - "Merke Ela's"	Dina & Lea Faygenboym	535
We Shall Remember Them	Benyamin Shafir (Shishko)	536
Volozhin in the Shadow of the Holocaust	Bela Saliternik (Kramnik)	542

The Soviet Regime Period

The Soviet Period	Rachel & Reuven Rogovin	546
Volozhin Under the Soviet regime	Mendl Goldshmit	549
During the Soviet Rule in Our City	Pnina Hayat (Potashnik)	551
The Destruction of Volozhin	Yosef Shvarzberg	555

Name Index - Volume I 560

VOLUME I
Volozhin; the Book of the City and of the Etz Chaim Yeshiva (Valozhyn, Belarus)

54°05' / 26°32'

Translation of
Wolozyn; sefer shel ha-ir-shel yeshivat "Etz Chaim"

Edited by: E. Leoni

Published in Tel-Aviv, 1970

Acknowledgments:

Coordinator

Anita Frishman Gabbay

Emeritus Coordinator: Moshe Porat (Perlman) z"l

This is a translation from: *Wolozyn; sefer shel ha-ir-shel yeshivat "Etz Chaim"*;
Wolozin; the book of the city and of the Etz Chaim Yeshiva.
Ed. E. Leoni. Tel-Aviv, former residents of Wolozin in Israel and the USA, 1970 (H,Y,E)

[Page 3]

Volozhin

by Isser Yehuda Unterman, Chief Rabbi of Israel[1]

Translated by Jerrold Landau

A.

During that era when I basked in the holy Yeshiva there, under the protection and influence of our rabbi, the Gaon and Tzadik, Rabbi Rafael Shapira, may the memory of the holy be blessed, approximately 55 years ago, the Yeshiva flourished greatly. A very precious group of great, excellent scholars, sublime young men and lads, were gathered there, occupying themselves in Torah with great diligence. A spirit of brotherhood and friendship pervaded them all. Among the adult scholars, there were some who were permanent residents of Volozhin, who lived there with their families. They served as a sort of connecting bridge in matters of the spirit between the Yeshiva and the city. There is no doubt that the spirit of the Yeshiva influenced the city in a recognizable fashion, causing the residents to aspire to raise their sons in Torah, and to choose husbands for their daughters from among the students.

In this manner, Volozhin merited to have a large number of scholars amongst its householders, raising the spiritual level of the city in general. I remember that an important guest, who was a respected merchant and quite learned, came at that time from Łódź to visit his sons in the Yeshiva, and he told "great things" about the wagon drivers of Volozhin. When he traveled to the city from the Polochany station, a journey of about three hours, he listened to explanations and sections of Biblical verses from the wagon driver as he was guiding the horses. This astounded him. This man had been accustomed to traveling from city to city in Poland on wagons, and within the previous decade, he had never heard so much Torah from wagon drivers as he head on that journey to Volozhin.

B.

I wish to add something to the two points I mentioned above, regarding the spirit of diligence in Torah that pervaded in the Yeshiva at that time, and also regarding the feelings of brotherhood between the students. At that time, there was an active spiritual guide in the Yeshiva, the rabbi and Gaon Rabbi Avraham Droshkovitz of blessed memory, who had previously been the rabbi in the city of Shatt[2]. (He also wrote a book entitled "Shaarei Horaah" to be used by those who are studying *Yoreh Deah*[3]. At the end there are responsa

[Page 4]

on halacha.) In essence, he was especially active as a principal in the affairs of the Yeshiva, and he did not act at all as a spiritual guide in the usual sense of that term. This was because there was no need in supervising the younger students to ensure that they do not waste their time. A spirit of diligence pervaded everyone, and each person was careful to sit and study. In addition, there were greatly diligent people, who excelled in their concentration in matters with which they were occupied. There was a tradition there that the spirit of diligence rested upon all who came the Yeshiva, as a legacy of the wonderful diligence imbued in that place by the founders and sustainers of the Yeshiva – Gaonim of the generation, may the memory of the righteous and holy be a blessing. This also influenced the subsequent generations.

Rabbi Avraham Droshkovitz

Externally, there was a spirit of deliberateness and politeness in the life of the Yeshiva. The prayer and of course the study were without external noise and enthusiasm, but the concentration of thought was recognizable, without the running and jumping that was common in a congregation consisting primarily of young people. The debates in matters of study were also without great noise, even though there were at times cases of clashes between various manners of study. Those who came from Telz made efforts to analyze the reasoning down to the minutest point, and those who were used to a different style of study could not tolerate this; however everything was without a great storm.

At times, we saw a small group standing in one of the corners, asking questions of each other in issues that required deep study. Reb Yaakov, a diligent student, of blessed memory, of Białystok, was an expert in deep questions in *Orach Chaim*[3]. On the other hand, there were some who were more proficient in the laws related to *Choshen Mishpat*[3]. At times, one could hear sharp and deep matters discussed during these deliberations. All this added urgency to the in-depth study of the Talmudic passage. One young rabbi was very well endowed in questions of what is permitted and forbidden[4], demonstrating a great breadth of knowledge. There were also those, on the other hand, who could derive points from the depths of halacha. The relationship between the young men was definitively friendly. They discussed amongst themselves with respect, for the urge for victory was not very prevalent, and they generally did not "nullify" each other. The good relations made the life in the Yeshiva pleasant.

C.

One day, the young men of the Yeshiva gathered in the library to deal with a practical issue. They recognized that there was a great need to delve into matters of lore, to expound publicly and to lecture before a large crowd. They decided to practice together, and then to

[Page 5]

discuss manners of expression and appropriate oratory principles. The head of these speakers was Rabbi Zalman Sorotzkin[5] of blessed memory, who was referred to as "the young man from Telz" at that time. He later became the rabbi of Zhetl and Łuck, and became known as an excellent orator. In his introduction, he said something nice that became embedded in the minds of the community, and which is worthwhile to repeat here. He asked, why did Moses, peace be upon him, first give the reason to the Holy One Blessed Be He that he cannot speak to the Children of Israel regarding the redemption because they will not believe him[6]; then when the Holy One Blessed Be He gave him a sign and portent to prove that G-d had sent him, Moses of blessed memory said: "I am not a man of words"[7] – which should have been his first excuse? The answer is that had the community not believed in and awaited the redemption, there would be no need for him to be a man of words. There would have only been the need for the simple statement, "I am the emissary of G-d, who sent me to redeem you." However, when the faith was lacking and there was a desire to convince them that the redemption was nigh, there was a need for "a man of words." It is the same with the rabbinate: in generations where faith is sufficiently strong, one has to say that you must do so and so in accordance with the Torah. However, when the generation is weak in faith – we need the power of speech to convince the community to follow the path of Torah and the commandments.

D.

It is worthwhile to mention one important note regarding the wonderful atmosphere that pervaded in the Yeshiva of Volozhin, especially during the time of the Days of Awe, which left a strong impression on those who did not go home for the vacation period, but rather remained in the Yeshiva. They dedicated their entire time to Torah study of issues related to Rosh Hashanah and Yom Kippur, and they drew from the Torah itself an awakening to repentance and good deeds without any enthusiastic speeches from anyone else. I then understood the stories that I heard in Volozhin in the manner of the Gaon the Netziv, may the memory of the holy be blessed, and from the Gaon Rabbi Chaim Soloveitchik, may the memory of the holy be blessed, that when they were advised to set times for the study of *mussar* (moral lessons) in the manner that the great students of the Gaon and Tzadik Rabbi Yisrael Salanter, may the memory of the holy be blessed, did; they claimed that there was no need for such in Volozhin. There, the Torah itself served as a source of moral lessons and reproof, purifying the thoughts of the students, and refining the recesses of their hearts. Indeed, I saw this with my own eyes, that also in their private lives and even when the young men and older lads went out to stroll for a bit, their thoughts were immersed in matters of Torah and the purification of their character traits. In this atmosphere, it was possible for each one of the older students to develop in accordance with their aptitudes and talents, without any spiritual pressure from anyone who might try to forge their spirit in accordance with their inclinations. Indeed, it is not in every place that it was possible

[Page 6]

to forge such a pure spirit. Volozhin, which was a small town, with a large tradition of holiness spanning generations, excelled at this.

After Yom Kippur, I traveled home via Vishnyeva, where several of the heads of the town urged me to accept the position of Yeshiva head for the youths of their town. Prior to that, the scholars of the town deliberated together and decided to found a Yeshiva in their town for youths who were developed in the study of Torah. I accepted the offer, and I opened the Yeshiva at the beginning of the winter. It was very successful. It had precious, talented students who had already attained a significant level in their learning. On occasion, I meet some of my students from there. Some currently serve in the rabbinate, and in any case, continue with their Torah study. They are full of pleasant memories of the life in the Yeshiva there and their success in the study of Torah.

From time to time, I visited Volozhin, where excellent students remained with whom I had forged bonds of the soul until I accepted the rabbinical position in the town and left. The First World War brought deep changes throughout the entire district of Lithuania in Russia. Of course, the wellsprings of Torah in Volozhin came to a halt. After the interruption, when the land quieted and the area came under Polish rule, the Yeshiva was renewed. Then, the Gaon Rabbi Yaakov Shapira, may the memory of the holy be blessed, stood at the helm as the rabbi and Yeshiva head. (His father, Rabbi Rafael, died in Minsk, as is known.) The essence of the Yeshiva was renewed in accordance with its old tradition.

During the current time, those who lived there and participated in the life of the community and the Yeshiva have come forward and continued with the memories of those days. It is appropriate that this was done by those who studied there during that era. About 50 years ago, a Yeshiva was founded in the Holy Land by the son-in-law of the Gaon Rabbi Yaakov, may the memory of the holy be blessed, the rabbi and Gaon Rabbi Shimon Langbard, may he live long. It was originally in Tel Aviv, and then moved to Bnei Brak. There is no doubt that several large yeshivas that were established in various places were influenced to a large degree by the Yeshiva of Volozhin.

Translator's Footnotes:

1. See https://en.wikipedia.org/wiki/Isser_Yehuda_Unterman
2. Šéta, Lithuania.
3. One of the sections of the Code of Jewish Law.
4. Referring mainly to the laws of kashruth – whether a certain piece of food or utensils are permitted or forbidden.
5. See https://en.wikipedia.org/wiki/Zalman_Sorotzkin
6. Exodus 4:1
7. Exodus 4:10

[Page 7]

The Power of Volozhin

Written by Harav Moshe Zvi Neriya (Kfar Haroe)

Translated by Moshe Porat z"l

Edited by Jerrold Landau

The Volozhin Yeshiva was established through the pattern of three luminaries: Rabbi Chaim, Rabbi Itsele, and the Netzi'v. There were other great men, beginning with Rabbi Hillel from Horodno and Rabbi Avraham Simcha from Amtshislav [Mscislaw], and ending with Rabbi Rafael Shapira and Rabbi Chaim Soloveichik. Nevertheless, the most significant aspect, the authentic yeshiva essence, was carried by the three. As "fathers" we name only three.

The holy yeshiva! Rabbi Chaim, created the foundations, Reb Itsele increased its glory, and the Netziv strengthened the walls. Rabbi Chaim was an exceptional educator and a most erudite person; a mighty genius, and "a wise man who is valued more than the prophet"; a man of deeds; a talented leader; a profound and brilliant thinker. Yet chiefly he was a pedagogue. Rabbi Itsele resembled his father in many ways. He was a born leader brimming with wisdom, unique intelligence, and astute comprehension. He was also blessed with a golden heart, flowing with love for Jews far and near and with general concern for the entire community. He was prodigious and honest. He was not only the head of the yeshiva but also the leader of the entirety of the Diaspora. The Netzi'v had an iron will and a powerful character. He was a remarkable builder who established himself as a leader and the yeshiva as a prime Jewish center, with solid comprehensive ingenuity, with diligence, integrity, and devotion and love for the Torah, his people, and the Land.

Indeed, other people also shaped the totality of the yeshiva's image. Each one of the Volozhin greats and priests of its Torah contributed to its character and left his personal imprint. This included not only its leaders, but also the best of its students, the magnificent yeshiva boys who later turned out to be the great sages of Israel. When they left the yeshiva, they left no small measure of their imprint behind. Stories and facts, memories and traditions passed from mouth to mouth and were woven into the web of the great Yeshiva. In addition, mysterious figures selected the Yeshiva for residence. Many years later, stories circulated about the awesome, humble characters who passed by way of the Yeshiva in silence, and the warmth of their breath hovered over and commingled with her ambience.

The Yeshiva became the Torah center of the great Russian Jewry. It became a mighty power of diligence in Torah learning, of love of Torah, of respect for Torah, and of every good character trait. From year to year the Yeshiva grew; its frontiers expanded with students and more elevated learning. Thousands basked in its shelter, drank from its wellsprings, absorbed its spirit, and became intoxicated by its aroma. The Jewish lads, talented and strong-willed, scraped their feet walking from remote places to bask in the light of the Torah of Volozhin and to breathe her scholarly atmosphere. There were brilliant prodigies and modest, yet diligent, students; virtuous souls clinging to the wings of the Divine Presence; broken spirits, suffering from the tribulations of life; hidden *tsadikim* seeking the wonderful, and erudite scholars with high aspirations. All of these streamed toward the Volozhin Yeshiva. Here they looked to develop their raw brilliant talent, a sanctuary for their searching souls, a balm for their grieved hearts, a mystical place for their yearning psyches and for clarification of their questions.

[Pages 8-9]

Map of Volozhin

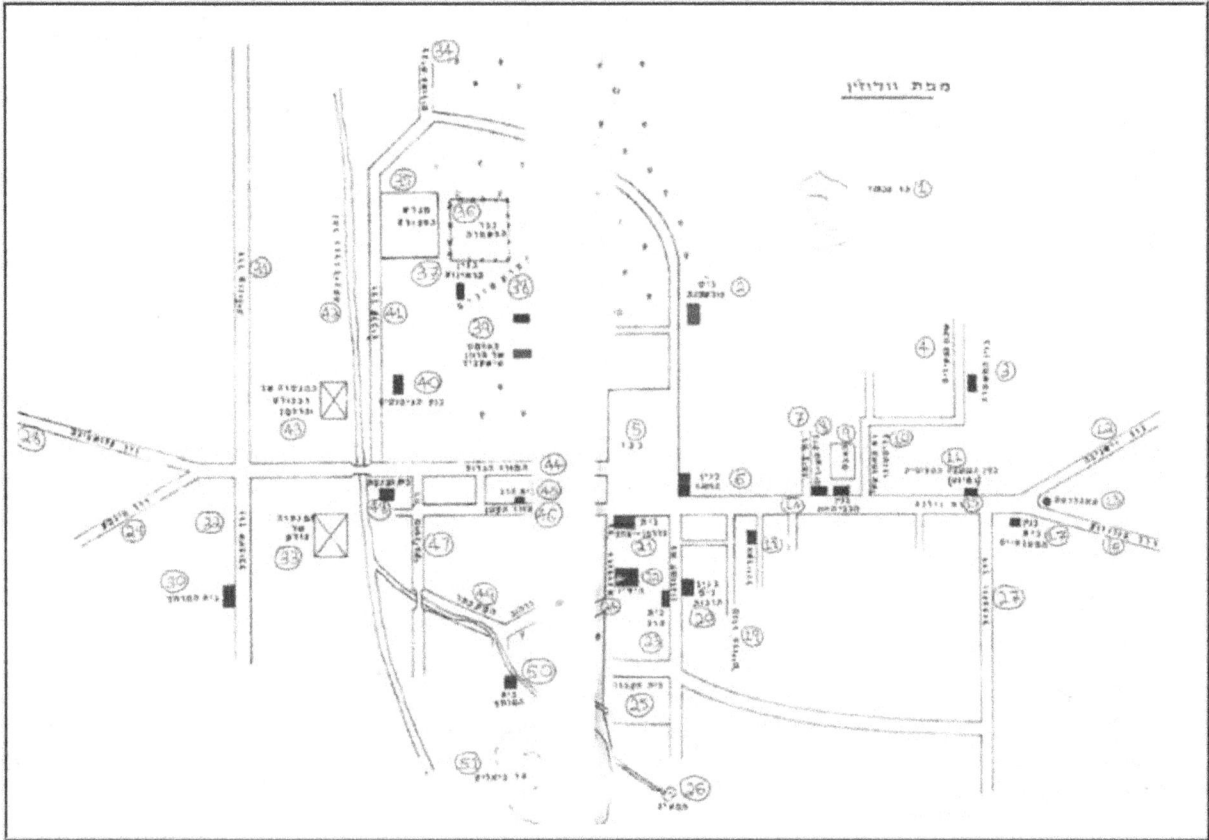

Legend[1]

1. Mount of the Priest	27. Jezobol Street (?)
2. Powszechna [Universal] School	28. Uroshchina Street
3. Police station	29. Minsk Street
4. The neighborhoods of the officials	30. Bathhouse
5. Plaza	31. Ponizia Street
6. Post office	32. Shopobel Street
7. Czychia Street	33. Bulak's sawmill
8. Armory	34. To the sand dunes
9. Pond	35. Sport field
10. 11 November Street	36. Field of the Guards
11. Town hall	37. Movie house
12. Vishnieva Street	38. Castle moats
13. The monument	39. Tyszkiewicz palace
14. Fire hall	40. High School

15.	Vilna Street	41.	Klevitz Street
16.	Horodok Street	42.	Volozhinka River
17.	Slaughterhouse	43.	Rapoport and Berlman's sawmill
18.	The Aliol (?)	44.	The Great Slope
19.	Slope to the Loim	45.	The rabbi's house
20.	Culture School Building (Street to the left of it is Smorgon Street)	46.	The Lesser Slope
21.	House of Bulman-Yitzchak	47.	Moshbitzki Street
22.	The Yeshiva	48.	Synagogue
23.	The Rabbi's house	49.	Winding Road
24.	De Gordona Street	50.	Bathhouse
25.	Cemetery	51.	Mount Bialia
26.	The well		

[Page 10]

There was a great concentration of the most outstanding people among the generation, wonderful and diligent disciples of Torah study and Divine service, a spirit of friendship, talent, and seriousness. All of these joined in creating an extraordinary reality, a mighty workshop of spiritual richness and charming legends, captivating hearts and souls.

No man left Volozhin empty-handed. Those who worked hard and laid the foundation departed with a great treasure. Volozhin fortified their image and strengthened whatever location they went to. Even those who struggled to find their way did not leave empty-handed: they took with them the Volozhin melody, which turned out to be their song of life, as a melody that played in the crevices of the soul, as well as the light of its Torah as a hidden light in the depths of the soul. Much later, after many days and years, they remembered the Yeshiva from afar; its memory refreshed the soul and reinforced the heart.

The dignity of Torah increased and multiplied from the Volozhin energy, and from the energy of its energy. This was accomplished due to the dozens of *Gaonim* and hundreds of rabbis who illuminated the entire land through their dignity, as well as through the thousands of householders who studied, the learned, outstanding scholars, erudite Talmudists, and virtuous personalities, people of bright opinions and plentiful good deeds. These people carried the Torah of Volozhin in their hearts and deriving their splendor from it. All of them expressed dignity. Above all, the core of the Yeshiva's influence was the spreading of its essence far away from its borders and from the sphere of her disciples. The Volozhin legend ascended above cities and towns, above Yeshivas and houses of study. It warmed and excited, encouraged and strengthened – and many, many followed its illumination.

(*Hatzofeh*, 15 Kislev, 5705 / 1944)

[Page 11]

The Story of Volozhin

Introduction

By Eliezer Leoni, editor

אֵלִיעֶזֶר לֵאוֹנִי (ליפֶּן) זַלְמַן (בּ״ר)

This Introduction appears in the original book in two versions, Hebrew & English -1970 Here we publish the English version edited by Eilat Levitan - 2001

What distinguishes Volozhin from other shtetls in Eastern Europe is obvious in this volume. It is not a single book, but an amalgamation of two. It is a description of a major Torah center and rabbinical learning academy; it is also the story of the Volozhin community.

The first section gives an account of those outstanding figures who were either born in the city, connected with the "Volozhin dynasty," or the select few who helped to maintain the Volozhin tradition. The main sections of the book are: the history of the Volozhin community, the Volozhin sages and scholars, and tales of the wise, who preserved the Volozhin tradition. These sections intend to develop a universal Jewish cultural source. The Volozhin sages and their disciples' deeds, teachings and casual conversations were insightful and educational. They had shaped not only the Volozhin community but also the entire Eastern European Jewry.

This book has been written not only for the Volozhin natives and its Yeshiva students but also for the tens of thousands for whom the Yeshiva influenced their way of life from afar. Rabbi Naftali Zvi Berlin wrote about this institution: "The Volozhin Yeshiva is renowned from one end of the Jewish world to the other one." However, writing this book involved considerable difficulties. The enormous amount of materials forced us to make selections, to eliminate a great part of the material ,and to shape a version which would be comprehensible to those who are not familiar with the Talmud. We tried not to be excessively grave and dry; we preferred to stress poetic aspects. We had chosen to display the Agada (fable) rather than Halacha (law), because the Agada is nearer to the heart of the common reader.

Concepts in Judaism could be articulated in diverse styles; they could be expressed through a philosophical discipline or by scientific methodology. And it can also be explained by using literary techniques. Some ideas can be displayed in a drawing, other by pictures or symbols, yet another can be expressed by a fables or legends. Rabbi Yohanan told about Rabbi Meir: "When Rabbi Meir expounded a Bible passage

[Page 12]

Eliezer Leoni, editor of the book

he would dedicate one third of his exposition to the laws it contained, another to the legends, and the last one to parables". He also remarked that Rabbi Meir knew three hundred "Fox Fables". Which goes to show that Rabbi Meir made full use of the fabulist art to make the legal side easier and more palatable to his students and listeners.

We adopted Rabbi Meir's method. Tales, anecdotes and legend were used to lead us to our objective: To understand the words, deeds and thoughts of the Volozhin scholars. We were very careful, Heaven forbid, not to write too much or too little, and not to misrepresent an entire spiritual world. Therefore, we hope that anyone studying our account on the Eytz Chaim Yeshiva will find it all praiseworthy and inspiring. It applies to all that was written about the three "patriarchs" --Rabbi Chaim Volozhiner; his son Rabbi Isaak – Reb Itsele; his son-in-law Harav Naftali Zvi Yehuda – Hanaziv; as well as to the sages of this spiritual center. We have done the best to tell our tale in an easy and simple manner, expressing their principles in a more popular style than the one they used.

I have reason to hope that this method is the correct one. I sent the chapters dealing with the community and Yeshiva history to Dr. Nathaniel Katzburg, history lecturer at the Bar-Ilan University, asking him to check and to verify facts and dates. In his letter dated 7th Tishri 5727, Dr. Katzburg wrote inter alia:

"The work in general seems suited to its purpose to provide a succinct but comprehensive literary description, on the basis of the available sources

[Page 13]

and literary material, while introducing passages from sources and memories, from which the intelligent reader and, particularly the younger generation, can obtain a comprehensive picture of this magnificent chapter in the Jewish history and Torah study during recent generations. Anybody who wishes to know more and to study the subject more deeply need only refer to the bibliography which you append".

In writing the Volozhin Community History we met distinct types of impediments. We had almost no one to assist us. There were no writers, rabbis, or scholars who would aid us to investigate the history of the community. Here lived some of the most outstanding figures of Jewry. They wrote about Volozhin for more than a century. Yet they were dedicated almost entirely to the Yeshiva and paid scarcely any attention to the congregation. And while the material on the Yeshiva is more than plentiful, there is next to nothing on what to base the general history essay. This forced us to engage in considerable research.

These features could be found in the second part, which deals with the ordinary life in the Volozhin community. It covers a period of 42 years, from the beginning of the twentieth century until the Volozhin entire Kehila destruction in 1942. Here we describe the ordinary Jews, their sufferings and struggles for existence. Here we find the intense background of the common Volozhin Jews. The Yeshiva left its spiritual impression on the shtetl inhabitants. Hanaziv, meeting the Volozhin water carrier would jokingly say, " And you shall draw water from the salvation springs." The Rabbi knew that the Volozhin regular natives were familiar with the Torah sources.

The principal Volozhin figures and the ordinary people suited each other. Peretz the Balegole (wagoner) in course of the journey used to test the Yeshiva students on various Talmud tractates. Rabbi Yohanan Rodkes, who would complete the entire Babylonian Talmud's study in cycles of nine months – an almost incredible feat. Freydele di Rebttzn (the Rabbi's wife, who knew the entire Bible by heart. It seems that the unique "Volozhin qualities" were found not only in Rabbi Chaim, his successors and disciples but also in Reb Peretz the Balegole. He was a real prodigy, "swimming" at ease in the entirety of the Talmud literature. However, financial circumstances compelled him to make a living with his horse and wagon. He reminds us of Abba the Builder, who could find an answer to the Greek philosopher Avnimos of Gadara, which demanded more acumen than the town Rabies could deliver.

The correspondence between the two parts of the book also finds a statement in this style. Here too are plenty of stories, tales and anecdotes from the lives

[Page 14]

of simple folk. This freshens the text, brings the past to life, and helps to familiarize us with the community's daily existence.

Preparing this text we were guided by the epithet: "multiple kinds of arts are good, except for those that are boring". We tried our best to avoid them.

Circumstances beyond our control compelled us to restrict our account to a few communal leaders and outstanding heads of households. We made every effort possible to obtain information that would enable us to extend the number of chronicles, but in many cases nothing could be done. Stories of other families have been forgotten and in many cases there is nobody left, to our knowledge, who could tell about them. And this we regret deeply.

Members of the editorial board and the active people
of the Organization of Volozhin in Israel

Standing (right to left): a) Pesach Berman b) Fruma Zwebner c) Dov Lavit d) Chaim Potshanik
Seated (right to left): a) Bella Slitarnik b) Binyamin Shapir (Shishko) c) Shoshana Neshri d) Mendel
Wlokowicz

[Page 15]

We have tried to be brief where brevity was called for, in order to be more expansive wherever possible and also to increase the number of those whom we recalled. But we did not succeed. So those whom we were able to describe, let them be the representatives of the entire Volozhin community.

* *

After years of dedicated endeavors by all the members of the editorial committee, we raised a memorial to the Etz Chaim Yeshiva and to the Volozhin community. Being engaged in this holy task the late Dr. Issaac Rivkind, blessed shall be his memory, was taken from us. He, who had helped us with his advice, guidance and discovery of sources, who considered Volozhin as his spiritual birthplace and home, he wrote me that every house, every tree and every Jew in Volozhin were dear to him, because they reminded him of the wonderful world which had enlightened his entire life. Dr. Rivkind looked forward to seeing the book and asked me about it. We regret his going from us, not seeing our work completed. But his memory is engraved in its pages.

The book deals also with the destruction and eradication of the Volozhin Kehila. The Volozhin Jews were burnt to death. In their reminiscences the survivors have tried to describe those horrors. Yet all we had succeeded to get from them is no more than a drop in the ocean of suffering. What really happened was far more blood curdling than has been told here. Those who were not on the spot; those who never saw how the life dried up and died away in the ghetto; those who never heard their moans and groans from evening to morning and morning to evening; those who never saw their sufferings; those who never experienced life lived at the risk of death at any moment; those who did not go along with the doomed; those who never heard the shots and the cries of the fallen; those who never saw the bleeding and dead; those who never saw them being hurt to death – those who never saw all of these things can never comprehend the depths of the tragedy.

* *

It is generally said that a memorial volume is a monument in memory of a city or a small town. But this does not apply to Volozhin. Neither the editor nor the editorial committee members have regarded themselves as a Burial Society performing the last kindness to all those who have gone. We have not raised a memorial, for that would reduce our book's value. A memorial is something lifeless which may be indeed respected but from which people keep away. People remember a memorial on occasions for mourning and weeping. Memorials are remembered on the Ninth day of Av and during the Elul Month, when Jews go to the graves of their kinsfolk.

The Volozhin Yizkor Book is not a graveyard or the mark of the last kindness. It sets out to record life, it sets out to be a source of pleasure, of inspiration and of physical exaltation. The words and thoughts of the Volozhin sages deserve to be drunk with thirst all the year around.

[Page 16]

The warmth they engender can warm us in all times. Let us stand in awe before their Torah! And let us dedicate ourselves to the study of their teachings, go back to it again and again, even though we cannot claim that we give it all. For anyone who studies the Torah according to the Volozhin method the whole world will have a meaning. His life will have a flavor of its own. It will raise him high above the drabness of life. Or, to quote the words in the Father's Chapter: "When a man passes away he's not taking with him money, pearls or gold but only Torah and good deeds".

It is my pleasant duty to thank everyone who helped us to accomplish this holy task, by providing us with literary sources and material. Particularly I need to mention Mr. Yehiel Lavie, the Ahad Haam Library Director, who did not spare toil in providing all the material that we required.

Similarly, we thank Mr. Moshe Ungerfeld, the Bet Bialik director, for his assistance in order to find all necessary sources for the "Bialik in Volozhin" Chapter. I owe special thanks to the management and director of the Rambam library, Mr. Abraham Goldrat, and his staff. They provided me with familiar and unfamiliar sources to describe the Etz Chaim Yeshiva history. I am particularly grateful to them for supplying me with the photos of the Yeshiva students from the library's ample material. Finally, heartfelt thanks to my friend, Mr. Moshe Morgenstern, who provided me with much interesting material from his colorful and rich library.

Though helped by so many scholars and having done our best to ensure the accuracy of our work, we would be less than truthful if we claimed that the book is completely without errors. "And may it be the Holy and Ancient One's will to allow us to atone for any faults due to error, and may we never do wrong for a vicious purpose. Forgive the errors created for Thy sake."

We submit this book to the public for consideration with our full knowledge of its deficiencies. We have tried to satisfy the demands of many people to whom the name Volozhin is very dear due to its historical, spiritual and scholarly associations. The members of this public will treat us as strictly as the subject calls for. Yet, we hope that we have succeeded in presenting the inner spirit and essence of Volozhin sufficiently well to gain the approval of them all.

Translator's Footnote:

1.   Not all legend items were clear on the original. Some guesswork took place in translating.

[Page 17]

History of the Community of Volozhin

By E. Leoni

[Page 19]

The Volozhin Jewish Community Origins

Translated by M. Porat z"l **and edited by Mike Kalt and Jerrold Landau and donated by Anita Frishman Gabbay**

According to our sources, Volozhin was founded in the 15th Century[1]. The Volozhin estate belonged then to the Volozhin counts, who originated from the counts of Oshmiana. The village was a part of the Oshmiana district in Vilna Guberniya.

The creek Volozhinka (Wołożynka) crossed the town from north to south. The stream's name probably became the town's name. It is also told that oxen flocks encamped here on their way from Minsk to Vilna. It is claimed that "Vol" (Woł) is the origin of the name of the town – "Vol" in Russian means ox.[2] The shtetl is situated 56 km from Oshmiana, and 112 km from Vilna. The Volozhinka stream pours out into the Islotsh (Isłocz) River.

Jews settled there during the second half of the 16th century. 383 Jews lived there between 1764 and 1766, 590 in 1847. The population was 2,528 in 183 houses in 1867, and 2,466 in 523 houses (including two mansions) in 1893, of which 1,900 were Jews. 2,452 Jews lived there in 1897.

Fishel Schneerson describes its topographical shape: "Volozhin, a small little town, is situated on the Minsk to Vilna highway. It is surrounded on several sides by low mountains, which impart some measure of importance to the town. It seems that the mountains summoned the town to superior actions. The shtetl is divided in two parts; the upper one is situated on the hilltop and is called "Arooftsoo" – Up Hill. The second part, on the east, is positioned in the Volozhinka Valley, and it's called "Aroptsoo" – Down Hill."[3]

The Volozhin soil was excellent to raise cattle and horses and to cultivate flax. Those were the

[Page 20]

main products to sell at the bazaars that gathered 4 times each year at the town markets, as well as at the smaller weekly market days. (Translator's note: one of them uphill at the Market Square in the town center, the second one down hill at the Horses Market on the right shore of the Volozhinka.) At the end of the 19th century there existed in Volozhin a linen factory, owned by Rabbi Chaim of Volozhin. As Rabbi Meir Berlin explains, "It was not long before he (i.e. Rabbi Chaim) came to Volozhin and became… the owner of a textile factory. Forty years ago, it was still possible to see a ruin in Volozhin, which, as was told, was the place of this factory.[4]

The entrance to Volozhin
(The intersection of Vishnayava and Horochki Streets)

Similarly, the Jews earned their livelihoods from leasing from the landowners and purchasing grain from the villagers. This can be surmised from the sermon of Rabbi Chaim, which states, "And the rest of the people must understand that perhaps, Heaven forbid, they will stumble in the sin of competition. For, in our abundance of sins, it is very common in our times for people to go to the market to purchase grain from a gentile, as well as by adding to the lease fees. This matter seems permissible to the masses of the people, and people should lament this.[5].

[Page 21]

In time, Volozhin transferred to the ownership of the Czartoryski Counts. The Volozhin estate, including lands of the area containing 81 villages and hamlets, passed into the possession of count Jósef Tyszkiewicz in 1803, It passed to his son Jósef in 1839. His son Michal received a portion in 1844. From 1894, it transferred completely to the ownership of Michal Tyszkiewicz.

Jósef Tyszkiewicz transformed Volozhin from a big hamlet to a little, but nice, town. He planted a beautiful garden on the banks of the Volozhinka, as well as a small grove. In the garden, there were fruit trees non–fruit trees, all types of vegetables, flowers, animals, and birds brought from distant places. All this was tended appropriately by the servants and employees of Count Tyszkiewicz.[6]

It is interesting that the lands of Volozhin transferred to the ownership of Jósef Tyszkiewicz in the same year that Rabbi Chaim of Volozhin founded the Etz Chaim Yeshiva (5563– 1803). Rabbi Chaim built the

Yeshiva in 1807, and Count Tyszkiewicz helped him greatly. He cut trees from his forest, and his workers constructed the planks and boards for the building of the Yeshiva[7].

Friendly relations between the family of the count and "the household of the rabbi" became a tradition. Just

[Page 22]

as of Jósef Tyszkiewicz was friendly with Rabbi Chaim, relations between the count's son Michal and Rabbi Chaim's son Itsele (Yitzchak) were particularly strong, to the point that the count summoned a sculptor to Volozhin to make a porcelain bust of Rabbi Itsele, to place inside his palace.

A student of Volozhin from three generations ago testifies about this:

"I recall from my early youth, when I merited to be a student of the great Yeshiva of Volozhin, I was told that the there were old, valuable objects in the palace treasury of the Polish Count Tyszkiewicz, located in the large garden in that small city. There was a portrait of Rabbi Yitzchak Volozhiner sculpted from porcelain."[8]

The first Volozhin Community head was Rabbi Yitzchak, Rabbi Chaim of Volozhin's father. The Itskhakin family had settled in Volozhin in the 16th century, and were among the first Jews who settled there. They laid the foundations of the community.

We have testimony from Rabbi Yitzchak's son, Rabbi Chaim, regarding the effectiveness and essence of Rabbi Yitzchak as the head of the community

"Once on the Holy Sabbath during the meal, a statement of our sages (Tractate Rosh Hashanah, 1) was presented before our rabbi of the Diaspora, the Gaon and Hassid Rabbi Chaim, may the memory of the holy be blessed, of Volozhin. The Gaon Rabbi Chaim of blessed memory was surrounded by his primary students, that is, his son, the great Gaon, the prince of Israel, Rabbi Yitzchak, may the memory of the holy be blessed, as well as other honorable great people. The following is the statement of our sages: "Rabbi Yehuda said in the name of Rav: A communal administrator who raises himself with pride above the community not for the sake of Heaven, does not merit to have a son who is a scholar." The Gaon Rabbi Chaim of blessed memory said as follows: If a communal administrator rules proudly over the community for the sake of Heaven, he is blessed to have a son who is a scholar. Faithful testimony to this is the honor of my master, my father, of blessed memory, who was a communal servant. The people listened to his voice, and he conducted his communal service in a high fashion, as was the custom of our Jewish brethren of those times, when the leaders of the community, headed by the administrator (*parnas*), ran the city in accordance with Torah and the commandments, as well as in accordance with the law of the state. However, we also know that the community and its servants always looked out to not impinge of the honor of the great ones, but would not pay attention to the lowly householders and impoverished people, knowing that they would not dare to be brazen to their communal leader. However, my honored father, of blessed memory was very careful to avoid imposing upon them with fees and the like. Even though the people trembled before him, he ruled over them for the sake of Heaven, and therefore merited to have a son who was a scholar, and who would have been considered a scholar even during the times of the Mishnaic and Talmudic sages. This is my brother Rabbi Zelmele[9].

[Page 23]

Already from the first days of Volozhin, its children were educated in the spirit of the Torah and commandments. The head of the community was the father to the poor, and concerned himself with their needs.

Rabbi Yitzchak married a wife from the Rapoport family, one of the oldest families of European Jewry. The name Rapoport comes from the family of "Rofeh" [doctor] from the city of "Porto" in the Verona district of Italy. The heads of the Rapoport family escaped from Germany to the city of Porto in the year 5222 (1462) due to persecution and murder. There, they increased greatly. In the year 5227 (1467), we hear that the prominent Rabbi Chaim Katz "Rofeh" attempted to settle many Jews in the Holy Land. Rivka, the wife of Rabbi Yitzchak, was the daughter of Rabbi Yisrael HaKohen Rapoport, who died in Vilna on 12 Av, 5540 (1780). Her illustrious son, Rabbi Chaim, maintained a correspondence with her father regarding halachic questions and responsa. One responsa is published in "Chut Hameshulash"[10] (section 11, 27).

Rabbi Chaim of Volozhin – Great Teacher & Educator of the Community of Volozhin

Translated by Jerrold Landau and donated by Anita Frishman Gabbay

Rabbi Chaim, the rabbi and educator of the Jews of the Volozhin, was one of the great forgers of ideas in Jewry during the latter generations.

His son, Rabbi Itzele, describes the Torah oriented educational activity of Rabbi Chaim in the introduction to *Nefesh HaChaim*:

"Even though the majority of the words in his explanations stand in the high places of the world, based on the Zohar and the writings of the Ar'i [Rabbi Isaac Luria] of blessed memory – through his righteousness he would cloak them, simplify them and conceal them so as not to exalt his words as if he was explaining hidden [trans: i.e. mystical] ideas. He would sweeten them as honey and milk under his tongue and spice under his garments, so that he could explain them clearly to the masses. This was so that the many who had not filled themselves with Talmud could purify their deeds in the proper spirit of fear of G–d, and not stumble in emptiness and meaninglessness…

"He would not refrain from telling over a section of the weekly Torah portion on a daily basis after the morning prayers. All who entered the *Beis Midrash* would exit full of content, each one having absorbed in accordance with their way. Those who loved simple explanations would absorb the depth of his simple explanation of scripture, and those who expounded ideas (exegetes, who knew how to explain passages of scripture via innuendo) expounded on what they heard, on that which emanated from his mouth in brief. All the listeners rejoiced with the sweetness of his lips that spoke clearly, as one reading a section of Torah to school children. This good deed was so precious in his eyes, that he left any holy matter and ran to the *Beis Midrash* while the congregation was still worshiping, and young and old were there."

The pedagogy of Rabbi Chaim of Volozhin was based on the adage of our sages, "we give over to

[Page 24]

a person in accordance with his strength." That means, there must be correspondence between "the power of understanding" and the "depth of the idea." Rabbi Chaim did great things with this concepts – he planted the thirst for Torah in the hearts of the Jews of Volozhin. Rabbi Nisenbaum writes the following about this thirst in the latter generations:

"The students would also visit the home of Rabbi Chaim Soloveitchik and engage in didactic discussions with him on words of Torah. At times, they would bring in his name some question to the Yeshiva, where almost all the students would busy themselves with finding the answer for him. Then, they would disperse to the *Beis Midrash*es of the city to search in many books, for perhaps they might find something."[11]

Rabbi Chaim's educational principle was that half understanding, partial understanding that does not delve into the depths of the issue, is worse than no understanding. Let a person's learning always be clear and clean; that is, fundamental understanding. Rabbi Chaim applied this principle to himself. He learned and reviewed, and never stopped until the matter became clear to him. Reb Itzele writes the following in the introduction to *Nefesh HaChaim*:

"He would exert effort to contradict his own words. He would review his words and deliberate over them with the scale of his intellect, how to come to the truth with straight logic and proper consideration. Someone who sees this will understand the wisdom that is thereby expressed, how he would minimize his intellect in his eyes. He had a lowly spirit [translator: i.e. was humble], as our sages have said: The words of the Torah are retained only by a person of a lowly spirit (*Taanit* 7a)."

The teaching of Rabbi Chaim include the doctrines of godliness and of moral teaching, that demonstrate to a person how to attain wholesomeness. Rabbi Chaim brought his own proofs regarding Torah that were taught by the early sages, that G–d is not immanent, not immersed in the internals of the world, but rather transcendental, over and above the world. His words are as follows:

"Why do we use a euphemism for the name of the Holy One Blessed Be He, and call him "*Makom*" [trans: the place – i.e. the Omnipresent One], because He is the place of the world, and the world is not his place. Just as a place tolerates and holds some object placed upon it, in this ideation, the Creator and Master of All, His Name Be Blessed, is the true place, that bears and maintains the worlds and all of its creatures. If, Heaven forbid, He would remove his energy from them for even one moment – there would be no place for existence of all the worlds, as is stated: 'And You maintain them all.' This is the point of foundation cornerstone of the faith of Israel"[12].

In other words: spirituality is the decisive reality. Without it, it, things are inanimate matter and devoid of any meaning or purpose.

"Just as a vessel standing in some place, even though the vessel has its own reality – nevertheless, if the vessel did not have a place upon which to stand

[Page 25]

it is as if it never existed. Thus, even though the world itself is perceptible and seems as its own reality – He Whose Name Is Blessed is its place."[13]

On account of "The Place" as the essence of the Creator, there is a support for physical essence, and its reality is dependent on His reality. Regarding the essence of G–d, Rabbi Chaim testifies to the faith with the intuition of the soul, and its proof is based on a deep connection: the Creator exists without connection to the physical world, and His reality is metaphysical. He is the founding source of the human soul. The relationship of the soul to the body is like the relationship of the Creator to His world. That is, even though it (the soul) is not a body, but is rather has the concept of an independent vessel – it is "the place" of the body, and gives it a hold on reality. The transcendental reality of the soul of a person is guarantee of its eternity.

The faith in the influence of the soul is the actual reality with respect to the life of a human being, for the reward in the World To Come does not come in a box as a matter guaranteed from the outset, but is rather the result of good deeds and toil in Torah.

"Everyone is happy with his lot – says Rabbi Chaim in his explanation – and relies on the Mishnah:

"All of Israel has a share in the World To Come, as is said, 'Thy people also shall be all righteous, they shall inherit the land for ever; the branch of My planting, the work of My hands, wherein I glory.'[i].

"However, they do not pay attention to the continuation of that Mishnah, which states:

"And these are the ones who have no share in the World To Come: One who denies that the resurrection of the dead is in the Torah, that Torah is from heaven, and an *Apikoros* [heretic].

(Tractate Sanhedrin 10:1).

"And this is the matter of the reward of the World To Come, which is based on the deeds of man himself. This is what our rabbis of blessed memory stated: 'All Israel has a share for the World To Come' and not 'in the World To Come,' for the World To Come is the work of man himself, who broadens and prepares the share (that is the share in the World to Come) for himself through his deeds."

Rabbi Chaim devotes a large place in his teaching to the moral education of man, purifying his traits and way of life. A life of justice and righteousness is preferable to the study of Torah. A person who studies Torah and worships with devotion, but steals from people and occupies himself with theft and deceit after his study and prayers – the Torah denigrates him as someone "who immerses [in a ritual bath] with the unclean creature still in his hands." Separating from sin is the precondition for the study of Torah.

"Apparently we will be amazed when we see how many people confess with a whole heart and request

[Page 26]

forgiveness and atonement for sins, but it is worthless, for the main point of repentance is abandoning sin. However, there is no benefit to this matter, for the essence of repentance is abandoning sin, especially sins committed in a repeated fashion to the point where it seems to the person as something permissible, for he becomes very attached to it and it is difficult to abandon it. Regarding this it says, 'let the wicked person abandon his sins' [translator: Isaiah 55:7]. That means that the sin has already become consolidated with him, and he is then called a wicked person. Thus, he should first abandon his and then 'he will return to G–d.'

1. There is no value to confession without abandoning sin, for a person is liable to continue the sin even after the sin on account of being accustomed to it, as is stated 'as a dog returns to his vomit.' [translator: Proverbs 26:11]" (A sermon of the Mahara'ch [Rabbi Chaim].

Rabbi Chaim warned the Jews of Volozhin to keep away from inappropriate competition in business that might impinge on a person's livelihood:

"And the rest of the nation must understand, perhaps Heaven forbid they will stumble in the sin of competition, for, in our great sins, it is very common in our times when people go out to the marketplace to purchase food from a gentile. His friend may come and also wish to purchase the same merchandise about which the first person is still negotiating with the gentile, and does not want the second person, who is already discussing with the gentile, to get it. When the second person sees this, he becomes jealous of his friend who is purchasing it for a low price. Even though he knows that the merchandise will remain with the first person, he offers a price greater than the gentile himself asked. On account of this, the first person is forced to give the gentile this price. It is the same with regard to adding to leasing fees. This matter has turned into something regarded as permissible to the masses of the people. Let all moaners moan about this, for who shall say that my heart has merited this. (sermon of the Mahara'ch).

Just as every person is required to be of clean hands and a pure heart – there is a doubled and redoubled obligation on the communal activists and leaders:

"And the leaders must ascertain for themselves about whether, Heaven forbid, they are lording over the community not for the sake of Heaven. For even if they are occupied in a holy matter, if their intention is merely to increase their own honor, and not for the sake of Heaven – they are in the category of those who impose their fear in the land of the living, Heaven forbid." (sermon of the Mahara'ch)

The problem of reward and punishment is dependent on the importance and value of the person, for the greater the person – the more he is scrutinized, for his sins shake the "Throne of Glory." A very heavy responsibility rests upon those who occupy themselves in communal affairs. When they conduct their mission deceitfully, they endanger the wellbeing of the community.

"The damage is commensurate with the level of grandeur of the soul of the person. Someone who sullies the courtyard of the king is not comparable to someone who sullies his own home. This is even more so regarding the throne of the king, and especially his clothing. According to this, we see that even though people commit the same sin, their punishment is not equivalent. This one

[Page 27]

is judged in accordance with the level of his soul, and that one is judged in accordance with the level of his soul. This one sullied the courtyard of the king, and this one his throne – therefore his punishment is greater than that of his fellow.

"If one of the king's warriors is lazy and does not conduct himself appropriately in battle, and thereby endangers not only himself, it is not similar to someone who endangers himself, but does not cause damage or danger to the rest of the army. However, if the leader of a 50–person battalion is negligent and lazy, or the leader of a 1000–person battalion is so, he causes damage to their 50 or 1000 people who fall in battle due to his negligence, for he was supposed to be their protector. And if the chief commander is lazy, he causes the entire war to be lost." (sermon of the Mahara'ch)

Since the Jews of Volozhin were completely enveloped in the atmosphere of Torah, and regarded this as something self–evident – they did not display special excitement toward the Yeshiva and its *Gaonim*. Rabbi Naftali Tzvi Yehuda Berlin (the Netzi'v) explains this, as told in the following story:

"One, one of the Netziv's students asked him: Let our rabbi teach us, indeed everyone sees and knows that there is no searching for the level of soulful astonishment and sublime spirit in a person passing through Volozhin, on account of the honor of Torah pervading in every path and corner. Behold, it is as if the question arises on its own: Why is it with the dwellers of Volozhin itself, that is, its residents, citizens, elders, youth – that the see the preciousness of the Torah all day and night, yet nevertheless, it is as if they are cold as ice and frozen as a stone.

"The Netziv responded with a fine story told by one of the cantors that came to him on account of his cantorial position. The cantor told as follows: once on Simchat Torah, as I was leading the procession of the congregation in the *Hakafot* [trans: festive Torah processions on Simchat Torah] around the *bima*, with a Torah scroll in my arms, and in the arms of all those in the procession, as was the custom, with the younger and older children surrounding, circling us from all sides, pushing themselves to kiss the Torah scroll – I sensed and noticed a small girl standing throughout the entire seven processions. Not only did she not push her way through her friends to kiss the Torah scrolls, but she let her friends through, as if saying: Go yourselves, kiss the Torah scrolls as you desire. Whereas she herself did not move from her place, and one could not notice any amazement or feelings of joy with her. This seemed strange in my eyes. Since I am by nature a person of words, who loves to look into things, I called the girl and asked her: Why did you not move toward the Torah scrolls to kiss them, as your friends did?

"The girl responded: For me, a Torah scroll is nothing new, and I am not amazed by it, for I see it in my house, and I never stop looking and staring at Torah scrolls day and night. All the tables and benches in our house are virtually full

[Page 28]

of Torah scrolls and portion of Torah scrolls. I eat and a Torah scroll is beside me. I am quiet and a Torah scroll is before me. Anywhere I go, sit, or stand, I encounter a Torah scroll. I asked the girl: Whose daughter are you? She responded: The daughter of a scribe of Torah scrolls, tefillin, and *mezuzot*.

"The Netziv responded: The response of the girl solves the question of your friend regarding the apparent cold relationship, so to speak, of the Jews of Volozhin toward the Yeshiva, for they are immersed in this holy camp from their childhood, and they never cease to hear the sounds of Torah day and night. From this, their feelings cannot sense the holy feelings and the soulful enjoyment that the guests who pass through Volozhin for days or hour feel."[14]

Translator's Footnote:

1. The Mishnah is from Tractate Sanhedrin 10:1. I took the translation of the verse from Isaiah from Mechon Mamre: https://www.mechon–mamre.org/p/pt/pt1060.htm

Volozhin and Hassidism

Translated by Jerrold Landau and donated by Anita Frishman Gabbay

Volozhin was known in the world as a fortress of *Misnagdism* [i]. The ideology of *Misnagdism* was forged there, and not only in the Vilna of the Gr'a [Vilna Gaon]. *Nefesh HaChaim* by Rabbi Chaim of Volozhin is the book of principles of the Misnagdic world. This book was not especially pleasing to the

Hassidim, whereas the *Beit Harav* [House of the Rabbi] dynasty regarded it as the holy of holies. It is told that the granddaughter of Rabbi Chaim once listened to a discussion of Hassidim who were uttering accusations against *Nefesh HaChaim*. The granddaughter got involved in the conversation, and uttered a brief statement: It is forbidden to take the *Nefesh HaChaim* into one's hand. When the Hassidim heard this sharp statement, they thought that she agreed with them. She revealed her intent to them and stated, "It is forbidden to take this book into one's hand, for it is the holy of holies, and renders the hands impure."[15][ii]

Rabbi Chaim of Volozhin wished to draw the Hassidim close. He did not fight a boycott war as did his rabbi, the G'ra. In this area, he forged his own path, and he looked at Hassidism with his own lens[15a].

[Page 29]

According to his opinion, Hasidism as based on the Baal Shem Tov did not come to uproot Judaism, or to changes the accepted forms of religious customs. He only wished to bring life to the Nation of Israel in a new manner, which was good and effective according to his opinion – but about which he, Rabbi Chaim, did not agree with. He says the following in *Nefesh HaChaim*:

"And even some of those who aspire to draw close to G–d have chosen for themselves to dedicated their entire course of study to books regarding fear of Heaven and morality for all their days, without making the main part of their endeavor in the study of Torah to scripture and the great body of law. They never saw the light, and the light of Torah has never illuminated them. May G–d forgive them, for their intentions are appropriate, but this is not the path to acquire the light of Torah."[16]

Many Hassidim studied in his Yeshiva. Rabbi Chaim did not treat them badly, but rather drew them near with love and friendship. Even the Hassidim who passed through Volozhin and wanted to see his face – he would keep them with him for a few days so he could befriend them. His son, Rabbi Itzele, owned all the books of Hassidic greats. He delved into them, and he would include many statements of Hassidim in his sermons[17].

A great thing happened around the year 5568 (1808): Rabbi Chaim of Volozhin, Rabbi Yisrael Markish of Minsk, and Rabbi Aryeh Leib Katzenelbogen of Brisk all joined together with Rabbi Levi Yitzchak of Berdichev and gave their asset to the publication of the Talmud in Kopust [Kopustai][18].

After the death of the G'ra, Rabbi Chaim refused to sign the ban against Hasidim. When his friends expressed surprised and asked him how he was able to separate from the opinion of his rabbi, he responded that his rabbi, the G'ra, was literally an angel of G–d, but to slaughter another a Jew requires a command from the Holy One Blessed Be He Himself. He brought a proof from the Binding of Isaac[19].

Rabbi Chaim's tolerant attitude can be explained by his desire to increase peace in the world. The following is written in *Dor Deah*:

"Once, a conversation took place between Rabbi Chaim and one of the Hassidic greats. For the sake of peace, Rabbi Hayin proposed that the Hasidim worship in the Ashkenazic mode. The Hasid claimed that the changes are vital based on the hidden wisdom[iii] and their proper energy at the time of the acceptance of the prayers On High. Rabbi Chaim responded: If this is the only reason that the changes were made – it is best that both of us, both you and me, do not worship at all, so long as there is peace upon Israel and we do not divide ourselves into multiple factions.[20]

[Page 30]

Similarly, Rabbi Chaim was prepared to worship in Sephardic fashion[iv], so long as it does not increase controversy among Jews. As Rabbi Tzvi Hirsh Katzenelbogen writes in *Shaarei Rachamim*: "He ordered his student, Rabbi Yisrael of Shklov, who traveled from here to a place among the Sephardim, to not change their custom and to worship in their fashion."[21]

As the years went on, family ties were forged between the "House of the Rabbi" and the Hassidic world. Rabbi Chaim of Volozhin's great–grandson married the daughter of a Hassid, whose grandfather was a student of the "Great Maggid," Rabbi Dov–Ber of Mezritsh.

The following is told to Yitzchak Izak HaKohen in the book *Shaarei Yitzchak*:

"It is known that the Gaon Rabbi Chaim of Volozhin of blessed memory, the greatest of the students of the Gr'a, may he be remembered for life in the World To Come, married off his grandson grandson of Rabbi Eliezer, the paternal grandson of Rabbi Yosef of blessed memory, to the daughter of the Hassid Rabbi Tzvi Hirsch of blessed memory of Seimatis, the son of the Gaon and Hassid Rabbi Uziel Meizlish, the author of *Kerem Shlomo*, the student of the rabbi and Maggid Rabbi Dov–Ber, as is written in the introduction of the aforementioned book *Kerem Shlomo*.

"Their hatred and jealousy had already dissipated, and the students of the Gaon, the aforementioned great rabbi and Maggid, his friends, students, and students of students, great in Torah and Hassidism, famous Gaonim, authors of holy books both about the fear of G–d as well as about Halachic didactics and responsa spread out and grew in number. All of Israel relies on them as on the early and latter decisors, as is known and renown. Many of them are included in *The New Names of Gaonim*, printed recently for the third time with the approbation of the sages of our generations, may their Creator and Redeemer protect them. Most Jews, rabbis, and seekers of Torah in our country of Russia and Poland, as well as nearby countries, are attracted to them in all their customs, as is known and renown.

"And I saw one book published in the previous generation, at the time of the aforementioned dispute (that is, the dispute between the G'ra and Rabbi Shneur of Liadi), as well as many letters in the name of great ones. It is impossible to believe that these words emanated from their mouths, the mouths of those great in Torah and fear of Heaven, for they are full of words of mockery, riddles, and castigation, for which it is not worthwhile to respond to, and all their questions have no basis…"[22]

The writer continues on and provides details about the good relations of the great–grandson of Rabbi Chaim with the Hassidim in his city, and about his visit to their *Beis Midrash*. This scion of Hassidim tells about hidden aspects of Torah that were illuminated

[Page 31]

by the scion of the *Beit Harav*. He announced that he literally revived him with ideas that had been hidden to him to this point.

This closeness is attested to by the words of Berdichevski, who states:

"Everyone who is familiar with the pathways of the dispute between the Gaon Rabbi Eliahu of Vilna and Rabbi Shneur Zalman Schneerson of Liadi knows that the Gr'a did not have any reliable understanding of Hassidism at all. He did not know that the spirit of the captive nation gave birth to Hassidism, and that Hassidism did not come to turn the nation away from Torah, but rather to rectify it and to breathe into it a living spirit instead of a suppressed spirit, to return the hearts of the People of Israel to their Father in Heaven, and to direct them in the meanings of Judaism. The Gr'a considered them as a religious sect separate from the general masses, as a sect whose aim was to forge a path under the seat of Judaism. In his great isolation, he only knew Hassidism from the hearsay of those who slander, who brought the defamation of the Hassidism to him and attributed deeds that should not be done to them. Therefore, he shook up the world regarding them."[23]

Translator's Footnotes:

i.   The ideology of formal opposition to Hassidism.
ii.   In Jewish law, certain holy books are considered to render the hands ritually impure – the purpose being to prevent frivolous touching of such books.
iii.   A euphemism for mystical or Kabbalistic ideas – which form a significant basis of Hassidic philosophy.
iv.   The Hassidic mode of worship has many similarities with the Sephardic mode.
v.

The Role of Volozhin in the Poetry of Chaim Nachman Bialik

Translated by Jerrold Landau and donated by Anita Frishman Gabbay

Ch. N. Bialik during the *Hamatmid* period

Volozhin gave over Chaim Nachman Bialik to modern Hebrew literature. Had Bialik not studied in Volozhin – we would not have merited the powerful creativity of the chief of Hebrew poetry. His first poem, *El Hatzipor* [To the Bird], written on "Mount Bialik," and his great poem *Hamatmid*[i] are completely Volozhin. We find an impression of Volozhin in every one of Bialik's poems.

Even though Bialik only remained in Volozhin for one year and four months, he was bound to the city and its Yeshiva with his whole heart. The poet writes in *Hamatmid*:

Times have changed, and you are far from your borders
I set up my altar, I gave my threshold –
But I still remember you all, you all
Your picture accompanies me, it will not move from my heart. The writer Zalman Epstein expresses well the influence of Volozhin upon Bialik:

[Page 32]

"The soil of Volozhin was full of moisture and life, and fine, fruitful seeds were planted in the students of the Yeshiva. Later on, when the conditions for growth converged, they sprouted and yielded bountiful fruit. It is sufficient to read the name of the bright star – Bialik. The influence of Volozhin on his talent was great and for the good. The blend of the past with the future regarding the life of our people, the understanding of the internal content of the study hall in all its light and darkness, the richness of style and expressions from the Mishna and Talmud of which Bialik worked wonders – all of this he inherited from Volozhin. Had he not studied there, he would not have been the same Bialik that we now have. He would not have written poems like *Hamatmid*. The atmosphere of Volozhin was needed to moisten and water all of ancient Judaism with illuminating dew with his mighty talent, and to fill it with the spirit of ancient Israel from Babylon until now. From the wings of this eagle received their Jewish form in Volozhin, and sent out results to the portion of his nation."[24]

Bialik came to Volozhin, according to his own testimony, to study there "Seven wisdoms and seventy languages."

Bialik writes, "After many experiences that are difficult for me to touch at this point, I traveled to Volozhin at the age of 15, relying on news that spread in my town amount the lads, that in Volozhin they study both the revealed Torah and hidden Torah [ii] together with Gemara, as well as seven wisdoms and seventy languages. And between Volozhin and Berlin it is like one step."[25]

[Page 33]

Bialik quickly realized that he had made a mistake: aside from Gemara and rabbinic decisors, the Yeshiva of Volozhin did not have any of the "seven wisdoms" nor any language of the "seventy languages." Even the teaching of the Russian language, which was imposed on the Yeshiva by the government, was to fulfil the requirements. In the Yeshiva, they only studied Gemara, Gemara, Gemara.

Bialik slowly made his peace with the reality. The essence of the spacious Yeshiva and the light and voice of the 400 students who never ceased swaying over their Gemaras through all the hours of the day – influenced Bialik to make peace with the situation. "The "mighty one and ruler" of the Yeshiva in those days, the Netzi'v, undoubtedly also influenced him to come to terms with the situation. The Netzi'v was the elderly, wide–hearted man of love, whose attracted the hearts of the students to the Yeshiva with the light of his facial countenance, the pleasantness of his words, and his refined personality.

Bialik "delved into the Gemara with his full soul." His diligence was so great that it also astounded the Netzi'v. When he examined him after a few months, and realized his great proficiency in Talmud, he testified about him, "That this was the first time that I saw a lad from Volhynia who was diligent and knowledgeable in Gemara as he was."

The time that Bialik spent in the Volozhin Yeshiva was a blessing to his mighty talents. There, the spirit of poetry came upon him. From Yarmulke Mountain[25], the young poet appeared with the song of the bird on his mouth. Bialik would spend many hours alone on this Kippa, and many days with the poetry that began to pulsate within him. It was there that he wrote his first poem, *El Hatzipor*, in the year 5651 [1891][26].

[Page 34]

Bialik struggled through many struggles of creativity on the Kippa. This was known by only very few of the Yeshiva lads, the Maskilim from among them, who gathered around the Volozhin poet and cleaved to him from the first day he arrived in Volozhin. These friends felt almost subconsciously that, in the future, Bialik would lighten up the eyes of all of Israel with the precious light of his creativity. They copied for themselves, one person to the next, every new poem that Bialik wrote in Volozhin[27].

After a year and four months in Volozhin, Bialik decided to actualize the desires of his heart, and he set out for Russia to acquire modern education. His departure from Volozhin left a great impression, as Abba Blusher writes in his memoirs:

"One day, we accompanied Bialik a distance of two parasangs, along the path that leads to the Maladzyechna Station. A large number of people were accompanying him since Bialik was beloved and accepted by all who knew him. Everyone trusted that he would imbue honor upon the Yeshiva in days to come. The entourage sat to rest next to a small hill on the side of the path. Bialik sat in the middle, and his entourage sat around him in a semicircle, singing songs of Zion. The wagon driver began to call out. The entourage stood up from where they were sitting and shook off the dust. The farewells began, with hugs, kisses, handshakes, and blessings. Hands were raised. They placed Bialik on the wagon, and it began to move. Due to the crowding, Bialik fell from his seat and was standing on his knees, half sitting and half standing, as he bid farewell with a final blessing to those who accompanied him. With each turn of the wheels of the wagon, they became farther and farther away from him, until they completely disappeared from sight. When the wagon appeared as merely a small dot on the far horizon, the entourage returned to the city, full of the sadness of parting. After time, when Bialik became famous in the world, and it became known in Volozhin that Chaim Nachman of Zhitomir was Chaim Nachman Bialik, they named that hill upon which they bid farewell "Bialik Hill."[28]

Bialik recalled Volozhin with nostalgia all his life. Yaakov Pichman tells that at a party with his friends in his home in Homburg, Bialik told about his life in Volozhin all evening.

" In his book about far–off days, his heart was warm. Memories and images arise and come to life before us with such clarity that we literally breathe the air of the Volozhin Yeshiva. All the tenderness preserved in his heart from this precious refuge of youth is now poured out like a melody from his heart." Pichman continues and states: "This was a new edition of *Hamatmid* – a poem in prose, as if it was now recorded from the teller, as it was. It was perhaps also the sublime creation of *Hamatmid* in verse."[29]

[Page 35]

The Great Ones of Volozhin [30]

Some claim that the main uniqueness of Volozhin stems from the Etz Chaim Yeshiva that was founded therein. If you remove the Yeshiva, it becomes a town like all other town of Poland and Lithuania. The historical truth does not confirm this claim. The city of Volozhin has its own pedigree. The founding of the Yeshiva was a result of the presence of great Gaonim, natives of the city, as well as Gaonim born outside the city, who turned their wellsprings toward it.

Volozhin was famous and known amongst Jewish communities for may years before the founding of the Yeshiva. Micha Yosef Berdichevsky defines its positive traits very well:

The "Gr'a chose the small city of Volozhin to actualize his lofty idea, for two reasons: a) he regarded the city of Volozhin was dear to the people of Lithuania, for the famous Gaon, the author of *Shaagas Aryeh*, lived there, about whom they said that he was capable of organizing a summary of the entire Talmud in his mind in one hour; as well as the Gaon, compared to an angel of the L–rd of Hosts, Rabbi Zalman. These two Gaonim gave Volozhin a great name, to the point where it seemed to the people of Lithuania that the atmosphere of Volozhin generated wisdom. b) He saw that the Gaon Rabbi Chaim of blessed memory was by nature a sublime person, sitting in the shadow of Torah and the shadow of money. Therefore, he chose him and his city to found the cornerstone of the high–level Yeshiva."[31]

Translator's Footnotes:

i.   Generally translated as "The Talmud Student" although literally it means, "The diligent (or persistent) one".
ii.   The hidden Torah refers to mysticism and Kabbalah.
iii.   In the original text, the footnote numbering is off, and 25 is repeated.

The Shaagas Aryeh – Volozhin's Spiritual Father

Translated by Jerrold Landau based on an earlier translation by M. Porat z"l and Mike Kalt and donated by Anita Frishman Gabbay

The Shaagas Aryeh

There was already an important community in Volozhin during the second half of the 18th century, and a "Sinai and uprooter of mountains" [i] such as the Shaagas Aryeh served twice as the rabbi of the city.

Rabbi Aryeh Leib (the Ra'l), son of Reb Asher Gunzberg, was born near Minsk in the year 5455 (1695). He was known as "Shaagas Aryeh" ("The Roar of the Lion"), from the title of his book. We do not know anything about his Torah educators, and through which means he attained greatness in the Talmud and its commentaries. In the year 5493 (1733), at the age of 38, the rabbi of Minsk, Rabbi Yechiel Heilperin, author of *Seder Hadorot*, invited him to serve as head of the Minsk Yeshiva. During his first years in that city, the author of *Seder Hadorot* would walk together with him as a friend and brother. When they walked together in the marketplaces, people would whisper: Here is a Sinai with an uprooter of mountains.

[Page 36]

However, these friendly relations did not last long due to the hard character of the Shaagas Aryeh. He recognized his own greatness in Torah too well, and therefore refused to subordinate himself to those superior to him if he saw that they had made an error in some matter. He did not fear anybody. In cases where he did not find that the *halacha* [decisions on Jewish law] was built on the foundations of the Talmud, he would push it aside with his strong hand, and let people say what they may. He permitted himself to use sharp language in his responsa, even against the decisors such as the Rema, Rabbi Yoel Sirkis, and the Sha'ch. We find that he used expressions such as "there is no reason to his words, "he erred greatly in this," "I don't know what he is talking about," and "his words are mixed up and non–understandable," etc.

The Shaagas Aryeh nullified as the dust of the earth [iii] all the Torah giants, except for the Gr'a, whom he honored and revered. Only to him did he show favour, as he said, "All the sages of Israel seem to me like a garlic husk, with the exception of Rabbi Eliahu of Vilna." The Gr'a himself honored the Shaagas Aryeh greatly, and said that Rabbi Aryeh Leib is the Yeshiva head in revealed Torah. Therefore, he testified that the Shaagas Aryeh could organize the entire Talmud in his mind in one hour.

It was not long before the Shaagas Aryeh impinged upon the honor of Rabbi Yechiel Heilperin as well as the *parnassim* [administrators] of the community of Minsk. Many enemies rose against him, and he was obliged to leave Minsk in the year 5502 (1742). He cleared a place for his student, Rabbi Rafael HaCohen (Hamburger).

The Shaagas Aryeh was accepted as the rabbi of Volozhin in the year 5510 (1750), and occupied that seat until the year 5515 (1755). The Shaagas Aryeh had been invited by the head of the community, Rabbi Yitzchak, the father of Rabbi Chaim of Volozhin. The Shaagas Aryeh opened a large Yeshiva in Volozhin, and he was called Reb Leib the Rosh Yeshiva [Yeshiva Head] by the Jews of Volozhin. His choicest students were Rabbi Chaim and his elder brother Simcha. Reb Itzele, the son of Rabbi Chaim, writes regarding this in his introduction to *Nefesh Chaim*: "They (i.e. Rabbi Simcha and Rabbi Chaim) then accepted the Torah methodology of the rabbi of rabbis, the Gaon of Gaonim, the lion of the upper realms, Rabbi Aryeh Leib, may he rest in peace, the author of the Shaagas Aryeh."

The Yeshiva founded by the Shaagas Aryeh in Volozhin was unique in its kind, in that the study was in the manner of simple explanation and straight intellect. The Shaagas Aryeh was the father of the simple expositors of Volozhin. His student, Rabbi Chaim, used this methodology as the foundation stone of the Etz Chaim Yeshiva. The following is a story that verifies the methodology of the Shaagas Aryeh: Once on Shabbat Hagadol, he delivered a long lecture of deep didactics in the great synagogue of Minsk, proving with 150 reasons and 5,689 partial innuendos that chometz is permissible on Passover. All the Torah greats present were astonished at the great sharpness displayed by that Gaon. After the Sabbath, the Gaon took a candle in his hand and began to search through all the corners of the synagogue, and under the benches and the tables. When he was asked: "Our rabbi, what are you searching for?" He responded:

[Page 37]

"I am looking for the Jews of Minsk. Where are you, Jews of Minsk? Doesn't the Torah say: Do not eat any leaven (Exodus 12:20). Of what use are thousands of Shaagas Aryehs in their sharpness, questions and answers when the simple explanation of the scripture is before your eyes?! Isn't this vain didactics, making the straight crooked, and making the Torah into a bandage?!"

The community of Volozhin was poor at that time, and it did not have a complete set of Talmuds. Volumes of Talmud at that time were hard to find, especially in Russia and Lithuania. Only a few individuals of great wealth who loved Torah, or large, important communities succeeded in purchasing an Amsterdam edition of the entire Talmud, published in its entirety in the year 5512–5525 (1752–1765). The impoverished population of Volozhin was unable to obtain a complete set of Talmuds. The *parnas* Rabbi Yitzchak, the father of Rabbi Chaim, would travel outside Russia for his business. Once, his wife Rivka asked him to purchase a complete Amsterdam edition of the Talmud, the price of which was very high. Rabbi Yitzchak listened to his wife, and brought a fine, splendid set of Talmuds back with him to Volozhin. On account of his business and his role as communal *parnas*, he was not able to respond to all the scholars in Volozhin and nearby towns who wished to peruse one tractate or another. Therefore, he gave the keys to the volumes of Talmud to his wife, who would willingly permit the scholars to peruse the Talmud in her home. As is said, the Shaagas Aryeh, who was not able to obtain his own Talmud due to poverty, would also come frequently to look into the Talmud volumes of the communal *parnas*. However, Rivka could not bear to see him pound his feet from time to time to come to her home to look into the Talmud, so she offered to send him any tractate that he needs by way of his assistant, whether for his own perusal or to teach the Yeshiva students. Therefore, the Shaagas Aryeh blessed her that her sons become great in Torah. His blessing was fulfilled.

During the years that the Shaagas Aryeh lived in Volozhin, he collected all his Torah and *halachic* novellae that he wrote during those many years, and compiled them into a book called *Shaagas Aryeh*. This book contains many acronyms. It is said that this is due to the poverty of the author, who did not have enough paper on hand, so he utilized more acronyms than usual.

The Shaagas Aryeh earned his livelihood with difficulty in Volozhin, and lived a life of want, for his salary was three guilder per week. He wore an old *kapote* on weekdays as well as the Sabbath. His difficult situation caused bitterness, and he also got angry at his wife in his vexation. Once she said to him: "You are a bad man." He responded to her: "You are more correct than I! *Ada'm R'a* [ע"ר ם"אד – bad man] is the acronym for: אביון דך מך רש עני[iii] – and these are the sources of my vexation.

In her desire to help her husband, his wife kneaded dough in the homes of others and earned some coins. Nevertheless, the poverty was very great, and the Shaagas Aryeh could not bear his straits and observe the Torah in poverty. He requested from the city *parnassim* that they add a half a guilder to his salary. The city notables gathered and adjudicated seriously, but could not find any means of giving him a raise, for the communal coffers were meager and empty. Therefore, the Shaagas Aryeh was forced to leave Volozhin after living there for five

[Page 38]

years and disseminating Torah in his Yeshiva, from which world luminaries went forth. However, this was not his only reason for leaving Volozhin. The Shaagas Aryeh wanted to publish his book. There was no printing press yet in Lithuania and Poland in those days, so he was forced to wander far–off to Germany and publish his book in Frankfurt an der Oder.

The Shaagas Aryeh and his wife were housed in the *Hekdesh* [hostel for indigents] in Frankfurt. He sat in the *Hekdesh*, lit a candle, and began to study the Rambam aloud, as was his custom. Some of the paupers woke from their slumber and uttered sharp words and curses at the guest who was disturbing their sleep. He extinguished the candle, went outside, and studied by the moonlight. When morning broke, and the slumberers awoke from their sleep, they saw that someone was standing outside dancing from joy. His wife was also rejoicing with him.

The manager of the *Hekdesh* looked upon this scene. When the dance finished, the manager asked him: "What is the cause of your happiness?" The Shaagas Aryeh responded: "A great miracle happened to me last night, and therefore I am thanking the Blessed G–d and dancing in a circle from joy. I had a difficult question on the Rambam, which was bothering me for many days, and I could not find an answer. This past night, the Blessed G–d lit up my eyes and I was able to answer it completely. This is the reason for the joy."

After publishing his book, he returned to Russia, and reached the city of Smilovich, where Rabbi Rafael HaKohen was serving as the rabbi of the city. He remained there for some time, and returned to Volozhin in the year 5523 (1763). He remained there for one year, until the year 5524 (1764). That year was known as a year of special importance in the forging of the image of Volozhin, for that time, his greatest student, who later would become famous as the Gra'h (The Gaon Rabbi Chaim of Volozhin), studied there.

The heart of the Shaagas Aryeh was bad and bitter toward the Jews of Volozhin, who had forced him to leave the city on account of a half a guilder. Therefore, he decided to take revenge on them. It is told that he was once delivering a sermon in the *Beis Midrash* of Volozhin, and his sermon was so deep, to the point that the great studiers could not delve into its depths. When he finished his sermon, he said to the audience: "You are greater than the ministering angels."

"In what way?" wondered the audience.

"Why are you surprised," responded the Shaagas Aryeh. It says regarding the ministering angels: 'And their feet are like the feet of a calf' (Ezekiel 1:7). But as for you – also your heads are like the head of a calf."

The Jews of Volozhin did not forgo the disgrace of the Shaagas Aryeh. Even after he left Volozhin for the second time and was accepted as the rabbi of Metz, they sent messengers to appease him and bring him back to the city. It is told that when the Shaagas Aryeh was living in Metz, and the city greats were sitting before him, he heard the sound of footsteps on the stairs.

"Someone from Volozhin is walking," said the Shaagas Aryeh.

"How does our rabbi know?" they asked him.

The Shaagas Aryeh responded: "A Volozhin native is recognized from his brazen footsteps."

The Shaagas Aryeh left Volozhin around the year 5524 (1764), never to return.

[Page 39]

He was around 70 years old when he left Volozhin. He left for Vilna, and then he went to Metz. He found rest, wealth, and honor in Metz. His extended period of wandering through Lithuania, with his knapsack on his shoulder, filled with groats, a few objects, his tallis and tefillin, and a book of the Rambam, came to an end.

His eyes became dim as he passed the age of 80, but he continued diligently with his studies as previously, for diligence in Torah was second nature to him. He settled permanently in Metz. He amassed a bookcase full of books. He no longer depended on the power of his memory in his old age.

Once, as he was studying, he approached the bookcase to take out a book to peruse. The bookcase tottered and a pile of books fell upon him. He remained beneath the pile for about a half an hour, until the members of his household realized what happened and came to rescue him. As extricated him from there almost dead, he said in his clear language: "All the authors fell upon me and sentenced me to death because I did not consider them, and I disputed them. However, the entire time that I was under the heap of books, I begged forgiveness from them. They all forgave me, with the exception of the author of the *Levush* (Rabbi

Mordechai Jaffe), who was prone to anger. He did not want to forgive me on account of him, I was sentenced to immediate death, but as for me, my soul still desires Torah.

He died at an old age, around the age of 90, on the 25th of Tammuz, 5545 (July 3, 1785), and was buried in Metz.

Translator's Footnotes:

i.   A Talmudic term for a person with both breadth (Sinai) and depth (uprooter of mountains) in Torah study. (Based on tractate *Horayot* 14a–b).
ii. A formula of nullification used for the nullification of chometz [leavened products] before Passover.
iii. Five Hebrew synonyms for an indigent (e.g. poor person, indigent, mendicant, pauper, beggar).

Rabbi Shlomo Zalman, nicknamed Rav Zalmele

Translated by Jerrold Landau and donated by Anita Frishman Gabbay

Thus does the biographer Rabbi Yechezkel Feivel begin his book "this is the Book of the Annals of Man," which is the biography of Rabb Zalmele.

"There was a man in the city of Volozhin of Lithuania named Rabbi Yitzchak. He was a straightforward, upright man, G–d fearing and avoiding evil. He was wealthy, and conducted his business in a trustworthy fashion. A son was born to him on the 29th of Sivan, 5516 (1756) whose name was Zalman. From the cradle this child was different than the other children his age."

Rabbi Zalmele was the younger brother of Rabbi Chaim, the founder of the Etz Chaim Yeshiva of Volozhin. Through his name alone, there was already a hint and innuendo to the future, for "Shlomo" comes from the word *shalem* [complete or wholesome] – for when the child would grow up, he would be complete in his deeds and traits, and, above all, his learning would be wholesome. Rabbi Chaim testified that the face of his brother was like the face of the Shaagas Aryeh. While still in his cradle, it was realized that he had some unique gifts. His mother Rivka protected him from everything, as if the surety of the Jewish people was given over to her.

He entered the *cheder* of Volozhin before he reached the age of three. From that time, the child was not involved in children's games. He only occupied himself with Torah. Once, the rabbi of Ruzhany, the Gaon Rabbi Avigdor, was a guest in the home of Rabbi Yitzchak, Shlomo Zalman's father. When he saw the small child lying in the cradle with a holy book

[Page 40]

resting in his hands – he said that it is a disgrace for holy books to be given as toys to toddlers. Rabbi Yitzchak said to him: "This toddler is not like the others. For this toddler, this book is not a toy, but rather a book of study that he always looks into." Suddenly the child woke up, took the book and began to read it with great diligence. The Gaon stood in astonishment and said that he was certain that this child will become an example and sign in Israel, and many will aspire to his Torah.

When he was approximately four years old, his father made a celebration for the rabbis in honor of the great event that his older brother Simcha had learned the entire six orders of Mishnah by heart. Young Shlomole asked his father: "Why are you making this celebration? In what honor is all this fuss?" His father responded: "This day is very great in my eyes, for I have merited to see my son know all the six orders of Mishna by heart. May it be that I merit to see you attain this level as well." Zalmele responded: "Gather, your heart can be sure that, if G–d grants me length of days and a healthy body – I will know books by heart, even more than you hope for. My brother, Reb Simcha, knows this small book (a small book of Mishna with a clear translation was on the table) – and I will know by heart all books on the bookcase." As he spoke, he pointed with his finger to the large bookcase in the house.

When he was five years old, Zalmele already almost knew the five books of the Torah with Rashi's commentary by heart. He was like an overflowing wellspring. This was not with the help of a rebbe, but rather through his internal power that stormed and flowed within him at all times to know Torah. Already in his childhood he felt that Torah and wisdom are the true life of a person, illuminating with their light the material life, that is nothing other than vanity. True happiness is the love of Torah and wisdom.

Slowly, the wonder child became known throughout the area, and many people streamed to Volozhin to see him with their own eyes. A legend went around the elders of Volozhin of previous generations, that on the 15th of Elul 5525 (1765), a holy spirit from heaven descended upon the child Zalmanke of Volozhin, and he drew all of his spiritual nutrition from the upper source of wisdom.

Rabbi Zalmele's diligence and thirst for studies was beyond human means. He prepared his heart to be nothing other than a sanctuary for the service of G–d. When he was occupied with Torah, he was taken with and affected by its love so much, that his soul almost left his body. He was graced with two precious, rare traits: the power of memory and of diligence. When he was ill, he would read the book *Tzitzat Novel* by Rabbi Yaakov Sasportas. After his first reading, every little thing from the book, from top to bottom, was etched in his heart.

Leib, the son of Rabbi Ber of Vilna, said: "Once Reb Ber saw the *Tzadik* Rabbi Zalmele going to and fro in the house, studying and repeating a Torah statement with great gusto and strong love. He read and repeated the matter, three times, twenty–five times, and up to a hundred times, until one could not count. Reb Ber stood in awe and wonder, and said in his head: "Torah, Torah,

[Page 41]

how strong is your love in the heart of Reb Zalman. Fire is consuming you." Then he grasped Rabbi Zalmele's hand and asked him: "Tell me, how many times have you reviewed your studies?" He responded: "250 times." He asked him: "Did the sages not say, ' a person who studies his chapter 100 times is not the same as a person who studied his chapter 101 times.' And this is the highest point that the sages set regarding study and review. Rabbi Zalmele responded, stating that the measure mentioned by the sages is with respect to memory alone. However, to develop a love of Torah there is no measure to study. If one has time, one would review a single Torah issue for an entire year, for it is pleasant at all times.

He would wear gloves when he went to sleep so his hands would not touch his body while he was asleep. That way, he would be able to study immediately upon arising, without having to wash his hands. That was the extent to which Rabbi Zalmele was careful his time, so as to not lose even one minute of his life without Torah.

Rabbi Zalmele knew the preciousness of the supernal Torah, which was dearer to him than any of the pleasures of the earth. His soul was clear of all vain thoughts. Therefore, he did not forget anything that he learned, for the words of Torah were guarded and protected in his heart, in the way that people guard and protect things that their honor and lives depend upon. No natural affliction would keep him from occupying himself with Torah. He expounded the verse "'Let us go in throngs [בְּרָגֶשׁ *beragesh*] to the house of the L–rd'.[i]. בְּרָגֶשׁ [beraghesh] is the acronym for *barad* [hail], *ruach*[wind], *geshem* [rain], *sheleg* [snow]. "

Rabbi Chaim of Volozhin relates: Once, Rabbi Zalmele woke his assistant up from his sleep to study the regular lesson with him. He noticed that he was acting lazy. He began to reprove him and said: "It seems to me that you are lying on your bed on a rainy, dark night, and someone comes to you and informs you that a pouch full of money is lying on the road. Would you not immediately get over your laziness and run like a deer without sensing the stones and other obstacles on the way. All of this effort is for something that is nothing other than toil and wind. A person will not take it along when they die, and it will not glorify his memory. How much more so must a person run like a deer to study Torah, for its merchandise is greater than fine gold, and all the objects in the world cannot be equal to it. Someone occupying himself with Torah finds life in this world, and his righteousness goes before him in the World To Come.

These are the books that Rabbi Zalmele knew by heart at the age of 24: the Bible with its Targum translations, the Babylonian and Jerusalem Talmud, Tosefta, Mechilta, books of Midrash, and collections of Zohar and mystical rectifications, the books of Maimonides and his predecessors. All of these things were etched upon his heart, and fluent upon his mouth, as the *shekakol*[ii] blessing is known by all Jews.

Despite his great expertise, Rabbi Zalmele complained that the sources of knowledge were sealed before him. If he compares that which he knows with that which he does not know – it would be clear to him that he knows nothing. His brother, Rabbi Chaim, relates that Rabbi Zalmele would often groan and complain bitterly in a vexed spirit. Rabbi Chaim asked him: "Why are you groaning, my brother?" He responded, "Oh my brother! Would it be that it would be like previous months, during my youth, with the company of G–d upon me in my tent – when I was one day less than 39 months old. That day, all the wellsprings of deep knowledge and the portals of heavenly attainment opened up for me, and bountiful influence streamed to me, flooding me and passing over my soul with strength. Several

[Page 42]

items of knowledge and Torah attainments that I had been trying to achieve for many days, but could not, that remained like closed riddles to me, for I could not solve them through logic – at that time became revealed to me in all their mystique. I have no words to describe the great, wonderful achievements that came to me at that time. However, when I turned with extra love to understand the essence of my achievement – Woe! – it was no more, for G–d had taken it from me."

Rabbi Zalmele desired spiritual completeness all his life. At every moment, he made efforts to strengthen the powers of his soul. His level of expertise astonished people and reached superhuman proportions. Nevertheless, he was very modest, to the point that he considered himself to be a person devoid of Torah and wisdom. When he heard that those who loved him honored and praised him – it seemed to him as if fire and brimstone were streaming toward him. Everything that he learned and did was not for the purpose of imaginary honor, but rather for the honor of the G–dly soul in his nostrils. However, he did not suffice himself merely with the study of Torah, but he also worked to disseminate Torah in public, and to perform charitable and benevolent deeds. Study and knowledge alone do not bring a person to the level of a *Tzadik*. It is rather charitable deeds that do so. He interpreted the verse: "For man was born for toil [לעמל]" (Job 5:7) as an acronym: Study in order to do.

Rabbi Zalmele was very particular about reading the Bible. He said that it is our duty to know the grammar of the Hebrew language, for through it we can attain full understanding of the Bible. When he would hear some Bible teacher interchanging a word or a vowel, he would immediately point it out to him. Once, a person read a verse in the Torah and made an error in the verse "and I will lie [ושכבתי] with my fathers" (Genesis 47:30), and instead of "and I will lie" he read "and I will sleep [וישנתי] with my fathers." Rabbi Zalmele said that this exchange of words was not a simple error, but rather a contradiction of a major principle of the Jewish religion – the resurrection of the dead. Referring to death as "lying" is a hint to the resurrection of the dead, for a person who is lying will generally rise, other than those who were cursed, and about whom is stated "They lie and will never rise again" (Psalms 41:9). The word "with my fathers" is a great proof, deeper than all proofs in the world, regarding the survival of the soul. It proves that the fathers are alive and in existence in the eternal world, and did not disappear as flying dust. Through this, our faith is different than the faith of the idol worships, for Alexander of Macedon asked one of the philosophers: "Who are more numerous – the living of the dead?" The philosopher responded: "The living, for the dead are no longer in existence. Our faith states that even the dead are alive and in existence, and this is the interpretation of "and I will lie with my fathers."

One of the wealthy men of Vilna, Reb Yechiel Michel Pasils, set his eye upon Rabbi Zalmele and took him for a groom for his daughter. A great change in Rabbi Zalmele's life took place in Vilna: there he became friendly with the G'ra [Vilna Gaon]. When Rabbi Zalmele came before the G'ra, the Gaon was very impressed by the depth of knowledge of this young person, and called out in astonishment: "Wonder of wonders!" At that time, they became connected to each other, and it was not long before that Rabbi Zalmele was considered as a unique person among the students of the G'ra, who called him "My Rabbi Shlomo Zalman."

We can judge the relationship between the G'ra and Rabbi Zalmele from the following story: One day Rabbi

[Page 43]

Zalmele was sitting with the G'ra, studying together until late at night. Suddenly Rabbi Zalmele dozed off and fell asleep, with his head about to fall off the table. The G'ra stopped his studying and placed one had under Rabbi Zalmele's head so it would not move. One of those close to the G'ra, who entered the room at that time and witnessed the scene, wanted to help the G'ra and remove his hand. The G'ra silenced him and whispered, "Quiet! The entire Torah is now resting on the palm of my hand!"

It was told regarding Rabbi Zalmele that once, he traveled by wagon from Vilna to his native city of Volozhin. It was during the month of Shvat. Rabbi Zalmele fell off the winter wagon due to the trotting of the horses, and the wagon driver continued on without noticing. When he later saw that Rabbi Zalmele had fallen off the wagon, he returned and found him sitting, studying with a book in his hands. He did not sense his fall or the cold outside due to his enthusiasm in his learning.

He did not even feel pain when he was occupied with Torah. Once, two scholars were sitting and studying the *Tur* with the *Beis Yosef* commentary. Rabbi Zalmele was with them in the house. They presented their questions to him. Rabbi Zalmele paced to and fro, as was his manner. As he was walking, a nail injured his foot, and blood flowed, but he did not know what had happened. He continued on and recited the sections of *Tur* and the *Beis Yosef* related to the resolution of the questions. He recited an entire page by heart with love and great joy, as if nothing had happened to him. Had they not interrupted his studies when they saw that he was loosing a lot of blood, who knows for how long he would have floated in the world of Torah without stopping.

Once, he was sitting in the *Beis Midrash* of Volozhin, and his clothes caught fire. The fire also touched his body, but he did not feel it at all, since he was engrossed in his studies with great enthusiasm, and he did not feel the pain of his body. Even though he was always immersed in the upper worlds, if he was asked to perform a mitzva, he would not hesitate for even one moment. He would immediately descend from the sublime world to the practical world. He would run to bring joy to a bride and groom, or to perform a kind act for anyone in need. The rabbinic adage was always upon his lips – that the Holy One Blessed Be He was the groomsman for the first man – and from this we learn that it is proper for a great person to be a groomsman to a younger man.

Once, Rabbi Chaim invited his brother Rabbi Zalmele to a wedding celebration. All those gathered at the wedding went to greet Rabbi Zalmele. Rabbi Chaim wanted to make his brother happy, so he brought musical instruments to play before him. However, Rabbi Zalmele sat with his lips constantly uttering words of Torah, as was his way. After a short time, the Gaon Rabbi Chaim entered the room. Rabbi Zalmele asked him: "Did you not say that you would send musical instruments to play before me – why did you not send them?"

Once, after midnight, Rabbi Zalmele was sitting in the *Beis Midrash* in Shniposhik, and he needed a book that was hard to find, that dealt with that issue. He was anxious to look into the book. He knew that the book was located in the library of the *Beis Midrash* in Vilna. He put on his coat, and set out in the darkness of night. He went alone on the route, which was full of snow and ice, to go to the place he wanted. He arrived in Vilna in the morning, and immediately immersed himself in Vilna without resting at all.

We have with us the deep Torah doctrine of Rabbi Zalmele regarding the education of a person. His opinion was that

[Page 44]

one must educate a person immediately after birth. The great sins that a person transgresses as he gets older – are rooted from the outset, from his first day of life. Rabbi Zalmele said that the power of the beginning, and the root of all matter, when one is young, is very deep in essence. Therefore, errors that come at the outset are very great, for they develop and burst forth upward and upward.

The greats of the generation said that Rabbi Zalmele is second to the G'ra, and when the G'ra would be requisitioned to the heavenly court [i.e. when he passes away], he would take his place. However, this was not decreed from Heaven, and the generation did not merit this, for Rabbi Zalmele was taken back by G–d when he was 32 years old, ten years before the passing of the G'ra.

Immediately after becoming ill, Rabbi Zalmele sensed that his end was very near. This became clear to those close to him due to his frequent review of various statements regarding the day of death and passing away from the world. As he doubled over in his suffering, all of Vilna and Volozhin were in uproar, not wanting to believe that the time of his passing has arrived. Even though Rabbi Zalmele felt the footsteps of death approaching, the Book of Psalms did not depart from his hand, and he did not stop reading it with a sweet voice and silent enthusiasm even for a single moment, as if death was coming at that moment.

One of the rabbis who sat near his bed advised him to rest a bit from his reading. Rabbi Zalmele responded, "'This is the Torah of a man who dies in the tent'[liii]. Rabbi Yochanan said: A person should not keep away from the house of study and from words of Torah even at the time of death. (Tractate Shabbat 83b). Who knows if I too have reached this point as well?"

All those next to him wept secretly when they saw the crown of his head fall. The greats of Vilna who knew that such terrible news was liable to have a bad effect on the G'ra sought to hide from him the news of the passing of Rabbi Zalmele to the extent possible. However, when the G'ra complained about this when he found out.

The eulogizers from all corners of the land lamented and eulogized Rabbi Zalmele, saying:

You were born of a woman, but how similar you were to the sons of G–d [i.e. the angels]

When you were with us in the land, you were like the son of Amram [i.e. Moses] in heaven.

There is none like you, you are similar to an angel,

And you are like one of the ancient ones.

Rabbi Zalmele died on 9 Adar II, 5548 (1788). He is buried beside the G'ra and his father Rabbi Yitzchak[32].

[Page 45]

The corner of the G'ra in the Vilna cemetery

On the right–the grave of Rabbi Zalmele
On the left – the grave of rabbi Yitzchak – the father of Rabbi Zalmele and Rabbi Chaim of Volozhin
In the middle – the grave of the G'ra (from the collection of Dr. Yitzchak Rivkind of blessed memory)

Translator's Footnotes:

    i.   Psalms 54:15.
    ii.   A blessing made on many types of foods.
    iii.   Numbers 19:14.

[Page 46]

The Rabbinical Judge Rabbi Shimshon Rodenski

Translated by Jerrold Landau and donated by Anita Frishman Gabbay

Rabbi Shimshon served as the Rabbinical Judge in Volozhin during the period of the tenure of Rabbi Itzele, the son of Rabbi Chaim of Volozhin, as the head of the Etz Chaim Yeshiva. This position was given to him at the command of Rabbi Itzele. He served as the rabbinical judge in Volozhin for approximately ten years. Then, he was accepted as the rabbi of the city of Trab [Traby], Oshmiana District, where he served for approximately ten years. After the death of Rabbi Itzele in the year 5609 (1849), he was asked by his son–in–law Rabbi Eliezer Yitzchak Fried to return to his native city and serve as the head of the rabbinical court. Rabbi Shimshon knew that one does not refuse a great person. He returned to Volozhin, and served as the head of the rabbinical court of Volozhin for approximately 15 years, until the day of his death in the year 5626 (1866).

Rabbi Shimshon was known for his generous traits. The spirit of the Jews of Volozhin rested upon him, and they benefited from his advice and resourcefulness. Everyone revered him due to his deep fear of sin. He toiled greatly in Torah already from his youth. Even though he was sickly through all his days, he would toil in Torah day and night with his remaining strength. His modesty grew along with his diligence. He did not boast of his wisdom, did not seek greatness for himself, and did not covet honor, "for he was created for this."[i]

Rabbi Shimshon had a great character trait, in that he was very stringent with himself. Even if something was clear to him in all its depth, he would continue to study and research the topic until he found a reason for doubt, why it is thus and not something else. Before he was appointed as a judge, he would investigate, search and research the books of the early and great commentators. He would even ask the advice of lesser people, for even in their words, there is the trait of "making your teacher wiser"[iii]. He did all this so he would not err or stumble, heaven forbid. He would push off the verdict to the following day in case he find any cause for merit in the guilty party. This stringency had an additional aim: Rabbi Shimshon wanted to serve as an example to his students, for them to learn every matter in depth as he did, so their hearts will not be presumptuous in issuing decisions, so that they not explain Torah in ways that are not according to the *halacha*, and so that they issue true judgments.

When Rabbi Shimshon was informed that a certain case would be brought to him the following day, he would remain awake all night, studying the *halacha* books, checking and examining them. He did not let slumber pass over his eyes until he had clarified the matter sufficiently.

Rabbi Shimshon lived a life of difficulty and want, and he observed the Torah in poverty. Despite his bodily weakness, he tended to his four children and provided all their needs. His illness became more severe in his older age, to the point that the Jews of Volozhin would ask themselves every morning: "How is Rabbi Shimshon the Judge?" Despite all this, his deep toil in Torah and in educating his children never ceased.

Rabbi Shimshon studied Torah for its own sake. The commentary of Rabbi Chaim of Volozhin regarding the Mishnaic statement "love the work, but hate the position of domination"[liii] – love the job of the rabbinate, that is the essence of toiling in Torah, the satisfaction that comes with it, without concerning oneself with the result that it brings. Even though Rabbi Shimshon did not escape this "transgression," utilized the "crown"[liv], and served as a rabbi and rabbinical judge throughout his life – he only did this unwillingly, as if forced, so that

[Page 47]

he would be able to succeed in sustaining his household. However, in truth, he only loved the deep study itself, the cleaving to the truth of the important, eternal matters that have their source in the Torah.

The words of the sages were always before his eyes: "A Sanhedrin that executes the death penalty once in seven years is called a murderous court (Tractate *Makkot*, Mishna 10). This is true regarding a judge as well, who would be called a perpetrator of injury were he to render the accused guilty, even on rare occasions. Therefore, after he would issue a guilty verdict against the accused, he would not be able to sleep, lest he was overly stringent and there might have been room for leniency. Once, the litigants came before him, and he issued a guilty verdict against the guilty party. Several years later, a convention of Torah greats convened in Volozhin. Rabbi Shimshon summoned the litigant who was found guilty, and asked him to present his case to this convention of rabbis, for perhaps they would find him innocent. He wanted the case to be adjudicated truthfully, and he was not concerned lest the rabbis issue a different verdict, and his honor would therefore be impinged.

In his great modesty, Rabbi Shimshon refused to publish his Torah novellae in a book. He would write them himself, so that he would not forget the reasoning of a verdict, and so that he could later look into it. It was his custom that after issuing a verdict, he would review, study, and delve into the matter again to ensure that he had not erred, and to make sure that he had indeed delved deeply into the matter. He had another reason: to make the investigation easier if a similar case were to come before him in the future. He wrote most of his Torah novellae for these two reasons.

In his old age, many of those who knew and revered him urged him to publish his novellae. He indeed began to organize the material and prepare it for publication, but his bodily weakness overtook him, and prevented him from carrying this out – even though his Torah stood with him until his final day and issued a verdict on an issue regarding a lung[v] an hour before his death.

His eldest son Yehuda–Leib published his book *Zichron Shimshon* in the year 5539 (1879). The Netzi'v write the following in the introduction:

"I remember days of yore, when I was involved in the group of the rabbi, the great luminary, our teacher Shimshon of blessed memory, the head of the rabbinical port here in the community of Volozhin. He would delve deeply into words of Torah and raise precious pearls. He also inscribed the book to be a memorial for him."

The rabbinical judge Shimshon Rodenski was the son–in–law of the Volozhin Starosta Yosef–Yozel Perski. We learn this from the introduction of Rabbi Chaim Shimshon of Rakowice to his book *Imrei Chaim* (Keidiani, 5699 – 1938):

"I hereby extend a blessing to my dear father, the rabbi and Gaon Rabbi Zalman Tovia, may he live long, the son of the splendid scholar and honored research, famous throughout the land, Rabbi Moshe Markowicz of blessed memory, the author of *Shem Hagedolim Hashelisi* [The Third Names of Great Ones] and the book *Lekorot Arei Yisrael Verabaneihu* [The Annals of the Cities of Israel and their Rabbis], and to my dear mother, the Rebbetzin Itel may she live,

[Page 48]

the daughter of the honorable, splendid rabbi, Rabbi Yosef–Yozel Perski of blessed memory, an elder of the community of Volozhin, the son–in–law of the righteous Gaon, Rabbi Shimshon Rodenski of blessed memory, head of the rabbinical court of the holy community of Volozhin, the author of the book *Zichron Shimshon*."

Rabbi Shimshon died on 5 Shvat, 5626 (1866).

Translator's Footnotes:

i.   Pirkei Avot 2:8
ii. Pirkei Avot 6:6
iii. Pirkei Avot 1:10
iv. Pirkei Avot 1:14 – referring to making use of the "crown" of Torah learning for self–benefit.
v.   Regarding the types of blemishes on a lung that would render a slaughtered animal non–kosher.

Rabbi Aharon Bunimowitz the son of Rabbi Yitzchak, and the Great Storm in the Community of Volozhin

Translated by Jerrold Landau and donated by Anita Frishman Gabbay

The Gaon Rabbi Aharon Bunimowitz was numbered among the *Gaonim* and Torah giants of Volozhin. He was one of the veteran students of Rabbi Chaim of Volozhin, and one of the head rabbinical judges of Volozhin. He served as the scribe of Rabbi Chaim's rabbinical court. He was also involved in secular affairs over and above his holy service, for he served as the head of the community of Volozhin for many years.

During his time, an event took place in Volozhin that caused a storm among the Jews of the city, the echoes of which spread afar. After the death of the Gaon Rabbi Chaim of Volozhin, a question was brought before his son Rabbi Itzele regarding an adhesion [*sircha*] on the lung with a wound on the [thoracic] wall[i]. The lung has five lobes. If the lobes were compared to each other, this would be an adhesion and a sign of an injury to the lung. Rabbi Chaim was no stringent in matters such as this, relying on his great rabbi, the *Shaagas Aryeh*, who adjucaated the case permissively in accordance with the *Beis Yosef*, and established this as the practical *halachic* guideline in Volozhin. However, Rabbi Itzele did not accept the *halachic* decision of his father the Gaon in this matter. He did not want to permit or to forbid[ii].

The rabbinical judges of Volozhin gathered together and decided to ask the Torah greats of Vilna. They asked Rabbi Aharon to write the letter. This letter is a first–class historical document, for it surveys the cultural and economic situation of the community of Volozhin in the first half of the 19th century.

The following is the content of the letter:

"Cedars of Lebanon, mighty ones of Torah, protective shields (a flowery nickname for those who know how to defend their opinions and win debates), from whom Torah goes forth. They are the renowned, famous ones, sharp and expert, whom people are used to, intelligent and wise, fearing of Heaven and wholesome, pious, sublime holy ones, filling in the breaches, *Gaonim* of the land – they are the rabbis and teachers of righteousness of the holy community of Vilna, may G–d protect it, and its sages, may they live. The splendor of their light shall shine like the morning light. Each one of them excels with their sharpness.

"We must weep because the honor has been removed from us, and our joy has been exiled (this refers to the death of Rabbi Chaim of Volozhin), fairest of brides[iii] and splendor of the entire earth, from whom emanated the emanations of life, the wellspring of living waters. He would respond appropriately and clearly to anyone who asked a pointed question. Now, when our honor has been removed and the crown of our heads has fallen – who will give us the waters of Torah to drink, teach us the clear *halacha*. To which holy one shall we turn.

[Page 49]

if not to the honor of the name of our holy, glorious ones, who are the splendor of our times, the heads of the Diaspora, who will show us the path, the path of Torah, upon which we should walk, and the action we should take with regard to the adhesion with a wound on the chest wall, about which the elder here in our community, the great tamarisk, the late Gaon, author of *Shaagas Aryeh* of blessed memory has already rendered a decision when he served as the head of the rabbinical court here in our community. Regarding this, throughout the Jewish Diaspora they conduct themselves in accordance with the decision of the Rema (Rabbi Moshe Isserles), and the aforementioned elder Gaon issued a directive and decided the *halacha* in our community that it be permitted without any need at all to examine the lung. Later, when the High Priest, Rabbi Refael of blessed memory, the author of the book *Torat Yekutiel* served as head of the rabbinical court of our district, he also decided in accordance with the decision of the Rema of blessed memory. The Gaon and author of the *Shaagas Aryeh* of blessed memory served once again in our community, and it seemed as a laughing matter to him that he was asked this question once again. His response was that he had already issued a directive to permit this. He responded as follows with his sharp language: "Kosher! Kosher!" Our community has conducted itself in accordance with his aforementioned responsa for approximately 70 years now, that is even before the tenure of the late rabbi, the Gaon Rabbi Chaim of blessed memory. Throughout the life of the *Admor*[iv] the custom here was in accordance with the directive of the elder author of the *Shaagas Aryeh*, for he himself had heard the permissive decision from him.

"However, the heart of the *Admor* of blessed memory did not see fit to permit this in other places. Toward the end of his life, he would say to the shochtim of our community that he would command his children to no longer follow this permissive decision. He also told his renowned, honorable son, Rabbi Yitzchak, may his light shine, the head of the rabbinical court of our community that he intended to give him a directive on this matter. However, when G–d took him away suddenly, no directive was issued on this matter.

"We remain as a post atop the mountain now, in that his son who took his place, Rabbi Yitzchak, may his light shine, the head of the rabbinical court of our community, does not want to issue a decision on this subject one way or another. We have seen that, in the opinion of the rabbi of our community, this is because under no circumstances does he want to do anything against the will of his late father, may the memory of the holy be blessed, for he trained him to conduct himself with honor toward him all the days of his life. So we, what can we answer regarding this?

"Now, the entire city is perplexed, and the outcry is great. Because it is common (i.e. such a *sircha* is a common occurrence), and the loss would be great[v], we place our hope in the honor of your Torah knowledge. You will guide us on the path that we shall follow, and the actions we shall take in such a case – to determine the *halacha* clearly, and so we will not

[Page 50]

mislead in this issue, and so we can remove the complaints of the members of our community from the head of the rabbinical court and from us, for it is hard for the members of the community to change course in a *halachic* matter that has been established in a permissible manner here in our community for generations, in accordance with significant *Gaonim* from whose waters we drink. May we merit to cleave to the dust of their feet, and we await their lofty response to be sent through our representative who will give over this letter. We have sent a special representative to the honor of your Torah.

"Awaiting your response, we, who sit in judgment here in our community, we sign, with the participation of those that frequent the *Beis Midrash* of our community, on 23 Kislev 5582 (1822), here in the holy community of Volozhin, may its Rock and Redeemer protect it.

"Signed: Aharon the son of my father, my master Rabbi Yitzchak, may his memory be blessed for life in the World To Come

Asher the son of my father, my master Rabbi Kalonymus Kalman, may his memory be blessed for life in the World To Come

Yechiel Michel the son of my father, my master Rabbi Dov–Ber of blessed memory

Avraham Simcha the son of Rabbi Nachman, may his memory be blessed for Life in the World To Come

Menachem Nachum the son of our late rabbi Avraham Avli, of holy seed

Moshe the son of Rabbi Nisan

Meir the son of Rabbi Chaim Katz, may his memory be blessed for life in the World To Come

Naftali the son of my father, my master the elderly Rabbi Aryeh Leib, may his light shine

Tzvi Hirsch the son of Rabbi Mordechai of blessed memory"[33]

We do not know the response of the rabbis of Vilna regarding this matter: However, since this lenient practice was the custom in Volozhin throughout all the days – we can assume that a permissive directive was issued from Vilna. We can almost say that they relied on the fact that the Gaon Rabbi Chaim did not issue a command regarding this.

After his first wife died in Volozhin, Rabbi Aharon left for Vilna, where he was appointed as a rabbinical judge. His approbation on the Vilna and Horodno edition of the Talmud from the year 5595 (1835) as well as the Slavuta edition of the Talmud can be found among the approbations of the greats of the generation. His approbation is also printed in the book *Poel Tzedek* (Vilna 5597 – 1837) and in other books.

He lived in Vilna for approximately ten years, and died there on Adar 15, 5698 (1830). He left an only son, a scribe named Reb Hirsch Volozhiner[34].

Translator's Footnotes:

i.   Various internal injuries render an otherwise kosher animal non–kosher. A puncture in the lung is one such injury. Therefore, the lungs are inflated after slaughter to ensure that there is no puncture. Questions arise with various surface lesions or adhesions on the lung (known *halachic*ally as *sircha*). Some are considered to render an animal non–kosher, and others are not. The *halacha* becomes very complex in such cases. An animal with a completely smooth lung (no *sircha* at all) is called *glatt* (literally smooth) kosher. The question dealt with in this chapter is whether an injury to the thoracic wall of an animal is liable to cause damage to the lung, thereby rendering the animal non–kosher, and whether such an injury makes it necessary to check the lungs with extra care.

ii.   i.e. he was neutral on the subject.

iii. A euphemism for the Holy Temple, taken from the *Hoshanot* service of the second day of Sukkot. Here it is used as a nickname for glory.

iv.   This is usually an honorific for a Hassidic leader, but here is used for Rabbi Chaim.

v.   Determining an animal to be non–kosher due to such adhesions causes a loss of money, as the carcass would then be sold to a gentile butcher for a low price.

[Page 51]

The Scholars and Geniuses of Volozhin

Translated by Jerrold Landau and donated by Anita Frishman Gabbay

Rabbi Dov Aryeh Persky the son of Zelig Pinchas Persky was numbered among the learned people of Volozhin. He was descended from Rabbi Chaim of Volozhin. He earned his fame from the commentary that he published on *Keter Torah* of Rabbi David Vital. This demonstrated his greatness in Torah. Rabbi David Vital lived in Toledo, Spain during the 15th century. His work, *Keter Torah*, is a prose discourse on the 613 commandments of the Torah, along with the seven rabbinical commandments that are not mentioned in the Torah (such as the kindling of Sabbath and Chanuka lights, the reading of the Megilla, immersion[ii], and *eruv*), which all together number 620, which is numerogically equivalent with the word *keter* [כתר][iii]. The commentary of Rabbi Dov Aryeh Persky, published in Vilna in the year 5631 (1871) and 5640(1880), explains the details of the main principals and the reasoning of each commandment.

In his preface to the comment, the Netzi'v is effusive in praise of the author and his activities:

"The eminent rabbi, our teacher Rabbi Dov Aryeh may he live, from our community of Volozhin, a scion of the family of my grandfather–in–law the Gaon, the noble one of the shepherds, Rabbi Chaim, may the memory of the holy be blessed, the author of the holy book Nefesh HaChaim, has found it his place to define and broaden the thoughts of the Gaon Rabbi David Vital, may the memory of the holy be blessed, to publish crowns over the letters of the ten commandments, and to place beneath them all 613 commandments with innuendoes in explanatory rhetoric…

"This author has added splendor to the matter by treating the letters of the ten commandments as headings. This will encourage people to review them every week, so that the rhetoric can be illuminated. He went further than this by anthologizing all the sources in the work of Rabbi David Vital of blessed memory. The lads, who have the strength to do so, will be able to draw from them. It is appropriate to recognize this activity with a pleasant countenance."

Rabbi Yoel Dov–Ber HaKohen

He was born in Volozhin in the year 5585 (1825). He was the son of Rabbi Meir HaKohen, emissary of the Etz Chaim Yeshiva of Volozhin, descended from the Gaon, author of the Shel'a[liii]. He was the friend and confidant of Rabbi Yose Ber Soloveitchik, who served as the deputy to the Rosh yeshiva of Volozhin. He was a full treasury

[Page 52]

of wisdom and deep knowledge in Torah literature. He also knew many languages, and had the nickname "Telemach" because he translated Fénelon's "Telemachus" into Hebrew during his youth.[35].

His expertise in Talmud, rabbinical lore [*Agada*] and Midrash was very great. He knew how to explain statements of the sages in simple languages, thereby providing insights into Torah. He was also graced with oratory talent, and many Jews of Volozhin came to hear him and to enjoy the clarity and pleasantness of his words.

While still young, he published a commentary of the Passover Haggadah, called *Neveh Tehilla*, in Vilna in the year 5606 (1846). Aside from this he composed a commentary on the *Yalkut Shimoni* on the Book of *Bereishit* [Genesis], and the book *Batei Kehuna*, which is a commentary on the *Midrash Rabba* of *Bereishit* and *Shemot* [Exodus]. The sages of Vilna praised this book greatly. The greats of the generation nicknamed the author "the Great Rabbi, Fortress and Tower."

Many manuscripts on lofty and sublime matters, which were not published, remained in his legacy. He lived a life of poverty and suffering throughout all his days, but he never complained about his difficulties, for he found comfort in his life of fruitful creativity. He did not live a long life. He died in the ear 5641 (1881) at the age of 56 ("His days ended" [כלו] – the numerology of כלו is 56).

The Genius Zalman Minkowski

The 19th century, which was the most fruitful in the annals of creativity and Torah study in Volozhin, put forth a lad who was a genius, who in addition to is great knowledge in Torah, also acquired expertise in secular subjects, languages, and science. This lad, Zalman Minkowski, astounded the Netzi'v, who said of him that there are very few like him in his generation. We only have one piece of writing regarding this wonder child, published in *Hamelitz* on 22 Iyar 5630 (1870), as follows:

"An outcry of brokenness and weeping was aroused in our city (Minsk) at the news from Volozhin of the death of the rabbi, the great luminary, young in years but great in wisdom, a scion of a high–level family in Volozhin, Rabbi Zalman the son of the honorable Rabbi Moshe Shalom Minkowski.

"This flower was cut off while still in bloom, at the age of 23. The deceased dedicated all the days of his life on the altar of Torah and wisdom. Even to the extent that he gave himself over to the study of Torah with all his energy, he did not neglect the sciences, for which he had a great desire. He loved our holy language strongly, and he knew other languages

[Page 53]

well. He also earned a great name in grammar and logic. He chose to learn the Russian language, and was able to translate it. He delved deeply into arithmetic and geometry, broadening his knowledge without the help of a teacher. The rabbi and Gaon Rabbi Tzvi Yehuda, a Yeshiva head in Volozhin, lamented and sighed over his death, and said of him that he was one of the remnants, the likes of whom can be found only very rarely in our days."

The *Mashgiach* Rabbi Shlomo David Dinkin

Rabbi Shlomo David Dinkin was one of the great scholars of Volozhin. His expertise in Talmud, rabbinical decisors, and the responsa of the early sages was wondrous. He occupied the rabbinical seat of the city of Propojsk (Mohilev district) for two years. When the Netzi'v heard of this excellent man, he brought him to Volozhin, and appointed him as *Mashgiach* [spiritual guide] of the Yeshiva. He filled this role faithfully for twelve years. During that time, when the Netzi'v was away from Volozhin, he would teach the class to the Yeshiva students.

When the Yeshiva was closed and the Netzi'v left Volozhin, the community of Volozhin chose Rabbi Shlomo David as the chief rabbi of he city. He served in that position for six and a half years. He taught Torah publicly throughout that entire period, through his Gemara classes, given daily to the scholars of the city. He was very diligent to his learning, and his mouth never stopped uttering his studies until his final day. Aside from his greatness in Torah, he had generous character traits. He got along with his fellow, and greeted every person pleasantly. People who suffered difficulties and ill luck would pour their tears out to him. He knew how to gladden sad, oppressed hearts with his good heart. He was greatly loved by the Jews of Volozhin due to his great love for all people. Everyone loved him greatly.

Rabbi Dinkin died on the first day of Rosh Chodesh Tammuz [30 Sivan] 5658 [1898] at the age of 64. All the residents of Volozhin wept and mourned for their beloved, revered rabbi.

Rabbi Eliahu the son of Rabbi Shlomo Zalman Neuwedel, a great–grandson of Rabbi Zalmele

He was a great–grandson of Rabbi Zalmele. His character arouses special interest. Torah and general knowledge were blended together with him. Rabbi Zalmele left behind a seven–year–old orphan daughter who grew up in the house of her uncle, Rabbi Chaim of Volozhin. When she came of age, Rabbi Chaim married her off to Rabbi Moshe Yehoshua Rabinowicz, who presented classes on the *Code of Jewish Law* and *Yoreh Deah* in Volozhin.

Rabbi Eliahu Neuwedel was the grandson of Rabbi Moshe Yehoshua, born to his father Rabbi Shlomo Zalman in the year 5581 (1821) in the city of Neustat (Kovno district).

While still a lad, his father brought him to Volozhin to hear Torah from Rabbi Eliezer Yitzchak Fried, the son–in–law of Rabbi Itzele. The student excelled with his straight intellect and deep diligence. His teachers predicted a bright future in the world of Torah for him. However, while still in the Etz Chaim Yeshiva of Volozhin, he was taken

[Page 54]

by the *Haskalah*. His desire for *Haskalah* brought him to the city of Raseiniai, where he became friendly with young *Maskilim* who later became well–known. One of them was Shneur Zaks. Through them, he mastered Hebrew, German, and French. His difficult straits led him to Warsaw, where he earned his livelihood through private teaching. When he noticed that Hebrew education was suffering from a lack of useful books, he wrote the book "A Guide to the Hebrew Language," based on the theory of Ulendorf. This book was published in 1873. Later, he published the book "Father to Children" to guide the students in good traits and manners.

Rabbi Neuwedel was one of the remnants of the "House of the Rabbi" of Volozhin, who blended Torah with secular knowledge, with neither contradicting the other. His children followed in the path of their father, and attained great achievements in science and education. One of his daughters became well–known as a physician. Another graduated from the faculty of education in Peterburg.

He was run over by a horse in the month of Elul 5646 [1886] while walking on the street. He died on Thursday, 16 Elul 5646 after great suffering, at the age of 65. He is buried in the cemetery of Warsaw[36].

Translator's Footnotes:

i.   Immersion in a *mikva* is indeed a Torah commandment. I believe that the author intended the commandment of washing the hands upon arising in the morning and before eating, which is considered to be one of the seven rabbinical commandments.
ii. Keter means crown.
iii. See https://en.wikipedia.org/wiki/Isaiah_Horowitz

Reb Chaim's Contribution to Establish a Settlement of *Misnagdim* in the Land of Israel[i]

Translated by Jerrold Landau, based on an early translation by M. Porat z"l and edited by Judy Feinsilver Montel

Just as Rabbi Chaim of Volozhin planted the love of Torah in the hearts of the Jews of the city, so did he draw them near to the love of the Land of Israel. The connection to the Land of Israel was a great principle in his teachingsl[37]. Rabbi Chaim believed that he would yet merit to see the coming of the Messiah during his lifetime. The first Zionist orator during the era of the Return to Zion, Rabbi Natan Friedlandl[ii], tells in one of his orations about a teacher who had studied in the Volozhin Yeshiva in his youth, and who testified that he had heard from Rabbi Chaim that he was waiting every day for the Rebbetzin to knock on the door of his room, interrupting his studies with the news that the Messiah has arrivedl[38].

The connection between Volozhin and the Land of Israel was mutual, and emissaries from the Land visited several times to obtain help and support for the Jews of Jerusalem, whose situation was very difficult, and who were not able to sustain themselves without annual support and donations from Jews of the Diaspora. Two emissaries from Jerusalem visited Volozhin between the years 1781–1788 (5542–5544)[iii] – Avraham HaKohen of Lask[iv] and Rabbi Hillel Mizrachi. The former was an Ashkenazi who made *aliya* to

Jerusalem from Poland, and the latter was Sephardic. They organized an annual collection of set donations, and appointed special trustees for this purpose. The donation was not

[Page 55]

a one–time event. Despite the poverty, the community of Volozhin fulfilled its commitment and provided support for the Jews of Jerusalem in an honorable fashion[39].

Rabbi Chaim of Volozhin filled a leading role in the establishment of a settlement of *Misnagdim* in the Land of Israel. Thirty–one years after the *aliya* of a large contingent of Hassidim of the Baal Shem Tov in the year 5537 (1777), their opponents, students of the Gr'a, followed suit and made *aliya* to the Land of Israel. Their aim was to set up a Judaic center in the spirit of their rabbi. The referred to themselves as *Perushim*[v] (in contrast to Hassidim). The first contingent of students of the Gr'a, headed by Rabbi Menachem Mendel of Shklov, the son of Rabbi Baruch of Shklov, made *aliya* in the year 5568 (1808), and first settled in Tiberias. In the year 5576 (1815), Rabbi Menachem Mendel moved to Jerusalem in order to expand the *Misnagdic* Jewish settlement there, which he headed.

Rabbi Menachem Mendel decided to found a center in Lithuania for the support of the *Perushim*. He sent emissaries for this purpose. He sent two emissaries to Lithuania, Reb David Tabil and Rabbi Avraham HaLevi. Rabbi Menachem Mendel knew that one must place a Gaon of renown such as Rabbi Chaim of Volozhin as head of such an organization for it to succeed. The emissaries came to Volozhin together with Rabbi Yisrael of Shklov. Rabbi Yisrael tells the following in his memoirs:

"The Merciful One brought me to the house of the Gaon, the Light of Life, the Rabbi of Volozhin. He read all the words of the heads of our Kollel, and he strengthened and adorned me with his holy writing. I brought the Gaon of Volozhin to Vilna, and we organized everything properly for the Holy Land. Several sheets of writing paper would not be sufficient to accomplish that which the Gaon of Volozhin did with his great wisdom and wonderful righteousness. We succeeded in founding a new, independent settlement."[40]

Rabbi Chaim of Volozhin emphasized the importance of founding agricultural settlements in the Land. This can be surmised from the letter of Rabbi Chaim the son of Rabbi Tovia Katz, in which the following is written among the rest: "We have already purchased lands in accordance with our close friend, the true Gaon, the famous pious one, Rabbi Chaim of Volozhin, may his light shine. We will yet succeed in purchasing lands when the opportunity comes our way, at the right place and the right time."[41]

Translator's Footnotes:

i.   The original translator of this section, M. Porat z"l, included a lengthy preface at this point, as follows (Note from translator J. Landau: I left this footnote in its original form)
Foreword to the Zionist articles series by M. Porat z"l and edited by Judy Feinsilver Montel
The Volozhin Zionist movement was born with the birth of the Volozhin congregation. Rabbi Chaim emphasized the role of agricultural settlements in Erets Israel and filled a leading part in its establishment. The Volozhin congregation of his time committed itself to support the Jerusalem Kehila permanently, and each year fulfilled the commitment (page 54).
"A society for the benefit of Holy Land settlements has been established in Volozhin, which is headed by Hanaziv the prominent Eyts Chaim Yeshiva head" This was printed in "Hamaguid" Journal on December 1886 (page 56). It happened in the middle of the 19th Century: Seven times Rabbi Avrom Chaim Marshak took his walk from Volozhin to the Holy City and seven times he returned to his hometown beaten, wounded and robbed. From his eighth journey he did not return. R' Avrom Chaim was buried on the Mount of Olives in a grave that was designated for a great Sage.(read "Reb Avrom Chaim Marshak" page 510)

Inside "Eyts Chaim" Yeshiva, at the end of the 19th century, the Zionist organizations: "Hibat Zion", "Ness Ziyona" and "Netsah Isroel" were founded. Our national poet H.N. Bialik took part in the foundation of "Netsah Isroel" (page 120).

The Zionist organizations flourished from the beginning of the 20th Century until the outbreak of WWII. Hundreds of Volozhin youngsters were involved in activities as members or sympathizers of the many Zionist movements that grew up on the soil of the friendly Shtetl.

It began with the youngsters of "Tseyirey Zion" and "Liberty and Revival" (page 393) before and during the First World War. The Zionist organizations became bigger and more important in the nineteen twenties and thirties: Branches of "Hakhaluts" (page 396) and "Hamizrakhi" (page 405), preparation sites for Aliya in "Male Berki" in Rudnik and at the sawmills inside Volozhin, Nest of "Beytar" (page 410) and Hakhshara of "Hashomer Hatsayir" (page 422).

Young men and women, many of them made Aliya, and ignoring it they saved themselves from the terrible holocaust. They took part in creating Israel and contributed their energy and power enthusiastically for this purpose. Many of them ran away from the Nazi beasts into the wood ands joined the partisans and the Red Army. Some of them survived the war and made Aliya after the victory.

But the great majority perished. They were murdered together with their parents, brothers, sisters, colleagues and friends by the Germans and their local collaborators inside Volozhin.

ii.   See https://en.wikipedia.org/wiki/Natan_Friedland
iii.   Note: the end years of this period do not correspond between the Hebrew and the secular. 5544 would correspond to 1784.
iv.   See https://en.wikipedia.org/wiki/Abraham_ben_Samuel_Cohen_of_Lask
v.   Literally "Pharisees" – those who expound the Law. This is another term for Misnagdim – opponents of Hassidism. The implication may also be of those who follow the true halachic path, as opposed to what they viewed the Hassidim to be doing.

[Page 56]

Reb Chaim's Contribution to Establish a Settlement of *Misnagdim* in the Land of Israel

Translated by Jerrold Landau, based on an early translation by M. Porat z"l and edited by Judy Feinsilver Montel

Volozhin was one of the first cities in which a Hovevei Zion organization was established[42]. Feivel (Favi) Bunimovitch represented the Odessa Committee of the "Society supporting the Jewish farmers and craftsmen in Syria and the Holy Land" in Volozhin.

As in other cities and towns, the activities of Hovevei Zion in Volozhin were primarily the collecting of donations for Jewish workers in the Land of Israel and for the Hebrew School in Jaffa. An announcement was published in *Hamelitz* on 1 Shvat, 5753 [1893], as follows: "With the marriage of Mr. Gershon the son of Reb Aharon Polak to Esther, the daughter of Rabbi Yitzchak Yaakov Bunimovitch, which took place in Volozhin on Tuesday 15 Tevet 5653 [1893], the in–laws made mention of our brethren, the workers on the mountains of Zion, above their main joy, and pledged a sum of 18 silver rubles for the benefit of the hired day workers in the Holy Land."

The Netzi'v was the father of the Hovevei Zion in Volozhin, as N. Tz. wrote to the editor of *Hamagid*:

"We have news today for the readers of *Hamagid*. A society for the benefit of Holy Land settlements has been established here in Volozhin, headed by the great Gaon, the honorable Rabbi Naftali Tzvi Yehuda Berlin (Netzi'v), may his Rock and Redeemer protect him, the head of the Etz Chaim Yeshiva… This sublime idea, coming from Hovevei Zion in Volozhin, is that much more valuable because their rabbi, known for his good name and praiseworthy, stands at the head and among its founders."[43]

The Netzi'v published a letter to the Jews of Volozhin in *Hamagid* in Kislev, 5646 [1886] to arouse them to the support of the settlement of the Land.[44] Among other things, this letter states, "The groups should make *aliya*, settle and built the Land of Israel, and plant all sorts of fruit trees there." The writer Moshe Leib Lilienblum[i] wrote about this letter to ShP'R: "It seems to me that the letter of the Gaon of Volozhin is more valuable than ten statements by various writers."[45]

The Netzi'v believed that the Land would be built through the small donations of the masses of Jewish people – for the Hovevei Zion movement is a movement of the masses. Along with the rabbis Rabbi Yitzchak Elchanan[ii] and Rabbi Shmuel Mohilever[iii], he signed a proclamation to place collection plates in the synagogues on the Eve of Yom Kippur for the settlers of the Land. The proclamation was announced in all the synagogues of Russia. The custom of placing collection plates on the Eve of Yom Kippur for the benefit of the workers of the Land of Israel took place on the Eve of Yom Kippur 5655 [1894], and spread throughout

[Page 57]

the Jewish communities of Russia. A significant sum for this purpose was already donated in the year 5655.[46]

Micha Yosef Berdyczewski[iv] writes about the great dedication of the Netzi'v to the idea of the restoration of Israel:

"In one of the Netzi'v's orations to his students, as was his custom every year, he also touched on the idea of the settlement of the Land of Israel, and aroused the hearts of his audience to support the hands of the workers of the Holy Land. His eyes filled with incessant tears on account of his great enthusiasm when speaking about this topic. His words had a great effect on the hearts of the Yeshiva students, and many who were ambivalent to this point became firm supporters of the settlement of the Land of Israel."[47]

The following story from an earwitness proves the extent of the Netzi'v's love of the Land of Israel: Rabbi Yisrael David, a native of the Land of Israel, was one of the emissaries of the Yeshiva. Once, when he returned from a journey the Netzi'v asked him about news of the Land. He inquired and asked about the lives of the Jews there. This was the time of settlement and acquiring land, the era of Rishon Letzion[v]. As the emissary responded to the questions of the Netzi'v, he began to complain about the settlers and the new arrivals, as he spoke badly about the Land. The Netzi'v interrupted him, and, with a voice suffused with anger, ordered him, "Spy, leave the house!"[vi]

The emissary became quite perplexed and asked with great contrition: "Rabbi, what is my sin and what is my iniquity? Did I not respond to your request? Everything that I said is the truth."

The Netzi'v responded, "The spies also spoke the truth. However, one must not speak bad about the Land of Israel."[48]

Toward the end of his life, the Netzi'v decided to transfer over the running of the Yeshiva to his son Rabbi Chaim, and to make *aliya* to the land of Israel. The letter of Yechiel Michel Pines[vii] from 21 Kislev 5652 [1881] testifies to this.

"The daughter of Zion is still sobbing. Woe to her for she lacks a great man, the honorable rabbi and Gaon, Rabbi Mordechai Gimpel Jaffe[viii], may the memory of the holy be blessed. And behold a heavenly voice is roaring like a dove words of comfort saying, withhold your voice from weeping[ix], for here is your king, a *Tzadik* and saviour is coming to you. He is our honorable rabbi, may he live, who has decided to make *aliya* and dwell in your courtyards. Relying on this news, I have come to recommend matters before the honor of your holy Torah. For if he chose Zion – he desires his sanctuary in one of the settlements.

"This idea came to my heart after I saw with my own eyes the honorable activity done by the honorable, late Gaon (Rabbi Mordechai Gimpel) of blessed memory when he lived in Yahud. Aside from the fact that that settlement ensured that the Sabbatical year would not be violated in any detail, it also caused many to uphold the Torah and religion in all settlements.

[Page 58]

"Immediately after the passing of the *Tzadik* we took counsel to beg Rabbi Chaim to come here, but we were ambivalent, lest Rabbi Chaim does not want to leave his holy Yeshiva. Now that the news reaches my ear that Rabbi Chaim has decided firmly to make *aliya* to the Mount of G–d, I hasten to tell him what is on my heart. That it is his obligation to choose for himself a place for his Yeshiva in one of the settlements, and perhaps he may even find Yahud appropriate, as it is a secure, quite place, a place of Torah and prayer, and a small Yeshiva of young men prominent in Torah was set up there by the Degel Torah society. It is a place of clear air and sweet water. This will also promote the rebuilding of the ruins in that area, the inhabitants of which left because of a lack of soil. Yahud became the spiritual center of the physical Moshavim. In any case, whether he chooses Yahud or some other settlement – it is for this reason that he left the Diaspora, to set up his Yeshiva in one of the settlements."[49]

It is not known why the Netzi'v did not actualize his plan. Perhaps, the great burden of debts afflicted him. First and foremost, he girded the remnant of his strength to become free of his oppressors and to pay off all his debts.

After the death of the Netzi'v, the movement was inspired to increase the donations for Keren Hatorah [the Torah Fund] and for the workers of the Land. Several days after the death of the Netzi'v, a proclamation was published in *Hamelitz* with the signature of Michael Oriaszson and Shlomo Zalman Jaffe in Horodno [Grodno], calling for the giving "of honor and glory to the revered, sublime name of the Netzi'v"[50]

A Zionist organization was founded in Volozhin in the year 5662 [1902].The organization was founded by the preacher Rabbi Bezalel Zadikov[51]. Many Jews of Volozhin made *aliya* under the influence of the appeal by Rabbi Chaim of Volozhin to the Jews of his city to personally fulfil the commandment of building up the Land. There are many gravestones of Volozhin Jews on the Mount of Olives from the years 5622 (1862) and 5624 (1864). We do not know when they made *aliya* to the Land, but we can assume that they lived in the Land for many years[52]. [x]

Translator's Footnotes:

i.   See https://en.wikipedia.org/wiki/Moshe_Leib_Lilienblum
ii.   See https://en.wikipedia.org/wiki/Yitzchak_Elchanan_Spektor
iii. See https://en.wikipedia.org/wiki/Samuel_Mohilever
iv.   See https://en.wikipedia.org/wiki/Micha_Josef_Berdyczewski
v.   Rishon Letzion was funded in 1882. See https://en.wikipedia.org/wiki/Rishon_LeZion
vi.   A reference to the ten spies of the Book of Numbers who spoke badly of the Land of Israel.
vii. See https://en.wikipedia.org/wiki/Yechiel_Michel_Pines
viii. See https://www.jewishvirtuallibrary.org/jaffe–mordecai–gimpel

ix.   Jeremiah 31:16.
x.   The original translator, M. Porat, added a note here: See "Reb Avrom Chaim Marshak" VYB page 510.

[Page 59]

The Economic, Cultural, and Social Situation of the Jews of Volozhin

Translated by Jerrold Landau and donated by Anita Frishman Gabbay

Volozhin was a poor town. In an earlier chapter we noted that it was forced to forego the *Gaon*, the author of the *Shaagas Aryeh*, because it was unable to add a small amount to his salary. The economic situation of the Jews of Volozhin deteriorated further during the last quarter of the 19th century. Poverty increased, commerce quieted, and many reached the threshold of hunger.

One of the great tribulations that afflicted Volozhin were the fires that caused destruction. A large fire broke out in the year 5575 (1815). Rabbi Itzele wrote about it in his introduction to *Nefesh HaChaim*:

"Due to our great sins, many of the archived responsa that were hidden away (that is, that his father Rabbi Chaim hid away) were burned, due to our great sins, in the fire that was sent from Heaven on Wednesday, 14 Iyar 5575. Heaven help us, about half of the city was burned. The homes of many people were consumed by fire, and only His school (i.e. the Yeshiva building) was scorched by the fire that raged around it, but through the mercy of G–d was spared as a brand plucked from fire[i]. The books were also saved."

In the year 5640 (1880), a large fire broke out in Volozhin and consumed the part of the city next to the river. The recently–built *Beis Midrash* also went up in flames. They succeeded in saving some of the books and Torah scrolls. However, many rare books, including writings of Rabbi Chaim of Volozhin, were burnt. The situation of those who were afflicted by the fire was frightening and terrible. Almost all were left naked and bereft of everything[53].

A large fire spread in Volozhin on June 27, 1886. Two hundred houses were burnt. At least two families lived in each house. Only a few houses remained in the market and in the *Aroptzu* [area behind]. The Yeshiva building built by Rabbi Chaim in the year 5567 (1807), two *Beis Midrashes*, the *Gemilut Chasadim* room with all its contents valued at 2,000 rubles were all burnt in the fire. The contents included valuable household utensils, and Sabbath and festival clothing that the poor would borrow from the wealthy to serve as surety. According to the regulations of the *Gemilut Chasadim*, the surety must be worth at least three times the value of the loan. The poor people were completely destroyed, and almost all the residents of the city suffered the indignity of hunger and want. As there were no houses, the people affected by the fire were housed in the barns and grain storehouses of the farmers.

The community of Volozhin was destroyed to the foundations. The Jews had no place to worship on Sabbaths and festivals. The appearance of the burnt, destroyed city grieved all those who saw it. The writers raised their voices in *Hatzefira* and *Hamelitz*, and called upon the Jews to provide assistance to Volozhin, which had sunk to the depths. Indeed, the Jews of Vilna, Minsk, Rakov, Stowbtsy, Ivenets, Oshmyana, Vishneva, and Lebedovo girded themselves to help, and sustained the Jews of Volozhin for a period of two weeks. However, this assistance was not sufficient to provide for the many needs. Day by day, the number of recipients increased whereas the number of givers declined. The harvest season was approaching, and the Jews were afraid that the gentiles would throw them out of the storehouses, and they would be left out in the cold.

[Page 60]

During this time of trouble and tribulation, the Netzi'v arose as a savior to his community. He called out to the Jews of the world to help in the restoration of the Yeshiva and the city. Those asked responded immediately[54]. Within a short time, the Yeshiva was built upon its ruins as a large, fine, stone building. Even Count Michał Tyszkiewicz[ii] participated in the endeavor and donated 800 trees for the Yeshiva and *Beis Midrash* buildings. Prysewski, the commissar of Count Tyszkiewicz, donated eight rubles, and Nykarsiewicz, a Christian from Zaberzeze, donated ten rubles. This was a significant sum in those days.

The restoration of the Yeshiva influenced the general restoration of the community of Volozhin. The city earned all its livelihood from the Yeshiva, as the writer A. L. Lewinski writes:[55]

"Volozhin is the guesthouse of Torah, but a precious guesthouse, a living guesthouse on account of its guests. Israel has its Torah – and it has its livelihood from its Torah. The lads of the Yeshiva of Volozhin are like an army brigade in the district city, from which it finds its livelihood."

From the financial records published by the Netzi'v, we learn about the role of the Yeshiva in the economy of the city.[56] A special sector developed – guesthouses. Almost every house had a special wing to house Yeshiva students. The guesthouses of Volozhin were famous throughout Russia and Lithuania. The well–known writer A. Litwin perpetuated one of the guesthouse keepers in his story "Przychulczka." This was the only source of livelihood to sustain the entire family. The Jews of Volozhin loved and revered the Yeshiva students very much. The writer Menachem Mendel HaLevi Ish-Horowitz described some of this reverence:

"In Volozhin, they respect the Yeshiva lad as an angel and as a rabbi and *Gaon*, or a great sage. They love these tenants, who are great in Torah and wisdom, are talented, and have excellent character traits. When he would wake up, the mistress of the house would already be concerned with his needs. When he came home from the *Beis Midrash*, the small room would be clean, the table set, and the meal would be on the table. There was quiet in the entire house! 'The Yeshiva student is eating,' whispered the mother to the young children, so they should not make noise at this time."[57]

Rabbi Chaim of Volozhin would say that, were it not for the householders of Volozhin renting rooms to the Yeshiva lads, and had they not prepared the food for the lads, and had the entire town notregarded the Yeshiva with awe and respect – what would we do?

The Yeshiva lads paid about 30 kopecks a month for room and board. The payment was not

[Page 61]

in cash, but rather in "notes." Sunday was the "payment day" in the Yeshiva, when the hosts would receive payment for the notes. The housewives of Volozhin awaited that day all week. They would gather in the women's gallery in the Yeshiva building, where the Mashgiach [spiritual overseer] sat and distributed the money to each one according to a list that had been prepared on Saturday night. Many of them, who were very impoverished, would receive an advance for the next payment based on a special assent of the Netzi'v.

Despite its poverty, when a fire broke out in the city of Lebedovo, Volozhin sent three wagons laden with bread, food, and clothing.[58]

This lowly economic situation forced the communal heads to found institutions for social assistance. In Tishrei 5645 [1884], the *Mekabtei Nidachim* [Gatherers of the Displaced] organization was founded, with the aim of caring to the abandoned orphans and children of poor people whose parents could not feed or sustain them. This organization sent those children to school, where they learned a profession that would provide them with a livelihood. Mordechai Bunimovich and Aharon Milikowski headed that organization.

In the year 5655 [1895], the *Chonen Dalim* [Mercy upon the Poor] organization was founded through the efforts of the rabbi of the city, Rabbi Meir Noach Lewin. Its purpose was to provide bread and other provisions for free to respectable householders who had lost their livelihoods and were suffering from hunger, and who were embarrassed to go from door to door requesting donations.

The *Linat Hatzedek* organization was founded in 5659 [1899] to provide significant assistance to poor people who were sick. It was headed by the elderly Menachem Mendel Bunimovich, who was a great expert and very competent in charitable affairs. Aside from hospitalization, they provided money, chicken, wine, and other provisions to the poor sick people. In cases of need, the society gave money to the sick person, so he could travel to a large city to consult with physicians. During its first three months of existence, the organization conducted important and very effective efforts for the benefit of the poor sick people of Volozhin.

A guesthouse was also founded in Volozhin. However, this house exposed the terrible poverty of the Jews of the city during those days. The house was small and narrow, and the walls were covered with much dust. It only had two broken beds. Often, four or five guests showed up at this inn at one time, so two or three of them were forced to sleep on the floor. This house was open and exposed to every wind. Many of the guests who came to Volozhin and were forced to sleep in this inn were particularly important people, including rabbis who came to seek rabbinical posts, as well as famous preachers and authors who came to request approbations for their books from the Yeshiva heads.

The health and medical assistance situation was very bad. There was no physician in the city. The district physician, Dr. Sawicki, lived in *Aroptzu*, but he was always busy in the hospital for leprosy, and had no time to provide help to other sick people in the city. Therefore, the Jews of Volozhin were force to summon

[Page 62]

a physician from Vishneva. The price was high – ten rubles for a visit and three rubles for the wagon ride. The physician would be very tired from the journey, and his examination was perfunctory and hasty. He was forced to return immediately, since many sick people were waiting for him in his city. Only wealthy people who were able to afford such a price to a physician would allow themselves such "luxuries." What could the poor people, who did not have a coin to spend, do? The cries of these poor sick people came before the communal administrator. He stopped the Torah reading in the *Beis Midrash*[liii], but it did not help at all, for there was nothing with which to help them.

The issue of purchasing medicine was even more difficult. There was a pharmacy in the city, owned by a Russian, and he would flay the skin off the sick people. The poor people could not afford to purchase medicine, and many died prematurely of their illnesses. The pharmacy supervisor visited Volozhin on the Friday of the week of the Torah portion of *Behaalotecha* of the year 5654 [June 22, 1854]. The city notables came before him and asked his permission to open a pharmacy for the poor of Volozhin who could not afford to purchase medicine from the pharmacy due to the inflated prices. The supervisor acceded to them and gave them the requested permit. That Saturday night, the city notables, headed by Rabbi Meir Noach Lewin met together to figure out from where they could get money for that purpose. After an extensive deliberation, they decided to take 400 rubles from the Bikur Cholim coffers and to impose a duty upon every householder to donate what they could. All those present willingly pledged their donation. Mendel Bunimovich and Hillel Chaikin were the chief activists.

Regarding that inspector, it is fitting to say: "Cursed are the wicked people whose good is not complete." A place was set up for the pharmacy in the lepers' hospital, under the supervision of Dr. Savitsky, at some distance from the city. It was difficult for the people of the city to get there, especially when the sick person was in a serious state and required immediate assistance. The Russian owner of the pharmacy did not place his hand in the plate[liv]. He had connections with the "high windows." The plans for the Jewish pharmacy were shelved.

The Jews of Volozhin did not neglect the education of their children despite their poverty and difficult situation. A school was founded in the year 5647 (1887), which was to teach Russian and Hebrew in its curriculum. However, in the year 5654 [1894], seven years after the founding of the school, the students who graduated Hebrew had no competency in Hebrew, as there was no Hebrew teacher there. The students only learned secular subjects. When the parents saw that they are not teaching Hebrew in the school (even though Hebrew language was part of the curriculum), they stopped sending their children to the school, and rather gave them over to *melamdim* [the traditional cheder teachers of young children]. The teachers saw that the school was liable to close, so they threatened the *melamdim* that if they would not give over three students from each cheder to the school, the cheders would be closed by order of the authorities. A great fear fell upon the *melamdim*, and they met to figure out what to do. It was decided to give over to the school children with learning difficulties, who required a great deal of care and were not succeeding at their studies, and who were not destined to become rabbis or leaders of the generation. However the teachers refused to accept them, and a "culture war" broke out in Volozhin with full strength.

[Page 63]

There was already a Talmud Torah of an appropriate caliber in Volozhin in the year 5654 (1894). It was not housed in a single building, for there was not enough money to purchase a special building for the Talmud Torah. Therefore, they rented large, spacious rooms. The students were divided into three grades. Each grade had its own location, where the students were able to study without being disturbed. The *melamdim* knew their trade well, and were talented in the education of children. The main subject was the study of Bible with the abridged commentary of the Malbi'm. They learned the entire Bible, from beginning to end. When the students were competent in the Bible and its commentaries, and no longer required the assistance of the melamed, they began studying Gemara.

The trustees would come to the Talmud Torah along with three ordained young men every Sabbath to test the students. The trustees of the Talmud Torah concerned themselves with the students and their needs. They provided food, clothing, and shoes. There was an old custom in Volozhin that on *Shabbat Shuva*, a *Mi Shebeirach*[lv] for every householder would make a pledge on that occasion for the benefit of the Talmud Torah. The trustees would collect the donations throughout the year for the upkeep of the institution.

The *Beis Midrash* was the center of spiritual life of the Jews of the city. Life ran in the spirit of tradition and faith; however sparks of aspiration for secular matters could already be seen. Even though the Yeshiva did not regard secular knowledge with a good eye, one cannot ignore the fact that there were students in the Yeshiva who were occupied in "heretical subjects," in Jewish and general philosophy. It was even said about one of them that the pathways of Greek philosophy were as clear to him as the pathways of Volozhin.

However, these were rare occurrences, and there was no noticeable change in the spirit of the Jews of Volozhin until a much later period than we are currently discussing. Nobody in Volozhin would have thought seriously about breaking the boundaries and changing the values during the 1880s. A single spirit pulsated through the city. Children cleaved to the faith of their fathers, and fathers regarded their children as continuing their traditions and way of life.

Religion was the joy of life of the Jews of Volozhin, as Menahem Mendel HaLevi Horowitz writes:

"What is the goal that carries the soul of the Volozhin Jew on the Sabbath? – Not to be a person of wealth with a huge fortune, not to raise oneself above everyone, not to have a multitude of pleasures, in the ways that are the hopes, aspirations and desires of all other nations. No, none of these are of value to him, they are as nothing and a zero in his eyes. For what would they give him or gain him? His strong desire and aspiration was 'to see children and grandchildren occupying themselves with Torah and the commandments.' This is the spirit which fills us on this holy day."

"One must give only a bit of slumber to ones eyes to fulfill the commandment of 'sleep on the Sabbath is a pleasure.' Then, one should go to the House of the L–rd to listen to the lessons of the preachers. The sublime ideas delivered in precious style will attract his heart, fortify his soul

[Page 64]

sanctify him and raise him up to the heights of the heavens. He will be suffused with emotion, and his soul will barely perceive the strength of these feelings."[59]

The great enjoyment of a person of Volozhin was to listen to words of Torah in the synagogue on the Sabbath. The spirit of the Netzi'v and of Rabbi Chaim Soloveitchik suffused the city. Even the Valozhynka River was saturated with the *Emek Sheeila* and *Meishiv Davar*[vi]. It was not a businessman or wealthy person who served as educational role models, but rather the Netzi'v. His presence in the city was its call to greatness. The Jews of Volozhin aspired to learn Torah and good character traits from these exemplary people.

In the year 5656 (1896), 300 Jewish families, consisting of 1,200 individuals, lived in Volozhin. In the year 5657 (1897), the population of Volozhin and its neighboring villages was 4,500, including approximately 2,500 Jews. These are not exact figures, for they include deceased individuals who were listed in the registries as if they were alive, and vice versa. The registry of births and deaths was disorderly, and many of those who lived in the "world of truth" walked about healthy and hale in the outskirts of Volozhin, and many who were already deceased were considered alive. There were also boys and girls who had not been born yet according to the registry. Despite all this, the aforementioned number is not that far from the reality.

In the year 5656 [1896], there were a small number of wealthy people alongside the poor folk. These wealthy people worked in the grain, flax, flour, salt, sugar, and kerosene trades. A few were innkeepers, for one had to have a large room and expensive equipment to open an inn. On the other hand, there were many shopkeepers, and there was barely a house that did not have an adjacent store. One did not need special effort to open a store. Every householder could make a hole in the wall of his house, stick out his hand from the inside, and sell.

During those years, there was a change in the makeup of the Jewish population of the city: The power of the tradesmen and workers grew. They earned their livelihoods amply and respectably, and became the strong people of the city. The heads of the community would not lift a hand or a foot without them. No difficult question that was deliberated upon reached a solution without the agreement of the tradesmen and workers.

With the rise of power of the worker in Volozhin, an organization was founded called *Chevrat HaPoalim* [the Workers' Society], whose members were part of the young guard of workers. This society had its own prayer group [*minyan*], and wrote their own Torah scroll. They also had a rabbi, who would read from [i.e. teach them] the weekly Torah portion to them each week immediately following services. They would gather again in the evening, and the rabbi would teach them a chapter of the Code of Jewish Law.

In the year 5651 (1891), civilization began to penetrate Volozhin. The city was connected to the telephone network, and roads began to be paved. The road to Vilna, which was the main road of Volozhin, was laid first. The workers were not particularly competent, and the uncut rocks sunk into the ground, and were it was as if they never were[60].

[Page 65]

From a political perspective, the Jews of the city were subordinate to the Czarist government. The enslavement and degradation of the Jews of Volozhin was expressed in a "celebration" that was organized to celebrate the miracle that took place to the Czar when he was saved from a serious train accident on October 17, 1888. To this end, a large celebration was arranged in Volozhin, where praise was given to G–d for saving the life of the Czar, may his glory be raised, his wife and children. The Netzi'v preached that we are commanded to love the king who rules over us, and to be faithful servants. His intention was based on the words of the wisest of men[vii] "Fear G–d, my son, and the king" (Proverbs 24:21). The fear of a king is compared to the fear of G–d.

Signs of strengthening of the economic situation were noticed at the beginning of the 20th century. The most obvious of them was the founding of the Society for Loans and Credit. The writ for Volozhin opens with this matter.

"After great efforts, we succeeded in obtaining a permit to found a society for credit and loans, the lack of which was felt especially in recent times, when the large Christian shops began to compete with our small shops. Immediately after receiving the permit, approximately one hundred members joined the society. A general meeting was called to elect the leadership. The society granted its first loans, to the joy of all the members of the city, who hoped that it would ease their bitter situation."[61]

This strengthening was not sufficient to ease the economic straits of the Jews of Volozhin. Therefore, immigration to the United States increased. Approximately one hundred families left within a short period. Most of the emigres were small–scale merchants and shopkeepers whose economic situation had become worse due to the drought, and the earnings from the shops had declined.

It must be noted, however, that very few of the tradesmen emigrated, because they, especially the tailors and the cobblers, earned a good livelihood from the Yeshiva students. In this era (the first decade of the 20th century as in previous years, most of the householders earned their livelihoods from the Yeshiva students, for there was almost no house in Volozhin that did not host three or four Yeshiva lads.

Translator's Footnotes:

i.   Based on Zecharia 3:2.
ii.   See https://en.wikipedia.org/wiki/Micha%C5%82_Tyszkiewicz_(Egyptologist)

iii.   A common methodology in those days for conducting an urgent charitable appeal.

iv.   I.e. he did not cooperate.

v.   A prayer for the wellbeing a specific person or group of people. It is also the formula of a prayer for recovery from illness. In the current context, it requests Divine blessing and favor upon those who have undertaken a certain charitable act.

vi.   Works of the Netzi'v.

vii.   King Solomon, traditionally considered the author of the Book of Proverbs.

Original footnotes:

1.   Rabbi Chaim of Volozhin wrote the name of the city as "Vlozhin" (וולאזין), as would be written in documents of divorce or marriage. However, researchers studied and found that the gematria [numerology] of Volozhin is 110, the same as Sodom. Therefore, they added an aleph and wrote it as וואלאזין.

2.   See "Chaim Growitzer" by Fishel Schneerson, Volume II, p. 307.

3.   "Chaim Growitzer" Volume II, page 307.

4.   "From Volozhin to Jerusalem", p. 21.

5.   The printed sermon in the book "Neima Kedusha" by Rabbi Yosef Yaski, Vilna 5632 / 1872.

6.   See the article of Aba Baluter "Bialik in Volozhin" "Meoznaim" Vol IV, book II, Tammuz 5695 (1935).

7.   We have interesting legends regarding the relations between Count Tyszkiewicz and Rabbi Chaim. Fishel Schneerson writes: "It was already square, large, and wide. Three high, white buildings stood prominently in a row. In the light of morning, they appear closed, silent, and full of secrets." Count Tyszkiewicz, the count of Volozhin, built these already in the time of Rabbi Chaim Volozhiner. The innkeeper notes regarding the building that stands apart and separate in a different direction in the middle of rows of shops: this house was built by the Volozhiner Count for Rabbi Chaim. Some say that the count only provided the bricks for the building, but Rabbi Chaim's father himself built the house. In any case, the count has a great share in the house of Rabbi Chaim, for it is very similar in colour and appearance to the three white buildings. The house of the count and the house of the Yeshiva ahead stand side by side, as if they are the buildings of two leaders equal in stature.

I heard from an elderly Jew that, for a long time after the Polish revolution, the count hid himself from the government in the Yeshiva of Rabbi Chaim, and disguised himself as a Yeshiva lad ("Chaim Growiczer", Vol II, pp. 308–309).

Moshe Shalit brings the following legend from "Fun Naenten Eiver", year II (January–March, 1938), booklet I (V), p 33: "Rabbi Chaim would visit the house of Count Jósef Tyszkiewicz once a week for a general conversation. During this cconversation, the count would read to Rabbi Chaim from the newspapers about news and important events taking place in the world. Rabbi Chaim came one day, and the count read to him that a son was born to Czar Pavel, named Nikolai. Rabbi Chaim burst out crying at this news, "Why are you crying, my teacher and rabbi?" asked Count Tyszkiewicz. Rabbi Chaim responded: "I suspect that this Nikolai will be an enemy of the Jews, and will cause us bundles of tribulations." The count asked, "From where do you derive this?" Rabbi Chaim responded: "Because his name begins with the letter *nun*. We have a tradition that any king whose name starts with *nun* is an enemy of the Jews: Nimrod, Nebuchadnezzar, Nebuzaradan, Nero Caesar. Nikolai too will be like them."

8.   Unknown author: "And Research their Honor in Honor", "Hameilitz", 5 Iyar 5657 (April 17, 1887).

9.   "Michtav Yakar" (Precious Letter), by Rabbi Yehuda Yudel HaLevi Epstein in honor of Rabbi Shmuel Yevnin. Printed as an addendum to "Saarat Eliahu", page 38.

10. Regarding the history of the Rapoport family, see "Daat Kedoshim" by Yisrael Tovia Eisenstadt, Pressburg, 5657–58 (1897–98), pp. 136–180.

11. "*Alei Heldi*", pp. 43.

12. "*Nefesh HaChaim*", Volume III, Chapter I.

13. "*Nefesh HaChaim*", Volume III, Chapter II.

14. "*Mekor Baruch*" Volume IV, Section 4, Chapter 40, "Hunger and Satiety," pp. 1818–1819.

15. *From Volozhin to Jerusalem*, page 25.

    a.   15a. It is said that Rabbi Chaim of Voloshin related to the Hassidim with understanding, even though they fought about him and sated him with bitters. A story known to the students of the Gaon Rabbi Chaim, called "the story of the Yabam" [trans: Levirate], can serve as an example of this. Rabbi Chaim once found a reason for permission to a woman who was liable to a Levirate marriage to a brother–in–law, through a testimony that the brother–in–law had died, so the sister–in–law was exempt from *Chalitza* [translator: the ceremony of the removal of the shoe performed to sever the requirement to marry the brother–in–law]. What did the Hassidim do? They hired a corrupt man for a large sum of money and asked him to go from place to place, shouting out everywhere: "I am the brother–in–law regarding whom the Rabbi of Volozhin permitted my sister–in–law to get married without performing *Chalitza*, and I am intending to perform *Chalitza* with my sister–in–law.

The Gaon Rabbi Chaim mocked this entire tumult, and supported the husband who married the sister–in–law to not separate from his wife [trans: a woman connected to a brother–in–law through a requirement of Levirate marriage is not allowed to marry anyone else unless the brother–in–law performs *Chalitza*.], for there is no reason for concern. When the alleged brother–in–law approached Minsk, the Gaon Rabbi Chaim informed the heads of the community that this alleged brother–in–law is a forger. He requested that they interrogate him and demand signs and details regarding his late brother and the family.
Of course, the alleged brother–in–law was unable to respond to the questions of the members of the rabbinical court, and the lie was exposed. He was forced to admit the truth, and even revealed the name of the people who hired him, and how much they paid him (Rabbi Yaakov HaLevi Lipshitz, *Zichron Yaakov*, Section I, Chapter 4, "The Conflict" pp. 14–16).

16. *Nefesh HaChaim*, Section IV, chapter 1.
17. Rabbi Moshe Shmuel Shapira: *The Annals of our Rabbi Chaim of Volozhin*, chapter 4.
18. Rabbi Yosef Litwin: *Rabbi Chaim of Volozhin and the Dispute Regarding the Founding of the Yeshiva*, *HaDoar*, 3 Adar II, 5722 (1962).
19. Rabbi Yosef Litwin: *After the Slingshots Come the Cannons, HaDoar*, 21 Iyar 5722 (1962).
20. Yekutiel Kamelhar, *Dor Deah* [The Generation of Knowledge], Section III, page 137.
21. *Shaarei Rachamim*, page 9 (25).
22. *Shaarei Yitzchak*, by Izik HaKohen of holy blessed memory, known as Cohen Gadol [High Priest], written in the year 5588 (1728), and published in Warsaw in the year 5658 (1898).
23. Yb'm *Olam Haatzilut* [The World of Sublimity], Hakerem, 5648 (1888), pp. 63–64.
24. Forgotten Jubilee, *Hatzefira*, Elul 5663 (1903).
The writer M. Peker also writes in his memoirs about the influence of Berlin upon Bialik: "I am connected today to one book of the books of the "early ones," and I had a pleasant feeling to delve into the lower story of the Yeshiva building, where its library is located, and to examine our ancient literature there. The torn volumes of the thick books, along with the layer of dust on some of the shelves imbued in me some sort of silent angst. I felt the great sense of abandonment pervading our eternal property. With embarrassment and great care, I examined each and every book that came to my hands, as a remnant of our vast treasury. As I was feeling my way around, my hand touched a certain thin book, bound in black cloth and torn at the bottom. When I opened it, I saw that it was nothing other than the [Talmudic] tractate *Nazir*, I wanted to return it to its place. However, at that moment, a small note in the corner of the tablet at the top appeared before me. I looked at it and read, "This tractate belongs to Ch. N. Bialik, from the year 5650 [1889–1890]. " A surge of warm feelings flowed over those words. This was a living impression of our great poet, who, in his time, absorbed the spirit of our fundamental, pure culture." M. Peker, *In the Volozhin Yeshiva*, *Hator*, edited by Y. L. Hakohen–Fishman, Jerusalem, 30 Sivan 5684 [1924], issue 40.
25. Autobiographical sections, version 3, *Kneset*, book six, pp. 14–15, Tel Aviv, 5701 [1941]. During the middle ages, general sciences were divided into seven main branches: arithmetic, engineering, music, astronomy, nature, divinity, and politics. The expression "seven wisdoms" is based on the verse in Proverbs (9:1), "Wisdom has built her house, and hewn out her seven pillars."
26. [iii] Mount Yarmulke, called by that name because of the Kippa [skullcap] over its head, is located outside of Volozhin, near the city. It served as a place of strolling for the native of the city during the summer. There is a tradition among the people of Volozhin that Bialik wrote his poem *El Hatzipor* [To the Bird] on Mount Yarmulke.
27. Mr. M. Ungerfeld determined that the date of the writing of *El Hatzipor* must be brought forward one year earlier. These are his words: "It is generally accepted that Bialik entered the halls of poetry with the publication of his first poem, *El Hatzipor*, in 5651 [1891]. However, a document has been found that proves that Bialik began to write *El Hatzipor* one year earlier, and its first expressions were already written in Iyar of 5650 [1890].
Mr. Ungerfeld brought the words of Bialik, whose hopes to obtain *Haskala* education in Volozhin were

dashed, and he was immersed in Gemara alone, and "through the duration of three months, I studied almost all of Tractate *Ketubot* with all of its *Tosafot* commentaries by heard." He then continues: "But Bialik did not suffice himself with that, but also looked into other commentaries on this tractate, including the *Pnei Yehoshua* of Rabbi Yehoshua. As was the custom of *Beis Midrash* lads in those days, the lad Bialik wrote various writing exercises on the inside pages of the volume, such as: "This belongs to the library of the Etz Chaim Yeshiva of Volozhin" – six times… Among these notations, there was the form of a draft of a letter in which he informs his friends that he finished writing the poem Maskil LiYehuda, and that he intends to write another poem called *El Hatzipor*. He wrote a few other notations. He wrote the date under this letter: 23 Iyar 5650, here in Volozhin: indicating: about two or three weeks after he arrived in the Volozhin Yeshiva. This changes that which was accepted about the annals of the creativity of Ch. N. Bialik that he wrote his first published poem, *El Hatzipor*, in Nisan 5651. According to the draft of the aforementioned letter, the date of the writing of his first "official poem" *El Hatzipor* must be brought forward one full year." (M. Ungerfeld: *El Hatzipor* was written in the year 5650 (A *New Light On the Beginning of the Creativity of Ch. N. Bialik*), Davar, 20 Tammuz 5726, July 7, 1966).

28. See *Ein–Hakoreh*, 2–3, Nissan Elul, 5683 [1923], page 103.

29. Abba Blusher: *Bialik in Volozhin, Meoznaim*, Tammuz 5695 [1935], Volume IV, Book 2 (20).

30. Yaakov Pichman: *Am Bialik, Knesset*, Book II, page 85, Tel Aviv, 5696 [1936].

31. This chapter does not include the sages of Volozhin connected to the Etz Chaim Yeshiva of Volozhin. They will be described in the annals of the Yeshiva.

32. Yb'm, *Olam Haatzilut, Hakerem*, 5648 [1888], page 64.

33. See picture on page 45.

34. The letter was published in *Ir Vilna* by Hillel Noach Magid–Steinschneider, Vilna 5660 (1900), pp 108–109 (with notes).

35. The rabbinical judge Rabbi Heshel Efron lived in Volozhin during the era of Rabbi Itzele. Rabbi Baruch HaLevi Epstein writes the following about him: "I recall that when I studied in the Volozhin Yeshiva during my youth, I heard some idea there in the name of one of the rabbinical judges of the previous generation, Rabbi Heshel Efron, who was called Rabbi Heshel Ivnitzer. He gave up on issuing rabbinic decisions, giving the reason that he was afraid that his decisions would permit that which is forbidden. [footnote continues on page 51] Furthermore, he was considered that he might forbid that which is permitted. He gave a reason for his extra concern on the last detail, in that if one permits something that is forbidden, one sins only against Heaven for issuing a decision that is not in accordance with *halacha*. But if one forbids that which is permitted, his sin is double: One sins against Heaven for issuing a decision that is not in accordance with *halacha*, and one sins against one's fellow for causing damage to the owners and causing them to lose money." (*Mekor Baruch*, Section I, Chapter II, *Dover Shalom*, paragraph I, pp 735–736).

36. Fénelon's "Telemachus" was published in 1699. Its content is based on a Greek legend. In Homer's Odyssey, Telemachus (the son of Ulysses and Penelope) sets out on a journey to find his father. Telemachus' many troubles improve his character and turn him into a wise man with pleasant mannerisms. The Hebrew translation was published in 1851–1853 (volumes I and II) by the Zamtheir publishing house of Königsberg, and a second time in Vilna by the Romm Publishers in the year 5613 (1853). There is a brief introduction to the Hebrew translation by Avraham the son of Chaim HaKohen, explaining the great benefits of the book.

37. Sources for the biography of Rabbi Neuwedel: a) *Ha'asif*, 5647 [1887], page 124. b) "The City of Vilna," page 175. C) A. Tz'm "Zion for a Pure Soul" (In memory of Rabbi Eliahu the son of Rabbi Shlomo Zalman Neuwedel), *Hatzefira*, 22 Elul 5646 (September 10, 1886), issue 131. d) *Kneset Yisrael*, 5646 [1886], page 1128.

38. Rabbi Chaim expressed his deep connection to the Land of Israel in a sermon that he delivered in Volozhin on the first day of *Selichot* of the year 5572 [1812]. The sermon is published in the book *Neima Kedosha* by Rabbi Yosef Jaski, Vilna 5632 [1872].

39. Rabbi Yitzchak Rivkind: "The Yeshiva in Volozhin and the National Renaissance," *Hatoren*, ninth year, booklet 10, Kislev 5683 [1922], pp 51–61.

40. Rabbi Avraham Yaari: "Emissaries of the Land of Israel," page 553, Jerusalem 5611 [1951].

41. Rabbi Aryeh Leib Frumkin: "History of the Sages of Jerusalem," Jerusalem 5699 [1939], section III, pp. 138–139.

42. Rabbi Avraham Yaari: "Legends of the Land of Israel," Tel Aviv, 5703 [1943], Letters of Rabbi Chaim the son of Rabbi Tovia Katz of Vilna, page 341.

43. The original members of the organization in Volozhin were: Avraham Bunimovitch, Yitzchak Yaakov Bunimovitch, Yishayahu Shmuel Bunimovitch, Moshe Bunimovitch, Sh. M. Bunimovitch, Rabbi Naftali

Hertz Eskind, Eliezer Leib Persky, Chaya Persky, Rivka Persky, Yosef Kramnik, and Moshe Yehoshua Rabinovitch.

44. Addendum to *Hamagid*, no. 47, first day of Chanukah, 5646 (December 3, 1885).

45. Addendum to *Hamagid*, no. 47, first day of Chanukah, 5646 (December 3, 1885).

46. Droyanov, "Writings Regarding the History of Hibbat Zion and the Settlement of the Land of Israel," Section I, page 684 (376), Odessa, 5679 [1819].

47. The proclamation was published in *Shivat Zion* by Avraham Yaakov Slutzki, Part II, pp. 28–30.

48. A the House of the Rabbi for One Day, *Hamelitz*, 5650 [1890], issue 120.

49. Rabbi Meir Berlin included this story in his book "From Volozhin to Jerusalem," page 105.

50. See Yitzchak Rivkind: "The Nezi'v and his Relationship to Hibbat Zion," Łódź, 5679 [1919].

51. See *Hamelitz*, 5 Elul 5653 (August 5, 1893), issue 176. Similarly, *Hamelitz*, 16 Cheshvan 5654 (October 14, 1893), issue 221. There, an article is published about the students of the Netzi'v in the land of Israel who decided to make a memorial monument to the Netzi'v.

52. See *Hamelitz*, 5 Kislev 5663 (November 22, 1902).

53. In the book *Chelkat Mechokek*, including all the gravestones on the Mount of Olives, the recorder Asher Leib Brisk includes several of these gravestones: Reb Mordechai Tzvi the son of Rabbi Eliezer (died in 5621 [1861]); Esther the daughter of Rabbi Shmuel (died in 5622 [1862]; Rachel the daughter of Rabbi Pinchas, the wife of Reb Gedalia (died in 5648 [1888]); Eliezer the son of Reb Shmuel (died in 5639 [1879]); Gedalia the son of Rabbi Avraham (died in 5640 [1880]); Rabbi Moshe the son of Rabbi Nisan (died in 5641 [1881]); Avraham Chaim the son of Rabbi Moshe (died in 5644 [1884]); Ezriel the Zelig the son of Rabbi Wolfe (died in 5624 [1864]).

54. Mordechai Binyamim Bunimovich, *Hatzefira*, 5640 [1880], issue 12.

55. See the Netzi'v: A significant announcement for Torah, *Hatzefira*, issue 125, 15 Elul 5646 (September 3, 1886); *Hamelitz*, issue 55, 16 Tammuz 5646 (July 6, 1886); *Hamelitz*, issue 149, 20 Cheshvan 5647 (November 6, 1886).

56. A. L. Lewinski, The Fires and Those Burnt, *Hamelitz*, 20 Tammuz 5655 [1895].

57. See *Hamelitz*, 1 Sivan, 5646 [1886].

58. "The Path to the Tree of Life," pp. 22, 54.

59. See *Hamelitz*, 5648 [188], issue 194.

60. *Derech Etz HaChaim* [The Path to the Tree of Life], pp 69.73.

61. See M. Zlotkin: "The Yeshiva of Volozhin during the Era of Bialik", *Shevivim*, year 1, booklet 1, Kislev 5715 [1954], pp 56–64.

62. Avi'a, *Hatzefira*, February 26, 1913, issue 49.

[Page 66]

Sources Regarding the History of the Jews in Volozhin

Translated by Jerrold Landau

Donated by Anita Frishman Gabbay

Articles and memoirs about Volozhin

Rabbi Avraham (the son of the Gr'a). *Peerat Eliahu*; Eulogy for the Gr'a. Brought to publication by Rabbi Shmuel Yevnin of Horodno, Warsaw, 5638 [1878].

Eisenstadt, Ben–Zion. *Rabbis and sages of Minsk*; History of the Torah greats who disseminated Torah in the city of Minsk (Lithuania) during the previous two hundred years, with copies of 75 gravestone inscriptions and lists of books that they published. Vilna 5659 [1899].

Eisenstat, Yisrael Tovia. *Daat Kedoshim*; Peterburg, 5657–5658 (1897–98), pp. 136–180, Berhman and Partners publishers.

Ish–Horowitz, Menachem Mendel HaLevi. *Derech Etz Chaim*; a portrait of life of the students of the holy Etz Chaim Yeshiva of Volozhin. Krakow, published by Emanuel Horowitz, 5655 [1895].

Bialik, Chaim Nachman. *Matters by Heart*; volume I, page 22 (about Cheder and the Talmud), Tel Aviv, 5695 [1935].

Brisk, Asher Leib. *Chelkat Mechokek*; A list of gravestones in the Mount of Olives Cemetery – Jerusalem.

Berlin (Bar–Ilan), Meir. *From Volozhin to Jerusalem*; Yalkut publishers, 5699 [1939].

Drianov, Alter. *Writings of the History of Hibbat Zion and the Settlement of the land of Israel*. Odessa, published by the Committee for the Settlement of the Land of Israel, 5679 [1919]. Volume I, page 684 (376). Volume II, Tel Aviv, Hapoel–Hatzair Publishing Cooperative, 5685 [1925], pp. 797–799.

HaKohen, Yitzchak Izak. *Shaarei Yitzchak*; written in the year 5588 [1828], published in Warsaw, Efraim Baumerister Publishers, 5658 [1898], pp. 111–112.

Zichron, Shimshon. *Words of Rabbi Shimshon the rabbinical judge*, published by his eldest son Yehuda Leib, Vilna, 5639 [1879].

Rabbi Chaim of Volozhin. *Sermon of our rabbi Rabbi Chaim*, delivered on the first day of Selichot, 5572 [1812]. The sermon was published in the book *Neima Kedosha* by Rabbi Yosef Jaski, Vilna, published by Reb Hillel the son of Reb Avraham Yitzchak Dworzec, 5632 [1872].

Yechezkel Feivel. *This is the Book of the History of Man*; History of Rabbi Shlomo Zalman, nicknamed Reb Zelmele (the younger brother of Rabbi Chaim of Volozhin). Bnei–Brak, Tifarteinu Book Publishers, 5722 [1962].

Yaari, Avraham. *Letters of the Land of Israel*. Published by the division of youth affairs of the Zionist Organization, Tel Aviv, 5703, pp. 341 and 503.

[Page 67]

Yaari, Avraham, *Emissaries of the Land of Israel*. Jerusalem, Mossad Harav Kook Publishers, 5711 [1951].

Magid, David, *History of the Ginzberg Families*. Peterburg, published by the author, 5659 [1899], pp. 35–50.

Magid (Steinsznajder), Hillel Noach, *City of Vilna*; Memories of the Jewish community and history of the lives of its greats. Vilna. Published by the Romm Widow and Brothers, 5660 [1900], pp. 108–109 (with notes).

Slutzki, Avraham Yaakov, *Shivat Tzion*; An anthology of statements of the geniuses of the generation in praise of the settlement of the Land of Israel. Two volumes. First edition appeared in the year 5652 [1892]. Second edition, Warsaw, Reb Meir Yechiel Halter and Partner Publishing, 5660 [1900]. Volume I, pp. 17–18. Volume II, pp. 5–6, 5–9, 28–29.

Fein, Shmuel Yosef, *Kirya Neemana*; History of the Jewish community of Vilna, and memorials to the souls of its Gaonim, sages, scribes, and philanthropists. Vilna, Reb Yosef Reuven the son of Reb Menachem of Romm Publishers. 5620 [1860], pp. 156–158, 158–160.

Frumkin, Aryeh Leib, *History of the Sages of Jerusalem*. Jerusalem, Solomon Publishers, 5688–5690 [1928–1930], Volume II, pp. 138–139.

Kamelhar, Yekutiel Aryeh, *Dor Deah*; 5695 [1935].

Katzenelenbogen, Avraham Tzvi Hirsch, *Shaarei Rachamim* [Gates of Mercy]; Vilna. Reb Avraham Yitzchak and his son Reb Shalom Yosef Dworzec Publishers. 5631 [1871].

Rivkind, Yitzchak, *The Netzi'v and his Relationship to Hibbat Zion*; Łódź, 5679 [1919].

Rivkind, Yitzchak, *Letters of Zion*; Letters to the Netzi'v from Rabbi Shmuel Mohilever, Dr. Pinsker, Reb M. Erlanger–Lubetzki, Yechiel Michel Pines, and a letter from the Netzi'v to Dr. Pinsker. The letters were published in *Sefer Shmuel* in memory of Rabbi Shmuel Mohilever, at 25th anniversary of his death (19 Sivan 5658–19 Sivan 5683 – [1898–1923]). Edited by Rabbi Yehuda Leib HaKohen Fishman, Jerusalem 5683 [1923], pp. 73–103.

Shalit, Moshe (editor), *On the Ruins of Wars and Disturbances*; a ledger of the region. YEKOPO Committee in Vilna (1919–1931). Accountings, articles, explanations, material, and documents.

In the Vernacular

M. Balinski – Lipinski – StaroŻytna Polska.

S. Orgielbrand – Encyklopedja Powszechna

Slownik Geograficzny Królestwa Polskiego in innych Krajów Slowianskich.

[Page 68]

Daily Newspapers

Hameilitz
(edited by Erez–Alexander Cederbaum)

Holand, Zalman Yitzchak: Hamelitz, 5 Tishrei 5650 (September 12, 1879), issue 38.[1]

Erez: Hamelitz, 28 Tishrei 5652 (October 17, 1883), issue 80.

Robinson: Hamelitz, 24 Tishrei 5645 (October 1, 1884), issue 77.

The Netzi'v. Accounting of the Yeshiva expenditures. Hamelitz, 1 Sivan 5646 (May 23, 1886), issue 40.

Article from the Heads of the Community of Volozhin: Hamelitz, 24 Av 5646 (August 13, 1886), issue 88. The heads of the community of Volozhin issue a call for the providing of help to the Jews of Volozhin after the fire that broke out on June 27, 1886. Signatories of the article: Sh. G. Perski (Scribe of Operova), Yosef Eliezer, Rabbi Ezriel Zelig Rogovin, Yehuda the son of Rabbi Yeshaya Kahana, Yitzchak Yosef Broda, Starosta of Volozhin.

The Netzi'v: Hamelitz, 20 Cheshvan 5647 (November 6, 1886), issue 149. The Netzi'v acknowledges the donations received for those affected by the fire.

The Netzi'v: Hamelitz, 23 Cheshvan 5647 (November 9, 1886), issue 151. The Netzi'v published a long list of donors for the restoration of the Yeshiva and those affected by the fire.

P.B.P., A researcher of their honor in honor: Hamelitz: 5 Iyar 5647 (April 17, 1887), issue 85 (in a note). The writer tells that when he was studying in the Etz Chaim Yeshiva of Volozhin, he saw the statue of Rabbi Itzele, son of Rabbi Chaim of Volozhin, in the palace of Count Tyszkiewicz.

An Article from Volozhin: Hamelitz, 13 Iyar 5648 (April 12, 1888), issue 80. In the article, they announce that "it has been about eight days since the eating of meat has been cut off from the mouths of Jews of Volozhin because the butchers decided among themselves to no longer slaughter cattle until they are given a new *shochet* [ritual slaughterer]."

[Page 69]

Peli: Hamelitz, 28 Iyar 5648 (April 27, 1888), issue 91. The writer announces that "the town of Horodok went up in fire, and the Jews of Volozhin sent two wagonloads of bread to the hungry." Similarly he announces that "a few days ago, a new prayer leader arrived in Volozhin with seven choir singers."

Absh'r: Hameltz, 1 Shvat 5649 (December 22, 1888) issue 281.

Bar–Bei–Rav Dechad Yoma (Micha Yosef Berdichevski) : Hamelitz, 28 Sivan 5650 (June 1, 1890), issue 120. The writer describes the activities of the Netzi'v in Hovevei Tzion.

Bunimovich, Sh. M. : Hamelitz, 10 Sivan 5653 (May 13, 1893), issue 106. The writer describes the difficult situation of the sick Jews in Volozhin, and demands that a permanent physician come to Volozhin.

Ish Yehudi. Eulogy for the Netzi'v: Hamelitz, 1 Elul 5653 (August 1, 1893).

Uriaszson, Michael and Yafa, Shlomo Zalman: Article from Horodno, Hamelitz, 5 Elul 5653 (August 5, 1893), issue 176. It states in the article: "We wish to state several things in the spirit of the Yeshiva students of Volozhin, the students of our teacher and rabbi, the Gaon, Tzadik, and luminary of Israel, Rabbi Naftali Tzvi Yehuda Berlin, may the memory of the holy be blessed. I have informed you of the greatness of the love of our Rabbi and Gaon Tzvi Yehuda for the Land of our Forefathers. Who knows like us that all his days he bore it in his soul to plead for the soil of our Holy Land, and to placate its stones. He especially took the idea of the new settlement to his heart. He always talked about it and predicted a great, creative future for it. Therefore, dear brothers! If he did not merit to see with his own eyes the Land that he pined for and desired all the days, please bring satisfaction to his pure soul, and leave him an eternal memorial through your donations for the benefit of the workers in our Holy Land.

"We hereby begin this great commandment to memorialize his soul by donating two rubles for the workers, in accordance with receipt 719. Would it be that they see what we did, and all the students in every city do the same. This way, they will give honor and value to his revered, sublime name, as well as fulfil the wishes of his heart that he conceived of and thought about while still alive."

Perpetuation of the Memory of the Netzi'v: Hamelitz, 17 Cheshvan 5654 (October 14, 1893), issue 221.

[Page 70]

In the section of announcements in this issue, a list is printed of students of the Netzi'v who donated to perpetuate the name of their great rabbi.

Raski, Eliezer Leib: Hamelitz, 6 Tammuz 5654 (June 28, 1894), issue 144. The writer demands that a permit be issued to open a pharmacy under the direction of a Jewish pharmacist in Volozhin.

Raski, Eliezer Leib: Hamelitz, 11 Elul 5654 (August 31, 1894), issue 198. The writer describes the Talmud Torah of Volozhin.

Raski, Eliezer Leib: Hamelitz, 7 Shvat 5654 (January 2, 1894), issue 1. The writer announces the opening of the school for the study of the Hebrew language in Volozhin.

Winski, Elchanan Leib. The fires and those affected by the fires: Hamelitz, 20 Tammuz 5655 (June 30, 1895), issue 143. Lewinski writes, among the rest: "Volozhin is the host of Torah, but a precious host, a living host on the account of its guests. Its Torah comes from Israel, and it livelihood comes from Torah. The Yeshiva lads in Volozhin were like the army unit of the region, from which livelihood is derived."

Lodocha, Yehuda: Hamelitz, 15 Kislev 5659 (November 11, 1898), issue 254. The writer announces the founding of *Linat Tzedek* in Volozhin.

Perski, Eliezer Leib: Hamelitz, 6 Iyar 5659 (April 4, 1899), issue 75. In the announcements section, the writer announces that this issue contains a list of Volozhin Jews who donated for the benefit of the workers in the Holy Land.

Bunimovich, Moshe: Hamelitz, 5 Kislev 5663 (November 22, 1902), issue 257. The writer announces: "The honored preacher, Rabbi Betzalel Czodikow, founded a Zionist movement here."

[Page 71]

Hatzefira
(Edited by Chaim Zelig Slonimski, and later by Nachum Sokolow)

Robinson, Yisrael: Hatzefira, 15 Tevet 5640 (December 18, 1879), issue 49. The writer describes the difficult economic situation faced by the Jews of Volozhin with the following words: "Clouds of grief spread over the residents of this city this year. All faces have gathered blackness[2] and sighing from the heartfelt agony that bursts forth from the oppressed indigents, for these times are bad times. Commerce has quieted, the paths of business are in mourning, and those who earn are earning through a bundle of holes. Inflation is spreading through the city, and many are bearing the disgrace of hunger, to the point where one person has committed suicide from great pressure and poverty."

A. Tz'm, a memorial for a pure soul: Hatzefira, 22 Elul 5656 (September 10, 1886), issue 131. The writer portrays the life of Rabbi Eliahu, the son of Rabbi Shlomo Zalman Neuwedell, the great–grandson of Rabbi Zalmele, the younger brother of Rabbi Chaim of Volozhin.

Perski, Eliezer Leib: Hatzefira, 11 Iyar 5656 (April 12, 1896), issue 82. The writer describes the economic situation of the Jews of Volozhin, and announces the founding of the *Malbish Arumim* [Clothing the Poor] and *Chevrat Poalim* [Workers' Group] organizations.

Epstein, Zalman. A forgotten Jubilee: Hatzefira, 28 Menachem Av 5653 (August 8, 1903), issue 184; 30 Menachem Av 5663 (August 10, 1903), issue 185; 2 Elul 5663 (August 11, 1903), issue 186; 4 Elul 5663 (August 13, 1903), issue 188.

Zak, Y. L. , One day in Volozhin: Hatzefira, 22 Adar 5671 (March 9, 1911), issue 58. Mr. Zak describes his visit to Volozhin and writes, among everything else: "We are close to the small, remote city from which Torah and light emanates to the entire Jewish Diaspora. Our wagon drove with difficulty. The mare, beaten by the wagon driver's whip, pulled us between two rows of low, bent houses, with withering grass growing from their roofs. The people standing were somnolent, staring at us with curiosity. The triangular balconies, which were protruding from beneath the roofs and appeared as dovecotes, were also staring at us, as if in surprise, and asking: Why are you coming to this desolate place?

"They were in wonder, as we passed by them and arrived at the large marketplace. It was not paved with stones and had there not been walkways of boards in the center, one might simply drown in the mud and grime that covers everything. We passed in front of the pond, surrounded by reeds growing from within it.

[Page 72]

Bent, oppressed Jews passed before us, bearing the entire burden of the exile upon their shoulders. They wore belts on their wastes and heavy, coarse shoes on their feet.

"This is Volozhin, from which Torah has been emanating to Israel for more than a hundred years. This is the city that has been the host of Torah for hundreds of years. These houses hosted all those Gaonim and Torah luminaries, all the masses of scholars and studiers who disseminated Torah and knowledge throughout the nation."

Hayom
(Edited by Dr. Yehuda Leib Kantor)

Eldad: Hayom, 28 Menachem Av 5646 (August 18, 1886), issue 160. The writer describes the economic destruction of Volozhin after the fire in the following words: "The heart of every soul shall mourn, and the eye of everyone who loves his people is smitten when seeing the straits and tribulations that overtook the people of this city. Their faces are foaming from sadness and agony. Dark clous rest on their foreheads.

Their situation is terrible and frightful, for, aside from having been judged by G–d with fire, with their houses and all their wealthy and property having been burnt, leaving them naked and lacking everything, an additional disaster befell them, in that the sources of livelihood from which they drew to this point have dwindled and dried up. The majority of the residents of the city earned their livelihoods by hosting the Yeshiva students in their homes. They sustained themselves and their families in this manner. Now, however, when their houses have burnt down, and the Yeshiva was also burnt, and virtually all of the Yeshiva students have traveled to their own homes – now the defeat is complete. My pen does not have the strength to describe the poverty and pressure pervading in our city at this point. The residents of our city have never been known for wealth. Many lived in straits and meagerness. There were only a few who earned a comfortable, ample livelihood. Now, the wheel has turned even for those few, and we appear as an empty vessel. If assistance is not forthcoming from afar – then, Heaven forbid, our fate will be destruction."

Eldad: Hayom, 6 Cheshvan 5647 (October 26, 1886), issue 209. Eldad continues with his description of the severe economic situation of the Jews of Volozhin: "The eye seeing our city will witness a heartrending, mournful scene during this period of ruin and destruction. Dark clouds dwell upon the foreheads. Everyone walks about gloomy, with body–wracking sighs bursting forth from their hearts regarding the sources of livelihood that have dried up and dwindled, and the sources of food cut off from their mouths. Many women who used to do their work for the Yeshiva students,

[Page 73]

whom they hosted in their houses, now sit with their hands on their bosoms with nothing to do. One meets only hungry people at every footstep."

Metushelach: Hayom, 27 Menachem Av 5647 (August 5, 1887), issue 172. The writer describes the fire that broke out in Volozhin.

Annuals, Monthlies, Weeklies, and Anthologies

Bialik, Chaim Nachman. First letters. Knesset, in memory of Bialik, Book II, 5696 [1936], page 29, Tel Aviv.

Bialik, Chaim Nachman. Autobiographical sections. Knesset. Book VI, Tel Aviv, 5701 [1941], pp. 14–15.

Blusher, Abba. Bialik in Volozhin. Meoznaim, Tammuz 5695 [1935], Volume IV, Booklet II (20).

Berdichevski, Micha Yosef (Yaba'm). Olam Haatzilut [The World of Nobility], Hakerem, "The annual book for the research of Jewish history and literature." Edited by Elazar Atlas, Warsaw, Yitzchak Goldman Publishing, 5647 [1887], pp. 63–64.

Breinin, Reuven. The Gaon of Vilna. Hatoren, Monthly for science, literature, and Zionism. Edited by Reuven Breinin, Seventh year, 6 Iyar 5680 (April 30, 1920), issue 7, pp. 9–10.

Hamagid (edited by Eliezer Lipman Zilberman): Lyk, Rudolf Zibert Publishing, 5 Tevet 5632 (December 2, 1871), issue 49.

Hamagid, First day of Chanukah 5646 (December 3, 1885). Addendum to issue 47.

Zlotkin, M. *The Volozhin Yeshiva during the era of Bialik*: Shevivim, a quarterly on current issues, research, and literature. Published by Brit Haivrit Haolamit (French chapter), edited by Yaakov Yisrael Fink. Year 1, booklet I, Kislev 5615 [1855], pp. 56–64.

Turberg, P. *When I left Volozhin: Haivri*, A weekly newspaper (founded in Berlin in the year 5671 [1911]), Editor: Rabbi Meir Berlin. 28 Adar 5677 (February 23, 1917), issue 8.

[Page 74]

Litwin, Yosef. *Rabbi Chaim of Volozhin and the Dispute over the Founding of the Yeshiva*: Hadoar, 3 Adar II, 5722 [1962].

Litwin, Yosef. *After the Shots Came the Artillery*: Hadoar, 21 Iyar 5722 [1962].

Pichman, Yaakov. *With Bialik*: Knesset, Book II, page 85, Tel Aviv, 5697 [1937].

Rivkind, Yitzchak. *The Yeshiva in Volozhin and the National Renaissance*: Hatoren, 9th year, Kislev 5683 [1922]. Booklet 10, pp. 51–61.

Rivkind, Yitzchak. *Pathways of Volozhin, Clear and Not Clear*: Hadoar, 24 Adar II, 5722 [1962], issue 22, page 349; 2 Nisan 5722 [1962], issue 23, pp. 366–367.

Rivkind, Yitzchak. *Bialik's G–d*: Ein–Hakoreh, edited by D. A. Friedman, Berlin, Nisan–Elul 5683 [1923], pp. 3–35.

Translator's Footnotes:

1. In this, and all dates in this chapter, I notice a 12–day discrepancy between the Jewish and secular years. For example Sept 12, 1879 corresponds to 24 Elul 5639. I attribute this to the fact that the Russian Empire was still using the Julian calendar prior to 1918.
2. Joel 2:6.

[Page 75]

The History of the Etz Chaim Yeshiva of Volozhin, and its Heads

[Page 76][Blank][Page 77]

The History of the Etz Chaim Yeshiva of Volozhin, and its Heads

By Eliezer Leoni

"It is a Tree of Life [*Etz Chaim*] to those who grasp it, and fortunate are its supporters." (Proverbs 3:18)

"Rabbi Yitzchak the son of Abba says: Why is the Torah called a Tree of Life [*Etz Chaim*]? – Because it is pleasant for all those who live. Rabbi Yudan says: Why is the Torah called a Tree of Life? – Just as the Tree of Life is spread over all those who inhabit the world in the Garden of Eden – so is the Torah spread over all those who are alive, and brings them to the World To Come" (Midrash Tehillim, Psalm 1, paragraph 26)

Chapter I

The Era of Rabbi Chaim of Volozhin
The History of Rabbi Chaim of Volozhin

Translated by Jerrold Landau, based on an earlier translation by M. Porat z"l
that was edited by Judy Feinsilver Montel

Volozhin in the 19th century was honored to fulfill a role similar to that of Sura and Pumbeita during the period of the Talmudic sages[1]. This privilege was due to the Etz Chaim Yeshiva, founded in the year 5563 (1803) by its choicest son, Rabbi Chaim, born in Volozhin on Sivan 7th 5607 (1747) to his father Rabbi Yitzchak.

We do not have many sources on the life of Rabbi Chaim of Volozhin. Rabbi Yehuda Yudel HaLevi Epstein writes the following in his letter to Rabbi Shmuel Yevnin:[2]

"And behold, to explain the greatness of our rabbi of the Diaspora, the Gaon Rabbi Chaim of blessed memory of Volozhin, the splendor of his genius, his sharpness, and expertise, righteousness piety, and pure discussions – I

[Page 78]

do not have the power at this point, in my old age, for I would have to compose an entire book, which indeed would be very worthwhile to leave for the last generation, and would also be very useful for Torah, mannerisms, as well as proper character traits. However, this matter is not for me. It is a wonder why his rabbinical and Gaonic grandchildren have muzzled their mouths and pens at a time when people of that generation are still alive."

Rabbi Chaim's life is enwrapped in many legends. It was told in Volozhin that Rabbi Chaim's father was son of the bartender, who used to sell alcoholic beverages in the town. He married a woman from Piesk, a shtetl near Horodno. The matrimonial relations were bad, and they separated. The woman returned to her parents in Piesk. The husband remained at his father's house in Volozhin. Both towns belonged to Count Tyszkiewice. Once, when the count was visiting his estates, he entered the tavern of Volozhin and encountered a sorrowful young man. He asked his parents to explain the situation, and they told him that their son was married to a woman from Piesk but could not live with her in peace. Therefore, he is sad. The Count decreed that the woman is obligated to return to her husband in Volozhin. Since he was also the landlord of the town of Piesk and its taverns, they had to fulfil his decree. The woman returned to her husband. The couple merited five children, one of them being Rabbi Chaim.

From the age of twelve, the child was taught by Rabbi Rafael HaKohen of Hamburg, who served then as the official rabbi in Volozhin district. Rabbi Rafael designated Rabbi Chaim to be the rabbi of Volozhin, as Rabbi Yehuda Yudel writes in his aforementioned letter:

"From early on, the Gr'ch (Gaon Rabbi Chaim) studied with the great Gaon of his generation, Rabbi Rafael HaKohen, may the memory of the holy be blessed, of Hamburg, when he served as the rabbi of the district of Volozhin. He was appointed as the rabbi of Volozhin after the aforementioned Gaon Rabbi Rafael of blessed memory returned to Hamburg, in accordance with his [Rabbi Rafael's] directive to the community of Volozhin. This is what he said to that community and to the father of Rabbi Chaim: For the sake of G-d, see that your son Rabbi Chaim will be the rabbi in your city. Even as he was bidding his final farewell to Volozhin, when the wagon was already moving away from those who accompanied him, he stood up and issued the strong command once more: for the sake of G-d, Rabbi Chaim will be the rabbi in your city!"

At the age of fifteen, he studied from the *Shaagas Aryeh*, who served as the rabbi of Volozhin at that time. His great thirst for study is described in the words of his son Rabbi Itzele in his introduction to *Nefesh Hachaim*:

"From his youth, he bore the yoke of Torah with great diligence. When he was more than fourteen years old, he set his learning with his older brother our Rabbi Simcha of blessed memory and they would study day and night. Our grandfather told us that when the light of a candle was not available, the moonlight was sufficient for them to study at night. They received their ways in Torah from the rabbi of rabbis, the Gaon of Gaonim, the supernal lion, Rabbi Aryeh Leib, may he rest in peace, the author of *Shaagas Aryeh*."

[Page 79]

Rabbi Chaim of Volozhin and his rabbi, the Gaon Rabbi Eliyahu of Vilna

Rabbi Chaim was the first among all the students of the Gr'a. "The first was the Gaon and Tzadik, the luminary of the Diaspora, our Rabbi Chaim, may the memory of the righteous be a blessing, the head of the rabbinical court and head of the Yeshiva of Volozhin. He would wait and peer with open eyes at the beauty of the splendor of his Torah."[3]

The Gr'a (HaGaon Rabbi Eliyahu) of Vilna

Regarding the great influence of the G'ra upon Rabbi Chaim, Rabbi Yisrael of Shkov writes the following:[4]

"More than seeing the sun in its strength, is that not his veteran student, the splendor of the generation, the crown of the times, the true Gaon, the pious and modest one, renowned in his generation both in the revealed and hidden Torah [i.e. kabbalah], the honor of his holy name, our rabbi and teacher, may his light shine, the head of the rabbinical court and Yeshiva head of the holy community of Volozhin. He is upright in his actions, and judging in his ways, as for a long time he stood before his rabbi the Gaon, who taught him his ways, so that he knew what is proper and what is not proper, for nothing is lacking from his table from the traits through which, according to the sages, the Torah is acquired[i]. He had already mastered the entire Talmud with all its commentaries by the age of 23.

[Page 80]

Rabbi Itzele, Rabbi the Chaim's son, also wrote in his introduction to *Nefesh Hachaim* that during that period when his father stood before the G'ra, "He illuminated for him the paths of the revealed Torah, as well as the wonderful paths of the hidden [mystical] Torah, and revealed to him tractates and the light of wisdom. When he began discussing Jewish law [*halacha*] and mentioned the name of his rabbi, his entire body trembled. Father collected the fine flour from the entire house of his rabbi of blessed memory."

Rabbi Chaim used to visit his teacher in Vilna three to four times a year regarding communal affairs of Volozhin. He would remain for about a month in order to confer with the G'ra about all his uncertainties and questions. He would first note them on paper, forming a full list. The Gaon Rabbi Chaim would say: I would read before him (the Gr'a) and he would respond. I would ask, and he would answer, until within a brief time he had responded to all of my questions that I had brought with me."[5]

Rabbi Avraham, the son of the Gr'a, told that "each generation has two kinds of sages. The first are like a fountainhead that flows from their inside.They can be compared to the sun, in the secret of Moses. The second are not able to create something on their own. They only have the power to receive a great day. They might be compared to the moon."[6] Rabbi Chaim of Volozhin belongs to the first category. He was like an overflowing fountainhead, and his entire genius was of his own essence. Therefore, he was a student and comrade of the G'ra, and at times they would confer on matters of Torah. It is told that once arriving in Vilna Rabbi Chaim went to Vilna, and was informed that the G'ra was in a sad mood because of difficulties in clarifying an issue in the Jerusalem Talmud. Rabbi Chaim delved into the matter and found a way to explain it. He told it to the G'ra, whose face immediately lit up, and he was filled with happiness.[7]

Rabbi Chaim considered the Gaon of Vilna as one of the early sages, the first and foremost of the sages of that generation, who mastered the essence of the mysteries of the Torah.

"I have heard that the Gaon, Rabbi Chaim once stated in public: There are important people, whom, had my brother, the Gaon and Tzadik, Rabbi Shlomo Zalman, may he rest in peace, lived long – would have reached the level of our rabbi our rabbi the Gaon, may he rest in peace. It is not

[Page 81]

so. Rather, had he lived a thousand years twice over – he would not have reached his ankles. I also heard that he said that his brother the Tzadik, Rabbi Zalman, cast off matters of this world completely to the point where he became like an angel of G-d dressed in human form. However, our rabbi, the G'ra, of blessed memory, even though he acted as a human being, his powers were so sublime to the point where they were like the powers of the angels of G-d. This was the intention of the creation of this world: to act like a human being, and to purify the material essence like a Divine angel."[8]

Rabbi Chaim learned from the Gaon that Torah Study is a fruit of very hard toil of the mind. Once he expressed his grievance to the G'ra: "Rabbi, I have reviewed the Order of *Moed* nineteen times, and I am still not expert in it.

"Nineteen times," mused the G'ra, "and you want to be an expert.!"

"So how many," Rabbi Chaim asked again.

The G'ra responded, "A person must review and study again endlessly."

After the death of the G'ra, Rabbi Chaim felt orphaned, as he writes:[9]

"I have already been warned from my teacher, the holy one of Israel, our great rabbi, the Gaon and Chassid, Rabbi Eliyahu, may he rest in peace, of Vilna, to refrain from favoritism in issuing rabbinical decrees. Nevertheless, from my early days, I have been afraid of establishing the *halacha* in accordance with my poor and weak opinion. While the sun of our great aforementioned rabbi was still in this world – at times I merited presenting my words before him, and he would enlighten the concept to me. After the sun of that Tzadik set, I do not have a rabbi in the city, and to which of the holy ones should I turn?"

After the death of the G'ra[10], Rabbi Chaim took it upon himself to disseminate his Torah in public, as is written in *Aliyot Eliyahu*:[11]

"After the sun set (that is, after the death of the G'ra), his students spread out from their pastures and appointed a chief amongst themselves, the Gaon, the luminary of the Diaspora, our Rabbi Chaim of Volozhin, a student of the Gaon, who began to disseminate his Torah and to draw from the wellsprings of his Torah that he had drawn from Eliyahu. He merited to raise up and disseminate Torah and fear of G-d to all of Israel, for the great ones of the generation, whose intention was raised to teach amongst the Jewish people, gathered and came to him to learn from his mouth, as well as to take moral lessons from the ways of Divine service. They grew, succeeded, and went out to teach amongst the Jewish people."

Original footnotes:

1. This is how Dr. Shlomo Mandelkorn outlines the role of the Yeshiva: "This high and lofty Yeshiva was for many years the host of Torah, as one of the famous Yeshivos during the Talmudic period (Pumbedita, Nehardea, Sura, and Yavneh). See Dr. Mandelkorn: "The Distant Made Near" *Otzar Hasafrot*, 5648 (1848), page 43.
2. *Saarat Eliyahu*, 38.
3. *Aliyot Eliyahu*, page 55.
4. In his introduction to Taklin Chadtin – a commentary on Tractate *Shekalim*, published in Minsk in the year 5572 [1812]. Rabbi Yisrael of Shklov was one of the great students of the Gr'a. In his old age, he made *aliya* to the Land of Israel, and died in Tiberias on 1 Sivan, 5592 [1832].
5. See *Saarat Eliyahu*, pp 40-41, published by Levin-Epstein publishers, Jerusalem, 5723 [1963].
6. *Saarat Eliyahu*, page 36.
7. See *Aliyot Eliyahu*, page 65, note 95. This story is from what we have learned (Taanit 7): "Rabbi Chama says, as Rabbi Chanina says, why is it written iron and iron together. This is to teach you, that just as one piece of iron sharpens its fellow, so do two scholars sharpen each other in halacha. – – – Rabbi Nachman the son of Yitzchak says: Why are words of Torah compared to a tree. For it says, "It is a tree of life for those who take hold of it." This tells you, just as a small piece of wood can ignite a large one, so can small scholars sharpen greater ones. This is as Rabbi Chanina says: "I have learned a great deal from my rabbis, more from my friends than my rabbis, and from my students, more than them all."
   In his commentary to the words of Ben-Zoma: "Who is wise? He who learns from every person" (*Avot* 4:1),

Rabbi Chaim says: "A person should think that it is not through the power of his understanding and greatness that he has attained Torah, but rather through his toil that he found it. Therefore, he learns from every person, for even if his friend is lesser than he, nevertheless, a lesser person can find something just as a great one, and G-d can designate the lesser one to find that which the great one does not find." (*Ruach Chaim*, page 59).

8. *Aliyat Eliyahu*, page 44, note 20
9. *Chut Hameshulash*, setion 9, 20.
10. The G'ra was born in 1720, and died in Vilna in 1797.
11. *Aliyat Eliyahu*, page 76, and note 122 on that page.

Translator's footnote:

According to Pirkei Avot 6:6, there are 48 ways through which Torah expertise is acquired. See https://www.sefaria.org/Pirkei_Avot.6.6?lang=bi&with=all&lang2=en

[Page 82]

The Yeshiva in its First Days

Translated by Jerrold Landau, based on an earlier translation by M. Porat z"l and edited by Judy Feinsilver Montel

The factors that moved Rabbi Chaim of Volozhin to found the Yeshiva are related to the poor situation of Torah study in those days. Rabbi Yosef, the head of the rabbinical court of Krynki and one of the greater students of Rabbi Chaim, describes the situation from the year 5625 (1865):

"I observed that prior to founding of the House of G-d by the angel of G-d, our holy rabbi, neglect and chaos reigned in the world. Nobody even knew what a Yeshiva was and what takes place there. Nobody even knew the concept of public dissemination of Torah, for the world was desolate of Torah. Furthermore, no holy books, and books of the Talmud could be found in the world, other than with a few wealthy Jews of renown. There was not even a complete set of Talmuds in the *Beis Midrashes* of the large cities, for there was no demand for them because people did not occupy themselves with them. However, when our holy rabbi founded the Yeshiva, there was a demand for many Gemaras, and it was necessary to contact large towns and gather Gemara volumes for the purpose of the Yeshiva students.

"When the rabbi and Gaon of Slavita, may he rest in peace, realized that Talmudic volumes were needed in the world, he printed several hundred sets of Talmud of both large and small size. Since they were precious, they were spread throughout the entire world. During the first year of the house of G-d [i.e. the Yeshiva] was functioning in Volozhin, I noticed that many merchants arranged their routes to be in Volozhin, so they could see what the Yeshiva was. When they noticed several tens of distinguished Torah students sitting and studying day and night, they were very astonished, as they had never imagined such. Many merchants remained for several days and did not want to leave."[12]

As Rabbi Chaim of Volozhin was convinced that the world is based on Torah, he encouraged (with the support of several greats of that generation) the founding of a Torah center in Volozhin, which would illuminate the face of the Polish and Lithuanian Diasporas.

He did not undertake the founding of the Yeshiva lightheartedly. Although believing that Jewry risked peril if Torah study was not strengthened, he was not convinced that he was the man to reprove the Jewish people and shout out loud that Torah was declining rapidly day by day. He thought that this crown was not fitting for him, and that such an enormous undertaking requires forces larger than him. Even after the great ones of Lithuania saw that he was the person designated by providence to return the crown of Torah to its ancient status – he did not easily accept this mission. Only in the year 5563 (1803), six

[Page 83]

years after the death of the Gr'a, did Rabbi Chaim lay the foundation stone of the *Etz Chaim* Yeshiva in Volozhin[12a]. The legend goes that when Rabbi Chaim began to lay the cornerstone of the Yeshiva, he broke out in exceedingly great weeping and his hot tears were absorbed into the stone. The Yeshiva stood literally upon Rabbi Chaim's unforgettable tears. For generations, they protected the Yeshiva from all storms and tempests, and contributed to its magnificence.

With the founding of the Yeshiva, Rabbi Chaim was accepted as the Volozhin town rabbi at the young age of 25. This was in the year 5633-5634 (1773-1774). He served this position until approximately the year 5649 (1789). He was accepted as the Vilkomir town Rabbi in 5650 (1790) to replace the Gaon Rabbi Shlomo, called Rabbi Shlomo the Great, one of the students of the Gr'a. After Rabbi Shlomo they [the leaders of the Vilkomir community] put a black cover upon his chair in the rabbinical court, and refused to accept any rabbi to replace him, until Rabbi Chaim was accepted. Then, they removed the black cover, and placed him in the position of Rabbi Shlomo. He only served in this rabbinate for one year, because he refused to accept any salary for his service. He earned his living from his linen factory. Complaints were raised against him for this, causing him to leave the city and return to Volozhin. The residents of the city accepted him with great honor, and he serviced in that rabbinate until the day of his death.

The following is written in his writ of appointment as rabbi of Volozhin:

"When the heads of the holy nation, and the entire holy nation gathered together, we all agreed as one person, we, the leaders, heads, chiefs of our community, may G-d protect and redeem it, together with the leaders and heads of the settlements of our community, we have all unanimously agreed to accept the honorable rabbi, the great, renowned luminary, our teacher Rabbi Chaim, may his light shine and

[Page 84]

his name be praised, as the rabbi and head of the rabbinical court of our community and its environs from this day. All the ordinances and laws of the rabbinate will apply.

"As a proof, we the leaders, heads, and chiefs of the community have signed, together with certain special people, and in conjunction with the heads of the settlements of our community, today, Thursday 4 Iyar in the year mevaser[i], which is 5542 [1782], here in our holy community of Volozhin, may its Rock and Redeemer preserve it."[13]

During the Ten Days of Penitence of the year 5563 [1803][ii], Rabbi Chaim of Volozhin published his proclamation regarding the founding of the *Etz Chaim* Yeshiva of Volozhin. This aroused strong echoes in the Torah world[14]:

"I am the communal representative of the many, wholesome people, whose hearts are worried, and who moan and groan about the Torah that is being forgotten and diminished from the world. Heaven forbid that I speak against the nation of G-d, for indeed, they are not distancing from Torah due to rebellion or sacrilege, Heaven forbid. There are those who wish to study, but do not have a full measure of grain. Others wish to learn but they do not have a rabbi to teach them the true ways of logic, for already for a long time the Torah greats of our country each build their own room and state: I am saving myself as a unique one in the generation, for the learners do not find the Torah pleasant.

"And now I hear a loud voice behind me saying that the time has come for Torah to be made pleasant amongst the studiers, and the nation of Israel is hungry and thirsty as their souls pine for the Torah of G-d, to go from strength to strength to hear the words of G-d. However, from the time that they stopped maintaining Yeshivas in this country, all those who seek G-d and His Torah have dispersed from here like sheep who have no shepherd to tend to the nation of G-d whose desire is to rest in the depths of *halacha* and the truth of Torah. It has been a long time since the people great in fear of G-d in this city have approached me to work towards this mitzva.

"Truly, I am conscious of my small worth, for I have not reached the level where I can express my opinion in public. However, when I see that Torah is disappearing, Heaven forbid, and if I be silent at such a critical moment, it could be that our brethren of the House of Israel will be without a teacher, for if there are no young goats, there are no adult goats, and the walls of the Holy Temple will be locked, Heaven

[Page 85]

forbid. Therefore, I could no longer restrain myself from those around me, and I said: Let us arise and arouse the hearts of the pure ones. I no longer wish to ignore the words of my friends who are urging me in this matter. I decided in my heart to no longer push off their words that are spoken in truth from the depths of their hearts. I have also said as follows: As a young servant summoning [people] to the synagogue, I now come to summon and arouse the hearts of our brethren the House of Israel, beloved and pleasant, so that they will hear the truth, of all that call to them in truth. And you who cleave to G-d and his Torah, may He be blessed, believers the children of believers, for our holy Torah is the life force of our souls, and the world is founded on the breath of our mouths as we delve into it, and especially from the time we were exiled from our Land and lost all that is good – we have no measure other than the study of Torah, and the Holy One Blessed Be He has nothing other than the four ells [of *halacha*] in His world, etc. So how can we not be ashamed when we see that the Torah of G-d is placed in the dust, and that truth has been cast to the ground. The Holy One Blessed Be He weeps every day over the fact that we have abandoned the Torah, may His name be blessed forever, for he demonstrated his wondrous love for us by granting us his hidden delight, in which He, may He be blessed, enjoys every day. How could we have hardened our hearts an exchange enjoyment for weeping, Heaven forbid, for the Holy One Blessed Be He weeps every day over anyone who is capable of occupying [himself with Torah] but does not do so.

"Our brethren, children of Israel! Perhaps the time has come to fence this breach and to return to maintaining G-d's Torah with all our strength. Who will volunteer to teach the students, and who will volunteer to finance the Torah [endeavor]? Everyone approaching the Holy Torah will live a life of eternity, for the shadow of the funds and the shadow of the wisdom will bring life to its owners. Let me be the first volunteer in heart and soul to be among the teachers, and with the mercy of G-d, Who guided me amply from the beginning of my life, in Him do I trust, and I anticipate that He will enable me to amply provide for the students according to their needs.

"During the brief time since this started, I was able to gather a small group of the holy flock [i.e. Jewish children], praise to His Blessed Name. They tasted the taste of Torah and the vast majority of them took upon themselves the yoke of Torah in truth, blessed be G-d. And now that I have dared to jump in to be the first to volunteer to teach, I ask other men of my age to do as I have done, and even those older than me shall most certainly do so. Fortunate are the elders who heed the younger ones. I call you, Children of Israel, of holy seed, blessed of G-d, please accept the truth from he who spoke it, for at the end, truth is more precious than anything – not to abandon the eternal life planted through the supporters of the branch of life, planted in the heart of the seas – for if a person grasps on to it they will be raised from the deep waters, but if they do not grasp on to it, Heaven forbid, the deep waters will sweep them away, and they will be lost forever. Is there anyone in this world who would not grasp on to it? All of us, o brethren the Sons of Israel, we are not called alive unless we grasp on to the Tree of Life. If the students take upon themselves the yoke of Torah in truth, as an ox accepts a yoke and a donkey a burden,

[Page 86]

if the supporters uphold the weakened pillar of Torah from both sides, about them it is said: Blessed are they who uphold the words of this Torah[liii], and the scholars and supporters of Torah are fortunate, and will live eternal life in peace. Blessed are they before the Blessed G-d, in their comings and goings, with the blessing of Zevulun preceding the blessing of Issachar[liv] – and both together cleave to the canopy of life, and the blessing of goodness will come to them. According to their deeds will they eat in the World To Come, and together they will justly behold the pleasantness of G-d. These will see the Face of the Blessed Name through charity, and those will be sated with the fullness of the Face of the Blessed Name, for we have no life other than through those who occupy themselves with the light of the Torah, and through those who uphold and cleave to G-d. Let us just all be strong and strengthen each other, so that the scriptural verse will be fulfilled for us: Even though they hire amongst the nations, I will now gather them[lv], speedily in our days, Amen, may it be His will.

"The words of the proclaimer are with great embarrassment, as I speak with great subjugation before the nation of G-d. I do not believe that such a great merit will come through me. Nevertheless, I do not forgo the merit of the many, and I am supported with the trust in the Blessed Name, so that the Torah of G-d will not be forgotten by the true seed.

Sunday of the Ten Days of Penitence 5563 [1802], here in Volozhin, Signed by Chaim the son of my master, my father Rabbi Yitzchak, may the memory of the holy be blessed for life in the World To Come."

When Rabbi Chaim founded the Yeshiva, he owned a cloth factory in Volozhin. He used to sign his responsa letters modestly "**Chaim B'MoHarYtz (Ben Mor**einu **Har**av **Yitz**chak) – [our teacher Rabbi Yitzchak's son], *the Melamed* (teacher of young children) *from Volozhin*."[15] However, as rightfully noted by Rabbi Meir Bar-Ilan in his book "From Volozhin to Jerusalem" – even though Rabbi Chaim did not use the title of "Yeshiva Head" as his signature, he was still the head of all Yeshiva heads.

Initially a quorum [ten] of students were assembled in the Yeshiva, a nucleus of great talent. It was unusual for so many students with such great talent to be gathered in a single Yeshiva. We see from this how great Rabbi Chaim's name was in the world of Torah as a Gaon and a guide. Already from the beginning of the founding of the Yeshiva, Rabbi Chaim made an enactment that blocked entrance to the Yeshiva to people lacking talent. Every student who wished to be accepted to the Yeshiva had to pass a test to determine his level in Gemara. Therefore, the Yeshiva was comprised of talented lads.

Rabbi Chaim provided food and clothing for his students on his own account. Even when the number of students who were taken in from the area increased, he fed them amply, supervised their state of health, rejoiced in their happiness, and participated in their sorrows.

[Page 87]

The following folktale demonstrates the extent of his care for his students: Once, Rabbi Chaim ordered a pair of large, peasant boots. When the shoemaker brought him the boots, his family members wondered: Why does he, Rabbi Chaim, need such boots?

He answered nothing. At an early winter dawn, he was seen wearing the heavy boots and pacing back and forth after a snowy night. As the Jews of Volozhin were going to the Shacharit service, they found Rabbi Chaim trampling in the deep snow.

"Our rabbi, why are you walking and trampling in the snow?" – they asked.

"I am forging a path for the poor Yeshiva students," responded Rabbi Chaim.

Out of his love and concern for his students, Rabbi Chaim abolished the custom of "eating days"[vi], which had a taint of denigration for the honor of Torah and its students. He ensured that the lads would receive a stipend from the Yeshiva coffers to provide sufficiently for their living expenses. He also made an enactment that the student would not be referred to as a "Yeshiva lad" but rather "a Yeshiva man" – a term that raises the esteem of the student.

Rabbi Chaim's relation to the Yeshiva members stemmed from the rabbi to student relation. He regarded them as friends, from whom one could learn, as is stated in the Midrash on Psalms: "As with water, where the great are not ashamed to ask the small for some water to drink; so too in Torah matters, the great should not be ashamed to ask the small to teach him a chapter, or a law". (Psalm 1, section 25). In order to hear something from the mouths of the students regarding their rabbi on the subject of teaching style and the orders of the Yeshiva – he instituted, in accordance with tradition, the "Purim Rabbi." Since no student was so brazen as to alert the rabbi to untoward matters, he designated one day a year, the day of Purim – a day when even the sages permitted levity – when one student will be free all day to freely express through words and deeds, and would be the sole arbiter of Yeshiva matters and conduct. On this day, the "Single Day" Rabbi would speak openheartedly about untoward matters relating the year-round rabbi. Rabbi Chaim took the words of criticism with great seriousness. He would then rectify the matters, and make sure to not stumble in the future.

When the number of students grew, Rabbi Chaim was no longer able to support them from the income of his factory. Therefore, he approached the great rabbis to declare an aid effort for the Yeshiva, so that the Yeshiva could be sustained. On the 15th of Iyar, 5664 (1804) an appeal was issued, signed by the great ones of Vilna, directed to the far-off communities outside Lithuania, calling for support of the Yeshiva of Volozhin. The signatories included Rabbi Avraham the son of the Gr'a. The appeal was written in the second year after the founding of the Yeshiva. Its content is as follows:

"We have seen that many wholesome people have assembled for the holy task, to study Torah day and night and to take shelter under the great tree of the rabbi and Gaon, our teacher and rabbi, Rabbi Chaim, the head of the rabbinical court of Volozhin, may G-d protect it. We have already supported him with our hands, and have become supporters of Torah, to provide support for him from within our country. Now that we see that G-d desires him to succeed – we inform those far away that thus is the way of Torah, from afar one brings one's sustenance, and we must give thanks that such a great thing has happened in our times, in an orphaned generation

[Page 88]

such as ours. We here, and you there shall come together to strengthen their hands, so they will not be neglected, Heaven forbid, and the merit of Torah will stand for us and our descendants forever. For we will do what is good and proper in the eyes of G-d, to strengthen the weakened pillar of Torah. May G-d grant us merit to magnify the Torah and make it more powerful."[16]

The Value of Torah Study in the Etz Chaim Yeshiva of Volozhin

Translated by Jerrold Landau**, based on an earlier translation by** M. Porat z"l **and edited by** Judy Feinsilver Montel

The main pillar of the *Etz Chaim* Yeshiva was the study of Torah, which is a tree of life for those who grasp it. The existence of all worlds depends on it, including the private world of a person. However, Torah knowledge alone is not the primary point, but rather the essence of learning and the effort in Torah study, and the constant cleaving to Gemara. It is impossible to complete the study of Gemara. Rather, a person should learn and learn endlessly. As a person becomes more proficient in Torah, it is a greater command to delve into it. Those who study more will know more.

His conviction that Torah study is the sublime essence of life was the basis of Rabbi Chaim's foreword to *Sifra Detzniuta* [The Book of Modesty] of the Gr'a. There, he includes an interesting story in the name of his great rabbi, who was offered by a messenger to have the secrets of Torah revealed to him, thereby becoming complete in Torah knowledge without toil or effort. The Gr'a pushed off the messenger:

"Above everything is the strength and awesomeness of the Gr'a, for he did not see G-d for his soul other than in the effort that he expended in wisdom, knowledge, and aptitude. After his great efforts, and when he was granted mercy from Heaven and the wellsprings of the secrets of wisdom were revealed to him – this to him was a gift of G-d. If not for this manner, he did no want these. Even if they wished to grant him from Heaven without an effort or toil the sublime mysteries and secrets via preachers of mysteries and princes of Torah – he would not want this. For I have heard from his holy mouth that on many occasions, several preachers came to his door from Heaven with their request, imploring him that they wish to give him the secrets of the Torah without any effort. He did not pay attention to them at all. One of the preachers urged him greatly. Nevertheless, he did not look upon his lofty appearance, and he responded that he does not want his proficiency in the Torah of the Blessed One to come through any intermediary at all. My eyes are only raised to He, Blessed be His Name, for what He wishes to reveal to me and to grant my share in His Torah, Blessed be His Name, through my toil that comes through my effort with all my energy. He, Blessed be He, will give me wisdom from His mouth, knowledge, and understanding. My heart will understand, my kidneys will be like two wellsprings, and I will know that I found favor in His eyes.

[Page 89]

I want nothing other than what comes from His mouth. Concepts via angels, preachers, and princes of Torah that are not through my toil and not through my wisdom – I do not want them.

"It once happened that I was sent to my younger brother Rabbi Zalman to tell him in his name that he should not accept any angelic preacher who might come to him. The main thing is what a person attains in this world through toil and effort through which he will give satisfaction to his Creator. He would often say that He, may His Name be Blessed, only created sleep for this purpose, for anything that a person cannot attain while the soul is bound to the body, even after the effort and toil of the body, which acts as a separating partition – is revealed to him during sleep, when he is then separated from the body and cloaked in the supernal garb, the outfit of the sages."

Rabbi Chaim of Volozhin provides a theoretical basis for the necessity of constancy in the study of Torah:

"It is written in the Scriptures: "She is a tree of life for those who grasp her"[vii], for a person must set in his heart and imagine in his mind that even if he was drowning in a torrential river and he sees a strong tree in the river, he would certainly expend energy to grasp and cleave to it with all his might, and he would not let go even for one moment, for his very life depends on this. Who is foolish and does not understand that were he to let go, Heaven forbid, even for one moment and release his grasp, he would immediately drown? The Holy Torah is called a tree of Life [*Etz Chaim*]. Only during the time that a person grasps it with love and occupies himself with it constantly does he live a true, sublime life, tied and bound, so to speak, with the eternal life of the Blessed Name, for G-d and the Torah are one. If, Heaven forbid, he would neglect his study, separate from its constancy, and occupy himself with the vanities and enjoyments of the world, he would be cut off from the supernal life, and would drown in the wicked waters, heaven forbid."[17]

"If, Heaven forbid, the world would be completely devoid, even for a single moment, from the treasured nation and chosen people observing and learning our holy Torah, all the worlds would be completely destroyed and nullified from reality, Heaven forbid. Therefore, even a single Jewish person has great power to sustain all the worlds and creation in general through his occupation and study of our holy Torah for its own sake."[18]

We may conclude from above, that Torah learning is significant not only for the person learning it, but also for the existence of all the worlds, which only exist for the sake of Torah. Therefore, Rabbi Chaim made sure that the sound of Torah would never cease in the Yeshiva, even for a moment. The doors of the Yeshiva were not closed even for a moment.

[Page 90]

The sounds of the students never ceased. Rabbi Chaim instituted night shifts every night. One shift would leave, and another would enter. The shifts would not be interrupted even on Sabbath and festival nights. He himself would visit the Yeshiva on Sabbath eves to ensure that the lads were not idle from Torah, Heaven forbid. At the conclusion of Yom Kippur every year, Rabbi Chaim would study himself until midnight, for he was concerned that at such a time, when every student was tired and weary from the great holy day, there would be nobody learning. Therefore, he took this effort upon himself.

Rabbi Chaim's learning methodology, instituted in the Yeshiva, was that of "straightforward logic" rather than didactics and twisting of the texts. In this sense, he followed the path of his rabbi, the Gr'a, who emphasized the straightforward meaning, and studied the scriptures in the literal sense, without intermixing hints and secret meanings. He also studied the Talmud in its straightforward sense, without all sorts of didactics and divisions. He would rely only upon the source.

This methodology of study took root in the Volozhin Yeshiva, as well as in other Yeshivas that were influenced from it. Many of the Yeshiva students who were used the methodology of didactics and divisions would come for to the Yeshiva of Volozhin for a specific term to enjoy the unique learning style.

R' Chaim of Volozhin as Yeshiva Head and Great Educator

Translated by Jerrold Landau**, based on an earlier translation by** M. Porat z"l **and edited by** Judy Feinsilver Montel

The Etz Chaim Yeshiva was based on pedagogical principles. Rabbi Chaim was not only the Yeshiva head, but, first and foremost, he was a prominent educator. He dedicated the vast majority of *Nefesh HaChaim* to explaining the value of Torah study, which is the pinnacle of human wisdom. "For all the philosophers admit that all the wisdoms are like a drop in a bucket in relation to the wisdom of the Talmud." (*Ruach Chaim*, page 52). *Ruach Chaim* is his work on his doctrine of morality and character traits. In this book, Rabbi Chaim teaches the proper path for a Jewish person to follow in order to attain moral perfection and sublime spiritual levels. This book also includes may ideas on the relationship between the teacher and the student.

One of Rabbi Chaim of Volozhin's educational fundamentals was the trait of being satisfied [with less] and abstaining from worldly pleasures. He adopted this lifestyle from his rabbi, the Gr'a, about whom it was said that he did not wish to take benefit from this world, and "he ate meager, cold bread dipped in water, of the size of two olives. He would eat this evening and morning, and would not taste them on his palate, but rather swallow it whole." (*Aliyot Eliahu*, 51)

Regarding the adage "This is the way of Torah" (*Avot* 6:14)[viii], Rabbi Chaim said:

"For eating and drinking are the downfall of a person, as is explained from "And the L-rd caused a slumber to fall upon the man" (Genesis 2:21). Eating is similar. Therefore, to the extent that one minimizes the downfall, it is more praiseworthy, and he will have time left to study Torah. Even your eating should be such that you do not go immediately to eating, but rather delay it, and not set aside your learning for it immediately at the onset of your hunger. The day is still young, and there will be time to eat. Therefore, it says in the future tense "you shall eat bread with salt," but "in Torah you labor" is in the present tense. For, in truth, the matter of eating is a great disgrace for a person, for one takes physical matter

[Page 91]

and places it in one's entrails, and one's life depends on this; this is certainly an embarrassment for one's soul, the spiritual portion. Perforce, one should not be embarrassed. However, excess in eating is foolishness."

The trait of being satisfied with little brings with it the trait of humility, which takes an important place in Rabbi Chaim's educational teaching. Rabbi Chaim says regarding "be of an exceedingly humble spirit" (*Avot* 4:4): "Do not think that the commandment of humility is filled by being of a humble spirit in one's own eyes, but rather one should think that in truth that he is nothing, that the hope of a human is the worm, and that there is nothing at all to be proud about."

As a pedagogue, Rabbi Chaim did not hold the view of autodidacticism. In this way, he diverged from the Gr'a who had only studied with a rabbi for six years, and then about another quarter of a year with the Gaon Rabbi Moshe, the author of *Pnei Moshe*[ix]. At that point, he stopped taking lessons from teachers. Rabbi Chaim held the view that one must study Torah from a rabbi, because the rabbi imbues the spirit of life into the written word. Torah is not acquired without "listening with the ear"[x]. The studier himself will have nobody to clarify his uncertainties. Therefore "appoint for yourself a teacher, and avoid doubt"[xi], so that you can ask him anytime a doubt arises, and thereby reach the knowledge of the truth.

Therefore, Rabbi Chaim would lengthen his explanations so that the matter would be absorbed. If the words of the Gr'a in comparison to Rabbi Chaim are compared to stars that appear small because of their distance from us – the words of Rabbi Chaim are like large candelabras on the table.

Rabbi Chaim's secret of success as an educator is concealed in his knowledge of the student's soul. He understood that attaining his educational purposes requires care in order to avoid trampling the pupil's personality, but rather to preserve his personal freedom. Not only did he give room for questions, but he also encouraged the student through asking questions from his side in order to create a dialogue.

Regarding "an impatient person cannot teach" (*Avot* 2:5), Rabbi Chaim used to say "If the pupil asks once and [the teacher] gets angry with him, then he will not ask anymore, for he will be embarrassed. Even that time, the questioner will not accept his words." The teacher must be happy with the questions of the students, and see them as a benefit for himself, for "sometimes the truth is with the student, just as the small piece of wood may ignite the large one". It was not for naught that our rabbis enumerated "didactics with students" along with serving the sages and give and take with friends among the 48 ways of acquiring Torah[x], for the *halacha* becomes clear through their questions.

Rabbi Chaim took care to develop the self-opinion of his students, for "A human being without an opinion is not worthy of compassion." People who are not pedantic and stringent with opinions and deeds, paying attention to all possible contradictions are mediocre and of small character. Moreover, they are lacking moral character, for moral principles are based on distinction of opinions and on fixing relations upon them. However, a person must not denigrate the opinions of his fellow, for the truth is a blend of various opinions. Therefore, one must listen to the opinions of one's fellow, analyze them and clarify them. Only after listening and research can one select the proper opinion.

[Page 92]

Rabbi Chaim expresses this outlook in his explanation to the adage "the more counsel, the more understanding" (*Avot* 2:7):

"There is an adage in the mouths of people: ask advice, and do according to your intellect. According to this, what is the apparent use of advice? However, one can understand simply that a person cannot understand the internals of the matter from the outside regarding the advice he received. He can only understand a little. It would be the same with a second advice giver. Only the person asking advice himself understands the internals of the matter completely, but he is lacking the intellect and understanding of them all. Therefore, when he collects the advice and intelligence of each of them regarding the matter – then he can understand how and what to choose as common advice from amongst all the individual pieces of advice, from this one a bit and from the other one a bit."

In this way did Rabbi Chaim teach his students to regard every concept as a deposit, with the owner of the deposit liable to come and take it back at any moment. It is natural for a person to think flippantly of his achievement. A poor person desires wealth, but when he achieves his goal, his wealth becomes routine. He then treats it flippantly and desires more. However, if he knows that his wealth is not permanent, and that he might return to his former poverty at any moment – he will be happy with his lot.

Rabbi Chaim says the following in his explanation of the statement "Who is rich?" (*Avot* 4:1):

"It is forbidden for a student to accept the words of his teacher when he has questions on them. At times, the truth will be with the student, just as a small piece of wood can ignite a large one. This is what it means by "let your house be a gathering place for the sages," and "sit at the dust"[xii], where it uses the same language as "and a man wrestled with him" (Genesis 32:25)[xiv], which is referring to battle, to war, for it is an obligatory war. Therefore, this is about our holy rabbis in the land, whose souls are in the heavens above, who write and publish books, and their books are with us. Indeed, through the books in our homes, our homes become a gathering place for these sages, and we are also adjured and permitted to struggle and battle with their words, and to answer their questions – not to play favorites with anyone, but rather to love the truth. However, with all this, one should be careful to avoid speaking with pride and a boastful heart when one sees a place to differ, and it seems that a person might be greater than his teacher or than the author of a book that he

[Page 93]

has obtained. For he should know that at times, he will not understand his words and intentions. Therefore, he should have extra humility. This is what it means by "sit at the dust" as stated above, but with the condition of "the dust of their feet," meaning that one should do so with humility and submission, dealing with them on the ground."

Rabbi Chaim of Volozhin knew how to penetrate the interior of the soul of each of his students, and to know what aim he would choose in life. When students went to him to receive a parting blessing before traveling home, he would delineate the path of life of each one, stating how he would act in the future. His love for the students was very great. He would invite them to dine at his table each Sabbath. During the meal, he would tell them sublime adages of morality. He had mercy on them as a father has mercy on his children. He knew their pain of being distant from their homes, and therefore he attempted to comfort them in their loneliness. Rabbi Chaim regarded leaving one's parental home as an important factor in their success in their studies. "Exile yourself to a place of Torah" (*Avot* 4:14). In order to bring joy to their hearts, he would invite them to Passover Seders. He knew very well their longing for their homes all the days of the year, and the longing and sadness would be especially strong during the festivals, when everyone would normally rejoice in the company of their families. However, not only on festivals did he try to bring them joy, but also every day. He always knew that joy is one of the 48 ways through which the Torah is acquired. For "one who studies in joy for one hour will learn much more than one who studies several hours in sadness."

Translator's footnotes:

i. *Mevaser* [harbinger of good tidings] bears the same gematria as the year.
ii. The Ten Days of Penitence are the days between Rosh Hashanah and Yom Kippur inclusive. As the year changes at Rosh Hashanah, the secular year should have been listed as 1802 rather than 1803.
iii. Based on Deuteronomy 27:26 – although in the positive rather than negative form.
iv. Moses blessed Zevulun in his goings and Issachar in his comings. This is interpreted as a blessing for Zevulun in his business endeavours, the proceeds of which are used to support his brother Issachar in his Torah studies.
v. Hosea 8:10.
vi. The practice of having Yeshiva students eat at the homes of various householders on a rotational basis.
vii. Proverbs 3:18.
viii. The entire adage is as follows (translation from https://www.sefaria.org/Pirkei_Avot.6.4?lang=bi&with=all&lang2=en): Such is the way [of a life] of Torah: you shall eat bread with salt, and rationed water shall you drink; you shall sleep on the ground, your life will be one of privation, and in Torah shall you labor. If you do this, "Happy shall you be and it shall be good for you" (Psalms 128:2): "Happy shall you be" in this world, "and it shall be good for you" in the world to come. (Note, this is *Avot* 6:4, not 6:14).

ix.   https://en.wikipedia.org/wiki/Moses_Margolies
 x.   *Pirkei Avot* 6:6.
 xi.   *Pirkei Avot* 1:16.
 xii.   *Pirkei Avot* 1:4, "Sit at the dust of the feet of the scholars".
 xiii. The term for wrestle is מתאב ק – literally "to raise the dust." This verse refers to Jacob wrestling with the angel.

[Page 93]

The Moral Personality and Wisdom of Rabbi Chaim of Volozhin

Translated by Jerrold Landau

The sublime moral personality of Rabbi Chaim is emphasized in prominent lines by his son Rabbi Itzele in his introduction to *Nefesh HaChaim*.

"If he was insulted – he would not insult. He was of humble spirit before any person. He was concerned about even the minutes amount of physical pleasure, and he conducted himself such that he would not feel any pleasure. When he reached old age and was afflicted with afflictions of love[i] – he accepted them with joy in body and spirit (and with a joyous face, without uttering a sigh, and his spirit was happy all the years that he accepted the suffering). That *Tzadik* was only distressed that he was forced to nourish his body due to his illness. His eyes descended very deeply into mystery (and my eyes saw it, and it was not strange). Even though his heart was pained over this, he was happy in his suffering, which limited his feelings of pleasure to the point where he paid attention to neither pleasure nor affliction.

"Anyone who sees the sun in its strength, witness and are astonished that with all of his bodily humility and lowliness of spirit regarding matters of the world, his heart was opposite with regard to Divine matters, clothing himself in strength and splendor to the nth degree. His heart was focused upon making a pleasant dwelling for Torah, Divine service, and performance of good deeds. His heart was very proud in the ways of G-d to fight the battles of Torah. Every mitzva that he began with the spirit of wisdom and strength, he concluded in the spirit of knowledge and the fear of G-d.

[Page 94]

"In all his ways, he minimized his personal honor in order to increase the honor of Heaven, regarding communal affairs, and especially regarding public issues. It is known that he cast his soul forward and put in far more effort than he had energies for. Even though he was elderly, he held his hands steadfastly until the sun set[ii]. Even when his energy was diminished, may G-d protect us, even when he was lying in bed with his illness, his thoughts were clear and his eyes were raised toward Heaven, to include the Divine Name in the pains of the public and the individual, with sighs, moans, and broken loins. His many sighs over this would break the body of anyone who heard. (He used to chastise me when he saw that I did not participate in the pain of my fellow.) He always told me that man was not created for himself, but rather to provide benefit to others to the extent that it is within one's power." He judged and taught: Love peace, pursue peace, love one's fellow, and draw them close to Torah."[iii]

Not only was Rabbi Chaim famous for his intelligence and sharpness among the Jews, but he was also renowned in the gentile world. It is told that in the year 5572 (1812), Rabbi Chaim was asked by a captain during a conversation, "In the rabbi's opinion, who will win the war?" Rabbi Chaim requested at the outset that he not become angry, and he told him the following parable: Once, a government official travelled by a horse-drawn carriage. The horses were the finest Italian horses. When the horses reached the area of a bog, they stopped and could not move. The wagon driver tried all sort of ruses, but for naught. A farmer was travelling behind the government official in a loaded wagon hitched to small, thin horses. Since the wagon of the government official was blocking his route, he turned his wagon to the side and crossed the bog without stumbling. The government official was astonished at what had taken placed, and asked the farmer to explain him the reason. The farmer responded: "Indeed, your horses are better than mine in number and in power, but they have no friendly relations with each other. All of them are superior, and when you whip one of them, the others are happy, for the whip cannot whip them all at once. Therefore, only the whipped one makes an effort to continue on as a result of the blow, and the rest remain fixed in their places. My horses are not the same, for the grew up together from the womb and from birth. Their temperament and legs are similar. Every one of them feels the pain of his fellow. If I whip one of them, they will all gird their strength to pull the wagon. That is what gave them the ability to transport me across the bog in peace." The captain understood the parable very well.

Another trait of Rabbi Chaim's was his straightforwardness. Rabbi Chaim was a man of the people, who greatly loved his fellow Jew. One detail, which testifies to the popularity of Rabbi Chaim of Volozhin, is included in *Orchot Chaim* (final page):

"An honest, righteous man in Volozhin had no children (may G-d protect us). Upon his death, he had made a request to ask our rabbi to study *mishnayot* on his behalf, for the elevation of his soul. The rabbi did so, for it is a mitzva to fulfil the requests of the deceased. When he concluded the [*Mishnaic*] order of *Zeraim*, he went to his grave and said to him: "I have studied the Order of *Zeraim* for the elevation of your soul."

[Page 95]

Rabbi Chaim's Death; The Wonderful Legend of his Love for the Jews of Volozhin

Translated by Jerrold Landau, based on an earlier translation by M. Porat z"l and that was edited by Judy Feinsilver Montel

Rabbi Chaim was afflicted with difficult suffering and pain in his old age. Nevertheless, he was not bitter, and he did not curse the day he was born[iv]. He accepted everything with love. Legend states that on Rosh Hashanah 5591 (1820) approximately a half a year before his death, when he was given the honor of *Hagba*[v], the Torah scroll fell from his hands. Then he informed his acquaintances that his end was near.

His son, Rabbi Itzele, portrays the passing of Rabbi Chaim of Volozhin in his introduction to *Nefesh HaChaim*, as follows:

"Whomever has not seen (his) strength and humility on the day he was taken from us, has never seen strength and humility[vi]. You would hear the Shacharit service until his soul departed for Above. He renewed his strength at every hour. One moment he lowed his body with his words, when he felt that "the dust returns to the ground as it was," and his face turned black as a raven. Then he girded himself with wondrous strength and devotion, and his face lit up as the face of a living king, binding his soul to his spirit that will return to the G-d who had given it in purity, until his spirit and soul were gathered up to the Blessed One Be He with a kiss[vii], and were bound up in the bounds of life with G-d."

R' Chaim passed away on Sivan 14[th,] 5581 (1821) at the age of 72. He was brought to eternal rest in the Volozhin cemetery[viii]. The text on the monument over his grave is composed in a manner that the first letters of each line form [his name]: Chaim the son of Yitzchak, of blessed memory."[ix]

The wisdom of the Babylonian Talmud and the understanding of the Jerusalem Talmud are the source of **Life**[x].

The radiant beauty of the Kabbala, and the brilliant splendor of Aggada [Talmudic lore], choose **Life**.

The purity of awe of G-d's advice, resource, and strength, are in his lot of **Life**.

Mysteries of many Midrashim, and the hidden secrets of the Almighty, find **Life**

In his house of study, among his students are those who know the paths of **Life**.

Lamentation, weeping and eulogizing, for departed from them is the soul of **Life**.

Wail, moan, and cry whomever has the spirit of **Life**.

With shouting of angels, G-d's winds are blowing when carrying the soul of **Life**.

Grace, truth, and charity are walking before Him on high, in the lands of **Life**.

Holiness, modesty, and justice are filling the corners of the world through way of **Life**.

He is resplendent there, he aspires to his place, the tree of **Life**.

G-d has taken him, to see the goodness of G-d, in the land of **Life**.

The text engraved on Rabbi Haym's tomb

וזה נוסח המצבה של רבי חיים

חכמת תלמוד בבלי, ובינת תלמוד ירושלמי, מקור חיים

יופי זוהר הקבלה, ותפארת זיו האגדות, בחרו בחיים

יראת ה' טהורה, עצה ותושיה וגבורה, חלקם בחיים

מסתרי מדרשי רבים, וממטוני דעת אלקים, מצא חיים

בבית תלמודו ומדרשו, בין תלמידיו, יודעי ארחות חיים

נהי ובכי ומספד, כי עלה מהם נפש החיים

יללה וזהגה זהי, בכל אשר בו רוח חיים

צעקת אראלים, נשבה רוח ה', נשא רוח חיים

חסד ואמת וצדקה, מרום לפניו הלכו, בארצות החיים

קדושה וענוה וצדק, קצוי ארץ מלאה, דרך חיים

זורח הוא שם, אל מקומו שואף, עין החיים

לקח אותו ה', לראות בטוב ה', בארץ החיים

The text on R' Chaim's tomb in Hebrew

Who was waved and lifted[xi], the crown of our head, the breath of our nose, my father, my father, the chariot and horsemen of Israel[xii], the great, living Gaon, pious, modest, in the honor of glory of G-d, our Rabbi Chaim, may he rest in peace, the head of the rabbinical court and head of the Yeshiva of the holy community

[Page 96]

of Volozhin, who poured living water on the holy heavenly angel, the true Gaon, the light of the world, the rabbi of the entire Diaspora, in the honor and glory of G-d, our rabbi, the renowned, pious one, Rabbi Eliahu of Vilna. The brother of the head of the thousands of Israel, the holy Gaon, similar to angel, holy is said of him, our rabbi Shlomo Zalman, may he rest in peace. Departed from life on Thursday of the Torah portion of "And when the Ark set forth"[xiii], 14 Sivan, of the year "Everything is written about life"[xiv].

Legend tells that Rabbi Chaim refused to enter the Garden of Eden alone without the Volozhin Jews who had toiled and struggled on behalf of the Yeshiva. He desired to come inside with the entire People of Israel and the entire world. Fishel Schneerson relates this legend in his book *Chaim Grobitzer*[19]:

"Rabbi Chaim told the Heavenly Entourage: "I no longer have the strength to bear the honor which I do not deserve. I cannot enter the Garden of Eden. I wish to stay here and await the days of the Messiah, the generation that will be worthy of it, to open the gates of the Garden of Eden for all mankind, for the entire world. Then I will merit redemption along with the entire People of Israel. Our Father in Heaven, in his great mercy, should permit me to remain here and wait."

"The Heavenly Entourage acceded to his request, that emanated from the depths of his heart. To this day, Rabbi Chaim of Volozhin stands and waits at the border between Heaven and earth."

As for the tomb, Schneerson writes in his book:[20]

"(One of the elders relates) I was once at the Volozhin cemetery and I visited. There, over Rabbi Chaim's grave, there is a white stone cabin. On the inside wall of the cabin, holy words regarding Rabbi Chaim of blessed memory are etched in Hebrew. I looked and saw the drawing of the Polish eagle above the lines, hidden somewhat. I did not dare to ask anyone about the meaning of this but I had no doubt that Count Tyskiewicz helped build the white cabin over Rabbi Chaim's grave, just as he had previously helped to build the Rabbi Chaim's white house that stands in the market square."[xv]

[Page 97]

The Eulogy for Rabbi Chaim of Volozhin from Rabbi David of Novhorodok

There are many who eulogized Rabbi Chaim of Volozhin. The most comprehensive and precise was the eulogy of Rabbi David of Novhorodok. The following are several sections of the eulogy:

"It is appropriate to shed a river of tears and to mourn for, lament for, and eulogize a person such as he, who was equal in deeds and character to Rabbi Chanina and Rabbi Chiya[xvi], who was known as sharp and expert at didactics, great and mighty, precise to the hairbreadth, and famous for his response that he responded to the far-off edges of the land and sea. He had the power and might to review the entire Torah, just like Rabbi Chiya, lest it be forgotten, Heaven forbid. In this way as well he did not desist from grasping the trait of Rabbi Chiya – – – with his wonderful efforts to uphold the Torah students, and to teach them so that the Torah will not be forgotten from Israel, and also to provide them with all their needs… For his net was cast across all ends of the earth and the fullness thereof[xvii]. Everything he decreed he fulfilled. Even in his old age, when he could not gird the strength to give the class himself, he nevertheless increased his personal supervision to the community of Yeshiva students, in manners that cannot be fully described… Furthermore, every night they would set up watches of separate groups from among the Yeshiva students, so that there would be no gap in the learning, day and night, and so that there would be people learning at all times, day and night. I was told that, in truth, these watches did not stop even on Sabbath eves, and he himself would at times make an effort to come and go even on Sabbath eves, in order to ensure that it would not stop."[21]

Yaakov Halevi Lifshitz describes the activities of Rabbi Chaim Volozhin at length, in the following words:[22]

"The works of Rabbi Chaim and the greatness of his Torah, his holiness and wisdom stand alive before the eyes of the nation, and his refined spirit walks in our midst today. There is no *Beis Midrash* without a novel idea from him, there is no holy idea upon which his name is not mentioned, there is no good suggestion and activity in our midst that is not etched with his nature and stamp. His book *Nefesh HaChaim* was accepted in the nation as a book from the earliest of the early sages[xviii]. His letters and adages are also still borne on the lips of all of clean intellect, like the mundane speech of holy purity. The greats of the generation said about him "A scholar is better than a prophet." All his days, he dedicated his soul and resources only for his nation and its Torah.

"In truth, it can be said about him that he created an epoch in the life of the nation, with a new style based on the methodology of our rabbi the Gr'a who established an order of study, with love

[Page 98]

of Torah, to magnify it and make it mighty, with national feelings to revive the nation, so that everyone will recognize their obligation to be concerned for the benefit of the public."

These are the Books that Rabbi Chaim Left Behind

a. *Nefesh HaChaim* – in which Rabbi Chaim delves deeply into the mysteries of the souls in Kabbalistic fashion, and in the manner of theoretical research. (Published by his son Rabbi Itzele in the year 5584 [1824]).
b. *Ruach Chaim*, a commentary on Tractate *Avot*.
c. *Responsa*, published in the book *Chut Hameshulash*, by his great-grandson Rabbi Chaim Hillel Fried.
d. *Responsa*, published at the end of the book Beit Halevi, by his great-grandson Rabbi Yosef Dov Soloveitchik.

He also wrote the introduction to the book *Sifra Detzniuta* [Book of Modesty] by the Gr'a, and glosses on the book *Shnot Eliahu*.

Translator's footnotes:

i.   Traditionally, afflictions of love refer to human suffering that is not due to sin, but rather to a refinement of the person by G-d.
ii.   Based on Exodus 17:12
iii. *Avot* 1:12.

iv. See Job 3:1. Job's first reaction after his afflictions was to curse the day he was born.

v. Lifting the Torah after the Torah reading in the synagogue.

vi. This form of expression is based on the Mishna *Sukka* 5:1.

vii. A reference to a comfortable death through the kiss of G-d, as Moses and Aaron merited.

viii. Original translator M. Porat added: inside a stone cabin (Shtibl).

ix. Original translator M. Porat added the following here: R' Chaim's memorial, the stone cabin with the inscription were destroyed during the Fascist's occupation. Sorrowfully we could not find any picture of the tomb. In the Volozhin Yizkor Book page 45 is presented Rabbi Eliyahu's corner on the Vilna graveyard. R' Chaim's corner at the Volozhin cemetery was built in a similar style.

x. *Chaim* means life in Hebrew.

xi. This seems to be a continuation of the text of the gravestone, beyond the mnemonic line portion. The first words "who was waved and lifted" is based on Exodus 29:27.

xii. Based on II Kings 2:12, the lament of Elisha as Elijah was taken up to Heaven.

xiii. This is a portion of the verse in Numbers 10:35, of the Torah portion of Behaalotecha. In poetic style, a Torah portion is often hinted to through a prominent verse.

xiv. The numerical value (gematria) of these words is 581. The secular year was 1821, which corresponds to 5581.

xv. The original translator, M. Porat, added a section of the photo from page 317 here, focussing on the Rabbi's House, with the following commentary: Beys Horav– The Rabbi's house – page 317. This picture shows the southern façade of the Volozhin Rabbis' house, taken in the nineteen thirties. It was situated at the market square. Its northern façade overlooked the Yeshiva and the main Volozhin Synagogue, the Beys Medresh. The house was built in stone for Rabbi Chaim by the Volozhin Count Tishkevitsh. The big white house belonged during the first half of the 19th century to Ms. Malka Perlman, nee Itskhaykin, She was Eli-Zalman Itskhakin's granddaughter, who was Rabbi Chaim Volozhiner's grandson. The translator of the above article is Malka Perlman's grandson. Malka Perlman's house (Beys Horav) was nationalized by the Soviets in 1940. During the war the house burned out. Inside its reconstructed stone skeleton is situated now the Volozhin Univermag.

xvi. Talmudic sages.

xvii. Based on Psalm 24:1

xviii. The early sages are considered to have more authority than the latter sages.

[Page 99]

Chapter II

The Era of Rabbi Itzele and his son-in-law Rabbi Eliezer Yitzchak Fried

Translated by Jerrold Landau, based on an earlier translation by M. Porat z"l and edited by E. Levitan

Rabbi Itzele's personality, cleverness, and sharpness

After Rabbi Chaim's passing, the leadership of the Yeshiva passed to his son, Rabbi Yitzchak, who was nicknamed "Rabbi Itzele." Rabbi Yitzchak was born in the year 5540 (1780). His father guided him in the revealed and hidden [Torah]. He also had the privilege of accompanying him to see the face of the "rabbi who is compared to an angel of the L-rd of Hosts," that is the Gr'a of Vilna.

Rabbi Itzele told one of his students, the Gaon Rabbi Shmuel Salant, about his visit to the Gr'a:

"Once when my father was about to travel to the Gr'a, I told him: 'I too wish to travel to the rabbi.' Taken aback, my father said with apprehension: 'You too desire to travel to the rabbi.' I became frightened myself, but I was still determined, and I responded: 'Yes I want to go.' Father hesitated, but finally he agreed, and we set out. When we started our journey, I noticed that my father's face was pale from terror and fear. The closer the wagon got to Vilna, father's face became more and more drained of color. By the time we arrived to the town it was difficult to recognize him. He asked me again with trepidation: 'Are you sure that you would like to enter to the rabbi?' I made a great effort and said: 'Yes!' When we arrived at the front of the room of the Gr'a, my father's knees literally knocked together from the awe of his rabbi... . Quaking, he repeated to me again: 'Do you to wish to enter?' Thus did we enter the Gaon's room."[23]

Rabbi Moshe Shmuel describes that visit[24]. He states that this took place when Rabbi Itzele was about ten years old. The Gr'a suggested that his young guest recite some words Torah. Rabbi Itzele recited a brief explanation of one of the verses. The Gr'a was impressed by the child's wisdom and his pleasant words. He said to his father: " I am certain that the boy would become a great preacher in Israel.

In his generation, Rabbi Itzele was known as the rabbi of the entire Diaspora, and was nicknamed "The Leader of Israel," "The Rabbi of the Nation," and "The Spokesman of the People." He was greatly versed in Torah and wisdom. He was skilled and expert in the ways of the world, and had pleasant relations with people. He gave his approbation to the commentary and Torah translation of Ben-Menachem, published by Yitzchak Aizik the son of Yaakov and the poet Adam HaKohen Lebensohn, regarding which all the Gaonim of that generation battled, headed by the Gaon Rabbi Pinchas Horowitz of Frankfurt, the author of *Haflaah*[25].

[Page 100]

Rabbi Itzele did not restrict himself to the four ells of *halacha* only. It is told that Rabbi Itzele once sequestered himself in his room so as not to be disturbed during his studies. His father, Rabbi Chaim, came, knocked on his door and told him: "It is not appropriate for you, Itzele, to isolate yourself. Go out and take on your shoulders the public burden, the duties for which you were created." Therefore, Rabbi Itzele took the running of the Yeshiva upon himself, and all of its needs were determined through him. He guarded his father's staff to ensure that their lives were primarily dedicated to strengthening and glorifying the Yeshiva. He wrote in his introduction to *Nefesh HaChaim*: "I was only commanded about this clearly on the day that he ascended to Heaven, with strong words, to gird myself with all my energy and to strengthen his educational institution, so that Torah shall not be neglected, Heaven forbid."

Indeed, Rabbi Itzele fulfilled the command of his father, and his classes in the Yeshiva became famous. One of his students, Avraham Krupnik, describes Rabbi Itzele with the following words of praise and accolades:

"To this day, I will not forget the feelings of enjoyment when I saw the great, holy, enlightened Gaon, lofty over all the people of his generation, our teacher Rabbi Yitzchak, may he be remembered for life in the World To Come, of Volozhin , as he explained to us each morning a section of the weekly Torah portion in its straightforward manner, attracting the heart. Anyone who never saw the face of the aforementioned Gaon, whose countenance was like that of an angel of G-d, and anyone who never heard his words dripping like dew and rain, cannot imagine the pleasure of the soul and the feelings of a pure heart that G-d has created for us."[26]

The personality of Rabbi Itzele lived among the people, but not in writing. He did not leave behind writings, other than his introduction to *Nefesh HaChaim* and *Peh Kadosh* – from his statements and discussions, published by his student Dr. Yaakov Koplovich in the year 5650 [1890]. Rabbi Baruch Epstein describes aspects of his personality his book *Makor Baruch*:

"In general, the mannerisms of the Gri'tz (the Gaon Rabbi Yitzchak) were defined by love, honor, and glory. He spoke well, with pleasantness, purity, and politeness. Grace was upon his lips, and the mannerisms of kindness, modesty, and humbleness were upon his lips and in all the ways of his soul. Therefore, he was beloved and admired by all the people of the country – to them his words were Torah and his opinion was holy. Rabbi Itzele was so dedicated and faithful to his soul's path through the traits of morality and a modest way of life, to the point where he requested those close to him to grasp on to moral, proper behavior, to be measured in their words, and to speak with clean language and in the style of modesty, humbleness, simplicity, and politeness, with thinking in advance and organizing of what one is to say, and being careful and cautious with the honor of all people. Further regarding the traits of the soul, fine, refined traits such as this adorn their owners and cast their splendor on the human race in general. Anyone who bursts through the fences of such traits is

[Page 101]

punished harshly with difficult matters, so he will repent and attempt to fix the traits of his soul. He would not accept any excuse or pretext for breaking through the fence of refining and elevating the human soul. He said that excuses do not cover the sin of coarseness of the soul and disgusting traits, for anyone whose soul is clean and his traits are fine, will generally not come to a crooked path, and will therefore not need any excuses. Anyone who offers excuses testifies regarding himself that his soul has a weakness and he has a moral blemish.

"It was accepted by the elders of the generation that the ways of politeness, honor, morality, propriety, modesty, humbleness, and other traits of the spirit and the soul with which the Yeshiva students of Volozhin excel in – were saplings of the Gri'tz, who planted them and made them took root. When one grasps this principle, which is upheld by several clear-minded sages, that 'advancement in character precedes advancement in opinions,' one would have a united, sharp view of the mannerism of all of the Yeshiva students regarding the traits that we have noted. Anyone who is not refined with them, and even further, anyone who does not want to be refined with them, that is to say, to take hold of them and to live according to them – his soul will be wrenched from him, and his friends would also shun him. Therefore, he would find it necessary to force himself to be accustomed to living according to these traits, and slowly 'habit will become nature.' Later, when he will be satisfied with the positive change his soul, he will take hold of them and not let go of them throughout his entire life. In the Yeshiva, the acquisition of these traits flows from generation to generation to this day.

"In general, Rabbi Itzele was a man with high opinions and great feeling. He loved and tried to understand that which his eyes saw and his ears heard. He was eager to explore, research, think, know, compare, and evaluate every matter and idea at its source, so as to ensure their value and be able to approve them. His broad knowledge and strength of spirit enabled him to forge opinions on nations, on people, on countries, on regimes, on life values, on worldly ways, and on anything that took place in the larger world in general, and the Jewish world in particular. In general, he was a superior and excellent visionary in his time, and the honor and glory of the House of Israel was upon them."[27]

There was a tradition amongst the Volozhin elders that when Rabbi Chaim of Volozhin laid the cornerstone of the Yeshiva, he said to those standing around him: "I am investing the soul of my son Itzele in this building" (in his words: "*Ikh moyer do ayn mayn Itzelen*"). This is because Rabbi Itzele wanted to accept a rabbinic post in one of the cities of Germany, which was in those times a symbol of freedom and religious reforms. Rabbi Chaim was opposed to this with all his soul. Therefore, as he laid the cornerstone of the building, he hoped that this project would keep his son in Volozhin. Indeed, his prediction was realized.

[Page 102]

Rabbi Itzele was also a very active communal servant. His knowledge was great in secular matters as well. He knew languages and sciences, and medical knowledge was not foreign to him. He knew how to read Latin, and at various times, he also tried to be involved in practical medicine. Since he considered himself as knowledgeable in medical books, he would give medication to his ill students. This was often effective, but there were cases where this alone was not efficacious, and even made things worse. A situation such as that took place with his beloved student, the writer Kalman Shulman. Shulman had a problem with his eyes, and the Gri'tz tried to heal him with various medications. However, instead of helping, this harmed him. When he realized that his student's eyes were in danger, he advised him to travel to the well-known professor in his time, Purichinski in Vilna. Shulman arrived in Vilna in 1838 with a letter of introduction from his rabbi, and he was healed there.

Regarding his medical knowledge, it is told that once, one of his students became ill. They summoned and brought from nearby Ivyanets the medic who was known as an expert in all types of illnesses and symptoms. Rabbi Itzele investigated him and discovered that he was not an expert in medicine. Rabbi Itzele said: "I am surprised about yourself, that you live in Ivyanets, but are not concerned with the adage: 'a scholar is not permitted to live in any city that does not have a physician.' It seems that the residents of the city themselves rely on you and believe that there is a physician in their city. But you, you certainly know that there is no physician in your city, so how can a Jewish man transgress the words of the sages and live in a city that has no physician?…"

His dedicated care for Kalman Shulman was not an isolated incident. The Gri'tz loved his students with all his soul. During the summer, the custom of the Yeshiva was that the students would leave the Yeshiva after the *Mincha* service and scatter to all four corners of the city to breathe some fresh air and enjoy the natural beauty, so that they could be refreshed for the next day. Indeed, if any students remained in the Yeshiva to continue their studies, the Gri'tz himself would approach them, turn out the lights, and send them outside to breathe some fresh air.

Rabbi Itzele was very careful with his words. He guarded his tongue even from a taint of derogatory language. Once he had to say that a certain person was a liar, and that one should not rely on him. He did not want to utter a derogatory word, so he circumlocuted and said: "So and so has a wonderful memory. Some people remember what took place ten years ago. Above him is a person who remembers what took place twenty years ago. People with exceptional memories remember what happened fifty years ago. This person, on the other hand, remembers things that never happened..."

However, once Rabbi Itzele did not maintain his composure, and he responded sarcastically to one author who brought him a commentary on Song of Songs, Proverbs, and Job, requesting his approbation. He gave the approbation for Job, but refused to give an approbation for Provers and Song of Songs. The author was surprised, and asked the reason. Rabbi Itzele responded: "Job had a multitude of calamities, so there is makes no difference if one adds one more trouble. King Solomon, however, why are you dealing with him?..."

[Page 103]

Dr. Max Lilienthal – his Expedition to Volozhin

Translated by Jerrold Landau, **based on an earlier translation by** M. Porat z"l **and edited by** Judy Feinsilver Montel

Dr. Max Lilienthal[1]

Rabbi Itzele inscribed a splendid page in the history of Volozhin and in our own history of the latter years through his ardent opposition to *Haskala* (the Enlightenment movement). In so doing, he managed to thwart an inimical plot of Czar Alexander I.

In the 1840s, the Czarist government decided to make fundamental reforms in the Jewish education methodologies by establishing primary schools and rabbinical schools, which would replace the existing *Cheders* and *Yeshivas*. The Russian education minister Uvarov[ii] said that one must not annihilate nations, especially the Nation of Israel, whose modern history began under Mount Golgotha. The minister considered that it would be possible to draw the Jews to the religion of Golgotha through other means: namely, by opening schools for secular education.

Uvarov held the Jewish *Haskala* writers in esteem. Ryb'l (Reb Yitzchak Ber Levinsohn) wrote an epigram in his honor as follows:

Frightful clouds cover the sun of wisdom,
But at God's order the mighty savior came
Fresh winds had blown to bring light
And the people called: The cloud has passed [*Uvar Av*], the cloud has passed.[28][iii]

In order to prepare the Jews to absorb "the sun of *Haskala*h," Uvarov decided to send a Jewish preacher to the Pale of Settlement to inform this stiffnecked people of the "serious intentions of the government." The young Dr. Max Lilienthal was sent there for this purpose.

Dr. Lilienthal was born in Munich in 1815. He was educated in a German university and was a typical German-Jewish *Maskil*, fighting for moderate religious reforms. After graduating from the University of Munich, he was invited by a group of *Maskil im* in Vienna to serve as their preacher and to direct the Jewish school in their city. Within a short time, Dr. Lilienthal succeeded in raising the level of Hebrew studies in the school to the levels of the new times.[29]

Dr. Lilienthal was a straightforward man, and he did not realize the hidden intentions of Minister Uvarov. Therefore

[Page 104]

he accepted this mission very willingly. First, he visited Minsk and Vilna, but he failed badly in both places. Therefore, he decided to try his influence on one of the great Jewish religious leaders of the generation, on the person who all of Russian Jewry relies on for matters of religion – Rabb Itzele, the head of the Volozhin Yeshiva. He knew that if he gained the support of this Gaon for educational reforms for Jewish children, he would know that he fulfilled his task. Therefore, he arose and traveled to Volozhin.

Dr. Lilienthal arrived in Volozhin some days before Yom Kippur. Rabbi Itzele received him with great honor and even hosted him in his home. For three days and three nights, the two men discussed the topic of the proposal of the Russian government. The Holy Day arrived. On the eve of Yom Kippur after partaking of the final meal, the Jews of Volozhin assembled inside the synagogue, which was illuminated by hundreds wax candles. Everyone was enwrapped in their *tallises* and wearing their *kittels*. They stood crowded, and waited for Rabbi Itzele to arrive for the sermon that he would deliver annually prior to *Kol Nidre*. The Rabbi arrived with his guest and began his speech:

"Concerning the preparations of the High Priest for his Yom Kippur services in the Holy of Holies, we learn from the *Mishnah* of *Yoma* (chapter 1:5): The elder judges delivered him to the elders of the priesthood, who took him up to the House of Avtinas, and made him take an oath: Sir High Priest, we are the emissaries of the court, and you are our emissary and the emissary of the court. We adjure you by He Who caused His Name to dwell in this house, not to deviate in any way from anything we told you. He would leave and weep, and they would leave and weep.

"Is it not strange, gentlemen – asked Reb Itzele – is it not our sages, the sages of the *Mishna* and *Talmud*, who constantly warned us to not think evil about a person without any reason? Did they not say, 'One who shames his fellow in public is as if he spilled his blood,' and such a person has no share in the World To Come: They also stated 'Those who cast suspicion on innocents will be physically stricken.' There are many more such statements in the *Talmud* and *Midrash*. And this *Mishna* is teaching us the opposite of all the aforementioned warnings, that during the time of the Holy Temple, the elders of the priesthood cast suspicion – and upon whom? The High Priest, the anointed of G-d! And of what did they suspect him? – Of the heresy of the Sadducees, which is a denial of the Oral Law and the concept of reward and punishment. And where? – Inside the Holy Temple! – And when? – On the eve of the great, frightful Judgment Day!

"He asked and he answered: Indeed, it's true. When it concerns a private person and his private deeds, we are forbidden to suspect someone without any foundation, and until he is accused, he should be considered as innocent. The case of a public persona, an emissary of the people, is completely different. Not only is suspecting such a person permitted, but have an obligation to inspect carefully, to determine if his intentions are for the sake of Heaven, or whether his actions will, Heaven forbid, lead to a mishap amongst the Jewish people. Such a person, even if he would be the High Priest, must be examined

[Page 105]

over and over, and must be made to take an oath before the community to ensure that he not act as a Sadducee, and that his behavior not negatively affect our holy Torah and the traditions of our father."[30]

Dr. Lilienthal understood the allusion. He mounted on the stage and turned to the worshippers: "My masters, the sermon of the honorable rabbi was not directed to you, but rather to me. I took on myself this communal task at the behest of the government. Every Jewish person has the right to think about myself, and my thoughts and deeds. I swear:" – he added turning to the Holy Ark and removing a Torah scroll – "In the name of He Who invested His name in this sanctuary and in this Torah scroll, that my intentions in this work are for the sake of Heaven and for the good of the nation of Israel. I further swear that if it becomes clear that I was mistaken, and it becomes evident to my eyes that Uvarov is affecting our religion in any way – I will withdraw my hands from this work."

On his return from Volozhin, Dr. Lilienthal wrote to Nisan Rosenthal of Horodno the following words of wonder regarding Rabbi Itzele: "I met in Volozhin the renowned Gaon, our teacher Rabbi Yitzchak. I found in him a bright, wise, enlightened man who investigates the Divine. Upon him rests the spirit of wisdom and understanding, the spirit of council, knowledge, and fear of G-d[iv]. I have done all that I could to be accepted by him as a beloved son, for I called out "My father, my father, chariot of Israel and its horsemen"[v].

In his memoirs, Dr. Lilienthal gave over a fine parable about the Gri'tz: A villager came to one of the large towns of Germany. Suddenly, a fire broke out in the town. There was a custom there that they would beat a drum to gather together all the people to come and extinguish the fire. In his naivete, the villager thought that the drum was the sole implement for extinguishing the fire. When he returned home, he purchased a drum as a remedy for fires. Eventually a fire broke out in his courtyard. He began to beat the drum, but all his efforts were for naught. The flames spread further and further, and burnt everything in his courtyard.

The villager did not understand the simple matter that the drum was indeed useful as an alarm to summon the people to extinguish the fire. However, it is useless without water. This is like what happens on Yom Kippur: The prayers and the beatings of the heart are only like the beating of the drum to arouse the person to repentance. If true remorse does not follow – they are for naught.

Rabbi Itzele's Journey to the Rabbinic Conference

Translated by Jerrold Landau, **based on an earlier translation by** M. Porat z"l **and edited by** Judy Feinsilver Montel

Since Dr. Lilienthal's visit did not yield the desired results, the government changed its tactics, and summoned a "Rabbinic Conference" in Peterburg in the year 5602 (1842). The delegation was composed of Rabbi Itzele, Rabbi Menachem Mendel Schneerson of Lubavitch, Yisroel Halperin the manager of the bank in Berditchev, and the principal of a school in Odessa Betzalel Stern.

They set out to the capital city to discuss matters of Jewish education with the government leadership.

[Page 106]

Deep trepidation amongst the people accompanied their delegates to Peterburg. They engaged in many fasts and prayers. The delegates were faithful to those who sent them, and the efforts of the authorities were in vain. Rabbi Itzele's stance to the recommendation of the authorities was expressed in his pointed response to Uvarov's question: From what age, in his opinion, should the religious education of a Jewish education begin? Rabbi Itzele responded: "Twenty years before his birth".

During the Petersburg convention, Rabbi Itzele sat with a long *tallis katan* [ritual fringed undergarment], with long fringes that were quite visible. Uvarov asked Rabbi Itzele: "Why do you wear a large *tallis* with long fringes? Is it not possible to observe the religion by wearing a small *tallis* with short fringes? Dr. Lilienthal is also observant of the religion, and is a Jewish rabbi – and his *tallis* with fringes is not visible externally."

Rabbi Itzele replied: "The commandment of *tzitzit* [ritual fringes] was given to us as a reminder, through which to remember the commandments of G-d, as it says: 'And you shall look at them and remember'[vi]. And not everything is equal regarding memory. Dr. Lilienthal is well-educated, with a good mind and a good memory – so he only requires short fringes. I, however, am only a simple rabbi, and my memory has weakened with old age. Therefore, I require a large *tallis* with large, long fringes, in order to remember and fulfil the commandments of G-d."

Rabbi Itzele's sharpness and intelligence found expression in his felicitous answers to Uvarov and the anti-Semitic priest. During the gathering of rabbis, Uvarov conducted a discussion of wisdom, and said to Rabbi Itzele, among everything else: "I protest against you, Jews, for preaching hatred against the Gentiles, and instilling jealousy between yourselves and the nations of the world, for you recite the blessing every day 'Who has not created me as a Gentile.'"

Rabbi Itzele responded: "No, sir minister, it is not because of hatred that we recite this blessing. The proof is that we also daily recite the blessing: 'Who has not made me a woman,' and is there any Jewish man who hates his wife?"

It is told that during his stay in Peterburg, an anti-Semitic priest approached him and said: "It seems that the Jews suspect their daughters, and for this reason marry them off before reaching the age of majority, and you rabbis quietly overlook this."

Rabbi Itzele responded with a smile: "Indeed, for generations we marry off our girls before the age of majority, and the reason is, approximately 1,800 years ago, there was a Jewish girl who had come of age and was not married to a man. She caused us so much difficulty that we still feel it to this day…"

The priest was stung by this piquant response, and began to debate matters of religion and faith with Rabbi Itzele. Wanting to challenge and irritate him, he pulled out from his pocket a tobacco box, one side of which was engraved with a Jew on its other side, a dog. He began to rotate the box from side to side before the rabbi. Rabbi Itzele responded: "Apparently, you think that you have showed me some novel secret. However, even our young schoolchildren know: a Jew, when he 'turns about' and becomes a Gentile – is a dog…"

[Page 107]

That rabbinic conference ended with compromise: For the time being, the *cheders* would not be affected, but the government schools can compete openly with them. Aizik Meir Dik tells in one of his letters that Rabbi Itzele was satisfied with the results of the conference: "The Rabbi of Volozhin has arrived today in Vilna in joyous and content spirits for all the good that was done to his nation. What and how – he did not tell."

Rabbi Yaakov Halevi Lipschitz[vii] relates the words of Aizik Meir Dik differently. According to him, Rabbi Itzele was immersed in depression after he returned from the convention. Rabbi Lipschitz writes that when Rabbi Itzele returned from Peterburg, he spent one Sabbath in the city of Vilkomir. The city notables asked the Gaon to tell them about the conference.

"The rabbi responded: Believe me that there is nothing at all to tell. One does not respond to a downfall. No salvation was granted to the land. Would it be that no further multitude of evil decrees are hatched. A new destructive spirit pervades and is blowing over our nation. We are required only to pray for mercy. I have nothing more to tell you, my brethren."[30a]

According to Rabbi Lipschitz, Rabbi Itzele was very afraid of the results of the convention, to the point that he "asked that a woolen cloak be packed with his belongings, lest he, Heaven forbid, not be successful at his mission, and be exiled to the Siberian wasteland, where the woolen cloak would shield him against the cold." (*Zichron Yaakov*, Section I, page 101)

The government did not give up on its intention of assimilating the Jews. A secret order was disseminated, stating, "The purpose of educating the Jews is to draw them near to the Christian religion and to uproot their faulty views influenced by the *Talmud*." This secret directive reached Dr. Lilienthal's ears. He then began to understand that there was a basis for Rabbi Itzele's concerns. He escaped Peterburg and immigrated to the United States at the end of 1845. He served as a Reform rabbi in New York until 1850. That year, he left his position and founded a school in Cincinnati. He also published a newspaper in the German language called *Devora*. Dr. Lilienthal died on April 5, 1882 at the age of 67.

In the meantime, Rabbi Itzele's life was reaching its end. Legend states that Rabbi Itzele went to be healed in Minsk. He passed away on his way home, and the wagon carrying his body reached Ivyanets on the eve of the Sabbath. A dispute broke out between those accompanying him and the people of Ivyanets regarding where the Gaon should be laid to eternal rest. The judges issued a verdict that since the Gri'tz never traveled on Friday after midday, he should not be carried further. He was therefore buried in Ivyanets. Rabbi Itzele died on 26 Sivan 5609 (1849).

[Page 108]

In order to show the esteem of Rabbi Itzele's personality we will bring the words of Rabbi Yaakov HaLevi Lipschitz:

"My brethren and my people, we have known and still remember the Gaon, the eminent sage, the leader in Israel, Rabbi Yitzchak of Volozhin, may the memory of the holy be blessed. His memory is still engraved on the hearts of every person of Israel, as are his love and dedication to his people, his pure sentiments, and positive thoughts. The generation will still tell of he shrewd, firm, and sharp responses to his opponents at the meetings at which the deliberated regarding what to do to rectify the nation. His sharp, sublime adages will remain etched in the history book of Yeshurun[viii]until the final generation.[30b]

Translator's footnotes:

  i.   Later became a reform rabbi in the United States. See https://en.wikipedia.org/wiki/Max_Lilienthal
  ii.   See https://en.wikipedia.org/wiki/Sergey_Uvarov
  iii. *Uvar Av* means "The cloud has passed" in Hebrew.
  iv.   Based on Isaiah 11:2.
  v.   Based on II Kings 2:12 – What Elisha called out as Elijah was being transported to heaven.
  vi.   Numbers 15:39
  vii. See https://www.encyclopedia.com/religion/encyclopedias-almanacs-transcripts-and-maps/lipschitz-jacob-ha-levi
  viii. A poetic name for the Jewish people, based on Deuteronomy 32:15, 33:5, 33:26.

Rabbi Eliezer Yitzchak Fried

Translated by Jerrold Landau

Still in his lifetime, Rabbi Itzele appointed his son-in-law Rabbi Eliezer Yitzchak Fried as vice Rosh Yeshiva, and included him in his work. Rabbi Eliezer Yitzchak was the son of the daughter of Rabbi Chaim of Volozhin, who was married to Rabbi Hillel Fried of Horodno[31]. After the death of his great son-in-law, Rabbi

[Page 109]

Eliezer was appointed as the head of the Yeshiva, as the following letter of ordination testifies:

"Since the leader, the crown of our heads and the diadem of our glory, our late rabbi, the renowned Rabbi and Gaon Rabbi Yitzchak the son of our master and teacher the great, renowned Rabbi and Gaon Rabbi Chaim, may his memory be blessed for life in the World To Come, has been taken to Above from our community – who was the head of the rabbinical court in our community, it is fitting to appoint his descendent or relative in his place. Therefore, we were diligent, and we found his son-in-law, the great, renowned luminary Rabbi Eliezer Yitzchak the son of Rabbi Hillel, may he be remembered for life in the World To Come, who, with the help of the Blessed G-d, will take the place of his late father-in-law in all matters relevant to the rabbinate.

"Therefore, we accept the aforementioned Rabbi Eliezer Yitzchak to become the rabbi and head of the rabbinical court in our community, and also to be the rabbinic decisor in our community and for all who belong to our community. We are not permitted to refuse him or refute him, Heaven forbid, regarding anything that affects us as a rabbinical decision. We, our community and all who belong to it, are obligated to accept, observe, and perform any rabbinical decision that comes our way.

"We also accept upon ourselves to fulfil all details of things that are obligations of the public to fulfil regarding the rabbi, in accordance with that which is explained in the writ of the rabbinate that was given by our community to his father-in-law, the aforementioned Gaon. On the other hand, the aforementioned rabbi is also obliged to fulfil that which is required of him. The tenure of the rabbinate of the rabbi that we are accepting as per the above extends throughout his entire life. May the Blessed G-d extend his days and years."

The writ of appointment was signed by thirteen rabbis. It was signed in Volozhin on 28 Iyar, 5609 (1840).

His son, Rabbi Chaim Hillel wrote about him in his introduction to *Chut Hameshulash*:

"Sir, father, the Gaon and Tzadik of blessed memory, the depths of whose diligence is known and renowned to everyone. During the period of mourning for his father the Gaon and Tzadik of blessed memory, he would review the entire Talmud every 30 days. All the *Gaonim* of his time deliberated over various questions with him already from the time of his youth,

[Page 110]

in accordance with the extent of his sharpness and expertise that he demonstrated when he would deliver the class in the holy Yeshiva here in the holy community of Volozhin. Many wholesome people followed in the light of his Torah. He was cut off while still in his prime. He ascended to Heaven at the age of 44 (on Thursday, 19 Elul 5613 [1873]). He became ill with a severe illness, Heaven protect us, approximately 14 years prior to his death. Even though his health situation was very bad and the weakness was severe, his love and desire for Torah grew, and he did not leave its tent. He spared no effort to preach his words in the Yeshiva twice a week. Each time, the *Beis Midrash* was not without a novel idea in sharpness and expertise, for he always responded to his questioners with words relevant to the question at hand. Many of his novellae remained in the hands of his students who poured water on his hands. Even those that were not written down were still organized in the appropriate order as would be needed for publication. There are also some that he was not able to complete, and that were written in several versions."

The details of the life of Rabbi Eliezer Yitzchak are sparse, but his sublime moral personality, his internal spiritual world in matters of character traits and morality we learn from his wonderful sermon that he delivered in the *Beis Midrash* of Volozhin on the eve of Shavuot 5607 (1847). The main idea was the greatness of the concept of performing acts of kindness[32]. This sermon was rich in ideas, and aroused the soul to abandon perverted paths, and to cleave to the good, fine, moral, and sublime. It has words that can arouse our generation to their precious light.

Rabbi Eliezer Yitzchak asks why we read the Book of Ruth specifically on the Shavuot, which is the festival of the giving of the Torah? His response is:

"For the main idea of the book is to publicize the greatness of acts of kindness, which is the main principle in fulfilling the Torah. Therefore, when Ruth knew in her soul that she had already acquired those traits that are the beginning of the approach to our holy Torah – she then became a proselyte. Therefore, our early sages enacted that we should read this book on the Festival of Shavuot, the time of the giving of our holy Torah, so that we will recall the greatness of acts of kindness as we read it. This is in accordance with the words of Rabbi Zeira: This *Megilla* [scroll] does not deal with the concepts of impurity and purity or the concepts of what is forbidden and what is permitted. Why was it written? To teach you the great reward for acts of kindness."

Rabbi Eliezer Yitzchak taught that before one comes to study Torah, one must prepare the heart. This preparedness is only forged through acts of kindness and charitable deeds. A person who is unable to ascend to the moral level of doing good for his fellow, of helping his fellow during times of difficulty – such a person renders the Torah into a fraud and is denigrated by it. "A person cannot approach Torah if he does not cleave to these traits, just as one cannot built a building before laying

[Page 111]

a strong foundation below. These traits are the basis of Torah – to be merciful and gracious ."

A person reaches the level of a moral individual by acting in the ways of G-d, through performing His deeds:

"Just as He clothes the naked, as is written: "And the L-rd G-d made cloaks of skins for Adam and his wife to clothe them." (Genesis 3:21) – so you too should cloth the naked. G-d visits the sick as is written: "And G-d appeared to him in the Terebinths of Mamre (Genesis 18:1)[i] – so you too should visit the sick. G-d comforts mourners, as is written: "And after Abraham died, G-d blessed his son Isaac" (Genesis 25:11) – so you too should comfort the mourners. G-d buries the dead, as is written: "And he buried him in a ravine in the Land of Moab" (Deuteronomy 34:6) – so you too should bury the dead. Rabbi Simlai expounded: The Torah begins with an act of kindness, and concludes with an act of kindness. It begins with an act of kindness, as is written: "And G-d made cloaks of skin for Adam and his wife to clothe them." It concludes with an act of kindness, as is written: "And He buried him in a ravine.""

The teaching of Rabbi Eliezer Yitzchak is the rock of grace in the forging of the Gaonim of Volozhin. Aside from disseminating Torah among the nation, they desired to disseminate Jewish morality and to raise the spiritual level of the person. Volozhin also bequeathed to us books and wonderful people of morality, for truth and justice were the foundation of their lives and the candle at their feet throughout all the days.

The Text of the Gravestone of Rabbi Eliezer Yitzchak[ii]

א It will be called a foundation stone, this place is very awesome, here is buried the ark of G-d
ל The hearts of all passers-by will be torn, for this place is a home and grave, and the fear of G-d will descend
י The violin and the organ turn to mourning, song and the harp turn to sorrow, let there be the fear of G-d
ע A dirge on all lips, agony from all corners, all sons of G-d shout out
ז Screams and wailing to the heavens, and tears as a stream of water, come from the house of G-d
ר See and believe, the flask of manna, has been taken and hidden, and is no more for G-d has taken him
י His fear and wisdom lit up the faces, all who saw him recognized that the honor of G-d shone upon him
צ The beloved of Israel, the diadem and crown, exacting to the hair, when a person asks about the word of G-d
ח He wore out his life in the tents of Torah, he is praised with might, a Tzadik who rules with the fear of G-d
ק He was holy to G-d all his days, he had many students from his younger days, whom he taught the book of the Torah of G-d
ב The sun set at noon, darkness from the skies above, on the day that the candle of G-d was extinguished
נ It fell, wisdom and its persona, its foundations melted, when the leader of the House of G-d was gathered

in

ה He went to his rest, to enjoy in the pleasantness of the G-d of the winds, in Eden the garden of G-d

ל To teach the nation the righteous statues, ha! Who will fill the breach? To teach them the laws of G-d

ל Israel is no widower, for it will be redeemed at the time of the end, and all flesh will see visions of G-d

ו This *Tzadik*, the pride of our strength, Eliezer Yitzhak our master, he was a prince of G-d in our midst

ל Our eyes will be illuminated by the light of his wisdom, the splendor of his stature will comfort us, and we will be desired as one who sees the face of G-d

Translator's footnotes:

i.   This was after Abraham had circumcised himself.
ii.   The first letters of each line form the acrostic: Eliezer Yitzchak the son of Hillel of blessed memory. The last word of each line has one of the names of G-d: Elokim. The last few words of each line, with the name of G-d, are taken from various biblical verse.

[Page 112]

Chapter III

The Era of the Netzi'v, Rabbi Yosef Dov, and Rabbi Chaim Soloveitchik

Translated by Jerrold Landau, based on an earlier translation by M. Porat z"l and edited by Judy Montel

This period was the longest in the history of the Yeshiva. It lasted for around forty years and was different from the two earlier periods. During the time of Rabbi Chaim of Volozhin and his son Rabbi Itzele, the Yeshiva heads were well-known in the Jewish world, both in the area of Torah study and dissemination in public, as well as with respect to their blessed efforts in matters relating to the nation in general (especially Rabbi Itzele); whereas the students, aside from their diligence in the study of Talmud and its commentaries, were not active in any other activities. They did not become involved in the management of the Yeshiva. Their lives were quiet with their [faithfulness to] tradition. This changed during the period under discussion. The Yeshiva students began to display their energy and initiative, leaving their stamp on the life of the Yeshiva and its future development. The Yeshiva students, with their problems, life situations, questions, and struggles, began to take their appropriate place in the Yeshiva alongside its directors, and at times even in opposition to them.

The Torah and man are connected to the candle of G-d in the land. Torah is the flame that separates the spark of the dwellers from Heaven. Man, with his two parts, is the flame that draws its light – His body is the twisted wick, and his soul is the pure olive oil. With their agreement and connection, the house will become full of its light.

(*Bechinot Olam*, 15)

From the history of the Netzi'v
(Rabbi Naftali Tzvi Yehuda Berlin)

The Netzi'v was born to his father Rabbi Yaakov Berlin in Mir, District of Minsk on the eve of Rosh Chodesh Kislev, 5577 (1816). He was approximately ten years old when his father brought him to the Yeshiva of Volozhin. He was married to Rayna-Batya, Rabbi Itzele's daughter, about a half a year after he became Bar Mitzvah.

After his marriage, the Netzi'v continued to study with great diligence day and night in a small room within the Yeshiva. There were legends about his diligence in learning. It was said that he was able to study 20 hours a day. He would dip his feet in cold water to stay awake. He himself denied the story years later, saying: "I only studied 16 hours a day." He added, "I did this on Sunday, as well as Friday, the Sabbath, and festivals." This continued for 25 consecutive years. The diligence planted in his heart during his youth did not leave him even in his old age. It seemed that he never slept, because in the evening, in the middle of the night and at daybreak he could always be seen entering and leaving the Yeshiva.

[Page 113]

Harav Naftali Tzvi Yehuda Berlin – (The Netzi'v)

One of his choicest students, Rabbi Avraham Yitzchak HaKohen Kook, may the memory of the holy be blessed, writes about his rabbi the Netzi'v:[33]

"Already from the time of his youth, it was apparent that this man was created for greatness. His deep diligence, his distance from all pleasures of life, his wonderful persistence, and his straightforward inclination to delve deeply into any aspect of Torah, to turn away from the methodology of convoluted didactics [*pilpul*], and to delve into and know the proper truth in Torah – all this gives testimony that the future of this scholar is to be the illuminator of the ways of the Torah, and the forger of paths of Torah for many of his age. In those days, all those who grasped Torah made efforts to place all their efforts into didactics within Talmudic discussions, with novel ideas in Gemara, decisors, Tosafot, and the Maharsh'a (Rabbi Shmuel Eidelish), which were the interest of all those who delved into the Talmud."

At the age of thirty-six, twenty-five years after his arrival in Volozhin, the Netzi'v was nominated as the Yeshiva head. The following is written in his writ of appointment:[34]

"According to the authority and permission that we have from the rabbis and Gaonim, the heads of the communities in our country, and as their words have reached us in their letters, we have gathered together to appoint the great rabbi, our honorable rabbi and teacher Rabbi Tzvi Hirsh-Leib Berlin, the son-in-law of the Gaon Mohari'tz (Our teacher and rabbi, Rabbi Yitzchak), may he be remembered for life in the world to come, to be the head of the Yeshiva in this *Beis Midrash*, for we have seen him fit and capable for this, for he toiled greatly in the Torah of G-d with wonderful diligence, to the point that he is expert in the entire Talmud, and he can discuss *halacha* in accordance with his will to direct to true goal. It is said regarding him: "He who guards the fig tree will eat of its fruit' (Proverbs 27:18). Furthermore, he has been G-d fearing from his youth, and he already presented *halacha* to students during the time of the Gaon Rabbi Eliezer Yitzchak (E. Y.) may he be remembered for life in the World To Come. He is obligated to teach *halacha* to the students, and to watch over them with a watchful eye,

[Page 114]

that they will be diligent in their studies, and will not be engaged in other matters. He himself will be the final authority in all matters of the Yeshiva, in the acceptance of students, to decide whom to draw near and whom to keep away, as well as with all matters of expenses, both regular and occasional, usual, and unusual – all in accordance with what is required by the times."

Although the Netzi'v was occupied with Torah study day and night, he nevertheless found time to read secular Hebrew literature. All the editors of the Hebrew newspapers that were published in Russia and abroad would send him their weeklies or monthlies for free, and ask that he donate the fruits of his spirit – whether words of Torah or research into the Hebrew language. He would regularly read *Hamagid* and *Halevanon*. *Hamagid* would arrive at the home of the Netzi'v every Friday toward evening. The Netzi'v would not read it at night, for he dedicated every Sabbath night to reviewing the *Mishnayot* of *Shabbat* and *Eruvin* by heart. He read *Hamagid* on the Sabbath day. If *Hamagid* was ever late on the eve of the Sabbath, the Netzi'v would say that he felt as if something was missing on that Sabbath, just as a Jew feels on *Shabbat Chazon* [the Shabbat prior to Tisha B'Av] – for one goes to the bathhouse every Sabbath eve other than on the eve of *Shabbat Chazon*. He would say that the newspapers were very important to him, for they brought him greetings of peace from the entire world.[35]

Similarly, the Netzi'v loved Hebrew grammar. He once stated in jest: "It is not fitting at all for the Holy Tongue to be studied from Ben-Zeev, but one can one do? *Talmud Leshon Avar* is the final fundamental book on that subject. To our dismay, the only book authored by a kosher Jew, *Hamaslul*, is not of the better ones.

If the Netzi'v sometimes opposed the reading of secular Hebrew literature, he did so from the concern of impinging on Torah study. When a group of yeshiva students began to publish a journal on Yeshiva issues called *Boker Or* [Morning Light], and the Netzi'v saw that this took away from the study of Torah, he called one of the directors of the newspaper and said calmly: "If you produce *Boker Or* [Morning Light], I will make "And the People were sent away"… (An innuendo to the verse "At the morning light, the men were sent, they and their donkeys" (Genesis 44:3)

The Netzi'v Sets up the Building of "The Holy Yeshiva"

The building established by Rabbi Chaim of Volozhin in the year 5567 [1807] burnt down on July 27, 1886, eighty years after it was built. The Netzi'v understood that in order to grow the Yeshiva and make it more prominent, a fitting building must be built, which could house the hundreds of students. To this end, a large announcement regarding Torah[36] was published, requesting world Jewry to help him build a new building on the ruins of the burnt building.

[Page 115]

The Netzi'v became personally involved in fundraising for the Yeshiva building. A story is told regarding this, demonstrating his intelligence and sharpness. Once, he was working on behalf of the Yeshiva and there was a very wealthy but miserly man there who wanted to get away with a meager donation. The Netzi'v said to him: I, for example, am called "Rabbi and Gaon" by people. Therefore, I do what I do: I teach, respond to questions, write books, uphold the Yeshiva, and disseminate Torah so that at least there will be a bit of truth in the term. You are called *Gvir* [wealthy person]. Therefore, we are required to act as befits a *Gvir*, to be first of those asked and of those who give, to give charity generously for any purpose. If you do not act in that manner, it appears that you are misleading people…

After about three months, the school was already standing. During those months, the Netzi'v demonstrated all his mighty power. He abandoned his personal issues and toiled day and night to renew the honor of Torah.[37]

The Yeshiva building was a stone building with two stories, a basement, and large hall. It was spacious, supported by four pillars. The rich library of the Yeshiva was in the basement. Anyone who strolled in front of the Yeshiva on long winter nights would witness a wonderful sight – the light of many lamps shining upon the snow. The voices of hundreds of Yeshiva students studying with great enthusiasm could be heard from one end of Volozhin to the other. An awesome reverence would overtake the passer-by and leave him feeling in his heart that here, Judaism could be felt in its strength and purity.

During this period, the Yeshiva expanded greatly. The number of students approached four hundred. Students from Britain, Germany, Austria, the United States, all parts of Russia, Finland, Kurland, Kovkoz, and Siberia studied there. Volozhin became a great Torah center, with a beating heart, full of life and creating life. The central heart of Volozhin was "The Holy Yeshiva," which was the life of the spirit and the source of joy of the Netzi'v. He had nothing in his world other than the four ells of this great house in Volozhin from where Torah was disseminated.

[Page 116]

The Great Dedication of the Netzi'v to the Yeshiva Students

Translated by Jerrold Landau

The Netzi'v lived in the Yeshiva building from the time it was built until the house of the rabbi was built. The top floor was designated for the Yeshiva, where hundreds of students occupied themselves daily with Torah and prayer, as well as mundane conversation. Their voices wafted from one end of the Yeshiva to the other. The lower floor served as the residence for the Netzi'v and his family.

The Netzi'v was asked: "Tell us, our rabbi, how can you tolerate noise such as this above your head. What about your sleep and your rest?"

"I will tell you a parable," responded the Netzi'v. "What is this like? It is like someone grinding with his mill. A person passes by the mill and hears a loud noise. The wheels turn around and around. The millstones grind. The sifter sifts. The passer-by wonders and asks: 'how can the miller tolerate the noise of his mill? How does he sleep, and how does he rest?' However, what does that miller say? This noise is good for my sleep and rest. The more noise the mill makes, the sweeter is my sleep. When the mill is silent, and the wheels stand still – my sleep escapes my eyes and I have no rest."

We can deduce from this response the great love that the Netzi'v had for the people of the Yeshiva. It is said that one father brought the Netzi'v his only son and asked him to specially supervise him. The Netzi'v responded: "To you, he is your only son. To me, the 400 Yeshiva students are all like only sons to me." When the Netzi'v reproved his students, this was "outward reproof and hidden love."

The building of the "Etz Chaim" Yeshiva

[Page 117]

He was connected to his students with his full heart. He had mercy upon them as a father has mercy upon his children. He took interest in their concerns and needs. He even outlined the path that they should follow in the present and the future, for their benefit. He would be informed immediately if any student became ill, for he ordered the householders with whom the Yeshiva students lived that in any event of illness – even if a Yeshiva person simply does not feel well – he should be informed immediately. The Netzi'v would immediately visit the sick student, even twice a day if necessary. He did not stop taking interest the illness. He would discuss the situation with the physician and tell him to make sure he attends to the sick person properly and in a timely fashion. He would even instruct the host to provide the sick person with everything needed for him to recover. The Netzi'v did not suffice himself with his visits. He would also send a special emissary to concern himself with his situation. Even after the student would start to get better, he made sure that the host would ensure his full recovery. The Yeshiva paid for all medical and health expenses.

The Netzi'v would free himself from his various pursuits in order to enter the Yeshiva and look and his beloved students. In the winter, he would visit the Yeshiva two or three times during the latter half of the night. On weekdays, he would take a nap in his room in the Yeshiva, lying partly on the couch with his feet resting on the adjacent chair, and a small pillow under his head. He would barely spend two consecutive hours sleeping. He would visit the Yeshiva on Sabbath eves a half an hour after midnight and again before dawn. Anyone who has never seen the Netzi'v standing in the Yeshiva and peering at the rows of students as they were sitting bent over, connected to each other, and his eyes were radiating with joy – has never witnessed the joy of Torah in his days[1]. He would pace with vigorous steps along the rows, take note of those seated there, at times look at what they were learning, circle the entire Yeshiva, and then exit. Due to his great love of his students, he did not take kindly to afflictions and displays of extremism among the students. He would say: "Who is a diligent student? A diligent student is one who eats at the right time, sleeps at the right time, and studies at the right time."

This is how Chaim Nachman Bialik portrays the devotion of the Netzi'v to his students in *Hamatmid* [The Diligent Student].

> There is only one ear that is nearby to hear
> The hum of the lad who gets up early, the diligent one who remains late
> Is alert to be attentive to the bitter sighs
> That arrive to it on the wings of morning –
> He is the Yeshiva head, mighty and majesticv Who, with the call of the rooster –
> the voice of the first diligent one
> It defines the purpose of his weakened body
> The chirping of his birds does not let him sleep.
> And when he hears the voice of the diligent one arising in the morning
> He loves to listen attentively in silence,

[Page 118]

> And he hears the echo of the voice of his youth, and he remembers
> The long chain of life of the soul.
> And he remembers – and two tear drops fall
> And are absorbed into the silver gate of his white beard,
> The diligent one trembles in the light of the dim candle
> As two stones of fire from the golden squares.

Greater than Netzi'v's concern for the physical wellbeing of the students was his concern for their souls and future in life, so that they would not regard the Yeshiva as a passing period of life, but will rather continue teaching and disseminating their wellsprings outward. He would warn his students about "going beyond their personal boundaries." The Netzi'v would say: "There are two types of going beyond boundaries: one can impinge on the boundaries of others, and one can go beyond one's own boundaries. Impinging on the boundaries of others is known to everyone – it refers to someone who breaks through the bounds of his fellow and damages his livelihood.

"However, there is also going beyond one's personal bounds. Every country has military schools. We all know in our souls that a military person who has graduated from this school and has reached the rank of general – he has studied a great deal, and worked hard with serious diligence, and is known to everyone for his talents. However, after he reached that level, if he suddenly removes his uniform with all the medals of honor and splendor, and dons the garb of a simple person, the garb of a person of the market, and becomes a merchant, a shopkeeper, or an agent – this is what we refer to as 'going beyond his personal boundaries.'" This is what the Netzi'v called out greatly.

The Netzi'v's feelings of love and dedication were not restricted to his students, but applied to all people. He was never exacting, and was tolerant to all who turned to him. He always attempted to help to the extent that he could. He did not regard this as a going beyond moral expectations, but rather as something self-evident, something that was required by the letter of the law. Our sages have defined the level of patience required by a communal leader as follows: "To what extent must a parnas [communal administrator] bear the yoke of the community? To the extent that a nursing parent carries the suckling child[iii]." When a mother carries her suckling child on her shoulders, and, as happened with babies, he dirties her and her clothes, and he also become dirty and stained himself – what must she do? Should she cast her child off her shoulders in anger for something unseemly? Heaven forbid! Rather, she washes him with love and patience, cleans him and changes him into clean clothing. After that, she cleans her own clothes. She again takes the child into her arms and kisses him with love. She speaks softly and pleasantly to him, and calms him. This is the same with the Netzi'v. Even if someone from the community bothers him and causes him anguish, Heaven forbid that he should chase him away. On the contrary! His duty was to draw him close and respond to his issues.

Translator's footnotes:

i.   This form of expression is derived from Mishna Sukka 5:1
ii.   From Numbers 11:12.

[Page 119]

The Order of Studies in the Yeshiva

Translated by Jerrold Landau, based on an earlier translation by M. Porat z"l

The school day in the Yeshiva would begin at nine in the morning. The Netzi'v would teach his students the weekly Torah portion each day. The following story indicates the importance of this lecture. Once, one of the students arrived from Pinsk, the city of residence of the brother of the Netzi'v, Rabbi Avraham Meir Berlin. The Netzi'v asked the student if he had heard news from his brother. The student hesitated and did not answer. This happened a short while before the class. The Netzi'v did not inquire further. He entered the Yeshiva and began his teaching. After finishing the lecture, he sent for the student and continued to question him about his brother until he understood that his brother was no longer alive and he must begin the period of mourning. He removed his shoes, rent his garments, and sat on the ground. Already at their first encounter, hearing the student stammering, he understood what had happened; but until he heard it clearly, he was not obligated in the laws of mourning. He did not want to hear it explicitly until the end of the lecture, so as not to cancel the study of Torah.[i]

The Yeshiva students were not obliged to learn specific topics. Each one could make his choice regarding which Talmudic tractate to study. After the Netzi'v's daily lecture, they would study until 1:00 p.m. Then they went to their boarding houses for lunch. They returned at 4:00 p.m. prayed the afternoon *Minchah* service and studied until 10:00 p.m. Then after the evening *Maariv* service they went home to have dinner. The great majority returned to the Yeshiva to study until midnight. Some even remained until dawn. The Netzi'v, like Rabb Chaim of Volozhin, was careful about ensuring that the Yeshiva was not devoid of studiers for even one moment.

The Netzi'v did not look kindly upon solitary study. The study was to be with others, not only because of the [Talmudic] statement: "When two scholars sharpen each other in *halacha*, G-d grants them success, as is stated 'and the path will succeed' (Psalms 45:5). Don't read 'path' והדרך [*vehaderech*] but rather 'you will be sharpened' [*vechadrach*] והדרך (from the term חידוד [*chidud*] 'sharpening'" Tractate *Shabbat* 63a.) – but because it says regarding us "who can discern his errors"[ii], and it says regarding the gentiles "error – is a human matter." There is a minimum of error to which we accept with patience and understanding. However, anyone who studies for himself, anyone who clarifies *halacha* for himself without communicating with friends, it is close to certain that he will stumble and err a great deal more than the natural level of acceptable error. This is because there is nobody to catch him if he errs, so he wallows in his error and mistakes. Often, one error will lead to further error, and a minor error will lead to fundamental errors. This is not the case with someone who studies and clarifies *halacha* together with friends – the dialog will help clarify and purify the matters.

The thirst for study was very great among the Yeshiva students. Bialik writes about himself in *Hamatmid* that he stood "like a hammered nail, not moving from his place for an entire day and half the night." They studied with great interest and consistency, as they derived pleasure from the broad sea of Talmud, streaming and flowing in all directions, without beginning and without end.

Even though Y. L. G. [Yehuda Leib Gordon] was one of the great fighters for *Haskalah*, he could not close his eyes from seeing the great dedication of the Yeshiva students, and he wrote a poem about them:

[Page 120]

How you became great, how you became strong, the desire for knowledge
In the hearts of the youth of Israel, this is the nation of the worm![iii]
An eternal light on the burning altar!
If they study Torah, Gemara, and rabbinic decisors
Or if they occupy themselves in secular wisdom –
Their desires will overcome every obstacle and stumbling block.

* * *

Stand on the streets of Mir, Eishishok [Eišiškės] or Volozhin
And see impoverished lads making haste
With large steps on the routes.
To where are they going up? To sleep on the ground,
To live a life of discomfort, to be molded –[iv]
This is the doctrine of the person who dies in the tent.[v] (Two Yosef the son of Shimon)[vi]

Translator's footnotes:

i.   Removal of shoes and sitting on the ground are practices of shiva – the ritual period of mourning following the death of a close relative. The rending of garments takes place upon the hearing of the news, or at the funeral. Torah study is prohibited during the period of shiva.
ii.   Psalms 19:13
iii.   A poetic term for extreme modesty.
iv.   Based on *Pirkei Avot* 6:4
v.   Based on a homiletic interpretation of Numbers 19:14. Referring literally to the Red Heifer ritual, but homiletically referring to a person who suffers a life of deprivation in the tents of Torah.
vi.   I am unsure what the name and the number two is referring to here.

Original footnotes:

12.   Reb Simcha anthologized: "Sources for the History of Education in Israel" published by Mossad Harav Kook, Jerusalem, 5703 [1943], volume IV, page 178, section 149. The letter was also published in "The History of our Rabbi Chaim of Volozhin" by Rabbi Moshe Shmuel Shapira, Chapter VIII.
Rabbi Chaim regarded Hassidism as a non-insignificant factor in the diminishment of the study of Torah. See the articles in "History of the Jews of Volozhin" in the chapter "Volozhin and Hassidism."

12.   [a] A. Berdichevsky writes that a hundred students studied in the Yeshiva in that era, and that the Yeshiva building was made of wood: "And it was when his rabbi counted the students and their number

reached 100, he built a house of study out of wood, and used the Yeshiva treasury to hire a woman to cook a large cauldron of food, and to provide drink for the Yeshiva students. The students slept at night on the Yeshiva benches." (The History of the Etz Chaim Yeshiva, Hakerem, 5647 [1887], page 233).

Rabbi Chaim Berlin writes that nobody helped Rabbi Chaim of Volozhin in the founding of the Yeshiva, and the entire yoke fell upon him alone. His words are as follows: "During the time of the founding of the Yeshiva by the Gaon Rabbi Chaim of blessed memory, he had nobody to help him. He only succeeded in this great mitzva with the help of Heaven. I heard from my uncle, the Gaon Eliezer Yitzchak of blessed memory, that at the time of the beginning of the founding of the Yeshiva, the Gaon Rabbi Aryeh Leib Katzenelenbogen, the head of the rabbinical court of Brest Litovsk, was jealous of this mitzva, and sent the Gaon Rabbi Leib Brisker to ask that they could both be partners in this mitzva, and then he would have an assistant in monetary matters and in everything that was required. The Gaon Rabbi Chaim of blessed memory responded that if he wishes to take upon the leadership of the Yeshiva himself, then he can take it upon himself, and he would defer to him. However, he was not willing to have him join as a partner. The Gaon Rabbi Leib Brisker of blessed memory did not want to take this mitzva away from the Gaon Rabbi Chaim of blessed memory, who had already commenced this." (Rabbi Chaim Berlin, *Shichecha UPeah*, Regarding the History of the Gaon Rabbi Chaim of Volozhin, Beit-Hamidrash (dedicated to Torah and the wisdom of Israel), edited by Micha Yosef Berdichevsky, Krakow, 5648 [1888], page 73).

13.   Eight rabbis signed. The write of the rabbinate was published in *Kobetz Al Yad*, by Michel Rabinowitz, Book 5 (15), Jerusalem 5711 [1951].

14.   The proclamation was published in *HaPeles*, Berlin 5662 [1902], Year II, pp 140-143. Also see Simcha Asaf: "Sources for the History of Education in Israel" Volume IV, page 169, section 143. See Rabbi Moshe Shmuel Shapira: "History of Our Rabbi Chaim of Volozhin," chapter 9, which includes the proclamation with minor omissions.

15.   Rabbi Chaim uses this this naming formula in one of his responsa. See *Chut Hameshulash*, section 5, page 19, where Rabbi Chaim signed: Signed Chaim, the son of our teacher Rabbi Yitzchak, the *melamed*, with the help of the Blessed G-d, in Volozhin.

16.   The appeal was first published in *HaPeles*, year II, page 293. See Simcha Asaf: "Sources for the History of Education in Israel" volume IV, page 173, section 144.

17.   *Nefesh HaChaim*, Section IV, Chapter 33. Regarding the value of the study of Torah in the teachings of Rabbi Chaim of Volozhin, see the chapter on Rabbi Chaim as an educator of the community of Volozhin in the section "The History of the Jews of Volozhin."

18.   *Nefesh HaChaim*, Section IV, chapter 25.

19.   Section IV, pp 297-298.

20.   Section IV, page 309.

21.   *Galia Masechet*, Section II, Drushim, page 4.

22.   Yaakov HaLevi Lifschitz, *Dor Vesofrav* [A Generation and its Scribes], HaKerem, Warsaw, 5648 [1888], pp 179-180.

23.   Rabbi Moshe Tzvi Neria: "Chapters of Volozhin" page 21, Jerusalem 5724 [1964].

24.   *Hadoar*, 17 Kislev 5723 [1922].

25.   Reb Sh. L. Citron "The Dynastic Battle in the Volozhin Yeshiva," *Reshumot*, Volume I, page 126.

26.   A. Kupernik: "And Then the Third Statement Comes to Decide Between Them," Hamelitz, 23 Adar 5641 (February 10, 1881), issue 6, page 119.

27.   *Mekor Baruch*, pp. 1075, 1942, 1927.

28.   *Uvar Av* – sounds like Uvarov.

29.   Simon Dubnow, "The History of the Jewish People" vol. 9, fourth edition, published by Dvir, Tel Aviv, 5708 [1948], pp. 123-128.

30.   A. Papirna, "Memoirs, and News" *Reshumot*, Volume I, pp. 148-151. Papirna notes that he heard all this from Reb Sh. Y. Fein.

1.   A. Papirna, "Memoirs, and News" *Reshumot*, Volume I, pp. 148-151. Papirna notes that he heard all this from Reb Sh. Y. Fein.

2.   Yaakov HaLevi Lipschitz, *Peulat Sofrim*, Halevanon, issue 13, 21 Cheshvan 5637 (November 18, 1876), page 98.

31.   Rabbi Hillel Fried died on Thursday, 2 Adar 5593 (1833). This is the text of his gravestone:
Here is buried
Our father
The teacher of righteousness – the laws of G-d and his Torah
On the seat of his fathers – A *Tzadik* sat to take his place
For the holy flock – he drew from the wellspring of life
As he sheltered in the shadow – the beam of the soul of life
The paths of his fathers – he went in a modest spirit
He girded himself with joy – to the service of G-d, and his *halacha* and teaching were arranged
He always had refined life on his tongue – he gave of it in his sanctuary. He was lifted from us – and he lives forever in his dwelling. He is the rabbi, the great luminary, sharp and expert, the pious, the modest person renown for glory and greatness, Rabbi Hillel the son of the rabbi, the great luminary, Rabbi Simcha, may the memory of the holy be blessed, who sat on the seat of teaching and judgment in our community, the son-in-law of the rabbi and Gaon Rabbi Chaim of Volozhin, may the memory of the holy be blessed. He was lifted from us on Thursday, 2 Adar, 5593. May his soul be bound in the bonds of eternal life.
I copied the formula of the gravestone from Shimon Friedenstein's book "The Greats of Horodno" pp. 77-78. Rabbi Hillel Fried married Esther, the daughter of Rabbi Chaim of Volozhin. Legend states the following regarding that marriage. The Gaon Rabbi Chaim, when he heard of the good name of Rabbi Hillel, desired greatly to take him as a groom for his daughter. However Rabbi Hillel's mother opposed the match, because the bride did not find favor in her eyes. The Gra'h did not take his attention off of Rabbi Hillel, and he attempted to soften the heart of his future in-law. The wife of the Gra'h met Rabbi Hillel's mother at the fair in Zelwa in order to bring the match to fruition.
At that moment, the Gra'h was sitting with his friend Rabbi Chaim of Baksht. Suddenly, the Gra'h's face turned red. He turned to his friend and said to him with emotion: "Mazel Tov! Mazel Tov! Rabbi Hillel of Horodno will be my son-in-law." Rabbi Chaim Bakshter asked him: "How do you know? Has a secret been revealed to you from Heaven?" The Gra'h responded: "I never uttered a word of prophecy, but regarding this matter, it is clear to me that it is true."
Did our sages not say in *Avot*: "Nullify your will before His will, so that the will of others will be nullified for your will." [Trans: *Avot* 2:4] To this day, I was not able to remove my attention from Rabbi Hillel, for he is a great genius, and my desire for him was very great. However, at this moment I decided to give up completely on Rabbi Hillel, so that not a scintilla of desire for him remained in my heart. Therefore, I am certain that since I have nullified my own will, G-d has nullified the will of others in favor of my will, which will take precedence. (See "The History of our Rabbi Chaim of Volozhin" chapter 13, pp 197-198).

32.   The sermon is published at the beginning of *Chut Hameshulash*.

33.   The head of the Etz HaChaim Yeshiva (*Toldot HaNetzi'v*), Kneset Yisrael, 5648 [1888], pp 138-142.

34.   The citation from the document is in accordance with "Documents of the History of the Yeshiva of Volozhin" from the estate of Michel Rabinowitz of blessed memory, Kovetz Al Yad, Jerusalem 5711 [1951], page 226.

35.   Regarding the fact that the Netzi'v read *Hamagid* and *Halevanon*, see *Mekor Baruch*, Volume IV, Part 4, chapter 39, "Good are the Two" pp. 1794-1795.

36.   *Hatzefira*, 15 Elul 5646.

37.   Mr. Yitzchak Rivkind of blessed memory writes that Volozhin natives in the United States also donated to the restoration and strengthening of the Yeshiva. The following are his words: In the year 5646 [1886], the year of the great fire in Volozhin, natives of the town set up the "Etz Chaim Anshei Volozhin" organization. Aside from local needs and the needs of its members, the members of this organization took upon themselves, from the time of its initial founding, the duty of supporting the splendid Yeshiva in their city, and distributed charity boxes for the benefit of the Yeshiva. To this day, when you gather in the synagogue of Volozhin natives on 209 Madison, you see an announcement in Yiddish hanging on the wall: "Whomever wants a charity box for the Yeshiva of Volozhin should give his address to the synagogue via the shamash [beadle], or a member of the committee, and they will come to subscribe." Every year after Sukkot, a volunteer of the synagogue committee comes to visit and to take the money. The money is sent directly from the synagogue to the Yeshiva of Volozhin, and every donor receives a receipt from there. This continued until the outbreak of the Second World War." ("The Attempt to Found a Yeshiva in New York in the name of the Netzi'v Forty Years Ago." Scharfstein Books, page 245.)

[Page 120]

The Secret Societies "Nes Tziona" ("Netz") and "Netsach Yisrael"

Translated by Jerrold Landau, based on an earlier translation by M. Porat z"l that was edited by Judy Feinsilver Montel

The Netzi'v was devoted heart and soul to the "Chovevei Zion" movement, albeit the Yeshiva was the soul of his life. Therefore, he demanded one thing only from his students: to be devoted entirely to Torah study and not to divert their thoughts to other ideas. In one of his letters to the Chovevei Zion Committee in Warsaw, he apologized for not being active in the work for "The holy organization for the settlement of the Land of Israel," because all his time and energy was dedicated to the holy Yeshiva, of which he was the living spirit, and for which there was nobody else to bear its burden. If the Netzi'v, the Yeshiva's head, could not find any possibility to refer his attention to national activities, all the more so could he not agree that his students interrupt their studies, divert their attention from their efforts in the Yeshiva, and immerse themselves in work for Chibat Zion.

In any case, the national revival ideas penetrated through the Yeshiva walls and were implanted deeply in the students' hearts. The Volozhin Yeshiva became the center of the national movement among the *Beis Midrash* attendees, from where the idea of Chovevei Zion spread out into the important Torah centers of the Diaspora. A clandestine organization called Nes Tziona was founded in the Yeshiva. There was no other organization like it. The center of the organization was in Volozhin, and its emissaries spread out throughout the country. It conducted a great deal of publicity amongst Torah oriented Jewry for the upbuilding and revival of the Land.

A meeting was held by seven Yeshiva students in utmost discretion during the winter of 5645 [1885]: Moshe Barshak, Ben Zion Dante, Shimon Zlotoybke, Yakov Flakser, Menaham Fridman, Yosef Rozenkrantz and Yosef Rotshtayn. They laid the foundation of "Nes Tziona" [Banner of Zion] Society and pledged allegiance to its aims.

The goal of the organization was the settlement of the Land of Israel with the purity of holiness and Jewishness, and imbuing good, upright and sublime traits and feelings of charm and honor for everything good, effective, holy and precious to the House of Israel.

During the first year of its existence, the society listed more than fifty members. More members were added from time to time. Everything was conducted in complete secrecy. The organization also grew beyond the bounds of the Yeshiva. Its founders set their goal to educate diligent, faithful workers who would prepare to be dedicated to the movement of the settlement of the Land of Israel throughout their lives, and to accept upon themselves the role of disseminating the idea of the revival of the nation and its return to Zion through all the broad pathways of the nation throughout its Diaspora.

[Page 121]

Rabbi Yehoshua Heschel Levin

Sitting (right to left): Menachem Fridland, Menachem Mendl Nahumovski, Rabbi Moshe Mordechai
Epstein, Yaakov Mordechai Alperin
Standing (right to left): Rabbi Avraham Yaakov Flakser, , Yaakov Mordechai Zingman, Chaim Lerman
(The photo was received from the Russian Zionist Archives,
founded by Aryeh Rafael-Tzenzifer)

The organization found a broad array of willing human resources among the Yeshiva students. Most were young, and their hearts were alert to everything good and effective taking place in the community and in the nation. In order to protect their organization from the "evil eye," to secure its existence, to ensure the trustworthiness of its members and to strengthen the connection between them throughout all the days of their lives and to bring them in to the yoke of reality, the founders found no

[Page 122]

other way to ensure proper protection than imposing an oath upon every member as they entered Nes Tziona. The oath consisted of two ideas: faithfulness to the organization, and dedication to work throughout life; and maintaining the secret, so as not to disclose anything that was seen or heard within. The oath was as follows:

"In the name of our Holy Land and in the name of all that is dear and holy to me, I am swearing this oath of allegiance to be faithful to our Society's purposes and to make every effort throughout my life to accomplish the idea of settling the Land of Israel, and to refrain from disclosing anything to anyone until they too enter into the covenant with an oath."

One of the first activities of the society was to disseminate literature in praise of the settlement of the Land of Israel. The society disseminated the book *Doresh Tzion* [Inquiring about Zion] by Rabbi Ch. Y. Kramer, published in 5645 [1885], as well as other books. *Hamagid* and *Hameilitz* were also distributed by the members. In the year 5649 (1889), members of the society took the initiative of publishing a large anthology on the idea of the settlement of the Land of Israel. The anthology was supposed to include sections from our literature throughout all the generations relevant to the idea of the settlement of the Land of Israel and the love of Zion, aside from sections from the ancient literature, from the Bible, the Mishna, Talmud, and Midrash. Those involved also wanted to include items from the new era starting with Rabbi Kalisher and ending with the rabbis of Chovevei Zion of their generation.

However, the publication of the anthology never took place, because the existence of the society became known to the authorities at the beginning of the year 5650 [1890]. That year, a letter from a member of the society to a student of the University of Dorpat [trans: an old name for Tartu, Estonia], regarding the society in Volozhin was intercepted by the authorities. The police searched the student of the Yeshiva who had sent the letter and found with him the copying machine that printed the flyers. The lad was arrested. This matter disturbed the Netzi'v greatly. He had not known about the existence of the society. They did not do anything against the heads of the society, but the result was the disbandment of the society.

In the winter months of 5651 [1891], a second secret society "Netzach Yisrael" (The Eternity of Israel) was created inside the Yeshiva. Chaim Nachman Bialik played an active role in it. Bialik writes in his "Autobiographical Note":

"It happened during the publication days of Ahad Ha'am's first articles. The best and the "enlightened" Yeshiva students formed a society and vowed to dedicate their talents and their entire life to working for their people. The foundational idea of the society was indeed glorious. It was stated as follows: The Volozhin Yeshiva is the center of the best talents that will ultimately spread amongst the Jewish world, penetrate to its midst, and be absorbed into it, and become its leaders, as rabbis, doctors, and scholars, as well as administrators, communal heads, publicists and writers. Therefore, it would be sufficient for us to establish among the Volozhin students a permanent incubator for lovers of Zion. These would later turn the entire world into lovers of Zion, etc.

"The society was based on the cream of the crop of Yeshiva students, and of those with clear intellect. Every

[Page 123]

person accepted as a member was tested thoroughly from every side. Only those who were deemed to become a benefit to the cause in the future were chosen as members. I was considered as a future writer (that is how I was known) and this was the reason for my acceptance as a fellow in their company. I was one the first ones. At this very time, I wrote an article, as requested by my colleagues of the society. This was my first literary attempt. It was titled "The Idea of Settlement." It was published in *Hameilitz* of that year. That article was intended as a manifest of our society to publish its outlook to the world."[38]

What aroused the enlightened students in the Yeshiva to found the society? There is a theory that the chief factor in this was the article of Ahad Ha'am "The Priests and the Nation." In it, it is written that "Any new idea, whether religions, traditional, or social, will not stand and will not come to be unless there is a group of priests who will dedicate their lives to it, and work on it with their whole heart and whole personality."

The purpose of the organization was: "The settlement of the Land of Israel with the purity of holiness." The meaning of "purity of holiness" is not only the upkeep of the religion in its simple meaning, but also complete traditional renewal, rooted in all the praiseworthy traits of Judaism within the Hebrew nation. The settlement in the Land must be a national home in the traditional Jewish sense, to serve as a center for Jews and Judaism.

There were some twenty members who composed the Society. Despite their small number, they considered each activity as very important. They planned to establish a cooperative settlement for religious youth in the Land of Israel, which would be a showpiece not only of loving work but also of morality and religious ethics. An important letter remains from M. L. Lilienblum to Bialik and his friends, dated 3 Sivan 5651 [1891], in which he informs them that he received their letter: "May G-d, the L-rd of Zion, be with the mouths of the Jewish lads, and grant them grace and mercy before the philanthropist, to have mercy upon them and upon our Land." He blessed the writer of the letter, Bialik, with: "With all my heart that his good intentions become actualized."

The Yeshivah was closed in the winter of 5662 (1892). The students dispersed and that was the end of that society in Volozhin[39].

Original Footnotes:

38.   Ch. N. Bialik: "Autobiographical Notes" Knesset, Book VI, Tel Aviv, 5701 [1941], page 15.

39.   A. Droyanov published in "Writings on the History of Chibat Zion and the settlement of the Land of Israel" Volume II, pp. 797-799, a letter from "A group of students of the Volozhin Yeshiva" to K. Z. Wissotzki from the year 5649 [1889] regarding designating a plot of land for the founding of an agricultural settlement in the Land of Israel for students of the Volozhin Yeshiva. The letter is as follows: "The national movement is continually spreading throughout our brethren the House of Israel. Great is the commandment of actualizing the settlement of our Land, for the time of its mercy has come. The bitter situation of our brethren and their bad lot in their lands of dispersion also breathed into our hearts the idea of making *aliya* to Zion, of working its land, eating of its fruits, and satiating ourselves with its goodness. Approximately 100 people have forged a covenant and formed a society for the founding, with G-d's help, of a settlement in our Holy Land, so we can be tenders of vineyards and farmers upon the mountains of Israel. It has been acquired for us from our brethren, men of valor, who went out as pioneers and made *aliya* to Rishon Letzion to till its mountains and smooth outs its valleys. Their hope for the future, with the vine plantation, is that it shall blossom and bear fruit."

Later, they request from Wissotzky that he "Purchase the necessary land for our desire, stating that they are prepared to provide 5,000 rubles as an advanced payment, so that he would perhaps agree to give over the land, and they would pay interest according to an agreement."

The signatories: Reuven the son of Rabbi Dov Yaakov HaKohen Gordon, Eliyahu Aharon Milikowsky, Menachem the son of Tzvi Krakowski, Yaakov the son Rabbi Baruch Yosef Blidstein, Shalom Eliezer the son of Rabbi Y. Rogozin (or Rogovin), Yeshayahu Bunimowitz, Aharon Yaakov Perlman, Efraim Zamonov (the grandson of the Netzi'v, the husband of the daughter of Rabbi Chaim Berlin), Moshe Chaim… Yitzchak Yaakov Perski.

[Page 124]

The Dispute Between the Netzi'v and Rabbi Yosef Dov Soloveitchik

Translated by Jerrold Landau based on an earlier translation by M. Porat z"l

A leadership of pairs, consisting of the Yeshiva head and his deputy, has always been in effect at the Etz Chaim Yeshiva. During the era of Rabbi Itsele, his son-in-law Rabbi Eliezer Yitzchak served as his deputy. After Rabbi Itsele's death, Rabbi Eliezer Yitzchak served as the Yeshiva head, and the Netzi'v was his deputy. The Netzi'v was appointed as Yeshiva head after the death of Rabbi Eliezer Yitzchak. Rabbi Yosef Dov Soloveitchik, a great grandson of rabbi Chaim Volozhin through his daughter, was appointed as his deputy. It is written in the writ of rabbinate given to the Netzi'v: "And as his deputy, we have chosen to place the honor of the great, sharp, famous rabbi, Rabbi Yosef DovBer the son of Rabbi Yitzchak Zev HaLevi, a grandson of the *Gaon*, our teacher Rabbi Chaim, may the memory of the holy be blessed, to assist and support the aforementioned Yeshiva head by teaching *halacha* to the students – for he is good and effective in imparting his didactics [*pilpul*] to the students."

These two *Gaonim* had different opinions as to the methods of Talmud learning. The Netziv's son, rabbi Meir Berlin, describes the methodology of the Netzi'v:

"The Volozhin Yeshiva introduced the method of study that can be traced to the Gaon of Vilna. Through this, the students of this Yeshiva differ from those who learned their Torah from other Yeshivas. This method of study is not based on sharp didactics, sectional expertise, or exactitude of wording. Rather, it penetrates into the Talmudic discussion and everything stemming from it. The aspiration for truth, efforts in preparation, and the will to understand the clear meaning – that is the learning methodology of the Rabbi of Israel (the Netzi'v) in his books, and that was the learning methodology of his Yeshiva and his students. The first approach is toward understanding and depth. To determine whether the understanding is correct, or whether the digging in depth is distorted, one must find support in the words of the great early sages, and especially from Talmudic sections that deal with the same concept in general, for there are cases where words of Torah are poor in one place, but rich in another place."[40]

The Netzi'v fundamentally rejected *pilpul*, stating that "Just as it is impossible to discharge one's obligation of a set meal through delicacies and sweets alone, even if they are good and proper when they follow a full meal with bread, fish, and meat – similarly, sharp *pilpul* is good if it comes as

[Page 125]

accessories and sweet treats," after the set study of Talmud, decisors, and books of the early commentators, after the student reaches the level of complete, true acquisition of the fundamental treasures and virtues of the Torah.

In the eyes of the Netzi'v, Torah study alone was important. And the more a man increased his Torah knowledge the more his spiritual power would grow. The Netzi'v would explain the matter with a parable from life: A studier can be compared to a machine in a factory. As long as you add coals for fuel, it works with greater diligence and complete purpose, and produces proper products. This is not the case of a meager quantity of coals are provided. The machine will then function lazily, without the spirit of life, and the products it produces will be without form or glory.

Such is also the complete man who has acquired his Torah. The more Torah he acquires from Talmud, decisors, and the books of the early commentators – for all of these demonstrate the clear fundamental of every law and area of research, like coals in a machine – the more he will be able to research and answer every Torah matter that comes his way. He will find the sources and basis in his Torah that he has studied in breadth and depth.

For this reason, the Netzi'v did not look positively at those who elongated their prayers, for overly extended praying interferes with the study of Torah. Torah learning demands that the student be dedicated to it totally and at all times. Regarding this, the Netzi'v relates that during the times of Rabbi Chaim of Volozhin, a certain scholar studied in the Yeshiva, and took a great deal of his time from his studies to recite Psalms. Rabbi Chaim was pained that his student took away so many hours from the study of Torah, and he reproved him for this. His student told him: "Our rabbi, indeed, it says in the *agada* [Talmudic lore] that King David requested that everyone who occupies himself with the recitation of Psalms will be considered as if he is occupied with [the laws of] leprous legions and [impurity transmitted by] coverings." Rabbi Chaim responded: "It is indeed true that he requested, but we do not know how the matter was answered to him."

Rabbi Baruch Halevi Epstein describes the essence of the controversy between the Netzi'v and Rabbi Yosi Ber Soloveitchik in the following words:[41]

"As opposed to the Netzi'v, the Gaon Rabbi Yosi Ber considered sharp *pilpul* to be a precious tool to forge the young students' intellects, to sharpen their logic, and thereby to excite the rivalry of wisdom and to make them enjoy the competition.

The two methodologies, or two regimens, at opposite sides gave rise to a chasm between the Yeshiva students. Some followed the opinion and regime of my uncle (the Netzi'v) and revered his methodology as a true and sure path in the ways of Torah, and others enjoyed the path of sharpness of Rabbi Yosi Ber.

At first, the chasm was mild and light, and was only hidden in the hearts of those sages, the mighty ones of their methodologies and paths. However, after the chasm broadened and entered the public domain of the Yeshiva students, it was no longer possible to confine the winds in the hearts of these youths, each of whom, with the heat of their souls and emotions, attempted to prove the superiority of their leanings, methodologies, and pathways that they had chosen

[Page 126]

Slowly but surely, the question turned into a dispute, and the logic became a conflict. Those close to each other grew apart; friends became ideological adversaries. It had become a storm of tribulations. Furthermore, as time passed, the dispute broke forth from the confines of the walls of the Yeshiva, and moved on to towns near and far from Volozhin. Several students and Torah giants began to take interest in the difference of opinion."

To settle the controversy, four of the Torah greats of the generation were summoned to Volozhin: David Tevel, the head of the rabbinical court of Minsk, Rabbi Yosef from Slutsk, Rabbi Yitzchak Elchanan from Kovno, and Rabbi Zev Landau the preacher from Vilna. They were joined by the wealthy Rabbi Yehoshua Levin of Minsk.[42]

The following was their verdict from 4 Cheshvan, 5618 (1857):

"When we came together and gathered here in the holy community of Volozhin to investigate the issues of the great house in which Torah is nurtured for the masses by our rabbi and teacher, Rabbi Naftali Tzvi Yehuda, may his light shine, and our rabbi and teacher, Rabbi Yosef Dov, may his light shine – the following is what we the undersigned agreed and have recorded.

    a. First of all, we decree that there should be peace between the rabbis, and that any Yeshiva student who impinges upon the honor of one of the aforementioned rabbis, and the matter becomes known, both of them must distance him or punish him as they see fit.
    b. The accepting of students into the Yeshiva is dependent on the will of Rabbi Naftali Tzvi Yehuda, as it was until now. Only when a letter arrives specifically to Rabbi Yosef DovBer does he have the rights to accept him on his own."

[Page 127]

After the verdict, Rabbi Yosi Ber did not see a place for himself in the Yeshiva. He left it and accepted a rabbinical post in Slutsk. Rabbi Rafael Shapiro, a son-in-law of the Netzi'v, took his place. Despite this, the two great ones of the generation forged bonds of marriage between themselves. Rabbi Chaim Soloveitchik, the son of Rabbi Yosi Ber, married the granddaughter of the Netzi'v, the daughter of Rabbi Rafael Shapira.[43]

Original Footnotes:

40. *Rabban Shel Yisrael*, page 106.
41. *Mekor Baruch*, Section IV, chapter 37, "Between Holy and Holy" page 1694.
42. Rabbi Yaakov Halevi Lifschitz writes about the difference between the Netzi'v and Rabbi Yosi Ber, as well as the impression that the arrival of the delegation had on the Yeshiva students: "These holy *Gaonim* and *Tzadikim* were different from each other in the traits of their souls and their methodologies of study and delving into Torah, as well as their paths of life. Since they were different from each other, and could not agree on the methods of conducting the Yeshiva and methodologies of study, a dispute broke out regarding who was better in behavior." (*Toldot Yitzchak*, chapter 16, *Orach Latzadik*, page 58). He writes about the delegation: "Regarding the controversy between the two *Gaonim*, heads of the Yeshiva of Volozhin, that caused a great breach among their students, a difference of opinion among the supporters of the holy Yeshiva throughout the country, a division in ideology – the great *Gaonim* of the generation called for an increase of peace among the scholars, who increase peace in the world, with advice of peace and truth, advice that they would deliver with their love of truth and peace. They would calm the opinions of the entire community. Are these not the chief *Gaonim* of that generation, Rabbi David Tevel of Minsk, the author of Responsa *Beit David*; Rabbi Yosef Behmer of Slutsk; the famous preacher of righteousness, our rabbi and teacher Rabbi Zeev, may the memory of the righteous be blessed, of Vilna; and Rabbi Yitzchak Elchanan – to whom the Netzi'v of blessed memory traveled himself to visit in Novhorodok to request that he come to Volozhin to be counted among the elders of those Torah scholars in expressing his opinion, with holy awe and splendorous honor that no person can describe other than a person who has previously seen the honor of Torah in Israel. All the students of the Yeshiva with their variegated opinions, many of whom were wholesome in Torah and effectiveness, rejoiced and trembled. Some were sharp in wisdom and exacting in *halacha*, and later became luminaries among the Jewish people. All of them rejoiced and trembled upon the arrival of these great rabbis of Israel who had gathered together." (*Toldot Yitzchak*, chapter 17, "In the Council of the Righteous," pp. 61,62.
43. See my article in the chapter "Sages of Volozhin" regarding Rabbi Yosi Ber and his son Rabbi Chaim Soloveitchik.

Slander Oppresses the Netzi'v

Translated by Jerrold Landau

In the year 5639 [1879], a very difficult event took place in the Yeshiva, which grieved the heart of the Netzi'v greatly. One of the Yeshiva students gave over a bad report regarding the Netzi'v to the Russian authorities. This slander shook the foundation of the Yeshiva, and its echo spread afar.

I'sh Yemin'i writes the following in *Hameilitz*[441]:

"At noontime, many army men and captains in official uniforms and medals of excellence came to the quiet city of Volozhin. They set out for the sanctuary of Torah, and those who dwelled therein. The army men surrounded the building, and the ministers (captains) entered. A deathly pall fell upon the faces of the shepherds and their flock. The captains searched all corners of the building, through all the crates and closets, through all the utensils. They confiscated anything they wanted. The took letters, and ledgers of income and expenditures from previous years, and placed them in a crate. They closed and locked it, and placed a government seal upon it, and sent it to the capital city. Only the money they did not take, although they checked the paper bank notes carefully to see if they were forged. When they finished their work, they interrogated the elderly *Gaon*: Why do you send emissaries to all ends of the earth to collect a great fortune? For what purpose is it designated? Is this done at the behest of the government? – and other such questions. After the interrogation, the minister took out a letter, turned to the rabbi, and asked him: "Do you recognize this signature? Is it your handwriting?" At first the rabbi answered him, 'It is my signature and handwriting.' But then he regretted his words and said, 'It is not my handwriting. In truth it is similar.' He did not understand everything that was written in the letter. All the responses of the rabbi were recorded in a notebook."

The government emissaries left the Yeshiva and went to obtain testimony from the officials and Volozhin police chief regarding the activities of the Netzi'v. They responded unanimously that the Netzi'v is faithful to his country and king, and dedicates his days only to Torah. The went to summon the Netzi'v. They received him with great honor and showed him the letter again. The Netzi'v, who had somewhat calmed down from the search in the Yeshiva, looked again at the letter, and then realized to his great astonishment that the letter was forged. Some forger who had signed the letter with a forged signature of the Netzi'v, wrote

[Page 128]

a letter to Rabbi Yaakov Reinovich in London in the name of the Netzi'v, and sealed it with the stamp of the yeshiva. Apparently, the scoundrel knew that the Netzi'v maintained a correspondence with him regarding halachic questions and responsa. The contact of the letter was that the Netzi'v wrote that he had received a letter from Rabbi Reinovich along with 30,000 rubles, one third of which was given to the Yeshiva people, and a second third as a bribe to the judges and police of Volozhin so that they will remain silent, and the final third given to the ministers of the country so that they would avert their eyes from the deeds of the heads of the authorities in Volozhin. The letter further stated that the Netzi'v requested that Rabbi Reinovich send him forged bank notes. It also contained other similar falsehoods.

The Netzi'v came out clean in the judgement, for the investigators were convinced of his innocence. The Netzi'v suspected three Yeshiva students, one from Volozhin, one from Minsk, and one from Vilna, whom the Netzi'v had distanced from the Yeshiva.

The issue of the libel greatly stirred up Erez, the editor of *Hameilitz*. Among other things, he wrote the following in his article "The Rotating Sword"[45] [i]:

"We have seen enough of this, that a Jewish person was so brazen as to forge a letter in the name of a great rabbi in Israel, elderly, and occupied with Torah, and to attribute to him slanderous words that stir up the heart, and could easily affect the refined soul of the rabbi, who holds back from issues of this world, and could, Heaven forbid, snuff out the wick of his life. The slanderer himself informed the ministers of the state to pay attention to that letter. No sufficient words exist to express all the feelings of our spirit regarding such a terrible travesty."

Original Footnotes:

44. 3 Tammuz, 5639 (June 12, 1879).
45. *Mekor Baruch*, Section IV, chapter 37, "Between Holy and Holy" page 1694.

Translator's Footnote:

i. Based on Genesis 3:24.

Rabbi Yehoshua Heschel Levin's Rebellion

Translated by Jerrold Landau based on an earlier translation by M. Porat z"l

Rabbi Eliyahu Zalman, Rabbi Itsele's son, married off his daughter to Rabbi Yehoshua Heschel Levin, a grandson of the Maharsh'a (Our Teacher Rabbi Shmuel Eidels)[45a]. Rabbi Itsele was very pleased with him. He would say "This grandson shall have an inheritance in the Yeshiva along with my sons-in-law."

Rabbi Yehoshua Heschel was very pretentious. He used to say that since he was a descendent of the Maharsh'a, he deserved to become president of the Yeshiva. There was no peace between him and the Netzi'v and Rabbi Eliezer Yitzchak Fried. Things reached the point that Rabbi Yehoshua Heschel stopped visiting the Yeshiva, and set his regular place of worship in the *Beis Midrash*. Finally, he organized a *minyan* [prayer quorum] in his home. From then, he completely cut off his connection with the Yeshiva.

Word spread in Volozhin that Rabbi Yehoshua Heschel had started to give classes to those who came to worship at his house, and that the number of attendees continued to grow. Among them were students of the Yeshiva.

[Page 129]

Indeed, this was not a false rumor. Rabbi Yehoshua Heschel decided to forcefully remove the reins of leadership from the Netzi'v and Rabbi Eliezer Yitzchak, and to take the presidency for himself.

In order to attract students, he began to give Talmud classes in his home every morning. Between *Mincha* and *Maariv*, he would teach a chapter of Bible with the commentary of Mendelsohn.

Rabbi Yehoshua Heschel Levin

These classes aroused great interest among the Yeshiva students. They were greatly impressed by them. The number of attendees grew from day to day.

One night, a secret meeting took place in the home of Rabbi Yehoshua Heschel, with the participation of many of the Yeshiva students. At that meeting, Rabbi Yehoshua Heschel announced in public that the crown of Yeshiva head would come to him because he was a grandson of the Maharsh'a. On the spot, a detailed plan was hatched to began preparations for a transfer of the presidency of the Yeshiva.

The lads who participated in the meeting aroused a great tumult in the Yeshiva. This reached the point of an open revolt against the Netzi'v. The community of Volozhin was shaken up by this commotion, which placed the existence of the Yeshiva in danger. The communal heads called a meeting in the *Beis Midrash* in order to deliberate about what to do.

The matter reached the communal heads in Vilna and Minsk. Rabbi Yehoshua Heschel received a letter from Vilna, signed by several *gabbaim*, advising him, for his own good, to cease thinking about the presidency of the Yeshiva of Volozhin, for his glory would not come through that path.

One day, when those close to Rabbi Yehoshua Heschel gathered in his home for the *shacharit* service, they did not find him at home. He left Volozhin in haste, and set out in an unknown direction.

A legend spread through Volozhin that Rabbi Chaim of Volozhin appeared to Rabbi Yehoshua Heschel in a dream, and commanded him to leave the city quickly, for his actions were liable, Heaven forbid to destroy the Etz Chaim Yeshiva. Thus ended the revolt, which threatened to uproot the Yeshiva.

Original Footnote:

45.   Rabbi Yehoshua Heschel Levin was born in Vilna on 18 Tammuz 5578 (1817) to his father Rabbi Eliyahu Zev. In the year 5631, he was appointed as the rabbi of the Warsaw suburb of Praga, where he served for one year. At the end of his life, he served as the rabbi of the great *Beis Midrash* of the Jews of Russia and Poland in Paris. He died there on 15 Cheshvan, 5644 [1884]. Books that he authored include: "Glosses on *Midrash Rabba*," *Aliyat Eliyahu* (history of the Gr'a), *Maayanei Yehoshua, Tziun Yehoshua, Tosafot Tzion, Pleitat Sofrim*, and *Dvar Beito*.

The Moral Sublimity and Educational Excellence of the Netzi'v

Translated by Jerrold Landau based on an earlier translation by M. Porat z"l

On the eve of Shavuot, 5645 (1885), an event took place in the *Yeshiva* in which the Netzi'v was revealed as an exemplary moral-educational personality. During that period, the *Yeshiva* excelled with many prodigious students. However, the *mashgichim* [religious supervisors] began to look into them and to suspect that they were not fulfilling the commandment of public worship appropriately, and that many of them are failing to come for the *Yeshiva* for the *Shacharit* service. In order to suppress this "plague," the Netzi'v nominated a special supervisor to serve as vice principal. His official role

[Page 130]

was to oversee the Yeshiva library, and to give the students the required Gemara volumes. Secretly, however, his job was to investigate the deeds and behavior of the Yeshiva students outside the walls of the Yeshiva. The Netzi'v gave this role to a certain zealot, who would bring the bad reports of the students to the Yeshiva head. The students hated this man with a strong hatred. They nurtured their enmity, and waited for the day when they would be able to take their revenge.

On the morning of that Shavuot eve, this spy informed that many of the Yeshiva students cut their *peyos* when they took their haircuts on the *Shloshet Yemei Hagbalah*[i], when haircuts were permitted. The prayer service passed peacefully until the end of the *Shmone Esrei* prayer. However, at its conclusion, the Netzi'v began to circulate among the students, directing an angry stare at them. He withheld his anger, and did not touch any student during the time of prayer, less the head tefillin be displaced and fall due to the slap, leading to a desecration of the holy object.

At the conclusion of the services, the Netzi'v delivered his class on the weekly Torah portion, as was his custom. When he concluded his class and left the Yeshiva, he met along the way a prominent, well-known student, who was very diligent and consistent in his studies, and was also one of the wealthy ones. He was returning from his residence with a Gemara in his hands. He had bathed, and his *peyos* were completely cut off. He had not worshipped in the Yeshiva that day, and knew nothing at all of the "hunt" for *peyos* that the Netzi'v had conducted. When the Netzi'v saw him, he poured out all his concealed wrath at him, and even hit the student. The student was astonished and surprised, as he did not know what this was about. The Gemara fell to the ground, and he stood there beaten, and shocked from the great shame.

This deed caused a storm among all the Yeshiva students, who decided to take revenge for the embarrassment of their friend. When the students took their places and began to study, they began to bang the tabletops incessantly. This served as a sign for the beginning of the revolt. All the students sat in their places studying, while their hands rose and fell upon the shelves of the learning tables. In addition, all the windows were open wide. The wind came through, and the windowpanes shattered.

The vice principal entered during the revolt. His appearance was like fire to wood. The banging grew stronger. Four Yeshiva students rose from their places, approached him, and said, "Get out of here, you scoundrel and slanderer! From this day on, do not dare to cross the threshold of the Yeshiva, for your end will be bitter." They did not suffice themselves with this warning. They lifted him with their arms, placed him on their shoulders, and forcibly removed him from the *Yeshiva*.

At noontime, the Netzi'v came to the Yeshiva, as usual, to deliver his lesson. However, the students did not extend honor to their rabbi, and the tumult grew even stronger. He banged his hand on the small table many times, but it was for naught, as nobody listened to him. The Netzi'v circled the hall numerous times and asked the students to calm down, but to no avail. Angry and bitter, the Netzi'v left the Yeshiva without completing his class.

The time for the *Mincha* service approached. All the students came to the Yeshiva dressed in festive garb. The Netzi'v

[Page 131]

arrived and the service began. They recited the silent *Shmone Esrei* as if nothing had happened. However, when the prayer leader reached the word *kadosh* in the *kedusha*, the students pronounced the sh sound for a long time, until it sounded like an uninterrupted sound: *sh sh sh*. Furthermore, many students tossed onions and potatoes into the women's gallery.

On every Sabbath and festival, when things functioned normally, the students would approach the Netzi'v one by one after the services to wish him "Gut Yom Tov, Rabbi." However, when the service concluded that Shavuot eve, they did not move from their places, and stood as if mute. Silence pervaded in the Yeshiva hall.

When the Netzi'v saw all this, he decided to put the cure before the affliction, and began to shout out many times, one after another, "Gut Yom Tov, children!" However, the students stood silent, and did not return the greeting. The Netzi'v realized the extent of the stubbornness of the students, and the extent to which they were continuing with their revolt. He was afraid and perplexed lest this revolt lead to a neglect of Torah study on that Shavuot night, for on Shavuot, the Yeshiva students were accustomed to study all night. He sought a way to put an end to this terrible revolt, the likes of which had not taken place in the Yeshiva since the day of its founding.

He felt that this time, the students would not give in. A deep battle broke out in his heart, a battle between the love of Torah and his own conscience. This internal battle lasted several moments, until the love of Torah won out, and he submitted.

He banged his small table several times and said: "Wait, do not leave until you listen to my words!" He ascended the *bima*, and, with a frightened voice, began to deliver a lecture on the events of the day. The content of his lecture was that the students must also forgive the rabbi. He felt that he had erred. He begged forgiveness and pardon from the beaten student in the presence of the entire congregation. "Forgive my sin," he called out at the end, "Even though it is grievous." When he finished his words, the pillars of the Yeshiva shook from the voices of the students, calling out "Gut Yom Tov, Rabbi!"

Through this act of begging for forgiveness, the Netzi'v rose to a very great height as a great pedagogue, and a man of wonderful morality.

Translator's Footnote:

i.   Literally "three days of setting boundaries" – referring to the virtual boundaries set around Mount Sinai prior to the giving of the Torah, to prevent the people from ascending the mountain. This is a term for the three-day period of preparation prior to Shavuot. The time period is considered as festive in anticipation of Shavuot. Haircutting, forbidden during the Omer period, are permitted by all customs (customs vary as to the portion of the Omer period during which some mourning observances apply).

The Big Uprising at the Yeshiva

Translated by Jerrold Landau, based on an earlier translation by M. Porat z"l

In the last years of the Yeshiva's existence the Netzi'v felt his energy leaving him, and he was no longer able to deliver his class. Therefore, he decided to pass the mantle of Yeshiva leadership to his son, Rabbi Chaim Berlin. This decision aroused a great tumult in the Yeshiva, for the students claimed that the son's power was not like his father's.

This is how Abba Blusher described the uprising in his article "Bialik in Volozhin"[46]

"That year (that is, the final year of the existence of the Yeshiva), was a year of tumult in the Yeshiva, due to the desire of the Netzi'v to install his oldest son into his position.

[Page 132]

"The Yeshiva students were opposed to this, for the power of the son was not like the power of the father. This internal battle was difficult and stubborn from both sides. The weapons of the Netzi'v in this battle were tears and pleas, and the weapons of the students were their voices and hands. The voice was the voice of Jacob, angry and shouting, going from one end of the world to the other. The hands were the hands of Jacob. They too threw arrows and catapulted stones from behind the fence, from where their owners could see but not be seen.

"The Netzi'v received anonymous letters every day and every hour. Most were written with coarse hands, full of words as hard as sinews against him, impinging on his honor in a coarse manner, like the frogs of Egypt. In this manner, letters reached the Netzi'v in his bedroom and upon his bed, at the Holy Ark, at his podium, in his tallis bag, between the pages of his books and in the pockets of his clothing. There was no place devoid of them. The Yeshiva students followed after the footsteps of the old man, watching every step, in a cruel manner that only the youth could do, causing him great suffering.

"The image of the Yeshiva diminished during this time of emergency. His daily regimen was affected, and his supervision was weakened. The serious students left the Yeshiva and moved to the small *Beis Midrashes* in the city or convened together in their rooms with their Gemaras. Prisoners of the war circulated around the markets and the roads. They went from home to home and occupied themselves with politics.

"The Zhitomerer (that is Bialik) was not among the fighters, and certainly not among the prisoners of war, even though he too agreed that the words emanating from the Netzi'v, to impose his will upon the Yeshiva against the will of the students, was an error. He was angry about the disgrace that the Yeshiva students were casting upon their dear rabbi. He castigated the tactics of battle that they utilized. Nevertheless, he gave his share to the battle in the Yeshiva. He sat and wrote an anonymous letter to the Netzi'v. A messenger placed it in the podium of the Netzi'v It was related in the Yeshiva that when the Netzi'v read this letter, which was written in fine style, with politeness and respect, he enjoyed it greatly. This letter remained on his table. He would boast to guests that came to visit him, saying, 'See how they write Hebrew in the Volozhin Yeshiva.'"

Chaim Nachman Bialik writes about the uprising in the Yeshiva in his poem "On the Night of Uproar," in the following words:

> Then, the Yeshiva turned to a den of wild ones
> The armies of G-d fought with an outpouring of wrath
> Hidden powers broke forth like a strong wind…
> A hundred hands released the chains
> Suppressed anger was set free
> They shattered windows, extinguished candles
> And overturned benches and tables."

[Page 133]

Bialik himself did not interrupt his studies and did not participate in the battle. Rather, he continued to study with the light of the one candle that remained. The students were wreaking havoc and the Netzi'v protected them with his body:

> "However, one candle remained in the corner
> Even the wind did not dare to extinguish it.
>
> It occupied a space of two cubits, protecting the Divine Presence
> And her precious sons – may G-d protect it.
>
> "That was the place of our relative, the lad, and regarding him
> Full of mercy and grace, like a father to his only child,
> Like an eagle to its nest, to its surviving chicks.
>
> The pillaged ones – thus did the rabbi show concern for his student.";

With great faith, Bialik describes the great tragedy of the Netzi'v:

"Suddenly the old man rose up
And raised his lean hand and touched the shoulder
Of the thoughtful lad, and tears flowed like a stream
They flowed between the silver threads…
The shocked youngster turned his head
The lad was shocked, and he turned his head.

Ho, my teacher and rabbi! – Aha, my dear son
And the boy's eyes rose up to his teachers eyes
Like a child's to his father's.

"Had you seen what they've done, oh lad…?
They did not honor my age, they did not respect me…
They swallowed my holy things, they violated my sanctuary
For which I dedicated my life, my interest.

But you – the eyes of the old man penetrated
Stared at the lad and forever
He will not forget the penetrating gaze of his teacher
Penetrating to the soul of the pure lad."[47]

Bialik reacted to the uprising of the large majority of the students with such reverence, forgiveness, and love.

Original Footnotes:

46. *Meoznaim*, volume IV, booklet II (20). Tammuz 5695 (1935)
47. Chaim Nachman Bialik: "On the Night of Uproar" (A passage extracted from *Hamatmid*), *Knesset*, Dvir Publishing, Tel Aviv 5696 (1936), Book I, from Bialik's estate, pp. 4-8.

The Netzi'v is Saddened in his Heart

Translated by Jerrold Landau

The uprisings in the Yeshiva, particularly the one that broke out regarding the desire of the Yeshiva students to appoint Rabbi Chaim Soloveitchik as the Yeshiva head and to reject Rabbi Chaim Berlin for that position, depressed the spirit of the Netzi'v, which was in any case in a poor state due to his illness.

This is how Menachem Mendel HaLevi Ish-Horowitz, a student of the Yeshiva, describes the Netzi'v during those days[48]:

"And the Yeshiva head sat on a chair at the Eastern Wall, leaning his head and immersed in his thoughts. He was thinking various thoughts, worried about various concerns, and also hoping positive hopes. Everything that took place with him in his prime, the good as well as the bad, the toil and tribulations, was passing before him like sheep, event after event. What were the years of his live? Like twenty-five years. Immediately after his marriage, he studied Torah himself

[Page 134]

closed in a room in the "Ezrat Nashim" home, day and night without end. He never saw the day of light and knew no rest. This was his only rest and purpose. However, this made it possible to make a name for himself and to raise up many students – 20,000 or more. Was this not the entire life of his spirit and goal of his soul. He still remembers everything that happened to him in the home and outside: the hatred of his father-in-law's in-laws for him during his youth, when he was devoted to Torah study and did not turn to any worldly pleasures, and he was the source of half of their mockery. Then there were the tribulations of all the Yeshiva students, who surrounded him and circled him at all hours. Over and above all those, there were the edicts and decrees of the government, and the inquiries regarding the holy Yeshiva. This was over and above the yoke of many debts that surrounded his neck, and continually increased.

"With these thoughts, the cold deepened and saddened his heart. However, there was still a hope in the recesses of his heart, that his son would rule after him, and sit on his throne. Perhaps he would rectify the wrongs, even if the Yeshiva students do not accept the yoke of his awe and love. But, but… A few more days passed, several months passed… And he became elderly. His last day was perhaps approaching. Did he not accomplish a great deal during the years of his life. He pondered and pondered, and perhaps dozed off a bit. Without intention, he awoke and set his gaze upon the images of the Yeshiva building. It was already late, and the time for the *Maariv* service arrived. 'The wicked shall return to questioning' – he banged on the podium, all conversations stopped at the sound of *Vehu Rachum*[i] emanating from the prayer leader."

Original Footnote:

48.   *Derech Etz Hachaim*, pp. 103-104

Translator's Footnote:

i.   The opening words of the weekday *Maariv* service.

The Pinnacle Years of the Yeshiva

Translated by Jerrold Landau

The Yeshiva reached its pinnacle during the final years before its closing, both with respect to the number of students, as well as the level of talent of the students who studied there. Among the students who studied there were some of brilliant talents, who later appeared in Jewish life in Russia, and disseminated their Torah and wisdom, each one in his place of residence. These included: Rabbi Chaim Ozer Grodzinski, the Illuy [genius] of Iwye, who later became famous as one of the great ones of his generation; Rabbi Avraham Yitzchak HaKohen Kook, whom the Netzi'v loved very much, and called "My Avraham Itze"; Rabbi Moshe Mordechai Epstein, the Illuy of Baksht, who later served as the head of the Knesset Yisrael Yeshiva in Slobodka and later in Hebron; Zunia Mirer (that is what the Illuy of Mir was called in Volozhin), who studied in Volozhin for about seven years, was a friend of Rabbi Chaim Soloveitchik, and later became known as the Gaon Isser Zalman Meltzer, the rabbi in Slutsk and later the head of a Yeshiva in Jerusalem and the author of novellae on the Ramba'm; Beril Kobriner, the Illuy of Kobrin, who later became known as the Gaon Rabbi Avraham Dov Ber Shapira, the final rabbi of Kovno; Rabbi Baruch Berl, who later became the head of Yeshivat Knesset Beit Yitzchak in Slobodka, and continued in the methodology of his rabbi, Rabbi Chaim, with great exactitude, and authored deep books. Shimon of Turitz, who was the famous Gaon Rabbi Shimon Shkop, one of the

[Page 135]

great Yeshiva heads in Telz; Menachem Krakovski from Volkovisk, who later served as a rabbi in Novogrudek, and a preacher in Vilna. He authored a book called *Avodat Hamelech* on *Sefer Hamada* of the Ramba'm, written in a scientific fashion, which was a great innovation in rabbinical literature; Baruch of Lomza, who served as a rabbi in Krynki. He authored the book *Minchat Baruch* and became known as one of the great ones of the generation; Rabbi Moshe David, the Illuy of Utian [Utena], who later became the son-in-law of the Rogochover Gaon; Rabbi Shlomo of Maytchet, who later became famous in all the Yeshivas as the Illuy of Maytchet. He was brought to Volozhin at the age of twelve, celebrated his Bar Mitzvah in the home of Rabbi Chaim Soloveitchik, and delivered a lecture with sharp didactics [*pilpul*]; and finally – Chaim Nachman Bialik, the poet of the nation.

The Authorities Persecute the Yeshiva

Translated by Jerrold Landau, based on an earlier translation by M. Porat z"l

External troubles were added to the internal problems and disorder within the Yeshiva. The Czarist government authorities continually increased the pressure upon the Yeshiva. From the beginning of its existence, the Yeshiva was like a thorn in the eyes of the Russian government. As long as the mighty spiritual fortress known as the Etz Chaim Yeshiva existed in Volozhin, religious reforms regarding the Jewish could not be actualized. Therefore, they sought pretexts to shut the Yeshiva down.

When Minister Makov was appointed as Interior Minister of the Russian Empire in the year 5639 (1879), reports about the Yeshiva were submitted to his office by informants. They claimed that the Yeshiva had existed for more than eighty years while the authorities knew nothing about its functioning. Therefore, there is room for suspicion that clandestine activities against the government take place there. Based on this, the Yeshiva should be closed, and its directors should be punished. However, Minister Makov related to the Yeshiva with appreciation and stated that since it has existed for approximately eighty years as a high-level house of study, and it was founded by a *Gaon* and a *Tzadik*, if is certainly not a place for conspiracies and intent to revolt against the government. Since no iniquity has been found with the Yeshiva for all those years, one must conclude that this house of study serves as a protection against revolutionaries. After an investigation and inquiry, the Yeshiva was certified to function under the supervision of the curatorium of the Vilna district.

However, the government was not content for long. The supervisor of the schools in the district came to the Yeshiva in the year 5647 (1887) along with Yehoshua Steinberg, the superintendent of the school for Jewish teachers, as a special emissary from the district minister. They conducted an exacting investigation. They remained in the Yeshiva for a week. First, they verified the validity of the students' documents, for a rumor had spread that youngsters who were evading army service had gathered in the Yeshiva. All the documents were found to be in order. Then they investigated the procedures of the Yeshiva and its students. There was no matter that they did not thoroughly investigate. They visited the student dormitories to see if they followed sanitation standards. They did not find any fault. When they interrogated the students, each one was asked where they were before they came to Volozhin, and what were they doing there. They especially examined their knowledge of the Russian language. After the investigations and interrogations, they listed

[Page 136]

the Yeshiva students on a sheet of paper to check if their numbers correspond to that which was registered in the Yeshiva ledgers. Everything was in good order.

They cordially took leave of the Netzi'v and left the Yeshiva. However, the Netzi'v was saddened in his heart. He suspected that great changes were liable to come to the Yeshiva in the wake of this visit, which would be enveloped in darkness. Indeed, that which he suspected indeed came.

The Decree of the Minister of Education Delyanov [i]

Translated by Jerrold Landau, based on an earlier translation by M. Porat z"l

Mr. Delyanov, the Education Minister, confirmed for the Yeshiva a curriculum that the Netzi'v could not abide by. There were four sections in this decree, which spelled death for the Yeshiva.

1. Introducing secular studies every day from nine in the morning until three in the afternoon.
2. The school day should not exceed ten hours within a 24-hour period.
3. The learning should be interrupted in the evening and the building should be closed at night.
4. The Yeshiva head and all the teachers should be certified with diplomas.

The rule restricting the hours of study was the most difficult, for, as per Rabbi Chaim's spiritual heritage, if the study of Torah were to cease, Heaven forbid, even for one moment, the world would be destroyed. Therefore, this decree was in accordance with "if you cut off its head, will it not die?"[ii]

Some members of the Jewish community supported the government program for the Yeshiva. Erez, the editor of *Hameilitz*, attempted to explain the benefits that would come to the Yeshiva by introducing secular studies. In his article "The Supernal Yeshiva"[49], he writes the following:

"The main role of the Yeshiva is to instruct the students to swim in the sea of Talmud and halachic decisors, to sharpen their minds with sharp didactics [*pilpul*]. However, if until this generation, every Jewish man knew how to understand the vast majority of Torah even without knowing anything about world events – times and concepts have changed, and we see how great is the honor of those rabbis who have succeeded in acquiring broad knowledge. Such rabbis have a strong power to attract all factions toward them."

Erez recommended that the Netzi'v educate his students "To speak and write properly in the vernacular, and to understand it fluently, as well as to master arithmetic, and to learn the annals of the nations of the world, and especially the history of their homeland, the structure of the world in general, and especially of their native land, as well as other such vital knowledge, without which a person may stumble, especially a rabbi amongst our people."

The Netziv's response to Erez was that this is the way of Torah, that its toil and purpose are fulfilled

[Page 137]

only by those who devote their entire mind to it. It is impossible for a person to become great in Torah when he is occupied with other matters. All Torah giants who are also wise in secular studies are only those who occupied themselves with secular studies prior to immersing their minds in Torah, or after they already became great in Torah. However, when combined, it is impossible to attain the purpose of studies. Indeed, secular knowledge is worthwhile, but Volozhin was only created for Torah study.

The response, published in *Hameilitz* in 5645 [50], is written as follows:

"Even though his opinion differs from ours regarding how to reach the heights, I am not embarrassed to inform his honor and righteousness that he must learn that we understand the preciousness of the holy Talmud more than he does, and we know that just as pure secularity causes impurity to holy objects through contact[iii], likewise do secular studies, even though they have no trace of impurity or forbiddenness, disrupt the holiness of the Talmud and its successful [study] when they are blended under a single inn."

Nevertheless, the Netzi'v had no choice, and he was forced to institute the study of the Russian language. The question arose: Who would be the teacher? Certified teachers were required, and there were only three such people in Volozhin: two Jews who had completed their studies at the Seminary for Jewish Teachers in Vilna and served as teachers in Volozhin at the school for Jewish children, and one Christian teacher. The Christian teacher was at a significantly lower level of qualification than the Jewish teachers, but the Netzi'v was specifically worried about the Jewish teachers, lest their influence penetrate to the Yeshiva students. The influence of such people, who were public violators of the Sabbath, was not desired in the Yeshiva. They brought in a certified teacher from Minsk, a G-d fearing Jew. However, for various reasons, he did not teach for very long. He had to choose one of the local teachers, a Jew or a gentile. Rabbi Chaim Soloveitchik opposed a Jewish teacher, and they selected a Christian teacher.

Like all the Christian teachers in small towns who were involved with the children of the farmers, he was quite limited. His education was minimal, and his pedagogic talents quite lacking. He did not succeed in his job, and the students avoided his classes. The Netzi'v, who knew very well the meaning of such avoidance, pleaded

[Page 138]

with tears before the students to continue their studies, for the entire existence of the Yeshiva was dependent on this. However, they did not heed him.

Rabbi Yosef Dov Soloveitchik was among the great opponents of the institution secular education in the Yeshiva. His opinion was that if it is impossible to maintain the Yeshiva as it was supposed to be, it would be best if it were to be closed.

Rabbi Yosi Dov said, "It is not for us to worry about the concerns of the Holy One Blessed Be He and to set up Yeshivas for Him. If we can maintain Yeshivas in accordance with the traditions we have from our ancestors, we are required to maintain them. Otherwise, we have no responsibility. Let the Give of the Torah come and concern Himself with the existence of the Torah." [51]

Original Footnotes:

49. *Hameilitz*, issue 36, 19 Tevet 5651 (December 9, 1880), and *Hameilitz*, issue 9, 28 Shvat 5645 (February 1, 1885).

50. *Hameilitz*, 28 Shvat 5645. Issue 9, page 139.
Rabbi Kook brings a different version. He writes: "The Gaon the Netzi'v indeed demanded faithful erudition, and desired the honor of Torah, that a rabbi who is the pastor to the flock of G-d should be a man of generous traits, with manners, and worldly knowledge at a level necessary for the conditions of life. He should also

know the vernacular language. If he opposed setting times for secular study, it was because he was afraid that the students would make their education primary and their Torah secondary. In any case, he made a great enactment, and asked the students who had already internalized the knowledge of Torah, and have become immersed in it, to set certain times for the secular studies in a special room, and under the tutelage of expert teachers. (The head of the Etz Chaim Yeshiva, Knesset Yisrael, 5648 [1868], page 142).

51.   Rabbi Moshe Meir Yishai: "The Chofetz Chaim" volume I, page 334, published by Netzach, Tel Aviv, 5718 [1958]. Dr. Shlomo Mandelkorn recommended that the "Society of Disseminators of Haskalah" found a secular school alongside the Yeshiva. The following are his words: "Everyone knows that the Yeshiva of Volozhin is virtually the only one certified and confirmed by the government. From way back, it has disseminated Torah and the knowledge of Talmud and halachic decisors, etc., which are 'the life of Judaism and the guardian of Israel amongst the nations.' The only thing missing is secular studies, which are necessary for every person as a human being, and especially or a rabbi, who must be the mouthpiece of the community and fulfil the duties of the deeds imposed upon him by the government. Therefore, would it not be good if the society of "Disseminating Haskalah in Israel" found a school for such studies adjacent to the Yeshiva for the Yeshiva students, who will only spare a small amount of time to easily acquire the necessary knowledge, small in essence and quantity, from expert teachers.

"My heart is certain and sure that my recommendation will be actualized, to rectify a lacuna in the rabbinate, and to fill what is lacking in the community by the good connection between the Yeshiva under the supervision of the rabbi and Gaon, mighty in Torah, and a school under the supervision of the 'Society of Disseminators of Haskalah'." ("The Have Been Drawn Near," Literary Treasury, 5648 [1888], pp 41-43.)

Translator's Footnotes:

i.   See https://en.wikipedia.org/wiki/Ivan_Delyanov
ii.   A Talmudic and halachic principle indicating that the consequence of an action or a situation is certain rather than doubtful.
iii.   Based on the complex laws of *Tumah* and *Tahara* (ritual purity and impurity).

The Yeshiva Closure – "The Destruction of the Third Temple"

Translated by Jerrold Landau, based on an earlier translation by M. Porat z"l

"It was an ordinary winter morning. Little Volozhin woke up from its sleep that day, a chilly day in Shvat, and saw its stormy landscape covered in white. Deep snow covered its hills and slopes, and the wooden roofs of the rickety houses. Even the nearby pine forest was wrapped in a white blanket. The grey skies were low, almost touching the roof of the Yeshiva building that rose proudly over the hilltop, the pride of the scholars. The well-known local swamps were frozen beneath it. Sleighs full of passengers arrived from Molodechna, the railroad station several parasangs from the city, travelling at a high speed. The residents were going to and coming back from the synagogue. Shops were opening. Sleighs of the farmers appeared at the marketplace. Jews seeking a livelihood were scrutinizing the products, incidentally examining the straw, rubbing their hands that were blue from cold, and bargaining over the purchases. They haggled with the gentiles. After a brief time, they went home with a chicken, a sack of grain, etc.

[Page 139]

Rabbis and new Yeshiva students were loitering around Yosi Zelig's inn. Their gaze was still directed only to the legend of the wonderful Yeshiva. There were also householders from all around Russia who had come to see the great tent of Torah."

This is how Shee'n[52] describes the day of the closure of the Yeshiva. On that day at the beginning of the month of Shvat, 5652 (1892), all the Yeshiva students sat down after breakfast, and occupied themselves with Torah as usual. Suddenly the district governor, the mayor of the city, and policemen entered the Yeshiva. Behind them, a long row of farmers, and villagers remained outside. The emissaries of the government entered. As they entered, one of them told the students to be quiet and stop their studies. When everything grew silent, one official read aloud the edict of the authorities, stating that the Yeshiva was closed. The edict contained three commands: the closure of the Yeshiva, the deportation of the students from the city, and the deportation of the three Yeshiva heads from three districts of the region. The Yeshiva was closed. The building will be sealed. The students were required to come to receive their documents. They were all required to leave Volozhin within three days.

The Netzi'v, who did not understand Russian, asked for the meaning of this. When he heard the translation, he remained seated at his seat as if he fainted. The Yeshiva students removed from the Yeshiva everything that was possible to salvage. The building was evacuated, and the destruction was actualized in full force. The matter became known to all the Jews of Volozhin, and all of them, from young to old, hurried to the Yeshiva building and removed the Torah scrolls. The men banged their hands, and the women wept aloud. The children ran about as orphans, and heard only the words of eulogy, "The destruction of the Third Temple!" Everyone felt that the greatest place of Torah for more than eighty years, was to be destroyed, and there was nobody to save it.[53].

After the officials determined that there was nobody left in the Yeshiva, they locked the doors, and sealed the entrance gate with a large seal imprinted with the insignia of the government. It stated that anyone who breaks the seal was liable to a severe punishment. With this, the closing ceremony ended. The grief was very great and deep. The large congregation that gathered around the Yeshiva did not have the spirit to leave the place. The Netzi'v sat on his chair, with his tears choking his throat, and words were caught in his mouth.

The closure of the Yeshiva made a frightful impression not only upon those who were immersed in Torah, the Rabbis and scholars of Judaism, but also upon every Jew. Everyone understood that the destruction of the Yeshiva of Volozhin was a national disaster – a loss for all of Jewry, for anyone who had studied in the Yeshiva, even for a brief time, became a lifetime partner in the weaving of the golden chain of Judaism.

Original Footnotes:

52. "When the Gates Were Locked," *Hatzofeh*, 8 Shvat, 5702 [1942].
53. The idea that the Yeshiva disbanded from the inside, in accordance with "Thy destroyers and they that made thee waste shall go forth from thee" [Trans: Translation from Mechon Mamre, Isaiah, 49:17. https://mechon-mamre.org/p/pt/pt1049.htm], was proposed by the writer Meir Rivkin in his article in *Hamashkim*, "The Volozhin Yeshiva During its Final Years" Woschod, 1895.

[Page 140]

The Netzi'v Conducts Tikkun Chatzot Next to the Yeshiva Building[i]

Translated by Jerrold Landau, based on an earlier translation by M. Porat z"l

The Yeshiva students, depressed and humiliated, left town to return home in groups. Peasant with horse-harnessed carts gathered from the entire region to transport the Yeshiva students to the railroad station. Bitter cold reigned outdoors. A blizzard started, covering the face of the entire world. The lads sat in the wagons, doubled over, crowded between their clothes and their baggage. They were overcome with grief and eaten by agony. The wagons seemed like a row of corpses that winter night, along the route from Volozhin to Molodechna.

Toward evening, the *Mincha* service was conducted for the first time in a different place. The Netzi'v stood in his corner, praying in his usual manner, pronouncing each word aloud, as if he were threading pearls. In the middle of *Ashrei*, he could no longer restrain his emotions. He groaned deeply and peered through the window at the dark Yeshiva building, which appeared before his eyes as a corpse in front of the entire Jewish people. Suddenly, he raised his arms heavenward, regained his composure and justified the judgment. In the sad melody of the Yeshiva, he recited the verse: "G-d is just in all His ways, and gracious in all His deeds."[ii]

However, the Netzi'v was not calmed. He mourned over the Yeshiva. It was a winter day, and a heavy snowfall fell over Volozhin. The windows of the Yeshiva, which were illuminated all night for ninety years, were sealed shut and spread a pall. The local Jews were wary of approaching the building – out of sublime fear of the "deceased" – the death of the community of Israel. Only the Netzi'v remained in Volozhin. He was granted the permission to remain for several weeks. A few days after the closure, footsteps were noticed in the snow upon the Yeshiva path. People recognized the footsteps of the lonely Yeshiva head. Late at night, when the marketplace was deserted, he would leave his home, stand next to the lock door, and recite the *Tikkun Chatzot* service. There were snowstorms, cold that froze the blood, and the government ban, but he, the wonderful guardian, to whom the soul of the building had become his own soul, stood there. A heavenly voice emanated from his throat into the space of Volozhin: "Alas for my children who have been exiled from the center of their lives, and are wandering along seven paths." He was unable to part from his nest, which he protected under the shade of his wings for forty years. His footsteps were also found along the path leading to the gravesite of the rabbinical family [*Beit Harav*], where he used to go to supplicate at the grave of his grandfather, Rabbi Chaim of Volozhin, at any time of tribulation. He would prostrate himself and put forth his supplication and embrace the cold monument in which the holy body was interred.

Translator's Footnotes:

i. A midnight set of dirges recited in memory of the destruction of the temple. Generally, *Tikkun Chatzot* is recited by especially pious people, and is not part of the obligatory prayer rites. See https://en.wikipedia.org/wiki/Tikkun_Chatzot https://halachipedia.com/index.php?title=Tikkun_Chatzot

ii. This verse (Psalms 145:17) is part of the *Ashrei* prayer, recited three times daily, including as the opening of the *Mincha* service. The justification of the judgment (*Tzidduk Hadin*) is a blessing recited upon receiving very bad news, especially upon hearing the death of a close relative.

The Sunset of the Netzi'v Begins

Translated by Jerrold Landau, based on an earlier translation by M. Porat z"l

After the closure of the Yeshiva, the Netzi'v left for Pinsk, and then to Warsaw. On the last day of Passover, the Netzi'v ascended the *bima* to bid farewell to the people of his community. The departure from Volozhin, where he was raised and educated, and from where his fame spread throughout the world, was very difficult for him. Tears flowed from his eyes, and his voice could be heard with difficulty. Seeing the elderly *Gaon* weeping aroused great agony. He left the city the day after Passover. Many of the Volozhin residents accompanied him. Volozhin was left enveloped in grief, as its glory and splendor was taken away from it.

[Page 141]

In his memoirs, the preacher Tzvi Hirsch Maslianski described the Netzi'v during his declining months[54]:

"During that time, there was a convention of the local Chovevei Tzion in Warsaw. I too was present at that gathering. Suddenly, as I scanned the people gathered with my eyes, I saw before me the *Gaon*, the Netzi'v of Volozhin, sitting at the head of those summoned. How surprised was I to see the great change that had taken place in the look of his face and the build of his body, since four years previously,when I had seen him before me alive and fresh, alert, and full of spiritual energy. He, the elder, encouraged me, the youth. He spoke to my heart and strengthened my hands, encouraging me to continue to speak and encourage the revival of Israel in its land. Now, he sat before me depressed and bent over. His face was gaunt and pale, and he exuded weariness and exhaustion. I knew the reason for the change in this exalted man. During the four years, a terrible event had taken place, which destroyed the world of this *Gaon*, and forcefully severed the wick of his soul – the closure of the great Yeshiva of Volozhin, and the severing of the golden chain that had extended back from the days of Rabbi Chaim. His great, wide heart could not withstand the terrible destruction, and had been cut to pieces.

"After the gathering, I approached the Netzi'v to greet him. We stood and chatted for a period of time. When I parted from him, he hugged and kissed me, and spoke the following words to me in the presence of all those gathered: 'I know that I will no longer merit to make *aliya* to our Holy Land. May the G-d of Zion be with you , and when you come to the Land, bring my bones with you from here.'"

The Netzi'v intended to make *aliya* to the Land, but he was forced to defer it due to the debts that were upon him. In his letter of Monday, 21 Adar 5652 [1892], the Netzi'v complained to his student, Rabbi Eliyahu Aharon Milikowski, about the debts that he had incurred on account of the Yeshiva: "In truth, my close friend said to me that if I had not had debts, I would have set out immediately after the festival to our Holy Land to rest there after bearing the burden of the Yeshiva for 38 years, and to die there [and be buricd] at the grave of my father, may the memory of the righteous be blessed, in Jerusalem, may it be built up speedily in our days. However, the debts that I owe force me to leave my wife and children, may the live, and to remain in the Diaspora, to collect, through our great sins, and to disburse. All this affects my soul, and my head spins."

The decline of the Netzi'v began. Eliezer the son of Zeev Perski writes[55]:

"Volozhin, 14 Tammuz. Today, a telegram reached the honorable Rabbi Chaim Hillel.

[Page 142]

from the Rebbetzin, Mrs. Batya Mirl, the wife of the rabbi and *Gaon*, our rabbi Naftali Tzvi Yehuda Berlin. It stated that her husband is sick, and he requested that Psalms be recited for him. In the wake of this sad telegram, immediately all the residents of our city gathered in the Great Beis Midrash and recited Psalms with deep devotion, pouring out their words before the Healer Of All Flesh, that He should send a complete healing for his serous illness. Rivers of tears were shed. After the recitation of Psalms, Rabbi Ben Tzion Shu'b [the *shochet*], a great friend of the Rabbi and *Gaon* the Netzi'v, may he live long, ascended the *bima*, and recited the *Mi Sheberach* prayer for the benefit of the sick person. The entire congregation pledged on his behalf eighteen zloty to Bikkur Cholim, and eighteen zloty to the Talmud Torah. In this merit, may the Healer Of All Flesh grant him a complete recovery, strengthen him, grant him life, and extend his days and years in good spirit and pleasantness, as is the will of all residents of our city, his faithful admirers."

Original Footnotes:

54.   *Haivri*, issue 32, 6 Elul 5677 (July 24, 1917) [Trans: I believe something is incorrect on one of the dates, probably the English date, as the date is too early for 6 Elul, even according to the Julian calendar.]
55.   *Hameilitz*, Thursday, 22 Tammuz 5653 [1893].

The Death of the Netzi'v

Translated by Jerrold Landau, based on an earlier translation by M. Porat z"l

In *Hameilitz* of Friday, 29 Av, 5653 [1893], Fogel announced the following frightening news: "Warsaw, 28 Av (July 29, 1893), at 7:00 a.m. The rabbi, the great luminary, the former head of the Volozhin Yeshiva, our teacher Naftali Tzvi Yehuda Berlin, passed away today."

Ben-Tzion, the *shochet* of Volozhi , writes the following about the heavy mourning of the Jews of the city[56]:

"Alas over the news that has arrived, the terrible, vexing news that was brought to us today from Warsaw over the telegraph lines, that the crown of our heads, the splendor of Israel, the portent and glory of the generation, the great *Gaon*, the famous *Tzadik*, Rabbi Naftali Tzvi Yehuda, the son of Rabbi Yaakov Berlin, may the memory of the righteous be blessed for life in the world to come, has fallen. The head of the rabbinical court and the head of the Yeshiva of Volozhin has been taken from us today. This awful, saddening news, which brought sorrow to the House of Israel in general, and to the community of Volozhin in particular, the city in which he served for close to forty years, reached us toward evening. The entire city was flabbergasted, and everyone, from young to old, gathered in the Great Beis Midrash to eulogize him appropriately, and to weep for him. The weeping reached great heights, and the flood of tears grew like a flowing river breaking through the courtyard of the House of G-d. Mourning and sadness was great in Volozhin."

"The angels were victorious on the heights, and the Holy Ark has been captured. The Netzi'v was gathered unto his people." The Netzi'v was gathered to his people on the 29th of the month of Av, 5653, in the year of "my eye is poured out"[i]. The newspapers announced that his son, Rabbi Chaim Berlin, included in his eulogy for his father the words that our sages stated in *Yalkut Yeshayahu*, 21:

"Our rabbis taught that when the First Temple was destroyed, what did the youths of the Kohanim of that generation do? They gathered in groups, with the keys to the Temple courtyard in their hands, ascended the roof

[Page 143]

of the sanctuary, and said before the Holy One Blessed Be He: 'Master of the World! Since we did not merit to be the treasurers, here are your keys given back to you. They threw them upward. Immediately, a form of a hand came forth and accepted them.'"

Original Footnote:

56.   Tuesday, 10 Elul, 5653 [1993]

Translator's Footnote:

i.   A literary technique exists in which a Hebrew year is represented by a relevant Biblical verse, some of the words of which form an acronym of the year. The verse fragment here is from Lamentations 3:49 [עיני נגרת] – with the second word matching the year, albeit the original ה was interchanged with a ת.

The Moving Eulogies for the Netzi'v

Translated by Jerrold Landau

On the day of the funeral of the Netzi'v, Y. Ch. Zagorodski sent words of eulogy about the Netzi'v to *Hameilitz*, expressing the greatness and lofty value of the illustrious deceased. At the end of his words, he tells[57]:

"The terrible news of the death of the *Gaon* the Netzi'v flew through all corners of Warsaw like an arrow from a bow. From the morning, masses and masses came to the house of the deceased. People from all segments of the nation came to stand around the body of the deceased, and to ponder his greatness and the magnitude of the loss to our nation with the death of this great giant. The deceased was lying on straw on the ground, as per Jewish law. There was a black shroud atop him, and atop the shroud, many books and tractates, a large heap of books. Around this holy heap were tens of candles. Children and youths from the Talmud Torah were standing from the morning, with the Psalms of David the son of Jesse upon their lips. 'For You shall not abandon my soul to the netherworld, nor will You let your righteous one see the pit'[ii]. Indeed, people such as the Netzi'v do not die and do not descend to the netherworld, for their memory lives – lives forever in the hearts of the myriads who honor and revere them. Generations will pass, hundreds of years will go by, and the memory of the great *Gaon* will stand as it is.

"Toward evening, I arrived at the house where the body of the deceased was reposing. In one of the rooms, I found one of the doctors whom I knew, who had also studied from the deceased. The doctor stood, leaning on his arm. Sadness was etched upon his face, and tears welled up in his eyes. 'Aha,' lamented the doctor, 'There is no word on my tongue to describe to you the worth of this deceased man, and the magnitude of the pressure upon my heart, as I stand now in this place. Does death even afflict angels, and do the mighty die? Indeed, this *Gaon* in the midst of our land was like an angel, a holy being descended from Heaven. His soul was as pure as the essence of the sky. His spirit was noble beneath the throne on high.'"

The eulogy of Yitzchak Sobolski was no less moving[58]:

"Who will comfort us from our sadness, who can sense the magnitude of the loss, more than us, his students, we who saw the preciousness of Torah? The stylus of any scribe is for naught, and vain is the paint of an artist to draw the holy splendor and lofty emotions that were aroused in the hearts of anyone who saw our rabbi, this man of G-d, enwrapped in his tallis and crowed with his tefillin, running

[Page 144]

back and forth in the afternoon, between the pillars of the Yeshiva, with his lips moving and his voice not being hard, for he was reviewing the six orders of the Mishnah by heart.

"All faces have gathered darkness[ii], and all eyes shed tears, as they see the Torah scroll resting in a coffin, for our rabbi has taken all the precious things of the world and disappeared.

"Rest, o pure, holy soul, for you accomplished so much in your life in the world. Your children, these are your students, whom you raised like your own children, will spread the wellsprings of your Torah."

The Netzi'v was 75 years old when he died. His honorable burial place is in the cemetery of Warsaw.

Original Footnotes:

57. *Hameilitz*, 3 Elul 5653 (August 3, 1893), issue 174.
58. *Evel Yachid, Hatzefira*, 4 Elul 5653 (August 4, 1893), issue 174.

Translator's Footnotes:

i.   Psalms 16:10.
ii.   Joel 2:6.

The Works of the Netzi'v

Translated by Jerrold Landau

1. *Haemek Sheelah* – A large, broad explanation on the She'eltot of Rabbi Achai Gaon, incidentally on general Talmudic literature (five volumes).
2. *Haemek Davar* and *Harchav Davar* – Commentary on the Torah.
3. *Rina Shel Torah* – A commentary on the Song of Songs.
4. *Biur* – Commentary on the Passover Haggadah.
5. *Meishiv Davar* – Responsa on all areas of Torah (two volumes).
6. *Emek Hanetzi'v* – A commentary on the Sifrei (the Tannaic Midrash on the books of Numbers and Deuteronomy).

[Page 145]

Chapter IV

The Era of Rabbi Rafael Shapira

Translated by Jerrold Landau

The Yeshiva was closed for approximately three years. The Jews of Volozhin, and the Jews of Russia in general, did not make peace even for one moment with the decree of closure. Rabbi Chaim Hillel Fried[59], the son of Rabbi Eliezer Yitzchak, was especially active. Several people of action and special individuals in Vilna and Minsk interceded through many avenues to soften the harshness of the decree, and to reopen the doors of the Yeshiva once again. Even Rabbi Yitzchak Elchanan of Kovno, who was seriously ill, entered the thicket. On Monday, 3 Adar 5656 [1896], one of his friends, a great and famous rabbi, came to consult with him regarding opening the Yeshiva. Even though the rabbi felt very weak, he girded himself due to the preciousness and holiness of this matter, and wrote a letter to his acquaintances in Peterburg.

Rabbi Chaim Berlin, the son of the Netzi'v, who went to Amsterdam to collect money to cover the debts that were upon the Yeshiva and his father, wrote to Erez, the editor of *Hameilitz*. Among other things, he wrote the following[60]:

"Regarding the matter of the doors of the holy sanctuary that were closed, our hope strengthens us, the strong hope in the merit of the holy Torah, that G-d will help us through the rabbis, the Gaonim of the generation, may G-d protect and save them, and the gates will once gain raise their heads, and the everlasting doors will be raised[i], and a great, wise rabbi who knows the language of the state will go there, and the ministers of the government, may its glory be raised, shall give permission. Then the crown of Torah will be restored to what it was, under conditions that will also be acceptable to the government ministers. The good G-d will conclude it for good on our behalf, in the merit of our holy father and grandfather, the holy Gaon, our Rabbi Chaim of Volozhin, may the memory of the righteous be a blessing, will stand for it, that it will be rebuilt upon its ruins, for renown and praise, forever, Selah."

The news about the reopening of the Yeshiva aroused precious memories, memories of holiness and spiritual loftiness in the hearts of its students. One of its students describes this well[60a]:

"I hereby close my eyes, and voices emanate from the mouths of the studiers awaken

[Page 146]

within me memories from the past, precious memories, memories of Volozhin. Those days were days of spiritual pleasure in the full sense of the term. The love of Torah and the love of Zion joined together in the heart of our elderly rabbi (the Netzi'v), and his spirit was imbued upon the best of the students, who also bore Nes Tziona [literally: the banner of Zion]. How pleasant were the hours of study in the Yeshiva after hours of discussion at a meeting that warmed the heart, after hours of study that sharpened the mind. At time, life was wholesome, a life of development of emotions and intellect. The heart, the mind, the hopes, and the imaginations – how did the grow, how high they were raised! We studied with enthusiasm, and we debated with excitement. Life hummed along, bustled, and flowed around us in the marketplaces, but we lived a completely different life. Our head was in Babylonia, and our heart in Zion. That was the reality of Volozhin. Volozhin, how pleasant you were to me, and how great are my longings for you!"

The intercessors succeeded in having the decree revoked, and received a semi-official permit to open the Yeshiva. As a foundation for the reopening of the Yeshiva as a *Beis Midrash* of a Talmudic kibbutz [gathering], the institute functioned in the form of a Kolel [institute of high Talmudic study] for young men, named for Brodsky, which was founded already during the 1800s as a special branch of the Yeshiva of Volozhin. Through all sorts of memos and intercessions, the Russian authorities agreed that the decree of closure of the Yeshiva from the year 5652 [1892] did not apply to the "Avreichei Brodsky" group,[iii] ten in number, for this group was not subsumed officially under the Yeshiva. Rather, it was funded by a private individual, a wealthy Jew from Kyiv. At this opportunity, a second group of young men, consisting of thirty individuals were sent to Volozhin, under the auspices of Tomchei Torah [Supporters of Torah] of Minsk, which was headed by Rabbi Avraham Gershon Brenner. In order to more firmly root this renewed Talmudic kernel in Volozhin, these two groups of young men, among the known Torah greats, assisted greatly in raising the profile of Volozhin.

Word spread very quickly through Poland and Lithuania that the Yeshiva of Volozhin has reopened. The Yeshiva was once again bustling through a large stream of new lads, most of them from the Yeshiva of Telz, and the minority from Slobodka. Their numbers reached twenty. Regarding the character of these students, "Yehudi" writes in his article "Hosts of Torah": "It is said that the students of the Yeshiva are primarily Zionists."

The day of the opening of the Yeshiva was a day of unusual festivity and joy, which encompassed all the Jews of Volozhin, from young to old. This joy is described in the words of Rabbi Moshe Shmuel Shapira in the following words:

Yisrael Brodsky

[Page 147]

"Today, the day that the Yeshiva has opened, was a day of great festivity for all the residents of the town. Young and old women from all strata hastened to come to the Yeshiva with jugs full of water and sponges in their hands to clean and scrub the floor and the windows, which were covered in dust. All the windows were opened to ventilate the building, which was full of mildew and stifling air. The Yeshiva was full of visitors throughout the day, one leaving as another arrived. Everyone wanted to see with their own eyes whether the Yeshiva was left in its complete state, and whether the internal appearance had been damaged after having been closed for three years."[61]

The question of a Yeshiva head arose several weeks after the opening. At the time of its closing, they turned to the *Mashgiach* [spiritual overseer], Rabbi Shlomo David Dinkin, whom the Netzi'v recommended on the day of his departure from Volozhin. Nevertheless, they hesitated to appoint him as Yeshiva head, for the seat of the rabbinate in Volozhin was considered prestigious, and the householders of Volozhin desired one of the Torah greats who would be fitting to fill the role of the previous Gaonim.

Finally, the appropriate candidate for this position appeared. This was Rabbi Meir Noach Levin, the rabbi of Moscow. In those days, he had been deported from Moscow along with the general expulsion decreed upon the Jews of that city. Since he remained without a rabbinic position, his brother-in-law, Rabbi Chaim Hillel Fried, recommended that he be accepted as the rabbi in Volozhin. His recommendation received general agreement, but the tenure of Rabbi Meir Noach Levin only lasted for three years. In the year 5658 [1898], he left Volozhin for Vilna.

Rabbi Meir-Noach HaLevi Levin

After the departure of Rabbi Meir Noach Levin, the trustees of the Yeshiva convened in Minsk and Vilna, and decided that the time had come to restore the crown of the Yeshiva to its former situation. To this end, they sought a rabbi, a famous Gaon, whose name would attract a large conglomerate of students, and the appearance of the Yeshiva would be restored to what it was in former years. They decided to invite Rabbi Rafael Shapira, who served as the rabbi of the *Misnagdim* in Bobruisk.

Rabbi Rafael was not a new face in the Yeshiva. He had become a son-in-law of the Netzi'v at the age of fifteen. When he was supported at the table of the Netzi'v, he continued his work in Torah, and assisted his father-in-law in several places in his work *Haemek Sheela* and the She'iltot of Rabbi Achai Gaon. In the introduction in *Kidmat Haemek*, the Netzi'v mentions this son-in-law among those who assisted him in his work, stating "He sits with me in a group. His power is fine in Torah,

[Page 148]

and his opinion is clear to deliberate in *halacha* and clarify it. He also added several glosses with a great deal of research."

Rabbi Rafael gave classes in the Yeshiva from the year 5625 (1865) until 5650 (1880) alongside his father-in-law the Netzi'v. He became known in the world as an expert in delivering classes. Aside from that, his appointment formed a continuation of the dynasty of Beit Harav [The rabbinical family] in Volozhin.

From the time that Rabbi Rafael left Volozhin until his return about twenty years later, he occupied the rabbinical seat in two cities: first in Novoaleksandrovsk, and later in Bobruisk, where he arrived in the year 5646 [1886]. He served as the rabbi of Bobruisk for thirteen years, and merited the love of everybody. Even the Hassidim loved him. The day of his departure was a day of mourning for the Jews of Bobruisk. Many of them shed tears, for the departure of their beloved rabbi was difficult for them.

The character of the Yeshiva during the era of Rabbi Rafael Shapira remained as it was formerly. When requests came to him at times for various changes and innovations in the Yeshiva, he would respond: "Just as I received from my fathers, so it is my will to give over to the next generation." He regarded himself only as the guardian of a pledge. However, with all the conservatism that pervaded in the Yeshiva during the period of Rabbi Rafael, the Yeshiva students were very different from the students of other Yeshivot. Their horizons were not as restricted. They were familiar with what was going on in communal life, and they took proper interest in all current events.

During the period of Rabbi Rafael, the Yeshiva was disturbed by the attempt to institute the *mussar* methodology[iii]. One of the *mussar* greats came to Volozhin, sought to settle there, and to institute the *mussar* methodology in the Yeshiva. The Yeshiva leadership acceded to the request. However, when the students heard this, they immediately gathered in the Yeshiva library and decided to send this man away and save the Yeshiva from the *mussar* methodology. They presented their decision to Rabbi Rafael Shapira. When Rabbi Rafael saw the bitterness and stormy spirits of the Yeshiva students, he acceded to their demand and dismissed the man from Volozhin. Thus, the spirits were calmed, and the students returned to their studies.[62]

The image of Rabbi Rafael was portrayed by one of his students in a few, meager lines. This survey also illustrates the image of the Yeshiva during that period.

"He would worship in the Yeshiva with a loud voice and enthusiasm ever day, morning and evening. He would elongate his prayers, especially the recital of the *Shema*, which he would recite with special enthusiasm. He pronounced every syllable separately "*Shema Yis Ra El*" all the way through to the end. All of the lads, even those who were late in their prayers, had already concluded the recitation, whereas he had still not reached *Vehaya Im Shamoa*[iv]. The voice of the elderly rabbi, standing near the Holy Ark, echoed in the complete silence that pervaded in the Yeshiva hall at that time. His entire body was trembling, he was breathing through his nose, and splicing syllable after

[Page 149]

syllable: "*Uke – tav – tam... veli – madi – tem... leda – ber bam.*" All the worshippers stood with holy feelings, aspiring to learn the ways of awe from him. Even his prayer alone was a form of declaration: Yes, there is a Yeshiva head in the Yeshiva of Volozhin, and everyone feels his presence. Rabbi Rafael bore the burden of the Yeshiva on his shoulders even from a material standpoint, and even during his old age. On several occasions during the winter, he would dress himself in his long, broad, winter furs, direct his heart heavenward, and travel to cities near and far to influence the Jewish communities to send their support to the Yeshiva. His efforts bore fruit. He was known as a *Gaon* and *Tzadik.*"[63]

Rabbi Rafael Shapira was a continuation of the dynasty of great Yeshiva heads of the Etz Chaim Yeshiva of Volozhin. His knowledge was wondrous in its extent and precision. He was diligent in his Torah study all his life, and his mouth never stopped learning. He would never even go for a stroll outside his house lest it cause a neglect of Torah. Once they urged him to go for a short stroll, since such is healthy for the body. However, since he was concerned about a neglect of Torah, he responded with the wise retort: "What is the benefit in this? For someone who goes out for a stroll eventually comes back to his house…"

Rabbi Rafael adopted a methodology of studies that was called "in accordance with its theme" [*leshitato*] – that is, a connection between various *halachot* and opinions of a specific Mishnaic or Talmudic sage, to prove that all those *halachot* and opinions are based on a common foundation, relate to each other, and have an internal connection to each other.

Since Rabbi Rafael was a great expert, he would demonstrate that the novellae of the most important authors were already published in the books of sages of old. He would show that a certain matter was written in a certain book, and that a certain novel idea was already written in other books. He would speak at length of the need to conceive of novel Torah ideas that had not yet been revealed in the world of Torah.

Rabbi Moshe Shmuel Shapiro was involved in describing the value and image of the Yeshiva during the period of Rabbi Rafael Shapiro. Among other things, he wrote:

"During the period of Rabbi Rafael Shapira, the Yeshiva was lacking the glory and splendor of previous years. Even the number of students was smaller. It was missing the two great luminaries: The Netzi'v and Rabbi Chaim Soloveitchik. The seders on Passover eves, which brought great light to the Yeshiva, were also not renewed. However, after all this, many lads and young men, great in Torah, gathered under the banner of Rabbi Rafael. These included Rabbi Isser Yehuda Unterman and Rabbi Y. L. Zlotnik (Avida). Volozhin always had some form of attractive force, secret and hidden from all eyes, concealed and hidden

[Page 150]

within the walls of the Yeshiva. The Spirit of the Gr'ch [Gaon Rabbi Chaim], may the memory of the righteous be blessed, the founder of the Yeshiva, always hovered over it, and graced it with a special grace, which was not absent from it until the final day."[64]

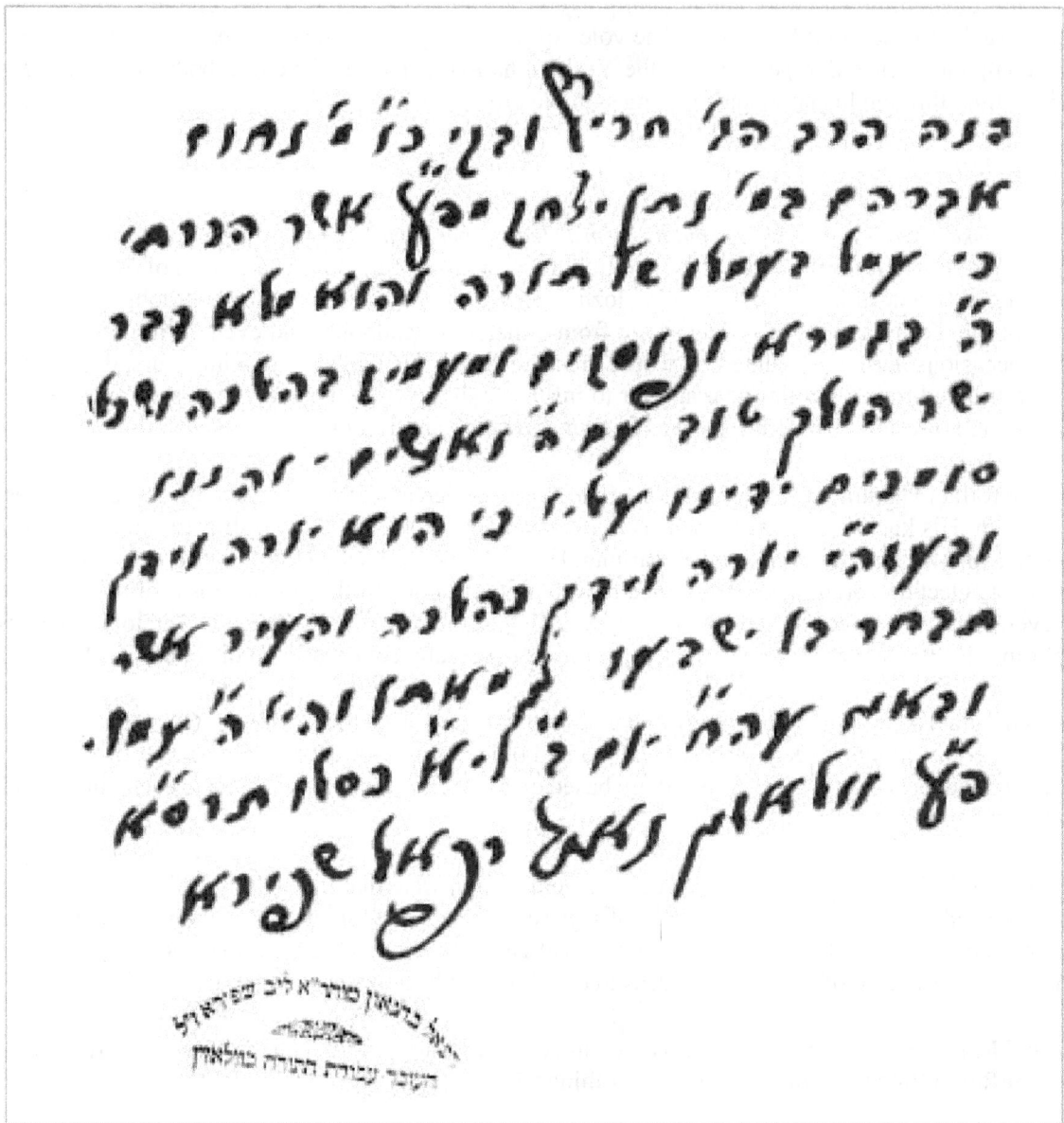

A handwritten note, sealed with the seal of Rafael the son of the Gaon Rabbi Leib Shapiro of blessed memory, who toils in the work of the Torah in Volozhin

A letter of ordination in the handwriting of Rabbi Rafael Shapira, given to Rabbi Nachum Avraham Golobnochich, a student of the Yeshiva: "with this, the Rabbi and Gaon, sharp and expert, fully and even more so, Mr. Nachum Avraham the son of our teacher Natan Yitzchak of the local holy community, whom I recognize to toil in the labor of Torah, fulfilling the word of G-d in Gemara and *halachic* decisors, delving deeply into *halacha*, with a sharp intellect, behaving properly with G-d and his fellow. We hereby place our hands upon him, that he can teach and judge. With the help of the Blessed G-d, he will teach and judge appropriately. A city that chooses him will be satisfied with him, and G-d will be with him. I sign, Monday, 11 Kislev, 5661 [1900], here in the holy community of Volozhin. Signed Rafael Shapira."

Rabbi Rafael's study room was illuminated for most of the night, as he sat and studied, delving into

[Page 151]

the Torah or writing his novellae. He produced many Torah novellae, which he organized in writing during the time he lived in Volozhin. These Torah novellae were on sections of both the Babylonian and Jerusalem Talmuds, the early and later sages, on all sections of the Code of Jewish Law, and even on novel ideas in *agada* [lore] and *Midrashim* of our sages. His book *Torat Rafael*, which was published by his two sons Rabbi Aryeh and Rabbi Yisrael Isser Shapira, in the year 5703 [1943] (in Jerusalem). He was one of the effective writers of Talmudic literature in the latter era.

The major events that took place in the second decade of the 20th century uprooted Rabbi Rafael from Volozhin. The Yeshiva was closed. The First World War also affected Volozhin, just as it affected the other Yeshivas of Poland and Lithuania. Many lads left Volozhin. Only a small group gathered around the Yeshiva head, Rabbi Rafael Shapira.

Volozhin became a very important strategic point when the front approached, and the city was flooded with the Russian army. The army expropriated many houses in the city, including the residence of Rabbi Rafael Shapira, which was the largest of all. The central military command stationed itself there. The army related politely to Rabbi Rafael, and left two large rooms for him and his family.

It is told that when Rabbi Rafael once stood up for the *Shmone Esrei* prayer, a bomb fell upon a nearby house. The explosion caused a panic in the city, and everyone was astonished when they found out that Rabbi Rafael was so immersed in his prayers that he did not hear this bomb. The Russian captains believed that as long as the rabbi was in the city, no disaster would happen. However, when a bullet once flew through the Yeshiva room, and Rabbi Rafael realized that it was dangerous to remain in this place, he left with his family for Minsk, the place of residence of his father-in-law Rabbi Chaim Soloveitchik at that time.

Rabbi Rafael lived with the hope that he would return to Volozhin at the end of the war, and re-establish the Yeshiva. However, he did not merit such. He died in Minsk on 23 Adar 5681 (March 3, 1921).

We will conclude our composition on the Etz Chaim Yeshiva with a legend told by Rabbi Yitzchak Rivkind of blessed memory:

"At the conclusion, it is worthwhile to relate one fine legend that went around Volozhin in the name of the Gaon Rabbi Chaim, which had the future redemption dependent upon the fate of the Yeshiva.

"The legend states that Rabbi Chaim, the founder of the Yeshiva, said that if, Heaven forbid, the Yeshiva of Volozhin shall cease to exist, the redemption would begin within two years.

"Apparently, the Volozhiners belied that only powerful world events and significant wars, from which the redemption would ensue, make the destruction and nullification of the Yeshiva possible."[65]

Original Footnotes:

59.   Regarding the death of Rabbi Chaim Hillel Fried, and on the impression it made on the Jews of Volozhin, we read the following sad words that move the heart: "Two days ago, the elderly Gaon Rabbi Chaim Hillel Fried died. He was one of the descendants of the Gaonim of Volozhin (the son of the Netzi'v's brother-in-law), who was of course connected to the Beit Harav.
"What terrible sadness pervaded in the town and the Yeshiva. The entire large congregation of Yeshiva

people accompanied him to his final rest, and eulogized him. When I returned home on the way back from this funeral, I drew in my imagination a large, thick tree, from its roots to its canopy, however the few leaves that covered it were turning yellow and falling. No new buds were yet seen beneath them, still not seen…" (M. Peker: "In the Yeshiva of Volozhin" *Hator*, Jerusalem 30 Sivan, 5694 (July 2, 1924), issue 40).

60.   *Hameilitz*, 23 Tammuz, 5652 (July 7, 1892), issue 151.

60a. Yehuda, "Hosts of Torah" *Hameilitz*, 28 Cheshvan 5660 (October 20, 1899), issue 229.

61.   Rabbi Moshe Shmuel and his Generation, An anthology of essays and letters, page 70.

62.   See *Hatzofeh*: "In the Yeshivot of Torah," "Echo of the Times.," 12 Tammuz 5670 (July 6, 1910), issue 150.

63.   Gedalyahu Pomerantz: "The Last Strike in the Yeshiva of Volozhin" *Hadoar*, 14 Shvat 5623 [1963], Year 42, issue 15.

64.   "The Yeshiva of Volozhin During its Years of Closure and Opening." From an anthology of essays and letters of Rabbi Moshe Shmuel Shapira.

65.   Yitzchak Rivkind of blessed memory: "The Yeshiva in Volozhin and National Revival," *Hatoren*, Kislev 5683 [1922], booklet 10, 9th year, page 54.

Translator's Footnotes:

i.   Based on Psalms 24:7,9
ii.   See https://en.wikipedia.org/wiki/Israel_Markovich_Brodsky
iii.   A methodology stressing teaching of morality. See https://en.wikipedia.org/wiki/Musar_movement
iv.   The beginning of the second of the three paragraphs of the *Shema*.

[Page 152]

The Volozhiner Family Tree [Beit Harav]

(Compiled by Eliezer Leoni)

Translator's note. Pages 152-159 include genealogical tables of Beit Harav. M. Porat originally translated these in a single-page table, including connections and dates, but missing some of the details. We have decided to preserve Mr. Porat's table, but also to provide a page-by-page translation with full detail. The boxes of the original page-by-page version have been converted to point form.

Translated by M. Porat-Perelman z"l

1700
- Israel Hakohen Rapport, Piesk Judge
- Rabbi Hayim, Volozhin Kehila Founder

1730
- Arye Leyb Ginzburg (Rabbi Leyb the Scribe)
- Rivka - born Rapoport
- R' Itskhak, Volozhin Kehila Head

1760
- Yosef, Poritsh Judge
- Nahmen, Pohost Judge
- Simkhe
- Sara - born Ginzburg
- Reb Hayim Volozhiner, Volozhin Yeshiva Founder, 1749 - 1821
- Shlomo Zalman "Zalmele", 1756 - 1788
- Wife Yehiel Mihal's daughter

1790
- R' Hilel Freed from Horodno
- Ester
- Yosef Reb Yosl Shershever
- Reb Itsele - Yeshiva Head, Rabbi Itskhak - Itskhakin, 1780 - 1849
- Relke
- Yosef Soloveytshik, S-nd husband: R' Moshke R' Artsiks
- Khasa
- Mordhe Kamenietski from Lida

1820
- Rehl
- Eliezer Itskhak Freed
- Rivka
- Rayne Bashe 1st wife
- Hanaziv - Yeshiva Head, Harav Naftali Zvi Ihuda Berlin, Mir, 1816 - 1893, Varsaw
- Bashe Mirl 2nd wife
- Ele Zalman Itskhakin
- Feygl "Di Bobe Feygl"
- Rabbi Zeev Soloveytshik

1850
- Yosef Duber Soloveytshik, 1820 - 1892
- Hayim Hilel Freed, 1833 - 1910
- Rafoel Shapiro, Yeshiva Head, 1837 - 1921
- Sara Rashe and Dreyzl
- Hayim Berlin, Volozhin 1832, 1912 Jerusalem
- R' Meir Berlin - Bar Elan, The University on his name, Volozhin 1880 - 1949 Jerusalem
- Haim Yosef Itskhaykin
- Yoshua Perlman, Vishnevo & Rehovot Rabbi

1880
- Hayim Soloveytshik, 1853 - 1918
- Freydele die Rebetzn
- R' Avigdor Derechinski
- Yaakov Shapiro, Yeshiva Head
- R' Hirsh Malkin & Haya-Riva born Marshak
- Malka Itskhakin
- Moyshe Perlman

1910
- Moshe Zalmn Ben Sasson, killed by Arab terrorist
- Prof. Hayim Ben Sasson
- Prof. Yona Ben Sasson
- Hayim Volkin, Yeshiva Head
- Rivka
- Etl born Malkin
- Yosif Perlman, lost in Soviet goulag
- Hay Dina
- Yani Garber, Vol Judenrat Head, Murdered 1941

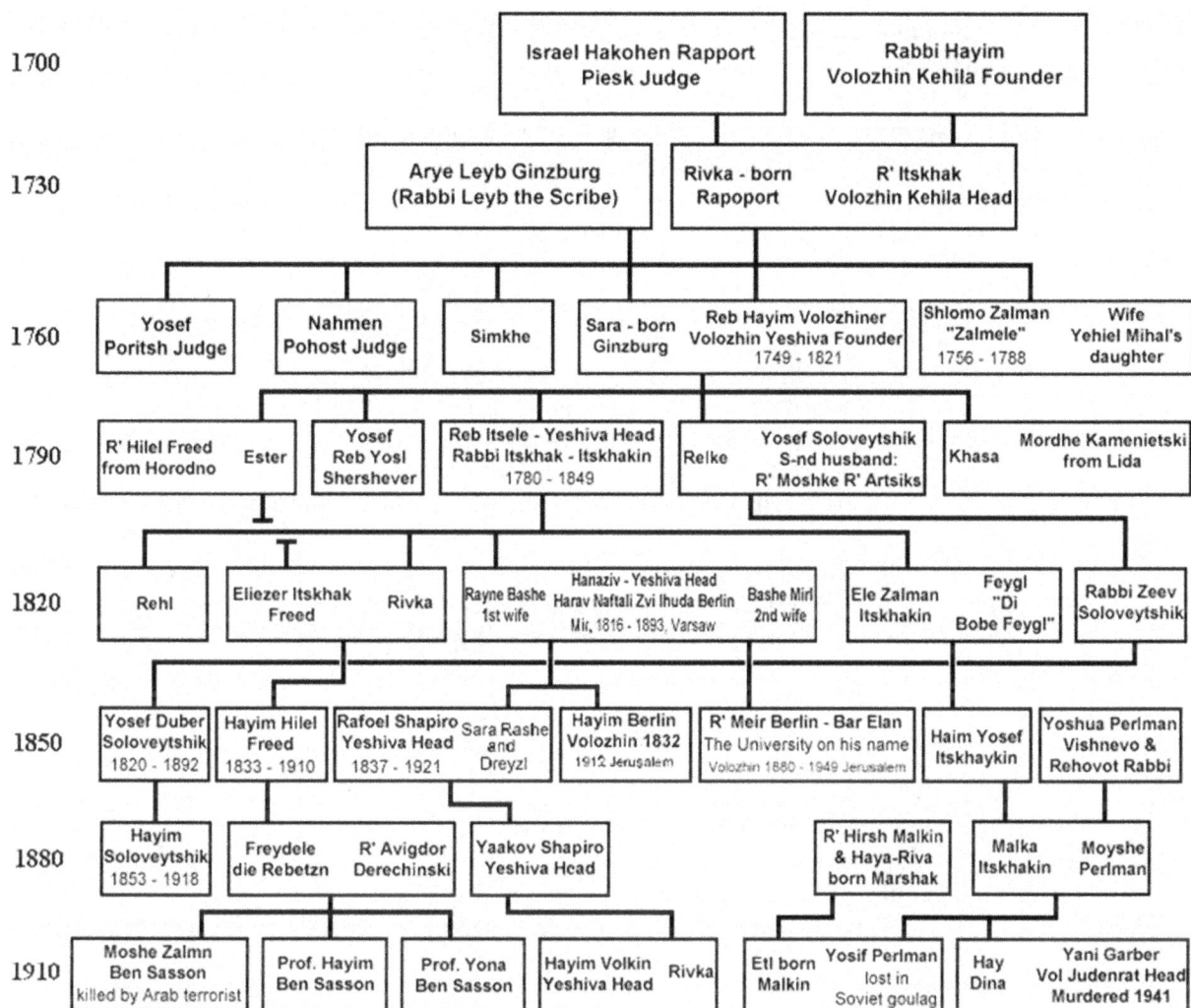

Translations by Jerrold Landau

- **Chaim** (Grandfather of Rabbi Chaim of Volozhin)

Parents of Rabbi Chaim of Volozhin

- **Yitzchak** (son of Rabbi Chaim)
- **Rivka** nee Rappoport (wife of Rabbi Yitzchak). Rivka's father was Yisrael Hakoehn Rappoport, head of the rabbinical court of Piesk, in-law of Rabbi Yitzchak. He died in Vilna on 12 Av, 5640 (1780)

Descendants of Rabbi Yitzchak and Rivka

- **Simcha**
- **Chaim** (Rabbi Chaim of Volozhin). Born in Volozhin on 7 Sivan 5509 (1749). Died in Volozhin on 12 Sivan 5581 (1821).

- **Shlomo Zalman** (Reb Zalmele). Born in Volozhin on 26 Sivan 5516 (1756). Died in Vilna on 9 Adar I 5548 (1788).
- **Yosef**, head of the rabbinical court of Poretsh.
- **Nachman** (head of the rabbinical court of Pohost), father of Rabbi Avraham Simcha, the head of the rabbinical court of Amtislav)

Descendants of Rabbi Zalmele and his wife (the daughter of Yechie Michel Psil's)

- **Their daughter** (orphaned at the age of 7 after her father died). She would say: Were I obligated in the study of Torah, I would not separate from the Torah even for one small moment. However, what shall I do in that G-d created me in accordance with His will… (Trans: reflecting the halacha that women are not formally obligated in Torah study). Her husband was Rabbi **Moshe Yehoshua Rabinowitz**, son-in-law of Rabbi Zalmele.
  - o **Shlomo Zalman**, grandson of Rabbi Zalmele
    - ▪ **Eliyahu Nayvedel**. Son of Shlomo Zalman, great-grandson of Rabbi Zalmele. Born in 5581) in Neustadt Sugind (Kovno district). Died in Warsaw on 16 Elul 5646 (1886)
  - o **Shalom** (head of the rabbinical court of Janishok [Joniškis]). Author of the book *Divrei Shalom VeEmet* – grandson of Rabbi Zalmele.

[Page 153]

The Father-in-law of Rabbi Chaim of Volozhin and his Daughter

- **Rabbi Aryeh Leib Ginzburg**, known as Rabbi Leib Katvan (Rabbi Leib the writer)
  - o **Sara**, daughter of Rabbi Leib Ginzburg (wife of Rabbi Chaim of Volozhin)

Descendants of Rabbi Chaim of Volozhin and his wife Sara

- **Yitzchak** (Rabbi Itzele), born in Volozhin in 5540 (1780), died in Ivanetz on 26 Sivan 5609 (1849)
- **Yosef** "Rabbi Yosel Shershover" died at a young age
- **Esther**
- **Chasa** (Rabbi Chaim was particular that her name be written as "Chasa" as is written in the Gemara, for he said that the name is based on mercy, in accordance with the language *Dechas Rachmana Alan* [G-dwas merciful to her].
- **Relka**

Sons-in-law of Rabbi Chaim of Volozhin

- **Hillel Fried** (Esther's husband) born in Horodna, died in Horodna on 2 Adar 5583 (1833)

Descendants of Relka

- **Rabbi Zeev Solovitchik** (born from her first husband), father of Rabbi Yosi Ber Soloveitchik
- **Rabbi Yankele of Volozhin** (born from her second husband), father of the Gaon Rabbi Zalman-Sender Shapira, rabbi of Krynki.

[Page 154]

Descendants of Rabbi Itzele (grandchildren of Rabbi Chaim Soloveitchik)

- **Eliyahu Zalman**
- **Rivka**
- **Reina Batya**
- **Rechel**
- ?
- ?

Son-in-law of Eliyahu Zalman

- **Yehoshua Heshel Levin** (author of *Aliyat Eliyahu*), born in Vilna on 18 Tammuz 5578 (1818), died in Paris on 15 Cheshvan 5644 (1884)[1].

Sons-in-law of Rabbi Itzele

- **Eliezer Yitzchak Fried** (son of Rabbi Hillel Fried), husband of Rivka. Born in Volozhin in 1809, died in Volozhin on 19 Ell 5613 (1853).
- **The Netzi'v** (Rabbi Naftali Tzvi Yehuda Berlin), husband of Reina Batya. Born in Mir on 29 Cheshvan 5576 (November 20, 1816 [1]), died in Warsaw 28 Av 5653 (August 11, 1893).

Descendants of Rabbi Eliezer Yitzchak Fried

- **Chaim Hillel Fried** (author of Chut Hameshulash). Born in Volozhin on 26 Cheshvan 5683 (1833) [1]. Died in Volozhin on 3 Kislev 5671 (December 4, 1910).
- Wife of Avraham Ber
- Reina, wife of Meir Noach Levin

Descendants of Rabbi Chaim Hillel Fried

- **Eliezer Yitzchak**
- **Shmuel**
- **Freidele**
- **Rechel** (Rachel)
- **Esther**
- **Batya**

[Page 155]

Son of Rebbetzin Freidele from her first marriage

- **Moshe Zalman Ben-Sasson**. Born in Volozhin in 5661 (1901). Killed on way to Yavne'el on 2 Nissan, 5697 (March 14, 1937)

Descendants of Rebbetzin Freidele from her second marriage, to Rabbi Shmuel Avigdor Derechinski

- **Chaim Hillel Ben-Sasson**
- **Yona Ben-Sasson**

Children of Shmuel Fried

- **Chaim Hillel Fried**
- **Shaul Fried**

Descendants of the Netzi'v from his first wife (Reina Batya)

- **Chaim Berlin**. Born in Volozhin on 5 Shvat, 5592 (1832), died in Jerusalem 13 Tishrei 5673 (September 24, 1912)
- **Michael**
- **Sara Rasha**, first wife of Rabbi Rafael Shapira
- **Dreizel**, second wife of Rabbi Rafael Shapira. Born in Volozhin, died in Minsk on 23 Kislev 5679 (November 27, 1918).

Wives of Rabbi Chaim Berlin

- **Rivka nee Ceitlin**

- **Tila nee Shachor**
- **Eiga Levin-Epstein**
- **Matlia nee Rokach**

[Page 156]

Descendants of Rabbi Chaim Berlin

- **Sara**
- **Dreizel Malka**
- **Esther**
- **Rechel**
- **Tema**
- **Rashel**
- **Moshe Yitzchak**

Son-in-law of the Netzi'v

- **Rafael Shapira** (who married Sara-Rasha and Dreizel one after the other). Born in Smargon, Adar 5597 (1837). Died in Minsk on 23 Adar 5681 (March 3, 1921)

Descendants of Rabbi Rafael Shapira and Sara Rasha

- **Yitzchak**
- **Lifsha**

In-laws of Rabbi Rafael Shapira and his son-in-law

- **Yosef Dovber HaLevi Soloveitchik** (author of *Beit Halevi*). In-law of Rabbi Rafael, father of Rabbi Chaim Soloveitchik, and great-grandson of Rabbi Chaim of Volozhin. Born in Nieshez, 5580 (1820). Died in Brisk, 4 Iyar 5652 (1892).
- **Chaim Soloveitchik** (son of Yosi Ber), son-in-law of Rabbi Rafael Shapira, husband of Lifsha. Born in Volozhin on Shushan Purim 5613 (1853). Died in Otwock 21 Av 568 (July 30, 1918).

Descendants of Rabbi Chaim Soloveitchik and Lifsha

- **Yisrael Gershon Soloveitchik**
- **Moshe Soloveitchik**

- **Yitzchak Zeev Soloveitchik**
- **Sara Rasha Soloveitchik**

[Page 157]

Descendants of Rabbi Moshe Soloveitchik

- **Yosef Dov Soloveitchik**
- **Aharon Soloveitchik**
- **Shmuel Yaakov Soloveitchik**
- **Chana** (wife of Shamai Gara)
- **Sheindel** (wife of Meiselman)

Descendants of Rabbi Yitzchak Zeev Soloveitchik

- **Yosef Dov Soloveitchik**
- **David Soloveitchik**
- **Rafael Soloveitchik**
- **Meir Soloveitchik**
- **Lifsha** (wife of Rabbi Michel Feinstein)
- **Rivka** (wife of Rabbi Yaakov Schiff)

Descendants of Rabbi Rafael Shapira and Dreizel (nee Berlin)

- **Yaakov Shapira**
- **Menachem Zundel Shapira**
- **Aryeh Shapira**
- **Levi Shapira**
- **Yisrael Isser Shapira**
- **Mirl Shapira**

Son-in-law of Rabbi Rafael Shapira, and his grandson

- **Yisrael Riff** (husband of Mirl)
  - **Naftali Tzvi Yehuda Riff** (son of Mirl and Yisrael), grandson of Rabbi Rafael and great-grandson of the Netzi'v

[Page 158]

Descendants of Aryeh Shapira

- **Tzvi Shapira**
- **Lipa Shapira**
- **David Shapira**
- **Moshe-Shmuel Shapira**
- **Rafael Shapira**
- **Yocheved Shapira**

Descendants of Yisrael Isser Shapira

- **Eliyahu Chaim Shapira**
- **Tzvi Shapira**
- **Rafael Shapira**
- **Yekutiel Shapira**
- **Dreizel** (wife of Rabbi Tzvi Kaplan)
- **Rivka** (wife of Rabbi Yosef Shaul Weingarten)

Descendants of Yaakov Shapira, his sons-in-law and grandchildren

- **Yitzchak Moshe Shapira**
- **Zalman Yosef Shapira**
- **Pesia Shapira**
- **Beila Shapira**
- **Rivka** (wife of Rabbi Chaim Wolkin)
- **Chana** (wife of Rabbi Shimon Langbart)
- **Dreizel and Chaya Leah** (daughters of Rabbi Wolkin)

[Page 159]

Descendants of the Netzi'v from his second wife, Batya Mirl (daughter of Rabbi Yechiel Michel Epstein)

- **Yaakov Berlin**
- **Meir Bar-Ilan** (Berlin). Born in Volozhin 29 Nissan 5640 (April 10, 1840). Died in Jerusalem, 19 Nissan 5709 (April 18, 1949).

Descendants of Meir Bar-Ilan (Berlin) and his wife Beila

- **Yehudit** (wife of Shaul Liberman)
- **Shulamit** (wife of Avraham Shlomo Halkin)
- **Tuvia Bar-Ilan** (Berlin)

Translator's Footnote:

1. The corresponding secular year during the months of Tishrei, Cheshvan, and much of Kislev should be one year earlier than listed, as the Hebrew year moves forward at Rosh Hashanah. Several dates here are given in Cheshvan, and the secular year should be one year earlier to correspond with the Hebrew year.

[Page 160]

Among the Prominent "Etz Chaim" Yeshiva Students

a) Rabbis and Yeshiva Leaders

Grodzenski, Chaim Oyzer
The Vilna town Rabbi

Elishberg, Mordkhay
Rabbi Itsele's student, and
Hanatzsiv's friend.

Hanaziv's student. Born in 5622 (1863) on Elul 9, in Ivye. Educated in Volozhin from Bar-Mitsva age. He was renowned as the Ivye Prodigy. Practiced as the Vilna Rabbi. Died in the month of Av 5th, 5700 (1940) in Vilna.

Born in Eysishok, Kovno district, 1st Adar 5577 (16/2/1817). He was one of the first Rabbis, which joined the "Hovvey Zion" (Lovers of Zion) movement. His book "The Golden Path" deals with the problems of Eretz Israel settlement. Died in Boysk (Leetonia), 18th Kislev, 5660 (11/12/1889). – For article see Table of contents, code 22.02.

Don Ikhya, Ihuda Leyb
Rabbi of Shklov, Drissa & Chernigov

Epstein, Moshe Mordekhay
Head of the Slobodka Yeshiva

Studied in the Volozhin Yeshiva As Hanatsiv's disciple from 5649 (1888) until 5652 (1892). Born in Drissa 1868. Practiced as Rabbi in Shklov, Viyatka, Drissa and Tshernigov. Was member in the committee of "Netsakh Israel" (the Eternal of Israel) movement. Among his books: "The Israel seniors" (Jewish religious laws novelties with questions and answers, accompanied by Chaim Soloveytshik's novelties). Published in Lutsk 5693 (1933). The second part was published, with his biography, in Tel-Aviv 5699 (1939). He also published incognito a pamphlet "Zionism from religious point of view". Died in Tel Aviv in 1941. For article see Table of contents, code 22.04.

Known as one of the best Hanatziv's students. Born in Baksht, close to Volozhin, in the month of Adar 5636, (1866). He was called "The Baksht Prodigy". Became head of the "Knesset Israel" Yeshiva in Slobodka. He transferred his Yeshiva to Hevron and was its leader. He was active among the Hedera founders. His Torah novelties were published in his book "Mordekhay's dress". Died in Jerusalem 10th Kislev 5694 (28/11/1933). – For article see Table of contents, code 22.03.

[Page 161]

**Kahana, Shlomo David
The Warsaw town Rabbi**

Hanaziv's student. Born in Peguir (Lithuania) in 5626 (1866). His father, Chaim Ben Zion, was son in law of Rabbi Shmuel Zanvill Klappish, who was married to Rabbi Chaim Volozhiner's great granddaughter. He practiced as the Warsaw Rabbi for forty eight years, and thirteen years as Rabbi of Jerusalem (the Old and the New one). Known as "Father of the abandoned" because of his care for the abandoned wives. Died Kislev, 28th 5714 (5.12.1953) in Jerusalem.

Halevi Epstein, Yechiel Michal

Rabbi Itsele's student. Brother in law and father in law of Hanaziv (he married Hanaziv's sister and Hanaziv married Halevi Epstein's daughter Bashe-Mirl- Meir Bar-Ilan's mother). Born in Bobruysk on Shevat 20th, 5589 (1829). He's the Author of the "Aruch Ha'shulchan". Died in Novoharodok , on Adar B 22nd , 5668 (1908).

Levinson, Zvi-Hirsh
Head of the Radin Yeshiva

Hanaziv's student. Born in Volozhin in 5623 (1863). Son in law of the "Hafets Chaim". Practiced as Head of the Radin Yeshiva. Died in the year 5681 (1921).

Kahana-Shapiro, Avraham Duber

Hanaziv's student. Born in Kobrin on Yom Kippur, in 5631 (1870). His father, Shlomo Zalmen was Rabbi Chaim Volozhiner's descendant. As student in the Volozhin Yeshiva he was known as the "Kobrin Prodigy". Was member in the "Netsakh Israel" (Israel's Eternity) movement. The last Rabbi of Kovno. Died in the Slobodka Ghetto on the Sabbath, Adar A 22nd , 5703 (29/3/1943).

[Page 162]

Leybovitsh, Boruh Dov
Head of the Slobodka Yeshiva

Student of Hanaziv and son in law of Bunimovitsh from Volozhin. Born in Mitava (Leetonia) in 5634 (1864). The pages 213-221 in his book "Yaakov's tents" are dedicated to Volozhin. Died In Jerusalem in 5707, Sivan 16th(4.6.1947).

Halevi Epstein, Yechiel Michal

Student of Rabbi Chaim Soloveytshik. Born in Slutsk, in 5624 (1864). Still infant he was introduced in the Volozhin Yeshiva. Despite his young age Boruh Dov was recognized for his capabilities. He practiced as Head of the Slobodka Yeshiva "Knesset Beyt Yaakov". Died in Vilna in 5700 Heahvan 25th (7.11.39).

Melzer, Issar Zalman
Head of the "Etz Chaim" Yeshiva in
Jerusalem

Student of Rabbi Chaim Soloveytshik.
Born in Mir, in 5640 (1870). Was called
"Zonie der Mirer". Wrote the book "The
precious Stone" about the Rambam.
Practised as head of the "Etz Chaim" Yeshiva
in Jerusalem. Died in 5714 Kislev
10th (17.11.1953), in Jerusalem.

Mohaliver, Shmuel

Student of Rabbi Itsele and son in law of
Rabbi Eliezer Fried. Born in Halovka, (Vilna
region) in 5584 (1824) Nissan 27th.
Mohaliver was one of the first "Hovvey Zion"
(Zion Lovers) members. Be friended with
Hanaziv and with Rabbi Yosi Ber
Soloveytshik. Died, in 5658 (1898), on Sivan
19 in Bialistok. For article see Table of
contents, code 22.09.

[Page 163]

**Salant, Shmuel
Jerusalem town Rabbi**

**Nahum (Nohemke) from Horodno
The Orphans Father**

Rabbi Itsele's student. Born in 5596 Shevat 2nd (1816), in Bialistok. As a young boy he joined the Volozhin Yeshiva and amazed his teachers by his Torah-study diligence. In 1841 he made Aliya to the Land of Israel and settled in the courtyard of Rabbi Yehuda Hosid's "Hurva" (synagogue). Acted as The Jerusalem Rabbi for 70 years. Died in 5669 Av 29th (16.8.1909), in Jerusalem. For article see Table of contents, code 22.14.

Rabbi Eliezer Fried's student. Born in 5572 (1812) in Beisegol (Shavli region). Known as a Torah studious and a God-fearing religious Jew. All his life he was considered as an orphans and widows protector and as a good helping friend of the poor, ill and oppressed persons. The "Hafets Chaim" used to say, that Nohemke reached the highest level of grace and charity. Died in 5630 (Heshvan 5th 1880), in Grodno.

Polatshek, Shlomo
The N.Y. Itskhak Elhanan Yeshiva head

Nissenboym, Isaak
writer

Student of Hanaziv. He Was called "The Maytshat Prodigy". Born in 5848 (1878), in Sinitsenits (a hamlet close to Maytshat). Rabbi Chaim Soloveytshik used to say, "Here is a prodigy without equals". Rabbi Meir Bar-Ilan (Berlin) invited him to be the Yeshiva head of the Itskhak Elhanan Yeshiva in New York. Died in 5688, Tamuz 21st, in New York.

Hanaziv's student. Born in 5639 Tishrey 25th (1869), in Bobruysk. A chapter in his book "My world" is dedicated to Volozhin. He was killed in 5703 (1943), on the month of Menahem-Av in Warsaw Ghetto. For article see Table of contents, code 22.12.

[Page 164]

Rubinshteyn, Itshak
Head of the "Elhanan" Yeshiva in NY

Student of Rabbi Refoel Shapiro. Born in 5640 (1880), in Datnivo (Lithuania). As member of the Polish Senate, he fought ardently to receive equal rights for the Jewish population in Poland. Rubinshteyn founded and headed the "Yavne" net of Jewish religious Schools in Poland. In the last years of his life he became head of the Itshak Elkhanan Yeshiva in New York. Died in 5706 Heshvan 24th (31.10.1945) in New York.

Faymer, Yosef (Yosl Slutsker)
One of Rabbi Chaim Volozhiner's best students

Born in Shklov. He was member in the delegation, that that came in Volozhin, to settle the dispute between Hanaziv and Yosi Ber Soloveytshik. The Delegation participants were R' Isaac Elkhanan from Kovno, David Tabil the Minsk Chief Dayan (Judge), the Vilna "Magid" (Narrator) Zeev Lande and Yehoshua Levin the Minsk rich-man Died in 5634 Sivan 30th , (31.10.1864), in Slutsk.

**Koock, Avraham Hakohen
The first chief Rabbi of Eretz Israel**

The most estimated Student of Hanaziv, who called him "Mine Avrom Itshe". He became the first chief Rabbi of Eretz Israel. Born in 5625 Elul 16th (1865), in Grayevo. Harav Koock wrote his excellent essay on Hanaziv "The Yeshiva "Etz Chaim" head", published in "Knesset Israel" 5648 (1888). Died in 5695 Elul 3rd (1.9.1935) in Jerusalem.
For article see Table of contents, code 22.15.

[Page 165]

Shkop, Shimon
The Teltz Yeshiva Head

Rayness, Itskhak Yaakov
The Mizrakhi party founder

Student of Hanaziv. Born in 5620 (1860), in Tortz. At the age of fourteen he went to Volozhin where he studied six years. His teachers were Hanaziv and Rabbi Chaim Soloveytshik. In 6644 (1884) he was accepted to lead the Teltz Yeshiva, and acted on that post for eighteen years. He published his essay "The Gates of Honesty" in 5685 (1925). Died in 1940 Heshvan 9th (23/10/1939) in Grodno.

Student of Rabbi Itsele. Born in 5600 Heshvan 9th (17.10.1839), in Karelin. He joined the Volozhin Yeshiva at the age of sixteen. Harav Rayness founded in 1902 the religious Zionist Mizrakhi party. In 1904 he founded in Lida (Vilna region) the "Torah Vadaat" (Torah & Knowledge) Yeshiva. Died in 5675 Elul 10th (20.8.1915) in Lida.

For article see Table of contents, code 22.17.

[Page 166]

b) Poets, Writers, Scholars, Public Figures

Bialik, Haim Nahman
Modern Hebrew most prominent Poet

Hanaziv's great Student. (Hanaziv was proud showing Bialik's letter to his guests. He said: "look, what Hebrew they write in Volozhin Yeshiva"). Born in 5643 Tevet 10th (11.1.1873), in Rady (Volyn'). Bialik's poetry was highly influenced by Volozhin. "Hamatmid" is entirely Volozhin. In his poem "The Scroll of Fire" Hanaziv is described as "The Old Man from Judea". The Yeshiva with the Students Bialik described in the words "And I saw the Temple, with the splendor of its Scholars and priests". Volozhin also influences many other Bialik's works. Died in 5694 Tamuz 21st (4.7.1934), in Vienna.- For article, see Table of contents, code 4.03.

Epstein, Zalman
Publicist and writer

Hanaziv's Student. Born in 5620 on Elul 19 (16.9.1860), in Luban (Minsk Region). Epstein contributed very much to the Volozhin Yeshiva study in his essay "The forgotten Jubilee", published in "Hatzfira" magazin, in 5663 (1903). Died in 5697, on Kislev 7 (21.11.1936), in Ramat Gan.

Droyanov, Alter Asher
Writer & publicist

Berditshevski, Miha Yosef
Publicist

Student of Hanaziv. Born in 5650, Tamuz 7th (6.7.1870), in Droya (Vilna region). In his book "Scripts on the Hovvey Zion movement history", is found material about the movement in Volozhin. Died in 5698 Iyar 17th(10.5.1938) in Tel Aviv - For article, see Table of contents, code 4.05.

Hanaziv's Student. Was born in 5625 Av 27th (19.8.1865), in Mezibozh (Podolye). Berdichevski contributed to the Volozhin "Etz Chaim" Yeshiva study in his excellent articles: a) "The Volozhin Tree of Life-Yeshiva's history", published in "Haassif, 5647 (1887) b) "The world of Noblesse", published in "Hakerem" 5648 (1888), c) "A bundle of letters from Volozhin", published in "Hameylitz". Died in 5682 Heshvan 17th (18.11.1921), in Berlin.

[Page 167]

Yoffe, Leyb
Poet, writer

Harkabi, Avraham Eliyahu
Researcher & writer

Student of Hanaziv (made his studies two years before the Yeshiva was closed, 1891-1892). Born in 5635 Sivan 13th (16.6.1875), in Grodno. Devoted Zionist, he was chosen to lead the Keren Hakayemet Organization since it was founded (thirty years). Yoffe found dead at the national institutions explosion in Jerusalem (5718 Adar 30th (11.3.1948). In his memories book "From the Spring Days" a chapter is dedicated to his Yeshiva-years in Volozhin. He wrote there also about his lodging in Peretz the coachman's house. - For article, see Table of contents, code 22.07.

Student of Rabbi Eliezer Isak Fried and Hanaziv. Born in 5600 Heshvan 22nd (30.10.1839), in Novogrudok (Minsk region). He made important researches in Israel ancient literature. He was educated in Volozhin. Among his books he wrote: "Memories to the first and to the last ones" and "The Jews and the Slavic languages". Died in 5679 Adar 2nd (15.3.1919) in Petersburg.

Rivkind, Isaak
Bibliograph & researcher

Hurgin, Pinkhas
Founder of The Bar-Ilan Yeshiva

Rivkind was Rabbi Raphael Shapiro's student. Born in 5655 Adar 21st (17.3.1895), in Lodzh. He dedicated most of his time to research the Volozhin Yeshiva history. Died in 5728 Shevat 20th (19.2.1968), in New York. Was brought to rest in Tel-Aviv on the Nahlat Itskhak cemetery. - For article, see Table of contents, code 22.16.

P. Hurgin was Rabbi Raphael Shapiro's student. Born in 5655 Heshvan 26th (25.11.1894), in Host (close to Pinsk). He studied for four years in Volozhin. Founded the Bar–Ilan University (on the name of Meir Bar-Ilan – Berlin, Hanaziv's son) in Ramat Gan and served as its first president. "Researches on the Second Temple's Time" is well known among his books. Died in 5718 Kislev 4th (28.11.1957), in New York.

Shulman, Kalman
Writer

He was Rabbi Itsele's cherished student. Born in 5579 Av 18th (9.8.1819), in old Bikhov (Mohilev Region - Belarus). He was a remarkable "haskala" (Enlightenment) writer. "The world History" is known among his important books. Shulman also had translated and edited the "Mysteries of Paris". He died in 5659 Shvat 5th (15.1.1899), in Vilna.

c) Activists

Nakhmany, Mordkhay
Public personality

Visotski, Klonimus Zeev
Donator

He was Hanaziv's and Rabbi Chaim Soloveytshyk's student (studied in Volozhin for four years). Born in 5638 (1867), Kislev 28, in Nisvizh (Belarus, Minsk region). He made Aliya in 5650 (1890) and was active in the Rehovot founding. He was active in the village council, in the agriculture committee and in the area of religious education. Died in 5710, at the first day of Shvat (19.1.1949), in Rehovot. - For article, see Table of contents, code 22.11.

Studied in Volozhin for three years, as Rabbi Itsele's student. Born in Old Sand (Kovno region). He became very rich from dealing with tea. A part of his wealth was dedicated for the Eretz Israel settlement. An important part of his inheritance enabled the establishment of the Haifa Technion (Engineers School). He also invested money in the foundation of Petah-Tikvah. Died in 5664 (1904) in Moscow.

[Page 169]

Sources for the History
of the Etz Chaim Yeshiva of Volozhin

Writings on the Etz Chaim Yeshiva and its Heads

Translated by Jerrold Landau

Ovsi, Yehoshua. Rabbi Rafael Shapira: From an anthology of his works "Mamarim Vereshimot", New York, Published by Ohel, 5706 [1946], p. 136.

Ish-Horowitz, Menachem Mendel HaLevi. Derech Etz Chaim: A portrait from the lives of the students of the Holy Yeshiva Etz Chaim of Volozhin, Krakow, Published by Shmuel Horowitz, 5655 [1895].

The book contains a very wonderful description of the building of the Yeshiva and its students. "This is the gate of G-d – to the great school – Yeshivat Etz Chaim. Even from afar, this splendid building will attract the eye of its viewers with its difference from all the other houses of the city, which are small, wooden houses. It stands alone, and it is like a cedar planted between rows of bushes and brambles, as a rose amongst the thistles. However, when the viewer approaches this sanctuary of G-d, all such simple feelings already dissipate and disappear, and he becomes entwined in a network of other more serious and lofty feelings. His heart is taken captive by the enchantment that overtakes him. A voice is heard from on high. The voice is the voice of Jacob – both a mighty and pleasant voice attracting hearts and capturing souls. The voice of the rejoicing of a crowd blended together – these are the dear sons of Zion, knowledgeable of G-d, who study with great emotion, reading pleasantly and learning with a melody. – – –

"I will also mention the enjoyment and pleasure, the enjoyment of the soul and pleasure of the spirit, that also satiated me at that time as my soul was overcome with emotion, such as during the long winter nights when the Yeshiva students would study for about six consecutive hours, from 4:00 p.m. right after *mincha* until 10:00 p.m. Many candelabras cast precious light upon the many desks and benches. The Yeshiva hall was filled to the brim with Yeshiva students studying and toiling with their bodies and souls, with might and mind, with the G-dly voices ascending and descending. Many were sitting, many others were standing, and a few were pacing back and forth. No sound could be heard there other than the powerful sound of G-d. The faces and clothing of the students varied, each in accordance with their birthplace.

Volozhin, o! I will remember you once more, and I will also remember your dear children, sons who were learned of G-d, and all their ways of life in holiness and regular life, all the toil of their spirit, efforts of their souls, and their joys. Their work filled them with pleasure, happiness, joy, and gladness, so that they could forget all their tribulations in the present and worries for the future, and life in goodness."

Asaf, Simcha. Sources for the History of Education in Israel, Tel Aviv, Dvir Publishing, 5705 [1945], volume IV, pp. 167, 169, 172, 173, 174, 176, 177, 180, 244.

Berlin [Bar-Ilan], Meir. From Volozhin to Jerusalem, Yalkut Publishing, 5699 [1939].

[Page 170]

Berlin [Bar-Ilan], **Meir. The Rabbi of Israel.** Rabbi Naftali Tzvi Yehuda Berlin (the Netzi'v), his history, events, and outlook. New York, 5703 [1943].

Dubnow, Shimon, History of the Jewish People. Tel Aviv. Dvir Publishng, 5708 [1948], volume IX (fourth edition), section 23, chapter "Education According to the Government" (1840-1944), pp 123-128.

David of Novhorodok. Galia Masechet. Vilna, Published by Reb Menachem the son of Reb Baruch of blessed memory, and Rabbi Simcha Zisel the son of Reb Nachum of blessed memory, 5644 [1884], section II, pp. 65-66.

And these are the name of the Jews of Volozhin who were pre-subscribers to the book "Galia Masechet.":

Rabbi Naftali Tzvi Yehuda the son of Rabbi Yaakov Berlin (the Netzi'v)
Reb Shmuel the son of Rabbi Yaakov Avraham Landau
Reb David Teitelbaum the son of Reb Nachum from Z'r
Reb Yisrael Shmuel the son of Reb Avraham
Reb Yisrael Shilem the son of Reb Eliahu HaLevi
Reb Shmuel the son of Reb Yehuda Leib Freinkel from Hlybokaye
Reb Tzvi Hirsch Yaakov the son of Reb M. Ch'r Yitzchak Chr'f
Reb Eliezer the son of Rabbi Sh. Zalman
Reb Yehuda Meir the son of Reb Shlomo from Denberg.

Hakohen, Asher. Orchot Chaim. Known as Keter Rosh, through the words of which, I tied a crown upon my head, so that these words will light up in front of my eyes as a constant memorial, that which I have heard from the Admor and Gaon, the rabbi of the entire Diaspora, etc., our Rabbi Chaim, may the memory of the holy be blessed, may he rest in the Garden of Eden, from Volozhin. Various stories that he heard from the mouth of his rabbi, the angel of the L-rd of Hosts, our rabbi Rabbi Eliahu, may the memory of the holy be blessed, of Vilna, and several things that I knew and saw with my eyes. Also that which I heard said about the Admor Rabbi Chaim, may he rest in the Garden of Eden.

His student, who merited to serve Rabbi Chaim, may the memory of the holy be blessed, for three consecutive years, and who imbued upon me of the splendor of his Torah and righteousness, Asher Hakohen, the author of the book "Birchat Rosh" on Tractates Nazir and Brachot, the head of the rabbinical court of Tyktin and Szarszow. These words were written as a memorial here in the holy community of Volozhin, may it be upheld, in the year 5579 [1819]. Edited by me, Rabbi Eliahu Landau, the grandson of the Gr'a, may he be remembered for eternal life, in the holy city of Jerusalem, where there is Torah and greatness together.

Halevi-Epstein, Baruch. Mekor Baruch. Published in four volumes. "Including memories of the author from life in the generation preceding him, of the lives of our rabbis and sages, scribes and preachers, administrators and wealthy people, from the class of Torah and wisdom, and from life of the nation in general." The fourth volume is dedicated primarily to the Netzi'v. Vilna, 5688 [1928].

Halevi-Lipshitz, Yaakov. Zichron Yaakov. Jewish history from the life of the Jews in Russia and Poland, in three volumes. The first volume was published in Frankfurt am Main in 5684 [1924]. The second volume in Kovno, 5687 [1927]. The third volume in Kovno, 5690 [1930].

[Page 171]

The dispute between Rabbi Yosi Ber Soloveitchik and the Netzi'v is described in the chapter "The Dispute Regarding the Leadership of the Volozhin Yeshiva," volume II, chapter 13, pp 33-37. In volume III there are chapters dealing with the Yeshiva of Volozhin, with the following titles: "The Yeshiva of Volozhin"; "The Yeshiva of Volozhin after its Closing"; "Musar Haskel"; "General Outlook of the Yeshiva of Volozhin."

Halevi-Lifschitz, Yaakov. Sefer Toldot Yitzchak; "It is the history of our rabbi, the true great Gaon, the rabbi of the entire Diaspora, the pious and modest, honor to the holiness of the Name and its glory, Rabbi Yitzchak Elchanan, may the memory of the righteous be a blessing, for life in the world to come, the head of the rabbinical court of the community of Kovno, may its Rock and Redeemer protect it. Warsaw, published by Reb Meir Yitzchak Halter and Reb Meir Ajzenstat, 5657 [1897].

Zevin, Shlomo Yosef. People and Methodologies; A series of articles about Halachic personalities and their methodologies in Torah. Tel Aviv, Beitan Hasefer Publishers, 5712 [1952]. See pp. 23-37, and about Rabbi Chaim Soloveitchik, see pp. 43-70.

Rabbi Chaim of Volozhin. Nefesh Hachaim. Vilna, Rabbi Yehuda Leib the son of Eliezer Lipman, 5634 [1874].

Rabbi Chaim of Volozhin. Ruach Chaim; Commentary on Pirkei Avot, Vilna, 5619 [1859].

Rabbi Chaim of Volozhin. Introduction to Sifra Detzniuta of the Gr'a.

Rabbi Chaim of Volozhin (a legend about Rabbi Chaim of Volozhin). **Fun Naenten Avar** [From the Recent Past], edited by Moshe Shalot. Year 2 (January-March 1938), issue 1 (V), p. 33.

Yaavet'z, Zeev. History of Israel. Tel Aviv, Achiezer Publishing, 5700 [1940], Section 14, p. 69.

The Yaavet'z writes the following about the Etz Chaim Yeshiva of Volozhin (page 69): "It seems to be that it was the intention of the Gr'a toward his choicest students – to turn his students away from the hidden aspects [i.e. mystical aspects] of Torah study, and to turn their hearts toward the straightforward explanation only, to study scriptures in a straightforward fashion according to its grammar, without any intermingling of innuendoes and mystery. The Talmud and everything dependent upon it [is also to be studied] in its straightforward fashion according to definitive grammar, without any type of didactics and divisions, and to investigate the sources of all laws in the books of the decisors only in accordance with the sources in the Talmud.

The Yeshiva of Volozhin was prepared to be such a center of refined Torah.

Yashar, Moshe Meir. The Chofetz Chaim. Tel Aviv, Netzach Publishers, 5718 [1958], volume I, p. 223.

Rabbi Yisrael of Shklov. Hakdama Letaklin Chadatin [Introduction to Sharp Shekels]. Commentary on Tractate Shekalim. Minsk, 5572 [1812].

Levin, Yehoshua Heshel. Aliyat Eliahu (Biography of the Gr'a).

Lachover, Fishel. Bialik, his Life and Works. Tel Aviv, 5697 [1937]. First publication, Volume I, chapters: "To Volozhin", "The Masmid", "In the Yeshiva", Between Torah and Haskalah" "The First Poems

[Page 172]

and the First Article", "To the Bird", "Upon his Leaving of Volozhin", pp. 32-58.

Mikikovski-Samonov, Eliahu Aharon. Oholei Aharon. Tel Aviv, 5696 [1936], volume II, pp. 213-221.

Mirsky, Sh. K. Torah Institutions in Europe as they Existed and in their Destruction. New York, 5617 [1957].

Mandelstam, Binyamin (Binyamin the son of Yosef of Mateh Hashkeidim), **Chazon Lamoed**: "The burden that he bore during his travels in his native country. Includes a report on the state of the Jews of Russia before the light of science and knowledge shone upon them, and they sat as Nazirites below them, very distant from a lofty person." Vienna, Georg Breg and his partner P. Smolniskin Publishers, 5637 [1877], volume II, letters from the city of Vilna (most of that volume describes the journey of Dr. Max Lilienthal in Russia).

Nisenbaum, Yitzchak. Alei Cheldi. Wrsaw, Grafit Publishers, 5689 [1929], pp. 14-21.

Frumkin, Aryeh Leib. History of the Sages of Jerusalem. Jerusalem, 5688-5690 [1928-1930].

Fried, Chaim Hillel. Chut Hameshulash: Questions and responsa from Rabbi Chaim of Volozhin \, his son-in-law Rabbi Hillel of Horodna, and his grandson Rabbi Eliezer Yitzchak Fried. Vilna 5640 [1880].

Klausner, Yisrael. History of the Nes Ziona Organization of Volozhin. Jerusalem, published by Mossad Harav Kook, 5714 [1954].

Katzenelbogen, Avraham Tzvi Hirsch. Shaarei Rachamim. The book is "an anthology of pure articles, several laws and modes of behavior, pleasant things regarding Divine service and the topic of blessings and prayers. By our rabbi, Rabbi Eliahu, may the memory of the holy be blessed, of Vilna, and from his students, the pious Gaon the light of the Exile, Rabbi Chaim of Volozhin, may the memory of the holy be blessed."

Keshet, Yeshurun. Micha Yosef Berdichevski (Ben-Gurion), his Life and Activities. Jerusalem, 5718 [1958], Chapter II "In the Yeshiva of Volozhin" pp 53-56.

Rabinowitz, Michel. Kobetz Al-Yad. Jerusalem, 5711 [1951], new edition, Book V (15), documents on the history of the Yeshiva of Volozhin, pp. 221-233.

Scharfstein, Tzvi. History of Jewish Education During the Latter Years. New York, Ogen Publishers, 5705 [1945], pp. 324-337.

Schneurson, Fishel. Chaim Growitzer. Tel Aviv, Avraham Tzioni Publishers, 5615 [1955], second edition, Volume IV.

Shapira, Moshe Shmuel. Biography of our rabbi, Rabbi Chaim of Volozhin. Vilna, 5669 [1909].

Shapira, Moshe Shmuel. Rabbi Moshe Shmuel and his Generation. An anthology of essays and letters (from his estate). New York, 5624 [1964].

[Page 173]

Daily Newspapers

Hamelitz
(Edited by Erez – Alexander Cederbaum)

I'sh Yemi'ni. Hamelitz, 5 Tammuz 5639 (June 12, 1879), issue 25.

In the section "Everyday Deeds" the writer tells about the search conducted in the Etz Chaim Yeshiva.

Erez. Hacherev Hamithpechet: Hamelitz, 24 Tammuz 5639 (June 3, 1879), issue 28.

In his article, Erez deals with slanders against the Netzi'v and the search conducted in the Yeshiva. Among other things, he states: "It was too much for us to see that a Jew was so brazen as to forge a letter from a rabbi, who was great among the Jewish people, elderly and occupied in Torah, and to ascribe to him libels that shake up the heart, which could easily have had an effect on such a refined soul as the rabbi who distances himself from worldly affairs, and to cut off the strand of his life, Heaven forbid. The accuser himself informed the ministers of the state to pay attention to that letter. There are not sufficient words to express all the feelings of our spirit regarding such a terrible travesty. In our opinion, it would be appropriate for the rabbi and Gaon to ask the government to tell him the name of this evil person, so that he could be put on trial."

Erez. The Supernal Yeshiva: Hamelitz 19 Tevet 5641 (December 9, 1880), issue 36.

In this article, Erez deals with the methodology of secular studies in the Yeshiva, and expresses his opinion that this will be to the benefit of the Yeshiva.

Fridenstein, Shimon. Aleh Nidaf: Hamelitz, 23 Adar 5641 (February 10, 1881), issue 6.

The writer gives over memories of Rabbi Chaim of Volozhin

Krupnik, A. And the third statement comes to decide between them: Hamelitz, 23 Adar 5641 (February 10, 1881), issue 6.

The writer proposes a compromise in the matter of the conduct of secular studies in the Yeshiva, and states: "In my opinion, it is right and proper that the G-dly studiers in the Yeshiva – who are excellent, and dedicate their days to the Torah and the law, to become rabbis and teachers of Jewish law in the communities of Israel – shall dedicate at least an hour or two during the study day to the proper study of the vernacular (if they cannot grab more), so that when they conclude their course of studies and go out with their ordination to become leaders of communities and teachers of law among the Jewish people, they will, at least, not be embarrassed to speak in official capacity to our judges and ministers when necessary. Perhaps in days to come, they will be able to wear on their heads two

[Page 174]

crowns together, the crown of a rabbinical teacher and the crown of a government rabbi, so that our enlightened sons do not look upon us as tongue challenged and lacking in personality, and the Divine name will be desecrated by them. In particular, these are among the things that a Torah scholar is obligated to know."

Erez. Yeshiva Shel Maalah [Supernal Yeshiva]: Hamelitz, 28 Shvat, 5645 (February 1, 1885), issue 9.

Erez takes issue with the Netzi'v in the matter of secular studies in the Yeshiva, and states: "A rabbi such as this, to whom the pathways of Haskala are clear and who knows how to speak and write in the vernacular, will function more effectively in his community in general, and with respect to the youth in particular, to stop them from abandoning their paths. If the up-and-coming rabbis do not learn what is necessary while they are still in Yeshiva, they will no longer be able to devote time to this after they finish their curriculum of study there, when they go out to seek a source of livelihood through a position in one of the cities of Judah.

"We hope that our words that emanate from the heart will go before the rabbi and Gaon, the Yeshiva head, and inspire his heart to fill this lacuna, and to ensure that this rabbinical seminary blend the necessities of faith and life together. Such students will be a blessing for Israel."

Bunimovich, Menachem Mendel. Masa Volozhin: Hamelitz, 12 Tishrei, 5646 (September 9, 1885), issue 68.

The writer devotes his column to the Yeshiva of Volozhin and opens with the following words: "The city of Volozhin is small, but is known in a lofty manner through its rabbis and sages who have been disseminating Torah in public already for many generations. It has organizations for charitable deeds, and now the members of our community are attempting to found an organization for the settlement of the Land of Israel. However, the primary charity, equal to them all, in which all the communities of Jacob participate – is the Yeshiva that is known throughout our country as "The Great School" and the Etz Chaim Yeshiva, which was founded by the great Gaon, the rabbi of the entire Diaspora, the chief of pastors, our rabbi, Rabbi Chaim of Volozhin of blessed memory, the author of the book "Nefesh HaChaim."

Dinkin, Shlomo David: Hamelitz, 2 Iyar 5646 (April 25, 1886), issue 32.

The writer, who in his time was the Masgiach [religious supervisor of a Yeshiva] for the Netzi'v, announced that lads who do not know how to study a page of Gemara with Tosafot and the halachic decisors will not be accepted to the Yeshiva.

The Netzi'v: Hamelitz, 16 Tammuz 5646 (July 6, 1886), issue 55.

The Netzi'v writes: "Volozhin, Sunday of the Torah portion of Pinchas, 5646 [1886]. On the eve of the Torah portion of Balak, G-d judged our city with fire, which consumed more than half of the city, including the large building in which Torah has been raised up for more than 80 years, the name of which extends from one end of the Jewish world to the other. Due to our great sins, it has been burnt from its foundations to the top, as has the Beis Midrash built

[Page 175]

in splendor at its side, in which the holy flock also crouch – for the holy Yeshiva did not have enough room for them. Also, more than 300 scholars, who lived in Volozhin were swallowed up by G-d on the day of his wrath, when he had no mercy.

Regarding this, I asked those who preserve the faith of Israel in the name of our holy Torah: arise, gird yourselves to restore the holy Yeshiva upon its foundations. Go from city to city wherever the Children of Israel live to ask them to help, for we have no other remnant of our precious things other than this Torah, and there is no limit to discussing this. I have faith in the love of Torah burning in the hearts of the Israelite people, that our words will bear fruit, and the righteousness of the will shine upon them in this world and the World To Come. Here I am, burdened with a great task, crouched under the burden of the Yeshiva."

Dinkin, Shlomo David: Hamelitz, 12 Tishrei 5647 (September 29, 1886), issue 125.

Dinkin announces that the "Wealthy Israelite Brodski from Kyiv gave 25,000 rubles of his wealth and purchased 60 shares that pay a dividend of 2,000 rubles annually in order to support ten prominent scholars to learn in the Yeshiva of Volozhin and prepare themselves to be rabbis, for no less than three years and no more than five years. Following that, their places will be taken by ten other prominent students."

Bar-Bei-Rav (Micha Yosef Berdichevski). A Bundle of Letters from Volozhin: Hamelitz, 23 Shvat 5648 (January 24, 1888), issue 19.

In this letter, Berdichevski writes that there are many Yeshiva students who are expert in secular knowledge and various languages, people who strive for that which is above and that which is below, that which is in front and that which is behind. He describes one student for whom philosophy did not remove him from his faith, and he is observant about the word of G-d: "In the midst of the Yeshiva, there was a small, poor lad, sitting and occupying himself with Torah. His bones were worn and his cheeks were wrinkled before their time, but in this weak physical frame was hidden a sublime, lofty soul. In his wrinkled forehead dwelt a sharp, deep intellect, penetrating into the depths.

"This young man already attained expertise in all subjects of teaching, and had he wished to make Torah his profession, he would already be partaking of its fruits in this world. However, he fled from leadership positions, for his soul desired Torah, and he dwelt in its doors day and night. However, for him, Torah was only a part of his ways. He also studied the wonders. He delved into the mystical chariot and Sefer Yetzira [Kabalistic concepts] and also entered into Divine secrets.

"All books of philosophy were fluent in his mouth, and the paths of Greek philosophy were as clear to him as the paths of his city. All sublime research that came to his heart he put on paper, and with great expertise, he edited the fruits of his research, with lofty order and awesome, sublime depth;

[Page 176]

to the point where when we read them, it seemed as if we were reading the books of Shlomo Maimon[1]. Philosophy did not lead him to doubt and despair. It was only the food for his soul, for the chain of faith never left him, and he feared the word of G-d, and was careful in both the easy and the difficult commandments."

Dement, Yosef Ben-Zion: Hamelitz, 28 Sivan 5648 (May 26, 1888), issue 113.

The writer announces that on My 15, the day that the royal crown was placed upon the head of our master, the Kaiser, may his glory be raised (in the year 1883), all the residents of the city gathered in the Beis Midrash to pray for the well-being of the Kaiser and his lofty household. The Gaon and Admor, the head of the Yeshiva, the rabbi Netzi'v, may he live long, delivered a speech on the issues of the day, and proved to the audience that it is a Torah commandment for us to be faithful children to our lofty king, and to love our native land."

Dement, Yosef Ben-Zion: Hamelitz, 17 Tammuz 5648 (June 14, 1888), issue 128.

The writer describes the visit of the district minister to Volozhin.

Av'sr: Hamelitz, 1 Shvat 5659 (December 22, 1888), issue 281.

The writer announces that the students of the Yeshiva gathered in the Yeshiva, wearing their Sabbath clothes, to give praise and accolades to the Creator for saving the life of the Kaiser, his wife and children from the danger of death.

Bron, Eliezer (from Minsk): Hamelitz, 26 Adar I, 5651 (February 22, 1891), issue 45.

The writer announces: "During recent times, our city has become a fortress, a hill toward which everyone turns, for rabbis and high level Gaonim have gathered there for a consultation meeting to improve the material and moral state of the Yeshiva of Volozhin – the sole university in our country set up to raise rabbis. They are also appointing a Yeshiva head, for the elderly rabbi, the Gaon of our generation, Rabbi Naftali Tzvi Berlin, may G-d protect and save him, a true lover of Zion who demonstrates his love for Zion through his action, has left his honorable post, his holy guard, and is preparing to set his steps toward our Holy Land, to spend his remaining years there (may G-d prolong them), in Torah, Divine Service, and fear of G-d. He will also be moving his family to the Holy Land. As he leaves his post, the Yeshiva is left as a ship without a captain, and its students are abandoned as sheep without a shepherd.

"Books and letters were sent to all the rabbis of the region to come to our town to deliberate with our rabbi, the Gaon, the rabbi of the city. Thus, the convention was convened. After an extensive deliberation, his son, the Gaon Rabbi Chaim, may he live long, who had been the rabbi and preacher in the capital city of Moscow, was unanimously appointed by all those gathered as the head of the Yeshiva of Volozhin. They will be collecting money from the philanthropists of our nation to sustain the Yeshiva, from which Torah and light emanate, and to fill its empty coffers and discharge its debts from bygone days. It is appropriate that

[Page 177]

the philanthropists of our people in all their places of residence will now arise with a generous heart and an open hand to become a support of this praiseworthy Yeshiva, that disseminates rays of light to our entire region, to support it, help it, and set up its foundations on a firm basis, so that it can stand forever in the honor and glory of our nation."

Gamzu, Mordecha Ber. Who is at the Head? Hamelitz, 7 Adar II, 5651 (March 5, 1891), issue 54.

The writer deals with the issue of the appointment of Rabbi Chaim Berlin, the son of the Netzi'v, as head of the Yeshiva. He opposed the choice of this rabbi, and said, "According to my small opinion, the appointment of the head of the Yeshiva is not the type of thing made in haste, behind the oven and stove, within a single night. It is clear and known that everything goes after the head, and the honor of the entire Yeshiva is dependent upon his honor. Therefore it is incumbent upon us to appoint a Yeshiva head about whom the entire people would say, this is he; and regarding whom our brethren in the Diaspora, myriads of thousands of Israelites, will know and recognize that he is the select one of all the sages of the time, that they searched and found nobody better than he."

Ravkash, Yitzchak (from Vilna): Hamelitz, 25 Iyar, 5651 (May 25, 1891), issue 112.

The writer complains that, in his old age, it is as if the Netzi'v had been forgotten, and nobody is helping him ease the burden of debts hovering over the Yeshiva. He writes: "The great rabbi and Gaon, the Netzi'v, the head of the Yeshiva and principal of the Yeshiva of Volozhin in our region, due to old age (may G-d lengthen his years), has stopped presenting his class before the students who cleave to the dust of his feet, and has given his place over to his son, the rabbi and Gaon Rabbi Chaim, and to his grandson, the rabbi and Gaon Rabbi Chaim Soloveitchik. It is the custom of the world that when great people descend from the stage, the people extend a pleasant face and tokens of honors to him, to fulfil their desires and to ease their mindset, so that they will know that their deeds are accepted, and the people follow after them. Since that aforementioned Gaon, who was the right pillar in the leadership of the Yeshiva, and the living spirit in its character for more than 30 years, and he never rested or become silent until he raised to a high and lofty structure, and if we take into account his students and students of his students who drew from his wellsprings, perhaps they will approach the number of students that Rabbi Akiva had – then the hearts of every person will grant honor to this great individual.

"Many rabbis, the Gaonim of our time, poured water upon his hands. Many maskilim learned Torah from his mouth, gaining knowledge and goodness. Also, many wealthy merchants, in whom the Jewish people take pride, cleaved to the dust of his feet. Who is it that has not seen the toil of the rabbi and Gaon, the Netzi'v in his Torah and supervision of his students – for in one glance, he surveyed them and his eyes discerned who was diligent in his studies.

1.   "And behold, after all this, have we recompensed him for all the goodness he gave to us? Aside from his private situation which is poor, and his lot is not fat, his heart and soul will yet weep and lament in silence over him, for the accumulated debts are large, and have burdened the neck of he who extended assistance and distributed money to the poor people, from whom Torah emanates."

[Page 178]

Greier, Moshe Chaim: Hamelitz, 7 Tevet, 5652 (February 3, 1892), issue 28.

The writer, who was one of the students of the Yeshiva, includes the announcement of the closing of the Yeshiva in his article: "The Yeshiva of Volozhin has been closed and locked by the government this past Wednesday, January 22. We, the students of the Yeshiva, have been sent back to our native cities. On the morning of January 22, minister of the city of Oshmana [Ashmyany] (the regional capital) and the vice prosecutor from that city came to the Yeshiva along with many policemen. Farmers from the villages were also called on order of the regional minister. The officer of the region demanded of the Netzi'v that he prepare all passports for the Yeshiva students which were guarded by him as of that day. After that, he asked the Yeshiva head whether all the students were currently present in the Yeshiva. When the Yeshiva head responded that nobody was missing, he issued a command that nobody dare to exit until he finished his words. The regional minister read from a book the government order regarding the Yeshiva and its students, as follows: 'From this day and henceforth, the Yeshiva shall be closed in accordance with the laws of the state, because it does not observe the law regarding schools. The students must leave the city within three days. Documents of the Yeshiva students, such as passports and certificates that they have fulfilled their army duty, will not be given to them, but will rather be sent to the offices of the police officials in their places of residence, from where they will be returned to them.'"

Erez. The Yeshiva of Volozhin: Hamelitz, 9 Adar, 5652 (February 25, 1892). Issue 47.

Erez accused the Netzi'v of failing to fulfil the command of the government, and thereby causing the closing of the Yeshiva: "The Netzi'v from the Yeshiva of Volozhin, pardon his honor, did not want to, or due to his conscience, was unable to fulfil these laws. Therefore, the commissioner of the Vilna region ordered to put a stop to the Yeshiva.

Anyone who knows what the times demand realizes that the laws were issued only due to the refusal of the Yeshiva directors to do what was commanded of them from the year 1889 until now. They do not affect at all the foundations of our faith, and are not intermixed with religious studies. They are only to create law and order, and they demand from the Yeshiva head and the students that they be familiar with the language of the state and the subject of arithmetic."

Regarding the Yeshiva of Volozhin: Hamelitz. 12 Adar 5652 (February 28, 1892), issue 50.

(A continuation of issue 48.)

Regarding the Yeshiva: Hamelitz, 19 Adar 5652 (March 6, 1892). Issue 55

[Page 179]

Berlin, Chaim: Hamelitz, 24 Tammuz 5642 (July 7, 1892), issue 151.

Rabbi Chaim Berlin, who went to Amsterdam to collect donations to ease the burden of debt that hovered over his father the Netzi'v, expressed his hope that the Yeshiva would develop shortly: "And regarding the impossible matter of the closing of the holiness, our hope strengthens us with a strong faith in the merit of the holy Torah, that G-d will help us through the rabbis, the Gaonim of the generation, may G-d protect and keep them, and the gates will yet be raised over their heads, and the eternal doors will be raised up, and a great rabbi, a sage, who knows the language of the state and how to deal with government ministers will raise its splendor and return the crown of Torah to its previous state, in ways that will also be acceptable to the ministers of the state, may their honor be raised. The good G-d will complete this on our behalf for the good, and the merits of the holy father and grandfather, the holy Gaon, Rabbi Chaim of Volozhin, may the memory of the righteous be a blessing, shall stand for it, that it will be built upon its foundations, for renown and praise, forever, Selah."

Zgorodski, Y. Ch. Eulogy for the Netzi'v: Hamelitz, 3 Elul 5653 (August 3, 1893), issue 174.

Luria, Mordechai Yona: Hamelitz, 10 Tammuz 5659 (June 6, 1899), issue 125.

The writer deals with the appointment of Rabbi Rafael Shapira as the head of the Etz Chaim Yeshiva of Volozhin. Among the rest, he says, "Bobruisk, the local head of the rabbinical court, Rabbi Rafael Shapira, may he live long, has been accept in honor to the city of Volozhin, the host of Torah and the place of its advancement. For the hearts of the philanthropists of Minsk felt a good thing, that is: to reopen the great educational institution there and to return the crown to its former state. They took the aforementioned Gaon to be the teacher and principal of this institution, to make Torah great and mighty."

Yehudi. Hosts of Torah: Hamelitz, 28 Cheshvan, 5660 (October 20, 1889), issue 229.

The writer expresses his wonder at the opening of the Yeshiva and begins with the following emotional words: "Behold, I close my eyes, and the voices emanating from the mouths of the studiers arouse old memories within me, precious memories, memories of Volozhin. Those days were days of spiritual pleasure in the full sense of the term. The lover of Torah and love of Zion together captured the heart of our elderly rabbi, and his spirit rested upon the best of the students, who also raised up Nes Tziona" [The Banner Toward Zion]. How pleasant were the hours of study in the Yeshiva after hours of speaking in a meeting, and how pleasant were the hours of a meeting that warmed the hearts after hours of study that sharpened the mind! Then, life was wholesome, developing the intellect and the emotions, the mind and the heart, hopes, and imaginations. How great were they and how lofty! We studied with enthusiasm and debated actively. Life bustled, hummed, and flowed around us in the marketplace, whereas we were living a completely different life. The head was in Babylonia, and the heart in Zion!

"O Volozhin, Volozhin, how pleasant you were to me, and how great is my longing for you! Behold, the gates of your Yeshiva have opened. Torah has returned to its host. Behold the voice of Jacob is heard again "between the pillars"…

[Page 180]

The Netzi'v. A Significant Announcement for the Torah: Hatzefira, 15 Elul 5646 (September 3, 1886). Issue 125.

The Netzi'v announces the renovation of the Yeshiva, and wrote among everything else: "Behold, immediately after the fire, blessed be G-d, we have strengthened and begun to rebuild the ruins of the holy Yeshiva upon its foundations. We further paid attention to enlarge its width and height, and to add splendor and glory to the entire plan of the house with additional expenditures, for it is a sanctuary of Torah and also property of all of Israel. Our hearts are certain that it will be desirable to all Israel, to honor the word of G-d regarding Halacha, and to prepare its place in the best possible fashion, so it will be fitting as the dwelling place of the masses in great crowds."

Sach, Peretz Shalom: Hatzefira, 20 Adar 5647 (March 4, 1887), issue 53.

The writer tells about the visit to the school of the regional superintendent and Mrs. Steinberg, the superintendent of Hebrew teachers.

Publication of New Regulations Regarding the Yeshiva: Hatzefira, 19 Adar, 5652 (March 6, 1892), issue 56.

The regulations regarding the Yeshiva that were certified on December 22, 1891 by the minister of education Baron Vielanov are announced in this issue.

The Conclusion of the Publication of the Laws Regarding the Yeshiva: Hatzefira, 21 Adar 5652 (March 8, 1892), issue 57.

Necrology About the Death of the Netzi'v: Hatzefira: 28 Av 5653 (July 29, 1893), issue 169.

The following is written in the necrology: "Before the finalization of this edition, the terrible news reached us that at 4:00 a.m. today, the elder of the Gaonim of Israel, the portent of the generation and the right pillar of the sanctuary of Torah in Russia, our rabbi and teacher, Rabbi Naftali Tzvi Yehuda Berlin, who was the head of the Yeshiva of Volozhin, has been summoned to the Yeshiva on high. He worked great things and wonders, and stood at his post for very many years, to make Torah great and mighty through his books, classes, intercession and efforts. Woe, such a great loss the House of Israel has endured, and who will give us a replacement!

The funeral will take place tomorrow, Friday, the eve of the Sabbath, at 12:00 noon.

Sobolski, Yitzchak: Mourning of an Individual (a eulogy for the Netzi'v): Hatzefira, 4 Elul, 5653 (August 4, 1893), issue 174.

Epstein, Zalman: A Forgotten Jubilee: Hatzefira, 28 Av, 5663 (August 8, 1903), issue 184; 30 Av 5663 (August 10, 1903) issue 185; 2 Elul 5663 (August 11, 1903), issue 186; 4 Elul 5663 (August 13, 1903) issue 188.

[Page 181]

Zalman Epstein points out that the year 5663 [1903] marked 100 years since the founding of the Etz Chaim Yeshiva of Volozhin (founded in 5563), and asked: "How can we celebrate the 100-year jubilee of our spiritual birthplace in the field of Judaism? We must publish a memorial book for the occasion of the completion of 100 years of the Yeshiva of Volozhin. The history of the Yeshiva since its founding would be included in this anthology, as well as memories and illustrations from the life of the Yeshiva during different eras; the characters of the Yeshiva heads, their history and pictures; lists of students according to their years of study in the Yeshiva. – – – This anthology will present a full, clear picture of the life of 100 years of the Yeshiva both materially and spiritually. We will leave it as a memento for the coming generation. – – – We, the last ones from the era of the greatness of the Yeshiva of Volozhin in its old style, must produce such a memorial book of this period of original life as hastily as possible, so that that their names and memory will not be wiped out from the community of the nation of G-d."

Eistenstat, M. Revolution in the Yeshiva: Hatzefira, 1 Sivan 5676 (June 2, 1916), issue 124.

The author describes the revolt that broke out in the Yeshiva on the eve of Shavuot 5645 [1886] because the Netzi'v slapped one of the students.

Hatzofeh (Tel Aviv)
(editor: Rabbi Meir Bar-Ilan (Berlin))

Shin. When the Gates were Locked: Hatzofeh, 5 Tevet, 5702 [1942].

On the 50th Anniversary of the Death of the Netzi'v: Hatzofeh: 26 Av, 5703 [1943].

Cinowitz, M. The Yeshiva of Volozhin During the Era of Rabbi Rafael Shapira: Hatzofeh 4 Nisan 5706 [1946].

Yearbooks, Anthologies, Collections, Monthlies, and Weeklies
(Ordered by the Aleph Beit by names of the authors)

Berkman, Yehoshua. On the Netzi'v and Rabbi Rafael Shapiro: Halevanon (edited by Yechiel Beril) 9 Kislev 5635 (November 17, 1874), issue 14.

Berkerman writes: "The large Yeshiva here, from which light emanates to all of Israel, from then until now, will not diminish in the level of brightness (into the future). The sun shall yet shine as in the days of Creation, and its rays will illuminate with the light of the Torah. The Divine flow will still emanate

[Page 182]

filled with wisdom and knowledge to give drink to the young sheep who are thirsty for the word of G-d, who will stream here in their masses. When they come, they will quench their thirst in the pathways and wellsprings of the Torah of the Admor and his son-in-law, the rabbi and Gaon, sharp and deep, pious and modest, the honor of his glorious name, our rabbi and teacher, Rabbi Rafael Shapiro, may his light shine, the son of that Tzadik, the great rabbi and Gaon, our rabbi Aryeh Leib Shapiro, the head of the rabbinical court of Kovno."

Rabbi Yehoshua Bekerman writes about the Netzi'v: "Our hand is too short to express before you one one-thousandth of the feelings of gratitude and blessing that our heart feels toward you regarding eternal life, and the benefit that you do for us. Now he is a faithful pastor, through the pride of your Torah you lead us, and through your mighty wellsprings of Torah you cause us to drink in abundance. Who is like you who raises the horn of Torah, our dear father, who is like you who dedicates your time night and day. Your hands are full of work, only to raise the horn of Torah and make it mighty."

Bekerman, Yehoshua: Halevanon, 8 Tevet 5635 (December 16, 1874), issue 18.

The writer announces the death of Yitzchak Eliezer Rabinowitz, who oversaw the Yeshiva coffers.

Bialik, Chaim Nachman. On the Night of the Earthquake (A hidden section from Hamatmid): Kneset, Dvir Publishing, Tel Aviv, 5696 [1836]. Book I, pp 4-7.

Bialik, Chaim Nachman. Autobiographical Sections: Kneset, Tel-Aviv, 5701 [1941], Book VI, page 15.

Blusher, Abba. Bialik in Volozhin: Meoznaim (monthly), Tammuz 5695 [1935], volume IV. Booklet II (20).

Berdichevski, Micha Yosef. The History of the Etz Chaim Yeshiva: Haasif (edited by Nachum Sokolow), Warsaw, Reb Yitzchak Goldman Publisher, third year, 5647 [1887], pp 231-242.

In this article, Berdichevski describes the building of the Yeshiva with the following words: "In the year 5625 [1865], when the Netzi'v saw that the Yeshiva had reached a period of decline, he spared no effort and traveled to many cities to collect money so that a splendid, strong building could be built, which stands in splendor to this day. The Yeshiva is like a wonderful palace built with a lower, second, and third floor. It has a large, wide hall, supported by four large pillars. Its walls are as white as snow and shiny wool. Its ceiling is clean and pure. That hall is the hall of Talmud. It also has a large corridor in which the students read during the summer. It also has a fine room in which the Gema'ch, the

[Page 183]

large charitable fund, functions, from which all the Yeshiva students can borrow during times of difficulty. (Its treasury consists of approximately 500 rubles.) There is also a clean room from which the principal, Rabbi Lipman, distributes the tractates required for study, and a smoking room (for it is forbidden to smoke tobacco in the Yeshiva).

"The Mashgiach and principal are on the lower floor, and the Yeshiva's large library is on the third floor. A person walking by the yard of the Yeshiva, paved with stones, on the long nights of Tevet will witness a wonderful, sublime sight. The lights of many candelabras will cast their shining rays upon the even snow. The voices of 300 individuals studying with serious feeling and deep enthusiasm can be heard as a great noise from one end of the yard to the other. Here, a visionary lad walks in a tapping fashion, with a Gemara under his noble hands, as his feet walk fast, for his soul desires Torah; here sit a few school lads, for sleep has already overtaken them, and their soul mourns that they have interrupted their studies. Here one sees Jewry in its image and form. We can state without exaggeration: Whomever has not seen such a wonderful display – has never seen beauty in his life."[2]

Berdichevski, Micha Yosef (Yb'm). The World of Nobility: Hakerem (Edited by Elazar Atlas). "A yearly book for the research of Israel and its literature." Warsaw, Yitzchak Goldman publishing, 5648 [1888].

Berdichevski, Micha Yosef (Yerubaal). The Authority of the Individual for the Many: Otzar Hasafrut, 5652 [1892], page 30.

Gil. In the Yeshivot of Torah: Echoes of the Times (edited and published by P. Margolin), 18 Iyar, 5670 (May 15, 1910), issue 110.

Hatzofeh. In the Yeshivot of Torah: Echoes of the Times. 12 Tammuz, 5670 (July 6, 1910).

Hatzofeh writes about the attempt to carry out the mussar methodology [methodology of stressing moral behavior] in Volozhin.

Zak, Shimon. The Yeshiva of Volozhin: The Book of Lithuanian Jewry, 5620 [1860], Published by Am Hasefer, pp. 206-213.

Zak, Shimon. From the World of the Spirit: : Hatoren (New York), 14 Tishrei, 5679 [1918], issue 27, fifth year, pp. 3-8.

The writer dedicates his words to the character of the studies in the Yeshiva of Volozhin, and the quality of the Yeshiva students. He states: "This Yeshiva, the first in time and quality, was never attracted to acute sharpness in the sense as is known in Yeshivas – or after the fervor of didactics [pilpul] where the leaf "floats on the head of a needle." In this Yeshiva, a spirit of

[Page 184]

simplicity and naturalness pervaded in the later years, the spirit of its founders, the early ones, the students and spiritual heirs of the Gaon of Vilna, the vast majority of whom inherited the methodology of straightforwardness and direct understanding in the study of Talmud and its commentaries. Even the thread of grace and the splendor of the soul that was stretched over the Yeshiva of Volozhin, and the ancient charm

– the charm of the tradition of days of yore and the spirit of generations – that hovered over it, influenced the soul of the youths who came there in a relaxed manner.

A person educated in Volozhin would have a straightforward understanding, and clear knowledge in his spirit. He was calm and deliberate in his knowledge, pleasant with other people and honored and dear to them – – – The Volozhiner was always a desired and dear guest even amongst the regular householders, who related to him as flesh of their flesh and bone of their bones, even though they knew and recognized that he was above them in the talents of his young spirit, the imagination of his intellect, the uprightness of his heart, and his spiritual development in general.

Therefore, they revered him, honored him, and loved him with the love of a parent. His opinion was accepted even in matters of the city and its needs. – – – The heart of the Volozhiner was as broad as the opening of the hall, alert to everything transpiring, sensitive of his environment, and knowing how to enjoy the wonderful, beautiful views of nature of which the town of Volozhin excelled. Anyone who did not see the youth and young men of Volozhin going out on summer evenings to stroll around this town, enjoying the beauty of nature, benefiting from the radiance of the world of the Holy One Blessed Be He between the pure meadows and paths of grain, discussing during their stroll matters that stand at the upper heights of the world and Jewry – has never seen a heart-arousing scene in his days."

Dr. Shmuel Yona. Rabbi Chaim of Volozhin as a Pedagogue: Pathways of Education (edited by Sh. B. Maksimon), Cheshvan 5689 [1928], (fourth year), booklet VI (21), pp. 209-217.

Yaavetz, Wolf. Migdal Hameah: The Nation of Israel (edited by Shalom Pinchas Rabinowitz), Warsaw, 5646 [1886], pp. 89-151 (about Rabbi Chaim of Volozhin, see page 133).

Kahana, David. Lilienthal and the Education of the Jews of Russia: Hashiloach (edited by Dr. Yosef Klausner) Odessa, Av 5672 [1912] – Tevet 5673 [1923], volume 27, pp 314-322; 546-556.

Lifshitz, Yaakov Halevi. A Generation and its Administrators: Hakerem, Warsaw, 5648 [1888], pp. 179-180.

Mandelkorn, Dr. Shlomo. The Distant Drew Close: Otzar Hasafrut, 5648 [1888], pp. 41-44.

Maslianski, Tz. Ch. Memoirs: Haivri (edited by Rabbi Meir Berlin), 6 Elul 5677 (July 24, 1917), issue 32.

[Page 185]

Neria, Moshe Tzvi. Chapters of Volozhin: Heichal Shlomo, 5723 [1963], pp. 525-544.

Neria, Moshe Tzvi. The Netzi'v of Volozhin: The Book of Lithuanian Jewry, pp 365-369.

Pomerantz, Gedalia. The First Strike in the Yeshiva of Volozhin: Hadoar, 14 Shvat, 5723 [1963], year 42, issue 15.

Fin, Sh. Y. Kneset Yisrael (Memories of the history of the Greats of Israel, renown for their Torah, wisdom and deeds from the days of the Mishnaic sages until this generation). Warsaw, Efraim Baumriter and his son-in-law Naftali Gonshar Publishers, 5647 [1887]. For Rabbi Chaim of Volozhin, see pp. 347-349; for Rabbi Itzele, see page 610.

Spirno, A. Memories and News: Reshimot (collected from memoirs, ethnography, and folklore in Israel), edited by E. Droyanov, with the participation of Y. Ch. Rabnitzki and Chaim Nachman Bialik. Odessa, published by Moriya, 5678 [1918], volume I, pp. 148-151.

Peker, M. From the Yeshiva of Volozhin: Hator (Mizrachi weekly, edited by Rabbi Y. L. Hakohen Fishman), 30 Sivan 5684 [July 2, 1924], issue 40.

Friedland, Pesach (Chad Min Chevraya). Chibat Tzion in Volozhin: Hator, Jerusalem, 5684. Issues 40, 44, 45, 47.

Cytron, Sh. L. The Dynastic Battle in the Yeshiva of Volozhin: Reshimot, volume I, pp. 123-135.

Cytron, Sh. L. The Old Purim Constitution of the Volozhin Yeshiva: Three literary generations (Literary memoirs, characteristics and personal experiences), Warsaw, "Central" society, fourth section, pages 160-165.

Kook, Avraham Yitzchak Hakohen. Head of Etz Chaim Yeshiva (History of the Netziv). Kneset Yisrael, Warsaw, Yehoshua Yehuda Ish-Horowic Publishing, pp 138-142.

Rabbi Kook writes about the Netzi'v, among other things: "Already during the days of his youth, it seems that this man was created for greatness. His strong eagerness, distance from all pleasantries of life, wonderful diligence, and straightforward inclination to delve deep into the question in all aspects of Torah, to turn away from the path of tortuous didactics and to dig and know the proper truth of Torah – all these bear witness that the future of this scholar was to be a luminary for the paths of Torah, and to clarify the paths of study for many of

[Page 186]

his age cohort. In those days, all those who grasped Torah made efforts to put all their energy to the didactics of Talmudic discussions, to the novellae of the Gemara, decisors, Tosafot, and the Maharsh'ah, to whom all studiers of Talmud turned their attention at that time.

Rivkin, M. The Last Years of the Yeshiva of Volozhin Waschod (Russian, edited by A. Landau). Peterburg, 5655 [1895], January-February issues.

Rivkind, Yitzchak. Miyalkutei Volozhin: Reshimot, volume V, pp. 362-381.

Rivkind, Yitzchak. A Certain Yeshiva Head of Volozhin (Rabbi Yechiel Michel of Nyasvizh): Sefer Turov (edited by Yitzchak Zylberszlag and Yochanan Twerski). Published by Beit Hamidrash Lamorim, 5698 [1938], pp 232-239.

In this article, Mr. Rivkind writes about a certain Yeshiva head who was not from the Volozhin dynasty, who was not known at all to the writers about the history of the high-level Beis Midrash for Torah during the first, critical years of its existence. The name of this certain Yeshiva head was Rabbi Yechiel Michel the son of Rabbi Tzvi Hirsch of Nyasvizh.

The year of his birth is not known. In my estimation, he was born during the 5530s [1770s]. He studied from the rabbi of Kapyla, Rabbi Yom-Tov Lipman, during his youth, and also merited to bask in the radiance of the Gaon of Vilna. Later, he served his [i.e. the Vilna Gaon's] great student Rabbi Chaim of

Volozhin. He taught and learned before him. "When his high-level Yeshiva was founded, I studied before him with the students who came to bask under his wings, for approximately seven years." In another place, he repeats, and writes: "And I learned before him with many students for approximately six years."

Even some of those who gave approbations to his book noted that "The deeds he does are great, so that Torah is not forgotten in Israel, and he teaches the sons of Judea the bow[3] in the large Yeshiva in the holy community of Volozhin." They note that "he was the first of the founders of the important Yeshiva in the holy community of Volozhin ." Among those who gave testimony was Rabbi Hillel, the son-in-law of the Gaon Rabbi Chaim, who himself had delivered classes in the Yeshiva for a decade. In his approbation, written three days before his death, he wrote about Rabbi Yechiel Michel: "Through his hand, the Yeshiva of the holy community of Volozhin was founded. He learned and taught many students before the Admor, my father-in-law Rabbi Chaim of blessed memory."

Rivkind, Yitzchak. An Attempt to Found a Yeshiva in New York in the name of the Netzi'v, Forty Years Ago. Sefer Scharfstein (edited by Yochanan Twerski, Kalman Weitman, and Avraham Epstein). Published by the Committee of Shvilei Hachinuch, pp. 243-249.

Rivkind, Yitzchak. Was there a Purim Rabbi in the Yeshiva of Volozhin? Hadoar, 12 Adar 5620 [1960], issue 19, pp. 337-338.

[Page 187]

Mr. Rivkind expresses his opinion that the custom of a "Purim Rabbi" existed in the Yeshiva. He states: "We attribute the establishment of the custom of a Purim Rabbi in the Volozhin Yeshiva to its first founder, Rabbi Chaim, a student of the Gr'a. He was a talented pedagogue, and he did a great deed in choosing "a rabbi for a day." He opened a pipeline for the students to criticize the ways of the Yeshiva. He developed their self-awareness, their self-esteem, and their personal value."

As proof of this, Mr. Rivkind cites the article by M. Eisenstant "Purim Rabbi" (Hatzefira, 5676 [1916], issue 66), which states: "It was in accordance with the tradition of Rabbi Chaim that the custom of a Purim Rabbi was established. He made it into a regulation in the Yeshiva. His reasoning was that he wanted to know the issues regarding the running of the Yeshiva about which he was not aware, and about which no student would dare to point out to him. Therefore, he established one day a year, the day of Purim, where even our sages permitted levity – upon which one of the students would be free to his own accord all day and would be the sole arbiter of matters of the Yeshiva and its running. Of course, the improper deeds of the "all year rabbi" would be clarified that day. He would know and understand later how to fix the issues and to be careful about them for the future."

Reines, Moshe. Achsaniot Shel Torah: Otzar Hasafrut, Krakow, Shealtiel Grober Publisher, 5649-50 [1889-90].

Shapira, Moshe Shmuel. Rabbi Itzele of Volozhin (on the 120th anniversary of his death): 17 Kislev, 5763 [1963], issue 7.

Translator's footnotes:

1. See https://en.wikipedia.org/wiki/Salomon_Maimon
2. A paraphrase of Mishna Sukka 5:1.
3. Based on II Samuel 1:18

[Page 188]

The Great Etz Chaim School of Volozhin

by Rabbi Shimon Langbort
(the head of the Volozhin Yeshiva of Bnei Brak)

Translated by Jerrold Landau

A.

The community of the city of Volozhin merited to be the host of Torah for a period of close to 150 years. It hosted Torah in the wonderful, praiseworthy Yeshiva called: "Beit Ulpana Rabta Etz Chaim DeVolozhin" [The Great Etz Chaim School of Volozhin], which stood gloriously in the center of the city, and disseminated Torah and light to afar. This Yeshiva registered a splendid chapter in the history of the nation of Israel in the Diaspora of Russia, Poland, and Lithuania for more than 100 years, during the period from before the First World War until the terrible destruction by the enemy.

Writers have written books and articles, and poets have composed songs of praise to the greatness and splendor of this mighty center of Torah, about the Divine presence that dwelt in that miniature sanctuary, and of the great light that illuminated and served as a beacon of light to the entire Diaspora. Booklets and articles about the greatness of the illustrious Yeshiva heads, giants of the spirit, and of their statue and image in Torah and spirituality, of their nobility and the fine traits of their soul with which they have been graced with supernal grace – to steer the ship in the midst of the sea and to infuse an influence of blessing on the knowledge and understanding of both the written and the oral Torah to their thousands of students who streamed in from the ends of the earth to receive Torah and refinement of the soul from their illustrious teachers. In addition, it was also a bastion [Tel Talpiot][1], for all mouths turned to them to resolve their doubts and to answer their questions on all subjects of the written and oral Torah, and in all areas of fundamental Jewish life.

Similarly, feelings of reverence and honor are expressed to the students of the Yeshiva, who came to dwell in the midst of and warm themselves from the light of the mighty ones of Torah in Volozhin, among them studious geniuses with excellent talents, who made their nights like days in their toil of Torah, as they drank with thirst the words of the living G-d. They grew, succeeded, and bore praiseworthy fruit in this great home of Talmud, splendid and infused with holiness. The vast majority of the Yeshiva students later developed into great rabbis, illustrious leaders, talented scribes, and heads of Jewish communities.

The first and foremost of the dynasty of *Beit Harav* [the rabbinical household] of Volozhin, the founder of the Yeshiva, was the pious Gaon, our rabbi Chaim, may the memory of the righteous be blessed, who was called the Great Rabbi Chaim. He was a prime student of the Gaon of Vilna (the Gr'a, may the memory of the righteous be blessed) who continued with his methodology and ways in holiness, and founded the Yeshiva of Volozhin in accordance with his directives and advice. He placed a cornerstone on the three pillars of the world: Torah, Divine service, and good deeds, and declared that without the study of Torah, the world could not even exist for a moment. Were the study of Torah to stop for a moment throughout the entire world – the world would be destroyed in a moment. If we see that the world exists

[Page 189]

and stands, it is proof that in some far-off place, scholars are sitting and occupying themselves in Torah. They strengthen and uphold the world and keep it from faltering. Therefore, he set up a watch [*Mishmar*] in his Yeshiva to study Torah without a break. One watch exists and another enters, day and night, at all times and every moment. Wonderful legends spread about Rabbi Chaim, who was a worker of portents, a holy, pure man, their teacher from the nation, both in Torah and in refinement and humility, in the revealed and hidden aspects of Torah. Several details about him are written in the booklet "Rabbi Chaim of Volozhin, may his memory be a blessing." From great modesty and purity of the heart, he would sign his name on his responses to questions on matters of religion and law: "Chaim Bmrhy'tz (the son of our teacher, Rabbi Yitzchak), may the memory of the righteous be blessed, the teacher [*melamed*] of Volozhin."

After him, his son, the praiseworthy Gaon Rabbi Yitzchak, may the memory of the righteous be blessed, served. He became known as "Chachima Diyehudai" (the sage of the Jews), and gained renown through the world through his wise and sharp responses that he issued to the Minister of Education of the Kingdom of Russia when he was summoned by him to the capital of Peterburg with other greats and choice people of the nation to take council together and influence them to introduce changes to religion. His wise responses that emanated from his holy mouth were powerful in front of the destroyers and uprooters, and they went forth with a splendorous victory, sanctifying the Divine Name in public, even in the eyes of the gentiles. He directed the Yeshiva in the same direction and methodology forged by his great father. After his death, the leadership of the Yeshiva was given over to his two great sons-in-law, the Gaon Rabbi Eliezer Yitzchak Fried of blessed memory, and the Gaon the Netzi'v of blessed memory. Both were cedars of Lebanon, mighty in Torah[2]. His first son-in-law did not live long. After Rabbi Eliezer Yitzchak died in his prime, the leadership of the Yeshiva was transferred to the faithful hands of the Gaon the Netzi'v of blessed memory, who ran it with great success. In addition to the Netzi'v of blessed memory, classes in the Yeshiva were given by the mighty Gaon, Rabbi Yosef Dov Halevi Soloveitchik of blessed memory.

The Netzi'v of blessed memory ran the Yeshiva and raised it to its pinnacle. His era was considered the glorious era in the annals of the existence of the Yeshiva. During his time, the Yeshiva grew in numbers and essence. Up to 500 students basked in its shade, and its influence was great throughout the Diaspora of Israel, to the point where the Russian government became jealous of it, and the ministry of education began to afflict the Netzi'v of blessed memory and limit his steps, demanding that the Yeshiva head introduce a curriculum in the Yeshiva that would be satisfactory to its desires, and under government supervision. Our rabbi, the Netzi'v of blessed memory, arose and strongly pushed off the intermixture of the government in its internal spiritual matters. Thanks to his glorious steadfastness, the Yeshiva did not change its fundamental content and style – however, it led to its exile, as the government closed the Yeshiva for several years and dismissed its students. After a short time, it arose again in its holiness and wholesomeness.

Several stories about his manner and ways spread in Volozhin; however, this is not the place to detail them and dwell upon them. The Netzi'v of blessed memory was also known for his great studiousness, toiling and wearying himself with Torah day and night. He published many books on the written and oral Torah, including books of responsa that he responded to questioners throughout the entire world. He would sign his letters: "Burdened with work."

[Page 190]

A great deal has been told about the suffering and tribulation of the Yeshiva heads, who were exiled by the government to districts far off from the Yeshiva; about the wanderings of the students who were uprooted from their place of flourishing, and especially about their depressed spirit, on the pain and agony of the people of the city of Volozhin who were bereaved and wept bitterly over the closing of the Yeshiva, similar to the destruction of the Holy Temple, and did not find comfort for their stormy spirits, until the Yeshiva reopened several years later. Then, it was called the Talmudic Beis Midrash and Library, and was headed by the great Gaon in his generation, Rabbi Rafael Shapira, may the memory of the righteous be blessed, the son-in-law of the Netzi'v may the memory of the righteous be blessed. He restored its crown to its former status, albeit not to the same extent and essence as it was during the period of the Netzi'v, may the memory of the righteous be blessed.

The elders of Volozhin would speak with deep wonder about the Seders on Passover nights conducted by the Netzi'v, may the memory of the righteous be blessed, in the presence of hundreds of his students. The Seders were conducted with everyone together, were wondrous to the eye and joyous to the hearts and continued until dawn. After the people of Volozhin concluded the Seders in their houses, they would stream to the House of the Rabbi to look, hear, and enjoy the splendor of the Divine presence that pervaded there. A special, sublime influence was felt when he delivered his novel Torah ideas. The joy of the festival, with the recital of the Haggadah and the songs was wonderful. Fortunate is the eye that witnessed this!

In addition to the books of the Netzi'v that were published during his lifetime and shortly after his passing – his holy manuscripts on the entire Talmud, on the Mechilta, and other works were recently published. His sermons, guarded by his son Rabbi Meir Berlin (Bar-Ilan) of blessed memory, were organized, edited, and published in a splendid fashion by his grandson Rabbi Yisrael Isser Shapira, may he live long, of Tel Aviv, and with the assistance of the grandson of the Netzi'v, Rabbi Naftali Tzvi Yehuda Riff, may he live long, in America, and the president of the Volozhin Yeshiva of Bnei Brak.

B.

The years of the existence of the Yeshiva after the era of Rabbi Chaim of Volozhin and his son Rabbi Itzele can be divided into three eras.

i. *The era of the Netzi'v.* During his days, the Yeshiva reached its pinnacle, and attained worldwide influence. Its existence continued until the closing of the yeshiva by the government of Russia in the year 5652 [1892].
ii. *The era of Rabbi Rafael.* When the Yeshiva was reopened through the efforts of the faithful of the Yeshiva and the trustees in Vilna and Minsk, and with the approval of the administrators of Volozhin, Rabbi Rafael Shapira, may the memory of the righteous be blessed, was invited to serve as the head of the rabbinical court and head of the Yeshiva of Volozhin. He opened the Yeshiva in the year 5659 [1899] and stood at its helm until the First World War reached Volozhin, and the aforementioned Gaon was forced to move to Minsk with his household and the Yeshiva. He died there and was buried in honor. May his soul be bound in the bonds of eternal life.
iii. *The era of Rabbi Yaakov Shapira the son of Rabbi Rafael.* He took the place of his father as the head of the rabbinical court and head of the Yeshiva of Volozhin. He opened the gates of the Yeshiva when he returned from Minsk after the war in the year 5681 [1921].

[Page 191]

and stood at its head until close to the Second World War. When he died in the year 5696 [1936], the leadership of the Yeshiva passed to his son-in-law Rabbi Chaim, the son of Rabbi Aharon Wolkin, may G-d avenge his blood, and to Rabbi Yitzchak Moshe, may G-d avenge his blood, and Rabbi Zalman Yosef, may G-d avenge his blood, sons of Rabbi Yaakov Shapira, may the memory of the righteous be blessed. However, destruction quickly overtook them and the entire *Beit Harav* of Volozhin, as well as all its holy students who basked in the shade of Etz Chaim, along with all the people of Volozhin, may G-d venge their blood. All were murdered with cruel deaths, through great physical and spiritual torture, and gave up their pure souls to Heaven, may G-d avenge their blood. May their souls be bound in the bonds of eternal life. Thus concluded the era of the existence of the Yeshiva in its sanctuary in Volozhin, which disseminated Torah and light to Israel through the years 5567-5699 [1807-1939]. "The enemy cast its hand upon all its precious ones," the treasury of the preciousness of the House of Israel. The wellsprings of Torah and knowledge of G-d ceased. The world became dark for us. May   G-d have mercy!

We must mention two other of the lions of the group who served in splendid fashion as heads of the Yeshiva during the era of the Netzi'v, may the memory of the righteous be blessed. They are the great Gaon Rabbi Chaim Berlin, the son of the Gaon the Netzi'v. He made *aliya* to the Holy Land at the end of his days and was numbered among the heads of the rabbis of Jerusalem, where he was buried in honor. The second is the mighty Gaon Rabbi Chaim Halevi Soloveitchik, the son of the Gaon Rabbi Yosef Dov Halevi, may the memory of the righteous be blessed. He was considered as one of the unique ones in the world of Torah. He created a new methodology in the understanding of Torah and forged a new path in the sea of Talmud. He lit up a path between the waves of the great sea and illuminated the eyes of the sages in all hidden, concealed matters in the Talmud and halachic decision of the Rambam of blessed memory. His way and methodology were accepted as proper in the great centers of Torah in Israel. In addition to the greatness and loftiness of these Gaonim in Torah, they were also known for their charity, abstinence, pureness of character, and pleasant ways.

When I now come to describe to a small degree the stature of the heads of the Yeshiva during the second and third eras, with the illustrious father and son, princes of Torah, Gaonim and Tzadikim, Rabbi Rafael and his son Rabbi Yaakov Shapira, may the memory of the Holy be blessed – "I am in awe as I open my mouth to speak, I lack knowledge, so how can I hope"[3]. In order to extend proper appreciation, it is necessary to recognize and discuss the fine traits of their high-level souls, their nobility and righteousness. One must understand and delve into the depths of their intellect, the breadth of their hearts, and the purity of their souls. We must give proper expression to the dedication of their souls to learn, teach, observe, perform, and fulfil. Everything that we will write about them will not fulfil our obligation toward our holy rabbis, may they rest in peace, who are beyond our conceptualization. The words of the *Nefesh Hahayim* portray them as follows: "The flame of the love of our holy Torah burned in their hearts like a fire burning with the love and fear of the pure G-d. Their entire desire was to aggrandize and glorify its honor, and to expand their bounds through many proper students, so that the land will be filled with understanding."

Who is so great for us as our rabbi, Rabbi Chaim of Volozhin, may he rest in peace. When he would mention the name of his rabbi, the holy Gaon the Gr'a of Vilna, may the memory of the righteous be a blessing, "my entire body would shake, and my hands would tremble from the holiness of his wonderful Torah and the awe of the sublimity of the Torah on his face." As for us, what can we answer after him? For our sages have said, "Let the fear of your rabbi be like the fear of Heaven!" But, in order to enter into the tents of the holy ones: during the lives of the martyrs of Volozhin "who were beloved and pleasant during their lives, and not parted in their deaths." [II Samuel, 1:23] – I hereby write some brief lines about the greatness and activities of these martyrs,

[Page 192]

to the extent that my weak hand and my meager pen can reach, and I pray that I do not, Heaven forbid, damage their high and lofty honor, may they rest in peace.

Our rabbi, Rabbi Rafael of blessed memory, is known and famous in the world of Torah for his classes in *halacha* that he gave in the Yeshiva, as the architect of the methodology of "in accordance with its methodology [*beshitato*]." Thanks to his wonderful expertise in all aspects of Torah, and in the hidden vaults, in the Babylonian and Jerusalem Talmuds, Tosefta, Mechilta, Sifra, Sifrei, and books by the greats of the early decisors, as well as his knowledge of the masters of tradition, his power was good and he had the ability to straighten out the crooked, and to explain difficult matters in the realities of Abayey and Rabba [Talmudic sages], and to resolve Talmudic passages in accordance with Maimonides of blessed memory in "his methodology." With all his wonderful expertise, he had a depth of diligence all his life. He did the majority of his studying and wrote his responsa during the nights, when the issues of the city and the Yeshiva did not disturb him. His students relate that early in the morning, after a night of study, near sunrise, he would recite the morning *Shema* with its melody and special enunciation. The students who had studied "*Mishmar*" [an all-night study session] would gather around the windows to hear the recitation of the *Shema* from their rabbi. They were moved, and this was more effective than may reproofs, for they had seen a living Torah scroll and a living book of morality.

Rabbi Rafael was also known as taciturn. He would hold back from speaking an extra word. He would even limit his speaking during rabbinical gatherings which took place several times in his presence in his house. When a young Yeshiva man came to him to receive his rabbinical ordination, or a rabbinical author came to receive an approbation for his work, and custom would have it that he would request to present before the rabbi some novel idea or explanation of a difficult Talmudic passage, with the verdict of the decisors, he would not debate or engage in didactics with the speaker. Rather, after hearing his words, he would immediately approach the bookshelf, remove a book, and show him his novel ideas on the debate regarding the issue at hand.

His brilliance covered his charitable and benevolent deeds that he performed quietly and discreetly. Only certain special people and members of his household knew of his activities in the realm of salvation for the individual and the community. When the economic and material situation in the Yeshiva was bad, and the debts began to afflict and oppress, Rabbi Rafael spared no effort or toil. He would gird himself like a lion, and travel to visit our philanthropist brethren, sometimes along with his son-in-law Rabbi Chaim Soloveitchik or one of the talented young men of the Yeshiva. In this manner, he would assure the continued existence of the Yeshiva. Through he wrote many holy manuscripts on the entire Talmud, as well as many responsa to his questioners on issues of religion and law (which he would write with a feather pen, due to the commandment, "you shall not lift an iron [tool] upon it."[4]) – only a small portion were published, on matters related to the Orach Chayim [section of the Code of Jewish Law]. These were published by his great children – the Gaon Rabbi Aryeh Shapira, may the memory of the holy be blessed, and may he be granted good life, the Gaon Rabbi Yisrael Isser Shapira of Tel Aviv. This was called *Torat Rafael*. He would sign his letters as "He who performs the work of the Torah in Volozhin."

The son, the Gaon and Tzadik Rabbi Yaakov Shapira, may the memory of the righteous be blessed, was like the father. When he returned to Volozhin from Minsk after the war, having endured all the tribulations of the journey (he was imprisoned by the Yevseka [KGB division responsible for Jews], was given a harsh sentence, and was saved through a miracle) – when he arrived in Volozhin, he found a desolate world, and was forced to create something from nothing.

[Page 193]

Through the mercies of G-d, he opened the gates of the Yeshiva, restored the crown to its former status, and disseminated the light of Torah. His classes excelled in clarity and proper explanation, in breadth of expertise, and in understanding. His words were illuminating and brought joy. Through his nobility, refined personality, and splendor of countenance, he would evoke honor and reverence in the eyes of all who saw him and would influence his hundreds of students to dwell at the gates of Torah and fear of Heaven, and to acquire wholesomeness of the soul through toiling in Torah. He also led his community in Volozhin with a pleasant staff. He followed the footsteps of his father and other rabbinical ancestors, of the cream of the crop, in all his ways and actions.

Rabbi Yaakov Shapira

It is appropriate to point out that the gentiles in Volozhin and the area recognized him as a symbol of justice and uprightness and revered him greatly. When they had disputes in matters of business or the like with Jews, they preferred to go to the rabbi, and did not want to rely on their own courts. The words of the rabbi were holy in their eyes, for they knew that he had no tendency to self-interest or to give preference to any side. This was a sanctification of the Divine Name.

The writer of these lines – who is the son-in-law of the Gaon and Tzadik, of blessed memory – sat in his presence and perfumed himself with his perfume. He saw him in various situations during the course of his life – whether standing at the heights of his splendor as a teacher and rabbinical judge, or during his difficult illness and oppressive suffering – and merited to hear his classes in *halacha* at the Yeshiva, his sermons and statements before his community, and even took note of his care and diligence in the observance of the commandments of the Torah with all details and embellishments. He saw his piety and responsibility as a pastor and a leader, and participated with him in his worries, efforts, and intercessions to strengthen the pillars of Etz Chaim, so it would not falter, Heaven forbid. Afterward, he saw him convulsing with his tribulations. I am the man who saw his suffering[5] as he was lying on the operating table in Vienna and on his sickbed in Warsaw, in his suffering and difficulties. There are no words in my mouth to express the raging of the stormy heart and the feelings of agony to the depths of the soul when, during his suffering and pain, he would read the verses "I will raise up the cup of salvation and call out in the name of G-d"; "I find difficulty and agony – and I will call out in the name of G-d"; "I will sing of graciousness and judgment"; "He tore, and He will heal me – He struck, and will bind me." During all circumstances and times, his hands were steadfast to guard the Yeshiva, the focus of his splendor, until the sun set. Regarding him, they said,

"The life of a sage is a long prayer." He died at the age of 62 in Warsaw and was brought to the burial canopy of his grandfather, our Rabbi Chaim, in the cemetery of Volozhin. He commanded that it be declared in all the synagogues of the city that he hereby requests forgiveness from anyone who has some complaint against him or feels that their honor or money was damaged. Thus, he ascended to Heaven holy and pure as the splendor of the firmament.

[Page 194]

The minutest amount of his classes that he disseminated among his students were published by the writer of these lines, with the title *Gaon Yaakov*. A bit about his methodology, his holy ways, and his life story are described in the introduction to that book. The rest of his holy manuscripts that he wrote about the Talmud were destroyed by the murderers.

Rabbi Chaim Wolkin

As had been said above, after his death, the Yeshiva passed to the leadership of his son-in-law, the Gaon Rabbi Chaim Wolkin, may G-d avenge his blood, may his memory be a blessing, and to his two illustrious sons, Rabbi Moshe Yitzchak, may G-d avenge his blood, and Rabbi Zalman Yosef, may G-d avenge his blood, who hoped to continue the dynasty in the rule of Torah in Volozhin. Both were cut off in their prime, as they were sprouting and growing, and did not merit to see their world in their lifetime. Rabbi Chaim Wolkin ran the Yeshiva and concerned himself for its spiritual and physical wellbeing for about two years in Volozhin, and for some time afterwards when it was exiled to Vilna at the beginning of the war. Many details about his prominent personality are not known to the writer of these lines, for I made *aliya* to the Land of Israel still in the lifetime of my father-in-law the Gaon Rabbi Yaakov Shapira, may the memory of the righteous be blessed. It is known that Rabbi Chaim Wolkin was educated in the *Beis Midrash* of the Mussar greats and was a veteran student of the Gaon and Tzadik Rabbi Yerucham, of blessed memory, the spiritual director of the Mir Yeshiva, and would travel to him to confer. He also led the Yeshiva in that direction. He was honored by all who knew him. It is known that he gave up his holy soul to the Heavens through terrible torments, in the common grave in the fields of Ponary in Vilna, as he was standing guard for Torah and fear of Heaven, in holiness and purity, along with his wife the Rebbetzin Beila, the daughter of the Gaon Rabbi Yaakov Shapira, may the memory of the righteous be blessed, and their two young daughters Dreizel and Chaya Leah, may G-d avenge their blood. The words of the liturgical poet apply to him: "Woe regarding the tongue that hastened to instruct with beautiful words – how you lick the dust due to sins."[6] It is very sorrowful and bitter for us regarding these two beautiful Shapiras [in the original: *Shofrei Shapira*] whom the ground swallowed up, from the family of "The House of the Rabbi" in Volozhin. The prominent woman of valor, the G-d fearing Rebbetzin Sheina Disha the son of Rabbi Zalman Yosef, may G-d avenge her blood, and her daughters Esther of blessed memory, Rivka, may G-d avenge her blood, and Pesia, may G-d avenge her blood – the righteous daughters, wholesome in all lofty traits – all of them were cut off before their time, holy and pure like the splendor of the firmament, they were murdered in sanctification of the Divine Name. May G-d avenge their blood, may G-d remember them for the good with all the martyrs of this prominent family of Israel. May their memories be holy and blessed forever.

Among the great rabbis who lived and exerted influence during the era of our Rabbi Yaakov Shapira, may the memory of the righteous be blessed, we should also mention the rabbi and Gaon Rabbi Shmuel Avigdor Halevi Derechinski, the honorable son-in-law of the praiseworthy rabbi and Gaon, Rabbi Hillel Fried, may the memory of the righteous be blessed, one of the grandchildren of the "House of the Rabbi" of Volozhin. He served for a time

[Page 195]

as the *mashgiach* [spiritual overseer] in the Yeshiva and was later appointed as the rabbinical judge and teacher of righteousness in Volozhin. He made *aliya* with his family to the Land of Israel at the end of his days and is buried in honor in Jerusalem. Two compositions of Torah novellae were published by his wife the Rebbetzin, peace be upon her.

We should also note the elderly, venerable rabbi, Rabbi Yehuda Avraham of blessed memory, who was a *shochet* in Volozhin also in the era of our rabbi the Netzi'v of blessed memory. He was one of the faithful ones of the House of the Rabbi, and was involved with the Yeshiva students, as he was an expert in the laws of *shechita* [ritual slaughter] and *treifot* [slaughtered animals with defects]. He died a few years before the Second World War. [We also note] Rabbi Yosef the son of Rabbi Chaim Tabchowitz, may G-d avenge his blood, and his family. He was one of the veterans of the Yeshiva and city notables.

Thus ends the glorious history of the great, ancient host of Torah in its dwelling place in Volozhin.

C.

The building of the Volozhin Yeshiva in Bnei Brak

The merit of the fathers and the merit of the martyrs, may they rest in peace stand with us to guard the coal, so it won't extinguish, and on the eternal light so its light won't falter. With the manifold mercies of G-d, we have succeeded in setting up a candle, a name and a remnant for the holy, fine Yeshiva to continue the golden chain in the Holy Land. We merited to set up the building of the Yeshiva of Volozhin in Bnei Brak, fluttering in its splendor as a center and fortress of Torah. It includes a Kollel for young men [Kollel Avreichim] with excellent scholars. There is also a Yeshiva for youths. They all immerse themselves in Torah with success, blessed be G-d. It disseminates Torah and light in a praiseworthy and blessed fashion.

[Page 196]

It is run by the writer of these lines, the son-in-law of our rabbi, head of the rabbinical court and final Yeshiva head of Volozhin. Its honorable president is Rabbi Naftali Tzvi Yehuda Riff, may he live long, the rabbi and head of the rabbinical court in Camden (U.S.A.), a grandson of the Gaon Rabbi Rafael Shapira, may the memory of the holy be blessed. He bears the burden of the Yeshiva and is diligent with maintaining it in a blessed fashion, as the benevolent hand of G-d.

The Yeshiva of Volozhin in the Land of Israel also contains a memorial monument to the Yeshiva Heads, their descendants, as well as to the martyrs of the city of Volozhin, who were their hosts for several generations. May it be His will that they have spiritual contentment and elevation of their souls. We pray that their merit shall stand with us to strengthen the pillars of Etz Chaim, so that they shall not weaken, Heaven forbid, and that they be good intercessors and presenters of merits that we may succeed in expanding its bounds, in firming up its existence, in aggrandizing Torah and disseminating its light.

Here is the place to express appreciation and recognition to our brethren-friends, Volozhin natives in the United States, and to all the members of the Etz Chaim Anshei Volozhin Synagogue in New York, headed by its honorable president, and especially to our honorable friends, active and excellent, who maintain the faith in the holy, ancient Yeshiva, and extend to us a hand of assistance in a generous fashion – that is Rabbi Nachman Rothstein, may he live long, and Mr. Dr. Avraham Jablis, may his light shine, who work faithfully and with dedication to ensure the existence and strengthening of the Yeshiva of Volozhin. May G-d remember them for the good!

Translator's footnotes:

1. A poetic term for the Temple. There is a play on words here as the word mouth *pi* is embedded in the word *Talpiot*.
2. See Kina 20 of Tisha B'av Morning (from Sefaria: https://www.sefaria.org/Kinnot_for_Tisha_B'Av_(Ashkenaz)%2C_Kinot_for_Tisha_B'Av_Day.2 1.2?lang=bi) Where the term "Cedars of Lebanon, Mighty in Torah" is used to describe great Torah scholars.
3. From the opening of the chazzan's repetition of the *Shacharit Amida* on the first day of Rosh Hashanah.
4. Deuteronomy 27:5, referring to the sacrificial altar. He obviously considered his Torah writings as a form of offering.
5. Based on Lamentations 3:1.
6. From the hymn of the Ten Martyrs from *Musaf* of Yom Kippur.

[Page 197]

The Yeshiva of Volozhin During the Period of the Gaon Rabbi Rafael Shapira

by Dr. Hirsh-Leib Gordon, New York

Translated by Jerrold Landau

After the Passover holiday of 5670 (1910), I set out on a journey. I set out to the Etz Chaim Yeshiva of Volozhin. The train was full of travelers, laden with baskets and cases. The tumult was great. However, when the train started to move, a feeling of calm fell upon me, and I was like a daydreamer, enchanted from vision of the past that wove in my imagination. With the eyes of my spirit, I saw Rabbi Chaim, the founder of the Yeshiva. I knew that they go to supplicate at the grave of Rabbi Chaim every Lag B'Omer, and shoot decorated wooden arrows there as a symbolic memorial.

The conductor called aloud "Stacja Mołodeczno" [Mołodeczno Station]. A woke up as if from a deep sleep. I quickly took my straw suitcase and transferred to another train that went to Połłoczany. From there, I traveled to the city of Volozhin itself by wagon, laden with several Yeshiva students with their suitcases. This was the adorned Volozhin to which my father came in the year 1892, 18 years previously, before my birth. It was the same road, the same destination, the same holy awe…

Someone prepared a dwelling for me at the residence of the Yeshiva students. The mistress of the house was a simple woman named Sara, who was married to the stepson of the assistant mail carrier. Ozer was well placed, for he had been one of the Cantonists, a military man who had served Nikolai for 40 years, and remained faithful to his religion and family. Like the rest of the Cantonists, he was prone to anger and unpleasant toward his fellow. The elderly soldier, with a yellow beard that had turned white, already stopped carrying and distributing the mail. His work was done by his yellow-haired granddaughter. Not only did she distribute the mail, but she also opened the letters and gave them over to the *Mashgiach* [spiritual supervisor] of the Yeshiva. She did the same with the letters that the Yeshiva students were sending from Volozhin to their parents. Due to this stringent supervision, the Yeshiva students were always prepared to take advantage of various contradictions and excuses if something improper was found in their letters.

When I arrived at the residence that they had chosen for me, and before I was able to open the door, a crazy man, grown wildly, stopped me. Later I was informed that this was Antoni, the town fool. He removed his hat and offered me a petition for the Czar. He turned to me in Russian, "Honorable sir, here I have a request to his majesty the Czar, to have mercy upon me and not send me to Siberia as a criminal. In the petition, I outlined all the details of the accusation that they placed upon my head. Now, sir, please save me and copy my petition in clear handwriting, so that his majesty the Czar will see that I am innocent of guilt." Someone winked at me with one eye that this person is not of sane mind. In any case, I was forced to copy the petition without delay in order to free myself from this evil affliction.

At lunchtime, I got to know the Yeshiva students who lived in my residence.

Among the group of residents was Meir Bogdanovski of Ashmyany, an intelligent, enthusiastic lad.

[Page 198]

He revealed to me the secret that he was intending to travel to the Land of Israel at the end of the term, in order to study at the teachers seminary there. When I came to the Land of Israel in 1914 and was hospitalized in the Shaarei Zion hospital of Jaffa, Bogdanovski came to visit me. When I asked him whether he intended to return to Russia, he answered me in a serious fashion, "Under no circumstances. You see, a Hebrew republic will yet be established, and my fervent desire is that I be part of the government." A prophecy came forth from his mouth...

After I got to know my neighbors in the inn, I walked together with them to the Yeshiva building, which was close to our residence. We first reached the "House of the Rabbi" [*Beit Harav*], which was the official dwelling place of the Yeshiva head and his family. On the right of the lane with the *Beit Harav*, there was a poor bookseller. From there, we went down and reached the Yeshiva itself, which made a strong impression upon me. It was a spacious building with two large gates. Next to the right gate, there was an inscription "Established in the year 5563" (1803). That was the year of the founding of the Yeshiva.

The impression of the inside of the Yeshiva was even greater than that of the outside. As soon as I opened the large door, hundreds of voices echoed in my ears. These were the voices of the lads who were not official students of the Yeshiva, and were studying from the older lads (called "*Talmidim*" [students]), as well as the voices of the older students. Some were monotonous and others had a pleasant melody. Most of the Yeshiva students did not pay attention to the new people who entered the hall, for they were immersed in their studies. However, some greeted the newcomers.

In the large hall, there were four strong, square pillars. There were long tables and benches along the length of the walls. I was advised to choose a seat. I chose a place next to the left pillar, opposite the place of the Yeshiva head. That is where I sat during my entire time at the Yeshiva. They explained to me that the rabbi, Rabbi Rafael, did not give a class on account of his age, for he was 79 years old. However, it was possible for the Yeshiva students to go to *Beit Harav* to ask him a question. Rabbi Rafael only entered the

Yeshiva during the time of the prayer services. He would elongate his recitation of the *Shema*, as he pronounced it syllable by syllable, as someone counting gold. He was careful with the enunciation of the words, with the dots and silent vowels, and was careful to pause in places that one is supposed to pause. It was quiet throughout the entire hall when the rabbi recited the *Shema*, especially when he repeated several times, with emphasis, "And you shall speak about them"[1].

I must mention here Yehuda Avrahamel the *shochet*, who would serve as the prayer leader in the Yeshiva for decades. He was a tall Jew, and he served as the prayer leader during my entire time in Volozhin. He would raise his long arms before his Creator and pray with enthusiasm. We, the Yeshiva students, would also look into an open Gemara during the times of prayers, for the words of Torah are "eternal life." We should note that the Yeshiva had a sort of autonomy, and it was forbidden for anyone who was not a student to enter its threshold other than for the *Simchat Beit Shoeva*[Sukkot night celebrations]. However, this Yehuda Avrahamel was an exception. (Incidentally, he was a relative of Daniel Perski of blessed memory and of Shimon Peres.)

Near the pillar close to the place that I chose as my seat, I met a lad from Novoborisov named Ben-Zion Peker,

[Page 199]

from New York. He now serves as the director of the United Jewish Appeal. He was secretly enlightened, and would constantly read Zionist periodicals in the Russian language, *Rozsvyet, Vyshgod,* and *Yevreiskaya Starina,* which he guarded as the apple of his eye. In America, he was the deputy editor of the *Haivri* weekly, and authored an important article, "The Volozhin Yeshiva" in the Anthology of Lithuania, 1951.

I purchased a new desk from the *shamash*, which had a special compartment with a yarmulka, and *Sav Shmatta*, a small book by the author of *Ketzot Hachoshen*, which was dear to me and the other lads. The author wrote it while he was still a lad below the age of thirteen. This was a good portent for a Yeshiva student to evoke novel ideas during his studies. The jealousy of scribes increases wisdom.

The sounds of Torah in the Yeshiva of Volozhin never ceased from the day of its founding, neither during the day or the night, neither during the winter or the summer. The lads whose turn it was to be on *mishmar* at night would come at 8:00 p.m. and study with great diligence until the light of the morning. The Rebbetzin or the *shamash* would bring servings of apples to the students on *mishmar*. There were lads who studied during the night after the regular evening study session even when it was not their turn. During these quiet hours of the night the students would not study in a methodological fashion or deal with difficulties, but would rather study for breadth expertise [*bekiyut*]. The tractate that as dear to us, that we studied during the hours of *mishmar*, was generally *Makkot*, on account of its brevity.

The freedom in Volozhin to choose any tractate and study it slowly or quickly encouraged us to try several experiments in study methodology. The stress on the straightforward meaning and the distancing from didactics [*pilpul*] was the way of the Gr'a, and was the regulation in the Yeshiva of Volozhin. The customs of worship were also according to the Gr'a. For example, on the High Holidays, they would minimise the recital of hymns and poetry. Even on Yom Kippur, we would have several free hours, which we dedicated to the study of Gemara. I recall that on Yom Kippur, an elderly, weak Jew stood near the left pillar and worshiped in a low, heartbreaking voice. This was Rabbi Chaim Hillel Fried, the great-grandson of Rabbi Chaim of Volozhin.

They would primarily study Gemara in the Yeshiva of Volozhin. We did not study Mishna as a separate subject. We also only heard about *Baraita* (*Tosefta*, *Mechilta*, *Sifra*, and *Sifri*) on an incidental basis. I do not recall whether I saw a Yeshiva student dealing with the *Sheiltot* of Rabbi Achai Gaon, which was published with a commentary by the Netzi'v. Certain special people would study all the tractates of the Talmud, but for the most part, we would focus on the three *Bavas*, *Ketuvot*, *Nedarim*, *Gittin*, *Kiddushin*, and then restart that cycle. We would study these seven tractates, and no others. I never saw the Jerusalem Talmud at all.

The Yeshiva students never looked into the *Ein Yaakov* or the *Zohar*, but the *Yad Chazaka* of Maimonides and the *Shulchan Aruch* of Rabbi Yosef Caro were often on our desks. More than we occupied ourselves with the *Tur* and *Shulchan Aruch* [Code of Jewish Law], we were diligent with several of their commentators, such as the *Ketzot Hachoshen* (by Rabbi Aryeh Leib Hakohen), *Netivot Hamishpat* (by Rabbi Yaakov of Lissa), *Turei Zahav* (by Rabbi David the son of Rabbi Shmuel Halevi), *Siftei Kohen* (by Rabbi Shabtai Hakohen), *Chatam Sofer* (by Rabbi Moshe Sofer), and *Shita Mekubetzet* (by Rabbi Betzalel Ashkenazi). Also precious to us

[Page 200]

was *Hateshuvot* [the responsa] of Rabbi Akiva Eiger and *Chidushav* [his novellae], and the books of Rabbi Yitzchak Elchanan Spector (*Nachal Yitzchak*, *Beer Yitzchak*, and *Ein Yitzchak*). However, most precious of them all was *Ketzot Hachoshen*, due to its sharpness and depth of penetration.

Volozhin was divided into two parts, like uptown and downtown in American cities. The upper area was known as *Aroiftzu* in Yiddish. That is where the Yeshiva and residences for the Yeshiva students were located. The most important road in this part was Vilna Street. There was also the orchard of Baron Tyskiwiecz, which enchanted the eye with its treasury of colors and tropical fruits. The majority of the town in size and in structure was *Aroptzu* (the lower part of the city). Most of the shops, workshops, tradespeople and regular householders were there. This was almost a unique community with its own rabbi. I recall that once I heard a sort of concert sound from one of the houses. I surmised that this the melody of a student of the Grodno Courses, which was founded in 1907 under the direction of the well-known pedagogue Aharon the son of Moshe Kahanstam. I knocked on the door and if I was not mistaken, the player was Bunimowicz, a student of the courses.

There was a round hill with an abundance of flowers next to Volozhin. It was called Yarmulka on account of its shape. We would stroll there on Sabbaths, chat, sing, and also do all sorts of physical exercise. The Double Mountain Summit was next to this hill. It was called that because every voice or sound made in the area would be head with a double echo.

My circle of acquaintances slowly grew. Among the first was the son of the rabbi of Pohost (Pinchas Churgin of blessed memory), who was nicknamed "The miniature Jerusalem." He sat immersed in his Gemara next to the last pillar on the left side, with a goodhearted smile on his lips. He belonged to our narrow circle that met in the cellar after the studies, where we enjoyed youthful games – like actual boys and not like students of the Yeshiva of Volozhin.

After four years, we made a big jump, from Volozhin to the University of Y.Y.L., from which we graduated in 1922. Churgin was highly active in the Mizrachi movement. He led the teachers seminary and later Bar-Ilan University until his untimely death. A lad from Rochwalow, David Cohen, the "Grandfather" of Hanaar Haoved [Working Youth] was also part of our group He wore a long Hassidic mantle, and wrote *Sipurei Hassidim* [Stories of Hassidim] in Tel Aviv.

There was a young Yeshiva student who always searched through books, and always strolled in the large hall among the older Yeshiva students. He was called the Warsawer and the Lodzer (Yitzchak Rivkind of blessed memory). He subscribed to *Hashiloach* and *Haolam*, aside from *Hatzefira* and *Hed Hazman*. He was an expert in the history of the Volozhin Yeshiva. His interest in the Mizrachi movement brought him close to a great person, who later married the daughter of his wife's brother. I refer to the rabbi of Gombin [Gąbin], Rabbi Y. L. Zlotnick, later Avida. I remember him as a young man, with a long beard, wearing a Hassidic hat on his head and a rabbinical cloak. He was very diligent in his studies, and did not want to spend a moment without learning. He stood near

[Page 201]

his desk, studying without stop. It seemed as if he had nothing in his world other than the four ells of *halacha*. However, when he left Volozhin, we were surprised to read his articles in Hatzefira, which he signed with the pseudonym "Bar Bei Rav De Chad Yoma" [Rabbi for one day] (winter of 5671 [1911]). He lived in the United States and Canada, and later was the director of Jewish education in South Africa (1938). At the end, he settled in Jerusalem (1940), where he immersed himself in Torah and Divine service. He wrote a great deal about folklore, like an overflowing wellspring. He died a few days ago.

In the diary that I kept while I was studying in Volozhin, there were novel ideas on Torah, technical derivations (such as the theory of instruction for telegraph officials), games of chess, and... a constant toothache. The pain did not stop even though the city doctor extracted an inflamed tooth with simple tongs. Once, when the pain was unbearable, and I could not find any remedy in the middle of the night, I went outside to ask for advice. This was on a summer night when the rays of dawn were lighting up the east. I suddenly remembered that in a small enclosure next to the house there was a chicken coop with one- or two-day old chicks. I took a lovely, tiny chick and placed it on my chest. The tiny creature fell asleep because he trusted me. The image of the tiny, weak chick sleeping on my chest gave me so much pleasure that my toothache stopped. I did that several times, and the ruse was effective.

Translator's footnote:

1. Deuteronomy 6:7. One of the Biblical sources for the commandment of studying Torah.

[Page 202]

About Rabbi Rafael Shapira

Translated by Jerrold Landau

"And I remember that during the days of my youth, when I studied Torah in the Yeshiva of Volozhin for a few years during the time of the Gaon and Tzadik, Rabbi Rafael, may the memory of the righteous be blessed – we had no need for books on fear of G-d or morality in order to merit such traits, for our teacher and rabbi served for us, through his Torah and righteousness, as a sort of living Torah school, a book with everything in it. His straightforwardness and great enthusiasm themselves taught us the ways of awe and morality. – – –

Whomever has not seen the great diligence of the Gaon Rabbi Rafael, may the memory of the righteous be blessed, does not now what diligence in Torah is. The dedication of his soul to Torah, and his true righteousness cannot be described. Every lad or young man of the Yeshiva was beloved and dear to him, somewhat like the love of fathers to their only sons.

Most of the Yeshiva students who were then in the Yeshiva of Volozhin would learn for 18 hours each day. The sounds of Torah never stopped in the Yeshiva for a moment, for every night there were students who studied *mishmar* throughout the entire night. Even on the night of Passover, the night of the Seder, the *mishmar* of studiers in the Yeshiva did not stop. After one *mishmar* round finished conducting their Passover Seder, they immediately came to the Yeshiva to switch with their friends who were learning up to that time, so that they too could conduct the Seder. Even at the conclusion of the *Maariv* service on the night following Yom Kippur, a number of students remained in the Yeshiva to study rather than going to their dwellings to break their fast, until their friends who had already broken their fast arrived at the Yeshiva to swap places with them. Thus, the Yeshiva students studied Torah day and night, without any interruption in the sounds of Torah even for a minute."

(Yosef Segal Halevi, *Chazon Yosef* book, pp. 6, 7)

"When I bring to my memory the era of life in the Yeshiva of Volozhin, an internal joy fills all the crevices of my heart, like a person who feels some important event in his life. Immediately the central, noble image in the Yeshiva stands before me, the great, righteous, pure Gaon, Rabbi Rafael Shapira, may he memory of the righteous be blessed. He was the symbol of holiness and pure straightforwardness, which is hard to describe in words. However, to hear his prayers or his recitation of the *Shema* was sufficient to be influenced deeply by him and attracted to him, to bind oneself with thousands of strands of the soul. He especially left a great impression upon those who studied all night, and were able to be witnesses to his remaining awake all night, by way of the light in his house that was next to the Yeshiva. Someone looking in could see that he was awake and studying for almost the entire night. Sometimes, he would enter the Yeshiva in the middle of the night, and would walk back and forth several times, and then leave, wearing his tallit and tefillin. He would remain for an hour after the services in the morning, and the students would have a good opportunity to discuss their studies with him."

(Rabbi Aryeh Leib Jochet, *Mishnat Aryeh*, "With the Yeshivot" page 271.)

[Page 203]

The Volozhin Scholars

[Page 204]Blank [Page 205]

Three Torah Pillars in Volozhin

by Eliezer Leoni (Tel Aviv)

Translated by Jerrold Landau

A.

Rabbi Yosef Dov HaLevi Soloveitchik

Rabbi Yosef Dov Soloveitchik was one of the supporting pillars in the pantheon of Volozhin sages. He was the great-grandson of Rabbi Chaim of Volozhin. He was born in Nesvizh in the year 5590 (1820). Already from his childhood, it became clear that he was created for greatness, that he was thoroughly sharp, that he had a deep power of memory, that he was diligent to the point where he knew no rest, and that he had the ability to penetrate the depths of *halacha*. All this portended that a bright star was passing through the skies of Talmudic Jewry.

At the age of thirteen, his father sent him to the Etz Chaim Yeshiva of Volozhin. At first he studied Torah from the rabbinical judge Rabbi Shimshon Rodanski, and later from his rabbis Rabbi Itzele (his father's uncle) and his [i.e. Rabbi Itzele's] son-in-law Rabbi Eliezer-Yitzchak Fried. His hidden talents began to develop in the Yeshiva of Volozhin. He separated himself from the pleasures of life and strove day and night in Torah. By the age of fifteen he was renown as a genius with great knowledge. Rabbi Itzele predicted that he will become a Gaon in Israel, and through his sharpness, he would reach the level of the Shaagas Aryeh.

When the Gaon Rabbi Gershon Tanchum, the head of the Blumke Yeshiva of Minsk, became ill, he approached Rabbi Itzele with the request that he send him one of his greatest students to deliver the class to the lads. Rabbi Itzele chose his sister's grandson, the young Rabbi Yosi Ber, for this task. His classes in the Yeshiva granted renown to his name, and he became known as one of the Torah greats.

At the age of Bar Mitzvah [thirteen] he married the daughter of one of the wealthy people, but the match did not work out well, and his father-in-law forced his daughter to separate from her husband, even though she had borne him a daughter. Rabbi Yosi-Ber[1] left Minsk with a heavy heart, and set out for Brod to study Torah from the Gaon Rabbi Shlomo Kluger.

Rabbi Yosi-Ber set out without a coin in his pocket. He used various means to arrive at his destination without paying. When nothing worked, the young Gaon dressed up as the assistant of one of the wagon drivers traveling to Brod. Rabbi Yosi-Ber sat in the cabin of the wagon for three days, with the whip in his right hand and the reins in his left hand. However, since he was not expert in this trade, his work did not find

[Page 206]

favor with his boss, who denigrated him, cursed him, and even beat him. The Gaon accepted the blows and was silent. They arrived at a hotel at the border of Galicia, where a young man who studied at the Yeshiva of Volozhin was staying. He was very shocked at the sight before his eyes, seeing the Gaon Rabbi Yosef Dov driving horses. He disclosed the identity of "the lad assistant" to the wagon driver. The wagon driver approached him and begged forgiveness for the blows. Rabbi Yosi-Ber responded with his great wisdom: "Had I been beaten for words of Torah, I would have felt it unjust. However, you have beaten me over the theory of wagon driving. In that matter, you are my teacher and rabbi."

Rabbi Shlomo Kluger was very astounded at Rabbi Yosi-Ber's depth of understanding, and drew him close. However, for various reasons, he did not stay there for long. He returned to Volozhin after much wandering, and married the daughter of the rabbi of Volozhin, Rabbi Yitzchak Efron.

After the death of Rabbi Eliezer Yitzchak, the Gaonim of the generation decided to appoint Rabbi Yosi-Ber as his successor in the Etz Chaim Yeshiva of Volozhin. Rabbi Yosi-Ber had a writ of the rabbinate from Telz, but the community of Volozhin and all the people of the Yeshiva stopped him, and did not let him leave Volozhin. The two cities presented their cases before a rabbinical court of great rabbis, and the community of Volozhin won the case.

After Rabbi Itzele died, his son-in-law the Netzi'v was appointed as head of the Yeshiva, and Rabbi Yosi-Ber served as second in command. He disseminated Torah in the Yeshiva for approximately twelve years. He demonstrated his powers of didactics [*pilpul*] and sharpness, and the students drank his words with thirst.

Due to the dispute that broke out between Rabbi Yosi-Ber and the Netzi'v, he left Volozhin in the year 5625 (1865) and served as the rabbi of Slutsk. The dispute was based on the fact that Rabbi Yosi-Ber, as a grandson of one of the daughters of Rabbi Chaim of Volozhin, demanded the right to serve as the primary Yeshiva head, whereas the great rabbis determined that the primary Yeshiva head must be the Netzi'v. Rabbi Yosi-Ber did not want to serve as the deputy Yeshiva head, so he left the Yeshiva. However, he did not alienate himself from the Yeshiva. After a few years, his son, Rabbi Chaim, married the granddaughter of the Netzi'v, and was made deputy to the Yeshiva head.

It is told that on the day of the marriage of Rabbi Chaim, the Netzi'v invited his in-law Rabbi Yosi-Ber to dance the Kozak dance with him. In that dance, one dances opposite the other. Rabbi Yosi-Ber responded: "I already tried to dance opposite you one time, my in-law, and I did not succeed."

Rabbi Yosi-Ber occupied the rabbinical seat of Slutsk for approximately ten years. He left the city in the year 5635 (1875) and moved to Warsaw. Many of the greats of Warsaw wished to choose him as the rabbi of the city, but for various reasons they could not actualize their intention. He was chosen as the head of Chevrat Sha's of Warsaw.

He left Warsaw in the year 5638 (1878) and was accepted as rabbi of Brisk, where he served in the rabbinate for approximately 14 years. He was laid to eternal rest in that city. He died through the death of a kiss[ii]. He left his house at the end of the Sabbath to perform the sanctification of the moon, and occupied himself with Torah until after midnight. He felt no pain. However, when he went to bed, he suffered a stroke. Rabbi Yosi-Ber died on 4 Iyar,

[Page 207]

5652 (1892) at the age of 72.

Rabbi Yosi-Ber's death was the cause of heavy mourning even in the community of Jerusalem. The Jews of the city conducted a eulogy for him in the large Beis Yaakov synagogue in the courtyard of Rabbi Yehuda Chassid. The place was filled to the brim.

Rabbi Avraham Abba Yaakov Senderovich was honored with delivering the eulogy for the deceased. He concluded his remarks with an explanation of the verse: "And David slept with his fathers." (I Kings 2:10). "David, left behind a son to take his place, so his death was not felt to a great extent – therefore the term 'and he slept' was used. This tells you that he only went to sleep with his fathers. We can say the same about Rabbi Yosi-Ber, that he went to sleep with his fathers, since he left a son who can take his place – is that not the Gaon Rabbi Chaim Soloveitchik."

Rabbi Baruch HaLevi Epstein writes the following regarding the personality of Rabbi Yosi-Ber:

" Aside from his greatness and excellence in Torah, this great man also excelled with a wise heart. He spoke with clarity and sharpness. His secular speech was spiced with wisdom of the heart, logic of the mind, and pleasant aptitude that attracted the heart, to the point that the ear of the listener was not sated by listening. Further, he was a man of friendship, with a good heart, a fine soul, and a proper spirit within him. These feelings were recognizable every place where he stood, walked, and sat. In general, he was a good man with a pleasant temperament. With all this, his company was beloved and pleasant to different people from a variety of factions…"[1].

Rabbi Yosi-Ber's intelligence and sharpness of mind became famous in the world. We will bring only two examples of this sharpness. One Sabbath, the challahs were missing at the time of the third Sabbath meal, and two challahs could not be found for the double loaves required for the meal. One of those near him said: "Is it not said that one can fulfil the obligation of the third Sabbath meal through words of Torah. If so, what is all the noise about? Can our rabbi not tell us words of Torah, and we will have double enjoyment from this. You will fulfil the obligation of the third Sabbath meal, and we will enjoy the pleasantness of your words of Torah."

Rabbi Yosi-Ber responded: "It is true that this is possible, but this is only possible and not certain, for it could be that one of the listeners will contradict my words. Then, I will be left without Torah and without a third Sabbath meal…"

Once, a Maskil said to Rabbi Yosi-Ber: "From such a great and intelligent rabbi as yourself, one might expect that you will be somewhat lenient in these laws, and not stringent."[iii] Rabbi Yosi-Ber responded: "You have hit the mark. In my books that that I published, and in those that I have in manuscript form, I tend toward leniency and not to stringency. I am very happy that this Maskil has requested that Rabbi-Yosi Ber inform him the reason for these leniencies." He responded, and read out the seven "leniencies," which are as follows:

[Page 208]

1.   Some are stringent to limit the time of the *Maariv* service to midnight, but I am lenient, stating that it is possible to recite the service until dawn.
2.   Some are stringent regarding the tefillin of Rabbeinu Tam[iv], saying that only Torah greats should don them. I am lenient, saying it is permitted for any person to don them.
3.   Some are stringent to not recite *piyyutim* [liturgical poetry] during the prayers, as this might be considered an interruption in the prayers. I am lenient, that is permitted to recite them, and this is not considered an interruption.
4.   Some are stringent with regard to the counting of the Omer, that if a person forgot to count one night, one can no longer count with a blessing. I have decided leniently that one is permitted to count with a blessing.
5.   Some are stringent to avoid studying Torah on the eve of Tisha B'Av that falls on the Sabbath. I have decided leniently, that is permitted to study.
6.   Some are stringent to not fast on Rosh Hashanah. I have decided leniently that it is permitted to fast.
7.   Some are stringent to not observe two days of Yom Kippur[v]. I have decided leniently that one is permitted to observe two days of Yom Kippur.

Rabbi Yosi-Ber was one of the first ones of Chovevei Zion, and worked a great day to disseminate the idea of the return to Zion.

In the year 5625 [1865], he published his first book, titled *Beit HaLevi*, which is a commentary on several isolated chapters of *Choshen Mishpat* [one of the four sections of the Code of Jewish Law] and on several sections of the Talmud. This book brought Rabbi Yosi-Ber fame. Rabbis from far-off places turned to him with difficult, complex questions of *halacha*.

He published his second book, also titled *Beit HaLevi*, in the year 5634 [1874]. In that book, he delved very deeply into the complexities of the Sea of Talmud, and he reveals great depth. Rabbi Ezriel Meir Braude writes , "We do not exaggerate if we state that no precious book, full of sharpness as this one, has appeared on the horizon of the skies of Talmudic literature since the days of the Shaagas Aryeh."

The third section of *Beit HaLevi*, explanations on the books of Genesis and Exodus, was published in the year 5644 [1884]. Rabbi Yosi-Ber displayed his exegetical prowess in this book.

The final book of *Beit HaLevi* appeared in the year 5651 [1891]. In it, he deals primarily with the question of the Sabbatical Year [*shmita*] in all its details and nuances.

Sources

Chaim Dov HaLevi Lewicki: "Deep Mourning," *Hameilitz*, 8 Iyar 5652 [1892], issue 90. Chaim Dov HaLevi Lewicki: "The Tzadik will be an Eternal Memory," *Hameilitz*, 4 Sivan 5652 [1892], issue 111, and *Hameilitz*, 11 Sivan 5652, issue 114.
HaAsif, 5654 [1894], pp. 150-152.

[Page 209]

Ezriel Meir Braude, History of the Gaon Rabbi Yosef Dov HaLevi Soloveitchik, *Hatzefira*, 5 Sivan 5652 (May 19, 1892), issue 111.
Rabbi Baruch HaLevi Epstein, *Mekor Baruch*, Volume IV, chapter 38, *Leil Shimurim*, pp. 1703-1725.
Yisrael HaKohen, *Hameilitz*, 17 Sivan 5652 [1892], issue 119.
Regarding the intelligence and sharpness of Rabbi Yosi Ber, see Meshichot Chachamim. Regarding the dispute between him and the Netzi'v, see the chapter on the Yeshiva.

B.

What is the straight path to which a person must cleave? Rabbi Eliezer says: a good heart. (*Avot*, 2:9)

A good heart, "for peace is the causative factor of all other powers, and the source from which all activity flows" (Rabbi Ovadia of Bartenura)

Rabbi Chaim Soloveitchik

Rabbi Chaim Soloveitchik was born in Volozhin in the year 5613 (1853) to his father the Gaon Rabbi Yosef Dov, who was serving then as the deputy to the head of the Yeshiva of Volozhin. Rabbi Chaim was already noted for his intelligence in his youth. It is told that his mother once saw him with dirty hands. She reproved him, saying: "Chaimke, are you not embarrassed with such dirty hands? Did you ever see such dirty hands with your mother?" The child responded: "No, I did not see, but your mother surely saw…"

Rabbi Chaim was still a baby when Rabbi Yosi Ber occupied the rabbinical seat of Slutsk. He was alert and deft, and was not diligent in the study of Torah. Once, the elderly rabbinical judge was sitting with Rabbi Yosi Ber, and saw the child neglecting Torah. He began to reprove him: "Come and see, your father, whose soul desires

[Page 210]

Torah and makes his nights like days, has become a great person in Israel. Whereas you, as you do not occupy yourself with Torah, will eventually be an ignoramus[vi]. And what will you end up as? Chaimke responded with a stinging retort: "In the end, I will be a rabbinical judge in Israel."

Rabbi Chaim's external appearance was unique, and also attracted the non-curious eye. His large head, out of proportion to his low stature, his wide forehead, and large, dark, prominent eyes, made a strong impression. Everyone immediately realized that they were standing before a great, unusual personality. He conducted himself modestly despite his great talents and extensive knowledge. When he went on an excursion, he would hide his *peyos* and wear a simple hat like someone from the marketplace rather than the broad hat that he wore in Volozhin. He would not study a book when he sat on a train, and he did not stand at the eastern side when he entered the synagogue. When he was sitting down to a meal with people he did not know, he would discuss their issues with them – business, trivial matters, and general conversation with people of the marketplace. Despite this, everyone, even those who did not know him, immediately recognized that one of the great ones of Israel was before them.

When he was about 20 years old, he married the daughter of the Gaon Rabbi Rafael Shapira, who at that time was the deputy to the head of the Yeshiva of Volozhin, who was his father-in-law the Netzi'v. He set up his permanent residence in Volozhin. His great influence upon the people of the Yeshiva was felt immediately. In the year 5640 (1880) he was appointed as the deputy to the head of the Volozhin Yeshiva. From that time, he began to deliver his Talmud classes, which immediately gained him a great name in the world of Torah. He delivered his classes in the Yeshiva for twelve consecutive years. Thousands of students studied with him during those year, many of whom later became renown as great ones of Israel. The Netzi'v even involved Rabbi Chaim in the running of the affairs of the Yeshiva.

The words of one of his choicest students, the writer Micha Yosef Berdichevsky, testifies to the level of reverence afforded to Rabbi Chaim Soloveitchik by the Yeshiva people:

"The brightest image of all the souls who are acting in our small world, is the countenance of the deputy Yeshiva head, Rabbi Chaim Soloveitchik. From the day I met him, I saw him as one of the excellent sublime people whom the Holy One Blessed Be He places in each generation. This man has a very great, sharp, and deep intellect. He penetrates and delves into the essence of each and every issue. It is no exaggeration to state that I, who was already used to delving into the deep waters and resting in the depths of the minutest of minute concepts, to the point where the minutest matters of Spinoza and Kant did not confuse me – any time I heard him speaking and dissecting matters with his sharp, penetrating knowledge, it is virtually difficult for me to grasp his words and to understand the fundamentals of the matter in all its great minutiae.

"Our rabbi never dealt with books of logic. Nevertheless, when he delved deeply into major *halachot*, he uncovered connections through his very great natural powers of logic. I would be surprised if there is any genius like him in this generation. In addition to his clear, sharp intellect, he is a good man who does good. He is a great philanthropist, who speaks peacefully to every person and judges

[Page 211]

everyone favorably. I never heard one of the students or any other person complain about him."

Rabbi Chaim's classes became an event in the life of the Yeshiva. They enthralled the students. His student M. Eisenstat writes:

"Rabbi Chaimke delivered his classes, and his words dripped like dew. All the students of the Yeshiva stood on their feet the entire time of the class, without touching arm or leg. There was silence in the Yeshiva. It seemed as if even the large, old clock of the Yeshiva was quiet, without sounding its tick-tock. Enchanted, people absorbed every word and expression that emanated from his mouth, that exuded pearls.

"There was a custom among the two Yeshiva heads, the Netzi'v and Rabbi Chaim, that if one of them was not present in the Yeshiva at that time, the other would deliver his class. Once, at the time of the conclusion of the tractate *Baba Batra*, it fell to Rabbi Chaim to conduct the concluding [*hadran*] ceremony. The next day, the Netzi'v snuck quietly into the Yeshiva, to the surprise of all the students, hid in one of the corners, and stood the entire time until the conclusion of the *hadran*. The students heard the Netzi'v talking to himself: "Indeed he relates to the Torah as one of the early sages – and I did not know!"

Another of Rabbi Chaim's students, Abba Blusher, rights about the analytical Rabbi Chaim and his unusual talents of analysis:

"Rabbi Chaim Soloveitchik would dissect a difficult section of the Talmud into the minutest pieces with the sharp chisel of his mind. He would take apart each of its links, expose its limbs, sinews, filaments, and bones, turn it about and about, and demonstrate the foundations of its structure to the students – its main floor and attic, from ground to roof. He would then return each part to its place, join together all the separate links, sew up the tears, and reconstruct the Talmudic passage once again, as he explained its logic according to the *halachic* tradition that has been accepted for generations – the *halacha* as explained in the *Yad Chazaka*[vii]. He would resolve all the questions of the Raava'd[viii] and other commentators of the Rambam [Maimonides] and prove "That our Rabbi Moses is true and his Torah is true[ix]". The students learned the art of analysis from him, the act of construction and separating, and the secret of creativity. The veteran students, those who were preparing to make Torah their profession, would constantly follow after him and surround him in every place to hear Torah from his mouth."

The great fame of Rabbi Chaim Soloveitchik in Volozhin and in the Torah world came to him through his great personality. He was not only great as a rabbi, but also as a teacher. From the day he began to teach in the Yeshiva of Volozhin, he was surrounded by many students who cleaved to the dust of his feet. He loved placing his hand on the necks of those who adored him, his sharp students, and take long or short walks with them.

[Page 212]

Rabbi Chaim did not provide many sources, and was not wont to say, "accept my opinion!" Rather, he would sit in a group as if the matter was not sufficiently clear to him. Thus, through mutual discussion, through cleaving to friends, the great teacher would join together word with word, rhyme idea with idea, and the complex, difficult matter would become self-clarified.

Day and night, at times also for entire weeks, Rabbi Chaim Soloveitchik would occupy himself with a single issue until he clarified it well, and decided that the matter was already clear and understood through the truth of the Torah. It was said of him: What is the difference between Rabbi Chaim and such and such a Gaon who was famous for his novel ideas? It would make sense that the Gaon would also say what Rabbi Chaim said, but the greatness of Rabbi Chaim was that he did not say what he [i.e. the Gaon] would have said. All of his words were measured and weighed. He would not utter even a single syllable for naught. Not one sound was scattered in the wind. His words were cutting in their sharp logic and clear content.

As a great pedagogue, Rabbi Chaim expressed great love to children and toddlers. When he met a child, he would enter into conversation with him, ask him about his home, his family, his teacher, and his studies, and he would test him on the weekly Torah portion. He was great not only with older people, but also with young people. When he spoke to a child, he would find common language with him. He knew how to talk to children.

A fire broke out in Volozhin in the year 5646 [1886]. The Yeshiva building, the synagogue, and the rabbi's house all went up in flames. Almost all the people of the city went out to the fields. Suddenly, they realized that Rabbi Chaim was not with them. They went to search for him, and found him running while carrying two babies in his arms. He went with them from street to street until he brought them to a secure place.

We will not speak here of Rabbi Chaim as a genius in *halacha*, of his vast knowledge that amazed the masses, but rather of his dedicated personality, of his love of his fellow. First and foremost, Rabbi Chaim was a great lover of his fellow Jew. His entire way of life was to look favorably upon the deeds of people. He did not look for a person's sins, but he rather always tried to expose the good in the person, the light in him. He was also understanding of people who were sullied in sin. He did not look at their faults, but rather at their life conditions and the and the circumstances over which a person does not always have control.

Rabbi Chaim had mercy in his heart, boundless mercy, a good heart, a pure, soft heart, open always to anyone suffering difficulties or in a bitter, depressed spirit. Anyone suffering from melancholy, any forlorn, sighing soul found comfort, calm, help and assistance from Rabbi Chaim.

Once, scholars were sitting in his house and discussing the concept of "a head that has not put on tefillin." Some were stringent and said that anyone who does not put on tefillin is not part of the Jewish people. Others were lenient and said: A Jew, even if he sins, is a Jew. They agreed to ask Rabbi Chaim. Rabbi Chaim responded: "I am surprised – is there really a Jewish man who does not put on tefillin?"

Here is an additional fact: They came and told hm that a Jewish lad had been captured by the government and was sentenced to hanging. Rabbi Chaim started to search for ways to save the lad from death. On the eve of Yom Kippur

[Page 213]

when the congregation gathered for the *Kol Nidre* prayer and everyone was standing with awe and fear as they recited *Tefilla Zaka*, Rabbi Chaim ascended the *bima*. Everyone looked at hm, for they thought that the rabbi would expound on issues of the holy day. However, instead of a sermon, Rabbi Chaim gestured to the *shamash*, who brought out a piece of paper, an inkwell, and ink. Rabbi Chaim signed his name and said to the congregation: "See what I did and do the same. Everyone must sign their name on this petition to the government to annul the verdict." Everyone ascended to the *bima* and signed their names. In the interim, it became dark. Some members of the congregation began to grumble: Yom Kippur has already begun. However Rabbi Chaim did not pay attention to the noise, and he ordered the entire congregation to sign. Rabbi Chaim only began to chant *Kol Nidre* when the last one signed.[x].

In 1905, when a series of strikes broke out in all the cities of Russia, and the factory workers of Brisk approached the employers with various demands, threatening a strike, Rabbi Chaim became involved and influenced the factory owners to give in to the workers. They willingly accepted Rabbi Chaim's intervention.

When the Yeshiva of Volozhin was closed in the year 5652 (1892), Rabbi Chaim went to Brisk, where his father Rabbi Yosef Dov had served as rabbi. Rabbi Yosef Dov had died that year, and Rabbi Chaim was accepted as his successor. As the rabbi of the city, he made efforts to help and improve the situation of the poor. The community provided Rabbi Chaim with the needs of his household, including candles for light and wood for heat. Once, the administrators felt that the rabbi's household expenses for firewood were very large. They investigated and discovered that the woodshed in the rabbi's house was not locked, and the poor of the city would come and take what they needed. They locked the shed and gave the key to the *shamash*. When Rabbi Chaim realized this, he ordered that the lock immediately be removed. The woodshed was again wide open, and the poor of the city came and took what they needed. The city administrators complained to Rabbi Chaim: "The communal funds do not have the ability to provide wood to all the poor of the city." "If so," Rabbi Chaim responded, "then I will not heat my house either. How can I sit in warmth while the poor are freezing from cold?"

When the large fire broke out in Brisk in the year 5655 (1855), Rabbi Chaim did not rest and remain silent. Day and night, he gave all his efforts to restoring the ruins of those affected by the fire. Rabbi Chaim did not sleep in his home during all those days after the fire. Rather, he went to the synagogue corridor and slept on the floor there. All urgings from his household that he rest in his house and on his bed were for naught. He responded to them, "I cannot sleep on my bed when so many Jews do not have a roof over their heads."

Once, two wealthy Jews came to him and gave him a sealed envelope with a sum of money. Those wealthy people joined their families together in marriage, and Rabbi Chaim conducted the wedding ceremony. Therefore, they brought him payment for serving as the officiant. In the meantime, a proper poor person entered his house and requested a donation. Rabbi Chaim took the sealed envelope and gave it to the poor person in the presence of those wealthy people, without even finding out how much was inside.

[Page 214]

Rabbi Chaim Soloveitchik had great authority in the world of Torah. He participated in several large conventions and gatherings of rabbis in Vilna, Peterburg, Katowice, and other places. He was the chief spokesman in every place, not only through his speeches, but through his logical, sharp opinions and his remarks that hit the target. He disseminated the Torah he obtained in Volozhin in every place where he had influence.

He was recognized as the Gaon of the generation and the teacher of the generation. Many Yeshiva students would come specially to Brisk to benefit from his Torah and life wisdom. He served as the rabbi of Brisk for more than 20 years. When the First World War broke out, and the residents of Brisk were forced to leave the city, Rabbi Chaim Soloveitchik went to Minsk. Despite the great material straits in which he lived in Minsk, he did not want to take benefit from any person, and he declined the offers of several wealthy people and communal institutions that wished to support in various ways. In the year 5678 (1918), he was given permission from the authorities to travel to Warsaw. From there, under doctor's orders, he went to Otwock. He died at the age of 65 on the 21st of Av of that year.

Sources

Rabbi Meir Berlin: "The Great One in his Generation" (*HaIvri*, 5678 [1918], issues 30, 31, 33). Bar-Bei-Rav (Micha Yosef Berdichevsky), "A Bundle of Letters from Volozhin" (*Hameilitz*, 8 Nisan 5648 (March 8, 1888), issue 56.)[xi]
Abba Blusher, "Bialik in Volozhin" (*Meoznaim*, Tammuz 5695 [1935], volume IV, booklet II.
M. Eisenstat, "Rabbi Chaimke Volozhiner" (*Hatzefira*, 21 Elul 5678 [1918], issue 35)
N'M: "The Grandfather and Grandson" (*Hatzefira*, 6 Tishrei 5679 [1918], issue 37)

[Page 215]

Rabbi Chaim Berlin

Rabbi Chaim Berlin was the eldest son of the Netzi'v from his first wife, Rebbetzin Reina Batya, the daughter of Rabbi Itzele. He was a scion of the splendid Volozhin dynasty from his mother's side. He was born in Volozhin on 8 Shvat 5592 (1832).

From his childhood, he was raised in the atmosphere of Torah – the atmosphere of his father the Gaon and the atmosphere of the Yeshiva. His father educated him in accordance with his spirit until the age of nine, when he became expert in three orders of the Mishna: *Moed*, *Nashim*, and *Nezikin*. Similarly, he knew the Bible thoroughly – something unusual in those days. The genius began to attend the Yeshiva at the age of nine, and heard classes from his maternal grandfather, the Gaon Rabbi Itzele. He studied in the Yeshiva for six years. During that period, he completed the entire Talmud and began to write Torah novellae and responsa to rabbis.

Rabbi Chaim was handsome. When he walked with his father the Netzi'v through the streets of Volozhin after the third meal of the Sabbath, the gentile passers-by would stand and be astonished at the beauty of the father and son. They would say to each other in amazement: "*Ati Rabini*" (these are rabbis). He also excelled from his youth as a great preacher. The *Beis Midrash* in Volozhin was filled to the brim when he would deliver a lecture. Many of his statements and adages served as topics of conversation for the masses.

The name of Rabbi Chaim was praised as wholesome in all traits. When he was 15 years old, the very wealthy people began to seek him out as a groom for their daughters. Out of all of them, the Netzi'v chose a well-connected family from Shklov, and made a match with the wealthy activist Reb Moshe Zeitlin, whose daughter Rivka was beautiful and intelligent. This match helped a great deal in Rabbi Chaim's spiritual development. Since he was the son-in-law of wealthy people, he was able to amass a large library of approximately 10,000 volumes, from the earliest of the early sages to the latest of the latter sages. Since he was free from worries of livelihood, he lived years of happiness in the study of Torah. His mouth never desisted from learning. His knowledge of Talmud became so deep that Rabbi Kook, may the memory of the holy be blessed, said of him: "His powers are like the powers of the father." (See "Head of the Etz Chaim Yeshiva")

Rabbi Chaim became renown as one of the great ones of the generation. Emissaries from communities came to him to offer him rabbinical posts. However, he pushed them off due to his modesty, saying that he must still

[Page 216]

learn much Torah before he would be fitting to serve as a rabbi in Israel. In truth, however, Rabbi Chaim was not attracted to the rabbinate. He wanted to live as a private individual, only under the yoke of the Kingdom of Heaven, and to only bear the burden of Torah.

However, with time, the financial situation of his wealthy father-in-law weakened, and the source of his wealth dwindled. Rabbi Chaim reached the point of material straits. Then he was forced to search for a source of livelihood, so he responded to the community of Moscow, to serve as a rabbi there. He was accepted as the rabbi of Moscow on 26 Adar 5625 (1865).

Rabbi Chaim did not find his appropriate place in that community. The charm of the place was not upon him. Ignorance pervaded there, and the community did not need such a great rabbi as he. Therefore, he restricted himself to the four ells of *halacha* and rabbinic decisions. His wife of his youth died on 23 Cheshvan 5643 (1883). Her death, along with the feelings of loneliness that eked at him when he lived in Moscow, affected him greatly. This attempt that did not succeed aroused in Rabbi Chaim the desire to separate from rabbinical service and live as a private person in the shadow of Torah and wisdom. He regarded his post as "forsaking the eternal life and living in temporal life." Then, a match with a wealthy person from Biała, district of Siedlce, was proposed to him – Tila the daughter of Rabbi Yitzchak Izak Shachor of Mir. Rabbi Chaim left Moscow in the year 5644 [1884] and moved to Biała – to live in the shadow of money and in the light of Torah. With him, the opposite of the adage of sages was fulfilled – it is hard to ascend the stage and easy to descend.

His exit caused a great storm amongst the Jews of Russia. Biała was known as a firmly Hassidic town. His father-in-law, Reb Yitzchak Izak, was Hassid of Kock and Gur. This seemed like a match with a different kind. Erez, the editor of *Hameilitz*, wrote the following about this period: The rabbi and great luminary, our Rabbi Chaim Berlin, the rabbi of the *Misnagdim* and deputy rabbi of government appointment, is it correct to leave this community, and to follow the wife whom G-d had designated for him in Biała? Since she refused to be a Rebbetzin, he removed from his head the crown of the rabbinate, in which he had served for 29 years. All the communal notables with whom he was in contact were sorry over the desire of the rabbi to leave their midst, since they had already become accustomed to him. He knew how to travel through life and to make peace with all factions. There was peace between him and the government rabbi.

"A man such as he, who had the tradition of his fathers with him, the great-grandson of the rabbi of the generation, the head of the Volozhin Yeshiva, Rabbi Chaim Volozhiner who was known as sublime, and in whose heart was rooted a feeling of strangeness to the Hasidic way, and he pursued them all his life – he will be one of the righteous converts of the Gerrer Tzadik and will worship in the long *kloiz* in Biała named for him? He will exchange the crown of the rabbinate with the holiness of Hassidim in the Sephardic rite?"" (*Hameilitz*, 28 Tishrei 5644 [1884], issue 80).

Rabbi Chaim lived in Biała for five years, until the year 5659 [1899]. Tila, his second wife, died in the month of Nissan. He returned to Volozhin to be the assistant of his father, the Netzi'v, in his old age, and delivered the classes along with his brother-in-law Rabbi Chaim Soloveitchik.

The Netzi'v, who sensed that his energies were dwindling and disappearing, concerned himself with a successor while still alive.

[Page 217]

He designated his son Rabbi Chaim as his successor. This decision was fateful in the existence of the Yeshiva, and led to its closing in the month of Shvat 5652 [1892][*] The students rebelled against the Netzi'v (see the details of the revolt in the chapter on the Yeshiva), and did not want to accept upon themselves Rabbi Chaim as the head of the Yeshiva. They indeed admitted to his greatness, but claimed that not every rabbi who is great in Torah is able to be the head of the Yeshiva of Volozhin, which at that time was at the pinnacle of its development.

The outrage that took place in the Yeshiva spread outside its walls, and turned into a matter of public adjudication. Rabbi Mordechai the son of Gamzo was among those opposed to the decision of the Netzi'v. He writes as follows in his article in *Hameilitz*: "Is there room for a judgment of the inheritance of Israel in this matter as well? The *Misnagdim* fill their mouths with laughter regarding the Hassidic Tzadikim who pass on their Tzadik status to their children after them. And now it affects them, and they are confused. They grasp on to the cloak-tails of Rabbi Chaim, saying 'You are the son of a Yeshiva head, so it coming to you that you will be our captain, the head of the Yeshiva of Volozhin.'

"I do not wish, Heaven forbid, to cast aspersion on the honor of Rabbi Chaim Berlin and state that he is not fitting for that position. However, the appointing of a Yeshiva head is not one of the things done without deliberation, behind the oven and stove, during the course of a single night. It is known that everything follows after the head, and the honor of the entire Yeshiva is dependent on his honor. Therefore, we must appoint a Yeshiva head about whom the entire people can state that this is he, and that all our brethren in the Diaspora can recognize that he is chosen from amongst all the sages of the era." (*Hameilitz*, 7 Adar II, 5651 [1891], issue 54).

We have sources stating that it is not the Netzi'v alone who designated his son Rabbi Chaim as his heir. Rather, this was based on a decision of the Torah greats who gathered in Minsk to deliberate over the question of a successor for the Netzi'v. "After a long period of deliberation, his son the Gaon Rabbi Chaim was chosen unanimously by all those gathered as the head of the Yeshiva of Volozhin." (Reb Eliezer Bron, *Hameilitz*, issue 45, 26 Adar I, 5651 [1891]).

Rabbi Chaim married his third wife Eiga after he returned to Volozhin. She was

[Page 218]

formerly the Levin-Epstein widow who was famous for book publishing. However, she died suddenly on a Friday night a few months after the wedding. At that time, Rabbi Chaim Berlin was in Vilna for Yeshiva business. All of Volozhin including the Yeshiva was immersed in mourning. The only one who did not feel it was the Netzi'v. The spirit of the Sabbath pervaded him. He was filled with internal joy and his face radiated holiness. When one of the family members, moved by the tragedy, shed a tear, the Netzi'v scolded him, saying: "Today is the Sabbath. There is no mourning on the Sabbath!" However, after Havdalah, the Netzi'v entered his room, wept out loud, and could not be comforted. (See "From Volozhin to Jerusalem," 54, 55).

In 5652 [1892], after the closing of the Yeshiva, Rabbi Chaim Berlin left Volozhin and was accepted as the head of the rabbinical court of Kobrin – a completely Hassidic city. There as well, he did not find the peace in his soul to which he aspired all the days of his life. Rabbi Chaim lived in that city until the year 5655 [1895]. That year, he was accepted as the rabbi of Yelisavetgrad[lxiii]. Rabbi Chaim arrived there on August 15, 1895. All the gabbaim [trustees] of the synagogues came to greet him at the railway station.

From there, they went to the *Beis Midrash* which was filled to the brim. Rabbi Berlin preached about issues of the day and the purpose of his coming.

In that city, Rabbi Chaim was also active in issues of Chibat Zion. He signed his name on the announcement of the placing of charitable plates in every synagogue on the eve of Yom Kippur for donations for the benefit of the workers in the Land of Israel. Thereby, he helped firm the foundations and the development of Chovevei Zion in the place he was serving.

He lived in Yelisavetgrad for about ten years. During those years, he decided to abandon rabbinical service completely, to leave the Diaspora, and to make *aliya* to the Land of Israel. He made *aliya* to the Jerusalem in the year 5666 (1906), and married Rebbetzin Matlia, the daughter of the Gaon Ephraim Rokach. He lived in the Land as a private individual. He brought a portion of his large library with him, numbering about 4,000 volumes. Rabbi Chaim sought to rest from the work of the rabbinate that he had borne all the days of his life in various communities in Russia. However, his wish was not to be. The Gaon Rabbi Shmuel Salant, the rabbi of Jerusalem, concerned himself during his lifetime with a fitting successor, and he chose Rabbi Chaim as his partner in the running of the Jewish community of the Holy City. He took this task upon himself against his will, as he wrote to Rabbi Ben-Zion Eisenstat in the year 5670 [1910]: "Due to the softness of my nature and my temperament, I cannot refuse the heads of the community." After the death of Rabbi Salant, all the needs of the Jews of Jerusalem were placed upon Rabbi Chaim. Even though he did not serve officially as the rabbi of the city, he headed the general committee and directed the Talmud Torah and the hospital.

He conducted this communal work, imposed upon him in his old age, with love and dedication. He was admired and loved by all circles of the Jewish community of Jerusalem. He excelled with his tender temperament, his love of his fellow, and in promoting peace between people. He was given the nickname *Zaken Harabanim* [the Elder of the Rabbis] and *Saba Deara Kadisha* [Grandfather of the Holy City].

Even with the burden of communal activity, Rabbi Chaim occupied himself with Torah novellae, and left

בשנת הטר מגוע נאני לפק
.. ע הרבע ה מרנא ם ..
אאאמם.. א מרנא ם עפ..
.ר בי חיים זללהה.
ברלין
בנו של הגאון הגדול אדמור
ובנפתלי צבי יהודא זללהה
רם דוואלאזין
ונין ונכד להגאון מאור הגולה
ר בי חיים זללהה
אבד ורם דוואלאזין
נולד בוואלאזין יום ה שבט שנת
ועך אתה נולד
וינבם פעיהק אור ליום יג תשרי
שנת תר עג בן שמונים שנה
ושמונה חדשים ושבעה ימים
תנצבה

The gravestone of Rabbi Chaim Berlin
in the Mount of Olives Cemetery in Jerusalem

Text of the gravestone is as follows:

In the year

Woe that a scion of the root of the Gaonim of the world[xiv]

The famous rabbi

Rabbi Chaim, may he be remembered for life in the World To Come, Berlin

The son of the great Gaon, the Admor

Rabbi Naftali Tzvi Yehuda, may he be remembered for life in the World To Come

The head of the Yeshiva of Volozhin

A Descendent of the luminary of the Diaspora

Rabbi Chaim, may he be remembered for life in the World To Come

Head of the rabbinical court and head of the Yeshiva of Volozhin.

Born in Volozhin on 5 Shvat of the year

And thus you were born[xv]

Died here in the Holy City on the evening of the 13th of Tishrei

Of the year 5673 [1912] at the age of 80, 8 months and 7 days.

May his soul be bound in the bonds of eternal life.

[Page 219-220]

behind many manuscripts of that nature. He also made efforts to establish a large Torah library in Jerusalem. He bequeathed his private library to the Etz Chaim Yeshiva of Jerusalem.

Rabbi Chaim did not live long in the Land. He died on 13 Tishrei 5673 (September 24, 1912), in his 81st year. The residents of Jerusalem gave him his final honor without eulogies, as per his desire and his will.

Rabbi Chaim Berlin was a very tragic figure. He went through a long journey in his life. With everything, he remained at the outset. This tragedy was expressed by Rabbi Moshe Shapira in the following words: "There are great people who are granted talent and spiritual riches by Divine providence, and could influence their generation to give over to them something of their spiritual treasure. However, it is as if some sort of evil angel accompanies them on their journey, and disturbs them from publishing their great thoughts. It is only when they reach old age, when life becomes more difficult, that they find the task that is appropriate for them, and for the attributes of their soul. But then, the works are not done with the appropriate, required wholesomeness, for they are lacking the power and freshness of the days of youth. One such tragic soul was the Gaon Rabbi Chaim Berlin, may the memory of the holy be blessed (See "Moshe Shmuel and his Generation" page 65).

Sources

a.   Levi Ochinski, *Nachalat Avot*, Vilna 5654 [1894], point 8, page 22.

b.   Shmuel Noach Gotlieb: *Oholei Shem* [Tents of Shem], Pinsk 5672 [1902], pp. 493-494.

c.   Avraham Moshe Luntz: "The Rabbi and Gaon Rabbi Chaim Berlin, may the memory of the holy be blessed," Luach Eretz Yisrael, Jerusalem, year 19 (5674 1913/14), pp 161-162.

d.   Rabbi Moshe Shapira: "Rabbi Moshe Shmuel and his Generation" New York 5724 [1964], page 65.

e.   Rabbi A. Y. Bromberg: "The Gaon Rabbi Chaim Berlin" Areas of Religious Jewish Thought, booklet 5727 [1967] (25), pp 110-116.

f.   Ben-Zion Eisenstat: "Latter Generations" New York, 5673 [1913], Book I, pp. 71-73.

g.   Ben-Zion Eisenstat: "The Gaon Rabbi Chaim Berlin" the full life story of the great one of the generation, his life and activity as rabbi and as communal activist. Der Amerikaner, 1912, Volume I, number 40.

h.   Rabbi Meir Berlin: "From Volozhin to Jerusalem".

i.   Erez: "A Writing from Moscow," *Hameilitz*, 28 Tishrei 5644 (October 17, 1883), issue 80.

j.   Mordechai Bar Gamzu: "Who is at the Head?" *Hameilitz*, 7 Adar II 5651 [1891], issue 54.

k.   Shmuel David the son of Reb Zeev Zaks (Shkod, Kovno District), *Hameilitz*, 19 Adar II 5651 [1891], issue 63.

l.   Eliezer Bron of Minsk, *Hameilitz*, issue 45, 26 Adar I 5651 (February 22, 1891).

m.   *Hameilitz*, 26 Tishrei 5656 [1895], issue 212.

Original Footnotes:

1.   *Mekor Baruch*, Section IV, page 1720.

2.   [footnote on page 217, not designated by a number] Rabbi Ben-Zion Yadler (the Maggid of Jerusalem) writes that Rabbi Chaim Berlin told him, in the name of his father the Netzi'v, the true reason for the closing of the Yeshiva. These are the words of Rabbi Chaim: " In memory of what my father, the Gaon, may the memory of the holy be blessed for life in the world to come, behold I am the atonement for his soul – told me before his death, that I should not bring into it (i.e. the Yeshiva) any secular studies. It was for this reason that the

Yeshiva was closed. This is the heritage from his sickness, from which he did not arise, as he commanded me with a warning that I do not agree under any circumstance, without any leniency in the world, for the Holy One Blessed Be He hinted to all this in the Torah, where it says, "to differentiate between holy and secular"[xii]. That means that when any secular matter mixes with holy, not only do the secular studies not obtain holiness, but furthermore, the holy studies are ruined by them. Therefore, it should not seem bad to you, my son, that this matter caused me to exit the world and to close the Yeshiva, for it was worthwhile for me to give up my soul for this matter." (Rabbi Ben-Zion Yadler (the Maggid of Jerusalem), in *Tuv Yerushalaim* (Memoirs from the life in Jerusalem and its greatness in the previous [i.e. 19th] century), published by *Netzach*, Bnei-Brak, page 373.

Translator's footnotes:

i.   Generally pronounced "Rabbi Yoshe Ber." I preserved the pronunciation of the spelling used in the original Hebrew – Yosi.

ii.   Referring to a sudden, painless death, as per the deaths of Moses and Aaron in the Torah.

iii.   It is generally considered more intellectually difficult to find a leniency in Jewish law than a stringency.

iv.   Rabbeinu Tam tefillin [phylacteries] are made slightly differently than other phylacteries. Some have the custom of using both sets of phylacteries every day, to remove the doubt regarding which is the correct form.

v.   All other biblical festivals are observed for two days in the Diaspora.

vi.   The term here is somewhat ambiguous. *Am Haaretz* – literally "a person of the land." It can be used with a neutral connotation for a regular, non-scholarly individual. It can also be used with a derogatory connotation (to varying degrees depending on the circumstance) to refer to an unlearned individual, a boor, or an ignoramus.

vii.   The 14-volume *halachic* work of Maimonides.

viii.   A commentator on the *Yad Chazaka* of Maimonides, who often points out inconsistencies in the text.

ix.   Here referring to Rabbi Moses Maimonides, and not the biblical Moses.

x.   Although it is forbidden to write on a holy day such as Yom Kippur, the prohibition is pushed aside in situations where life is at stake.

xi.   The secular date is too early for 8 Nisan according to the Gregorian Calendar. As this was the Russian Empire, the Julian Calendar would have still been in effect.

xii.   Leviticus 10:10

xiii.   Today https://en.wikipedia.org/wiki/Kropyvnytskyi

xiv.   The numerology [gematria] of the Hebrew letters of this phrase add up to 673, which would correspond to the year 1912 (he died on September 24, 1912).

xv.   The gematria of this phrase is 592, corresponding to 1832, the year of his birth.

The Gaon Rabbi Chaim Hillel Fried[1]

by Chaikel Lunsky of blessed memory
(Librarian at the Strashun Library of Vilna)

Translated by Jerrold Landau

Rabbi Chaim Hillel Fried was born in Volozhin on 25 Cheshvan 5593 (1833)[i] to his father Rabbi Eliezer Yitzchak the son of Rabbi Hillel of Horodno (Rabbi Hillel was the son-in-law of Rabbi Chaim of Volozhin). Rabbi Chaim Hillel's mother was also a granddaughter of Rabbi Chaim of Volozhin (the daughter of his son and successor as head of the Volozhin Yeshiva, Rabbi Itzele Volozhiner). Already in his youth, Rabbi Chaim Hillel excelled with sublime talents. He studied in the Yeshiva of Volozhin and became known as a genius. His father died when he was 17 years old. His mother married him off to Sara Beila, the daughter of Rabbi Shmuel Landau (of the family of Rabbi Yechezkel Landau, the author of the *Noda BiYehuda*, and son-in-law of Rabbi Itzele[iii]) .

The Land of Israel was the desire of the soul of Rabbi Chaim Hillel. After he married, he decided to actualize this. His mother and wife were opposed to such an imaginative journey. The seat of the Yeshiva head was awaiting him (as the heir of his father Rabbi Eliezer Yitzchak who served in that role), and he should have been preparing for it. However, they acceded when they realized that they could not budge him. Rabbi Chaim Hillel set out for Odessa and waited for the ship to transport him to the Holy Land. However, this ship sunk. Rabbi Chaim Hillel regarded this as a portent from G-d, and returned to Volozhin.

When Rabbi Yosi Ber Soloveitchik left to serve as the rabbi of Slutsk, Rabbi Chaim Hillel ascended to his seat as the head of the Volozhin Yeshiva. The state of his health forced him to give up this role after a few years, and he earned his livelihood from his wife's manufacturing shop. She conducted business, and he studied Torah day and night[2]. In addition to his genius, Rabbi Chaim Hillel excelled in his understanding of interpersonal relationships. He was also important in the eyes of the government, and people turned to him to work on annulling decrees against the Jews. Even the prince of the city, Tyskiewicz, related to him with honor and acceded to his requests to do good for the Jews of the city.

[Page 222]

The residents of the city would often ask for his advice in communal and individual matters: business, marriage, etc. His words would also often be heard off the stage. The man was very modest and pious. He did not wear a rabbinical hat (*streimel*), but rather a simple velvet hat. He stood behind the *bima* in the synagogue. When he would come to Vilna for communal matters, he would worship in the Zanvil Synagogue behind the *bima*. The *gabbaim* would say that Rabbi Chaim Hillel would transfer the "eastern wall" to near the door.

From when he was 14 years old, his life was dedicated to helping the poor and tormented, especially with benevolent acts. His house was filled with peddlers every Saturday night (this was the most common source of livelihood in Volozhin) who had come to request loans for merchandise for Sunday. He gave to all of them with a pleasant countenance and good wishes. He extended an appropriate blessing to everyone. His house was open to visitors. There was no meal without guests. Rabbi Chaim Hillel fulfilled the commandment of visiting the sick in the literal fashion. He would bring amulets that he had inherited from his grandfather Rabbi Chaim to women in difficult labor.

He was completely dedicated to helping others. When a fire broke out – a common occurrence in Volozhin – Rabbi Chaim Hillel hurried to save the babies and elderly people. From his own house he would only save the Torah scroll that he inherited from Rabbi Itzele, and the "Jewish symbol" – the tzitzit garment that Rabbi Itzele had worn when he stood before the heads of the state of Russia to deal with the problems of the people. Therefore, when the great fire consumed most of the buildings of the city, including the Yeshiva, and Rabbi Chaim's house remained standing – some elders regarded this as a reward for his dedication in saving people during the times of fires. After this fire, the Yeshiva moved to Rabbi Chaim Hillel's house.

His behavior toward G-d was as meticulous as his interpersonal relationships. He would get up early to immerse himself in a ritual bath before prayer, and he bathed in the bathhouse in honor of the Sabbath.

Sabbaths and festivals in the home of Rabbi Chaim Hillel were very nice. The table was surrounded by a quorum of guests, and he was meticulous about reciting the Grace After Meals with a minyan, and with a cup of wine. Rabbi Chaim Hillel broke out in traditional melodies and hymns, a heritage from his grandfather Rabbi Itzele. The occasion of the baking of matzos mitzvah[iii] on the afternoon of the eve of Passover was a celebration unto itself. Rabbi Chaim Hillel himself poured the flour. Others from the rabbi's family poured the "water that had stayed overnight"[iv]. His daughters-in-law would roll the dough. The rest of the tasks were given to scholars. The house bustled with the chant "for the sake of the commandment of matzo" and "crumbs are considered ownerless" (for it was after the time of the burning of the leaven, and it was necessary to nullify any crumb that might have become leavened)…

It was the custom in Volozhin that on the eve of Yom Kippur, the entire city, from young to old, would come to receive a blessing from Rabbi Chaim Hillel[c]. On Sukkot, he slept in the Sukka together with his children. Once, when Rabbi Chaim Hillel was sick,

[Page 223]

the doctor forbade him to sleep in the Sukka. Rabbi Chaim Hillel was distressed. The doctor saw his distress and permitted him to do so, lest he come to harm from the agony. Indeed, the mitzva did not injure him. He recovered quickly.

Rabbi Chaim Hillel had the finest etrog, and those meticulous in commandments recited the blessing only on that one. Simchat Torah was observed as a day of gladness, in accordance with tradition: The home was full of light. The prayer services took place in his home. The participants were the people of the Yeshiva and important people of the city. During the *hakafot*, Rabbi Hillel, surrounded by the crowd of worshippers, would dance with sublime enthusiasm. He himself would read the Torah with a holy melody. At the conclusion of the festival, Rabbi Chaim Hillel would change his clothes as they were full of sweat.

All the people of the Yeshiva participate in his Purim feast. The joy took place in the dwelling, bustling with song and dance. When Rabbi Chaim Hillel was old, he would take out the book *Chut Hameshulash*: Novel ideas on Torah from his ancestor the Yeshiva heads – Rabbi Chaim of Volozhin, his son-in-law Rabbi Hillel, and his grandson Rabbi Eliezer Yitzchak. His modesty ensured that his name would not be explicitly mentioned in the book, but would rather be hinted to as follows: "And as long as Hillel is alive"[v]. He wrote the introduction to the book himself. His style was fine and modest. He expressed a prayer to G-d that he would send him a full recovery, so that he would be able to publish the rest of his father's books – for he was acquainted with sickness and pain all his life.

Rabbi Chaim Hillel died on 3 Kislev 5671 [1902] at the age of 78. He was not eulogized, for he had commanded thus in his will. He was buried in the grave canopy of his father Rabbi Eliezer Yitzchak and his grandfather Rabbi Chaim of Volozhin.

Original Footnotes:

1. This article was published in the Vilna Weekly *Dos Yiddishe Vort*, 2 Tammuz 5697 (June 11, 1937), number 657, translated to Hebrew by Yonah Ben-Sasson.
2. His Love for the Yeshiva, the forging house of the nation and the forger of the life of his ancestors never diminished. He wandered and toiled a great deal in order to have the decree of the closure of the Yeshiva repealed. It was reopened thanks to his efforts. – a note from the translator [the translator to Hebrew in the original – not the translator to English – JL]
3. I was told by a certain great person in Jerusalem who used to frequent the home of the grandfather when he studied in the Yeshiva of Volozhin, that anyone who did not see Rabbi Chaim Hillel recite the Grace After Meals on the eve of Yom Kippur has never witnessed emotion, love, and awe. He would drown in a sea of tears. – a note from the translator [the translator to Hebrew in the original – not the translator to English – JL].

Translator's footnotes:

i. Cheshvan 5593 would actually correspond to 1834.
ii. The son-in-law of Rabbi Itzele would be Rabbi Shmuel Landau.
iii. The matzos to be used for performing the commandment of eating matzo at the Seder. Some have the custom of baking these matzos on the afternoon of the eve of Passover, at the time the Passover offering would have been brought during the time of the Temple.

iv.   Matzos are baked with water that had remained overnight (*mayim shelanu*) to ensure that the water would be somewhat chilled (pre-refrigeration era) so as to not hasten the leavening process.

v.   The word "alive" is *Chaim* in Hebrew. Thus, the name Chaim Hillel is hinted to in this phrase.

[Page 224]

> And indeed your lives – the best of your visions
> And your splendor – the essence of your being;
> You are the faithful guardians
> Of the image of G-d in the world!

(Chaim Nachman Bialik: May My Portion be with You)

The Rabbi and Gaon Rabbi Rafael Shapira,
may the memory of the holy be blessed

by Yitzchak Rivkind of blessed memory[1]

Translated by Jerrold Landau

(The last of an era)

One by one, the last of the Mohawks, the *Gaonim* of the generation, the bearers of the banner of the Torah, the luminaries of Judaism the noble spirits, pure hearts, soulful individuals, and paradigms of morality have been leaving us.

During the years of evil, the years of the world war, destruction, and eternal revolutions, the *Tzadikim* of our generation have been gathered in, and the remnants of the hearts of our great ones and rabbis have been burst. Long is the list, the list of those who have died, the loss of the Gaonic personalities, holy and pure, cedars of the Torah in the latter era. Not only is their loss a loss for a portion of the nation, the Torah studiers, but it is a loss for the entire nation, for they were the guardians of the heritage of the nation, the bearers of the Torah and spirit of Israel. They were creative through the essence of their being. They influenced through their essence and discussions – they were the lengthy song of the soul of faith and purity, sublime and supernal, in glory and holiness, great splendor, spreading holy, modest light to their surroundings like the stars.

In recent days, we have added one more to that list of great losses. The sad news arrived from Minsk that our elder rabbi, the head of the Volozhin Yeshiva in its final period, Rabbi Rafael Shapira, is no more!

Again, we weep over a loss that will not return. We stand with bowed heads before a new grave, of a great and holy person, the grave of the *Tzadik* of the generation, the pure one of the generation, and the chaste one of the generation.

[Page 225]

With the death of our late rabbi, we, his students of the orphaned generation, weep not only over the death of the unique, excellent personality among the great ones and *Gaonim* of his period, but we also feel like it was the death of our second father. We see this as a severing of the golden chain of the Volozhin dynasty that continued for five successive generations. The final scion of the ancient root of the Etz Chaim Yeshiva has been cut off.

A distance of only 100 years separates the first creator and the final concluder. The death of the latter also marks a full century since the death of the first. However, the thread that connected two jubilees of years was a single thread, the unique Volozhin thread, that continued and was woven through these generations without interruption, and without a change of hue, style, and quality.

In his spiritual image and his traditional essence, our late rabbi was the faithful spiritual heir of his fathers who preceded him. He was an appropriate link in the golden chain of "the rabbinical house."

With the personality of Rabbi Rafael, Lithuanian Jewry consolidated in a practical manner in decisive wholesomeness. The *weltanschauung* [worldview] of the Volozhin *Beis Midrash*, the creation of the spirit and fruit of the thought of the author of *Nefesh HaChaim*, came to fruition. The primary principles and fulcrum of this outlook was: the Torah of Israel "that only it imparts the influence, the life, the holiness, and the light of all the worlds because it is above everything." (*Nefesh HaChaim*, section IV, chapter 26). "The holy Torah is called the tree of life, for only at times when a person grasps it with love and occupies himself with it and studies it regularly does he live the true, sublime life, connected and bound, so to speak, to the eternal life of the Blessed Name, for the Holy One Blessed Be He and the Torah are one" (*Nefesh HaChaim*, section IV, chapter 33).

Here perhaps is the secret of the essence of the founding of the Yeshiva, the source of devotion and dedication of its leaders to the study of Torah, the secret of their exemplary consistency and Volozhin style diligence.

All the days of the life of our rabbi were a life of study, a devotion to learning, to fulfil that which is said "and you shall occupy yourself with it day and night"[i]. He was not, however, as consistent in study as his father-in-law the Netzi'v, the author of *Sefel Hamyim*, with the wax candle glued between his fingers. Similarly, he did not reach his level of scholarship or fame. This was not only because he was by nature modest amongst the great ones of his times, but rather that that he was different from his father-in-law in his character, temperament, talents, energy, and will.

Above all, the Netzi'v was an exemplary Yeshiva head, as if he was created for that purpose. More that being a Yeshiva head, Rabbi Rafael, at the time of the "pairs" when he was the Yeshiva head along with his father-in-law from the years 5630-5641 (1870-1881), and when he was the sole Yeshiva head during the latter period – he himself was the archetype of the eternal Yeshiva head, the diligent Gaon.

Every generation has its Yeshiva heads. The Volozhin Yeshiva had many Yeshiva heads during its period of existence. Furthermore, for almost the entire period from the founding of the Yeshiva until its closing in the year 5652 [1892], aside from brief interruptions, its heads were pairs: Rabbi Chaim and his son-in-law Rabbi Hillel; Rabbi Itzele and his son-in-law Rabbi Eliezer Yitzchak; the Netzi'v and Rabbi Yosef Dov Ber; the Netzi'v and Rabbi Rafael and afterward Rabbi Chaim of Brisk, Rabbi Chaim Berlin – and each personality had a unique form of influence, through which his spirit

[Page 226]

soul, and the beauty of his traditions was imparted to the institution. Rabbi Rafael was a unique Yeshiva head. He was – "the toiler."

His letterhead, "a worker for the labor of Torah in Volozhin " accurately notes the character of his soul, the foundation of his essence, and his spiritual composition. He gave the impression of "a worker in the labor of Torah" also through his personality and external appearance. "Torah and service" in the normative sense of the term – "the service of Torah" was the style innovated by Rabbi Rafael.

His fundamental Torah novellae were also fitting for his style. They had more of the creativity of a worker than that of an initiator. The creation was the essence of the form. The style was fundamental, and the internal content was all about labor. In general, his learning style was appropriate to his outlook, with sharpness, breadth of expertise, and quantitative depth, and was not in sync with the usual outlook of the Volozhin style. His high quality novellae had the simplicity of a "Sinai"[ii]. In contrast, the fundamental Volozhin learning tradition, the style of the Gr'a, stresses straightforward investigation. The source itself, through the wellspring of creativity, exposes the genius in simplicity. The Netzi'v, the creative Yeshiva head, was faithful to this style. He was the teacher, the educator, the guide, the leader, and the spokesman. The era of Rabbi Rafael was merely a continuation of the tradition, the tradition of the fathers, the guarding of the existence of the essence. But it did not have the novel creativity or development and progress. He was a faithful guardian of the treasures of his fathers, the forger of the spirit and soul of the Yeshiva. He considered himself as a guardian, and nothing more. When he was approached with a demand for some rectification or innovation, his response was: "just as I received from my fathers, I wish to give over to the coming generation." This response highlights for us his conservative essence in general. Rabbi Rafael utilized this character strongly until his last days…"

He excelled in one thing over and above all the other *Gaonim* of his generation – in his integrity [perhaps simplicity or innocence]. He truly had the paradigm of integrity of the generation. His integrity was a form of beauty of the soul and pureness of the spirit and heart. The trait of integrity in his personality was especially prominent at light-hearted moments. He loved to laugh, and I never have seen such pure-hearted laughter as that of our late rabbi.

Several episodes exemplify his integrity. It is told that on the day of the wedding of his daughter to Rabbi Chaimke, Rabbi Rafael sat in his room, occupying himself with Torah as was his custom. All the needs of the wedding and the couple fell upon the Netzi'v and his wife. They toiled and prepared all the needs of the wedding. When the time of the *chupa* [wedding ceremony] came, they sent for him to come to the wedding of his daughter. In his haste to get ready, the buttons of his cloak fell off as he was getting dressed. He groaned and said: "Oh, the agonies of raising children…"

Another episode: "Once, when he was sitting in his house studying Torah, he wished to eat, but there was nobody home. He searched around and found a pot filled with seeds. They appeared doubled – a food that he liked very much. He made a blessing, ate, and enjoyed. When the Rebbetzin returned, he said: "The beans that you cooked today were very tasty." The Rebbetzin said: "They were almonds!" The rabbi responded: "If that is the case, I made an error and recited the improper blessing"

During the time that I was studying in Yeshiva, Rabbi Rafael traveled to Vilna to participate in a rabbinical convention, that took place in the summer

[Page 227]

of 5669 or 5670 [1909-1910]. I recall that the Yeshiva then found out about another typical episode. However, I cannot verify whether it was true or it was the fruit of the imagination of the Yeshiva students. An important question arose regarding the order of the day, which was dependent on the fluidity of the opinion of each participant. They asked Rabbi Rafael: "Rabbi, where do you hold?"[liii] He responded innocently: "I am holding in such and such a tractate, at such and such a page."

As is known, the Yeshiva was open in an illegal manner during the time of Rabbi Rafael. Some time after the final closing, during the time of the Netzi'v, great efforts were made to open the Yeshiva with government permission, but only as a *Beis Midrash* and not an educational institution. The "Yeshiva" existed during it final era as a *Beis Midrash*. The city policemen and government officials knew of its existence, of course, and the hundreds of young students who came from the entire Diaspora were not unknown to them, but they received remuneration for "not doing anything" as was the custom in those days…

In the summer of 5672 [1912] the district supervisor came to investigate and find out about the activities of the Yeshiva. He visited the house of the rabbi, and sat there for a period of time, interrogating, and asking him questions. The rabbi was not fluent in the Russian language, so a Yeshiva student translated. Among other things, the supervisor asked: "Why do so many people come to study in Volozhin?" The rabbi told [the translator] to respond: "Everyone who studies in Volozhin sees a blessing in his studies.."

Such were many of the general conversations of Rabbi Rafael, showing the great level of his integrity.

Indeed, during the period of his leadership, there were also disputes and arguments between the leadership of the Yeshiva and the students, some of which led to strikes and disruptions in the protocols of the Yeshiva. However, these conflicts were the fault of the *mashgiach* [spiritual supervisor of the Yeshiva] who was a follower of "*Musar*"[iv], and used the integrity[v] to conquer the "Volozhin fortress" for "*Musar*." He began with a ban on reading newspapers and literature, which was against the traditional internal freedom that pervaded in the Yeshiva of Volozhin. This "enactment" was reenacted in 5667 [1907] and led to a dispute between the Yeshiva students and the leadership. Rabbi Rafael then saw it as his duty to publish a letter clarifying the situation[2]. The *mashgiach* renewed his "enactment" in the year 5672 [1912] and further added that every Yeshiva student must sign on to the writ of ban, stating that they must not read newspapers or books from the new literature. Then, a strike broke out lasting for about three months. The Yeshiva students demanded the repeal of the writ and proposed from their side a "writ of obligation" to be signed by the *mashgiach*. The battle was heavy. Suddenly the rabbi left the city together with the *mashgiach* and went to the baths [i.e. spa] in Duvlin. The Yeshiva students publicized their opinion in the Hebrew newspapers. At the end, the Yeshiva students won. The *mashgiach* was forced to sign the writ of obligation.

The behavior of Rabbi Rafael at that time was very characteristic, for all the winds were

[Page 228]

storming, and the ferment was growing from day to day. The Yeshiva students came to him en masse. He was silent and they were silent. Finally, the Yeshiva students presented their complaint, and proposed their demand and claim. The rabbi was silent. The students murmured, lamented, and complained – and he remained silent. He only uttered some word or some truncated phrase on occasion. The "negotiations" continued in this manner for several hours until the rabbi rose and said: "The time for the *Mincha* service has come." He walked between the rows of students and repeated in a remonstrating voice "and you should fear your G-d, and you should fear your G-d"... – for not only was he a man of great integrity, but he was also taciturn. They said of regarding him: he was silent until he got tired of all the silence. He then rested a bit and continued with his silence…

Rabbi Rafael was born in Smorgon the 5590s in accordance with our counting[3]. He was educated by his father the expert Gaon Rabbi Leibele Kovner until the age of 15. At around that age, the Netzi'v took him as a groom for his daughter Sara Rasha. He spent his nights and days studying Torah being supported at the table of his father-in-law.

In his commentary *Haemek Sheeila* on the *Sheiltot* of Rabbi Achai Gaon (5521 [1761], the Netzi'v mentions his son-in-law in the introduction to *Kadmat Haemek* among those who helped in the effort. He states that "He sat with me in the group. His power is great in Torah, and his intellect is clear to delve into the depths of *halacha* and clarify it. He also added several glosses with great research depth." In his introduction to the second part, *Vayikra*, he again emphasizes the contribution of his son-in-law and notes his great help in organizing the book, in making corrections and refining the style of language: "And also to fix errors in places where his eyes saw it appropriate, and he dealt intelligently with the matter so it will also be understood for others." This was aside from many additions, Torah novellae, notes, and pointers that came from him in all of the volumes. He was young at the time of the publication of the book of the Netzi'v. At that time, his first wife died, and he married the Netzi'v's daughter Dreizel in 5625 [1865]. They [i.e. he and his first wife] had lived together for two years, and then she died during their wanderings in Minsk[vi].

He was appointed as the Yeshiva head, second to his father-in-law the Netzi'v, in the year 5630 [1870], replacing the late Rabbi Yosef Dov Ber Soloveitchik, who had been accepted as the rabbi in Slutsk. He served in this position for about ten years, until the year 5641 [1881], when he ascended the rabbinical seat of Novoaleksandrovsk. He became the rabbi of Bobruisk in 5656 [1886]. His son-in-law Rabbi Chaim Soloveitchik was appointed in his place as Yeshiva head. It is told that this was on the recommendation of Rabbi Rafael, who once told the Netzi'v: "The competency of my son-in-law (Rabbi Chaim) is superior to the competency of your son-in-law (referring to himself)."

He was accepted as the head of the rabbinical court and Yeshiva head of Volozhin in the year 5659 [1899], after making great efforts to reopen the Yeshiva, and to return Torah to its rightful place. He would give his class

[Page 229]

on rare occasions, and only in his home, for it was forbidden by law to do so at the Yeshiva. However, the Yeshiva students would come to his home and discuss Torah and *halacha* with him. The married students who were in the process of becoming rabbis and wished to receive the ordination of the rabbi would visit him frequently. Despite his old age, he bore the yoke of the Yeshiva. From time to time, he would go out on a journey for several weeks on Yeshiva business to collect money and strengthen its situation.

On festivals, the Yeshiva students would greet their rabbi in his home, as was the custom in Volozhin. He would come to join in at the public celebrations that the students arranged in the Yeshiva, especially at the *Simchat Beit HaShoeva*. The Yeshiva students extended great honor to him. They danced in his honor, and he, with his pure smile, stood in the middle clapping his hands.

He would worship only in the Yeshiva. If on occasion he worshipped in the *Beis Midrash*, he would go to the Yeshiva after the services to greet the people. His room was lit all night as he sat and studied, delving into the Torah, or writing a novella. Thus, did our elderly rabbi live his holy, peaceful life until the year 5674 [1914], the year the First World War broke out. Then, he and his family went into exile, and the Yeshiva was exiled with him. They went to the same place where his father-in-law the Netzi'v went after the closing of the Yeshiva in Volozhin – to Minsk. His son-in-law Rabbi Chaim was with him in exile because of the difficulties of the time and the weight of the war. Thus began his terrible period of wandering, and years of agony and tribulation. The Rebbetzin died in Minsk. Then, his son-in-law Rabbi Chaim died. He remained alone, abandoned, and forlorn. He suffered very greatly toward the end of his life… During the latter days, they tried to encourage his spirit with the hope of reestablishing the Yeshiva and setting it up again in Volozhin – the source of his life. However, in the interim, his great, pure, holy soul departed to the G-d of the spirit, and he was laid to rest in the city of his wandering.

Original Footnotes:

1. Published in *HaIvri*, 25 Nisan 5681 (May 6, 1921).
2. The letter was published in *Aspaklaria* by Ben-Zion Eisenstat, booklet IV, 5669 [1909].
3. According to *Oholei Shem*, he was born in the year 5597 [1837]. In "The Generations of our Rabbis and Scribes" (Vilna 5660 [1900], page 49), Ben-Zion Eisenstat states that the year of his birth was later, in 5598 [1838]. According to his brother-in-law Rabbi Meir Berlin, he was born at the beginning of the 5590s, around the time of the birth of his brother Rabbi Chaim Berlin on 5 Shvat 5592.

Translator's footnotes:

i. Joshua 1:8
ii. This refers to one of the two styles of Torah study: A "Sinai" stresses breadth at the expense of depth, and "an uprooter of mountains" stressed depth at the expense of breadth.
iii. Meaning, "What is your opinion?"

iv.   See https://en.wikipedia.org/wiki/*Musar*_movement
v.   The term may refer to integrity to the point of naivete.
vi.   Rabbi Rafael's first wife Sara Rasha and his second wife Dreizel were sisters.

[Page 230]

Rabbi Moshe Shmuel Shapiro

by Shimon Zak (Tel Aviv)

Translated by Jerrold Landau

A.

Rabbi Moshe Shmuel Shapiro was born in Volozhin on the second day of Sukkot 5640 [1879] to his father Reb Yeshaya and his mother Sara. During his childhood, he studied writing and arithmetic along with the religious subjects, but from the age of 12 and beyond, he only studied Gemara from expert Torah teachers, especially from his rabbi, Rabbi Ziskind.

In those days, a public school for Jewish children was opened in Volozhin by the Russian authorities, as was the case in other Russian cities. The child Moshe Shmuel, wishing to also become educated in secular subjects, registered as a student at the new school. However, Rabbi Ziskind summoned the child's mother and warned her that if Moshe Shmuel does not leave the school, he will be "removed from his *cheder*." In accordance with the demands of his mother – a typical Jewish mother who excelled in her natural intelligence and love and reverence for Torah masters and students, and who played a great role in the education of her three sons in the study of Torah and the fear of Heaven – the lad left the school.

During his childhood, Moshe Shmuel witnessed all the difficulties that afflicted the famous Yeshiva in his native city, and the changes that took place in its leadership: the closing of the Yeshiva by the Russian government in the year 5652 [1892], and its reopening in the year 5655 [1895] when Rabbi Meir Levin, who had been the rabbi of Moscow, was accepted as rabbi in Volozhin. The lives of the residents of the city of Volozhin were connected with the life of the Yeshiva in many ways, and the closing of the Yeshiva was a cause for heavy mourning in the city. This event also greatly moved the heart and tender soul of the lad Moshe Shmuel.

In the year 5663 [1903], Rabbi Moshe Shmuel married Chaya, the daughter of the Rabbi and Gaon Rabbi Avraham Abba Zak, may G-d avenge his blood, the rabbi of Olshad (Alsėdžiai) in the Lithuanian area of Zamot [Zhemaitiya]. Both in the time he studied in Yeshiva, and after his marriage, Rabbi Moshe Shmuel excelled in his diligence and dedication to the study of Torah. With this, he also felt himself comfortable in world culture and the new Hebrew literature. However, he would only peer into the Haskalah books incidentally, literally at a time that was not day or night[i]. His primary world was with the Talmud, and its early and later commentators. His true love of Torah burned inside him, and that was his entire

[Page 231]

interest, in accordance with the ancient poet: "Your Torah is my desire."[ii] His broad and deep Torah knowledge was not a source of income, or a means of any practical application. He satisfied himself with a life of simplicity and modesty both at that time, as well as in later years. A desire for an expansive life was foreign to him. However, he was one of those who grasped a great deal in matters of the spirit: his occupation in such gave purpose to his life and was the source of his happiness. This is the sublime meaning of "Torah for its own sake" – if one says "Torah" – it says everything.

B.

After several years, Rabbi Yisrael Moshe traveled to Kovno and studied in the Kollel there for one year. There, he was ordained to the rabbinate by Rabbi Tzvi Hirsh of Kovno and Rabbi Moshe Danishevski of Slobodka. Then, he studied for a period in the Kollel of Rabbi Chaim Ozer in Vilna. He collected material for his book "Our Rabbi Chaim of Volozhin" while he was in Vilna. Then, Rabbi Moshe Shmuel studied for about three years in the Kibbutz of Rabbi Itzele of Ponevezh. After his marriage, Moshe Shmuel fulfilled the words of our sages: "Exile yourself to a place of Torah"[iii]. Until his marriage, he had only studied in Volozhin. In the year 5674 [1914], Rabbi Moshe Shmuel was invited to give classes in the Yeshiva that was founded in the town of Aniksht [Anykštis]. However, the First World War broke out at the end of the year, and the Yeshiva was closed.

The Yeshiva of Volozhin remained his spiritual birthplace throughout all his wanderings to places of Torah. Even though at times he expressed his dismay over the lack of direction in the study paths of the Yeshiva heads during a specific period, it remains a fact that it was not only his fundamental knowledge in Talmud and its commentaries that he obtained from the Volozhin Yeshiva, which he later deepened and broadened through diligence and dedication throughout the years until he became one of the Torah greats – but this Yeshiva also forged his moral personality and his spiritual image. The years of his study and education in Volozhin were decisive years in his life, the light of which shone in him until his last day. The warmth that his soul absorbed during those early years of his life remained etched in the fire of love for the Yeshiva of Volozhin and its Torah. Its influence never ceased throughout all the days of his life. The physical uprooting from the world of Volozhin in the midst of difficult life conditions – and later also from the world of scholarly Lithuania – did not cause a spiritual uprooting from that world. He remained faithful to the tradition and spirit of Volozhin. Typical of his soulful connection to the Yeshiva of Volozhin is the fact that his Torah-oriented literary efforts began with his book "The History of our Rabbi Chaim of Volozhin," and the final article that he wrote was about Rabbi Itzele of Volozhin (published in *HaDoar* approximately two weeks after the death of the author).

C.

The Jews of Lithuania were never pampered with enjoyments and lives of excess. They were satisfied with little. However, even this little amount was not readily available in every house. There were many whose lot was a measure of carobs from eve of Sabbath to eve of Sabbath[iv]. Many of the marred Yeshiva students, Torah scholars, and Yeshiva educated people in every city and town who managed to gain a role in the world of commerce, and found some source of livelihood for themselves and their families,

[Page 232]

were unable to get accustomed to the ways of commerce and awaited a rabbinical seat. If a rabbinical position became open, many would leap forward, and the competition was great among the young rabbis. This would be the case even in a small, poor town that could barely provide a meager livelihood for their rabbi. Furthermore, even in scholarly Lithuania, the bumptious ones who knew how to promote themselves had the upper hand over the more reticent, modest ones whose souls were disgusted by cheap, loud, publicity.

Rabbi Moshe Shmuel, with his generous traits and sublime character, with a noble spirit and refined soul, could not get accustomed to the demands of this cruel reality. After much doubt and hesitation, he decided to part from his family for a while and to move to the United States. With a heavy heart full of sorrow, his family members, acquaintances, and friends parted from him. This decisive step frightened them: would he succeed in overcoming the difficulties of acclimatizing to that far-off, strange world? Would he succeed in finding a firm basis under his feet in the new world, whose principles, lifestyle, and spirit were so different than what he was used to?

He indeed stumbled across many difficulties during his first period in America. Only after many difficulties was he appointed to the honorable position of principal of the Rabbi Chaim Berlin Yeshiva. He served in that position for approximately 25 years. However, that did not bring him to complete rest. There as well, there were petty, narrow-minded trustees who embittered his life, to the point where he was forced to turn to the Agudas Rabbonim [Rabbinical Union] to protect his rights. He endured much suffering throughout his life. However, his difficult experiences and bitter trials did not crush his spirit or affect his integrity. Those who came in contact with him benefited from his good spirit, the light of his face, and pleasant demeanor, and enjoyed his great knowledge and personal charm. He found his comfort in the study of Torah and in his literary pursuits. It seems that during the difficult moments of his life, he felt the need to distance himself from the environment and to unite with the spiritual world of the Torah great and luminaries, the sparks of whose souls also burned within his soul. From time to time, he would publish articles that exhibited great analytical depth and deep sharpness in the Torah of our sages of his generation and of previous generations.

In his article "One of the Superior People"[1], Dr. Yitzchak Rivkind of blessed memory writes about the great contribution of Rabbi Moshe Shmuel to Volozhin research.

"He was 29 years old when he published "The History of the Gaon Rabbi Chaim of Volozhin" in the year 5669 [1909]. This first work brought attention to the author and his research. Rabbi Moshe Shmuel had all the talents of the soul to become the historian of the supernal Volozhin. He was a native of Volozhin, and remained a man of Volozhin until his final day. Volozhin was in him, and he lived as Volozhin."

He revered the greatness of the Yeshiva from his youth until his final day. His work

[Page 233]

"The Yeshiva of Volozhin During the Years of its Closing and its Opening"[2] concludes with an ode to the Yeshiva.

"Volozhin always had some sort of attractive force, lofty and hidden from the eyes of everyone, secluded and enclosed within the walls of the Yeshiva. The spirit of the Gaon Rabbi Chaim, may the memory of the holy be blessed, the founder of the Yeshiva, hovered within it always and adorned it with a unique charm, which never left it until its last day."

Rabbi Moshe Shmuel died in Brooklyn (United States) on 9 Cheshvan, 5623 (November 6, 1962)[v].

Original Footnotes:

1. *HaDoar*, 7 Kislev 5623 [1922], and in the anthology of writings of Rabbi Moshe Shmuel, "Rabbi Moshe Shmuel and his Generation" pp 23-31.
2. *HaDoar* 5622 [1922], issue 36.

Translator's footnotes:

i.   A common expression for devoting a very small amount of time to something.
ii.   Psalm 119:92. The ancient poet is King David.
iii. *Pirkei Avot* 4:14
iv.   A Talmudic expression for a meager amount of food, based on Tractate *Taanit* 24b.
v.   For more information, and his gravestone, see http://kevarim.com/rabbi-moshe-shmuel-shapiro/

Rabbi Meir Bar-Ilan (Berlin)

by Shimon Zak (Tel Aviv)

Translated by Jerrold Landau

"The nobleman of the house of Volozhin" – Rabbi Meir Bar-Ilan was called that by his acquaintances and those who appreciated him. He was born in Volozhin on 29 Nissan 5640 (April 10, 1880). The unique methodology of the Yeshiva of Volozhin found its full, sublime expression in his personality. A wonderful blend of broad Lithuanian scholarship, Israelite intelligence, populist simplicity, trappings of nobility, paternal tenderness and warmth, the strength of a spokesman and leader, the flame of a deep soul, and the sharp depth of analytical skills consolidated within him. He also studied in the Telz Yeshiva for a certain period during his youth. This Yeshiva greatly strengthened his vitality, which was embedded within his soul already from his early youth.

After his marriage, he worked for a short period in business. (His father-in-law Reb Tovia Rabinowitz was one of the large-scale merchants in the Zamot district of Lithuania – a wonderful character of a Lithuanian Jew who merged Torah and greatness). He settled in Vilna during his period of business. However, Rabbi Bar-Ilan did not find satisfaction for his soul in the world of commerce. He was a man of vision and internal drive, and he aspired to a different field of endeavor that would find release for his great aspirations and many talents. He moved to Berlin after a brief period and founded the *HaIvri* weekly, which became the mouthpiece of the Mizrachi organization. The newspaper continued to fill that role afterward, even when its editor moved it to New York at the beginning of the First World War.

In the United States, Rabbi Bar-Ilan became known as a talented leader and first-class organizer.

[Page 234]

He travelled the length and the breadth of the United States, and with his enthusiastic, fiery speeches, he agitated religious Jewry and the circles close to it in America. He was received everywhere with love and reverence. His audience of thousands was influenced by his enthusiasm, and was drawn by him to Zionist national activity. He literally reeducated our Orthodox brethren in America. He aroused them from their frozen state and indifference, and exposed them to the path of the renaissance movement, which was strange to them to that point. The Mizrachi organization, which was founded in all Jewish communities of the United States through his influence, attracted many who had previously been far from issues of Jewry. Throughout many years, it served as the most vibrant and active foundation of the Zionist movement in America, both from a national-cultural perspective, as well as from a practical perspective. From that time, a bridge was formed over the abyss that separated American Jewry from that of the old world. The feeling of common fate between American Jewry and the Jewish nation in general was implanted in the hearts of our brethren in America. Their hearts were opened to help their brethren in the Diaspora, and toward the building of the homeland in the Land of Israel. Rabbi Bar-Ilan played a great role in this revolution, which took place at that time within American Jewry and continues to that day .

His Literary Activities

"From Volozhin to Jerusalem" – this was the way of life of Rabbi Meir Bar-Ilan. This was a long path strewn with obstacles, but it was completely filled with activity and deeds, and illuminated by the ancient lights. In his memoirs between the two volumes of "From Volozhin to Jerusalem" Rabbi Meir Bar-Ilan brings to life an entire era, and presents to us a long row of rabbis, *Gaonim*, activists, scholarly householders, mighty in Torah and with many deeds, wonderful characters revered in the eyes of the people, with whom the author felt himself at home in their company already during his youth. With a faithful hand, he portrays the people of that era, with their temperaments, essence, and talents. Through this, we become familiar with the environment in which they acted, and the place that each of them took in the Israelite world. The research abilities of the author, developed already from his early youth, are astounding. His portrayals testify to a fine sense of psychology, which enabled him to penetrate into the nature and understand the character of anyone with whom he came into contact. Light, hearty humor can be sensed between the lines, as well as a relationship of honor and reverence toward the personalities he describes. The personal weaknesses of some of them is also not lost upon us. Rabbi Bar-Ilan's memoirs will serve the historian as a valuable source of Jewry of the 70 past years.

Rabbi Meir Bar-Ilan's literary activity over 35 years was broad and variegated. He published hundreds of articles on the issues of the times in periodicals published by himself, as well as in those published by others. There was no cultural, political, or communal issue within our world that was not subject to his analysis, via his clarifications and explanations according to his unique methodology, and fitting with his weltanschauung. A small portion of his articles and essay are collected in the *Bishvilei Hatechiya* [On the Paths of the Renaissance] anthology, published by the "World Covenant for the Torah V'Avoda Movement" on the 60th birthday of the late author. Aside from articles on current events, some of his essays on personalities were also published in that anthology. These essays excel in deep analysis of

[Page 235]

the personalities of many of those who laid the foundation of our revival movement, especially from the world of rabbis and Torah greats, the chief spokespeople of the Chovevei Zion era, some of whom later stood at the right hand of Herzl

Rabbi Bar-Ilan's third book is *Rabban Shel Yisrael* [Rabbi of Israel], a comprehensive biography of his father the Gaon, the Netzi'v of Volozhin – his personality, influence, and activities in the fields of Torah and the Chovevei Zion movement.

His style was fundamental and influential. He would create and forge his own sentences and connections with a wonderful voice. Their root was from the Bible, which lived inside him, and gave expression to his thoughts, moving his lips voluntarily and involuntarily. The words were flavored and spiced with adages from our sages from the world of *halacha* and *Aggadah*. Rabbi Bar-Ilan did not like the concise, summarizing style. Rather, he loved to expand broadly. He would add many accompanying statements, and connections and comparisons from the world of thought and culture, over and above the central matter. However, these "additions" were a form of "from issue to issue in the same issue." They were not of the form of "extraneous material detracts," but rather the opposite: they enlightened the eyes of the reader and broadened his knowledge and outlook.

The crowning achievement in his Torah-literary efforts was the publication of the Talmudic Encyclopedia, which he edited along with Rabbi Shlomo Yosef Zevin. This significant Torah endeavor was carried out from that time, according to plans, by Rabbi Zevin, may he live long. Twelve volumes have already been published.

Rabbi Bar-Ilan's literary work and national-communal activities were like two sides of one coin: the thought and deeds blended inside him in a full, harmonic blend. He was not only the greatest innovator in the ideology of Mizrachi, the explicator and commentator of the fundamentals and ideas of the movement that he headed, but he was also the decisor in all practical matters. The great enterprise that clothed his ideas and opinions in the form of a multitude of literary and nationalist activities, the concern for the spiritual and moral situation of the people in the Land and the Diaspora, and the internal impetus for unceasing activity, accompanied by a deep internal flame, did not permit him to restrict himself to the world of study and ideas. They took him out to the expanses of life that demanded his responses and reactions day by day and hour by hour.

"The obligating situation that we should be active, that we should at least feel ourselves that our days do not pass idly… we have lost a great deal as long as we ourselves do not sense the constant activities, unceasing achievements, whether small or large – as long as we do not stop progressing and going from task to task, from deed to deed." (*Bishvilei Hatechiya* [On the Paths of Revival], page 147)

His Educational Activities

For many years, the heads of the Zionist movement displayed an attitude of indifference to the questions of Hebrew culture, and ignored issues of Hebrew education and the need to develop such. The unfortunate results of this attitude were assimilation, national denigration, and the distancing of a significant portion of the younger generation of Jews

[Page 236]

in the Diaspora from Jewish values and national appreciation. This situation aroused fear in the hearts of the leaders of the nation. This was deliberated at the conventions and Zionist Congresses of recent years, and resolutions were accepted obligating the Zionist movement to dedicate its finest powers and energy to the strengthening of Hebrew education and nurturing Jewish consciousness.

Rabbi Bar-Ilan was one of the prominent personalities of Mizrachi who delved deeply into questions of education. He even reached set, firm opinions in this realm. "Study is not the main thing, but rather education" – Rabbi Bar-Ilan stressed in his speech at the convention a few days before his death, "to clarify the educational questions of Mizrachi. We must educate toward Torah and its commandments. And what are the commandments of the Torah if they are not fulfilled? The question comes to the fore today especially, can we rejuvenate life, and not a slow rejuvenation, but one with great energy and fire; our aspiration is not only to continue with what we have, but rather to renovate values and habits." (*Hatzofeh*, 16 Nissan, 5709 [1949])

The Kirya (Campus) of Bar-Ilan University

From right to left: 1) The Stollman Administration Building.
2) The Wurzweiler Library.
3) the Goodman Tower and the Polak Building

Rabbi Bar-Ilan regarded the crisis of the generation as the crisis of education, which misappropriated its role. In our educational efforts, we must especially pay attention to improving the moral makeup and composition of the generation. This task is much more difficult than the imparting of knowledge. "In recent years, we have seen how entire nations, millions of people can turn crazy: humans can become worse than beasts of the field…"

[Page 237]

"This is not only because of wantonness and coarseness in the world, not only because of errors and crimes around us, but rather travesties in the full sense of the term." (*Bishvilei Hatechiya*, page 172).

Rabbi Bar-Ilan saw the vision of everything within the Torah, in accordance with the adage "Turn it over and over, as everything is in it"[i]. Simultaneous with his national and Zionist activities, he toiled and worked all his days to raise the splendor of Torah and its students. For this purpose, he founded Mifal Hatorah [Torah Project] to provide assistance to the Yeshivot and to publish a complete Israeli set of Talmuds, as well as the institute for Torah research. He also participated in founding the Yeshiva of the New Settlement, the agricultural Yeshiva, and others. Rabbi Bar-Ilan merited to have the religious Bar-Ilan University named for him.

The Hebrew village was not only a strong physical fortress in Rabbi Bar-Ilan's eyes, but also a shelter and eternal stronghold of the spirit of Israel and love of the Land. How great was Rabbi Bar-Ilan's joy when he lid the cornerstone for the agricultural Yeshiva in Kfar Haroeh. He regarded this blend of Torah and agriculture as a blend of two fundamental values of great influence from an educational and moral perspective.

With great sharpness and words filled with agony and pain, Rabbi Bar-Ilan spoke out against those who permitted themselves to display an indifferent and hesitant attitude toward the State of Israel because the outlooks of its heads and leaders were not on par with those of Mizrachi. "It is forbidden to bring such thoughts to mind. I stand by my opinion that the State of Israel is an obligation regarding the Torah and commandments. The State of Israel is a Heavenly phenomenon, the footsteps of the Messiah and the beginning of the redemption. With the founding of the State of Israel, we must also introduce the study of the laws of citizenship into the school curriculum. We must instill into the hearts of the students the spirit of the state and a recognition of national consciousness, not only of the past, but also regarding that which we are doing in the present. We are creating history at every moment..." (From the concluding speech at the convention of educational matters – *Hatzofeh*, 30 Nissan 5709 [1949]).

Rabbi Meir Bar-Ilan, the spokesman for religious Jewry, the leader and statesman, the talented writer, the man of vision and deed, the wonderful orator, who brought news of the renaissance to the dispersed of Israel in the many countries of the world, the initiator and creator of many varied literary Torah and national endeavors in the United States and in our country – embodied with his personality an image of great glory and splendor, overflowing with light and wisdom. This was the noble image of the "family of the rabbi"[ii], and the last Mohawk of the splendid Volozhin tradition.

He died in Jerusalem on the 19th of Nisan, 5609 (April 18, 1949)

Translator's footnotes:

i.   *Pirkei Avot* 5:22.
ii.   *Beit Harav* – a term for the rabbinical family stemming from Rabbi Chaim of Volozhin.

[Page 238]

The Home of Rabbi Shmuel Avigdor Derechinski

(Memories and Impressions)

by Yona Ben-Sasson, Jerusalem

Translated by Jerrold Landau

In the Shadow of the Cedars of the Dynasty of the Household of the Rabbi

In the Volozhin Cemetery, aside from the regular monuments, there were two or three canopies of the early founders of the Etz Chaim Yeshiva in the city – the canopies of Rabbi Chaim of Volozhin and his dynasty. These canopies did not serve as regular venues of pilgrimage for wailing and making petitions. Indeed, on occasion, someone with hard luck would come to pray at the grave. However, the primary uniqueness of these canopies was that they marked the chain of sages who imparted to Volozhin a status of importance within Eastern European Jewry of the 19th century.

The canopies were part of the landscape of the city. The praiseworthy rabbinical house, wise women, rabbis, greats in Torah, and Yeshiva heads were part of the character of Volozhin in every generation. The city, from young to old, including the area, treated the Household of the Rabbi with the status of spiritual aristocracy, independent of role and title.

There are several items in the archives of my maternal grandfather, Rabbi Chaim Hillel Fried, that typify the character of Rabbi Chaim of Volozhin, his son Rabbi Itzele, and his grandson Rabbi Eliezer Yitzchak Fried. There is an article of clothing that is fully a tallis, with which Rabbi Itzele would enwrap himself when he stood before ministers in Peterburg. From Rabbi Eliezer Yitzchak, there remains holy objects and covers of holy books made in artistic fashion from silver, as well as manuscripts copied with decorative script by a scribe who was employed specially for this purpose.

From Grandfather, Rabbi Chaim Hillel Fried, there remains many bundles of diaries, each page beginning with the heading "the graces of G-d." Their content includes the details of loans that he obtained, and sums lent to those in need. He would borrow from others in order to lend, since his own funds were limited. He wrote the events of his days on these pages. This diary, which could form an entire book, was in our possession. When he made *aliya* to the Land, he left it with my uncle, Rabbi Shmuel Fried, a rabbi in Vilna.

These three tangible remnants of three generations apparently signify the paths of the ways of life of these three great ones of Volozhin: communal conduct is signified by the tallis; the beauty and pleasantness of a person's spiritual life is symbolized by the art on the private objects of Rabbi Eliezer Yitzchak, and the practical concern for the fate of each and every individual in the community, without being commanded to do so

[Page 239]

by the power of official office, and without the personal ability to respond to the needs of the public, is expressed by the diary "Graces of G-d" of Rabbi Chaim Hillel Fried

The Remnants of the Household of the Rabbi[a]

My mother, Freidele, was the daughter of Rabbi Chaim Hillel Fried. The rest of the sons and daughters of Rabbi Chaim Hillel spread out through various cities in Russia and Lithuania. One of the sons, Rabbi Shmuel Fried, served as a rabbi in Vilna. He was also known by the masses for his good heart and his concern for the public and the individual. Another son, Rabbi Eliezer Yitzchak, was occupied with the lumber trade, at first in Russia and later in the area of Danzig. However, he set times aside to study Torah even when he was fully immersed in the world of business. His day-to-day comportment guarded the family tradition. The other daughters of Rabbi Chaim Hillel, Rechel (Rachel) the eldest and her sisters Esther and Batya, married men from the area of Volozhin and from Minsk. The connection with the sister Esther and her family was severed at the time of the ascent of the Soviet regime.

This article is dedicated to describing the character and life of my father and mother, and of Moshe Zalman.

My father, Rabbi Shmuel Avigdor Derechinski

"This was his teaching. He found everything in the Gemara. He only taught Gemara in his class. Everything was proper and exact. All didactic questions were answered in an incidental fashion. He fulfilled the principle: One should always teach one's students in a concise fashion. In his teaching methodology, he worked to develop the straightforward logic of his students."

These words, written by the editor of HaMelitz, L. Rabinowitz, regarding Rabbi Chaim Tyktinski, may G-d preserve him forever, the head of the famous Yeshiva of Mir, are a perfect definition of Father, Rabbi Shmuel Avigdor Derechinski of blessed memory, as a Torah great and a teacher in the Yeshiva. As you traverse Vilna Street, the main street of Volozhin, during the evening, you would meet an elderly rabbi strolling leisurely, leaning on his cane, accompanied by a family member or someone from the Yeshiva, discussing words of Torah.

[Page 240]

He would greet the passers-by with *Shalom*. They would move aside to clear the way for him. A shopkeeper or tradesman would rise from their place. This would express the respect of the householders of the city toward their rabbi. This respect was expressed not only due to their personal connection with a scholar, but also to the honor given to a representative of the Household of the Rabbi.

If, during the summer, you would veer off in one direction to the path leading to Mount Bialik and the forest behind it – Father would also be accompanied there, as in the city, by family members or students, and would be occupied with words of Torah. Even the gentiles who lived on the road opposite the rabbi would display a level of honor and respect to him, just as did the Jewish residents of the city. This level of respect for the rabbi in his own right, and as a representative of a branch of the Household of the Rabbi, was also expressed with his connections to the secular and religious authorities – the Starostowa, district officials, the commander of the brigade stationed in the city, captains, the clergy, etc.

Among the halacha books that were in Father's house, there was one the content of which was different from the rest. In addition to the pages of the book, it included sheets of parchment cut along the length and width, and written in the script of a scribe. These were *gets* [divorce documents]. The day of a *get* was a day of complete gloom in Father's house. The mourning of separation and the loneliness of divorce oppressed Father the rabbi, and organizer of the *get* ceremony, as well as Mother. Father did not tire in his efforts to bring peace to the family until the tragic moment of separation. When that bitter moment arrived, Father, the organizer of the *get* ceremony, took responsibility along with Mother, who bore the yoke of comfort along with the divorced woman whose world had been lost. This sad ceremony expressed the responsibility that the Household of the Rabbi bore for the fate of the individual, and his tragedies.

Now we look at the image of Father from a different perspective. It was Sabbath in the synagogue. The *Shacharit* service had concluded, and one of the worshippers approached the Holy Ark to take out the Torah scroll. However, they prevented him. What happened? -- They are holding up the Torah reading![2] – Once time – it was the butchers whose meat the rabbi had declared non-kosher. They arose, defending their livelihoods, and did not permit the Torah to be taken out until

[Page 241]

a remedy was found for them. Another time, it was the recruits who were new draftees to the army, demanding reparations and assistance due to their draft to the army (apparently, a relic from the era of the czar, when those who went to the army freed others in a bodily fashion from serving).

The delaying of the Torah reading was a holy matter. The tumult would last for hours. The many would not dare impinge upon the rights of the few who were decrying injustice and demanding protection. Then the rabbi approached the Holy Ark, surrounded by a storm, as those bitter souls continued their screams and complaints. However, with all this, they cleared a path for the rabbi, and nobody was so brazen as to make any sort of physical contact with him. Father took out the Torah scroll and brought it to the *bima*, accompanied the entire time by those who were delaying the reading, and repeating their complaints.

The delay of the reading reached its end, and they began to read the Torah. However, this was not sufficient. During the time of the service or immediately thereafter, the rabbi began to deal with and adjudicate the complaints of those who stopped the reading, and ensured that justice would be done. This was the power of the rabbi within his community.

The concern of the rabbi was extended to every Jew, and not only to the Jews of his city. A unit of the border guard (K. O. P.) was stationed in Volozhin, which included Jewish soldiers. Father left his studies and classes at the Yeshiva, set out, convened meetings, and enlisted the philanthropists. As a result, "*Maachal Kasher*" [Kosher Food] – a kosher kitchen for Jewish soldiers – was set up. It was one of the few in Poland during those days. Father was busy with this mitzva for several years, and worked as the prime mover in this matter. He worked with the commander to grant the soldiers payment for kosher food, he supervised the workers of the kitchen, and he took interest in details, including the portion of food that would be appropriate for the army directives, etc.

In the times prior to his *aliya* to the Land in 1934, Father's strolls with family members in the city and the fields of the area were dedicated both to words of Torah as well as the commandment of settling in the Land of Israel, for Father was a true "*Chovev Tzion*" [Lover of Zion]. In the Yeshiva, he encouraged and supported the formation of a group of Yeshiva students who went out to agricultural *hachshara* in a farm in the area. This was perhaps the only *hachshara* group that stemmed from a Lithuanian Yeshiva and made *aliya* in organized fashion as a group of pioneers. On these strolls, the conversation turned to *aliya* to Zion and to the life of the farmers who were working the ground, benefiting from the toil of their hands.

His pining for Zion was emotional. He ignored his old age, and believed that he would literally fulfil the commandment of settling in the Land of Israel with his own body. Father of blessed memory did indeed merit such, and he served as the rabbi of the farmers who were working the land in the Moshava of Yavne'el, where his son Moshe Zalman lived. As a great one in Torah, as a scion of the family tree of the Household of the Rabbi, and as a lover of Zion and its builders – Father earned a relationship of esteem in this Moshava of veteran workers of the soil.

Father's relationship to the upbuilding of the Land was expressed in his Torah works – with a full pamphlet at the end of his book *Ohel Moshe*, bringing a halachic solution to the bitter question for agricultural farms in the Land – milking on the Sabbath.

Even in his final days, when he was serving as a rabbi in West Jerusalem, he earned for himself a status of honor and esteem among the residents of the area. The characteristics of a great scholar and continuer of the tradition

[Page 242]

of Torah authority were an essential part of his personality, and stood for him wherever he went. Father never stopped studying despite the difficulties of the times and tribulations of life. A list of his Torah publications appears at the end of his book *Masa Levi*: two books in print, and a collection of novellae on the Talmud and responsa in manuscript. He also published more than twenty articles in Torah anthologies: *Sinai*, *Shaarei Zion*, and *Torat Eretz Yisrael*.

Rebbetzin Freidele Derechinski (nee Fried)

The following is etched on the gravestone of my mother, Rebbetzin Freidele, at the Sanhedria Cemetery in Jerusalem: "Here is buried a wise and righteous woman." This description of wisdom and righteousness was not just a cliché. It defined Mother's essence, as the residents of Volozhin knew her. Grandfather, may the memory of the holy be blessed, Rabbi Chaim Hillel Fried, once found under her pillow a note from mother, when she was a child. She requested her permission to study. A portion of her request was granted. They hired a private teacher for her to teach her Bible and the Hebrew language. She was successful at her studies, and she was well-known until her last days for her expertise in Bible and the treasury of the Hebrew language. This was wondrous in the eyes of the great ones and sages of Israel, such as Rabbi Chaim Ozer Grodzinski and Rabbi Meir Berlin, may the memory of the holy be blessed. Rabbi Bar-Ilan (Berlin) wrote in his book "From Volozhin to Jerusalem" that the women of the Household of the Rabbi played a central role in the Household of the Rabbi. They imparted character and direction to the Household, and were true partners with their husbands in the spiritual leadership and dissemination of Torah to the public. My mother was one of those women. However, in addition to her role in the Household of the Rabbi, she also had her own *mitzvot*. The blessed pen in her hand served as a mouthpiece to the poor and suffering people of the city. Her letters were sent on their behalf to relatives and friends of the families in the United States, and brought assistance to these afflicted families. The people of Volozhin knew that they had a mother who would present their requests with a full heart and honorable expression – and they would be answered. They also had utility closer by. Anyone in need of assistance in Vilna, the district city, received a letter from her to her brother, the rabbi there, and he helped anyone who was experiencing difficulty. She also wrote letters to Rabbi Chaim Ozer Grodzinski to help those in need, and he respected her requests.

Mother left behind her contribution, *Masa Laeifa*, an introduction to Father's work *Masa HaLevi*, published after his death. In it she writes with great emotion about the events of Father's life

[Page 243]

from his childhood, tracing the places he lived – Slonim, Białystok, Vilna, Sorotzk, Wyszków, Volozhin, Minsk, Yavne'el, and Jerusalem. It also details his activities in the study of Torah and communal affairs. *Masa Laeifa* is a testament to her talent of portrayal and editing, and the richness of her language and style.

A characteristic picture is etched in my memory: Mother did not love the rabbinate as a source of income. The following was an unusual scene in the house. The tables were set, and the city notables were sitting around them. "For a happy occasion, what does one do?" They brought a writ of the rabbinate to Father to serve among the rabbis of Volozhin. There was a tradition in the Household of the Rabbi still from the days of Rabbi Chaim of Volozhin, preferring the work of Torah and communal leadership over a salaried rabbinical position. Grandmother had a respectable store, and she supported the household and even paid with her money Grandfather's debts that he borrowed to lend to others. Mother continued this tradition and maintained the store, until the times changed and the and the wartime disruptions resulted in a diminishment of livelihood, which became insufficient to support the home. Only then did Father agree to accept the rabbinical post.

This celebration of giving over the writ of the rabbinate melted immediately after the last guest left the house. Then, Mother burst out crying, and the honor and joy turned to anguish. Mother was distressed, and now the entire family was distressed that they were forced to earn their livelihoods from the rabbinate rather than from the toil of their hands.

Mother served as the address for anyone immersed in distress and worry. She was like an unofficial institution for advice and support. Her wisdom and pleasant demeanor, and the discussion with a scholarly woman shone upon anyone who was searching for support, advice, and comfort. However, this was real, from her very essence. Mother was a shattered soul, for she had endured many crises throughout her life. She lost her first husband, Rabbi Menachem Luntz, when she was young, and her oldest son, Eliezer Yitzchak, when he was a young child. She suffered during the tribulations of the First World War. After she made *aliya* to the Land, she was broken by the tragedy of the murder of her son Moshe Zalman, may G-d avenge his death.

Mother was a Rebbetzin not through the power of the writ of the rabbinate, but rather due to her personality and the tradition of the Household of the Rabbi. The name Freidele exemplified her traits of wisdom, righteousness and good-heartedness.

Moshe Zalman Ben-Sasson (Luntz)

In the family album one can see the photo of a charming lad at the age of Bar Mitzvah, with a Gemara under his arms, and dreamy eyes peering at you. This is Moshe Zalman, Freidele's son. He was a tender and wise child. Father taught him Torah and was proud of his novellae. His Bar Mitzvah speech from *Emek Yehoshua* made an impression in its time. His Torah novellae are recalled in Father's book *Ohel Moshe,* that he dedicated as a memorial canopy to Moshe Zalman after he was murdered,

During the 1920s, a young lad was sitting on a train, inwardly turned, without uttering a word. Next to him sat a Polish captain who attempted

[Page 244]

to get him to speak, but to no avail. The captain said to him, "Tell me, young man, what can I give you so that you will at least tell me one word?" The lad did not respond. This was the quietude of Moshe Zalman on the day he parted from the family on route to the Land of Israel. His internal world during that journey was full of an accounting of the soul of two decades of life that had passed.

He regarded himself as Mother's protector. When Moshe Zalman was a young child, and mother required caresses, joy of life, and support – he had to serve as a support for mother during her illnesses that she suffered from on account of the crises she endured.

When he left the bench of study and Gemara, he became the living spirit of Cherut VeTechiya [Freedom and Renaissance], the movement of *chalutzim* [Zionist pioneers] in Volozhin. He was involved in the establishment of the movement and in the social conventions. He also served as the ideological spokesmen and the recognized counselor of that group. *Aliya* to the Land was the pinnacle of what he absorbed from the Household of the Rabbi and the movement. According to his nature, these were values that became part of his personality and essence, leaving no room in his thoughts for other matters. However, since the world of his childhood and youth in Volozhin was very dear to him, he united completely with that world, and his ear was inattentive to the question of the captain who sat next to him on the train.

Moshe Zalman made *aliya*, and we followed him in *aliya*. My brother Chaim Hillel and I came to Yavne'el to visit him. We heard that Moshe Zalman Luntz would lecture that night in Beit Ha'am. We found that Moshe Zalman the first to arrive at Beit Ha'am! He set up the lecture hall, placed the benches and lectern, and swept the floor. That was Moshe Zalman. No domination, but rather work and service. He did not seek honor. He was the lecturer, and other should have been serving him. However, he served the community with whatever the community required, from setting up the benches to delivering his lecture.

A scorpion stung him as he was looking after the defensive weapons that were hidden in "Salik" for he was responsible for security. Here too there was domination, but rather service. He was the one who cleaned the weapons in "Salik" and he did not demand recognition or fame. At that time, there was no antidote to snake bites in Yavne'el. The paralysis spread through Moshe Zalman's body, and he was only saved through the mercies of Heaven.

Moshe Zalman kept a diary, from which we learn about the areas that caught his interest. Issues that were of utmost importance to the group during that period are recorded in his diary alongside details of his work, family matters, etc. Feelings of responsibility and bearing the burden of the group and family needs were expressed in his diary.

Moshe Zalman was a *chalutz* [pioneer]. That is, he did not work solely for a need to earn a living, but rather due to his weltanschauung that connected to the problems of the group, to issues of the spirit, and questions of the nation and redemption. The factors that spurred on his work were ideological factors. This is the clear sign of a *chalutz*.

When settlement was taking place in the Beit Shean valley, Moshe Zalman decided that his place was in that place which called out to *chalutzim* – that is to those who responded to vital needs to which there was nobody else to take care of. He

[Page 245]

wanted to move to a pristine, desolate, and dangerous area. However, he did not merit such. He was murdered by an ambush of Arabs on his way to an evening farewell party that was arranged for him.

His final words before his soul departed were: "Mother! Mother!" Even though he was a *chalutz* concerned with the needs of the public – his first concern was for his mother. Nobody knew like him the suffering and tragedy, and he tried to ease her lot in life to the extent possible. He even took on the family name Ben-Sasson to keep up the faith of her mother (Freidel = Sasson)[3], and to impart continuity to the unity of the family so that the three brothers would be called by the same name[4].

There is a large monument in the Yavne'el cemetery, different than the rest. This is the monument of Moshe Zalman and his two friends who were killed together by the ambush. There is no special pilgrimage to this monument, but it speaks to the heart of people from both Yavne'el and Volozhin who knew Moshe Zalman face to face.

The canopy of the Household of the Rabbi, which is noted for its uniqueness in the Volozhin cemetery, found its continuation in the unique monument in the Yavne'el cemetery. Through his personal fine traits, his responsibility to the group, his concern for its fate and its establishment, his concern for the individual and his faithful group, Moshe Zalman was a continuation of the branch of the Household of the Rabbi, which began with his grandfather Rabbi Chaim Hillel and continued through his father and mother Freidele.

The grave of the three in Yavne'e
The grave of the three in Yavne'el. The grave of Yehuda Ilovich, Moshe Zalman Ben-Sasson, and Gedalyahu Geller, who were murdered on 2 Nisan 5697 (March 14, 1937) returning from a party that was organized in their honor in Bayit-Gan.
The following is engraved on the monument: "The three martyrs of Yavne'el, beloved and pleasant during their lives, and not separated in their deaths. Murdered on the evening of Monday [i.e. Sunday night] 2 Nissan, 5697."
The following is engraved on the monument of Moshe Zalman: "Moshe Zalman Luntz Ben-Sasson, a scion of the Gaon Rabbi Chaim of Volozhin, born 21 Elul, made aliya in 5683 [1923]."

Original footnote:

a. Rabbi Shmuel Avigdor HaLevi Derechinski was born in Slonim. (The exact year of birth is not known. Apparently it was around 5634 – 1874.) His family was related to the Gaon Rabbi Shmuel Avigdor of Karlin. He was the youngest of the five sons of the family. He lost his father when he was about ten years old. He studied Torah in Białystok, [Page 240] supported by his brother the Gaon Rabbi Yonah, a friend of Rabbi Meir Simcha HaKohen of Dvinsk [1]. From there he moved to his second place of Torah, Vilna, where he became known as a great and diligent studier.
He became connected with the family of the Etz Chaim Yeshiva heads when he got married to Freidel, the daughter of Rabbi Chaim Hillel Fried, may the memory of the holy be blessed. He occupied himself with Torah in the home of his father-in-law until the First World War. When the war broke out, he moved to Minsk, where he continued with the study of Torah. He became friendly with the great rabbis who lived in that city. The family returned to Volozhin after the First World War, and Rabbi Shmuel Avigdor was appointed as rabbi and Yeshiva head. The entire family

made *aliya* to the Land in the year 5692 [1932]. Rabbi Derechinski served as rabbi in Yavne'el, Israel. He loved Zion and was faithful to the house of Mizrachi throughout his entire life. He died on 12 Shvat 5704 [1944].

The works of Rabbi Derechinski include a) *Ohel Moshe*, dedicated to the memory of the martyred son Moshe Zalman (Jerusalem, 5699 [1939]); b) *Masa HaLevi* (Jerusalem 5704 [1944] with the volumes i) *Masa HaLevi* – novellae on the Talmud; ii) *Masa HaLevi* – Responsa. Furthermore, Rabbi Derechinski published articles in important periodicals.

Translator's footnotes:

i. See https://en.wikipedia.org/wiki/Meir_Simcha_of_Dvinsk
ii. This was a common form of protest to grab the attention of the community.
iii. *Freid* (Freida – of which Freidel is a diminutive) means joy in Yiddish, whereas *Sasson* means joy in Hebrew.
iv. Moshe Zalman was the son of a different father than the two younger brothers, one of whom is the author of this article.

[Page 246]

Conversations of the Sages

by Eliezer Leoni

Translated by Jerrold Landau

(From the treasuries of Volozhin wisdom, experiences, sharpness)

The regular conversations of the sages of Volozhin, spoken in aphoristic-anecdotal style, contain treasuries of educational and instructional Torah of life. From this treasury, we have gleaned valuable pearls, pleasant in their sharpness and directness. They form wonderful reading material, enjoyable and educational for both youth and adults.

The Wisdom of Rivka, the Mother of Rabbi Chaim of Volozhin

When the scholars of the city would gather in the home of her father, the rabbi of Piesk, to study together a chapter of Mishna or a page of Gemara, she would sit at the side and listen to the studies. Once, during the month of Elul, she heard them studying a Mishna from [Tractate] *Rosh Hashana* (23:b) "Even a wise one who comes to deliver…" The explanation of "a wise one" is a midwife. She stood up and asked politely and modestly: "Teach me, my rabbis. Why is a midwife called 'a wise one'"? The listeners were quiet, but her father the rabbi responded that a midwife serves in place of a physician, and a physician is called *chakim* [a wise one] in the language of the sages (see *Bava Metzia* 86:a). Therefore a midwife is also called *chachma* [a wise one in the feminine].

She continued: "My revered father should forgive me if I state that in my opinion, a midwife is called 'a wise one' because it states in Tractate *Tamid* (32:a) 'Who is wise? – One who can see what is to come' [note: the terminology for 'what is to come' is *nolad* – i.e. what is born]. Since the midwife is the first to see the child who is born, she is called 'a wise one.'"

(From Rabbi Maimon, *Sarei Hameah*, part II, p. 122)

A Sharp Response from Rabbi Chaim of Volozhin

There were times when lads from all parts of the world, even from the Caucasus, came to study in Volozhin. Rabbi Chaim loved his students, and had mercy upon them like a father has mercy upon his children. There were rumors that the lads from the Caucasus were talking to girls during the evenings.

When this matter reached Rabbi Chaim's ears, he asked the zealots: "And how do the lads from Volozhin and the nearby towns behave?" They responded: "They too stroll with girls during the evenings."

"If that is the case," Rabbi Chaim responded, "Then the lads from the Caucasus are no worse than other lads. Their only 'sin' is that they are studying in Yeshiva. That sin I take upon myself."

(Naftali Gross, "Stories and Parables" pp 127-128)

"And the King of Egypt Died, and the Children of Israel Sighed" (Exodus 2:23)

Rabbi Itzele of Volozhin asked: "And before that, when the king was alive, was their lot any better? Their situation was better? – However, as long as the king was alive, they thought that only that Pharaoh was cruel

[Page 247]

to the Jews, and when the king would die and a new king would arise – they would be able to breathe a sigh of relief. However now "the king of Egypt died" and the situation did not improve Therefore – "The Children of Israel sighed and cried out." They realized that their hope was for naught, for all the kings of Egypt are similar to each other.

(B. Joashson 'From Our Old Treasury'; vol II, p. 21)

The Title *Iluy* [Genius] in Volozhin

In Volozhin, they referred to only those who excelled in unusual talents as an *Iluy*. However, there were also semi-*Iluys*, and that term also testified to a high level.

The following joke went around Volozhin: An *Iluy* is someone who has a sharp mind, a great deal of knowledge, and is slightly crazy. What does a semi-*Iluy* mean? – Indeed, he is crazy, but he does not know Torah.

(Ibid. Vol III, page 208)

The Sharp Explanation of Rabbi Zalmele

It is written: "And Machla, Tirzah, Chagla, Malka, and Noa, the daughters of Zelaphechad, married their cousins." (Numbers 36:11). Rashi states: "Here they are listed by their age, and they got married in chronological order. Everywhere else in scripture, they are listed by their level of wisdom, to show that they are equal to each other."

Rabbi Zalmele asks: What is the reason that they are listed by wisdom throughout the scripture, and only in this place "they are listed by age"? The Gemara states the following regarding the daughters of Zelaphechad: "Even the youngest of them did not get married when they were less than 40 years old" (*Bava Batra* 119), therefore it was not their desire that they be enumerated by age. However, here, in the Torah portion of *Masai*, they are mentioned after their marriage: "And Machla, Tirzah, etc.... married their cousins." After the wedding, it was already permitted to reveal the secret of their ages…

(Ibid, Vol IV, p. 175)

The Deeds of our Father in Heaven and the Deeds of Man

A former student who rose to greatness and became very wealthy came to the Netzi'v (some say to Rabbi Yosi Ber).

"What are you occupied with?" the Netzi'v asked him.

"Thank G-d, Rabbi, I am healthy and whole, and I also have livelihood."

The Netzi'v sat and chatted with his student about this and that. Suddenly, he asked him again, "What are you occupied with" – "Did I not answer the honorable rabbi that I, thank G-d, am healthy and also have a good livelihood?"

They continued their conversation. A few minutes later, the Netzi'v asked his student for a third time: "And so, what are you occupied with?"

"Let the honorable rabbi not get angry," he expressed in surprise. "This is the third time that the honorable rabbi has repeated himself and asked the same question. I have already told our rabbi, thanks to our G-d that He has blessed me with physical health and ample livelihood."

[Page 248]

"You are not answering me according to the question," said the Netzi'v. "I have asked you: What do you do? You are currently answering me about your physical health and livelihood. All these are deeds of the Almighty, and not of your own. He gives health and He gives livelihood. Now I want to know: What are your own deeds? Do you set aside times for Torah? Do you give charity? Do you do acts of benevolence to the poor?…"

(Ibid., ibid. p. 236-237)

The Shadar'im (Shada'r = Emissary of the Rabbis) of the Yeshiva of Volozhin

When the Yeshiva of Volozhin was standing, the *Shadar'im* went out throughout the Jewish Diaspora to ask for donations for the needs of the Yeshiva. A *Shada'r* from Volozhin would go to the ends of the earth and the distant seas. There is a story of Shmuel Simchovich, who was a *maskil* and great in Torah, as he sat with a group of *maskilim*. The question was asked: Where are the Mountains of Darkness? Simchovich responded: "Sirs, it is known that the Mountains of Darkness do not exist and were never created. A proof: Had they existed, the *Shada'r* of Volozhin would have gone there."

(M. Lipson, "From Generation to Generation" vol II, paragraph 1274)

The Life Wisdom of Rabbi Hillel Fried

There is a story of Rabbi Hillel Fried, the son-in-law of Rabbi Chaim of Volozhin, that he saw him on Friday Night walking with a lit lantern in his hand. He wondered. He followed after him until he entered a certain house, remained there for a little while, and left without the lantern.

"Our Rabbi," they asked him, "What is this about?" Rabbi Hillel responded, "The essence of the deed is such. There is a dangerously ill person in this house, and the members of the household fear sin, and do not light a candle or do anything for the needs of the sick. I demonstrated the actual *halacha* to them: When there is a dangerously ill person, it is a mitzvah to violate the Sabbath for him…"

(Ibid. vol III, paragraph 2048)

The Sons-in-law of Rabbi Itzele of Volozhin

Rabbi Itzele of Volozhin had two sons-in-law: Rabbi Eliezer Yitzchak Fried and Rabbi Naftali Tzvi Yehuda Berlin (the Netzi'v).

Once, on the night following Yom Kippur, after midnight, Rabbi Eliezer Yitzchak said to Rabbi Itzele, "Tell me, my father-in-law, what is my duty and I will do it at this time, after the fast?"

"Come," Rabbi Itzele said to him, "And I'll show you what to do." They entered a second room of the Yeshiva. Rabbi Naftali Tzvi Yehuda standing with his feet immersed in cold water, as he was diligently occupying himself with Torah.

(Ibid. ibid. paragraph 2237)

[Page 249]

The Response of Rabbi Eliezer Yitzchak Fried to a Nice Parable

Once Rabbi Eliezer Yitzchak saw one of the Yeshiva students reciting his prayers in rapid fashion. He invited him in and began to talk words of reproof to him regarding prayer. A person is required to pray in a leisurely fashion, as if he is counting money. A prayer without proper intention is like a body without a soul.

The Yeshiva student responded "I say to our rabbi, what is this compared to? To a person traveling in a carriage. When he drives slowly, *shkotzim* [gentiles] jump onto his carriage. It is not the same when he drives fast. They cannot ascend. Prayer is the same. If one prays quickly, the evil inclination cannot take hold of one's prayers, and foreign thoughts separate from him."

"I suspect," Rabbi Eliezer Yitzchak said with a smile, "That you drive so quickly that even one *shegetz*, you yourself, is not able to ascend the carriage.

(Ibid. ibid. paragraph 555)

How Did Rabbi Zalmele Demand the Needs of his Body?

Thus was the way of Rabbi Zalmele of Volozhin: He never asked out loud for the needs of his body, such as food, drink, and sleep. If he was hungry, he would begin to recite by heart verses and adages regarding eating, and the members of the household would fulfil his will and prepare his meal. If he was thirsty, he would begin to recite verses and adages regarding drinking, and the members of his household would give him something to drink. It was the same with sleeping, bathing, etc.

(Ibid. ibid. paragraph 587)

The Innocence of Rabbi Zalmele

Rabbi Zalmele was a complete Gaon, Tzadik and pure. Once when he was in the bathhouse on the eve of the Sabbath, his cloak was stolen. Rabbi Zalmele did not say anything, and he returned home.

His wife asked, "Zalmele, where is your cloak?"

Rabbi Zalmele responded, "One of the bathers switched it with his."

His wife responded by asking, "If so, where is that person's cloak?"

Responded Rabbi Zalmele, "It seems, that he forgot to leave his…"

(Ibid. vol III, paragraph 1825)

The Opinion of Rabbi Chaim of Volozhin of his Brother Rabbi Zalmele

The Gr'a of Vilna was expert in the entire Torah, both written and oral. Rabbi Zalmele of Volozhin was also expert in all areas of Torah.

Rabbi Chaim of Volozhin said of them: What is the difference between our holy rabbi and my brother Zalmele regarding expertise [in Torah]? My brother Zalmele is expert in the entire Torah in a straightforward manner, whereas our holy rabbi is expert in all of Torah in a straightforward manner and backwards…"

(Ibid. ibid. paragraph 2516)

[Page 250]

Be Careful Even About a Dispute for the Sake of Heaven

Regarding the statement of the sages "What is a dispute for the sake of Heaven, this is the dispute between Hillel and Shamai"[1], Rabbi Chaim of Volozhin said: "Only people such as Hillel and Shamai themselves are permitted to conduct a dispute for the sake of Heaven. However, petty people such as ourselves, simple mortals – we need to avoid such disputes.

(B. Joashson, "From Our Old Treasury" vol. III, page 248)

The Rejoicing of the Water Drawing[2] in the Yeshiva

In Volozhin, Yeshiva students fulfilled the commandment of the Rejoicing of the Water Drawing properly: they would rejoice and be glad, dance, and also drink until a very late hour at night, sometimes until dawn. The Netzi'v also used to participate in the rejoicing of the Yeshiva students, and would stay awake with them all night. After the energies of those rejoicing and dancing weakened, and the joy was extinguished by weariness, the Netzi'v would open the holy ark, and the Yeshiva students would sing *aleinu* in the melody of the High Holy Days. When they reached "and we bend our knees" they would bend their knees, bow, and prostrate themselves along with the Netzi'v. Apparently this custom is based on the verse, "And when the rotation of parties was over, Job sent word to them to sanctify themselves… for Job said, perhaps my children have sinned" (Job 1, 5).

(Lists, vol I, 4685 [1825], pp 353-362)

Eating "Kodke Blintzes" on the Festival of Shavuot

During the years 5646-5649 [1886-1889] the students of the Yeshiva of Volozhin would go to the house of the Rosh Yeshiva, the Netzi'v, on the first day of Shavuot immediately after the morning services, where they would all be fed dairy pancakes and breads. These Volozhin pancakes were called "Kodke Blintzes" because they would be prepared in large number, so that there would be enough for all the Yeshiva students, and placed in barrels (Kodke is a barrel in Russian).

(Ibid. page 340, note 4)

The Passover Seder in Jerusalem

The large, eight-room house, the home of the Yeshiva head (the Netzi'v) was lit up with many candles. Tablecloths white as snow were spread over the tables, upon which there were bottles and tens of cups. The reclining couch of the Yeshiva head stood at the edge of the first table next to the bedroom, where the Rebbetzin sat dressed splendidly. Approximately 200 students sat around the tables, with festive appearance on their faces. Al were joyous and glad, speaking and discussing Torah matters as well as general chat.

Suddenly the Yeshiva head entered, wearing his silk cloak, with a snow-white kittel on top.

[Page 251]

On his head, he wore a white cap with a silver garland around it. He blessed the students with the blessing of the festival, and reclined on his couch. A deep silence pervaded in the house. The Yeshiva head surveyed all the tables to ensure that everything was in place. Then he recited kiddush and began to read the Haggadah. It was the Yeshiva head's custom to give each Yeshiva student his own Haggadah with his *Imrei Shefer* commentary. The Haggadash were given as a present, as a memento. Each student read from their Haggadahs section by section, and waited. The Yeshiva head would explain, comment, and translate each section based on sources from the Talmud, and the early and latter sages. The students would listen. A spirit of the holiness of the festival and of freedom of the soul pervaded the entire house.

The meal and the reading of the Haggadah continued until two hours after midnight. Then, the true joy began. The Yeshiva head, who was a good singer, began singing *Ata Bechartanu*[3], and all the students would respond in chorus. The faces were splendorous, the hearts were full of emotion, the voices were sublime, as were the feet. The Yeshiva head would stand in the middle, as his students would dance around him and sing. They would conclude *Ata Bechartanu*, and start singing *Baruch Elokeinu*. They would continue dancing and singing until dawn.

(Z. Heller, "The Volozhin Yeshiva", *HaIvri*, issue 8, Rosh Chodesh Adar 5677, February 2, 1923)

The Tobacco Box of Rabbi Yosi Ber Soloveitchik

The Tobacco box never left Rabbi Yosi Ber's table. When he was talking with someone he would open the box, peer inside, and then start the conversation.

One of his relatives could not control his curiosity, and peeked into the box. He found etched therein: שפושמ"נ . He did not know the acronym, so he asked Rabbi Yosi Ber. Rabbi Yosi Ber explained that this is the acronym of the verse: One who guards his mouth and tongue, guards his soul from tribulations (Proverbs 21:23).

(M. Lipson, Midor Ledor, vol. 20, paragraph 1619)

Rabbi Chaim of Volozhin's "Faith" in Physicians

Rabbi Chaim of Volozhin did not believe in the new doctors, who were educated in [the spirit of *Haskala*] – or in their medicine. Once, he felt ill. His family members summoned the city physician, who was a gentile. The physician came, examined the ill person, and prescribed a course of medicine. Rabbi Chaim said to him, "Cures have nothing to them."

The physician said, "Medicine has no benefit for the sick person unless he believes in the physician with full faith, like our lord Jesus."

Rabbi Chaim smiled and said, "I too believe in the physician just as I do in Jesus, and the medicine is not effective for me…"

(Ibid. vol I, paragraph 152)

[Page 252]

What is the Difference between the Netzi'v and Rabbi Yosi Ber?

Rabbi Yosi Ber Soloveitchik was one of the stringent ones, whereas the Netzi'v was lenient. The Netzi'v said, "What is the difference between me and Rabbi Yosi Ber? I, when I recline at the Passover Seder and see a large bundle of matzos, I have fulfilled: the search for chometz, the eating of matzo, the four cups, the celebration of the festival. My heart is full of joy within me, and I bless, 'He Who has kept us alive, preserved us, and brought us to this occasion.'[4]

"In contrast, when Rabbi Yosi Ber reclines at the Seder, he is full of fear and his heart was pained and full of worry, lest he has not fulfilled his obligation: lest he has not gotten rid of chometz completely, lest his portion of matzo had not been guarded in accordance with the law, lest the wine for the four cups was not complexly kosher – lest the bundle of mitzvot has turned, Heaven forbid, into a bundle of sins…"

(B. Joashson, "From Our Old Treasury" Festivals, Five Megillot, page 97)

Even G-d Has given Precedence to "We shall do" over "We shall listen"[5]

Rabbi Yaakov Aharon of Volozhin said, "The giving of the Torah was the marriage between the Blessed G-d and us. Every match obligates both sides. Therefore, we are also entitled to ask the Creator, just as we had faith in Him and preceded 'we shall do' with 'we shall listen' – that He too bestows upon us in that manner, and fulfils 'we shall do' by sending us help before the 'shall listen' – even before he hears our promise to fulfil his Torah."

(Ibid. ibid. pp. 132-133)

The Response of the Netzi'v to a Certain Maskil

A certain *Maskil* was one chatting with the Netzi'v about politics and the Hebrew language. The Netzi'v responded to him "Certainly, I accept all these things. For we indeed recite during the festival kiddush, 'and He chose us above all other nations.' Therefore, we must be proud of our faith. 'And He exalted us over all tongues' – we must bless with our Hebrew language. However, that is insufficient. We must fulfil an additional thing, 'and He sanctified us with His commandments.' We must also fulfil the Torah and guard His commandments."

(Ibid. ibid. page 164)

[Page 253]

Rabbi Chaim Soloveitchik's Opinion about Chibat Tzion

Rabbi Chaim Soloveitchik was a staunch opponent of Chibat Tzion and Zionism. He regarded them as a form of bringing nigh the end of times[6]. Furthermore, they were headed by people who were not fearers of Heaven.

He was asked, "Our rabbi, are they not occupied with the settlement of the Land of Israel and its upbuilding. Is it possible for the Land of Israel to be built up while those who keep the commandments are sitting and waiting for the arrival of the Messiah, in a form of 'sit and do not act'[7]?"

Rabbi Chaim responded, "I say to you, it is the way of the world that regarding how the bride and the groom enter the wedding canopy. The brats ran before them, pass by the musicians, and come first to the place of the wedding canopy. The in-laws, the bride and groom themselves come last."

(M. Lipson, *Midor LeDor*, vol. I, paragraph 65)

The Faith of Rabbi Yosi Ber Soloveitchik in the Upbuilding of the Land

One of the simple folk asked Rabbi Yosi Ber Soloveitchik, "Let our rabbi teach us, this mourning that the Jewish people observe 'between the straits'[8] and on Tisha B'Av, what is the reason for it?"

Rabbi Yosi Ber responded, "I say to you, what is this like? It is like a fire that broke out in the city, and several householders emerge clean from their houses. Those that pay attention to the fire, dig through the mounds of ash and gather whatever they can, believing that they will soon rebuild their houses. Those who do not pay attention to the fire renounce ownership of the remnants, and it is obvious that they are not thinking about rebuilding."

Rabbi Yosi Ber concluded, "This situation is the same. As long as we mourn over the destruction of Jerusalem and the burning of the Holy Temple, we are assured that it will be rebuilt speedily in our days."

(Ibid. ibid. vol III, paragraph 2142)

A Person is Obligated to See the Providence of the Creator Every Day

There is a story about Rabbi Chaim of Volozhin, regarding one of the large-scale merchants coming to him and discussing his troubles: "Our rabbi, I am in great trouble. I have sent barges on the water to Prussia, and the border guards are not letting them pass. Now I will lose all my money and be cleaned out of my possessions."

Rabbi Chaim told him, "Don't fret or be worried. G-d will help you." In the interim, the price of lumber rose, and the merchant profited by several thousands.

He returned to Rabbi Chaim and told him with joy, "Our rabbi, your blessing has been fulfilled with me. Now I clearly see the providence of the Creator."

Rabbi Chaim said to him, "Come and see the difference between a wealthy person and a poor person. A poor person sees the providence of the Creator every day, every moment, and every hour, whereas a wealthy person only sees it once in several years…"

(Ibid. vol II, paragraph 1740)

[Page 254]

"The Tribulations of Childrearing" of Rabbi Rafael Shapira

Rabbi Rafael sat and occupied himself with Torah all his days. He studied, taught, guided, and judged. His mind was not on the affairs of the home. His wife, the mistress of the house, was marrying off sons and daughters. Her dowry and livelihood ran dry, and Rabbi Rafael did not realize her difficulties. On the wedding day of a son or a daughter, they would come to him an hour before the wedding ceremony and inform him, "Our rabbi, the time has come to bring the groom and bride to the wedding canopy."

Rabbi Rafael would close his Gemara, don his Sabbath clothing, and go to the ceremony. Once, when he was getting dressed in his Sabbath clothing for the wedding of his son, his hand got caught in the sleeve, and it was difficult to put on the garment.

"Oy," groaned Rabbi Rafael, "How difficult are the tribulations of raising children…"

(Ibid. vol III, paragraph 1870)

The Preserved Cheese of a Villager…

When Rabbi Yosi Ber Soloveitchik, the great-grandson of Rabbi Chaim of Volozhin, brought his son Rabbi Chaim to the wedding ceremony, where he married the maternal granddaughter of the Netzi'v, the jester at the wedding feast was Elyakum Tzunzer, one of the greatest jesters in his time. He starting jesting, and joined several verses of Torah and the prophets with statements from the Mishna and Gemara, and forged them into rhymes.

When he finished, Rabbi Yosi Ber said to Elyakum, "You know, my sir, what your jesting is compared to? To the cheese of that villager.

There is a story of a villager who entered the *Beis Midrash*. He went to the bookshelf and began to remove books. He took out tractate after tractate, until he laid down the entire Talmud. He still was not satisfied, and he began to take out and place down books of Alfasi, Maimonides, Turim, and responsa. Those who stood at the side saw and wondered: How great must this person be in Torah. He uses so many books at one time. After the villager had amassed a pile of books, he stood upon it, reached the top of the bookcase, and took down preserved cheese…

(Ibid. ibid. paragraph 1868)

The Father and Child

Rabbi Naftali-Tzvi-Yehuda (the Netzi'v) said about Rabbi Chaim Soloveitchik, the son of Rabbi Yosi Ber, "The power of the son is stronger than the power of the father. This one is a genius, and that one is a genius, but Rabbi Yosi Ber did not have the type of father that Rabbi Chaim has…"

(Ibid. ibid paragraph 1939)

Witticisms from Volozhin

a.   Is it your desire to be a rabbi among the Jewish people – and you Maimonides with *Lechem Mishne* [a commentary on the 14-volume *halachic* work of Maimonides];

[Page 255]

and even if you are the *Magid Mishne* [another commentary on Maimonides – but here a play on words – a preacher] (a proper expositor) – in any case you still require the *Kesef Mishne* [yet another commentary on Maimonides – and another play on words, as *Kesef* means money] (to bribe the city activists).
(*Reshimot*, vol I, 5685 [1925], page 389)

b.   Regarding one of the people of the Yeshiva, it is told that at the time when he came to the Yeshiva and told the *mashgiach* [Yeshiva supervisor] that he was 18 years old, the *mashgiach* responded, "I in your years was already 28." One student aspired to be a great expert. Someone who loved witticisms said about him, "He is expert in two sections of the Talmud, but he does not know which of them…"
(HaLevi Ish-Horowitz, *Derech Etz-Hachaim*)

The Power of the Dead is Greater than the Power of the Living…

When the Netzi'v went abroad for recuperation, he noticed to his surprise that all the worshippers were reciting kaddish. He called to the shamash and asked him whether, Heaven forbid, such a severe plague had befallen the city that all the worshippers had become orphaned, let it not happen to us.

The shamash laughed and explained to the Netzi'v that no plague had happened, but the explanation is as follows: the Jews have no great desire to come to worship in the synagogue. They only come when they are obligated to say kaddish.

The Netzi'v smiled and said, "Now the meaning of the verse in Kohelet [Ecclesiastes] is clear to me "Then I accounted those who died long since more fortunate than those who are still living;"[9]. Now I see that the dead are on a higher level than the living. The proof is that the living fathers do not have the power to bring their children to the synagogue, but the deceased fathers – they have the power…"

(B. Joashson, "From Our Old Treasury" Festivals, Five Megillot, pp. 201-202)

Anecdotes about Rabbi Rafael Shapira

a.   Rabbi Rafael Shapira was diligent in the study of Torah. He did not even go out to stroll outside his home out of concern for his time. Once, he was enticed through many words to go out and stroll a bit, for a walk is good for the body   .
Rabbi Rafael said with his simplicity, "What is the benefit? A person who goes for a walk ends up returning to his home."

[Page 256]

b.   Rabbi Rafael was so diligent in Torah study to the point where he ignored the ways of the world. Once, a platter full of cherry fragrances was placed before him. Rabbi Rafael, who loved sweets, ate and did not leave anything over. He wiped his mouth and said, "How tasty were these beans."

c.   Rabbi Rafael was quiet about the ways of the world. He barely opened his mouth amongst people. They said about him: Rabbi Rafael is very quiet. When he gets tired of his quietude, he rests – and then gets quiet again." He would say, "People think that I do not know how to speak. It is not that, rather, it is that I know how to be silent…"

d.   Once Rabbi Rafael was at a rabbinical conference. He sat among them and was silent as usual. There was a difference of opinion regarding one of the items on the agenda. One said, "My opinion is so-and-so," and the other said, "My opinion is so-and-so."

They asked Rabbi Rafael, "And what is your opinion?" Rabbi Rafael responded in innocence, "My opinion is regarding such and such tractate, such and such a page, and such and such a Talmudic discussion…"

e.   Rabbi Rafael would use the "common opinion" methodology with regard to Torah novellae. He joined together several statements from a single person regarding different *halachot*, and would blend them into a single logical unit.

The following joke spread through Volozhin: "Rabbi Chisda was seen walking through the markets of Volozhin. They asked him, 'Rabbi Chisda, what are you doing here?' Rabbi Chisda responded, 'Rabbi Rafael brought me here for the purpose of the "common opinion" methodology.'"[10] (M. Lipson, "From Generation to Generation" vol III, paragraphs 1844, 1845, 1846, 1847, 1848, vol. II, paragraph 1260)

The Mark of Recognition in Volozhin between a Kosher Book and a Forbidden Book

In the Yeshiva of Volozhin, they would prevent students from reading secular books. This was given to the hands of Hershel-Yeshaya the shamash, one of the common people who did not know Bible or Mishna. His eyes were on each and every student. He would even make the rounds to the hosts of the Yeshiva students and check through the windows.

Once, he was looking through the window and saw a student sitting and perusing *Ahavat Zion*. He had heard that *Ahavat Zion* by Mapu was one of the secular books. He hastened into the house, removed the *Ahavat Zion* book from the hands of the reader, and ran to the Netzi'v, the head of the Yeshiva. "See, my rabbi, what I found in the hands of such-and-such a student – *Ahavat Zion* by Mapu."

[Page 257]

The Netzi'v looked and realized that the book was *Ahavat Zion* by the Noda BiYehuda. The Netzi'v told him, "This sign should be in your hand: A book the pages of which are marked by the letters of the *aleph beit* is one of the kosher books. If the pages are marked in the gentile numbers, it is one of the forbidden ones…"

(ibid. II, p. 963)

Very Important and a Small Thing

There is a story regarding Rabbi Chaim Soloveitchik who was in a place together with one of the famous ones. That rabbi was talkative by nature. He sat and talked incessantly the entire time. Rabbi Chaim was silent more than he spoke.

After he left, those around the table asked Rabbi Chaim, "Our rabbi, why were you quiet the entire time, and did you let so-and-so speak incessantly?" Rabbi Chaim responded, "I say to you, so-and-so can speak 23 hours' worth in one hour, however, for me, I require 23 hours to speak one hour's worth.

(Ibid. I, paragraph 802)

The Response of Rabbi Yosi Ber Soloveitchik to a Certain Hassid

One Hassid came to Rabbi Yosi Ber and said to him, "Rabbi, I dreamed a dream in which groups of Hassidim made me a Rebbe."

Rabbi Yosi Ber said, "Great fool, what benefit is there to your dream? Had the Hassidim dreamed about you, the dream would have been good for you. Now that you dreamed about them, these are only meaningless matters…"

Rabbi Yosi Ber would say, "The rabbis of the Hassidim greatly mislead the masses, and from now, there is a need for them…"

(Ibid. I, paragraphs 138, 195)

The Sharp Response of Rabbi Chaim Soloveitchik to his Brother-in-law

During his childhood, Rabbi Chaim Soloveitchik would neglect his studies, distract others, and burn them with his breath. When he left Volozhin, his brother-in-law, Rabbi Yitzchak, the grandson of the Netzi'v said to him, "Rabbi Chaim, let us write Torah novellae to each other."

Rabbi Chaim responded, "No. you and I are not partners. If I write my own Torah novellae, they will say that they are from Father (Rabbi Yosi Ber). If you write Torah novellae of Grandfather (the Netzi'v), they will say that they are your own…"

(Ibid I, paragraph 914)

[Page 258]

Regarding Poor Compositions that have Many Sources

Rabbi Yosi Ber was not pleased with authors who include a plethora of sources: look here and look there.

He would say: "As is customary in the world, one money changer issues a check to his fellow money changer regarding such-and-such a payment. The checks pass to the merchant and are as good as actual cash. Why all this? Because that money changer is wealthy, and he has money to support the checks. If he were poor, and had no coins to pay, his checks would be as a candle to a rock on top of a plate."

Rabbi Yosi Ber continued, "This situation is similar. Sources are like checks. It is like each author issues a check against his fellow author. This can only work when the author himself has content to support the sources. This is not the cause with an author who is poor in knowledge and does not have his own content. In such a case, what is the value of the sources?..."

(ibid. I, paragraph 756)

Rabbi Chaim Soloveitchik has Mercy on a Crazy Girl

'Once a Jewish girl came to Rabbi Chaim and whispered to him with eyes lowered to the ground that she has a secret for him. When Rabbi Chaim removed all people from is presence, the girl burst out crying and said through her sobs that she had erred, and she was pregnant (and was due shortly, and had no recourse). Rabbi Chaim did not chastise or reprove her, but rather spoke to her gently, encouraged her, and calmed her. She did not leave him before he gave her money for her sustenance during her latter days of pregnancy. He asked her to bring the child to him when it was born. He himself would take the child from her hands, and nobody would know about it.

Not long after, at midnight, as Rabbi Chaim was sitting by himself studying Torah, he heard a light knock on the door. He went to the anteroom and saw that girl standing before him with a basket in her hands. He took the basket and brought it into the house. He woke up his wife the Rebbetzin and told her to take care of the baby. In the morning, he sent for a nurse. He paid her wages and gave the foundling to her to nurse and raise.

From that time, that was not the only foundling in the anteroom of the house of the rabbi. Rabbi Chaim would give over the foundlings to a nurse and pay the wages from his own funds.'

Rabbi Chaim – the Patron of Foundlings

Once, a foundling was found in the anteroom of a certain wealthy person. When Rabbi Chaim heard about this, he summoned the wealthy person and told him, "You should know that I have been taking care of this mitzva for some time. However, since you merited from Heaven, I wish to participate in the mitzva with you. The wages of the nurse should be paid half by me and half by you..."

[Page 259]

Rabbi Chaim Concerns Himself with the Wellbeing of a Foundling

Once, a nurse to whom Rabbi Chaim had given over a foundling came to him to demand her wages. Rabbi Chaim felt all his pockets and did not find a coin. He told a nurse to come back the next day, and he would give her. She, who was one of the lowly ones, got angry and shouted, "I will not move from here until I receive my wages. I cannot raise foundlings for free!"

Rabbi Chaim borrowed money from one of the rabbinical judges who was present and paid the nurse. After she left, Rabbi Chaim caught himself and asked her to return. When she returned, Rabbi Chaim said to her, "Be careful, woman, to not nurse the baby immediately after you return home. You were angry, and your milk will cause harm to the baby, Heaven forbid…"

(Ibid. I, paragraphs 794, 795)

The Netzi'v Honors Simple Folk

The Netzi'v was careful in honoring scholars. When he met Avrahamel Moshe Cohen's the water drawer on occasion along the way, who was a scholar, to appease hm, the Netzi'v would greet him first by saying, "And you shall draw water with joy…" [Isaiah 12:3]

(From one of the elders of Volozhin)

And "The People Were Sent"…

When a group of Yeshiva students began to publish a newspaper on Yeshiva matters called *Boker Or* [The Light of the Morning], and the Netzi'v saw that this was causing neglect of Torah, he called one of the directors of the newspaper and said to me, If you make *Haboker Or*, then I will do "And the People Were Sent" (A hint from the verse "The morning was light, and the people were sent, them and their donkeys" Genesis 44:3)

Rabbi Chaim On His Neck

The Netzi'v would constantly reprove the lads who were not overly diligent. He did not even exonerate the geniuses among them. His second in command, the Gaon Rabbi Chaim Soloveitchik, loved to caress the necks of his favorite, sharp students, and go for long or short strolls with them. Even though only the excellent ones merited this honor, the Netzi'v still reproved them, saying, "Rabbi Chaim on his necks, and they are occupied with Torah"? (Based on the Talmudic statement, "With a millstone on his neck he shall occupy himself with Torah?" *Kiddushin* 29).

(*Zichron Lachronim*, by Binyamin Goldberg, pp 22-25)

[Page 260]

The Atmosphere of the Yeshiva Brings Wisdom

There was a wise man in the Yeshiva of Volozhin who excelled in his jokes and wise responses that he gave. The students decided that if he brought them empty letters, they would not give him anything, but if he gave them letters of money, they would give him a payment.

One day, he gave a letter with money to one of the students, but the student did not give him anything. A few days later, he met him in the marketplace and demanded his due. The lad told him: "I suspect that you drank three cups, and therefore you are making your demand in the marketplace." He retorted, "I did not drink three cups, but four cups, therefore I demand like a donkey…"

(Ibid, page 24-25)

(This retort is based on what is written in *Sanhedrin* 65b: "One cup is fitting for a woman, two is a disgrace, with three she demands by mouth, and with four she demands even from a donkey…"[11])

The Netzi'v and Dr. Yehuda Leib Pinsker

When Dr. Yehuda Leib Pinsker died, the Chovevei Zion committee in Odessa sent a telegram to all Chovevei Zion activists in every place throughout the Diaspora.

Rabbi Naftali Tzvi Yehuda Berlin, the Netzi'v of Volozhin also received a telegram. There were two Russian words in the telegram: Pinsker finished.

"No," said the Netzi'v, "This concept is a gentile concept. To them, the death of a person is his end and conclusion. To us, the death of a person is nothing other than his beginning and outset…"

The Netzi'v Has Mercy on Fowl…

The Netzi'v would not eat until the fowl were first given their food, in order to fulfil that which is written: "And I shall give the grass of your fields to your animals, and you shall eat and be sated." (Deuteronomy 11: 15).

Once on *Rosh Hashanah* afternoon, the Netzi'v returned from the synagogue and waited to recite Kiddush until the fowl were given their food. They could not find the key to the coup in the house. They searched and looked, and the key could not be found. The Netzi'v ordered that the lock be broken by a gentile. They went to fetch a gentile from town.

In the meantime, it was getting late. Most of the day had passed, and the members of the household had not yet had anything to eat or drink. The Netzi'v, was elderly, and tired from the service of the day, but he would not make Kiddush. They waited.

When the gentile came, the lock was broken, and the fowl were given their food, the Netzi'v recited Kiddush and feasted at the table…

(M. Lipson, "From Generation to Generation" section III, paragraph 2184)

[Page 261]

The Modesty of Rabbi Chaim Soloveitchik

Once, two of the excellent students of the Yeshiva were debating some Talmudic idea, and they could not compromise. It was the third hour of the night, and without thinking too much, they went to Rabbi Chaim's house to ask that he decide between them. Of course, the door was closed, and they knocked loudly. All the members of the household were perplexed to hear such loud knocks at such a late hour, and thought that some sort of disaster must certainly have occurred. How great was their surprise and anger when they opened the door and heard what they wanted. However, Rabbi Chaim did not get angry. On the contrary, he received them as usual in a pleasant fashion. After forging peace between the two disputants by explaining to them who was correct – they left with glad hearts.

(M. Eisenstat, "Reb Chaimke Volozhiner" *Hatzefira*, 21 Elul 5678, issue 35.)

In the Merit of the Torah

(A legend about Rabbi Chaim of Volozhin)

When the Gaon Rabbi Chaim of Volozhin, of blessed memory, was ready to found his great Yeshiva, he went to the Gaon of Vilna of blessed memory to receive a blessing from him.

The Gr'a was happy to meet him, and told him, "Know, my student, that you are about to do a great thing that is of inestimable value. I see that evil winds will come to uproot the Jewish people, Heaven forbid. From one side there is the spirit of heresy, Heaven forbid, coming to destroy the supernal Jerusalem. From the other side is the spirit of folly that comes to sully the hearts. The equal side between them is that they all are coming to uproot the tree. However, as long as Torah is not forgotten from Israel, I am certain that all the winds of the world will not move it from Israel. From the day that I gained understanding, I realized that only Torah differentiates between Israel and the nations of the world. Therefore, Chaim my student, supervise your Yeshiva to ensure that they occupy themselves day and night with Torah, for is it not said, 'Talmud Torah is equal to them all'[12]."

Rabbi Chaim of Volozhin guarded these matters in his heart for all his days. During the time of Rabbi Chaim of Volozhin, there were three students from among the excellent students in the Yeshiva, about whom it was predicted that they would eventually become great luminaries in Israel. One was a scion of good pedigree; the second had a good heart; and the third was an incomparably wonderfully diligent person. He sat and studied Torah day and night not interrupting his learning for even one minute.

Rabbi Chaim believed that these three were created for greatness, and he prayed about them: May it be His will that the evil eye not rule over them. However, Rabbi Chaim's hopes were for naught. After time, the three lads left the Yeshiva and went out to bad company, for at that time the intelligentsia of Berlin was passing through the camp of Israel, hunting for the best of the Jewish lads.

After many years, Rabbi Chaim of Volozhin investigated to see what was the fate of the three

[Page 262]

students who had strayed from the path. The first one arrived in a large city and had become a heretic. The second one studied philosophy and gave public speeches speaking folly about Jews. He eventually converted his religion and became an accuser of Jews. The third entered a Christian school where he studied all seven wisdoms, to the point where all wise people would come to his door to ask him questions.

A short time later, he was appointed as a professor. When he was lecturing from the podium, the hall was filled to the brim, and his name reached the court of the king. One day, two ministers came to his house and said to him, "There is none as wise and understanding as you in the entire country, and they are looking toward you to give the running of the country over to you. However, you would be required to abandon your religion." He requested three days to deliberate over the matter.

That night, his sleep fled. The next day, he arose, escaped from the city, and decided to make *aliya* to the Land of Israel. On his way, he stopped in Volozhin, enter Rabbi Chaim's home, and told him everything that had happened. When Rabbi Chaim asked him, "What saved you from sin?" that student responded, "I passed by a Jewish home and the voices of Torah came to my ears. It seemed to me that the Torah was weeping. Thoughts of repentance immediately arose in my heart..."

(Ben-Eliezer, "Merit of the Torah" (from the conversations of elders) *Hatzefira*, 1914 ,issue 113, 6 Sivan 5674 [1914])

The Difference between Trust and Shelter

(a Midrash about Rabbi Chaim of Volozhin)

The issue is that there are two parts of trust. One is that G-d promises a person to give him great wealth, as we see that the blessed G-d promised Abraham that he would become wealthy. That is called trust [*bitachon*]. The second is that G-d does not promise, but a person himself places his faith in G-d. This is called shelter [*chisayon*], as is stated "the rock in which they took refuge" (Deuteronomy 32:37). The rock is what shelters a person from downpours and rain when he rests there himself, but the rock does not promise him to be his shelter.

(*Shaarei Rachamim*, page 40)

A Maskil in Volozhin Style...

There were still a large number of Yeshiva students with the character of Maskilim. The fundamental form and style remained with each and every such person. It is said that one of them studied in two weeks the entire *Maarachei Leshon Ever* by Steinberg with all the punctuation, dots, roots, and examples noted in the right place. From that time and on, this lad continued on and became a great, unparalleled linguist.

(M. Peker, "In the Yeshiva of Volozhin" *Hator*, 30 Sivan 5684 (July 2, 1924), issue 40)

[Page 263]

"The Minister of Routes" of Volozhin…

One lad, known for his great memory as a pitched cistern that does not lose a drop[13], also wanted to learn external wisdom. He went and absorbed the entire… instruction book of the railroad and their tracks throughout the entire expanse of Russia, with the schedule of hours and minutes of the departure and arrival of every transport in every city. From that time, they called him the Minister of Routes. If any Yeshiva student had to travel home, he would turn to this "Minister" who would explain to him the details of the route to even the farthest place. The "Minister" never erred or made the minutest mistake…

(M. Peker, "In the Yeshiva of Volozhin")

The Acronym of Rabbi Chaim of Volozhin

Rabbi Chaim of Volozhin did not institute from the outset the custom of partaking of meals on a rotation basis. He concerned himself with the needs of his beloved students. For this purpose, he circled the world to collect donations for the upkeep of the Yeshiva. Once Rabbi Chaim traveled with his assistant to Baron Edmund (Anshel) Rothschild. He entered the Baron's office during the morning hours and requested an appointment. The secretary asked him, "Who are you that you are requesting to see the Baron?" He responded, "I am Rabbi Chaim Volozhiner." The secretary went into the Baron and told him that the rabbi from Volozhin has requested to speak with him. The Baron responded that he would gladly receive the rabbi, but he is not free at this moment, and he is prepared to meet him in the evening. The secretary informed Rabbi Chaim of the response of the Baron. Rabbi Chaim became despondent and requested from the secretary that he inform the honorable Baron that he wishes to tell him only one word. The secretary entered the office of the Baron and transmitted Rabbi Chaim's request. The Baron immediately sent out all the people who were with him in the room, and asked that the rabbi be brought in.

Rabbi Chaim entered and said "Gemara!" The Baron asked Rabbi Chaim if he wanted to teach him a chapter of Gemara. Rabbi Chaim responded that Gemara is an acronym for "Good morning Reb Anshel [*Gut Morgen Reb Anshel*]. "And what is the request of the Rabbi, that I may fulfil it?" asked the Baron. Rabbi Chaim responded "Gemara!" The Baron did not understand the meaning. Rabbi Chaim told him: "I will explain the secret to the honorable Baron: "Give Money Reb Anshel" [*Git Maos Reb Anshel*].

The Baron liked this acronym and directed his secretary to give a check for the Volozhin Yeshiva. The Baron noticed that Rabbi Chaim's face was exuding dissatisfaction. The Baron asked him once again to explain, and Rabbi Chaim responded again, "Gemara." To the great confusion of the Baron, Rabbi Chaim responded, "This time, honorable Baron, the explanation of the acronym is, Give More Reb Anshel" [*Git Mehr Reb Anshel*].

(From Mr. Pesch Berman)

[Page 264]

How Did Rabbi Chaim of Volozhin Wait for the Coming of the Messiah?

Rabbi Nathan Friedland, the first Zionist orator in the era of Shivat Zion, related: "And it came to pass that there was a nobleman of the shepherds, a teacher, sharp, learned, and wise, who made sure to learn from the spirit of every person, and who studied in the Yeshiva of Volozhin during his youth. He stated as testimony that he had heard from Rabbi Chaim of Volozhin, may the memory of the righteous be a blessing and may his merit protect us, that thus it will be at the time of the coming of the Messiah. That is, just as he sits in his room alone and studies, the Rebbetzin will suddenly enter and say, "O Chaim you are sitting, and learning? Behold the Messiah has come!" He would then become confused, spit three times, and tell her, "Who told you?" She would say, "Go outside and see that there is not even a child in the cradle left in the city, for all have gone out to greet the Messiah."

(Reb Yitzchak Rivkind, "The Yeshiva of Volozhin and National Renaissance")

Rabbi Chaim of Volozhin's Great Love for the Land of Israel

"And Judah said to his brothers, what profit will we have if we kill our brother and cover his blood. Let us sell him to the Ishmaelites, and our hand will not be upon him, for he is our brother and our flesh. And his brothers heeded" (Genesis 37:26-27). The Sages state (*Sanhedrin* 6) that one who blesses Judah is cursing. Apparently, Judah's recommendation was better than Reuben's recommendation to cast him into a pit. "And the pit was empty, without water – but were there snakes and scorpions therein?"[14] Reuben, however, said to cast him into a pit in the Land of Israel, whereas Judah said to sell him to the Ishmaelites [to go] outside the Land. From this is a proof: a pit in the Land of Israel is better than being "free" in the exile.

(Shlomo Yahalomi (Diment), *Pninei Torah*, pp. 72-73.)

The Explanation of Rabbi Chaim Soloveitchik on *Urva Parach*

"And he sent out the raven, and it went to and fro" (Genesis 8:7). From this we understand that which we find several times in the Talmud, when one Talmudic sage asks another about something, and the other has no response, he said "*Urva Parach*" [literally: the raven flew away].

This response does not make sense, but the meaning is: Just as the raven that Noah sent did not return with an answer, so you will not hear an answer from me on this matter.

(Shmuel Eliezer, *Likutei Batar Likutei*, page 26)

A Sharp Explanation of Rabbi Yosi Ber Soloveitchik

"And now do not fear. I will sustain you and your children. And he comforted them and spoke to their hearts" (Genesis 50:21). "Do not be afraid – I will sustain you," that is, you need not be afraid that I will punish you for your sin against me, for the punishment of "I will sustain you" is sufficient. That is, the world is dark for someone who depends on someone else's table.

(Ibid. page 143)

[Page 265]

A Pleasant Sermon of the Netzi'v

Regarding the statement of our sages: "Poverty is good for Jews as is a red bridle for a white horse" (*Chagiga* 9b), the Netzi'v said: "Only then will be poverty be good for Israel, if it is "a red bridle" which everyone can see that they decorate the horse, and not when it is standing in the barn. If we are poor when we go out, and wealthy in our own tents, and all our honor is within our homes – only then will the evil eye not affect us. However, to our dismay, our Jewish brethren do not heed the advice of our sages of blessed memory and do the opposite of their words. Inside their houses – the teeth are clean and there is a lack of bread. Whereas outside, there is no call for help before the poor, and everyone is wealthy, everyone is dressed splendidly. This brings great, evil tribulations upon us and brings upon us the hatred of the nations amongst whom we dwell.

(Nachman HaLevi Levitan, *Hameilitz*, 17 Av 5651 [1891] issue 178)

Several Pearls of Wisdom from Rabbi Chaim Volozhin

a.   "Anyone whose deeds are greater than his words" (*Avot* 3:9) – some study for love of wisdom, for all philosophers know that all wisdoms are like a drop in the bucket compared to the depth of the wisdom of the Talmud (*Ruach Chaim*, page 52)

b.   "Very much be lowly in spirit" (*Avot* 4:4) – and one should not think that he fulfils the commandment of modesty by being of lowly spirit in his own eyes. Rather, he must think that he is nothing, "that the hope of man is the worm" and he has nothing in which to take pride. (Ibid. page 64)

c.   "And if he does not add, he detracts" (*Avot* 1:13) – everyone must go higher and add to his perfection, and anyone who wishes to remain at his level and not to aspire to something higher – will end up falling. (Ibid. page 67)

d.   "Everyone who occupies himself in Torah for its own sake" (*Avot* 6:1) – to the extent that one continues to learn, one should desire to learn more. He should become crazy and think, would it be that I would not need to sleep or eat, and only delve into Torah day and night, and drink its words with thirst. (Ibid, page 87)

e.   Rabbi Chaim said: Whomever is careful to study Torah for three hours a night for its own sake – all of his sins are forgiven, with the exception of sins between man and his fellow, for the energy of the soul does not return and become rectified other than through the study of Torah. (Avraham Tzvi Hirsh Katzenelbogen, *Shaarei Chaim*)

[Page 266]

f.   Our sages have already said in *Avot*, "All their words are like fiery coals" [*Avot* 2:10], that just like only a spark of fire is seen in a coal -- if you make the effort to turn it over and blow it – the more you blow it the more it will flame and the spark will spread, until it fully burns and you can derive benefit from it, use its light, and warm yourself near it. Similarly, all the words of the sages are like this, for even if the words seem short and simple, they can break things like a hammer. For the more that a person turns them over and delves into them – his eyes will be lit up from the flame, and their light will be great, for deep matters will be found within them. (*Nefesh HaChaim*, section III, chapter I).

A Nice Parable About Rabbi Itzele

Every person can reach his level if he finds his hidden abilities. Rabbi Itzele expressed this idea with the following parable: A wealthy tycoon, a large-scale merchant came to a town where the people were poor and indigent and asked for several people to help him with his merchandise, and they would become successful like him. However, due to a lack of self-confidence and laziness, they did not respond to the tycoon. There was a wise person among them who said to the tycoon, "Here I am, for you called me."

After a few years, that townsperson became very wealthy. The two of them, he and the large-scale merchant, came to that town. When the townspeople saw their towns-fellow who rose to greatness, they hid their faces from shame, and were embarrassed to look at his face.

He asked them, "Why are you embarrassed, but you are not embarrassed in front of my master, who is a thousand times wealthier than I?" They answered him, "The level of your master is a gift of G-d, and we cannot reach it. However, we could have reached your level, as you did, had we not been lazy and lethargic."

(*Ruach Chaim* of Rabbi Chaim of Volozhin, chapter I, page 8 (in a footnote), published by Kerem Shlomo, Jerusalem, 5718)

Rabbi Itzele's Opinion on Colored Patriots

Rabbi Itzele once went to the city of Ustronė (Vilna District) and spent the Sabbath there. Following the Sabbath morning service, before the reading of the Torah, a melancholic woman burst into the synagogue and began to weep bitterly: "Merciful ones the children of merciful ones, have mercy on a poor widow. My only child has been snatched for the army due to the fault of the head of the community of Ustronė."

The head of the community, who was present, rebuked the woman, "The law of the land is the law." The head of the community apologized to Rabbi Itzele – we are obligated to be faithful to the government.

Rabbi Itzele recognized the head of the community and knew that he was childless. Therefore, when he ascended the *bima* to deliver his sermon, he opened by saying, "All my days, I did not understand that which is written in the Book of Kings (II4, 13-14)

[Page 267]

that when Elisha asked the Shunamite 'Shall I intercede regarding you to the king of the captain of the army?' she responded, 'I live amongst my people.' Gehazi completed her statement by saying, 'But she has no child.' The response of the Shunamite cannot be understood. The words of Gehazi are also a mystery, for what connection is there between the fact that she has no child to the question of Elisha, regarding whether he should intercede on her behalf to the king of the captain of the army?"

Rabbi Itzele continued his words, "However, from the events today, I have come to understand these versions. Elisha asked the Shunamite, 'Shall I intercede on your behalf to the king or the captain of the army?' That is, perhaps they have given your child over to army service, and you wish that I intercede to the king or the captain of the army to free him. To this the Shunamite responded, 'I live amongst my people,' and I must be faithful to my nation and my country and fulfil the obligations of the king.' Gehazi came and elaborated upon her words, 'But she has no child.' She is speaking words of patriotism and faithfulness to the regime because she has no child. Were she to have a child, she would have spoken differently."

(Rabbi Yehuda Leib HaKohen Maimon, *Sarei HaMeah*, section IV, page 23)

Rabbi Itzele Wishes to Give a Blessing to Those Who Have No Bread in the House...

When Rabbi Itzele prepared for a trip frin Volozhin to Brody, he took leave from all the students of the Yeshiva with a blessing and warm handshake. He said to them, "I request of you that, during the vacation time, when each of you will return to your cities and your families, that you give my blessing to all those who have no bread at home..."

The students did not understand Rabbi Itzele's meaning. He wanted to explain his intention to them, but his father, Rabbi Chaim, preceded him and told the students, "The House of Israel bless G-d... The House of Levi bless G-d, those that fear G-d bless G-d[15]. It is that those who fear G-d have no bread at home, and it is to those that my son sends a blessing through you before his journey..."

(Ibid, page 211)

"Wonder of Wonders..."

All the time that Rabbi Itzele lived in the city of Brody, several authors from Galicia would come to him to receive an approbation for their books. However, it was not the way of Rabbi Itzele of Volozhin to give approbations to new books, so he would deflect the authors with various excuses, and would not give his approbation.

Once, an author from a small town came to him and did not give him any rest. He requested that he peruse his book, and express his opinion in writing, or at least orally.

[Page 268]

Rabbi Itzele could not free himself from him, so he took the book, leafed through several pages, and read here and there some verbose novellae and meaningless didactics.

Rabbi Itzele told the author, "I cannot give you an approbation, for I have vowed to myself to not give approbations to books. However, after reading several pages, I recommend that you call your book 'Wonder of Wonders.'"

The author rejoiced in his heart that Rabbi Itzele considered his book to be a wonder of wonders, but he acted modestly and said, "I do not know if my book is worthy of such a praiseworthy title."

Rabbi Itzele responded to him, "This is the meaning of my words that I said: To this point, I knew that paper is made of rags, and it was a wonder in my eyes. Now I see that the pages of paper can be returned to their original source, and can be made into rags once again. This to me is a 'wonder of wonders'"…

(Ibid, pp. 212-213)

The Works of Man and the Works of the Creator

Rabbi Chaim of Volozhin based Divine providence in the following manner: The ways of G-d are not like the ways of flesh and blood. As a parable, when a man builds a building of wood, the builder does not create the wood of his own power. Rather, he takes wood that had already been created and forms it into a building. After he already arranges the wood and builds the house according to his will, the building exists even though he does not continue to supervise and care for the house. The works of the Creator, Blessed Be His Name, are not the same. Since he created them all[16] at the time of the creation of the world, they depend on the energy of the Creator. This is the way it always was, literally every day and every moment – their entire force of existence and order is dependent solely on what He Blessed Be He bestows upon them with His Blessed will – a new influence at every moment. Were He Blessed Be He to remove His force of influence from them for even one moment – everything would turn to naught and nothingness within a moment.

(*Nefesh HaChaim*, section I, chapter II)

The Coming of the Messiah in the Eyes of Rabbi Chaim of Volozhin

Rabbi Chaim of Volozhin once sat with his students and spoke about the redemption and the coming of the Messiah. One student said to him, "Our rabbi, I looked into *Avkat Rochel* and saw that tribulations and disasters will eventually come upon the Jews at the time of the birth pangs of the Messiah, and I wonder whether a person will be able to withstand them."[17]

Rabbi Chaim smiled and said, "Do you think that during the times of the Messiah, the Holy One Blessed Be He will stand and leaf through every page of *Avkat Rochel*?"

(M. Lipson, *Midor Ledor*, volume IV, paragraph 2728)

An Ignoramus in the Entire Talmud…

Rabbi Chaim Soloveitchik said about a certain person who made himself out to be a scholar, "So-and-so is a complete ignoramus."

[Page 269]

They asked him, "Our rabbi, this person has studied the entire Talmud."

Rabbi Chaim smiled, "That is the way it is. Had he only completed one tractate, he would only be an ignoramus regarding that tractate. However, now that he completed the entire Talmud, he is an ignoramus regarding the entire Talmud."

(Ibid. ibid. paragraph 2926)

Who is Exempt from the Tribulations of Raising Children?

There is a story regarding Rabbi Chaim Soloveitchik that a person once came to him and complained, "Our rabbi, the tribulations of raising children are difficult for me. There is no day in which the concerns and worries are not more than the previous."

Rabbi Chaim responded, "You know, who is a person who does not have the tribulations of raising children? Someone who is childless, may it not befall us…"

(Ibid. ibid. paragraph 3323)

"And all the Magicians of Egypt Did So" (Exodus 7:22)

Rabbi Itzele expounded on this verse: The sign was to turn the rivers to blood. The magicians of Egypt knew to wait for the contemptible thing. The Jew haters excelled in these matters from time immemorial. This is their ancient expertise…

(B. Joashson, "From Our Old Treasury" section II, page 46)

Rabbi Yosi Ber Soloveitchik Denigrates Neutrality…

A great dispute broke out during the period that Rabbi Yosi Ber Soloveitchik served as rabbi of Brisk. Rabbi Yosi Ber approached several of the city notables whose opinion was acceptable to the community, asking them to influence the disputants to quench the fire of controversy. However, they refused the request of the rabbi, claiming that they do not want to enter into the foray, and therefore they would take a neutral stance.

Rabbi Yosi Ber told them, "This neutrality reminds me of the neutrality of the dogs of Egypt. For our sages have said, 'If dogs cry, the Angel of Death is coming to the city. If dogs play, Elijah the Prophet is coming to the city.' (Bava Kama 60b) Since the Angel of Death was in Egypt at the time to smite the firstborn in the Land of Egypt, as was Elijah the Prophet the redeemer, who came to redeem Israel – the dogs did not know what to do. Therefore, 'and not even a dog made any noise amongst the Children of Israel' (Exodus 11:7). The dogs decided to be 'neutral' and did not open their mouths…"

(From B. Joashson, "From Our Old Treasury" volume II, page 64)

Rabbi Yosef Dov Soloveitchik Changes the Name of his Book

Rabbi Yosef Dov called his first book *Yad HaLevi* (Y'D is the acronym for:

[Page 270]

Yosef Dov)[18]. He sent this book to the printing house of Yitzchak Goldman in Warsaw, who was considered to be one of the *maskilim*.

The typesetters had already begun their work. Once, the author went to the printing house. When he saw the printer, he said to him that if he finds any errors in the language, he is permitted to fix them. Goldman then said to him, "If the rabbi permits, I will first fix the name of the book." "Why?" called out the rabbi in astonishment. The printer replied, "For the words *Yad HaLevi* appear only once in the Bible, with regard to the Statue of Micah ("Micah inducted the Levite, and the young man became his priest and remained in Micah's shrine.", Judges 17:12[19]).

Rabbi Yosef Dov agreed that he was correct and called the book *Beit HaLevi*.

(Rabbi Yitzchak Nissenbaum, *Alei Cheldi*, page 86)

The Sharpness of Rabbi Rafael Shapira

Once, one of the wealthy people came to Rabbi Rafael and placed two rubles and 70 kopecks on the table before him. Rabbi Rafael lifted his eyes and looked at the man, asking, "What is this money for?" The man understood the glance and responded, "I recited the *Mi Sheberach* for my sick son, and pledged 18 gold coins for charitable purposes. Now I have brought this money to the rabbi to do with it according to his will." Rabbi Rafael shrugged his shoulders and said, "There is destiny for Israel! For the Jews, in Hebrew, *Chai* means life, and Met means death. This wealthy Jew exempted himself with the smallest sum of life: 18. Had *Chai* meant death, and Met meant life – he would not have been able to exempt himself with this sum…"

(Ibid. ibid. page 67)

Every Good Prayer Was in the Eyes of Rabbi Rafael

When Rabbi Rafael came to sit on the rabbinical seat of Bobruisk, he attempted to erase the traces of the dispute that broke out in that city several years previously between the *Misnagdim* and the Hassidim.

He went to visit Rabbi Shmarya Noach Schneerson, the rabbi of the Hassidim, in his house. Rabbi Shmarya honored him with words of Hassidism, the essence of which was that the prayer "O L-rd, grant us success" is at a higher level than the prayer "O L-rd, save us"[20].

Rabbi Rafael sat, listened, and was silent. When the Rabbi of the Hassidim finished his words of Torah, he asked Rabbi Rafael when he thought of it. Rabbi Rafael shrugged his shoulders and responded innocently, "The prayer 'O L-rd save us' is also a good prayer."

(Based on *Alei Cheldi*, pp. 67-68)

[Page 271]

"When you take a census of the Israelite men according to their army enrollment, each shall pay G-d a ransom for himself on being enrolled, that no plague may come upon them through their being enrolled." (Exodus 30:12)[21]

Rabbi Yosi Ber Soloveitchik said: When Moses our Teacher heard that the Holy One Blessed Be He commanded him to count the Jews, he became worried in his heart. It is a minor matter! Sixty myriads of Jews will hasten to "enter the records" [Exodus 30: 13] and fulfil the commandment. Everyone wants to be first. They will push and shove each other, and this is liable to end in a tragedy, Heaven forbid.

The Holy One Blessed Be He comforted him: Calm down, my servant Moses. When the Jews will hear the end of the commandment "each person… a ransom for himself" – that will cost a half a shekel, and they realize that the census will cost money, I will then promise you "and there will be no plague." They will not run, hurry, or hasten, and will not trample each other. The commotion will not be so great…

(From B. Josefson, "From Our Old Treasury" Part II, page 195)

What is the Difference Between the Grave of Misnagdim and the Grave of a Hassidic Rebbe

An elderly Hassid came to the cemetery in the city of Brisk to supplicate over the grave of the Maggid of Turisk. Incidentally, he also visited the grave of Rabbi Yosi Ber Soloveitchik. He noticed that the grave of the Maggid was clear on all sides. The other graves were a distance away. However, the grave of Rabbi Yosi Ber was surrounded on all sides by other graves, right next to it.

That day, the teller [of the story] was together on a train with the Ridba'z (Rabbi Yaakov David the son of Zeev Wilovsky – who is known for his commentary *Peirush Haridva'z* on the Jerusalem Talmud) and told him what he had seen with his eyes in the Brisk cemetery.

The Ridva'z, who was an enthusiastic Misnaged, told the elderly Hassid, "In this matter, you Hassidim are above us *Misnagdim*. With you, as long as your Rebbe is alive, you cleave to him and come close to him, whereas after his death, you distance yourself from his grave. With us *Misnagdim*, it is the opposite. As long as the rabbi is alive, we keep away from him, and only after his death do we come close to him and wish to be buried next to him…

(Yitzchak Nisenbaum, Alei Halevi, page 213)

"The People Sat Down to Eat and Drink, and then Rose to Revel." (Exodus 32:6)

Once, Rabbi Yosi Ber Soloveitchik said when he was in a jocular mood: Everyone knows that there is a big difference between the *Misnagdim* and Hassidim. The *Misnagdim* fast on the yahrzeit of their rabbi, and on that day, they are in a mournful mood. On the other hand, Hassidim drink liquor on the anniversary of the death of their Rebbe and organize celebrations and festivities.

However, there is nothing new under the sun "it has been like this forever." This difference already existed when Israel was in the desert, as we learn from that which is written in the Torah: Before the giving of the Torah, before the Jews

[Page 272]

knew how to study – they maintained the custom of the Hassidim. When Moshe went up to the upper heights and they thought – as the sages teach – that he was no longer alive, they conducted a feast "And the people sat to eat and drink." However, when "And Moses died there" [Deuteronomy 34:5], when Moses really died, and this was after the giving of the Torah when the Jews already knew how to study – they acted in accordance with the custom of the Misnagdim: "And the Children of Israel wept for Moses" (Deuteronomy 34:8).

(From B. Joashson, "From Our Old Treasury" Section II, page 207)

"Anyone who appoints over the community a judge who is not fit, it is as though he plants a tree used as part of idolatrous rites [*ashera*] among the Jewish people" (*Sanhedrin* 7a)[22]

Rabbi Chaim Soloveitchik asked: Why is a judge who is not fit compared to an idolatrous tree? When a statue, an idol, one can immediately see that this is idolatry, and there is no room for error.

This is not the case with an idolatrous tree [*ashera*]: From the outside, it is beautiful in appearance and pleasant to look at. However, from the inside, it is nothing other than idolatry. This is the same with a judge who is not fit…

(B. Joashson, "From Our Old Treasury" Section IV, page 272)

Righteous People of Sodom

Rabbi Itzele once spent some time in the medicinal springs outside of Russia. [He was concerned] lest they tell about the famous "son of holy ones" that he plays the role of Tzadik in his home, but in another country, he casts off the yoke of the fear of Heaven, and that people would spread rumors about him.

Rabbi Itzele responded, "Now the meaning of the verse 'Fifty righteous ones in the city' (Genesis 18:26) is clear to me. Apparently, the righteous ones of Sodom were G-d fearing only in their city, but when they left their city, not a shred or memory of their righteousness remained…"

(Ibid. Volume I, page 91)

"You shall say, It is from your servant Jacob, a gift sent to my master Esau" (Genesis 32:19)[23]

"A gift – to Esau" Rabbi Yosi Ber Soloveitchik was once traveling in a train car in which several Jews were sitting. When the time for the *Mincha* prayer arrived, they checked to see if there was a *minyan* [prayer quorum], so they could conduct the service with a quorum. Two "progressive" youths were sitting in the car, and they were asked to join the *minyan*. However, they responded that they are not connected with "such matters" and disappeared from the car. They returned to their places when they finished praying. Rabbi Yosi Ber said out loud so that the two youths will also hear, "You know, sirs, now you have answered a difficult question for me. In the gift[24] that Jacob sent to Esau, there were flocks of he-goats, she-goats, ewes, rams, camels, she-asses and he-asses. I have always had the question: why did Jacob not also send several dogs to guard the flocks? Now, as you see," said Rabbi Yosi Ber, pointing to the lads, "The question is no longer a question. The nature of dogs is that when they detect the aroma of *"Mincha"* [which also means a gift] – they immediately disappear…"

(ibid. ibid. Section I, page 180)

[Page 273]

The "Permissible Ruling" of Rabbi Yosi Ber Soloveitchik

Once, a Jew entered the home of Rabbi Yosi Ber Soloveitchik on the eve of Passover, with the question: "Our rabbi, is it permissible to fulfil the commandment of the four cups with milk?"

"Are you sick, Heaven forbid," Rabbi Yosi Ber asked him.

"I am healthy, praised be G-d," responded the Jew. " But the wine, as the honorable rabbi knows, is very expensive this year, and I am unable to purchase it."

Rabbi Yosi Ber told the Jew that, in accordance with the law, it is permissible to fulfil the commandment of the four cups also with milk, and he placed a check for 25 rubles in the hands of the asker.

When the Jew left his home, the Rebbetzin asked in surprise, "Why did you give the Jew a cheque for 25 rubles? Two or three rubles would be sufficient to purchase [wine for] the four cups."

Rabbi Yosi Ber answered her, "From the question of the Jew regarding whether it is permissible to fulfil the obligation of the four cups with milk, it is obvious that he was not only lacking wine. He was missing 'something else.' He was missing chicken soup and a piece of meat. For if he had soup and meat, how would it be permissible for him to drink dairy for the four cups?…"

(From B. Yoashson, "From Our Old Treasury" Festivals, Five Megillot, pp. 101-102.)

"And let Pharaoh take steps to appoint overseers over the land" (Genesis 41:34)[25]

During the years of the drought in Russia, a heavy famine pervaded, from which the Jews suffered especially. Aid committees were set up in every city and town, the effectiveness of which was not apparent at all. As the number of committees increased, so did the famine.

Rabbi Yosi Ber Soloveitchik said, "From here, the trust in the words of Josef 'And seven years of hunger will come' (Genesis 41:36) are clear to me. Did not the asker ask: From where did Joseph have the faith that in truth there will be 'seven years of hunger'? Is not G-d omnipotent, and if He wished, He could annul this decree, and there would not be famine in the land of Egypt.

"However, it is fitting to realize that his words were not for naught. Joseph advised Pharaoh: 'And let Pharaoh take steps to appoint overseers over the land.' When he would start immediately to appoint committees and councils, he would appoint a legion of officials, accountants, and secretaries to gather all the food of the good years and store up grain as a guarantee for food assistance for the needy when the time comes. Then, he was certain that 'and seven years of hunger will arise' – that indeed, there will be a famine in the land.

(Ibid. Vol I, page 232)

"Gather for me seventy men of the elders of Israel" (Numbers 11:16)

Rabbi Yosi Ber Soloveitchik was invited to a town to settle a dispute that broke out regarding

[Page 274]

the choosing of a rabbi. Each side wanted their own rabbi, and the fire of dispute burned and became a godly fire.

"Now," said Rabbi Yosi Ber, seeing that the entire town was immersed in the dispute of the choosing of a rabbi, "Now, answer the following difficult question for me: Why, after the children of Israel complained about the manna and the quail, did the Holy One Blessed Be He suddenly say to Moses: 'Gather for me seventy men'? Apparently, this is a complete mystery. What does this have to do with the complaint that the Children of Israel complained to Moses, 'And now our souls are parched, without anything other than the manna before our eyes'? (Numbers 11:6) How is this an answer to Moses' question, 'From where will I get meat to give to this entire nation, for they cried to me saying, give us meant to eat' (Numbers 11:13)?

"However, if we think about this matter well," said Rabbi Yosi Ber, "we will prove that this was the only result. When the Holy One Blessed Be He saw that the Jews were complaining and arguing amongst themselves regarding matters of livelihood, and Moses, Heaven forbid, was wearing himself out for the matter was too difficult to give the Children of Israel the fish, cucumbers, melons, leeks, onions, and garlic [based on Numbers 11:5] – He offered him advice, 'Gather for me seventy men of the elders of Israel, etc. take them to the Tent of Meeting, and let them be there with you.' Prepare a list of 70 new leaders of seventy rabbis and find out of the Jews will be happy. The Jews will begin to argue amongst themselves, and they will immediately forget the worries of livelihood, the worries of the manna, the worries of the quail, and other mundane concerns…"

(From B. Joashson, "From Our Old Treasury" Volume IV, pp. 50-51)

How Did Rabbi Chaim of Volozhin Behave Toward his Students?

The great rabbi, the famous Hassid, Rabbi Meir Shalom the son of Rabbi Shmaryahu HaKohen, may the memory of the holy be blessed, a native of the city of Karelitz, one of the students of the Gaon Rabbi Chaim of Volozhin of blessed memory, served with him in holiness and purity for close to 14 years. After that, he sent the aforementioned rabbi to Vilna to supervise the Yeshiva building of great scholars. He was first and the head of them all, where they established students who became luminaries amongst Israel.

Many of the students of Rabbi Chaim of Volozhin were jealous of this honor, and they sometimes defeated him in *halacha*, as they did not know his lofty value. When our rabbi, the Gaon, found out that he was immersed in agony regarding this, the Gaon Rabbi Chaim of blessed memory traveled to Vilna himself and remained there for about two months. During those days, our teacher the Gaon of blessed memory remained enwrapped in his tallis and tefillin, as was his custom always, leaning and standing in the Yeshiva of his aforementioned great student, discussing *halacha* with him, asking questions like one of the students. Rabbi Meir Shalom of blessed memory would discuss didactics with him, teach, and explain every difficult matter to him.

(Aryeh Leib Frunkim, "History of the Sages of Jerusalem" Part III, chapter V, page 176)

Translator's footnotes:

1. *Pirkei Avot* 5:17.
2. A type of celebration on the nights of Sukkot commemorating the water drawing festivities during the time of the Temple.
3. "You have chosen us" – the opening words of the middle section of the festival *amida*, which is often put to a variety of melodies.
4. The *Shehecheyanu* blessing.
5. See Exodus 24:7. The common interpretation is that the Children of Israel agreed to fulfil the mitzvot even before fully understanding them – and this was considered meritorious.
6. In opposition to the notion that one should wait for G-d to bring about the Messianic era and do nothing to artificially hasten it.
7. A *halachic* concept of being instructed to refrain from fulfilling a positive commandment.
8. The term for the period between 17th of Tammuz and the 9th of Av.
9. Kohelet 4:2. Translation from Sefaria:
https://www.sefaria.org/Ecclesiastes.4.2?ven=Tanakh:_The_Holy_Scriptures,_published_by_JPS&vhe=Mi qra_according_to_the_Masorah&lang=bi&with=all&lang2=en
10. Rabbi Chisda was a Talmudic sage. The methodology *leshitateha* [literally, 'according to his opinion'] brings together disparate Talmudic statements from a single individual.
11. There is an error here in that the Talmudic quote is not from *Sanhedrin* 65, but rather *Ketubot* 65a:
https://www.sefaria.org/*Ketubot*.65a.7?ven=William_Davidson_Edition_-_English&vhe=William_Davidson_Edition_-_Vocalized_Aramaic&lang=bi
12. *Mishnah Peah* 1:1:
https://www.sefaria.org/Mishnah_Peah.1.1?ven=Mishnah_Yomit_by_Dr._Joshua_Kulp&vhe=Torat_Emet_357&lang=bi
13. *Pirkei Avot* 2:8.
14. Based on Rashi's commentary on Genesis 37:24
15. Psalm 135:19-20.

16. i.e. the raw materials.
17. According to tradition, the period prior to the coming of the Messiah will be a period of great tribulation.
18. Yosef Dov is the Hebrew version of the Yiddishized Yoshe (or Yosi) Ber.
19. Translation from Sefaria:
    https://www.sefaria.org/Judges.17.12?ven=Tanakh:_The_Holy_Scriptures,_published_by_JPS&vhe=Miqra_according_to_the_Masorah&lang=bi&with=all&lang2=en
20. Both prayers are from Psalm 118:25, which is part of the *Hallel* service.
21. Translation taken from Sefaria:
    https://www.sefaria.org/Exodus.30.12?ven=The_Contemporary_Torah,_Jewish_Publication_Society,_2006&vhe=Miqra_according_to_the_Masorah&lang=bi&with=all&lang2=en
22. Translation taken from Sefaria:
    https://www.sefaria.org/*Sanhedrin*.7b.8?ven=William_Davidson_Edition_-_English&vhe=Wikisource_Talmud_Bavli&lang=bi&with=all&lang2=en
23. The original says this is Genesis 32:15, but it is actually 32:19.
24. *Mincha* is the name of the afternoon service, but it can also mean 'a gift', and is the word used in the verse.
25. Translation from Sefaria:
    https://www.sefaria.org/Genesis.41.34?ven=The_Contemporary_Torah,_Jewish_Publication_Society,_2006&vhe=Miqra_according_to_the_Masorah&lang=bi&with=all&lang2=en Note, the original had an error in the reference. It said Numbers 11:16 rather than Genesis 41:34. The incorrect reference from Numbers was evidently copied from the subsequent vignette, where it is correct.

[Page 275]

Of Those Who Continued the Tradition of Volozhin

Translated by Jerrold Landau

[Page 276] Blank [Page277]

Of Those Who Continued the Tradition of Volozhin

by Eliezer Leoni

(according to the alphabet)

The essence of this group was the pride of Volozhi . Volozhin was their spiritual birthplace. From it they drew their ideology regarding the value of the study of Torah and the renaissance of the Jewish people. They gave birth to the image and form of Volozhin. Their learning was drawn from the Torah of Rabbi Chaim of Volozhin, with the Torah of the Netzi'v and the Torah of Rabbi Yosef Dov Soloveitchik. Their words form chapters of Volozhin. When we examine the ideologies of Rabbi Shmuel Mohilewer or of Rabbi Mordechai Eliasberg – we recognize in them the insignia and seal of Rabbi Chaim of Volozhin and the Netzi'v. This speaks of Volozhin, and it makes no difference that Rabbi Mohilewer was born in the town of Hlybokaye and Rabbi Eliasberg in Cikishok [Čekiškė].

They were the faithful continuers of the Volozhin tradition. They planted "saplings" of Volozhin in every pace that they lived. Rabbi Mordechai Gimpel Yaffe planted the Torah of Volozhin in Yehud, Rabbi Mordechai Epstein in Hebron, and Rabbi Isser Zalman Meltzer in the Etz Chaim Yeshiva of Jerusalem. The modest *chalutz* of mild thoughts, Rabbi Mordechai Nachmani, planted the Torah of Volozhin in the Beit Midrash of Rehovot.

One strand joined most of them: patience. They were moderate in their ideology, masters of the "golden path" and tolerant of the views of others. They believe in "togetherness" and "dwelling together" – joint action among the religious and the non-observant, for only through this means will the redemption be completed and will Zion be built.

In this way, the students were faithful to Rabbi Chaim of Volozhin, for he too was not extreme in his views. He did not declare a war of boycott against Hassidism. On the contrary, he drew Hassidim near and brought the writings of the Hassidic greats into the Yeshiva library[*]. He dreamt of a blend of Hassidism and *Misnagdut* [the ideology of opposition to Hassidism], and thought in the recesses of his heart that if the two great cedars, the Gr'a [Vilna Gaon] and the Besh't [Baal Shem Tov] would have met – the redemption would come.

[Page 278]

This group takes a place of honor in our book, and we are proud of it. Out of concern for space, we were forced to only present a small portion of their many words and deeds.

Mordechai Eliasberg

Rabbi Eliasberg was 13 years old when he went to study in the Yeshiva of Volozhin. There, he was one of the choicest students of Rabbi Itzele, and a friend of the Netzi'v. He attained renown for his greatness in Torah. He made his nights like day [i.e. he studied day and night] and astounded his great rabbi with his diligence and desire for Torah.

The Torah that he studied in Volozhin, as well as the pogroms against the Jews in Russia during the 1880s, aroused the idea of settlement in the Land of Israel in the heart of Rabbi Eliasberg, and he gave himself over to that with heart and soul. He began to take interest in the needs of the community already during his youth. His example in this arena was his rabbi, Rabbi Itzele, who also worked greatly for communal needs, and was often absent from the Yeshiva due to his travels for the benefit of the Jewish people.

Rabbi Eliasberg regarded the revival of the desolation of the Land by Jews as the main thing. He said, "We must increase the settlement in the Land of Israel by purchasing properties there and settling a large gathering of our people there, to work the land and built it up with fields and vineyards."

Rabbi Eliasberg differentiated between religions nationalists and natural naturalists. For the first, religion bound them to the Land of Israel, and for the latter, a natural love tied them to the nation and the Land. The source of differences of opinion between them stems from the source from where their national arousal stemmed. The arousal of the first comes from the words of the Torah and the Prophets, whereas the love of the nation and the Land of their fathers for the latter stems from the source of wisdom that they learned from the great ones of the nation.[1]

According to Rabbi Eliasberg, the success of the upbuilding of the Land stems from the creation of "alignment" (in current lingo) between the "nationalists" and the "natural ones" He writes in his letter to Dr. Pinsker, "When we need to do something for the benefit of the nation, we must bind two wisdoms together (i.e. the wisdom of the nationalists, and the wisdom of the natural ones) by two separate individuals, one great in Torah and the other in wisdom. When they are bound together, the first completeness that shone in Israel from ancient days has already been restored." The essence of the name of his book "The Golden Path" testifies to the intention of Rabbi Eliasberg to find the middle path through which the nation will go to greet its renaissance.

Even before Dr. Herzl, Rabbi Eliasberg said that our redemption would come with the help of the nations. He opposed Messianism that happens "against the will of the nations and kingdoms." Our redemption must come in a natural manner, in a "secular" fashion and not through miracles – "the way of holiness"[2].

Rabbi Eliasberg wanted to see the Land of Israel, the land of life, the land of creation and of

[Page 279]

youthful renewal, and not the place of refuge for the elderly and poor who come to be buried in the Holy Land so as to be freed from rolling through the tunnels.[*1]

He said, "Until when will the Land only be a place of refuge for the poor of Israel, or for scholars who distance themselves from the ways of the world, whose conduct is solely in holiness, or for the elderly who come alive from the Diaspora to dig their graves in the Holy Land, and live the rest of their lives from the wealth that they earned in the land in which they lived[3].

Ahad Ha'am held Rabbi Eliasberg in very high esteem. He dedicated an article to him titled "Rabbi Mordechai Eliasberg"[4] in which he calls him "the Enlightened Rabbi."

Even in his work *Divrei Shalom* [Words of Peace] (page 56), Ahad Ha'am writes: "In my eyes, finding such a rabbi among the lovers of Zion is a faithful testimony to the wonderful power in Chibat Tzion to straighten the crookedness and to draw near those far." Further, he writes, "The Rabbi and Gaon speaks words of peace, and his heart is full of love to the entire nation as it is, without differentiation by class."

For his entire life, Rabbi Eliasberg desired to fulfil the commandment of building up the land with his own body. In his old age, he said, "May the Merciful One grant me the merit of making *aliya* to our Holy Land, to work its soil as a simple works." They asked him, "Our rabbi, your energy is to work the land?" Rabbi Eliasberg responded, "It is no big deal. I will be a guardian of gourds…"

Rabbi Avraham Yitzchak Kook said that Rabbi Eliasberg was one of the few of the sublime people who penetrated to the depth of true Zionist thought.

Zalman Epstein

The Volozhin Yeshiva enriched the spirit of the writer Zalman Epstein. It created within him the basis for humane culture, which was a blend of the Torah of Judaism and of secular wisdom. The Netzi'v planted the love of Zion within him.

Zalman Epstein writes about the Yeshiva: "Through the influence of the youthful life that filled the Yeshiva, the study of Talmud and its commentaries also received some special lifeforce, of feeling and movement, of joy in the present, if it is possible to say so. The dry, wrinkled, aged face of that study was as if it was no more. They studied Torah, Gemara, and the early commentators, not out of fear of Heaven or because it was a mitzva, but only because it was something real, a science, wisdom – – – The cold was not great, and they did not worry about a purpose in life, just like the European youth completed himself with general and classical studies, without worrying about is future and asking himself what purpose the poetry of Homer and the rhetoric of Cicero would have in his life.

[Page 280]

" – – – When someone from a small city studied in Volozhin for several years, he turned into another person from the perspective of his external appearance, his clothing, his manner of speaking, and his movements. He would attract the attention of everyone when he returned to his home, and he would become an example for the rest of the youths of his city. When a young man studied in Volozhin, that itself was a sort of diploma regarding the knowledge of Torah and scholarship."[5]

The nationalist doctrine of Zalman Epstein is based on the idea of unity and drawing from the source of Judaism. Zalman Epstein based the idea of unity on the verses in the Torah portion of *Vayishlach*: "And he arose that night, took his two wives, two maidservants, and eleven children, etc. and brought them across the river, etc. And Jacob remained alone, and a man fought with him." These verses are bound with words of lore, that Jacob remained because he had not yet taken over small flasks, and the man who fought with him was the ministering angel of Esau.

Zalman Epstein states that this story is completely difficult based on the simple understanding of scripture, for when the entire family approached the river crossing, Jacob should have crossed together with them. But he did not do so, as the Torah states: "And Jacob remained alone." At times, there are difficult incidents in life that led to the separation between fathers and sons. Here, however, according to tradition, Jacob remained alone only because of small flasks that do not take any special place among household objects. – The bitter results were not long in coming: Since Jacob remained alone, the ministering angel of Esau fought with him. At times when the father is separate and the children are separate – then Esau comes to fight with Israel. Had Jacob not concerned himself with the small flasks and instead crossed and advanced along with his children – the ministering angel of Esau would not have dared fight with Jacob. When there is disunity among the people, especially due to small flasks – then life is damaged and limping[6].

Zalman Epstein opined that had the Nation of Israel remained with its full, unique national character, despite the bitter, dark exile of 2,000 years, and despite the lack of a homeland and national life – this is thanks to Judaism, and thanks to the Torah of Moses and the Prophets. If there is division among the nation, who do not find satisfaction with this Judaism – they [i.e. the national character] leaves the nation forever, and is lost from among the community of the people of Israel. For, without this Judaism – there is no longer a place for Jews. "Judaism is the reason for the existence of the Nation of Israel."

Zalman Epstein states: "Judaism is one of the most precious, excellent stones that are found in the spiritual treasury of the human race. The eternal curse, down to the dust, would fall upon that nation who has such a precious gem, who purchased it with the blood of its mighty forefathers, and gets up one cloudless morning and casts it off as an undesirable object, giving over its birthright to the wilting sprout, to the day-old gourd, to the passing shade."[7]

However, Epstein does not only preach Judaism, but also that one should be immersed in the culture of the nations. However, the main thing is: the holiness of Israel, faithfulness to our ancient world, guarding the pillars of "the Tents of Jacob" that they do not move from their place.

[Page 281]

Zalman Epstein regarded secular wisdom as solely the sheets of the tent, where there is no issue if their colors change or are swapped. This was the same situation as with the tent of the tabernacle that Moses constructed. "Its foundation was built of standing acacia wood, but the covers atop the tent were of various types: some were of goats, others were of rams, and some of *tachash*."[*2] [8]

There is no doubt that new generations will arise among Israel who will remove the old in favor of the new in many corners of life, and life on the soil of the homeland will receive a new color – this is the process that is bound with reality, and we cannot stand in its way, for this is the doctrine of life. "However," says Zalman Epstein, "There is one vital factor, unique and special, that Israel will stand at its full stature in the center of the renaissance, along with the renewed land and the renewed human being."[9]

Moshe Mordechai Epstein

He was one of the great and wonderful personalities that emanated from the Etz Chaim Yeshiva of Volozhin. Rabbi Moshe Mordechai Epstein earned the title "the Ilui [genius] of Baksht." This title was not easily given in the Yeshiva of Volozhin. It would only come after great investigation and examination, with which they used to examine the most excellent of the students. They would then nickname them in accordance with their great talents and qualities.

Along with Torah, the Netzi'v implanted the love of Zion in the heart of Rabbi Moshe Mordechai. He was one of the initiators and founders of the Nes Ziona organization – a secret organization that operated clandestinely and even kept its activities away from the eyes of the Netzi'v.

The insignia of Nes Ziona

[Page 282]

Rabbi Moshe Mordechai Epstein left the Volozhin Yeshiva in the year 5648 (1888). He moved to Aleksoto (adjacent to Kovno), and married a daughter of the Frank family, who were faithful to the Mussar [morality] doctrine of Rabbi Yisrael Salanter. The Volozhiner student accepted the doctrine of Mussar, and later became one of its pillars.

Rabbi Moshe Mordechai influenced the family of his father-in-law with the spirit of the love of Zion. With this influence, the house turned into a center of publicity for the settlement of the Land of Israel. In the year 5650 (1890) an organization for purchasing land and settling in the Land of Israel was founded in Aleksoto. The name of the organization was Nez Ziona. With its founding, it was explicitly noted that its members wished to live in the Land of Israel in the spirit of Nes Ziona of Volozhin.

Rabbi Moshe Mordechai Epstein traveled to the Land of Israel in the year 5650 [1890] as a delegate of the organization, along with Yehuda David Botkowski (a merchant and Chovevei Tzion member from Suwałki) to actualize the purchase of land. They purchased 30,000 dunam of land upon which Hadera was founded.

The news of the purchase of Hadera immediately spread in the Diaspora (and of course, reached Volozhin as well). Every lover of Zion saw it as their duty to bless the translation. Rabbi Shmuel Mohilewer and Rabbi Yitzchak Elchanan Spector blessed the translation and those involved with it.

In the year 5651 (1891), Rabbi Moshe Mordechai Epstein traveled to the Land of Israel once again. He had a bundle of money in his hand to complete the details of the purchase of the land, which was very complicated in those days. Menachem Mendel Nachumowski, also a student of Volozhin and a member of Nes Ziona, also joined him. However, they encountered great obstacles. The seller refused to fulfil the conditions related to the drying of the marches and the malaria. This was the cause of great disappointment to the directors as well as to Rabbi Moshe Mordechai Epstein.

Rabbi Moshe Mordechai immersed himself in his spiritual world. He felt that a different yoke was pushing atop him, not the yoke of obtaining property, but rather the yoke of Torah. He would not be able to occupy himself with the purchasing of land and founding of settlements, but rather, a different task of "building and planting" was awaiting him – the work of building Judaism.

A great tragedy occurred in the year 5652 (1892) – the Volozhin Yeshiva closed. However, then the sun of the Slobodka Yeshiva shone. Many of the students of the Volozhin Yeshiva found a place in that Yeshiva so they could continue their Torah studies.

The head of the Slobodka Yeshiva, Rabbi Nosson Tzvi Finkel ("The Saba of Slobodka") was seeking a young Gaon who could develop the Yeshiva. He found Rabbi Moshe Mordechai Epstein fitting for this position. In the year 5654 (1894), Rabbi Moshe Mordechai was appointed by the Saba of Slobodka as head of the Yeshiva, which was one of the largest wellsprings of Torah at that time.

Indeed, this choice succeeded. The young Gaon, aged 25, dedicated himself to his high position with the entire warmth of his heart. Thousands of students streamed to this new Nehardea[*3].

When he was serving as head of the Yeshiva of Slobodka, his great book *Levush Mordechai* on Tractate *Bava Kama* was published at the beginning of the year 5661 (1900). It was accepted with honor and reverence in the world of studiers. This book,

[Page 283]

like all his other books, was accepted in all Yeshivas as a fundamental book to attain the proper path in direct understanding and extra depth in the study of Torah.

The First World War moved Mordechai Epstein and his Yeshiva to Minsk, and from there to the district of Poltava. These wanderings proved clearly to him that there is no longer a place for a Torah center in the Diaspora, and he began to dream of moving the Slobodka Yeshiva to the Land of Israel.

In the summer of 5684 (1924), the first group of students arrived in the Land of Israel, and the cornerstone of the Slobodka Yeshiva in Hebron was laid in Elul of that year.

Rabbi Epstein made *aliya* to the Land of Israel in 5685 (1925) after being away from it for 45 years. His first stop was Hadera. That settlement, which caused him so much disappointment and bitterness during its early years, as if Hadera rendered its residents bereaved – was now flourishing and sprouting up. Rabbi Epstein enjoyed the vision before his eyes, for his efforts were not for naught.

In Hebron, the city of the patriarchs, the golden chain that began in the hills of Volozhin and continued to the summits of the Mountains of Jerusalem and Hebron was once again tied to the soul of Rabbi Moshe Mordechai Epstein. That which he received and inherited in Voloshin he bequeathed to the Yeshiva of Slobodka, both in the Diaspora and in Hebron. Even though the Slobodka Yeshiva was conducted in accordance with the Mussar methodology (which was not the way things were in Volozhin), the "pillar of Torah" that was the fundamental foundation of the Yeshiva of Volozhin was transplanted to Slobodka. Thus, Rabbi Moshe Mordechai Epstein continued the chain of Rabbi Chaim of Volozhin, of the Netzi'v and of Rabbi Chaim Soloveitchik.

Rabbi Moshe Mordechai Epstein only taught Torah in Hebron for four years. Disturbances broke out in the Land in the year 5689 (1929). Twenty-four of Rabbi Moshe Mordechai's students, great in Torah, were slaughtered before his eyes. The Yeshiva in Hebron was destroyed, and its survivors moved to Jerusalem.

The frightful disturbances and terrible destruction crushed Rabbi Epstein's soul and destroyed his health. He died in holiness and purity after disseminating Torah in his Yeshiva for 40 years.

One of Rabbi Moshe Mordechai Epstein's students writes about his rabbi: "He was one of the last of the early Gaonim of Israel. This type of Gaon revealed and opened the storehouses of Torah in all aspects. These were the type of people in whose hands were the keys to the treasuries of Torah in all its types and subjects. They felt as if everything emanated from themselves, for everything was open and revealed to them."[10]

[Page 284]

Yehuda Leib Don-Yechia

Rabbi Yehuda Leib Don-Yechia as one of the rare students of Volozhin who left an interesting chapter of memoirs about the Yeshiva. In his memoires[11], he relates that he was 19 years old when he decided to move to a place of Torah, "To the praiseworthy Volozhin Yeshiva." The Yeshiva left a strong impression on him. He was especially impressed by the Netzi'v and Rabbi Chaim Soloveitchik. He describes the Netzi'v as "short, with white hairs on his head and beard, and his entire body filled with energy and action."

Rabbi Chaim Soloveitchik especially attracted his heart. He is described as, "Having the head of an aged lion, connected to deep brain power. His image is etched forever in the memories of all who saw him."

As Rabbi Don-Yechia writes, his classes gave satisfaction to the audience, also due to their unique manner of expression. Rabbi Chaim Soloveitchik knew how to express the finest of reasoning in a logical fashion. "He was the statue of Talmudic logic. He knew the character and soul of the Talmudic rock very well."

His classes were free of the taint of didactics. Rather, they were replete with fundamental depth. In the Yeshiva, they said that Rabbi Chaim Soloveitchik could "split a hair into two." Rabbi Don-Yechia writes, "Indeed, there was a need for special effort in order to understand the fine details of his explanation. However, anyone who merited to understand him would go forth with a great bounty. The rabbi writes, "Rabbi Soloveitchik's head functioned endlessly like a steam engine."

In Volozhin, Rabbi Don-Yechia was among the members of the Netzach Yisrael organization. This was the organization that bore the news of the advent of Zionism. Members who excelled in the knowledge of Torah, in the fear of Heaven, and in literary talents were accepted into this organization. When they recommended that he join this organization, he made the condition that the organization must ensure that the idea of the love of Zion be expressed with holy purity, as "a step toward the coming of the righteous redeemer." The organization disseminated the books of Sh. R. Hirsch and the brief history of Zeev Javitz to the Yeshiva lads.

Rabbi Don-Yechia studied at the Volozhin Yeshiva for three years. When it closed, he moved to Brisk to continue studying Torah from Rabbi Chaim Soloveitchik, who had been appointed as rabbi of that city.

After he married the daughter of the Gaon Rabbi Shlomo HaKohen, the elder of the rabbis of Vilna – Rabbi Don-Yechia got to know from up close the activists of Chovevei Tzion, headed by Zeev Javitz. The religious Zionists in Vilna founded an organization called Shaarei Zion, the members of which gathered in the Strashun library and occupied themselves with Torah and the ways of religious Zionism. Rabbi Don-Yechia gave the classes in *Halacha*.

Rabbi Don-Yechia saw the eternal path of the nation of Israel within religious Zionism. He published a booklet called "Zionism Based on Religious Outlook" that served as important publicity material for religious Zionism. Among other things, this booklet states, "Not only does the Zionist idea not contradict religion,

[Page 285]

but, on the contrary, it is in accordance with religion, based on the words of the prophets and the Talmud. Anyone who places obstacles in the path of Zionism will eventually have to give account." In another place in that booklet, he writes: "Supernal providence has provided us with the idea of Zionism as a balm and cure for all the ills of our nation at this time."

Rabbi Don-Yechia believed that "The Jew – the sublime person, according to the image of the Torah" will arise in the Land of Israel.

Alter Droyanow

Droyanow was one of the few of the students of Yeshivat Etz Chaim of Volozhin who remembered Volozhin and pined for it all the days of their lives. The grace of Volozhin was never erased from his heart. In the year 5691 (1931), when he came to Poland on a mission of the Jewish National Fund, he was invited to Białystok for a celebration hosted by the students of the sevenths grade of the Hebrew gymnasja. At that celebration, Droyanow presented memories of Volozhin for an extended period.

He went to study in the Volozhin Yeshiva when he was 16 years old (in the year 5646 – 1886). When he arrived, he joined the Chovevei Zion group of the Yeshiva students. He as examined for the first time by the Netzi'v several months after he entered the Yeshiva. Droyanow relates that he entered the library of the Netzi'v. The rabbi placed one of the sharp didactic books before him, showed him a section, and asked him to study it for an hour or two, and then present its contents. Droyanow delved deep into the section, and when he was sure that the topic was clear to himself, he presented the section to the Netzi'v. After he finished his words, the Netzi'v said to him that he indeed fully understood the intention of the author, but he did not succeed. The Netzi'v asked Droyanow to take out Tractate *Chullin* from the bookshelf, from which was the source of the Talmudic discussion that formed the topic of the sharp didactics. When Droyanow looked into the source, he noticed that the author added the word "no" to the Talmudic source, and if one uses the original version of the Talmudic source, the didactic argument falls apart completely.

The Netzi'v said to Droyanow, "You see, my son, had you started with this, that is by looking into the source of the Talmud statement – you would not have had to exert effort for naught. This lesson that Droyanow learned from the Netzi'v, that is that one must always go to the original source and not suffice oneself with a secondary or tertiary source – served as the candle for him in his wide-branched literary work.

Droyanow testified about himself that he learned about pioneering [*chalutziut*] itself in its sublime meaning from the Volozhin Yeshiva. Droyanow said, "A *chalutz* [Zionist pioneer] is our *kloiznik* [someone who frequents a *kloiz*], our kabbalist, who dedicates his soul to the supernal awakening, to the unification of worlds, someone who dedicates his entire soul to the holiness of his work and the holiness of his life."[12]

[Page 286]

Droyanow regarded the Volozhin Yeshiva as a mighty fortress that guarded Judaism and Jews from all sorts of usual and unusual winds. When he studied in the Yeshiva, one elder, they told him about one of the heads of the Etz Chaim Yeshiva who was afraid of lightning and thunder. When he saw the sky darken and thunder threatening, he would immediately leave his home and enter the Yeshiva building. He would not move from there until the sky cleared, and the thunder and lightning ceased. That elder would say, "Here, in the tent of Torah – I am not afraid of any tribulations in the world."[13]

Droyanow learned from the Netzi'v that the condition of living in our Holy Land is going back to the sources. When ne repents and returns to the source – only then can he stop wandering through the world. The words of the Netzi'v are based on the legend that is told about the Holy Ar'I (The G-dly Ashkenazi Rabbi Yitzchak). It is told about the Ar'I that he once went out of the city to isolate himself, and saw all the trees, fields, and the entire river – all filled with wandering souls. He asked them, "What are you doing here?" They responded, "We had not repented during our lifetimes, when we were in the world of humans, and we did not strengthen the hands of our friends to repent. This is our punishment: We have been pushed outside the bounds, and we are wandering through the world." The Ar'i answered them: "Repentance is great in that it reaches the Throne of Honor. No gate is locked in the face of repentance. Every time is its time. Repent, and you will stop being wanderers."

Droyanow saw the Archimedean Point in the Zionist Movement. "What Archimedes did not succeed in – we have succeeded. He searched for a point outside the world, in order to turn the entire world around it – and could not find it. We have found it. We have found our homeland, the Land of Israel, which was outside of our world for a prolonged period.[14]

In the year 5691 (1931), he went on a mission for the Jewish National Fund of Poland. During this mission, he studied and researched Polish Jewry. He reached very dark conclusions. In every corner, he saw "the cloud of degrading poverty, where begging for bread was widespread in its entire fierceness."

He describes the Jewish Street in Vilna: "Male and female shopkeepers, sitting like mourners at the doors of their empty shops, with no customers. Tailors and shoemakers murmuring like autumn flies at their machines and workshops, silent with no work.[15]

Already then, Droyanow foresaw the destruction of the Jewish town, and the following words escaped his mouth: "My precious town! In you I was born, raised, and educated, and in you

[Page 287]

I spent the days of my youth. How great is my longing for you. And from these longings I hear that you are forlorn, dying, and passing away, for your end is nigh."[16]

Droyanow saw a special depth in Zionism. This is not merely a return to the homeland. This is not merely a return to a life of independence and a life of creativity. This is much more. This is a blend of a supernal awakening with an earthly awakening. When the students of Rabbi Akiva entered the Pardes[*4] he said to them: "When you enter toward the pure marble stones, and it seems to you like water – be careful not to say: Water, water! Because the pure marble stones have some other essence, a different depth than simple water. That is the same with Zionism, which cannot be regarded as a simple path."

Droyanow made his biggest contribution to the Zionist movement in his book "Writings about the history of Chibat Zion and the Settlement of the Land of Israel" which is a veritable source to understand the Chovevei Zion movement.

Droyanow earned a name for himself in his "Book of Jokes and Sharpness," which was published in three parts. Volozhin plays a significant role in this book. The jokes in Volume II, sections 2274 to 2296 are Volozhin jokes. I will include some of them:

a.   During the time of the leadership of Rabbi Eliezer Yitzchak Fried, the son-in-law of Rabbi Itzele, an intelligent *mashgiach* [spiritual supervisor] named Rabbi Elyakum served in the Etz Chaim Yeshiva. Once a bearded lad came to him to be accepted to the Yeshiva. Rabbi Elyakum asked him, "How old are you?" The lad responded, "I am 17 years old." Rabbi Elyakum looked at the grown beard of the lad and said to him, "How the generations have changed! In its time, when I was your age – I was already twenty years old… (Volume III, section 2283)

b.   A wealthy woman named Miriam Sharla't (acronym for Much Peace to the Lovers of Your Torah) [שָׁלוֹם רָב, לְאֹהֲבֵי תוֹרָתֶךְ] lived in an estate near Volozhin. Once during a harsh winter, she sent to the Netzi'v several wagons laden with wood as a gift for the poor. The Netzi'v sent her a letter of thanks, and wrote at the top: "To the prominent woman, Mrs. Miriam Sharla'd) (with a *daled* rather than a *tav*)." Everyone wondered: The Netzi'v is very precise – why did he make such an error?

One of the sharp people of the Yeshiva said, "The Netzi'v did not make an error. On the contrary, he was very precise. He was intending the acrostic, "Now she is troubled for three years (that is: Vespasian Caesar came and caused trouble for Jerusalem for three years.) There were three very wealthy people there… etc. One said to the other, 'I can feed everyone in the city with wheat and barley.' The second said, "With wine, salt and oil.' Another said, 'With wood.' The rabbis praised the

[Page 288]

owner of the wood. Rabbi Hisda said, 'One storehouse of wheat is worth sixty storehouses of wood.'"

c.   Rabbi Yosi Ber Soloveitchik had a dispute with a certain man. When they both came for judgment, Rabbi Yosi Ber erred in his claim. One of those being judged said, "I am surprised that a foolish claim could be made by such an intelligent man as yourself."

Rabbi Yosi Ber responded, "And according to you, when the Holy One Blessed Be He seeks to fulfil the verse 'He turns the wise back and renders their knowledge foolish' (Isaiah 44:25), with whom will He fulfil 'Perhaps with a fool like you?'" (Volume III, section 2294).

d.   One of Rabbi Yosi Ber Soloveitchik's sons got engaged, and the father of the bride specified a dowry of 3,000. He became proud, and began to boast in front of his friends. Rabbi Yosi Ber said to him, "You are making a mistake my son, and you are boasting for nothing. They designated the dowry for me and not for you." The son was embarrassed and said to him, "Father, perhaps there is a proof from here that you are only worth 3,000?"

Rabbi Yosi Ber responded, "You are again making a mistake, my son. I am worth much more. Why did I get less? Because there is a match in the middle…" (Volume III, section 2295)

e.   Rabbi Itzele was afraid of thunder. Once during a storm, he said to one of his students, "I really enjoy thunder!" The students were surprised, and one of them asked, 'Rabbi, how is it that you enjoy it, when we all know that your honor is afraid.' Rabbi Itzele responded, "And if I do not enjoy, will there be no thunder? Therefore, it is better that I enjoy…" (Volume III, section 2282)

Kalonymus Zeev Wissotzky

He was the son of poor parents. During his youth, he went to settle in a village founded by Jews around Dunaburg [Dvinsk or Daugavpils]. He settled in Moscow in the year 5614 (1854) and became wealthy through the tea trade. As he became wealthier, he did a great deal of charitable deeds.

His love for Zion was implanted in his heart at the Etz Chaim Yeshiva of Volozhin, where he had studied for three years. Already in the year 5633 (1872), when Rabbi Kalisher began his work for the benefit of the settlement of the Land of Israel, Wissotzky was one of the first to offer generous donations. His independent, fruitful work for the settlement of the Land of Israel, which bore much fruit, began in the year 5644 (1884). From that time, he was the first for anything good and effective that was to be done for the revival of the Land of Israel.

He disseminated the idea of the love of Zion among the wealthy Jews of Moscow. With their participation, he founded a group for the settlement of the Land of Israel, which would send significant sums of money for the benefit of those who settled in the Land of Israel. He assisted the members of the Balkind family to purchase land in Gedera (Qatra, as it was called in those days).

Wissotzky extended great assistance to Petach Tikva during its first years, He made sure that the residents

[Page 289]

would not be dependent on the table of the "philanthropist" but would rather become independent. He was of the opinion that the upbuilding of the Land would not come from donations alone, and he thought of other sources to raise funds. He was influenced by the words of Smolenskin, that the movement to settle the Land of Israel could not wait for centuries or even decades. If the Jews do not succeed in working toward the settlement of the Land of Israel within one or two decades – there will be no hope of reaching their goal in a natural fashion, for German settlers and others have set their eyes on the Land of Israel, and have begun to settle it and to purchase land there.

In order to advance the building of the Land, Smolenskin recommended the development of business, trades, and manufacturing in the Land of Israel. In the fashion of the countries of Europe, in which manufacturing brings livelihood to the majority of the residents, trade and manufacturing can absorb a large population in the Land of Israel as well. Wissotzky was prepared to contribute a tenth of the needed funds at the outset to begin manufacturing efforts in the Land.

At the Katowice Convention, Wissotzky expressed his willingness to invest 3,000 rubles himself, and he also wanted others to do the same. He also was interested in the Land of Israel turning into a spiritual center that will enlighten the entire Jewish Diaspora.

In his will, he left a sum of close to a million rubles for the benefit of the founding of a *Beis Midrash* for Torah and wisdom in the Land of Israel. He obligated his heirs to give over this sum through the course of fifty years, and the rate of 20,000 rubles a year. In his will, Wissotzky appointed Ahad-Ha'am and Rabbi Mza'h as trustees of this bequest. A portion of this bequest enabled the establishment of the Technion in Haifa[*5].

Leib Yaffe

Leib Yaffe, the well-known Zionist emissary, was the grandson of Rabbi Mordechai Gimpel Yaffe (see later on about him). He went to study in the Yeshiva of Volozhin at the age of 18. His older brother Zalman was already studying there. He live in the house of Peretz the wagon driver, who would bring the residents of Volozhin and the Yeshiva students from the Molodchana stop to Volozhin.

Leib Yaffe was accustomed to isolating himself on the hills that surrounded Volozhin. There, his Zionist poems already began to form. He and his brother would get up while it was still night and go to the Yeshiva, as Bialik writes in *Hamatmid*:

"In the morning, in the morning, before one can distinguish
Between blue and white, between a wolf and a dog,
At the time that from the silent darkness sparkle
All the stars of the morning, a host of myriads."

He pours out his longing for Zion in his poem "There is no *Beis Midrash*"[17], in which he doubtlessly describes the night of Tisha B'Av in the *Beis Midrash* of Volozhin:

[Page 290]

In the darkness of the small *Beis Midrash*
One can only recognize the dark faces –
The congregation listens sadly to *Eicha*
And laments and sighs through the dirges…

I do not recite, I do not weep, I only look
With tired, with dry eyes
Around at the people, who are sitting
In stockings, as they twist about and bend over.

How dull is the glow of the lights
That fall from the old candelabras…
They lament on the ground, as is the custom
As they have already lamented for tens of generations.

They weep over the ruins of the past
Of good fortune, long confused and lost,
The children of the people, who in exile
Have also become a ruin.

It is dark… The holy ark
Is bare, without the *parochet* [ark cover]…
I am silent, but I am in the synagogue along with the congregation
Who sigh and lament, without energy.

It could be that I am the only one who feels
How terrible is the suffering
Of the people who are far from their homes
How great is the destruction of us both.

Leib Yaffe writes that Chibat Tzion was a part of his essence from his childhood days. He was connected to the Land of Israel in a natural manner. His maternal grandmother, Rabbi Fishel HaKohen Lapin, and his paternal grandfather Rabbi Mordechai Gimpel Yaffe made *aliya* to the Land.

As a guideline for his nationalist activity, he took the well-known statement of Dr. Herzl: "Our activity

[Page 291]

is so sublime, to the point that we must speak about it in the simplest words." Leib Yaffe conquered the masses with his straightforwardness, with words uttered in a simplest fashion. He strove for a blend of the doctrine of Ahad Ha'am and the political Zionism of Herzl – a synthesis of Jews and Judaism. The wonderful expression of Menachem Sheinkin always stood next to his eyes: "Had the Besh't [Baal Shem Tov] and the Gaon of Vilna united – the Messiah would have come." The Messiah will therefore come as a result of the unity of Herzl and Ahad Ha'am.

Leib Yaffe knew how to find pathways also in the hearts of opponents of Zionism. He told of a visit with one *Tzadik*, a great Hassid, who was so influenced by the words of Leib Yaffe, that he said to him, "Indeed, our paths are separate, but we will enter the redemption together."[18]

Leib Yaffe did not believe that the redemption of Israel would come through the liberation of enslaved nations. These are not dependent on each other. He brought words from the speech of Adam Mickiewicz about Slavic literature: "It is for naught that you seek to tie the Jewish question with the Polish question by promises of land purchases and a good physical future for the Jews. Is it possible for the Jewish nation to forget all the tribulations it endured through centuries? Can they forget their bright past for a morsel of bread? How great was the tragedy of the world that it was so treacherous against the remnants of the ancient people, who never lost their faith in Divine providence."[19]

Leib Yaffe concerned himself with the traditional purity of our national endeavor. He said, "It is typical regarding the internal feelings of our nation, for already from ancient days, when darkness covered the land and a fog the nations, King David was not able fight the wars of G-d and to build G-d's sanctuary, for he had spilled blood."[20]

Leib Yaffe was fundamentally a great national poet. He wrote many poems, the finest of which was "Behold, We are the Generation," which radiated with longing for the nation and the homeland:

> Behold, we are the generation to which Heaven decreed
> The path sought through longing for the fire,
> And it did not reach the peak,
> And the hunger of the heart did not satiate.
>
> We have a Land whose rocks are scaled
> With the marrow of bones, and with blood,
> The paths of its deserts will be scaled by youth,
> Every rock drips red.

[Page 292]

> And everyone who lives and breathes in it
> Will be wasted from a placid life
> And his soul will be cut off in calm…
>
> And we – we shall grab without stop
> In agony and happiness
>
> Despair and hope
> We will fall and rise up,

> And go on to be raise
> To the heights of the peak Where the light is blinding."

This was the fruits of Leib Yaffe's education in Volozhin, as he strolled on Mount Bialik and walked through the alleyways of Volozhin at the end of the 19th century.

Mordechai Gimpel Yaffe

Rabbi Mordechai Gimpel's father, Rabbi Dov Ber, was one of the great students of Rabbi Chaim of Volozhin. He was one of the first group who studied in Volozhin. Rabbi Chaim was exuberant in his praise of this student, and said that he as "awesome like one of the early sages."

Rabbi Mordechai Gimpel Yaffe was born in Ruzhany in the year 5580 (1820). At a young age, he went to study at the Etz Chaim Yeshiva, which was, according to the words of Bialik, "A foundry for the souls of our nation." The Yeshiva of Volozhin forged the spiritual character of Rabbi Mordechai Gimpel throughout all the days of his life.

He was from the second generation of students of the Volozhin Yeshiva, and studied Torah from the mouth of Rabbi Itzele. Rabbi Shmuel Salant, Rabbi Mordechai Eliasberg, Rabbi Shmuel Mohilewer, and the Netzi'v were his friends during his studies.

At the Yeshiva, Rabbi Mordechai Gimpel was considered to be sharp and precise. When Purim arrived, his friends sought to select him as the "Purim Rabbi" – a custom that had taken root already from the time of Rabbi Chaim of Volozhin. According to this custom, the Yeshiva students selected a "Yeshiva Head" [Rosh Yeshiva] to serve for one day in place of the true Yeshiva head who was "fired" from his position for that day. The lads would choose the sharpest and most incisive student as the Purim Rabbi. In his "writ of the rabbinate" they would write that "he is the rabbi for one day" and that all his Torah lessons and lectures must be "random sharpness" without a scintilla of truth.

When Rabbi Mordechai Gimpel Yaffe was chosen as the Purim Rabbi, all the students gathered

[Page 293]

together, including the Yeshiva head, Rabbi Itzele. The Purim Rabbi "stumbled" and delivered a speech of deep didactics in order to solve a certain question regarding a contradiction between the Jerusalem Talmud and Maimonides – and the didactics was close to the truth.

The students turned to Rabbi Itzele and asked him to judge the Purim Rabbi, who changed the condition that was set with him, that it was forbidden to give a lesson that had even a scintilla of the truth. Rabbi Itzele smiled and said, "Indeed it is so, the didactics themselves were true, but this is the problem: Maimonides and the Jerusalem Talmud upon which these didactics were built – neither existed or were created, but rather they were formed in the mind of the sharp, incisive Purim Rabbi.

A deep love of Zion was awakened in the heart of Rabbi Mordechai Gimpel Yaffe already when he heard Torah from the mouth of Rabbi Itzele. One evening, when he was sitting in the Yeshiva of Volozhin, Rabbi Mordechai Gimpel delved deeply into the verse "Your clothing did not wear out" (Deuteronomy 8:4). He saw in this verse an expression of our life in the Diaspora. In the Diaspora, we are forced to live through miracles, with "Miriam's well," with "and your clothing did not wear out.," and similar miracles.

The time came to return to "the settled land" to our land and homeland. There, we will not live a life dependent on miracles. Rather, we will live in a natural fashion, as is the way of all people.

Rabbi Mordechai Gimpel connected himself to the Land of Israel with strong love, not merely from the traditional points of connection, but rather because he felt and believed with full faith that there is no other place in the world aside from the Land of Israel that can serve as a place of refuge for our nation. He expressed his faith in Zion with his unique sharpness. He said, "Three festivals you shall observe for me each year" (Exodus 23:14), namely "The season of our freedom," "the season of the giving of our Torah," and "the season of our joy." We should add a fourth season: "the season of our refuge" – that is "to make refuge" and to escape the Diaspora.

He was hitched to the yoke of Chibat Zion from an early time. In the year 5643 (1883) he became the assistant of Rabbi Yechiel Berl, the owner of *Halevanon*, to choose eleven families of Jewish farmers from one of the settlements near Ruzhany (his hometown), and bring them to the Land of Israel. These families were the one that founded the Moshav of Ekron.

In the year 5642 (1882), Rabbi Mordechai Gimpel Yaffe published an article in *Halevanon* (issue 13) in which he spoke against immigration to America, and in favor of *aliya* to the Land of Israel. Among everything, he wrote in this article that anyone immigrating to America would indeed find livelihood in that land, but in such, only the individual would be saved, and not the nation as a whole. "Not so with our Holy Land, for it is a long, difficult path at first, but it is short, good and easy at the end. For it will be the guide to myriads of families. Jaffa, Akko, and Haifa will become commercial cities like Odessa and Livoy"[*6].

At the end of the year 5648 [1888], Rabbi Mordechai Gimpel Yaffe made *aliya* to the Land of Israel at the age of 68. He refused to settle in Jerusalem on account of the disputes that were taking place there at that time. He chose Yehud, to which the first ones of Petach Tikva moved in the year 5642 (1882) on account of the malaria that spread there. Rabbi Mordechai Gimpel brought his student Rabbi Yechiel Michel Pines and the historian Zev Javitz with him to Yehud.

[Page 294]

Yehud became the first agricultural settlement of Torah oriented people through the influence of Rabbi Mordechai Gimpel Yaffe. The Chevel Torah organization of Jerusalem decided to found a sort of permanent *Beis Midrash* for rabbis in Yehud. This organization sent to Yehud on its own account young men to study Torah from Rabbi Mordechai Gimpel Yaffe.

After he visited Yehud, Rabbi Shmuel Mohilewer said that anyone who wants to attain some sort of concept of the World To Come should go to Yehud and see the world of Rabbi Mordechai Gimpel Yaffe there. This is a world where there is no jealousy, hatred, or competition, but rather of righteous people sitting, with their crowns on their heads, basking in the radiance of the Divine Presence[*7]

Rabbi Meir Gimple was also known for his sharpness and incisiveness, as is demonstrated by the following story: He built up a large library. His way was to lend books from his library to anyone who asked, but he made two conditions – that the borrower will not write any notes or glosses in the book, and that he will not sign his name in the book. Once, an unsophisticated Jew came to him and asked him to lend him the Mishna of Order *Moed*. Rabbi Mordechai Gimpel fulfilled his request, but he repeated the aforementioned conditions. The person took the Mishna and began to study. When he reached the Mishna in Tractate *Eruvin*: "Rabbi Meir and Rabbi Yehuda say: this is a donkey driver and a camel driver"[21] [*8] (chapter 3 Mishna 4), he did not understand the meaning of this Mishna. He thought that there might have been a printers error, and it should have said: He is certainly a donkey driver. He liked this theory, and he wrote on the page: "fully a donkey driver."

When he returned to the Mishna book to Rabbi Mordechai Gimpel, he showed him his emendation of the Mishna. Rabbi Mordechai Gimpel said to him with a smile: "You did not fulfil my two conditions: You wrote a gloss in my book, and you also signed your name on the book."

Rabbi Mordechai Gimpel Yaffe became ill with malaria three years after his *aliya* to the Land. He died on 25 Cheshvan 5652 (1892). Rabbi Meir Gimpel continued the tradition of the Etz Chaim Yeshiva of Volozhin in Yehud. In order to continue this tradition, Rabbi Yechiel Michel Pines approached the Netzi'v and asked him to serve as the head of the Yeshiva of Yehud. The Netzi'v refused for reasons that we described on page 58 (see there).

Shmuel Mohilewer

Rabbi Shmuel Mohilewer was one of the great students of the Etz Chaim Yeshiva of Volozhin, who was attracted to the idea of the settlement of the Land of Israel. He spoke explicitly about a Jewish state that would soon gather in the dispersed of Israel. Regarding the verse: "And you shall return each person to his estate and each person to his family

[Page 295]

he shall return" (Leviticus 25:10) Rabbi Mohilewer expounded: When we will return to our land, to our old estate, then "each person will return to his family." Then, we will find our lost children, our family that we have lost in the Diaspora.

Rabbi Shmuel Mohilewer's grandfather, Rabbi Yosef of Horodok, was a student of Rabbi Chaim of Volozhin. Rabbi Chaim called this student Yosef Daat. Rabbi Shmuel Mohilewer's father was also great in Torah. He taught his son Torah and Talmud, as well as The Guide For the Perplexed, the Kuzari, and other books of research and philosophy. Out of concern lest the research books might arouse doubt and uncertainties in the heart of the son – his father sent him to study in the Volozhin Yeshiva. Rabbi Itzele and his son-in-law Rabbi Eliezer Yitzchak received him with honor, for his name went before him. He was ordained as a rabbi by them.

The idea of settling the Land of Israel began to take hold of Rabbi Mohilewer while he was still living in Volozhin. He understood that the task of preparing the hearts would be difficult, because the nation is not prepared for redemption. He found references for his suspicions in the Torah. It is written, "And the sea returned to its strength toward morning" (Exodus 14:27). Rabbi Mohilewer asked: Why was the sea in such a hurry, such that it already returned to its strength toward morning? The answer is: because even with all the signs and omens, Moses was not sure that the Jews would not want to return to Egypt – to the fleshpots. Therefore, as the day was breaking, the sea hastened to returned to its full strength to block off the path for the Children of Israel.

At the Katowice Convention[22], Rabbi Mohilewer chose to speak about the vision of the Prophet Ezekiel regarding the dry bones (chapter 37). Rabbi Mohilewer said that it seemed that the dry bones were separated completely from the body of Community of Israel, and the Nation of Israel stopped being a nation like all the other nations of the world. Then the earthquake came, anti-Semitism came, affecting all Jews, whether religions or secular. This immediately led to a drawing close of the various sections of the nation. However, the drawing close was not sufficient until they will all be united with the common idea of the settlement of the Land of Israel.

Rabbi Mohilewer founded the first organization of Chovevei Zion in Warsaw in the year 5642 (1882), together with Rabbi Yosef Dov Soloveitchik and Rabbi Eliahu Chaim Meizel of Łódź. They issued a proclamation that was sent to every rabbi, to arouse them to work for the building of the Land in their cities and communities.

However, Rabbi Yosef Dov Soloveitchik thought of an even greater idea. Instead of turning to the people to donate their coins, he said it would be better to approach 100 very wealthy people, asking each to donate 10,000 rubles for the upbuilding of the Land. Then, they would have a million rubles at one time, and they could do great things.

Even though Rabbi Mohilewer was unsure whether they could find 100 such philanthropists, he nevertheless agreed

[Page 296]

to follow this path, and he told Rabbi Yosef Dov that he would begin by finding the first ten philanthropists. Then he, Rabbi Mohilewer, would complete the task by finding the remaining 90.

At the time that these Gaonim were searching for the philanthropists, and had already found two, a proclamation was issued about the founding of Bilu [acronym for] "House of Jacob, Let us Arise and Go") [from Isaiah 2:5]. When Rabbi Yosef Dov Soloveitchik and Rabbi Eliahu Chaim Meizel heard that "students," that is, secular individuals, were traveling to Israel – they were concerned due to the suspicion that the Holy Land would turn into a secular land. However, these two Gaonim remained with Chovevei Zion. When Rabbi Yechiel Brill, the owner of *Halevanon*, came to Russia in the year 5654 (1883) on behalf of the "well-known philanthropist"[*9] to search for Hebrew farmers to found a settlement in the Land of Israel, Rabbi Yosef Dov Soloveitchik helped him in this matter.

Rabbi Mohilewer first made use of "the tribulations of the Jews." He regarded the Land of Israel as a place in which the Nation of Israel would become a nation of farmers and laborers. When Chovevei Zion decided in Warsaw to found the Moshava of Rehovot, they sent from among themselves Rabbi Eliahu Zeev Levin-Epstein. He returned to Warsaw in order to give a report on the Moshava and what is happening there. The leaders of Chovevei Zion, Rabbi Shmuel Mohilewer among them, gathered together. Levin-Epstein rose up and spoke the praises of Rehovot: all of its residents set times to study Torah. Among them are those well versed in Bible, Mishna, and Gemara.

Rabbi Mohilewer stopped him and said, "Your mission was to found a Moshava in the Land of Israel in which the residents are occupied with agriculture, and not to found groups for Torah. We are not lacking in Talmud study groups even in the Diaspora."

Rabbi Shmuel Mohilewer also preached for a transfer to a life of labor and creativity in the Diaspora. He thundered against the Jewish factory owners who fulfil the blessing with which Jacob blessed Esau, "and you shall serve for your brother" (Genesis 27:40). He said mockingly and bitterly, "Would it be that the Jewish tycoons fulfil all the commandments of the Torah, just as they fulfil the commandment 'and you shall make your brother serve'"[*10] From this, it can be implied that the Jewish factories are open to tens of thousands of gentile workers, but are locked before our Jewish brethren.

The work of Rabbi Mohilewer in the field of Chibat Zion is connected to interesting episodes. We will tell about two of them: He once visited Kovno. When he was staying in the home of Rabbi Yitzchak Elchanan Spektor, who was his close friend, Rabbi Mohilewer asked Rabbi Yitzchak Elchanan to permit the convening of a meeting of Chovevei Zion in his home. Rabbi Yitzchak Elchanan, who was also a faithful lover of Zion, immediately agreed. However, Yaakov Lifschitz, a great detractor of Chovevei Zion was also in Rabbi Yitzchak Elchanan's home. He warned Rabbi Yitzchak Elchanan that a great danger could expected in his home due to this gathering.

Rabbi Yitzchak Elchanan sent a note to Rabbi Mohilewer, that "for various reasons, the meeting cannot take place in his home." The next day (this was a Friday), Rabbi Yitzchak Elchanan came to the hotel of Rabbi Mohilewer and invited him to dine at his table for the Sabbath. However Rabbi Mohilewer declined this invitation.

[Page 297]

In response to the astonishment of Rabbi Yitzchak Elchanan, Rabbi Mohilewer responded, "I am here in a hotel. If I order Sabbath meals here, I will be certain that the meals will be prepared, and I will have what to eat for the Sabbath. However, if I accept the invitation of your honor to eat in your house, and I do not order anything here, then I am afraid that your honor will send me a note that 'for various reasons, we cannot eat in my house,' and then I will remain hungry..."

This is the second episode: The founding meeting of the Zionist organization in Russia took place in Białystok, where Rabbi Mohilewer served as the city rabbi. Due to his weakness, the attendees of the convention came to his home. Rabbi Mohilewer requested two things of them: to have their heads covered and to speak in Yiddish. Dr. Bernstein got up and said, "We will do the first in honor of the rabbi. The second request is difficult to fulfil, because they are not fluent in the Yiddish language."

Rabbi Mohilewer responded to them, "It is not for me that I make this request, but rather for the benefit of the matter. You certainly know that Moses our Teacher was 'heavy of mouth and heavy of tongue.' Specifically this deficiency was a great benefit to the redemption, for had Moses been a great orator, then, when he would come to Pharaoh, he would certainly have delivered an enthusiastic speech about the value of human justice, world brotherhood, national freedom, etc. to the point where he would have forgotten the main point, the redemption of Israel. However, since he was 'heavy of mouth and heavy of tongue,' he did not elongate his words when he came to Pharaoh, but rather went directly to the point, 'Dismiss my nation.'

"It is the same here: You are all excellent orators, and if you speak in the language in which you are fluent, I fear that enthusiastic orations will be heard here about the value of our idea, and the need for our work, to the point where we will forget the crux of the matter – the founding of the Zionist organization..."

Rabbi Shmuel Mohilewer maintained a connection of discourse with the great ones of the nation. We will especially note his debate with Baron Hertz Ginzburg. In one of his discussions, he told the Baron that if the wealthy people invest their money for the benefit of the Land of Israel, we will merit to see, with G-d's help, a Jewish state in our day.

The Baron told him, "The state certainly needs a railway, a telegraph, and the like. How can we Jews observe the Sabbath and festivals if we have to make sure that the trains depart on time?" Rabbi Mohilewer responded to him, "First of all, let the wealthy people build the railway and set up the telegraph in our land. Regarding the observance of the Sabbaths and festivals, we, the rabbis, will concern ourselves..."

Another time, Rabbi Mohilewer debated with the Baron about the Land of Israel from the point of view of political and economic outlook. When the Baron saw that Rabbi Mohilewer was outsmarting him with his intelligence through his responses, he turned the conversation to another issue, and said to him: "Your Torah honor certainly believes that the Messiah will eventually come and return us to the Land of Israel. So how is it that a rabbi such as yourself is conducting publicity in order to force the end [of time], and does not wait until the coming of the Messiah?"

Rabbi Mohilewer responded, "Since My Master the Baron debates with me from a political and economic perspective, I thought in my heart that the Baron is perhaps more expert at this than I am. However, when he starts to speak to me about issues of faith in the Messiah – it would be appropriate if he left this question to me: a rabbi

[Page 298]

of Israel [i.e. among the Jewish people] is presumed to be more expert in matters of the Messiah than Baron Ginzburg.

Rabbi Mohilewer succeeded in winning over the heart of Baron Edmond Rothschild. The baron did not believe that the Jews were cut out for being diligent workers of the soil. However, he charged Rabbi Mohilewer with finding ten families of Jewish farmers, and to attempt to found a settlement in the Land of Israel. If this attempt succeeds, he would take the issue of the Land of Israel into his hands. Rabbi Mohilewer found Jewish farmers around Ruzhany, in the district of Grodno. They were brought to the Land of Israel, where they founded the Moshava of Ekron.

Rabbi Mohilewer continued to preach patience regarding the non-observant, and to draw them near to work together in the work of the nation. In his letter to the First Zionist Congress, he wrote, "We do not look at the firefighters who come to extinguish the fire" to determine whether they are proper and complete in their religious outlook. He held that the Land of Israel was given to the entire Hebrew nation. For according to the *Yalkut* of *Eicha*[*11], did not The Holy One Blessed Be He say that "Would it be that the children of my nation be in the Land of Israel, even if they impurify it." Rabbi Mohilewer said, "Rather, we must enlist all energies so that the Land will not be impurified, but rather that it be sanctified with greater force."

Rabbi Mohilewer greeted the First Zionist Congress with hidden trepidation. At the opening of the congress, he sent a letter to Dr. Herzl, beginning with the prayer: Be with the mouths of the representatives of your nation the House of Israel, guide them with what to say, make them understand what they should speak, that they should not falter in their tongue, and they should not stumble in their pronunciation[*12] This letter was read from the podium of the congress, and made a strong impression on those gathered. It was published in *Hameilitz*. Sholom Aleichem translated it into Yiddish in the booklet that was published by Professor Mandelstam about the First Congress in Basle.

Isser Zalman Meltzer ("Zunia Mirer")

His father sent him to the Yeshiva of Volozhin when he was of the age of Bar Mitzvah. The Netzi'v became very upset that they sent a child to his Yeshiva, which was designated for great scholars. However, after a few days, he was recognized in the Yeshiva as having great talent. He turned into a dandled child of the Yeshiva, and even the older students of the Yeshiva found it interesting to discuss words of Torah with him. They were amazed at the straightforwardness of his intellect, his quick grasp, and his refined behavior.

They said about him: There are many types of geniuses in Volozhin. There is a "half genius," a "great genius," an "excellent genius," and there is also a "genius of geniuses." However the genius with the definitive article is Isser Zalman.

Rabbi Chaim Soloveitchik liked this excellent student very much He drew him near. Despite his young age, he brought him in to the restricted circle of lads with whom he prepared and organized his lessons before he delivered them in the Yeshiva. Rabbi Chaim would say that when Zunia Mirer opens his mouth – the pathways of the mind are opened to him. He would further say that Zunia Mirer has a straightforward intellect, and if Zunia agrees with a straightforward explanation – it is correct.

[Page 299]

One day, the Netzi'v saw Rabbi Chaim Soloveitchik pacing and walking with his student Isser Zalman Meltzer, with Rabbi Chaim's arm hugging the shoulders of his student, as they were sharpening each other with Torah novellae. The Netzi'v smiled and said, "Rabbi Chaim on his neck, and they are occupied with Torah" (based on the Talmudic statement: millstone on his shoulder and he is occupied with Torah?" (*Kiddushin* 29) [millstone is *rechaim*, which sounds like *Reb Chaim*.]

Rabbi Isser Zalman Meltzer studied in the Volozhin Yeshiva for seven consecutive years (5644-5650 – 1883-1890). Then he went to study for a year in the Yeshiva of Radin, under the auspices of the Chofetz Chaim.

In the year 5654 (1894), Rabbi Isser Zalman Meltzer as appointed as the Rosh Yeshiva of Slobodka, along with his elder brother-in-law, Rabbi Moshe Mordechai Epstein. When a dispute broke out in that Yeshiva in the year 5657 (1897) regarding Mussar, Rabbi Isser Zalman moved to Slutsk, where he founded the Slutsk Yeshiva. Prominent students of the Yeshiva of Volozhin such as Rabbi Yosel Slutsker (one of the great students of Rabbi Chaim of Volozhin) and Rabbi Yosef Dov Soloveitchik (the great-grandson of Rabbi Chaim Soloveitchik), had formerly sat on the rabbinical seat of Slutsk.

In his Yeshiva classes, Rabbi Isser Zalman planted the Torah of Volozhin, based on the foundations of his rabbi, Rabbi Chaim Soloveitchik. His style of study was indeed very close to that of Rabbi Chaim, but with regard to his relationship to the Land of Israel and its renewed upbuilding, he was closer to his rabbi the Netzi'v. He loved Zion, and was a member of the Nes Tziona group.

Despite his great expertise in the two Talmuds, the Babylonian and Jerusalem, Rabbi Isser Zalman would always say, "I only recognize one page of Gemara, the page that I am currently studying." There are scholars whom, when you ask them what they are studying, respond: the six orders of Talmud. They think that they are studying the entire Talmud at one time. However, he, Rabbi Isser Zalman Meltzer, would say about himself, "I am only studying folio so-and-so, and no more."

Most of his novellae are collected in his book *Even Haezel*, based on the verse" And you shall sit near *Even Haezel*" (I Samuel, 20:19). According to the interpretation of Rashi there, *Even Haezel* is a stone [even] upon which there is a signpost for travelers." These are the explanations and novellae on the words of the Rambam [Maimonides].

In the year 5685 [1925], he made *aliya* to the Land of Israel, where he was invited by the Etz Chaim Yeshiva of Jerusalem to serve as its head. Here, he continued the tradition of Volozhin.

[Page 300]

Mordechai Nachmani

"May my lot be with you, the modest ones of the world, the silent souls
Who weave their lives in secret, discreet in thought and action,
Concealed dreaming, of few words, and great splendor;
The preciousness of your spirit is hidden within you as a pearl in the bottom of the ocean,
Your hearts – a holy sanctuary, and your lips – its closed gates."

(Ch. N. Bialik: May My Lot Be With Them)

Such was Reb Mordechai Nachmani, one of the layers of the foundation stone and founders of the settlement of Rehovot. He was modest in thought, dreaming secretly, and full of splendor.

He basked in the shadow of the Netzi'v and Rabbi Chaim Soloveitchik for about four years. The Bible and Mapu's "Love of Zion" led Reb Mordechai to Chibat Zion.

Almost directly from the Volozhin Yeshiva, he made *aliya* to the Land of Israel; in the year 5650 [1890] and worked in Ekron. He came to Rehovot on the intermediate days of Sukkot 5651, with preparations for the first plantings. From then he lived there in a life of Torah and work. The Moshava, which was then at its beginning, quickly learned to hold the value of this precious man in esteem, and everyone loved him.

In the year 5656 (1896), the "Ezra" Chovevei Zion organization of Berlin purchased 50 dunams of land in Rehovot, and divided it into five fields. A small house and barn was built on each field, and they were allotted to five workers in Rehovot. The candidates were chosen by the Moshava committee. Reb Mordechai Nachmani was chosen as one of them. In the year 5662 (1902), he was chosen to the "Committee of the Nine," which crafted the laws of the Moshava.

When the committee of farmers was first set up in the year 5682 (1923), Reb Mordechai Nachmani was chosen to the committee. His public work was conducted with modesty and dedication.

He regarded the Balfour Declaration as the "Beginning of the Redemption." From that time, he stopped reciting the *Tachanun* prayer[*13] as he regarded the era as the eve of a festival.

Reb Mordechai Nachmani was one of the few spiritual people in Rehovot, who never departed from the ways of the spirit throughout his life. The Torah of Volozhin was not forgotten from his heart. He was a faithful soldier for the revival of the Hebrew language. After the British conquest, he stopped speaking any other language, and only spoke Hebrew – at home, on the street, in the synagogue, and at gatherings.

[Page 301]

He was righteous and upright in all his ways and deeds throughout his life. These traits gave him the status of a spiritual guide in Rehovot.

Yitzchak Nissenbaum

Rabbi Yitzchak Nissenbaum went to study in the Volozhin Yeshiva at the beginning of the year 5644 (1883). In his words, he returned from the Yeshiva "expert in the three *Bavas*" – *Bava Kama*, *Bava Metzia*, and *Bava Batra*). Rabbi Nissenbaum described his methodology of study in the Etz Chaim Yeshiva of Volozhin, which, as he testifies, was also the methodology of study of the majority of the Yeshiva students in his day, in the following words, "Bread and tea morning and evening, bread and a hot dish at lunchtime, and a piece of meat each Sabbath. A straw sheet on the hard bed, and a pillow and blanket for sleeping. And Torah was our toil all day and for almost two watches of a winter night."[23]

When the Yeshiva closed, he wrote to Bialik the following emotional words, "Without doubt, the bad, terrible news that the holy Yeshiva has closed has reached your ears. We have been afflicted with a great misfortune. Our limbs have been crushed, our bones have been separated, over the destruction of the Holy Temple, for it was destroyed – my eyes are a source of tears, and on the destruction of the Holy Temple, for it is closed, my heart is torn within me."[24] [*14]

He was a member of the Netzach Yisrael organization when he studied in the Yeshiva. When the Yeshiva closed, Bialik went to Rabbi Nissenbaum in Minsk and asked him to take over the leadership of the organization. Bialik wrote to Rabbi Nissenbaum regarding this journey[25]: "Before my eyes arose that self-same evening when I passed through Minsk on my route from Volozhin to Odessa, and I went through the dark alleyways of that city to look for you, as a demon, to fulfil the mission of my comrades and to prepare your hearts to join the covenant of the Netzach Yisrael organization. I sought and I found you and your friends as a demon in one of the *Beis Midrash*es of Minsk, where we discussed long and short about Netzach Yisrael and its goals."

Rabbi Nissenbaum turned to the members and asked their opinion about the future of the organization. In the months of Elul 5652 and Tishrei 5653 (1892), Rabbi Nissenbaum received responses from 18 members who comprised the majority of the members. All of them agreed that Rabbi Nissenbaum together with Rabbi Don-Yechia would act as the central committee of the organization. Rabbi Nissenbaum served as the head of the committee. He continued to direct the headquarters of Netzach Yisrael for two years, until the organization disbanded in the year 5654 (1894).

Already in the year 5643 (1887), Rabbi Nissenbaum joined Chovevei Zion. He acted primarily in the realm of Hebrew culture. In the year 5651 (1891), he founded the Safa Berura organization in Minsk.

At the beginning of the year 5654 (1893), he began to serve as Rabbi Shmuel Mohilewer's secretary. In that year

[Page 302]

he was among those active in the planting of an etrog orchard, which was planted on the 27th of Nissan of that year, the 70th birthday of Rabbi Shmuel Mohilewer. The orchard occupied 50 dunams, and was meant to supply etrogim to the Jewish Diaspora, so that they will no longer have to purchase Corfu etrogim. The orchard was destroyed during the First World War, and a Kibbutz of Hashomer Hatzair was set up on the location.

As a token of recognition for Rabbi Nissenbaum for his great activity in the planting of Gan Shmuel, which formed the basis of Hadera, one of the neighborhoods of Hadera was given the name Shechunat Yitzchak [Neighborhood of Yitzchak] by the Hadera city council in the year 5698 (1938).

Rabbi Nissenbaum centralized the activities of Chovevei Zion throughout the cities of Russia and Poland. He visited many cities, and enlisted the activists for the settlement of the Land of Israel. He made it a principle to preach once a month in the Hebrew language – a great innovation in those days.

He believed that national work should be done with joy and enthusiasm. Only in this manner would it be successful. He explained the verse "those who sow in tears shall reap in joy" (Psalms 126:5) as follows, "All who sow, whether in tears or in joy – will reap. Both will reap. The difference is in 'they go forth in weeping.' Those who do their work with weeping, with lack of energy and sadness – will carry the load of the seed, he will harvest only that which he planted, and no more."

Yosef Zundel Salant

Rabbi Yosef Zundel was born in Salant [Salantai] in the year 5540 (1779). He was one of the first ten students of the Etz Chaim Yeshiva of Volozhin. As is known, Rabbi Chaim of Volozhin loved all his students, but he especially recognized Yosef Zundel because he displayed sparks of holiness and nobility. He would say of this student, "My Zundel is a man of full stature."

Rabbi Yaakov, the rabbi of Karlin (author of *Mishkenot Yaakov*), one of the great students of Rabbi Chaim of Volozhin, once said to the son-in-law of Rabbi Zundel, Rabbi Shmuel Salant, "Our great rabbi, Rabbi Chaim of Volozhin, loved his students. However, he loved your father-in-law Rabbi Yosef Zundel more than he loved all of us."

During the years of his study in Volozhin, Rabbi Yosef Zundel acquired for himself, through great diligence, great, deep expertise in all Torah subjects, in both the revealed and hidden [i.e. Kabbalistic] Torah. He would spend nights as days immersed in his studies, as he minimized his eating and drinking.

Rabbi Yosef Zundel especially won the heart of Rabbi Chaim of Volozhin on account of the deed that his student did with his mother. It is told that they found Yosef Zundel on a rainy day sweeping a path on his knees on one of the roads. He was thoroughly wet from rain and dirty with mud, as he was covering the road with stones. He did that in honor of his mother, who would pass through that street daily to worship in the synagogue – so that she would not step on the mud.

The following story is connected to the years of study of Rabbi Yosef Zundel in Volozhin: The students of the Yeshiva

[Page 303]

saw him walking every morning and evening on the gentile street with a pipe in his mouth – in general, an unseemly trait for a Yeshiva lad. They told this to Rabbi Chaim of Volozhin. Rabbi Chaim invited him to his house and said to him, "My Zundel, they say of you that you stroll in the morning and evening on the gentile street with a pipe in your mouth. Is there any truth to this rumor?"

Rabbi Zundel responded, "Everything is true and correct, but I am justified. Our rabbi surely knows that hunger pervades in Volozhin, and having no alternative, many Jews of the city are forced to eat 'gentile bread' – that is, bread baked in gentile bakeries. I have therefore decided to stroll morning and evening on the gentile street. Along the way, I enter the home of the gentile baker, and ask permission to take a coal from his stove in order to light my pipe. Incidentally I toss a toothpick into the burning oven, and I thereby save the Jews of Volozhin from eating gentile bread"[26]

As a student of Rabbi Chaim of Volozhin, Rabbi Yosef absorbed great love for the Land of Israel. The desire of his heart was to settle in Jerusalem. At the age of 52, he began to prepare for his journey to the Holy Land, and he arrived in Jerusalem in the year 5598 (1837).

He settled in the Hurva, and would circle the walls of Jerusalem from time to time, in order to fulfil the verse: "Circle Zion and go around it, and count its towers" (Psalms 48:13). Many houses were expanded and built in Jerusalem due to his influence. He was filled with joy and gladness each time he saw a new house being built in Jerusalem, to the point where he virtually danced on the streets out of great joy. He would say, "The land should be built by whomever builds it, and finally the land will belong to us."

Rabbi Yosef Zundel of Salant lived in Jerusalem for close to 28 years. An epidemic broke out in Jerusalem at the beginning of the year 5626 (1865), from which Rabbi Yosef Zundel of Salant also perished. He died on 3 Cheshvan of that year.

Shmuel Salant

Rabbi Shmuel Salant came to the Yeshiva of Volozhin with his Talmud. He had already become known as a genius. Rabbi Itzele, the Yeshiva head of that time, greeted Rabbi Shmuel Salant with great honor. He set aside a special room for him for his studies, and brought an entire set of Talmuds there, so that he would not have to move around to search for any point of halacha.

Rabbi Shmuel Salant expanded his knowledge and depth in Torah in the Volozhin Yeshiva. There was no bounds to his diligence and dedication to Torah. He would minimize his sleep, and delve into Torah during the nights.

Rabbi Itzele, who was quite amazed with the breadth of Talmudic knowledge of Rabbi Shmuel Salant

[Page 304]

appointed him to teach classes in the Yeshiva. This was his first step in the public dissemination of Torah. He merited special esteem from the great ones of the generation, who prophesied great things about him as a great halachic decisor of the generation.

When Rabbi Shmuel Salant was in the Yeshiva of Volozhin, he exchanged letters with Rabbi Yisrael of Shklov (one of the great students of the Gr'a), who was already living in the Land of Israel. In those letters, he expressed his strong desire to settle in Jerusalem.

His years of study at the Yeshiva of Volozhin were etched deeply in the heart of Rabbi Shmuel Salant. His spiritual life was greatly enriched. He rose on the ladder of Torah, and also drew his strong love of Zion from the Yeshiva.

He made *aliya* to the Land of Israel in the year 5601 (1840), and settled in a dwelling in the courtyard of Hurvat Rabbi Yehuda Hachasid in Jerusalem. This dwelling had no light and no ventilation. There were no windows in its walls, so light penetrated through the door. A Talmud Torah was founded in the Hurva. With time, the Etz Chaim Yeshiva (as a continuation of Etz Chaim of Volozhin) was founded alongside the Talmud Torah. It became a center of Torah education in the Land of Israel. This Yeshiva attained renown throughout the entire Diaspora.

Rabbi Shmuel Salant did not interpret love of Zion in in an abstract fashion. His opinion was that one does not love Zion (or is considered a supporter of Chovevei Zion) unless he makes *aliya* to the Land of Israel and settles there. The idea of working the ground enthused him greatly. He used to say, "Anyone who works as a laborer in planting the soil of the Land of Israel not only receives his daily salary, but also his worldly salary, for in this case he brings the redemption nearer." When he saw the laborers going out to their work, he would say to them, "May my lot be with you."

When they began to build dwellings in the Nachalat Shiva neighborhood in 5632 (1872), and there was an urgent need to complete them before the rainy season, , they asked to take 50 children from the Talmud Torah. They hesitated, for it is written, "one does not take school children away from their [Torah] studies even for the building of the Holy Temple" (Tractate *Shabbat* 119). However Rabbi Shmuel Salant decided to permit this, since the commandment of the upbuilding of Jerusalem draws the redemption closer.

During that period, the Jews of Jerusalem were very poor. It is told that once, a tourist visited Jerusalem. After he toured the various institution of the city, he asked Rabbi Shmuel Salant if all the residents of Jerusalem are poor. "Heaven forbid," responded Rabbi Salant. When the tourist asked him again, "And what about the rest of the residents?" Rabbi Salant responded, "they are indigents…"[*15]

Rabbi Shmuel Salant served as the rabbi of Jerusalem for 70 years. He was known for his good heart, and his dedication and concern for poor and those undergoing difficult times. It is said that once after he issued a judgment regarding monetary matters, the loser thundered and threatened to break all the windows in the home of Rabbi Salant.

Rabbi Salant turned to the people in his house and said, "And he thinks that I will hold back, will be silent, and will not do anything?" The litigant was afraid of the threats of the rabbi, and he fled. Later, the people asked him what he intended to do? Rabbi Shmuel Salant said, "I would immediately call the glassmaker to install new windows…"

---

* "His relationship with Hassidim was also very different than the relationship of his rabbi. Many Hassidim studied in his Yeshiva. They were pious and dedicated to Hassidic doctrine, and he drew them near in love and friendship. He even ensured that the many Hassidim who passed through Volozhin and came to greet him would stay for several days, so that he could become friendly with them. Once, the wise Rabbi Yisrael Jaffe, a publisher, passed through Volozhin, and the Gaon Rabbi Chaim kept him until the Sabbath. At a meal, he asked him to tell over some novel idea from his rabbi, the Gaon Rabbi Shneur Zalman of Liadi. His son, the Gaon Rabbi Yitzchak, possessed all the books of the Hassidic *Admorim*, as well as many sermons and Hassidic writings in manuscript. He would peruse them, and blend in many precious ideas of Hassidim in his lectures. Once, his father the Gaon Rabbi Chaim came during a lecture, and he liked the words of the lecture very much. He said, "My son is a great sermonizer – – – " Legend has it that after the death of the Gr'a, the Gaon Rabbi Chaim and Rabbi Shneur Zalman of Liadi came to Vilna to debate about Hassidism, and to quiet the fire of dispute. However, their journey did not yield results. (Rabbi Moshe Shmuel Shapira, The History of Our Rabbi Chaim of Volozhin, end of Chapter IV.).

Original footnotes:

1. See *Shivat Tzion*, Section II, page 36.
2. See "These and Those are the Words of the Living G-d", Chibat Tzion, Section II, page 103.
3. "These and Those are the Worlds of the Living G-d"
4. All the Writings of Ahad Ha'am, published by Dvir, Tel Aviv and Hotzaah Ivrit, Jerusalem 5707 [1947], pages 41-43.

5. *Yovel Nishkach* [Forgotten Jubilee], *Hatzefira*, 28 Av, 5663 (August 8, 1903).
6. See the Writings of Zalman Epstein, *MiYalkuti*, pp. 171, 172.
7. The Writings of Zalman Epstein, Optimal [*Lechatchila*] Judaism, and Ex Post Facto [*Bedieved*] Judaism, pp 3-13.
8. Writings of Zalman Epstein, *Myalkutai*, pp. 173-174.
9. *Miyalkutai*, page 186.
10. Nachman Malachi, Our Great Rabbi, may the memory of the holy be blessed, *HaYesod*, 6 Tevet 5694 [193].
11. See *Bikurei Yehuda*, section II.
12. See the speech on the 30th anniversary of the Minsk convention in All the Writings of A. Droyanow, page 877.
13. See "Zionism in Poland" Writings of A. Droyanow, page 548.
14. See "Zionism in Pain" Writings of Droyanow, page 663.
15. See "Zionism in Poland" Writings of Droyanow, page 520.
16. See Writings of Droyanow, page 204.
17. The poem was sent to us by Mr. Binyamin Yaffe, the son of Leib Yaffe of blessed memory.
18. *Tekufot*, page 280.
19. *Tekufot*, page 289.
20. *Tekufot*, pp 174-175.
21. This is a parable: He who drives the donkey prods from behind, and urges him on with a stick to run faster. He who drives a camel walks in front and pulls it leisurely by its reins. A person who drives a donkey and a camel together, and he is between them, cannot run after the donkey because of the camel who will pull him backward, and cannot lead the camel because of the donkey who will pull him forward. Therefore, he is forced to follow the middle path, not as a donkey driver and not as a camel driver.
22. It took place from 18-23 Cheshvan, 5645 (November 6, 1884), and was convened to choose a central committee for all the Chovevei Zion organizations.
23. *Alei Cheldi*, the chapter on the Yeshiva of Volozhin, page 43.
24. Letters of Rabbi Nissenbaum, page 2.
25. Letters of Chaim Nachman Bialik, Volume IV, page 198.
26. The Ramba'm writes that even if a Jew only tosses one piece of wood into the oven, all the bread therein is permitted." *Yoreh Deah*, 112, Laws of Gentile Bread.

Translator's footnotes:

1*. There is a Talmudic statement that, at the time of the resurrection of the dead, those who died outside of Israel will roll through underground tunnels to be resurrected in Israel. See
https://www.myjewishlearning.com/article/jewish-resurrection-of-the-dead/

2*. The top cover of the tabernacle, *tachash* hides, has no definitive translation in English. See
https://www.chabad.org/library/article_cdo/aid/4298548/jewish/What-Was-the-Mysterious-Tachash.htm where, among others things, it might be translated as a ermine, badger, seal, antelope, okapi, zebra and giraffe – or possibly even a mythical unicorn.

3*. A reference to an ancient Babylonian Yeshiva. See https://en.wikipedia.org/wiki/Nehardea_Academy

4*. Literally 'orchard' – but it means the garden of esoteric Torah study. See
https://en.wikipedia.org/wiki/Pardes_(legend)

5*. For Rabbi Maza'h see the Hebrew article:
https://he.wikipedia.org/wiki/%D7%99%D7%A2%D7%A7%D7%91_%D7%9E%D7%96%D7%90%22%D7%94 (you can translate it online).

6*. Perhaps Lwow.

7*. A quote from the Grace after Meals of the Seder night.

8*. For the quote in context, see https://www.sefaria.org/Mishnah_Eruvin.3.4?lang=bi

9*. Baron Edmond Rothschild

10*. Although the original verse is that 'you shall serve your brother', the Hebrew can be twisted to mean 'and you shall make your brother serve.'

11*. A commentary on the Book of Lamentations.

12*. This prayer is taken from the supplication recited by the prayer leader in the middle of the repetition of the *Musaf Amida* of the High Holy Days.

13*. A supplicatory portion of the daily prayers, omitted on festive occasions.
14*. These words are written in the style of the *kinot* [elegies] of Tisha B'Av.
15*. The two Hebrew words for poor people are different here – with the latter one, *evyonim* [indigents] indicating a deeper state of poverty than the former one, *aniyim*.

[Page 305]

Avraham Itskhok Hakohen Kook (the Raaya'h)

By E. Leoni

Originally translated by M. Porat z"l and edited by Mike Kalt

Edited further and refined by Jerrold Landau

[Photo and introductory paragraph added by translator M. Porat.]

The most esteemed Student of the Netziv; he became the first chief Rabbi of Eretz Israel. Born on 5625 Elul 16th (1865), in Griva, Latvia, Harav Kook wrote his excellent essay on Hanaziv "The Yeshiva "Etz Chaim" head", published in "*Knesset Israel*" 5648 (1888). Died in 5695 Elul 3rd (1.9.1935) in Jerusalem.

* * *

"My Avrom-Itshe" – So did the Netziv refer to his talented student, Avraham Itskhok Hakohen Kook. In Volozhin he was called "The Ponevezh Prodigy," because while in Volozhin, he became the son-in-law of R' Dovid Rabinovitch-Teomim from Ponevezh.

Harav Kook used to study in the Volozhin Yeshiva eighteen hours per day. Each day he learned sixty pages of Gemara. The Yeshiva men noticed once that the glass of his kerosene lamp, the light of which he used to study late in the night, disappeared. They discovered that at the end of his daily learning he dismantled and hid the glass. However, what was the reason? The reason was that he wrote verse "I keep G-d before me at all times" [Psalms 16:8] on the glass, in order that those words would be in front of him when he was learning.

Hanatziv liked Rav Kook to such a degree that he ordered the Yeshiva management to provide this young Prodigy with all his material needs. He said: "The Ponevezher is beyond the bounds of allocations." Rav Kook was also liked by all the students of the Yeshiva, who recognized his worth, and turned to him with various questions in Jewish law.

The article "Glory for the Righteous" [*Tzvi Latzadik*] was his first literary publication. He published it in 5646 (1886) the *Kol Machzikei Hadas* journal as a response to a criticism of Hanaziv's book Haemek Davar. Around the same time, he published in the *Knesset Israel* journal another article, "The Etz Chaim Yeshiva Head" (Hanaziv's Annals).

The Volozhin era was a time of happiness and pleasure in his life. He wrote then to his parents and friends: "The hours are very dear in Volozhin, in the large town where Torah is grown." He praised and thanked the Creator who "guided him in the true way and brought him to this place of Torah." He was full of pleasure from "the atmosphere of Volozhin, which makes those who seek wisdom and who are diligent in Torah wise."

In the year 5648 (1888), Harav Kook published an anthology called *Itur Sofrim*, a forum for the path of religious Jewry. Prominent Hassidim as well as Misnagdim took part in this anthology. Among them were the Netziv and the Rabbi Zeev Twerski, a scion of the Admorim of Chernobyl.

As for his life orientation, Harav Kook was a faithful student of Rabbi Chaim of Volozhin, which taught that the existence of the entire world is in the merit the Torah. In his article *Teudat Yisrael Uleumioto* [The Mission and Nationality of Israel][27], Harav Kook emphasized that Israel's mission, the study, and dissemination of Torah, "Exists and is constant like the days of the heavens upon the earth," for there is no existence of the Torah without the nation of Israel "which bears the signature of True Torah. Heaven forbid, if the nation of Israel would cease to exist, and Torah would be forgotten, humanity would revert to its boorishness and its idols."

Nevertheless, he wrote, the most important condition to accomplish our mission is the concentration of the Nation of Israel in the Land of Israel. Harav Kook states, "There is no doubt that it is impossible for us to fulfil our general mission

[Page 306]

unless we are a nation that resides in the Land of Israel, on the holy ground, for only there it is possible for the spirit of our nation to flourish and develop, to be the light of the world." Harav Kook sees in this national essence as "the foundation and essence of Judaism." Therefore, "A small group in the Land of Israel is better than large Sanhedrins in the Diaspora."[28]

Harav Kook once gave an interesting answer to a local Zionist who mocked those Jews who come to die in the Land of Israel and concern themselves with obtaining a grave in the Holy Land. He said that the very first settlement in the Land of Israel began with a grave [the Cave of Machpela in Hevron]. "Give me land for a family grave." (Genesis 23:4). Also, later during the exodus from Egypt, the children of Israel went into the Land of Israel carrying the bones of Joseph – once more a grave. In any case, on account of those graves and those buried there, the Land of Israel developed and flourished.

Harav Kook's love of the land of Israel was very strong. He was not able to breathe the air of the Diaspora. It is told that when he once went to the United States in order to collect money for the Yeshivas in the Land of Israel, he was hosted in the luxurious house of a wealthy person. In spite of that, his admirers who came to visit him found him in a state of sadness.

"Our Rabbi, why are you unhappy?" Harav Kook answered: "I will tell you a story: A king went out to sea on a ship with his ministers and servants. Of course, they took all the fine dishes which the king was accustomed to. They prepared all sorts of food and drink that are worthy to appear on a king's table. They invited a choir and a band to try to make the king happy. Nevertheless, the king remained sad.

"One of his ministers asked him, 'Our king, why are you constantly unhappy? Are you lacking something on the ship?' The king responded, 'No, I am not lacking anything, other than a bit of dry land…';"

Harav Kook finished by saying, "Thank G-d, I am not lacking anything. But I am lacking 'something. I am lacking the soil of the Land of Israel."

Since the building of the Land was the main thing to Harav Kook, he did not investigate the *tzitzit* [fringes – here a symbol for religiosity in general] of the builders. He would say, "The simples of the simple in the Land of Israel is more proper than the fittest of the fittest in the Diaspora." He understood the soul of the worker in the Land. Once, some religious people came to him and complained about the *chalutzim* [pioneers] and laborers who were occupied with the settlement and the upbuilding of the Land, stating that they were simple people who were lax about religious matters, and the land was the holy Land of Israel.

Harav Kook responded, "During the time that the Temple existed, a stranger did not enter the Holy of Holies, other than the High Priest. Even he would only enter once a year, on Yom Kippur Day, wearing the white priestly garb. However, at the time of the building of the Temple, every worker entered the site daily, wearing workaday clothes." When he received complaints that the *chalutzim* did not put on tefillin, he responded, "It is sufficient for them that they are placing bricks in the building."

The crown of Harav Kook's actions was the establishment of the Mercaz Harav, as a kernel for the central world Yeshiva in Jerusalem, from where Torah and the word of G-d would emanate to the entire nation.

Original Footnotes:

27.   Published in *Hapeles*, first year, in *Hamashkim*.
28.   Igrot Raaya'h, letter II.

[Page 307]

Yitzchak Rivkind

Translated by Jerrold Landau

Yitzchak Rivkind was the son of a well-pedigreed family rooted in Lithuania (the Gaon Rabbi Chaim Heller was his uncle). In his parental home, a home of Torah, he absorbed the love of Torah and its studiers, and a deep connection to the holiness of the nation.

His grandfather, Rabbi Sender Diskin, one of the great wealthy people of Łódź, set up a Yeshiva with his own money, which he conducted in the Lithuanian style.

This grandfather made *aliya* to the Land. He intended to establish a weaving enterprise, similar to the enterprises that he set up in Łódź. However this did not succeed. On the other hand, his brother, Rabbi Mordechai Diskin succeeded in setting up roots in the Land. He was one of the founders of Petach Tikva, and he also authored booklets on the love of Zion and the settlement of the Land.

Rivkind acquired the love of Zion from his grandfather. He became an active member of Chovevei Zion when he studied in the Yeshiva of Volozhin during the period of Rabbi Rafael Shapira. During that period, vibrant nationalist youth gathered in the Yeshiva, who dreamed and prepared for *aliya* to the Land of Israel.

Rivkind began to dedicate himself to Zionist activity at a young age. He was one of the heads of those who made efforts for political Zionism. He visited many cities and towns, appealing for *aliya* to the Land of Israel. His teacher and rabbi regarding Zionist publicity was the well-known Zionist preacher, Rabbi Yitzchak Nisenbaum.

In the year 5677 (1917), Rivkind participated in the founding of the Young Mizrachi organization of Łódź. The founders aspired toward a large movement. Indeed, Young Mizrachi became a wide-branched organization, from which Hapoel Hamizrachi later developed.

During that year, Rivkind was a delegate to the Mizrachi convention in Poland. Where he was elected to the leadership. Rivkind conducted publicity for Mizrachi in writing as well. He participated in the Hamizrachi weekly, of which he was also one of the founders. He published two booklets regarding national publicity: "The Netzi'v and his relation to the Land of Israel," and "The Mizrachi and its Outlook." He was sent by Mizrachi as a publicist to Vilna. Once, an Orthodox opponent of Mizrachi complained and asked him, "What is your purpose? To add another 'booklet of Mishna' to those that already exist?" Rivkind responded, "Indeed, we are another 'booklet of Mishna.' However what is the difference between us and you? We study the order of *Zeraim*, whereas you study the order of *Nezikin*."[1*]

Rivkind was invited by Rabbi Meir Berlin (Bar-Ilan) to come to the United States to set up the Mizrachi movement there. He came in the year 5680 (1920). However, he left his communal work after some time, especially after he was accepted to work in the library of the Shechter Theological Seminary[2*] in New York in the year 5683 (1921). Rivkind became involved in the bibliographic profession in that library, and was one of the great bibliographers of our generation.

During the period when Rivkind left his communal work and immersed himself completely in the world of the book, a strong longing for his "spiritual birthplace" of Volozhin was aroused in him. He began to gather material to write the history of the Etz Chaim Yeshiva of Volozhin. Until his great effort came to fruition, he published several

[Page 308]

articles about the Yeshiva in *Reshimot*, *Hadoar*, *Sefer Turov*, and other forums. His material was of great value to anyone researching the history of the Yeshiva.

Among the important items for a researcher of the history of the Etz Chaim Yeshiva of Volozhin, Rivkin published "The Drama of the Closing of the Yeshiva of Volozhin," which was written in Yiddish by a young student of the Telz Yeshiva who was very pained by the closing of the Etz Chaim Yeshiva. The active individuals in this drama were mainly abstractions – the Netzi'v and his students, the Talmud, the Torah, the Jewish nation, and the prophet Elijah. The content of this drama is: at the time of the closing of the Volozhin Yeshiva, a great danger awaited the Talmud, the source of Jewish life in the Diaspora. The Talmud got sick, and the Torah prayed to G-d for his only son. The first scene describes the closing of the Yeshiva. Later, there is a dialogue between the Netzi'v and his students. The fifth scene describes the Netzi'v going to the grave of Rabbi Chaim of Volozhin, as was always his custom when danger was lurking for the Jewish people.

The Netzi'v prostrates himself upon the grave of Rabbi Chaim and says with bitter weeping:

> Holy grandfather, I disturb your rest today
> With terrible news, that your Yeshiva is closed.
> There is nobody in your Yeshiva. It is silent
> From the Gemaras. And they have been driven out of learning.
> The Talmud is missing in the world. The well is dry.
> The soul of our people is in danger.
> Go, grandfather, plead before G-d in Heaven
> Go to the *pargod*[13*], prostate yourself before G-d, before his stool.
> Act, Grandfather, with your tears, your full measure of tears.
> Tell the Gaon, wake up Moses, that they should supplicate.
> Wake up the Patriarchs, that they should know, and they can save us.
> The Yeshiva that you hoped would remain forever,
> Has been shuttered and locked, one cannot enter.
> Awaken a merit for the People of Israel, they are immersed in tribulations,
> Supplicate for Torah, with your tears wash away the decree.
> I am weak. I do not know what to do
> To again raise the sacred banner.
> Do not sleep, Grandfather, your Yeshiva is closed.

Rivkind writes that on Seder nights, when all the Yeshiva students reclined together, the Yeshiva heads would sing *Chasal Siddur Pesach*in a special melody, at all times, and in all eras.

[Page 309]

Who was the composer of the melody? Two answers are given to this question. One states that Rabbi Chaim of Volozhin was the composer. The other states that his son Rabbi Itzele was the composer. Rivkind continues and says that when he was in Volozhin, he heard an additional legend that stated that when Rabbi Itzele traveled to Petersburg in the year 5604 [1844] regarding matters of the Jewish people, Jewish soldiers who were stationed in the capital of Russia came out to greet him with song, as was fitting for a great rabbi such as him, who was a leader of the generation. When Rabbi Itzele returned to Volozhin, he set the melody with which the Jewish soldiers greeted him to *Chasal Siddur Pesach*. From that time, this tune was accepted in Volozhin, and the heads of the Yeshiva and the students sung it every year[29].

Yitzchak Rivkin revealed an interesting thing, that in the year 5663 (1903), ten years after the death of the Netzi'v – two rabbis, students of the Etz Chaim Yeshiva of Volozhin, attempted to found a Yeshiva in New York named for the Netzi'v. The two rabbis were Rabbi Eliezer HaKohen Drucker, and Rabbi Michel Yehoshua Feinstein. Rabbi Drucker was not only a student of the Yeshiva of Volozhin, for he also married a woman from Volozhin, the daughter of Rabbi Dov Aryeh Perski, the author of the book Keter Torah. He was forced to leave Russia while his wife was still pregnant, and came to Montreal, Canada, where he was accepted as a rabbi. His wife sold her house in Volozhin, and prepared to travel to her husband, but she was forced to delay her departure because she loaned the proceeds of the house sale to the Netzi'v so that he would be able to discharge the debts of the Yeshiva.

Rivkind notes that students from the United States also studied in Volozhin. The Netzi'v valued greatly the power of the Russian immigrants in America, and foresaw their historic role as "for I was sent to preserve life" [Genesis 45:5]. When things were difficult for him and the Yeshiva, he called to "our brethren who live far away but are close in our thoughts."

Rivkind states that he does not know whether this attempt succeeded, and for how long the Netzi'v was in the United States. However, he expresses a personal connection to the attempt to found a Yeshiva such as this in New York, ten years after the death of the Netzi'v[30].

Yitzchak Yaakov Reines

Rabbi Reines was a scion of great ones of the Jewish People, a link in the long chain of *Gaonim* who descended from the minister Shaul Wohl[4*], and going further back, to Rashi and King David.

He was different from many of the students of Volozhin in that he attempted to blend the study of Talmud with rational principles, making them fit together. By chance, the book "Explanation of World of Logic" by Maimonides came to his hands.

[Page 310]

He read it several times, and swallowed every word, until the words were etched in and penetrated deep into his heart. From then, he became a master of logic.

Logic overtook him more and more when he was in Volozhin. He began to utilize it to "explain the methodology of the Talmud with a completely novel explanation." However, he did not suffice himself with this, and he made additional step. With is visionary eye, he realized that the Yeshiva of Volozhin as well as other Yeshivot had become old. Therefore, the command of the Torah and of the times is to rejuvenate the youths of the Yeshiva, to prepare them for the demands of the times, and to imbue them with the beauty of Japheth[5*]. This was a daring innovation at that time, almost considered to be an attack on the holy of holies with apostasy. Rabbi Reines explained his "revolution" with the following words: "There are times when the masses are wrong, and consider a true opinion to be invalid, and if someone holds such an opinion – they spread rumors about him and question his uprightness and correctness. However, a person for whom truth is more important than anything will support this opinion openly, without concern as to whether this mater will degrade his honor in the eyes of people. People such as this, who are fit to give their souls for the truth without concern for their own honor, are necessary for the existence of the world."

Therefore, the thought of founding a Yeshiva in which they would also teach the vernacular language and secular studies sprouted in his heart. However, he did not want to do this on his own accord, so he brought his proposal to a rabbinical convention that convened in Petersburg in accordance with the demands of the government. The Netzi'v and Rabbi Yosef Dov Soloveitchik also participated in that convention. They rejected his plans, for the Yeshiva of Volozhin had always fought against *Haskalah*, and this was the reason for its closing.

Rabbi Reines was among the first of the students of the Netzi'v who joined the ranks of Chibat Zion. He entered communication with Rabbi Kalisher, and proposed a comprehensive and imaginative plan of action, the aim of which was to establish the work of Chovevei Zion on a broad basis. Rabbi Kalisher immediately realized the level of energy and greatness of Rabbi Reines, and continued his correspondence with him.

Rabbi Reines knew that his work for Chibat Zion, which occupied a great deal of time, would result in his diminishment of his image as a Torah great. However, he felt that he was compelled to this by the Torah as well as a national command. He stated that Rabbi Shmuel Mohilever was one of the great ones of the generation, who would have surpassed all the great ones of the generation had he not immersed himself in the work for the Chovevei Zion movement. Chibat Zion darkened his genius, but it was impossible to free himself from it. He explained his words as follows: It is written in the book of Deuteronomy "And an iron yoke will be placed upon your neck" (28:48). Regarding this, the Jerusalem Talmud states: What is a yoke of iron? Rabbi Eleazar says, that is the idea. (Tractate Shabbat 84). The intention of the Jerusalem Talmud was that any idea that penetrates into the heart and mind of an individual is like a yoke of iron upon his neck, and it is impossible under any circumstance to free himself of the yoke."

Rabbi Reines rejected the Diaspora. He did not believe that we could exist among the gentiles, "for your descendants will be strangers in a land not theirs" [Genesis 15:13]. Rabbi Reines continues and explains: "God informed Abraham about this,

[Page 311]

that as long as they will be in other lands, and not in their holy land – they will be considered as strangers, and all efforts to win over the hearts of the nations to consider them as full citizens will be for naught."

He regarded the redemption as the purpose of the exile. Rabbi Reines said, "There are two types of exiles: an eternal exile, and an exile whose culmination will be redemption. Many nations who were exiled from their land died out and assimilated into other nations, without leaving a trace among the nations. An exile of this sort is an eternal exile. However, the culmination of the exile of Israel will be the redemption."

Rabbi Reines also believed that the redemption would come through manual labor, especially through agriculture. "Every intelligent person knows that all the good and fortunate traits can only exist and be preserved among workers of the land, and not among merchants and traders."

Similarly, he was in favor of mutual action with the non-observant people in the Chibat Zion movement. To those who denigrated him for enthusiastically speaking the praises of the new settlement [*Yishuv Hechadash*][6*], which was built up for the most part by those who had thrown off the yoke of Torah, he responded: "Our sages stated in the *Sifrei*: Everyone who dwells in the Land of Israel, recites the *Shema* morning and evening, and speaks the Holy Tongue is destined for the World To Come. From this it appears that neither the non-observant in the Land of Israel nor the Orthodox in the Diaspora are able to merit the World To Come, for they do not uphold these three things together. However, there is more hope for the non-observant, since they fulfil two things: they live in the Land of Israel and speak the Holy

Tongue. On the other hand, we only fulfil one thing – we recite the *Shema*. Let us make *aliya* to the Land of Israel, where we will fulfil the three things and merit the World To Come."

The crowning achievement of Rabbi Reines' nationalist activity was the creation of Mizrachi. In such, he removed the shame of standing aback from the question of questions in our lives from the vast majority of the Jewish community of those days.

Rabbi Reines wanted to make *aliya* to Israel during his final days. He wrote to Rabbi Maimon: "I want to see with my eyes the land for which I dedicated the best of my energies."

The Jews of Jerusalem perpetuated the name of Rabbi Reines when they founded in the north part of Jerusalem a neighborhood called Neve Yaakov, named for Rabbi Yitzchak Yaakov Reines.

Original Footnotes:

29. Reb Yitzchak Rivkin, *Miyalkutei HaVolozhin*, a) The closing of the Yeshiva of Volozhin; b) Melodies of Volozhin, *Reshimon*, Volume V, year 5687 [1927], pp 362-382.
30. Reb Yitzchak Rivkind, attempt to found a Yeshiva in New York named for the Netzi'v forty years ago. Scharfstein Book, New York, 5704 [1944], pp 243-249.

Translator's Footnotes:

1*. The Mishnaic order of *Zeraim* [seeds] deals primarily with agricultural laws, many relating to the Land of Israel. The Mishnaic order of *Nezikin* deals with tortes and monetary law, which is applicable everywhere.
2*. The Jewish Theological Seminary. Re Rivkind, see https://www.encyclopedia.com/religion/encyclopedias-almanacs-transcripts-and-maps/rivkind-isaac
3*. The figurative partition in Heaven that divides between the area comprehensible by angelic beings, and the area solely in G-d's domain. See footnote 207 in this translation of the *piyut* [liturgical hymn] of the ten martyrs for Yom Kippur, which mentions the term: https://www.sefaria.org/Machzor_Yom_Kippur_Ashkenaz%2C_Musaf_for_Yom_Kippur%2C_The_Ten_Martyrs.10?lang=bi
4*. See https://yivoencyclopedia.org/article.aspx/Wahl_Shaul
5*. The Biblical Japheth is considered to be the progenitor of the arts and beauty. There is a rabbinic statement that the beauty of Japheth is positive when subordinate to the tents [i.e. study halls] of Shem.
6*. The community in the Land of Israel that was built up through the waves of immigration in the late 19th century, as opposed to the older, original, primarily Orthodox community.

[Page 312]

Sources

(According to the *aleph beit* of the names of the authors)

Translated by Jerrold Landau

Ovsi, Yehoshua, "Tikkun Neshama" (about Rabbi Yitzchak Yaakov Reines), Hadoar, 25 Nisan, 5699 [1939], issue 22, pp. 394-395, New York, 5699.

Ahad Ha'am (Asher Tzvi the son of Yeshayahu Ginsberg). "Rabbi Mordechai Eliasberg", Complete Works of Ahad Ha'am, published by Dvir, Tel-Aviv, and Hotzaah Ivrit, pp 41-43, Jerusalem, 5707 [1947].

Eisenstein, Yehuda David (Editor), "Otzar Yisrael"l (Encyclopedia of all subjects of the Torah f Israel, its literature and history), published by Pardes Book Publishing, New York, 5712 [1952].

Epstein, Zalman. "Writings", published by the Oneg Shabbat Organization – Ohel Shem, Tel Aviv 5698 [1938].

Bialik, Chaim Nachman, "Letters", Volume V, Dvir Publishing, Tel Aviv, 5698 [1938].

Berdichevski, Micha Yosef (My'b), "Haeshkol" (History of the rabbi and Gaon Rabbi Yitzchak Yaakov Reines), Hakerem, 5648 [1888], pp 228-234.

Genchovski, A. M. "The Rabbi of Yehud" (Rabbi Mordechai Gimpel Jaffe), in Mishor, 24 Cheshvan, 5702 [1941], issue 87.

Genchovski, A. M. "Rabbi Mordechai Eliasberg", Yosef Sherberk Publishing, Tel Aviv, 5707 [1947].

Grajewski, Pinchas Ben-Tzvi, "In Memory of the First Chovevim" (Rabbi Mordechai Gimpel Jaffe, booklet 19), Jerusalem, 5687 [1927].

Don-Yechia, Rabbi Mahari'l, "Bikurei Yehuda", Section II, Published by Yitzchk Naiman (son-in-law of the author), and Avraham Yonish, Tel Aviv, 5699 [1939].

Droyanov, Alter, "Selected Writings", Volume I, 5703 [1943]; Vol II, 5708 [1948]. Published by Brit Rishonim, Tel Aviv.

Droyanov, Alter, "Writings on the History of Chibat Zion and the Settlement of the Land of Israel", Published by the Committee for the Settlement of the Land of Israel, Section I – Odessa 5679 [1919]; Section II – Tel Aviv, 5688 [1938]; Sectin III – Tel Aviv 5692 [1932].

Droyanov, Alter, "Book of Wit and Sharpness" (three volumes), Dvir Publishing, 5717 [1957].

Hadani, Ever, "Hadera" (sixty years of its history). Published by Masada and Organization of Founders of Hadera, 5711 [1951].

Chacham, Y. "Our Rabbi Moshe Mordechai Epstein", Hayesod (Weekly on issues of life, literature, and youth). Third year, 26 Kislev 5694 [1933], issue 8 (68), Tel Aviv.

Joashson, B. "From Our Old Treasury", published by Modiin Ltd., Jerusalem, 5715 [1955].

Yaari, Y. "Jubilee Book On the Fiftieth Anniversary of the Founding of Petach Tikva", Published by the Local Council of Petach Tikva, Tel Aviv, 5699 [1939].

[Page 313]

Jaffe, Binyamin, "The Rabbi of Yehud" (Rabbi Mordechai Gimpel Jaffe), Jerusalem, 5718 [1958].

Jaffe, Leib, "Tekufot", Published by Mesora, Tel Aviv, 5708 [1948].

Mozes, Sh. Z, "The Gaon Rabbi Moshe Mordechai Epstein, may the memory of the holy be blessed" (his story). Haderech (Agudas Yisroel weekly in the Land of Israel, published by Rabbi Moshe Bilevi), 12 Kislev 5704 [1943], issue 64.

Maimon (Fishman), Rabbi Yehuda Leib Hakohen (editor), "Book of Shmuel" (in memory of Rabbi Shmuel Mohilever) , published by the Mizrachi Organization, Jerusalem, 5683 [1923].

Maimon, Rabbi Yehuda Leib Hakohen, "The Raaya'h" (Rabbi Avraham Yitzchak Hakohen Kook), published by Mossad Harav Kook, Jerualem, 5725 [1965].

Maimon, Rabbi Yehuda Leib Hakohen, "For the Sake of Zion I Shall Not be Silent "(Chapters of memoirs on Zionism), published by Mossad Harav Kook, Jerusalem, 5714 [1954].

Maimon (Fishman), Rabbi Yehuda Leib Hakohen, "History of Rabbi Yitzchak Yaakov Reines" (introduction to the book Vale of Tears by Rabbi Reines), Jerusalem, 5694 [1934].

Maimon (Fishman), Rabbi Yehuda Leib Hakohen (editor), "Book of Mizrachi "(An anthology in memory of the Gaon Rabbi Yitzchak Yaakov Reines on the thirtieth anniversary of his death), Mossad Harav Kook, Jerusalem, 5706 [1946].

Maimon, Rabbi Yehuda Leib Hakohen, "Sarei Hameah", Mossad Harav Kook, by the Achiasaf Book publishers, Jerusalem, 5721 [1961].

Malachi, Eliezer Rafael, "Rabbi Shmuel Salant" (on the fiftieth anniversary of his death), Hadoar, 22 Elul 5719 [1959], pp. 685-686.

Malachi Eliezer Rafael, "Rabbi Yosef Zundel Salanter", Hadoar, 28 Shvat 5713 [1953], pp. 273-275.

Malchi, Nachman, "Our Great Rabbi, may the memory of the holy be blessed" (in memory of Rabbi Moshe Mordechi Epstein), Hayesod, 6 Tevet 5684 [1824], issue 10 (70).

Nissenbaum, Rabbi Yitzchak, "Alei Cheldi", Warsaw, 5699 [1939].

Nissenbaum, Rabbi Yitzchak, "Letters" (Collected and edited by Yisrael Shapira), Jerusalem, 5716 [1956].

Nissenbaum, Rabbi Yitzchak, "The Religion and National Revival", published by the Mizrachi organization of Poland. Printed by the Lewin-Epstein brothers, Warsaw, 5680 [1920].

Sorski, Aharon, "Images of Splendor", Rabbi Isser Zalman Meltzer, Hanetzach publishers, Bnei Brak.

Slovatitzky, **Rabbi Moshe Chaim**, "On the Torah Scroll that was Burnt" (on the thirtieth anniversary of the death of our great rabbi, the rabbi of the entire Diaspora, Rabbi M. M. Epstein, may the memory of the holy be blessed), Hayesod, 6 Tevet 5684 [1924], issue 10 (70).

Slutzki, Avraham Yaakov, "Shivat Zion", Warsaw, 5652 [1892].

Smilenski, Moshe, "Those Who Went to their World" (Rabbi Mordechai Nachmani of blessed memory), Haaretz, February 17, 1950.

PI'A, "From Volozhin to Slobodka" (A few lines about the personality of our rabbi, the Rabbi and Gaon M. M. Epstein, may the memory of the holy be blessed), Hayesod, 9 Shvat 5694 [1934], issue 13 (73).

Paltin, Rabbi Y. Z., "The History of the Admor the Gaon Rabbi M. M. (Rabbi Moshe Mordechai) Epstein, may the memory of the holy be blessed"

[Page 314]

Tvuna (Issues of Torah and Morality), published by Yisrael Zissel Paltin-Dvoretz, Tevet 5704 [1944], Volume IV (38); Nissan 5704, 7 – (41), Sivan 5704, 9 (43), Tammuz 5704; 10 – (44), Jerusalem.

Friedland, P., "The Gaon Rabbi Moshe Mordechai Epstein", Hator, Tevet 5694 [1934] issue II.

Pershal, Tovia, "From Youth to Old Age) (on the Jubilee of Yitzchak Rivkind), Hadoar, 29 Adar II, 5728 [1968].

Citron, Shmuel Leib, "Zionist Lexicon" (History of people of renown who excelled in the field of the Zionist idea), published by Sh. Sherberk, Warsaw, 5684.

Ceitlin, Aharon, "A Son with the Book" (on the 70th birthday of Yitzchak Rivkind), Hadoar, 29 Adar II, 5728 [1968].

Kloizner, Dr. Yisrael, "When the Nation Awoke", published by the Zionist Library, Jerusalem, 5722 [1962).

Kloizner, Dr. Yisrael, "History of the Nes-Ziona Organization of Volozhin" (documents and facts), Published by Mossad Harav Kook, Jerusalem, 5714 [1954].

Kressel, Getzel, "With the Moshavot of Petach Tivka" Published by the Petach Tikva City Council, 5613 [1953].

Kressel, Getzel, "Yitzchak Rivkind" (on his death), Davar, 22 Shvat 5728 [1968], Tel Aviv.

Rivlin, Eliezer, "The Tzadik Rabbi Zundel of Salant and his Rabbis", Jerusalem, 5687 [1927].

Rivlin Yosef Yoel, "Harama'g (Rabbi Mordechai Gimpel) Jaffe in the Land of Israel", in Mishor, 22 Cheshvan, 5702 [1941], issue 87.

Rimon, Yaakov, and Yosef Zundel Wasserman, "Shmuel in his Generation (Rabbi Shmuel Salant, may the memory of the holy be blessed, the rabbi of Jerusalem 5611-5649), Maslul Publishing, Tel Aviv 5721 [1961].

Rafael, Yitzchak (editor), "Encyclopedia of Religious Zionism (Personalities, Concepts, Enterprises), Published by Mossad Harav Kook, Jerusalem.

Shok Menachem, "On the Personality of the Gaon" (on the thirtieth anniversary of the death of Rabbi Isser Zalman Meltzer of blessed memory), Hadoar, 4 Shvat 5714 [1954], page 185.

Shurin, Aharon Ben-Zion, "Keshet Gvirim" (Images on the Jewish landscape of the previous generation), Rabbi Isser Zalman Meltzer – Mekorei Yerushalayim, pp. 169-174.

Shulman, Rabbi Sh. B., "Al Bamotayich Chalal" (in memory of Rabbi Moshe Mordechai Epstein), Hayesod, 6 Tevet, 5684 [1924], issue 10 (70).

Shapira, Rabbi M. Sh., "Yitzchak Yaakov Reines" Hadoar, 11 Iyar 5687 [1927], issue 28, pp 393-394.

[Page 315]

Memories

[Page 316] Blank [Page317]

A Bundle of Memories
- Prior to the First World War

By the Agronimist Asher Malkin of Holon

Translated by Jerrold Landau

based on an earlier translation by Moshe Porat z"l

Volozhin Topography

The marketplace was at the center of Volozhin. It was very large, and almost a square area. Only its northern section, near the shops, was paved. Vilna Street, through which one would travel to the train, extended from the west side. Fields and forests spread out at the end of the road.

Market Square

From the east side of the market, one would go downhill to the second side of Volozhin – to "Aroptzu." From the north side of Vilna Street and from the market, one would find several alleyways with Jewish residents. On the south side, there was the courtyard of Count Tyskiewicz. Parellel to Vilna Street at the north, a large village, Aroptzu, spread out. In the southern direction, there was a second large village –

[Page 318]

Ponizha, which led to the town of Baksht and to the forests of Count Tyskiewicz.

Jewish houses and shops were built in the middle of the town and in the streets and alleyways. Some Christians lived there as well: the pharmacist on the marketplace, and the owner of the liquor monopoly. The priest lived on Vilna Street. The police chief and others lived in Aroptzu.

In the southeastern corner of the market, there was an entrance to a large gate in the courtyard of Count Tyskiewitz. The entire administration there was Polish.

Livelihoods in Volozhin

The majority of the Jews of Volozhin Jews mostly earned their living from the Byelorussian peasants in the surrounding villages who were occupied with agriculture. The soil between the forests was not good, so they grew corn rather than wheat.

The peasants were poor, and they could not spend a lot of money in Volozhin. When Heller's office purchased an area of forest near the village of Belakorets (a verst from Volozhin) from Count Tyskiewicz at the end of the19th century, my father, who was the manager of the forest exploration (Heller himself lived and had his main office in Berlin), built a large house in Belakorets with workshop buildings, and set up a main office there.

Many Volozhiners were employed in the office. Heller's office was one of the sources that bought the orders into Volozhin. Volozhin earned a portion of its livelihood from this.

The peasants set up stalls and sold to the flax dealers of Volozhin. There were several flax dealers, including Weisbord. His house and workshop were on Vilna Road. There was a large press in his yard to pack the cut flax.

The second flax dealer was Abba Levin. His house and workshop were near the Yeshiva. With Weisbord as well, the workshop was in

[Page 319]

a large, wooden hut. Levin's had a separate large house with iron shutters to prevent fires. The press stood near the workshop. From the Yeshiva, one could see the flax being packed for transport by train.

Abba Levin was one of the enlightened Jews. He sent his children to study in a middle school in a big city. His manufacturing shop was located in Perelman's brick house in the market. He would keep the best textiles for the wealthy homeowners from Volozhin, the employees of Tyskiewicz' court, and the well-off citizens of the surrounding area.

The second source of income was from Count Tyskiewicz' possessions. The count, who owned the bathhouse in Volozhin, was the owner of much property. He owned many agricultural farms, such as the Volozhin farm, Andepolia, Kapustino, and large areas of the forests.

The count's office was also located in his courtyard, in the southeastern corner of the market. Within it stood large buildings constructed of brick and stone. The palace of the count was among them. The buildings were used for administration, the employees, and the workers.

The courtyard was beautified with a park, full of various trees, flowers, and greenhouses to cultivate plants that were moved to the gardens in the spring. Aside from decorative trees in a grove, there were also fruit orchards. The workers of the court cultivated the orchards, and Jewish lessees would purchase the fruit while it was still on the trees.

There were Jews in the city who rented gardens and cultivated vegetables, cucumbers, cabbage, and carrots. Others leased large agricultural farms. Two Bunimovitz brothers lived in Volozhin. One of them rented the Sakovshchina mill. He was a wealthy man. In 1905, his house was expropriated in the middle of the night by the Jewish anarchists who took money and valuables.

The second brother leased the Andopolia farm, three or four verst from Volozhin. Our family was friendly with the Bunimovitzes, and we would often visit Andopolia on our horses. To us, it seemed that this was not just a farm, but rather a Garden of Eden. It was a large house, as the wealthy people in Russia used to have (Pomeshtshike), with a huge yard filled with

[Page 320]

grass, a storehouse for wheat, a large barn for cattle and calves, as well as a large stable with red horses and for work.

Aside from wheat and cattle, they had large areas for the cultivation of industrial potatoes, which were delivered to a distillery near Volozhin. On their way to the Polochany railway station, butchers would stop before the plant to let the cattle enjoy the offal (the leftovers of the potatoes after squeezing out the spirits) so to fatten it before sending them on wagons for slaughter.

The second source of livelihood was the Yeshiva, in which several hundreds of lads studied. Almost all of them came from other cities towns. Many of them received supports from their parents, and Volozhin gained livelihood from the Yeshiva lads. In addition, emissaries who collected funds for the Yeshiva in all Jewish communities brought in money to Volozhin.

The economic basis of the town's inhabitants was commerce. There were many stores in the market square and in Aroptzu. Aside from commerce, Volozhin Jews were involved in various trades.

There were peddlers who used to travel through the villages, selling merchandise to the peasants and purchasing calves, grain, and flax from them.

Excluding the water driven mill and Kotler's soda water factory there was no small-scale industry in Volozhin. It is therefore easy to understand the great astonishment in the town when Michel Wand-Polak brought the first steam engine for his mill, which was situated on the left bank of the Volozhinka.

It happened on a summer evening, when many horses harnessed to a large platform on big strong wooden wheels carried the steam engine from the railway station through Vilna Street. Many children ran behind the engine. Young and old stared with curiosity at the great wonder.

A generator, installed in Polak's enterprise, generated electricity. It was the source of the first electrical light in Volozhin. On Friday before candle lighting, a whistle of the steam engine announced the onset of the beloved Sabbath.

[Page 321]

Post and telephone in Volozhin

There was a post office but no telephone in Volozhin. The post office was situated in Aroptzu, on the right side of the road, next to the Volozhinka. Every day around ten o'clock a horse driven cart arrived bringing the mail from Vishnyevo. On Fridays, the wagon would be escorted by an armed policeman, because, aside from regular mail and newspaper, it brought in registered mail, packages, and especially money.

The postman who served the Jewish population was Oyzer der Raznoshchik. For the entire year, aside from Simchas Torah, he was an easygoing Jew with a dark yellow beard. He was a reserved man and an ardent Hassid. Incidentally, it should be noted that almost all the Jews of Volozhin were *Misnagdim*. Hassidim could be counted on the fingers. The other Hassidim, apart from Oyzer, were Kukse the matzo baker, Shlomo the Hassid [Shepsenwol], and perhaps two or three others. On Simchas Torah, they would demonstrate the difference between Hassidim and *Misnagdim*.

Since Oyzer was an observant Jew, he of course went to the *Beis Midrash* on the Sabbath, and did not deliver mail. He would bring the mail on Sunday.

Many inhabitants, particularly the young ones, got together on Saturdays near the post office, hoping to receive some mail. Very few people actually received letters, but many gathered in the yard of the post office. They took the opportunity to take a stroll, meet with acquaintances, have a chat, and speak of Volozhin gossip and various news.

The first telephone in the area was in our home. We lived on Vilna Street, near the Sazhelke [pond]. Tyskiewicz' courtyard was connected with a telephone cable to his woodland horse mounted guards. My father took advantage of that cable to install a telephone connection between our home in town and his forest office in the village of Belakorets. That is how the first telephone in Volozhin was born.

Volozhin Barbers

Two barbers worked in Volozhin, Mosheke and Alterke. Mosheke was the first and most important. The important people of the city and the officers of Tyskiewicz' court went to him for haircuts.

Mosheke lived in Perelman's big brick house, which stood on the

[Page 322]

north side of the Market Square. Shops occupied the first floor, one of them was Mosheke's "salon".

The second barber, Alterke, a small, dark Jew lived in another small house on the narrow lane leading to the *Beis Midrash*. To get to Moshke's, one had to climb several stairs, but to Alterke, one had to go down, because his flat was in half a cellar with tiny windows, flush with the ground, through which one could see what was going on in his home.

Alterke did not have a special salon. In one room stood a chair, on the wall a mirror and beside it a small table with barber's tools. His clients were the common folk, laborers, tradespeople, and youth. I used to have my hair cut at Alterke's. One felt at home there and could fool around, mostly when Alterke suddenly left his client in the middle of a haircut to go to the second room, where there was a cradle with his crying child. There was always a child in the cradle, for one followed the other.

Alterke had a goat. Between Alterke's flat and the Beis Midrash was an empty lot surrounded by a fence. Alterke often took his goat to pasture there. We children would often let the goat into the synagogue, close the door behind it, and quickly run away.

Mutual Aid

An organized community did not yet exist in Volozhin prior to the First World War. There was only a poorhouse, where the transient indigents used to go. A hospital or a savings bank did not yet exit. Private individuals dealt with charitable endeavors. There were Jews in Volozhin who would borrow money for investment. However, several wealthy families would lend money without interest, for humanitarian purpose, and to fulfill the mitzvah.

My mother kept a special fund of few hundred rubles for this purpose. Before every fair or large market day, our home would be visited by small-scale merchants, especially manufacturing businessmen. My mother would lend everyone 30 - 50 rubles to buy merchandise. The loans were repaid after the fair.

The shopkeepers did not travel themselves to buy the goods. There were Jews who owned horses and carts. They traveled to Smorgon or Minsk immediately after the Sabbath to buy the merchandise for the shops.

[Page 323]

Shaker's "Private" Zionist Organization

As I recall, no Zionist organization existed at that time. In Volozhin, there was a shopkeeper named Shaker. In his shop on the market, one could buy all kind of goods, from small to large: manufactured items, haberdashery, tools for children, and even gramophones with records. On fair days, Shaker used to put a gramophone on the entrance steps of his shop and turned the handle. He aroused the attention of the crowd with the music. In those days, that was an excellent advertisement for his merchandise. Shaker was also the sole photographer in Volozhin

One of his sons (now in America, then a youth of my age) developed Zionist activity in the city. He wrote well and made contact with Zionists in Vilna. He possessed Keren Kayemet stamps, pictures of the Land of Israel, and sold them to his friends.

He obtained a significant number of shekels [tokens of membership in the Zionist movement] for one of the Zionist Congresses. I bought one shekel, even though I did not yet understand the procedure of the Congress elections.

Revolutionary Circles in Volozhin

During 1905, the year of the first Russian Revolution, revolutionary parties developed in Volozhin, as in many Jewish towns. These included the Bund, S.S. and Anarchists. I remember that it was said that Leizer the Baker's daughters and other lads and girls being members in an organization named "Siostry I Bracia" [Sisters and Brothers], in which both Jews and Christians were members. Various anecdotes spread around Volozhin at that time. It was said, for example, that Motke the Shoemaker's would transfer from the Bund to the S.S. for a glass of cocoa… This was probably just for fun, but this was characteristic of those times.

Melamdim, Learning Institutions and Theater

From among the *cheders*, which functioned from dawn to dusk with a midday break, there were a few in which the teachers [*melamdim*] were at a high level, and the number of students was limited.

My first rebbe was Nachum the Melamed, an easygoing man with a yellow beard. He used to speak slowly in a calm voice. However, he would beat the students without anger, as though he was washing his hands before eating.

[Page 324]

At first, my mother used to come to take me home from *cheder*. Once she complained to Reb Nachum about my naughtiness. Reb Nachum looked at me with his cold eyes and said in a florid style: "If your son is naughty, I am obliged to make a blessing over his challahs." He meant that he would beat me over my bare buttocks.

My mother did not understand Reb Nachum's innuendo, and answered that when she bakes challahs at home, she makes a special, small one for me, and she recites a blessing on it.

All the students burst out laughing. From then on, they would tease me, saying "a blessing on my challahs."

From Reb Nachum, the *melamed* of young children, I graduated to Gorelik. After he immigrated to America, I was transferred to Schwartzberg. Both Gorelik and Schwartzberg were higher level *melamdim*. Only eight to ten people studied in the cheder. The *cheder* and the rebbe's home were located in Perelman's house.

From my cheder year, the "Alef-Beit" [song] of Warshawsky is etched in my memory. I include a few stanzas of the song:[1]

> A fire burns on the hearth
> And it is warm in the little house.
> And the rabbi is teaching little children
> The alphabet.
>
> See, children, remember, dear ones,
> What you learn here;

Repeat and repeat yet again,
"Komets-alef: o!"

When you grow older, children,
You will understand by yourselves,
How many tears lie in these letters,
And how much lament.

[Page 325]

When you, children, will bear the exile,
And will be exhausted,
May you derive strength from these letters,
Look in at them!

Aside from the *cheders*, there was a Jewish primary school in Volozhin, founded by the "Jewish Society for Disseminating Education Among the Jews." The society was established during the Enlightenment [*Haskala*] Period. The headquarters were located in Petersburg. The primary school received a subsidy from the government, and the tuition was free.

The school had two grades. The curriculum included the Russian language, arithmetic, singing and hand crafts for girls. The majority of the pupils were girls. The building was placed opposite the Sazhelke [pond]. The manager's house was in the courtyard.

The manager, Director Freedman, was a graduate of a teacher's seminary. The society sent him especially to Volozhin to manage the school. The language he spoke with his wife was Russian. Freedman was a strange person. He was of medium height, of dark complexion, with marks of black hair. I say marks, because Freedman shaved not only his beard but also his whole head, during both summer and winter. He was a misanthrope. He had no friends, and he never visited anyone. He always walked alone, without his wife or any other acquaintances. He taught the children in the upper grade. He also taught singing, accompanied by his small, six-sided harmonica. His playing captured the hearts. Often during the evenings, when he played for himself, we would stand under the school windows to hear and to enjoy his delightful melodies.

His wife, on the other hand, knew everything that was going on in town. She had Jewish and Christian acquaintances. Freedman's wife came to our house often. Blustering into the house like a wind, she told all the stories she knew. Mother would serve her a glass of tea. She would drink a glass of tea and run to spread her gossips in another house.

There was a teacher named Bakshtanski in the first grade. Boys who learned in *cheders* and wanted to acquire general education would take lessons with a private teacher. All the teachers I had who prepared me to the secondary school were not native to Volozhin.

[Page 326]

They were itinerant teachers who were skilled in teaching arithmetic and the Russian language. They came to the town for a few years, earned a bit of money and moved on to another area. My last teacher was someone with the name Tekt. There was always only a single teacher, for the number of children who took private lessons was small.

There were no Jewish students in the city at that time, aside from Areh Polak's daughter, who studied and graduated in Peterburg. She did not return to Volozhin.

From among some of the Polish employees in Tyskiewicz' court as well as from the Polish pharmacists, there were children who had studied in Moscow. They came home for the summer vacations. They put on performances in a large attic. Many Jews frequented those events and enjoyed the performances, that were in Russian. The last show I saw was [Anton] Chekhov's " The Bear".

There was a Yiddish dramatic circle. One of its top artists was the blacksmith's son, a beautiful boy with a pleasant voice. His most significant role was in "The Sale of Joseph". The Yiddish language show was performed in the Firemen's barracks.

Important cantors would sometimes visit Volozhin as guests with several singers. Our cantor would criticize them harshly, but we youngsters enjoyed them greatly.

The Gaon Rabbi Rafael Shapira

When one talks about education and synagogue personalities in the city, one must recall in the first place the great religious pedagogue in that time, the Gaon Rabbi Rafael Shapira, who was the head of the Yeshiva in Volozhin. He was a wonderful man. I had opportunity to meet many rabbis during my long life, but none could be compared to our Rabbi Rafael. His standing for *Shmone Esrei*, and especially his worshipping, his face, his figure, and his entire demeanour remain before my eyes to this day. Just like the other great rabbis who were in Volozhin before Rabbi Rafael, and who were known by their first names, there were may Volozhin Jews who did not know the family name of our rabbi. It was enough to mention the name "Rabbi Rafael" for all of us, young and old, kith and

[Page 327]

kin, to know that they meant "him," our rabbi, the Gaon, the first among the firsts.

Rabbi Rafaelwas a tall, slightly bent man. His virtuous eyes radiated kindness. You could see in them the long day and night hours-spent on studying Torah.

My father worshipped in the same synagogue as Rabbi Rafael. As a small boy, I often used to leave my father to stay close by the rabbi, as I loved to listen to his prayers. He pronounced each sentence slowly, clearly, and with great devotion.

Volozhin Jews, who usually thought themselves as well pedigreed, had great awe for Rabbi Rafael. When he entered the *Beis Midrash*, it was so silent that one could hear a fly passing. All the worshippers looked upon him with great respect. It seemed to me that the High Priest used to be treated in such a manner as he entered the Holy Temple.

My father used to go to Rabbi Rafael Shapira's house at Shavuot, to hear the rabbi's sermons for specially invited Torah scholars. I remember my father later explaining to my mother the depth of Rabbi Rafael's thinking.

When you looked at Reb Rafael G-dly image, it seems as you were standing before a man not of this world, a man who was indeed created in the image of G-d.

Rabbi Rafael was the *sandek* at the *bris* of my brother Yitzchak (Izio), who currently practices a doctor in Paris. Anyone who saw Rabbi Rafael remained enchanted by his personality for his entire life.

The Perelman Family [2]

The Perelman family belonged to the Jewish intelligentsia in the city. Moshe Perelman's father was the rabbi of Vishnievo[3] Moshe married Malka Yitzchakin, who was related to Rabbi Chaim of Volozhin (as is known, the family name of Rabbi Chaim Volozhiner was Yitzchakin, after the name of his father Yitzchak). Malka was a beautiful, refined, and cultured lady.

Moshe Perelman's father left Vishnievo before the First World War

[Page 328]

and made *aliya* to the Land of Israel. He changed his surname to Margolis[4] and served as a rabbi in Rehovot.

All the Perelmans were talented, educated people. The two sisters never separated from their Russian books. The younger[5], later became a professor at the University of Moscow.

At that time, the Jews of Volozhin would receive the Jewish newspapers from Warsaw, *Heint*, and later *Moment*. Russian newspapers were seldom read. Moshe Perlman regularly received the Moscow daily newspaper "Dos Russishe Vort" [*Russkoye Slovo*].

The Perelman's brick house was built in 19th century. Count Tyskiewicz built it and gave it as a gift to Rabbi Chaim Volozhiner. Malka Perelman inherited the house. This house was similar to those in Count Tyskiewicz' estate. Behind, on the *Beis Midrash* side, there were dwellings. On the market side in front was a row of shops. To reach them you had to climb a few steps. There were dwellings behind the shops. On some of the houses, a second story was built. The Perelman family lived in one such second story. A large balcony extended out into the market from the house. This was the only balcony in Volozhin.

Steps descended from the left side into half a cellar in which the wine shop was located. Many bottles with a variety of colored labels were arranged on the shelves. The sales counter was located on the left side. Perelman's younger daughter, Chaya Dina, usually sat on a chair at the table, engrossed in a Russian novel. While she was reading, she was not aware of what was going on around her and it was possible to remove entire bottles of wine from the store.

Steps ran down from the shop to a second and then to a third, deep, underground cellar. Here the liquor was transferred from barrels to bottles.

A wooden building stood next to the brick house, close to the *Beis Midrash*. There one would pour out beer from barrels into bottles with a special pump, and cork them with a small hand-machine.

Moshe Perelman was one of the insurance agents in the city. He had a great deal of work as an agent, in Volozhin and in the entire area, because all the houses were made of wood, and fires broke out often. Time periods in Volozhin were reckoned according to the fires:

[Page 329]

"A few years have passed since the great fire," "So and so was born after the great fire."

Areh Polak

Areh Polak was the wealthy man of the town. He was of medium height, well dressed, with a "classic" belly, a gold chain, a French small beard and his hair parted in the middle. This all gave Areh Polak the appearance of a wealthy man. Everyone related to him with respect and always was the first to greet him with a "good morning."

As a widower, he lived by himself for long time in his large house on Vilna Street, opposite the Sazhelke [pond]. The house had many rooms, including a parlor with pictures on the walls and soft furniture.

We children were mostly interested in his collection of flies, insects, and butterflies. They were pierced and packed in boxes with glass covers, which hung on the wall. The scientific and common names of each one was marked beside each box.

In his elder years, Areh Polak married Mrs. Kromnik, the midwife of Volozhin. Her son, my friend, took me often to the parlor, and I could not look at the collection enough.

In Volozhin one did not say "I am not Rothschild" but rather "What if I was Areh Polak?"

Happy Childhood and Boyhood in Volozhin

Youth and adults had their best time spending at Sabbath evening walks on Vilna Street. The street was crowded. The strolls were far into the fields. We had no theater, movies, or concerts, but we were happy and joyful. We *cheder* boys sneaked into fruit orchards to taste the delicious apples and other fruit.

At the end of summer, when the sun was still warm but no longer too hot, it was such a pleasure to wander in the distant fields. We would dig potatoes, cook them in the fields, and then return home tired and exhausted.

In later years when I was a high school student, and would return home for the summer, I used to walk to Kapustina in the middle of the night, get Michel Polak's brother, and together sneak into the creamery to fry remnants of Holland

[Page 330]

cheese with butter. We would enjoy the taste of the Garden of Eden, and then return home with the first rays of dawn appearing in the east. At other times, we would go to to Kaldiki, a village about ten kilometers from Volozhin to bathe in the Byaroza River, and then walk in the forest to collect blackberries and strawberries. We might lie with a book, becoming intoxicated by reading Mapu and Mendele, Artsybashev and Tolstoy.

We would often walk at night to Stolb, at the end of Vilna Street, along the path that led to the forest, together with our sisters, and often with their friends. The first feelings of love were aroused in our hearts. This was the desire of the lads mixed with joy and happiness…

With longing and sorrow, I remember my happy young years, my hometown, and my home that was destroyed.

Translator's footnotes:

1. I took the lyrics for the stanzas of the *Oyfn Pripetshik* song from http://www.jewishfolksongs.com/en/oyfn-pripetshik The same translation is used in the Wikipedia article.
2. Note from the initial translator: Les parents de Yosef Perelman, pere de Sonia et Monia.
3. Note from the initial translator: Vishnievo - a small shtetl near Volozhin, in which Shimon Peres was born.
4. Margolis means pearl in Hebrew, so it is a Hebraization of the Yiddish surname.
5. The original translator identified her name as Fania.

[Page 330]

Inside Volozhin

by Avraham Halevy, Kiryat Tiv'on

Translated by Meir Razy

Donated by Anita Frishman Gabbay

The Kippa

On the hill behind the Volozhinka, about half a kilometer from the city, was a round pit. It was several meters wide and two meters deep. It looked like an upside-down kippah, wider at the top and narrower as you descended into it. This was how it got the name "Yarmulke". People said it was dug by the Army of Napoleon.

Sitting inside the pit, one would feel oneself floating between heaven and earth. You could see only the sky and the wall around the pit. It was that special place where one could be alone with G-d and feel very spiritual. It was said that the poet Chaim Nachman Bialik used to sit there and so became inspired. People said that this is where he wrote his song El Ha-Tzipor ("to the Bird" – Bialik's first published song).

The Livelihood of the Jews of Volozhin

Of course, not all the Jews of Volozhin earned their living in the same manner. As in most of the towns in the "Pale of Settlement", there were tradesmen, merchants, storekeepers and people with many other occupations. I want to describe the occupation of the forest Manager. Timber trading was a very common occupation among the residents of Volozhin.

[Page 331]

A rich landowner (a "Paritz") would sell the rights to a parcel of his forest land to a wood Merchant, who then hired a forest Manager to supervise that land. The Manager's job was to protect the area from illegal loggers and thieves, to hire laborers, to supervise them and to pay them for their work as cutters and haulers.

I remember one Manager who lived in Volozhin. He was responsible for a large forest and had many sub-managers reporting to him. He owned a beautifully embellished carriage and looked noble. His house stood on the main street near the lake.

Another Manager lived in Arapecho. He used to return home to Volozhin every week for Shabbat. He was liked by everyone in town but, unfortunately, he became ill with pneumonia while he was working in the forest. With no help, he died there and his family, a wife and two children, remained devastated and penniless. This was a time before pensions, compensation or life insurance. The employer had no responsibility towards the employee's family. The widow became a baker and provided for her family by baking and selling bread.

The Argument over the Secular School

Some of the town's people promoted the idea of creating a modern, secular school instead of the "Cheder". This was in 1910 and the leader of this group, a beer importer, was related to the richer families of the town.

As soon as the Yeshiva heard about this, they summoned Rabbi Elyakim Getzel, a famous leader in Bialystok. He arrived at Volozhin, went on stage, put his tallit over his head and spoke vehemently against the "Epicureans" and the idea of modern schools. He was known to be an anti-Zionist and he attacked the Zionist Movement in Volozhin. "If there are 'Sons of Zion' and 'Daughters of Zion' we must hope that their children will be 'children of Zion'". He made a great impression on the crowd. Some of the women in the crowd wept and Rabbi Elyakim Getzel left victorious. The idea of opening a secular school was thus summarily dismissed.

My Last Place Stay in Volozhin

For more than a year, I stayed in a big family home in Arapecho. The house had ten rooms and was the only hostel in town before it became a private home. At that time, some fifty years ago, it was the only place for traveling merchants to spend their nights. The property had a large stable, which made it very convenient for the traveling merchants.

The homeowner had good relations with the head of the local police and used his connections to assist Jews. That man was a sad and miserable man. He had lost his first wife and his second wife and, at the time I was staying with him, he was living with his third wife and all his children. The atmosphere in the home was that of melancholy and even today, when I think of this family, I feel sad.

[Page 332]

The Volozhin Yeshiva and Town
During the Time of Rabbi Raphael Schapiro

by Aharon Zvi Dudman-Dudayi, Tel Aviv

Translated by Meir Razy

Donated by Anita Frishman Gabbay

I studied at the Etz HaChaim (The Tree of Life) Yeshiva in Volozhin at the time of Rabbi Raphael Schapiro who was the son-in-law of HANAZIV (Rabbi Naftali Zvi Yehuda Berlin, 1816-1893). About 300 students attended the Yeshiva at that time and some of them married local women. Eliezer Kapuler married the daughter of Zalman, a flax merchant whose home and barn stood across from the Yeshiva. Rabbi Israel Lonin (he was later called "The Kazacker Rabbi") married the daughter of Feitche. The "Shaliver" married Reitche's daughter.

Volozhin benefited from the Yeshiva, which operated as a state within a state. The Yeshiva issued paper notes that carried the Yeshiva's stamp and local merchants accepted these notes as money. Once a month the merchants would redeem the Yeshiva notes for money.

The supervisor, Rabbi Avraham Drushkowitz, wanted to introduce the study of Ethics and Morals into the curriculum as a course similar to those available in other leading Yeshivas. However, he could not overcome the resistance from the other Rabbis and the Yeshiva continued focusing only on the Holy Texts.

Vilna Street

[Page 333]

The Yeshiva had a charity that lent money to its students. Students rented rooms in the homes of Exter, Stiker, Elka Ramza, Rivka Chaya Shoshes, Brodna, and others. I lived in the homes of Yaakov Weisbrod and Michael Kramnik. Later, I moved to Vilna Street and lived in the home of Rabbi Gertz Askind. He was a devoted student who studied while standing throughout the whole night while holding a candle.

Many of the Volozhin Jews were flax or wood traders. Mr. Heller's office stood next to the Yeshiva. Mr. Malkin was his office Manager.

Rabbi Chaim was the Yeshiva's tailor. Shoes and boots were made by the shoemaker, the son of Yekutiel. The town's physician was Rabbi Aharon Tzart, who was later succeeded by his son Avraham, the son-in-law of the baker Eliezer. The SHAMASH was Rabbi David.

I remember one of the water carriers. His name was "Pinye the Water Carrier". He owned a horse and wagon which had a large barrel on board. He would carry water from Aropecho [refers to going downhill] to Arufecho [refers to going uphill]. At times, the horse would not climb up the hill but just stood there. Good Jews gathered around and fulfilled the mitzvah of "help the animal" (Exodus 23, 5) and would help stop the wagon from rushing downhill.

The famous homeowners in Volozhin were Moshe Perlman, Itze Hillels, Yochanan Rootkas, Berl Romer, Eliezer Pini-Nettas, Yehuda Avraham'le the slaughterer, Ara Polack, Michael Polack, Avraham Berkowitz, Menachem-Yoel Potashnik and Uri Rapaport.

Volozhin, the mother of all Yeshivas in Russia, Lithuania and Poland – lost everything. The terrible Holocaust destroyed it. All our holy relatives were consumed by fire.

Let their memory be blessed.

Looking Back
(Memories From the Time of First World War)

by Yehuda Chaim Kotler, New York

Translated by Meir Razy

Donated by Anita Frishman Gabbay

I was one of the early "deserters" of Volozhin. Both Jewish and general studies played equal and important roles in my life.

My time at the Yeshiva "Etz HaChaim" (the Tree of Life) was the happiest time of my life. I remember the wagon driver Rabbi Peretz, an outstanding Yeshiva student who, following his marriage, bought a horse and a carriage and made his living by shuttling the Yeshiva students to and from the train station. He was an interesting character who was very knowledgeable in Mishna and Talmud but kept a modest, low profile.

[Page 334]

One time, on my way to Vilna, he was driving me to the train station. I intended to study in Vilna as an independent student, a student who did not need a teacher to instruct or supervise him. Independent students received a small stipend for their food from the Yeshiva. In contrast, the Yeshiva students were fed by local families on assigned days (this arrangement was called "Eating Days").

During the First World War
Standing (right to left): Velvele Persky, Avraham Gurewitz
Seating: Akiva Potashnick, Moshe Weisbard, Yehuda Chaim Kotler
Laying: Eliahu Malot

[Page 335]

I told Rabbi Peretz about my plans and he stopped the horse. "I am going to test your knowledge of Gemara to see if you are capable of independent study." He wanted to test me on NEDARIM, a portion of the Talmud. I asked him to test me on a different portion because NEDARIM was not explained by RASHI, and he said: "if you are not capable of studying TALMUD without the RASHI interpretation, it is as if you admit that you are not ready to be an independent student. You'd better stay here and continue with the arrangement of "Eating Days"."

Hunger in those days was prevalent in Volhynia and the only available food was potatoes. One Yeshiva student lived in a hostel where the property owner was feeding him plate after plate of potatoes. She used to listen to him blessing the meal and noticed once that he said, "Who brings forth bread from the stomach". She asked him why he did not say the common blessing of "who brings forth bread from the earth?" "You grow your potatoes in the earth but I grow them in my stomach."

A little later, I move to Vilna to study at the Epstein's TARBUT School during the days and at an Agriculture School in the evenings. In 1918, I returned to Volozhin to find it burning. We had a "tradition" that a major fire broke out once every seven years. My mother and sisters were pouring buckets of water on our burning house while I ran to the library to save the books. This heroic deed made me famous among the educated people of Volozhin who then selected me to manage the library.

The young people of Volozhin were idle during the years of the war because the Yeshiva and all the Talmud Torah Schools were closed. We instituted lessons in the library and taught people how to read. Another educational activity was the creation of an amateur theater troop. We did not have real actors but found several men who could act. It was, however, close to impossible to find an actress. Being an "actress" cast shame on her family so women refrained from the stage. Eventually, we found a married actress, Gitel, the daughter-in-law of Gershon "der bunir" and a sister of Sara Shlomovitz who now lives in Israel. Her husband approved of her participation only after we promised him that there would be no kissing on stage. We also had an all-female string quartet with Rashka Dubinsky, Chaya Feigle Malot, Tamar Tzart and Malka Rubinstein.

We selected "The Yeshiva Bucher" play. The leading actor was Moshe Veisbord who had a nice voice and his song "Mai Ka Mashma Lan" touched many hearts. The performances were successful and we collected several hundred rubles. We used the money for our activities and created a no-interest loan Bank. Leibel Shepsenwol was the treasurer and used to carry the whole "Bank" in his pocket. Later on, this "Bank" became the City Bank of Volozhin.

[Page 336]

We were enthusiastic and expanded our activities. We reorganized the community services with the financial aid we received from the Volozhin ex-patriates who were now living in the U.S.A. Mr. B. Persky (his name now is Harrison) lead the fundraising activity and Mr. Metzer brought the money to us. We used this money to repair the Mikva, to rebuild the fence around the cemetery, to support students in the Yeshiva and for other community needs.

The Flour Mill, Electricity and the First Movie House in Volozhin

by Michael Vand-Polack z"l

Translated by Meir Razy

Donated by Anita Frishman Gabbay

In 1910, I moved from my town of Halshany to Volozhin. I had married the daughter of Esther-Ethel who was the daughter of Yochanan Rodensky. My father-in-law was a flax merchant whose business took him to faraway cities, even to Germany, and he introduced new western technology to our town. One of these new inventions was a kerosene lamp which would hang from the ceiling and illuminate the whole room. Until then people used a little tin can that held a small amount of burning material. Matches were new and hard to find so people used to keep a smoldering piece of coal in the stove. Sometimes the coal was extinguished and people would go to a neighbor to light a piece of wood. People carried flint and cotton in their pockets so they could light a stove or a candle at will. Things improved in 1910 when they started importing matches from the town of Vyazma, Russia.

I had some experience operating a flour mill and I decided to build one in Volozhin. There was no flour mill in town. The nearest one was in the village of Sakovshchina, some eight kilometers away. That mill, which stood on the river Berzina and operated through the power of the water, belonged to Count Tishkivitz. It was leased by Yitzhak Yaakov Bunimovitz who lived next to it. The operation was slow and people had to wait up to eight days before their wheat became flour.

I decided to improve the life of the local farmers by building a mill in town. I imported old-style machines from Minsk and from Germany. My flour mill was operated by steam power.

Yitzhak Yaakov Bunimovitz predicted that my project was doomed even before I started. He had tried to build a flour mill in Volozhin and lost a bundle. He predicted that this too would be my fate.

[Page 337]

His words were "you will be trapped in this like a rooster in a ball of cotton". His warning did not deter me and the mill was working by the end of 1910. It worked around the clock at full steam and I was the Master Miller.

A disaster hit us right at the start. A big flood washed away all the wood I had prepared to burn in order to generate the steam. After the waters subsided, the Christian neighbors claimed that the wood, which was spread all over town, was theirs and I had to buy it back from them at full price. The mill was soon working again.

The First World War ended with Poland winning over Russia and major technological improvements followed. The new Governor of Volozhin ("Starosta niegrodowy") came to see me. He had previously been the Land Supervisor for Count Tishkivitz and was familiar with my abilities. He appointed me supervisor for the installation of an electric power grid. In addition, I was responsible for building a movie theater in town. I installed a large electric generator at the site of the flourmill and initially used it to operate the mill during the time period we were installing the new electric power grid. Having light and power in every house was a great achievement that changed the whole atmosphere of the town.

Then I set up the movie theater inside one of the Count's deserted barns. I renovated the barn and installed benches and electricity. Mr. Komay, a Jewish engineer from Vilna, was the Project Manager. Mr. Zvi Kershtein from Vilna became the theater's Manager and was also in charge of the projector.

The first movie ever shown in Volozhin was "Shulamis". A tragi-comic event at the premier night occurred with my mother–in-law, Sara Rodensky, who had very much wanted to see this new invention. It was her first-ever visit to a movie theater and she was sure she was seeing "real life" people and animals on the screen. When a horse galloped towards the audience, she started screaming and crying that she was afraid of the horse and wanted to go home.

When I came home later that night, she was happy and relaxed. "I did not know you are so rich! All those houses, the streets, the horses, the slaves, the princes and the princesses with their beautiful dresses are all yours!" After that, she thought very highly of me.

[Page 338]

Estate Owners in Volozhin

by Meir Shiff, Tel Aviv

Translated by Meir Razy

Donated by Anita Frishman Gabbay

Three Jewish families from Volozhin leased the estates of Count Tishkivitz. The Count liked the Jews and leased out all his 400 square kilometers in the villages of Adampol, Michalow, Chechovshchina and Sakovshchina to Jewish families.

The lessees were Avraham Moshe Shiff who leased the Chechovshchina estate, the family of Bunimovitz who leased the Adampol estate, and the family of Michael Weisbrod who leased the estate in Michalow.

At the time of Tsar Nikolay II, Jews were not allowed to live in villages and the leases were registered to Christian men. Each of the lessees had a nice house in Volozhin but they spent most of their time on the estates. They bribed the local official and he ignored the infraction.

They produced wheat, vegetables, milk and milk products for the residents of Volozhin.

Floating timber on the Berzina River
First person on the right: Chatzkel Glick)

[Page 339]

My family lived in Sakovshchina until 1914. When the war broke out, we move to Minsk and I was subsequently drafted into the army. After I was discharged, we moved to Volozhin and then to Sakovshchina. Before the war, the Bunimovitz family operated the flourmill they leased from Count Tishkivitz. Now however, the mill was burnt out and no longer functioning.

The flour mill of Yuzefpol [Estate] (1929)

Mr. Baruch Kuchevitzky lived in Sakovshchina and was an expert in operating flourmills. Together, we bought a plot of land in the Yuzefpol[Estate] and built a new flour mill. The flour was sold in Volozhin as well as among all the neighboring villages. The Jewish population preferred it for making matzahs for Passover. We built a sawmill, and as the business grew, we built a second one. The flourmill burnt down in 1929 and, within six months, we built an even bigger one. The sawmill produced wooden roof tiles, some of which we donated for the roof of the new synagogue in Zabrezhe.

My time in Yuzefpol[Estate] was very happy. When the Soviets invaded in 1940, I fled to Volozhin. This was the end of a beautiful period in my life.

[Page 340]

Flour and Torah in Volozhin

by Chaim Zvi Potashnik, Holon

Translated by Meir Razy

Donated by Anita Frishman Gabbay

Volozhin was not a particularly commercial town with a thriving economy. Living was not easy and there were no big factories or mines in the vicinity. Most of the Jews earned their living as "go-betweens". Some were storeowners, some peddlers and there were a few artisans as well. The largest segment of the economy stemmed from renting rooms to students from the Yeshiva, to travelling fund-raisers and to the messengers and representatives from Jewish Communities all over the Russian Pale of Settlement. This was the Volozhin's version of the "Tourist Industry".

The retailers bought wheat and flax from the local farmers and sold the products to the wholesalers – Yaakov Weisbrod, Moshke Weisbrod, Getzel Persky, and Berl Yoshkas.

Timber trading was an important part of the town's economy and many Jews worked as clerks in Mr. Heller's business. After the end of WW-I, the town came under Polish rule. The government moved many services from Galicia and Central Poland to Volozhin. There then began a housing boom to accommodate the needs of these government employees.

The government stationed a battalion of Border Guards in town and the army, too, helped drive its economic development. It needed a new military base and food supplies. Shneur Kivilevitz won the tender for supplying bread and built a new, modern bakery.

New co-operatives imported goods. Arie and Mussia Tofef imported beer from Vilna and from Lida. The preferred brands were Pupko, Zhivitzer and Filco. Velvele Persky and Shevach Rogovin were tanners and developed a business processing leather. Fruit and vegetables were sold both in and around the town.

Several families leased orchards and sold fruit. Many Jews found employment in the flour mills, sawmills and the power generator station of Michael Vand-Polack. Members of the Zionist training camps worked in these plants as well.

Work and material matters, however, were not the center of life in Volozhin. They provided the support needed for its spiritual life – learning the Torah. As soon as work was over, people hurried to their studies. In the morning, you could hear morning prayers coming out of the many synagogues and in the evening people gathered in groups to study the Talmud, "Ein Yaakov" or the weekly Torah portion. The sound of holiness filled the town.

In the years preceding the Second World War, Polish anti-Jewish sentiment grew. They organized themselves into co-operatives and distributed pamphlets to the peasants. They encouraged Polish peasants to boycott the Jews and sell their produce only to Polish merchants.

[Page 341]

All this negative anti-Semitic activity severely affected the economic condition of the Jewish community.

Young people were idle. They did not study nor could they find work. They were supported by their parents who did their best but could not change the circumstances. Those "idle" people were called "Engineers" – in reference to surveyors who walked and measured distances on the streets.

They invested their time and energy in Zionist activities. They helped to educate the older generation, they collected donations for national organizations, they sold "Shekels" for the Zionist Congress and were busy in discussions and arguments among themselves. All of this was done at night but during the day they were idle.

Free Embroidery Training Course by the Singer Company

Top Row (near the wall) right to left: a) a Christian woman b) Gittel Rogovin c) a Christian woman d) Zipora Kramnik e) The Company representation a Christian man
Second row: a) Fruma Kivilevich b) Levit c) Taybel Kivilevich d) Bella Kramnik e) a Christian woman
Third Row: a) a Christian woman b) a Christian woman
Fourth Row: Chaya Liba Shepsenvol

[Page 342]

A chance for improvement for young women was the opening of a Singer Sewing Machine Sales Office in town. The office, as a publicity stunt, ran a free Embroidery Training Course. Many women registered and acquired new skills that were not, however, very useful.

The Jews realized that there would be little or no economic improvement in Europe. Many immigrated across the oceans. Others decided to immigrate to Eretz-Israel and joined Zionist training camps.

No one saw the dark forces that would soon destroy their world.

[Page 342]

Market Days in Volozhin

by Israel Levinson, Ramat Gan

Translated by Meir Razy

Thursdays were market days in Volozhin. In the early morning hours, peasants from the nearby villages would arrive in their horse-drawn wagons full of milk products, fresh eggs, fruit, pig bristles, flax, different types of grain and more.

The peasants, after they sold their produce, would then buy herring, salt, sugar, oil, kerosene, cloth and shoes, kitchen utensils and other necessities at the Jewish-owned stores. They also spent generously in pubs and inns. Thursdays were good days for business.

Many people attended market days, especially towards the end of the summer. The nature of the trade changed as autumn approached. The villagers ordered winter clothing, boots and other necessities. The Jewish merchants went to Vilna or Warsaw and bought boots and cloth. The local artisans, the shoemakers, the tailors and even the carpenters filled orders for coats, boots and new furniture.

The market played an important role in the economy of Volozhin.

[Page 343]

Volozhin During and After the First World War

By Reuven Rogovin (Petach Tikva)

Translated by Jerrold Landau

based on an earlier translation by M. Porat z"l, and edited by Judy Montel

The "strategy specialists" debate the war in the kloiz

When the nationalist Serbs in Sarajevo shot and fatally wounded the Austro-Hungarian crown prince and his wife on July 28, 1914 – shots that shook up the foundations of the world and caused the First World War – Feive the tailor, Baruch Leib the tailor, Oizer the Raznostik (mailman), Naftali the bookbinder, Meir Pesha Yente's, and others sat in the *kleizl* (small *kloiz*) and debated the principles of strategy and warfare in stoic calm.

They reached the conclusion that the war would not reach us in Volozhin, and therefore, we should not be afraid or worry. Russia is vast. If it wishes, it can fight with the Germans in Siberia, and if it wishes, it can fight with the Austraks (Austrians) in the Caucasus. If it desires to torment its enemies, it could fight them in the large steppes and wildernesses of Ukraine, or it can fight in Manchuria, where Lipa the butcher was serving. "Everything depends on the decisions of the upper command" determined Oizer the, the great "Strategist."

Nahumke Telzer, a Yeshiva lad, who was reading a book the entire time, suddenly raised his head and said: "My masters, with your permission, I will tell you a true story." The audience became attentive, and Reb Nahumke began, saying: "A Jew, a poor lessee had six ugly daughters. Due to their ugliness, it was impossible to marry them off. A matchmaker arrived one day at the lessee's home, bearing the news that he has an excellent match for the eldest and ugliest daughter, but he could not reveal the groom's name fearing the lessee's anger. The Jew swore on his beard and *peyos*[sidelocks] that nothing bad would happen to him. The matchmaker became courageous and revealed the secret: the suggested bridegroom would be the only son of Count Tyskiewicz, who live near Volozhin, and owns large, vast estates.

"The lessee became very angry upon hearing to whom his daughter was suggested. He shouted, 'It could never be! I would never give my daughter over to apostasy!' The matchmaker went on his way, but the match began to irritate the lessee's mind like Titus' mosquito[1], giving him no rest. His wife too was giving him no rest. She told him, 'Had you agreed to the match, we would have ascended to greatness. Is having the Count as an in-law a small matter! We would marry off all our daughters in honor and wealth, and enjoy life in this world.'

"The lessee consulted with his friends and acquaintances. The unanimously advised him to hurry to the matchmaker and agree to the match. He called the matchmaker and told him, "After much inner conflict and unbearable deliberations, I have decided to give my daughter to be the wife of the count's only son.

"'Fine,' answered the matchmaker, 'but you must wait a bit, because your agreement alone is not enough. 'I must now receive the agreement of the Count and his only son.'"

[Page 344]

"The moral of this story is," continued Reb Nahumke, "you claim that, as per her desire, Russia would be able to lead the fights in Siberia, the Caucasus, Manchuria, and Harbin – but have you received the assent of Germany and Austria for this? Are you certain that they would agree to conduct the battles specifically in those places?"

The Torah Didactics of the Yeshiva Lads

(This subsection translated by Meir Razy)

While the guns thundered in the distance and many soldiers died, life in Volozhin continued uninterrupted. The Head of the Yeshiva was Rabbi Raphael Shapiro. Rabbi Kotick was the head of another school, and Naphtali Hertz Askind was the third rabbi in the town. Sounds of liturgical singing emanated from all the schools and the yeshivas. Many of the students were occupied in hair-splitting arguments about religious questions.

Reuven Ladzcher was the apprentice of Avreima'le the Slaughterer. He quoted the Talmud passage "All may slaughter, and their slaughtering is valid, except a deaf person, an imbecile or a minor, lest they invalidate their slaughtering; and if any of these slaughtered while others were standing over them." (Talmud - Chullin Chapter I, page 2A). he asked: if "All may slaughter" why should he pay for his training? And if only trained men are allowed to slaughter – why is this entry in the Talmud?

Kalman'ke "Der Zaslar", a well-dressed young man with dreamy eyes asked about the Talmud's topic of "an egg that was laid during a holiday".

Leibe'le Brisker was very intelligent and considered a philosopher. He wondered about the Bible but not the Talmud. The Bible tells the story of the Prophet Elisha who was walking back to the town of Beit El after his teacher, the Prophet Elijah, went up to the heavens. Small boys "mocked him, and said unto him, Go up, thou bald head; go up, thou bald head. And he turned back, and looked on them, and cursed them in the name of the LORD. And there came forth two she bears out of the wood, and tore forty and two children of them."

(Kings 2, Ch 2, 23-24). The prophet then continued on his way as if nothing had happened. Leibe'le Brisker asked: How could this be accepted? It is possible the Prophet was bald but how could he use G-d's name to cause the death of forty-two boys?

Continuing on, Leibe'le Brisker said "this might just be a story." He remembered another story: a Chassid and a Misnaged (an orthodox Jew opposing Chassidism). The Chassid praised his Rabbi whose Shabbat fish weighed more than a PUD (a Russian unit, 16Kg) and the person who delivered the fish to the Rabbi was the Prophet Elijah himself, dressed as a fisherman.

Then the Chassid asked the Misnaged what was so special about his Rabbi. The Misnaged answered, "My Rabbi is very skilled at playing cards. When you have two aces, he will show you three of them. When you have three, he will show you four, and when you have four he will show you five." "Wait a minute! There are only four aces in a deck."

[Page 345]

"When you reduce the size of the fish, then I will reduce the number of aces. This was just a 'story' and the story about the bears killing the boys was just a story too".

This was the nature of the discussions and arguments among the Yeshiva students during those long days of war with little food and no sleep.

Translator's Footnote:

1. For the Talmudic story of Titus and the mosquito or gnat, see https://www.chabad.org/library/article_cdo/aid/953573/jewish/Tituss-Death.htm

The Economic Situation in Volozhin Before the First World War

By Reuven Rogovin[1]

Translated by Jerrold Landau

based on an earlier translation by M. Porat z"l, and edited by Judy Montel

There were three synagogues in the city at that time: in the marketplace, in Aroptzu, and the small *kloiz* on Vilna Street. Itshke the Shamash served as the primary *shamash* in the synagogue in the marketplace. His deputy and the Torah reader was Leibe the Shamash (his daughter lives in Israel). Kopel Deretshnski served as the *shamash* and Torah reader in the synagogue in Aroptzu. Moshe Lavit (his grandson is in Israel) served as the *shamash* on the synagogue on Vilna Street, and Moshe Shlomo the Melamed [teacher] (his son is in Israel) served as the Torah reader. Rabbi Rafael Shapira, the *shochet* Yehuda Avrahamel Perski, and all the Yeshiva students worshipped in the Yeshiva. The Korovka [tax] for *shechita* [ritual slaughter], yeast and candles was in the hands of my uncle Leibe Eshkes (his daughter, Gitel Eshkes is in the United States). The *shochet* [ritual slaughterer] was Yehuda Avrahamel Perski. Velvel Bloch served as the cantor and *shochet*.

The butchers of the city were Yehuda Chaim, Chaim Yitzhak Zusia (his son Joel lived in the United States), and Areh the Koltun. Bread was provided by: Zlotke the baker (her son is in the United States), Elka the baker, Sorke the baker, Feytshe the baker (her daughter is in Israel), Fruma Leizer the baker, and Hershel the baker (his son is in Israel[2]).

Milk was provided by: Reuven the lessee[3] (his son is in Israel), Golda the lessee, and the lessee from Kopuschina. Yehuda Mordechai and Gershon Rogovin (both have sons in the United States) were involved in the fish business. I will especially discuss my uncle Yehuda Mordechai, for he was a very interesting person. He was short, and his voice was hoarse. He was already about sixty years old at the time, but nevertheless carried the heavy crates of fish on his shoulders.

We both worshipped in the *Kleizl*. He abstained from smoking in the synagogue, and did not even smoke in the anteroom, for it is forbidden to smoke in a holy place. He would smoke fine cigars from Havana. I surmise that half his income from the fish business went up in "smoke." He would be our guest on every holiday, and we honored him greatly.

Reb Yehuda Mordechai visited the United States several times. When he longed for Volozhin while he was in the United States, or for the United States while he was in Volozhin – he would take his suitcase and travel to Volozhin, and then after a short time, take the same suitcase and return to the United States

Volozhin and America were in his eyes like a room and its anteroom. He used to consider a two-way journey from New York to Volozhin as a journey on Avraham Leib Shmuel's horse and wagon from Volozhin to Minsk and back,

[Page 346]

or as Chaim the Galanterinchik's trip by foot from Volozhin to Rakow, a distance of 40 kilometers.

He prepared his burial shrouds while still alive. Leah Yoel Areh's took his measurements. He paid her generously. He purchased a burial plot, and paid good money to the Chevra Kadisha. He told me, "I want to arrange this during my lifetime, so that no dispute will arise after my death."

The following *melamedim* [*cheder* teachers] served in those days: Kalev the Melamed, Moshe Shlomo, Moshe Feive, Simcha and Nachum (the *melamed* from Grieva), and Eliyahu Yitzchak (who later served as the religion teacher in the Polish gymnasja). Avraham Goralik (who went with his entire family to the United States), Pesach Jeruzalimski, and Kaminstein of Mizeiki served as Hebrew teacher of the new style.

The following worked in the carpentry trade: Michael Garbiel and his son Hershel (the mute), Yudel Eli, Zalmanke, Moshel Shimon's, and Zalman Sheiva's. The shoemaker were: Leizer Itshe, Yitzchak Getzel, Alter Dvoshke's, Hershel the Large (Groiser), Avraham Yitzchak, Eliyahu Chaim, Izik Elke's, and Hershel Elke's (his son is in Israel). The blacksmiths were: the brothers Reuven, Avraham, and Zalman Wolf, Saneh the Zielaner (his son is in Israel), Moshe Yona, and Avrahamel (his daughters are in Israel). The tinsmiths were Ben Zion and his sons. Leibe Kaganovitch was the sole glazier. The builders were: the brothers Feive, Yehoshua and Matisyahu, and the Christian "Fulzhidkes)[4]. Pharmacy owners were: Yitzchak Shrira and Avraham Berkovitch (the daughter has a son and two daughters and the second one, a daughter[5] in Israel)[6].

Sheike the Potshter served as the postman. Aharon Tzart, who was also a medic, served as the mohel. The city physician was Polski the Pole. There was no electricity yet in Volozhin. The owner of the only steam driven mill was Michael Wand-Polak. (died in Israel at an old age). Wine could be bought in two stores; one owned by Moshe Perlman (his grandson lives in Isael, and the second from Yochanan Rodke's (the Rebbetzin Unterman of blessed memory[7]). There was no dentist in Volozhin. Dentists from Minsk would visit the city on occasion.

Merchants of manufactured goods who provided textiles to both the residents of the city and the residents of the villages were: Avraham Shaker, Bashke Mendel's and Rela Levin. Avraham Leib Kukse's and Avrahamke Ozer's owned the matzo factory. Itzia Tane and his son Areh, called Areh the Zavaznik, provided water to the Jews of the city.

Kushe the Amerikanietz, or Kusha Rode's managed the Talmud Torah. The only inn in the town was owned by Velvel Zelig Przchulska.[8] Yankel Yosel Skliot sold beer. Soda (seltzer water) was manufactured by Yaakof Shpetnicki (his son is in Israel). Eliahu Moshe Golda's sold grain. There were two liquor stores (Monopol) in the city: one in the marketplace and the other in Aroptzu that belonged to the Gendarme (government official) Buksztanowicz. Every year, a ruckus broke out next to those stores, when the "Prizivniki" (army conscripts)

[Page 347]

from Baksht, Nalibok, and Derevna would go to Oshmyana to present themselves before the conscription committee. When they arrived in Volozhin, there shops closed immediately by order of the command. The draftees wanted to break into them, but the Pristov (police chief) and officers guarded them with drawn swords.

In Volozhin, there're were two Pravoslavic churches and a Catholic church at that time. The relations between the Jews and the Pravoslavic and Catholic priests were good.

dThe castle (Palac) was in the center of the city, where Count Tyskiewicz's estate was located. The Grafshiks (nobility family members) lived with their grandmother near Vilna, and would visit Volozhin in the summer. They were still "kids" and only became "goats" – that is mighty counts – after the war. The castle was surrounded by a large fruit orchard. Several families leased that orchard in partnership. They were had inherited rights to this. Zwirko the guard only permitted special people to stroll therein.[9]

The Starosta Yosef Yozel Perski served as head of the community. His son, Shimshon Perski served as the government appointed rabbi of Volozhin (his son is in Israel).[10]

The tailors to whom the trade passed by heritage were: Chaim the Shneider, Yaakov the Blinder, Hillel Moshe Yudke's, Binyomke the Ainbinder's [bookbinder's son], and Izak Minke's. Yankel the Kirzhner was the sole hatmaker. Naftali Arotzker was the bookbinder. Shimon the Bord repaired the shingled roofs. Chaim Meir Shaya's was involved in the rag trade. The former Yeshiva student, the genius Peretz, and the Nikolaev soldier Itshe (Nikolayevsker Soldat) transported passengers to the railway station. There were two railway stations, Listopad and Polotshan, both located about 22 kilometers from the city. Even though the distance from Volozhin to Minsk was 70 kilometers and the distance to Vilna was 110 kilometers, 98% of the trade was conducted through Vilna. The sole dealer traveled the Volozhin -Minsk line to important merchandise for the shopkeepers of the city was Avraham Leib Shmuel's (Rogovin, his two sons are in Israel).

Mr. Heller, the renowned forest trader, had purchased a huge forest from Count Tyskiewicz. It served as an important source of livelihood for many lumber merchants of Volozhin. Among these specialists were Menachem Yoel HaKohen Potashnik (his grandchildren are in Israel), Yisroel Kaplan, Alter Bunimovitch, Yosef Kaganovitch, Moshe Rogovin, Eliyahu Brudna, Tsvi Eliashkevitch, Meir Levin, Chaim Shulman (his son is in Israel) and Hirsh Jozefovitch (his daughter is in Israel). Tsvi-Hirsh Malkin served as manager (his son Asher Malkin now lives in Israel)[11].

Translator's Footnote:

1. The original translator, M. Porat, indicates that this section was written in 1968-1969.
2. Note from the original translator, M. Porat: His son Beniyomke Kleynbord came to Israel on the Altalena and was member of the Volozhin Committee
3. M. Porat notes that the term for lessee in Yiddish (which would have been used as these people's nicknames) is Arendator (feminine: Arendatorke).
4. According to M. Porat, this refers to half Jews. M. Porat also notes that he was a stove mason.

5.   M. Porat identifies Berkovitch's daughter as Shoshana Nishri.

6.   M. Porat added the following at this point: Alter and Meyshke were the town barbers. There was no running water in Volozhin. Water was drawn from wells by a bucket on a rope and brought home in a pair of buckets suspended on a rod – "Koromislo", from the shoulders. But it was possible to buy the water at the door from Hirshl Der Wasser Feerer , Itshe Tane's and his son Ore who was called "Ore der zavoznik". Each one of them transported a barrel of water on a horse cart and sold it to the housewives.

7.   M. Porat indicates that the Rebbetzin's name was Chaya Feiga.

8.   M. Porat added the following this point: The brothers Mikhl and Moyshe Weisbord, Yankl Rudenski brothers and Levin were flax traders.

9.   M. Porat added the following at this point: A group of Volozhin children once discovered a brand new, until then unseen, red fruit growing inside the garden. It was a new plant in Russia, the tomato. The children were attracted by its color and beauty. They chose a dark night to sneak inside the garden and to flee with some fruits. After the escape they assembled to taste the fairy fruit. They divided and tasted the trophies. And as great as their expectations were, the frustration was just as large. They foresaw the sweetness of paradise, they found acidity and sourness. The tomato became known in Volozhin as the… "Khazershe Eppele"- "the piggish apple" (*I also heard this story told by my father, he was one of the children –translator's note*).

10.   M. Porat added the following at this point: Volozhin was situated at the intersection of the Vilna-Minsk road with the road to Novogrudek. The shtetl received an abundant number of visits from beggars and emissaries, so the Starosta's hands were full with work.

11.   M. Porat added the following note: Tsvi-Hirsh Malkin, the translator's Grandfather with his wife Haya-Riva were murdered by the Fascists in Volozhin on May 10, 1942. Osher Malkin, the Translator's uncle (his mother's brother) made aliya to Israel in 1952. He served 15 years as manager of Mikveh Israel, the famous agriculture school near Tel Aviv. Osher Malkin passed away during the fall 1973 Yom Kippur war in Holon, Israel.

The following sections were translated by Meir Razy

The War did not follow our "Masters of Strategy"

The war did not follow the plan that our "Masters of Strategy of the little synagogue" hashed out. Instead of fighting in Siberia and Ukraine, it took place in France, Belgium and East Prussia.

[Page 348]

The Russians, after three months of bloody battles in the Carpathian Mountains, retreated from Galicia and Poland and the front stabilized near Volozhin.

Groups of Russian officers arrived in Volozhin, surveyed the town and left without revealing their intentions. People were confused. Many Yeshiva students left town. Ivanov, the Governor, who had lived in the city of Ashmyany, moved his office to Volozhin.

A Russian General established his headquarters in the palace of Count Tishkivitz. The army placed three mortars on the roof of the palace. Armed soldiers guarded the gates around the clock while soldiers filled the streets. Officers confiscated the nicer homes for their quarters, and the synagogues became barracks for the soldiers. The town looked like a city under siege.

In 1916, Rabbi Raphael Shapiro moved to Minsk. The whole town came to see him off. Rabbi Naphtali Hertz Askind was then nominated as the new leader of the community.

New economic opportunities, such as supplying food to the soldiers, developed. The soldiers bought herring, bread, and any many other baked products. The demand was greater than the supply and the merchants profited. They placed barrels of herring and piles of fresh bread in front of their store and saw everything disappear very quickly. Every family baked bread, challah or bagels with the flour they had bought in Minsk.

Although the front was not far, only about 20 kilometers away, the town was quiet. The nights were silent; everyone, except for the guards, was asleep.

Tragic news started to come out. Alter the Barber was killed in a battle. Alter-Eli the paver returned from hospital with his leg amputated. Binyamin Rogovin returned, but with four fingers missing from his right hand. Then we heard that Yochanan Leibush was killed.

Some people were able to buy their way out of military service but most did not have the required sum of money. They literally went "underground". Chaim Kinkin, the son of Simcha the Melamed, dug a small room under his bedroom and stayed inside it for twenty hours each day. He came out at night for just a few hours. By the end of the war, his beard was very long, and after he shaved, his skin was as yellow as a leaf in fall.

[Page 349]

My mother, Batya, hid a Yeshiva student from Pinsk for five months before we smuggled him to Minsk. He lived in Minsk until the end of the war. He was murdered in 1920 by the hoodlums of Pilsudski.

During the holidays, the synagogues were filled with Jewish soldiers. We welcomed them warmly as guests in our homes. I did not encounter a single Jewish officer. Jews were 90% of the players in military bands. A soldier from Ukraine fell in love with Matla Chatzkels of Zbazaza [maybe Zbaraz] and married her. They moved to the Ukraine. Matla had a brother – Eliezer Yachas.

The Refugees are flooding Volozhin

Several dozen Jewish families came from Vilki to Volozhin in the second half of 1915. The local residents did their best to welcome and accommodate them. Some of them found apartments and others settled temporarily in the synagogues until they too were able to rent apartments. They returned to their town at the end of the war.

Another refugee family who arrived around the same time was the Rogovins with their son Avraham who was then a Bar Mitzvah boy. They settled in the home of Shmuel-Ytche "the angel" on Vilna Street. Chatzkel's "the Africaner" lived nearby and had two daughters, Grunia and Esther. The boy and the girls crossed paths many times a day but never said a word to each other. Years passed, the war was over and Poland became independent. Avraham Rogovin immigrated to the U.S.A. in search of a better life. The sisters, Grunia and Esther also move to America. One day Avraham and Grunia met in the street. They fell in love, got married and today are living in California.

Another family was the Meltzers from Vishneva. The father was Hersh, the mother – Alta. They had a son and a daughter, Yoseph and Sara. Sara was the mother of Shimon Peres. I remember them settling in the home of Velvel Zelig's and running a tavern where they would sell beer and soda.

I did not know then that Reb Hersh was a good cantor. On Rosh HaShana of 1916, the Beadle invited him to lead the "Musaf" Prayer. A few attendees started to express their frustration about calling on an unknown Cantor. The Beadle slammed his fist on the pulpit and Reb Hersh started to sing "I am the poorest of deeds ..". We have never heard such a touching prayer. The atmosphere became very joyous and reached its peak when he sang "Unetane Tokef". I have always attended his performances since that Rosh HaShana prayer.

[Page 350]

A terrible thing happened in Volozhin

I remember a tragic event from wartime. It happened on Tisha Be'Av of 1916. Many men were in the small synagogue waiting for Rabbi Naphtali Hertz Askind to join them for the Morning Prayer, but, unusual for him, he did not appear. One man asked what had happened to the Rabbi. Another answered, "You know the Rabbi is old and frail." After a few hours, someone said, "I am afraid the Rabbi is sick. I cannot remember a day he did not come to pray, no matter what was happening. Let us pray, then we shall read "The Book of Lamentations" and later we will go and call to check up on the Rabbi."

As soon as they started praying, the Rabbi, completely well, entered the synagogue. However, once he started praying people realized that he was also crying. At the end of the prayer, they asked him what had happened.

"I will tell you. Last night at midnight I was reading the book "Choshen Mishpat" (a fourteenth-century book explaining legal aspects of property) when someone knocked on my door. I opened it to see a young Russian officer. He apologized for coming at such a late hour and asked if I was the Rabbi of Volozhin. I told to him that I was temporarily filling in for Rabbi Raphael Shapiro. "I was ordered to bring you to General Lomakin. A horse and carriage are waiting for you outside." "What is it about?" I asked. "I do not know. I was just ordered to bring you.""

The journey took more than an hour and when we arrived, the officer led me into the General's office. He told me that I had been brought there for a humane reason. Yesterday, a Jewish soldier was sentenced to death for treason. The verdict would be carried out in three hours. We asked the condemned for his last wish and he asked to see and speak with a Rabbi. Please fulfill your duty.

An officer took me to the dark basement. He gave the password and an armed guard led me into the cell where they were keeping the condemned man.

[Page 351]

It was a small room with exposed concrete walls and a blocked window. A young man of about 25 years old with thick black hair was sitting on a mattress which was on the floor.

He gave the impression of being a Russian university student. He got up, greeted me and thanked me for coming so late at night. He said, "I want to die as a proud Jew. I wish to tell you everything. My name is X, my parents are X from town X. One of my brothers went to Eretz-Israel in the 1890s and still lives there. My sister is a well-known children's medical doctor in Petersburgh. My younger brother is a student and my mother a renowned singer. My father is a famous lawyer who dedicates a lot of his time to community affairs. He attended one of the Jewish Congresses with Herzel. I grew up in a Jewish home and was a student at the University. I volunteered to serve in the Army six months after the onset of the war. I behaved as a proud Jew in my military service and many people, especially Citnick, the Battalion Commander, did not like it. He ordered his staff to monitor me. They invented infractions I did not commit and when investigated, were proven false. Two days ago they summoned me to Headquarters where I saw several high-ranking officers present, including Battalion Commander Citnick.

They told me they were going to search my suitcase. When they opened it, I was shocked to see a wire-cutting tool and a pair of leather gloves. Citnik said, sarcastically, "These are the tools this Jew used yesterday when he tried to cut through our fence and desert to the Germans. However, he saw one of our soldiers so he came back to wait for another opportune time."

I told the Commander I did not recognize the cutter or the gloves. Someone had put them in my suitcase in order to incriminate me.

It did not help. They court-marshaled me yesterday. The cutter and the gloves were the evidence. The prosecutor asked for the death penalty and I got it.

The Rabbi continued: The verdict was sent to the Empress for approval (Alexandra Feodorovna was Empress of Russia. She was the spouse of Nicholas II—the last ruler of the Russian Empire). She read the document of the verdict and ordered him released. It was clear to her that this was a false plot, but it was too late. They had executed him by the time her order reached the army base.

The "February Revolution" started on February 27, 1917. This was the end of the three hundred year-long Romanov Dynasty. On April 6, 1917, Kerenski, the Minister of War, ordered the Russian Army to attack the Germans near Maladzyechna [Molodechno]-Vilna. We could see the bombing of Lask from the "Bialik Mountain". The attack failed, and the Bolshevik Revolution had that started on November 7 finally reached Volozhin.

Under the Bolshevik Rule

The first action of the Bolsheviks in Volozhin was to depose the leaders of the community and the town and to nominate "new leaders" from among the "working class".

[Page 352]

Some of the appointees were Neta the saddle maker, Fitel the shoemaker, Chaikel "the lip", Avram'ke the shoemaker, Alter-Leizer "of Itche", Hillel "the tailor" and alike. These men welcomed the Bolsheviks.

Volozhin was only a stop on the route of the Red Army moving westward. Two soldiers were left in town. They were members of the Communist Party and not "real" soldiers and their assignment was to establish Soviet rule in Volozhin. Their names were Mishzerski and Zotov and they used to walk around town wearing long military coats, carrying pistols. They nominated a Christian man named Balashko as the Superintendent of Police and he then hired several police officers. Most were Christian but he also hired Jews. The Jewish police officers were Benim'ke Itzkes (Benyamin son of Yitzhak Rogovin), a war veteran who had lost three fingers on his left-hand and Alter'ks Avraham Yashkas.

Mishzerski created the "Revkom" (A revolutionary committee) and nominated himself as Chairman with Zotov as Deputy. Zorkovich was nominated as Secretary and Marisha Radanovich was the clerk. Lawyer Sidorsky became the head of the Culture Department and Fidotov (who had been born in Siberia, moved to Volozhin and eventually was killed in 1941 by the Germans) was in charge of military relations.

The Head of the Social Services Department was Krastianov, a lawyer who served as a judge during the time of the Holocaust. He was sent to Siberia by the Soviets and died there.

Mishzerski nominated Neta Zimmerman, who could not even sign his name in Russian, to manage the City Council. Jewish members of the City Council were Feitel Rubinstein, Chaikel "the lip", Avram'ke the shoemaker, Hillel "the tailor" and Moshke "the glazier".

The new Soviet regime had no impact on the local economy or its religious life. People traded as before, brought merchandise from Minsk and prayed in synagogues as before.

Cultural activities flourished in the Byelorussian language. A retired actor named Chabayoff lived in a nearby village. He had organized a troop of amateur actors and they performed, free of charge, every two weeks. People stayed after the plays and danced until the early hours of the morning. All of the Volozhin young people attended these performances.

Visiting propagandists promoted the Soviet ideology daily until a war broke out between Poland and the USSR. The Red Army retreated and, following the Riga Accord of March 18, 1921, the whole region of Volozhin then became part of Poland.

[Page 353]

Self Defense

The Russian Army lost its discipline after the February 1917 Revolution. Soldiers did not obey their commanders' orders, the military police lacked authority and occasionally soldiers entered stores and "forgot" to pay for their purchases. Subsequently, towns set up their own local police forces to protect themselves.

Military units organized local town councils. Propagandists from Petersburg, Moscow and Minsk arrived and promoted the idea of making peace with Germany. The atmosphere in and around Volozhin was that of lawlessness.

One night, a small group of soldiers entered the town, robbed dozens of Jewish stores and killed one man, Nishka Glick. The situation forced the community to organize a self-defense group that would protect their life and property. The organizers were Avraham Berkovich, Michael Vand-Polack, Arka "der Feldshar" the Medic, Chaim Velvele Persky, Yehoshua Shmerkavich (a soldier from Dzhankoy in Crimea), Zvi Ziversko and many others. They all obtained rifles legally.

The town was divided into three defense sectors: the Market, Arapecho and Vilna Street. The command post for Arapecho was set at Michael Polack's home; the one for the Market was at the house of Chelem the shoemaker and in Moshe Perlman's stone house. The Vilna Street unit met at Velevle Zeligs'. Their leaders were Hershel "valick-macher" the wool merchant and his son Yoseph.

A General Headquarters, consisting of Avraham Berkowitz and Michael Vand-Polack, was set up at the Berkowitz house. They nominated a commander for each sector and issued instructions. They recruited all the able-bodied young men and assigned them to different sectors. The men were stationed in their command posts and they patrolled in three-hour shifts at night.

Thirty Jewish men, some of them parents of small children, carried weapons, protected property and defended the honor of the Jews of Volozhin.

This self-defense activity was effective and successfully deterred would-be thieves and murderers from carrying out more crimes. The streets of Volozhin were under control and the fear of the population subsided.

[Page 354]

Volozhin Jewish Defense Brigade

[Page 355]

The Fire Fighting Brigade

In the early years of independent Poland, towns in the regions of Vilna and Navogrudok competed with each other to establish Fire Fighting Brigades and marching bands. Both the fire fighters and the band players were Jews. Volozhin was enthusiastic about having a fire-fighting brigade for a good reason: the great fire of 1918 destroyed the fire station and all its equipment. In addition, the service lost many of its men. Some of them were killed in the war, others move to other towns, and only two fire fighters remained in Volozhin: Anton Mandrick, an over sixty years old Christian, and Simon Lapes, a little younger.

Four men started the project. Avraham Berkowitz was responsible for managing the project and recruiting the firefighters. Getzel Itche Beres (his name later was Getzel Perski) was in charge of organizing the band (he was a band member during his military service), Mota'le Yudels was in charge of procurement (pumps, ladders, axes, etc.) and Chaim Velvel Perski was looking for the land where the new station would be built. They reported their progress every Saturday at a meeting in the home of Chaim Velvel Perski.

The new building of the Fire Station stood across from Ara Polack and was ready in two years. They bought all the necessary equipment and the Brass Band was ready too. All the firefighters and the players were Jews except for Roman Horvachebski and Semion Zhorkovitz. Avraham Berkowitz was elected as the Fire Chief. He was the first Jewish Chief in independent Poland. The firefighters received uniform, a coat and a helmet.

Like the rest of Poland, Volozhin celebrated the Third of May (Poland Independence Day) and November 11(the Miracle on the Wisla[Vistula] - the 1920 victory over the Soviet Army). The town erected a large sitting platform for these holidays. The churches and the synagogues carried out special prayers for the state, followed by public celebrations. All the Christian town leaders (never a Jew) and government representatives, the town's elder (Starosta) and the Priest sat on the platform. The Band assembled near the platform.

[Page 356]

The Firefighting Brigade

[Page 357]

The parade started with the Band playing a March. The Police marched first. Police delegations from many surrounding towns participated in the March to give the impression of power. The Band followed the police and schoolchildren marched last.

The Fire Brigade operated for many years. Sundays were dedicated for training. More people got involved and the government provided a budget. The year 1925 marked the 50th year of the Brigade and a celebration was carefully planned. All the Fire Brigades from the nearby towns and cities were invited to join the parade that was set for a Sunday.

Guests started arriving already on the Friday before the parade. A forty men delegation that included a marching band came from Lida. Their leader was Moshe Dvoretzki, the principle of Lida's High School. A 35 strong team and a band came from Iwye with their leader Mr. Bakshet.

The list of the distinguished guests on the platform included the town Elder, members of City

The Community Leadership Committee (VAAD)

An emissary from the Ministry of the Interior visited Volozhin at the end of 1921. He called for a meeting with the leaders of the Jewish Community. In that meeting, which took place at the home of Chaim Aizers (Tzirolnik), he instructed the leaders to elect a democratic Leadership Committee. The leaders nominated Shlomo Chaim Brodno to manage the election process.

[Page 358]

Shlomo Chaim Brodno proposed a nine–man body, three delegates each from the three Jewish neighborhoods; the Arapecho, the market and Vilna Street.

Hershel "the Great" proposed Yoseph Simarnitzki, Yehuda Avraham Dubinski and Yaakov Tzadok Kantorovich as representatives of the Arapecho. They were voted in without any opposition.

Similarly, the members chosen from the market region were Chaim Meir Shayas, Meir Pesha Yentes and Naftali "the Bookbinder". The Vilna Street neighborhood elected Menachem Yoel Hacohen Potashnik, Chaim Rogovin and Israel Lonin. None of the nine members of the Committee had any experience in leading a community. However, they were all honest men.

Shlomo Chaim Brodno was elected as the Chairman. He appointed Moshe Weisbrod as his assistant. Their office was in a small room near the entrance of the synagogue on Vilna Street. The room had an iron door but no heating, so it was cold during winters.

The Committee worked without financial support or staff. Through the dedication of its members, it supported the poor, impoverished students, the library and other good causes.

Over time, Volozhin became the capital of the region and the nature of working with government agencies called for a more sophisticated community leadership. Younger and more active people were elected to the Committee and the Jewish Community continued its growth.

The new Chairman was Yaakov (Yani) Garber, a Zionist. He negotiated a large increase in the town's financial support and organized all the activities of the Committee with great efficiency.

A new election was called at the end of Garber's mandate and Reuven Rosenberg was elected Chairman. He, too, was a skillful and a very energetic man who dedicated his time to helping the poor and assisting Jews in their dealings with the government.

The next VAAD was led by Meir Chalopski, the husband of Mara Shrira. He was an officer in the Polish Army and a successful merchant in town.

A new election was called at the end of the mandate and Anie Rubin (from the town of Radashkovichy) became the new Chairman. Membership in the Committee was changed from a geographic base to economic and political affiliations. It included representatives from among artisans, merchants, Zionists and Revisionists.

[Page 359]

As a result, Committee meetings became a forum for infighting among the different groups, especially when the topic was allocating the Budget.

The Secretary–Treasurer was Chaim Krugman, who was a graduate of the Yeshiva.

The Red Army invaded on September 17, 1939. One of its first orders was to terminate the operation of the Community Leadership Committee. This was the end of eighteen years of the VAAD.

The following Committee members died naturally: Yaakov Tzadok Kantorovich, Hershel "the Great", Feive Yasha Simarnitzki, Yehuda Avraham Dubinski, Meir Pesha Yentes, Naftali "the Bookbinder", Chaim Rogovin, Shlomo Rosenberg, Mordechai Potashnik and Mosh'ke "the African".

The following Committee members were murdered in the Holocaust: Chaim Tzirolnik, Shlomo Chaim Brodno, Kopel Drachinski, Chaim Meir Klein, Israel Lonin, Yaakov Garber, Reuven Rosenberg, Mendel Alperovitch, Meir Chalopski, Moshe Wainer and Chaim Krugman.

The Founding of the Jewish bank

Until 1915, the only financial "Institution" in Volozhin was "Gmilut Chasadim", the traditional Jewish charity. The charity gave people small loans that they had to repay in tiny weekly installments every Saturday, after the end of the Shabbat. This modest organization operated from the home of Berka "Der Rimer". It was managed by Binyamin "the Store Owner", who was also known as "the Yellow Binyamin". Binyamin married Shprinza, the daughter of Rabbi Yoseph Yozel Perski who carried the title of the Elder of the Town (Starosta). Following Shprinza's death, Binyamin moved to the town of Dzwoneczek[Devenishkis].

Not a single financial institution operated in Volozhin during the First World War or during the Russian Revolution or during the Polish–Russian war. However, following the Riga Peace Treaty between Russia and Poland, aid started to arrive from American Jewish Organizations: ORT built schools in many towns, HIAS assisted in immigration affairs and YEKOPA opened Bank branches.

The YEKOPA's operated from Vilna. They called for a conference where they presented their plans for assisting the Jews of Poland. Shlomo Chaim Brodno was the delegate from Volozhin. After the conference, he reported to the community that a local Jewish Bank was being planned. The assembly elected him to become the Manager of the local branch.

[Page 360]

Each neighborhood selected their own delegates to the Management of the Bank: the delegates from the Arapecho were Feive "the horse trader", Natta "the saddle maker" (they were also the delegates to the Burial Society), Moshe–Yona "the blacksmith" and Israel "the pipe smoker". Meir "Pesha–Yentes" was the delegate from Braverna Street. The delegates from Vilna Street were the treasurers of the synagogue,

Chaim "the butcher" and Menachem–Yoel Potashnik. None of the Board Members possessed any knowledge of finance.

Shlomo Chaim Brodno, the Manager, rented a room in the home of Elka "Berka Dam Rimers". It was, in fact, only half a room as a large baking oven filled the other half.

Shortly after, Shlomo Chaim Brodno invited me to help him manage the Bank. Each borrower received a little booklet that listed the details of his miniscule loan and his payments.

Akiva Potashnik had studied accounting in Vilna. He could not find a position as an accountant and we invited him to "volunteer" at the Bank. Shlomo Chaim Brodno did not like the situation where I was salaried (although it was only a symbolic salary) while Akiva had been asked to volunteer. He proposed that Management increase my salary and pay Akiva too. Both Akiva and I were present at the Board Meeting but were asked to leave for that discussion. At the end of the discussion, we were called in only to hear that the proposal had been rejected because the Bank did not have enough profits.

This situation continued until I was offered a position at the company of Michael Vand-Polack and, subsequently, Akiva started to be paid.

Over time, the Jewish Bank became one of the most important financial institutions in town. It relocated to the home of Rykla Shepsenvol on Berko Yoselevich Street. Akiva became the General Manager and Sonia Zelzer was his assistant. Another employee was Dov–Ber Levit. The new Management included Israel Lonin, Avraham Zart, Shlomo Chaim Brodno, Yaakov Garber, Volf Perski and Chaim Tzirolnik. The "old guard" of undertakers and synagogue treasurers was no longer involved. I was nominated as the Chairman of a new Audit Committee. Many community leaders including Yaakov Zimernitzki, Michael Vand-Polack, Mendel Alperovitch, Shmuel Bunimovich and Shalom–Leib Rubinstein raised donations for the Bank, which continued to grow. People could receive loans of up to 1,500 Zloty.

[Page 361]

The Bank continued to flourish until September 17, 1939, when the Red Army entered the town. I do not know if the Soviets found any money in the safe. At that time I was detained in a political prison in Kartoz–Bereza.

A Nekrasov story in Volozhin

In 1861, Nikolay Nekrasov, the great Russian poet, published a poem called "A Merchant". The poem tells the story of an innocent man who spent twelve years in jail because of a small administrative error. A similar event happened in Volozhin exactly fifty years later.

Two Jewish women lived in Volozhin at that time. One was "the short" Chaya–Eska and the other – "the long" Chaya–Eska. "The short" Chaya–Eska was about sixty years old, married to a very religious man.

She earned her living for her family by making *samogon*, the Russian term for moonshine, an illegal occupation at the time. It was a very successful business until the day she insisted that one of her regular customers, a local drunk, pay his growing debt to her. He reported her illegal business to the local Police instead of paying up. She was sentenced to two months in a jail that was located in another town. The Chief of Police sent her a written order to appear at the Police Station on a given date in order to be sent to that jail. She, however, left town and hid on the farm of one of her acquaintances in a nearby village. When the Chief realized she had not obeyed his instructions, he decided to act.

The Chief did not hate Jews. In fact, he liked Jewish *gefilte* fish and *Chulent*. The head of the Jewish community, Rabbi Yoseph Yozel Perski, made sure that a regular supply of gefilte fish and Chulent reached the Chief in addition to the regular "peace and quiet" payments.

[Page 362]

At 2 PM, on the Friday of Shabbat Nachamu (the Shabbat that follows Tisha Be'av), the Police Chief instructed a police officer to go and arrest Chaya–Eska immediately and to keep her locked up until Sunday morning when she was to be sent to jail.

The police officer went to "the long" Chaya–Eska and told her to come immediately to the Chief. She went without suspecting anything. Two hours later, when the merchants were closing their stores and people started to gather in synagogues, her father, Yaakov Yosel and her husband started worrying. They went to see the head of the Jewish community, Rabbi Yoseph Yozel. As soon as he understood the severity of the situation, he told his family to continue their Sabbat meal without him. Rabbi Yoseph, Chaya's father and her husband all hurried to the police station. There they found only the police officer who would not tell them anything and just sent them away. They returned home very much worried about the fate of the woman.

The Shabbat services in all of the synagogues of Volozhin were disrupted. People discussed the arrest of Chaya–Eska. Ozer, the assistant mail carrier, told the crowd in the Market Synagogue that last week he had delivered a registered letter to the secretary of the Police Chief. That letter bore several wax stamps and looked very official. He believed the letter came from a "high place", maybe the Security Service in Saint Petersburg. He felt the letter carried bad news for someone but he had not guessed it was "the long" Chaya–Eska.

"The short" Chaya–Eska told the women around her that Chaya–Eska was not arrested without a valid reason and that they would soon find out why. Avraham Shaker shouted, "The Christians will say bad things about us!" Neta "the saddle maker" told the crowd in the synagogue of Arapecho that this may be a disaster for the Volozhin Jews and even Graff Tishkivitz, who was known to like Jews, might now stop hiring them as workers for his fields.

[Page 363]

People spread baseless rumors. Feive "the builder" told them that while he had been repairing the oven at her father's house, he saw her talking to a stranger that did not look Jewish. Leib "the philosopher" described a suspicious box that was delivered to her house very early in the morning. He was sure it was a printing press for forging money.

The Chief of Police was just returning to town and the crowd gathered around his house. Yaakov Yosel went in and told the Chief he had come about his daughter. When the Chief heard the name of Chaya–Eska, he exploded and shouted that she would stay in jail for a long time. Her father slipped a one hundred rubles note into the Chief's hand and the Chief then relaxed somewhat.

During the conversation that followed, the Chief began to understand the mistaken identity problem and instructed his men to release "the long" Chaya–Eska immediately. The policemen then hurried to the home of "the short" Chaya–Eska and instructed her to prepare herself in order to join the next day's convoy to the jail in Ashmyany.

And indeed, the following day, on a Sunday at 11 AM, a group of nine prisoners, including "the short" Chaya–Eska was on its way to jail.

[Page 364]

Volozhin at the end of World War One

by Sara Perski (Meltzer)

Translated by Meir Razy

Donated by Anita Frishman Gabbay

The year was 1915. The German Army was advancing towards my hometown of Vishneva and bombing it. The approaching front caused many Jews to move to Volozhin, which was some 18 kilometers farther from the front. My family of nine souls walked that distance and found a temporary refuge at the home of the "starosta" – the head of the Jewish community – Yoseph Yozel Perski. We all shared one room while other refugees and Russian soldiers lived in some of the other rooms.

The town was under war conditions and a blackout was enforced. At night, the Russian Army patrolled the streets, checking that no light was visible and no one was out in the streets.

One night a German Zeppelin flew over town but did not cause any damage. Airplanes, on the other hand, bombed the town many times. People had dug shallow shelters and hid in them during bombing.

All social and cultural activities stopped. The Yeshiva was deserted and its head, the Gaon Rabbi Raphael Shapiro, was yearning for the return of the days of its glorious past. The Community fed the hungry refugees and distributed warm meals. My family opened a teahouse.

Regardless of the war situation, children's education remained a priority, Elka Svirski managed the Russian Library. A Jewish school continued to operate with its teacher, Pesach Yarozlimski. In the evening, adult classes for Hebrew had many students as–well.

I witnessed the evolution of a new world. Russian soldiers spent many idle, boring days in their trenches. One day they left the trenches and their first action was shedding Jewish blood. They entered Volozhin, rioted in the streets and killed a young man named Glick. A few days later, we received the news that a Communist Revolution had started. The walls of the houses were covered with posters saying, "Comrades, the Tsar's rule is over. Freedom to all!" People were excited by the change and were hypnotized by public speakers who talked about equality and freedom. They sang the Marseillaise (the French anthem) in the streets, and silent movies were shown in open theatres. People believed the coming of the Messiah was near.

However, reality soon hit home. A local REVCOM (the Revolutionary Committee) settled in the home of the "starosta" Yoseph Yozel Perski and started confiscating the property of landowners. Rioters and thieves attacked, without fear, under the cover of the Revolution. Jews felt unsafe and started organizing a self–defense force.

[Page 365]

Volozhin Memories

Shoshana Nishri – Berkovich

Translated by Rivka Matz (Shoshana's daughter)

Edited by Mike Kalt

At the beginning of the 1930's Volozhin became the district (*poviat*) town of the region with close to six thousand inhabitants, among them four thousand Jews.

One part of our town was located on a hill. It was called *Arooftsoo* (uphill). The other part, located on the descent, was called Aroptsoo *(downhill)*. The market square, on the town's center, was in the upper part. It was a spacious square area, which contained mostly Jewish stores and the Catholic Church. All the national ceremonies of the non- Jewish population took place there. (See map in the section "Volozhin Childhood")

The Christians celebrated their holidays in the city streets. The Polish Independence Day, May 3rd, was very impressive and I don't have enough words to express our sense of jealousy when we saw the joy and happiness on the faces of the celebrants.

Close to the Market Square, on its northern side, were located the Etz Chaim Yeshiva, the Hebrew Tarbut School, and the main Synagogue. The public Christian school, the government offices, and military barracks were located on the its southern side

The market place was filled every Thursday. with harnessed horse carts in which the farmers brought their peasant products, fruits, and hand made fabrics to sell.

The farmers were White- Russians (Orthodox), primitive in their way of life and education. Their garments were unique. The women had long wide skirts, one on top of another. Obviously the nicest was the outside one. They banded their hair with colorful kerchiefs. The men wore embroidered shirts (known in Israel as Russian shirts) and trousers tucked in high boots.

They spent the market day earnings buying holiday clothes and other necessities. They ate their meals on the carts. The main nutrition was pork fat, bread, milk, and potatoes, accompanied with strong vodka.

During market day there were many drunkards who could hardly stay on their feet. Most of them kept quarrelling and cursing. Many times these exchanges ended in fights.

White Russians lived also in the suburbs; most of them in Ponizhe on the eastern side of the town.

[Page 366]

They were influenced by the city atmosphere and were more educated. The bureaucracy was composed of local and western Poles.

Most of the houses were single floor buildings constructed from wood. The houses were surrounded by vegetable gardens. Many houses had cowsheds in the yard and the cow's milk was consumed by the owners. The vegetables were stored in caves, kept fresh by the cool temperature. There were also a few two-story houses near the market. There were some buildings with a room in the attic. In one of them dwelled the musician Mr. Ratner, with his wife. He organized a string orchestra in the Tarbut School and the firemen's wind orchestra. In the other house lived my family. The nicest buildings in town were the Government and Military buildings. They once belonged to Graf Tishkevitsh, whose estate included Volozhin.

There was no running water in town. Water was carried in buckets from wells. A pair of buckets attached on a rod, which was carried on the shoulders, and brought home. The water was kept in barrels, which stood near the entrance during summer. In winter the barrels were placed in the kitchen, to prevent freezing. There was no bathroom, no bathtub, and no shower inside the house, so people bathed in the municipal public bath house. Once my father tried something unusual--he ordered a bathtub made of tin and we filled it with hot water from the stove. This procedure was very tiresome and long. That is why a few family members bathed in the same water, first the women, later the men. Finally we decided that it wasn't worthwhile and for the time being, we continued to visit the public bath-house.

Mr. Ratner the musician
(in a firefighters uniform)

Market Square South-West corner in the nineteen thirties
Berkovitsh's (author parents) house the fourth from left

[Page 367]

The stoves were built from bricks. One stove "Aristocrat" was covered with china, and was used to heat the appartment. The second, a simpler one, was in the kitchen and was used for cooking and baking. The housewife, even though she dedicated much time to raise the family and contribute to the income, found time to bake during the end of the week. A special homemade bake was the "Bonda" kind of bread made of chopped potatoes with flour and yeast. They baked the "Bondas" in special baking boxes, and to prevent sticking, they used to spread big yellow leaves at the bottom.

Some families baked regular bread. The ingredients they baked with were eggs, flour, milk, butter and sometimes jam. We never knew chocolate or cream cakes. The jams were made by the housewife herself. In the forest fruit seasons, the female farmers came with buckets full of raspberries and black berries, which they picked in the forests.

In those times the housewives stood near the stoves in front of the "Mednitzes" (wide, flat brass bowls specially made to fry jams). Those bowls had a stand (Dreifus) ,and they stirred the fruit mixed with sugar.

We didn't know about refrigirators or ice coolers. It was necessary to cook daily. Truly our mothers' lives were tough. We, their sons and daughters, often wonder about their diligence and work ability.

Electricity was introduced only in 1925. Before it, the houses were lit by kerosene lamps, and the main streets were lit by kerosene lanterns. Hand lights were made with candles and only few had battery-operated lights.

The city had a large public park; a large part of it contained fruit trees. A small shallow creek ran through the city, it was called Volozhinka. The townspeople enjoyed dipping and swimming in it. The bushes around it were used as "changing rooms". On the side of the main street was a nice lake which was frozen in winter; its surface was used for ice skating. People skied also on the surrounding hills. Sleds were used at the crossroads of the streets that connected the upper and the lower part. It filled the Jewish youth with joyous occupation. It was a small low sled for two riders with their feet outside from both sides of the sled. The feet guided the sled like oars of a boat. A third person pushed the sled down.

The main street was called Vilna; it started from the center in the direction of Vilna,

[Page 368]

the nearest big city. The streets were covered with irregular unpolished cobblestones and walking or riding on them was difficult. The sidewalks were made from wood. The building owners themselves kept the sidewalks and the adjacent roads clean. The public places, like the market, were cleaned by workers. The shopkeepers who sat in their open stores got warm by the "fire top" - a pot full with burning coals.

Few buses and cars appeared; and then only in the thirties. Before that, the horse cart was the only means of transport. The train station was 17 km away, and people went there by horse carts. Any ride to the near cities and villages was by cart, because there was no train or bus service.

The climate was almost northern. Rain fell also in summer. Fall rains were heavy. In winter snow fell frequently. Deep snow covered the earth. People wore warm leather boots to keep their bodies warm.

Commerce was the main source of Jewish income. Most shops were owned by Jews. The trade in linen was important economically. Flax grew in the fields near Volozhin. The businessmen sent it as raw material to the big cities.

Cultural life in this time was scarce, despite the thirst for knowledge. Youth education usually ended in elementary school; only a few went to Vilna to continue their studies, because tuition and life in the city were expensive, far beyond the possibilities of many.

Very pleasant memories are bound with the Matzah baking. The baking took place in private homes, which were evacuated during the days between Purim and Passover. In one room was prepared the dough. In the big room of the apartment, girls sat on two sides of a long table and used to round the dough and cut it into Matzot. The Matzot were baked cooperatively. The work was done precisely and the Matzot were tasty. A part of the Matzot was prepared to make Matze-Mell (Flour) mostly for kneydlakh (dumplings). These Mazot were crushed with a pestle in the "Stupe", a wooden recepticle of conic shape. The ones who were lazy were threatened by not having Kneidleich.

Volozhin Jews were united in times of mourning and trouble. As I said before, the houses were built of wood. The roofs were made from wood tiles. Some roofs were of straw. When a fire broke out (a most difficult and frequent disaster) it spread quickly. Its location and extinguishing was difficult.

[Page 369]

It required quick action of many people. Our city people always acted with devotion to save human life and property.

When a person died, almost all the town inhabitants participated at the funeral. Crying and wailing, they accompanied the dead. As much as mourning was everywhere, so was also the joy. A wedding in the town was a source of joy for everyone. The wedding started generally in the big room of the bride's parents. The bride would sit in a chair, on her head a white veil, and on both her sides stood women who were relatives and friends. The groom, who waited at his parents' house, went to the bride's place accompanied by his nearest men. There they greeted him with "Mazel Tov". After that, the bride and groom walked at the head of the crowd, accompanied by musicians (Kleizmers) to the chupa ceremony. At the end of the ceremony, the couple went to the "party house". At the entrance, two women raised trays above their heads. On each tray were candles and large cakes. Inside the house, tables were set with all kinds of homemade delicacies. Food and delicacies were also distributed among the kids who gathered around the house. On Saturday, the bride went to the Synagogue. In the evening there was a dance ball; most of the young people participated in it. They danced until dawn. For seven days ("Seven Blessing") the participants continued to celebrate among the family.

The feeling of a common destiny and mutual assistance was one of the most admired qualities which our parents possessed. Their descendants desire to imprint those superb qualities among their children.

[Page 370]

I Shall Remember You, Volozhin

Pesach Berman

Translated by Meir Razy

Donated by Anita Frishman Gabbay

"I will remember and pour out my soul":Psalms 2:5

"I had tears in my eyes day and night":Psalms 2:4

The Volozhin legend

At times, I think of it as if it were all an illusion and Volozhin itself some lost mirage. It appears as a noble world where reality existed in a different dimension. Then, the pain stabs my heart, reminding me of all that was lost; the Torah sages, the Torah learners and all the simple, ordinary, everyday people.

Now, after everything has literally gone up in smoke, their lives came back to me as if in a dream. I see them and hear their plea to set down their lives in writing so that their existence once filled with so many joys and sorrow, will not just disappear. Therefore, I shall write the Volozhin story for everyone, a legend for both adults and children.

Rabbi Yaakov Shapiro and Simchat Beit Hashoeva in the Yeshiva

Whenever I think of Volozhin I remember the enlightened personality of Rabbi Yaakov Shapiro z"l, who was loved by everyone in town. He was a member of the Volozhin rabbinical dynasty that had started with Rabbi Chaim of Volozhin. Rabbi Yaakov was the son of Rabbi Raphael Shapiro who married, in succession, Sara, Resha and Dreizel, the three daughters of the NATZIV (Rabbi Naftali Zvi Yehuda Berlin).

The festival of Simchat Beir HaShoeva was a happy celebration, indelibly linked to Rabbi Yaakov in my mind. We, the students of the Yeshiva, used to go to his home, carrying lamps at night, to bring him to the Yeshiva. We carried him on our shoulders, a Chuppah–like canopy over his head, singing and dancing all the way. The entire town's Jewish population celebrated with us and the Rabbi's face shone with happiness.

My heart still pounds when I think of the celebrations that followed inside the Yeshiva. The teachers and the students were singing during the HAKAFOT (dancing with the Torah) and I remember the voices of Motel Traber, Leibel Klachker, and that of my cousin, Rabbi Shlomo Kozlowski, who had made a special trip from his own Yeshiva in the town of Mir.

The celebration peaked when Chaim "the tailor" gave everyone an apple. He had the "right" for doing so. He used to buy apples from the owners of the apple orchard, hide the apple boxes inside the synagogue and finally, distribute them to everyone.

[Page 371]

Rabbi Chaim was a remarkable person. He participated in all the charities, was a member of many committees and was the Treasurer of the Burial Society.

Groups of Scholars

A group of Etz–Chaim Yeshiva Students – 1925

Standing (right to left): Moshe Golob, Motel Traber, Moshe–Simcha Traber, Shmidt (from Vilna), Margolin, Chaim Bergman, a Student from Slabotka

Sitting: Herchel (from Rakov), Yoseph Goldstein, a Student from Lomza, Meir Berniker, Tkatch (from Grodno), Arie Charutz, Leinel Perski (from Klatzk)

I would like to mention some of the students of the Yeshiva. The head of the Yeshiva at that time was The Gaon Rabbi Yitzhak Weinstein (we wish him a long life), and under him studied groups of scholars. One of them was Motel Traber from the town of Trab (Traip). He was one of the outstanding graduates of the Yeshiva.

Another important person was Rabbi Yehuda Avraham the Slaughterer, who was very old. As a young man, he met the NATZIV. The walls would tremble when he raised his voice, calling "holy" during prayers.

[Page 372]

I remember the visit of Daniel Perski z"l, a famous writer who was a relative of the slaughterer. Rabbi Avraham welcomed him with the "Shehecheyanu" blessing, thus greeting his relative who had just come from Eretz Israel.

R'Yehuda Avraham Persky

I remember the beautiful sundial that was built on the East wall of the Yeshiva building. It had a large hand and black numerals. Over time, the outside of the building deteriorated. One day Mr. Yoseph Sochobolski of Bialystok, who had once been a student in the Yeshiva and later on became a prosperous contractor in the U.S.A., revisited our town. Seeing the condition of the building he paid for the necessary renovations, including its outside appearance. This made the sundial even more striking and distinctive.

The Great Synagogue stood on the east side of the Yeshiva while the house of Rabbi Yaakov Shapiro stood on a hill to the north. Next were the homes of both Naphtali Arotzker, a bookbinder and owner of the stationery and newspaper store, and of Pesia Bakshet, whose food store fed the students of the Yeshiva.

Rabbi Yaakov Shapiro's House, his Death and Funeral

We all remember the wedding celebration of Rivka, the daughter of Rabbi Yaakov Shapiro, to Rabbi Chaim Walkin, a son of the rabbi of Pinsk. We remember the groomsmen, dancing in the streets, accompanying the couple on their way to the wedding ceremony. The wedding party included a non–Jewish couple dancing in front of the wedding couple, holding two buckets of water. The young couple was both tossing coins into the water for good luck and happiness.

The Rabbi's house was large and spacious and when I entered, I felt the holiness and awe of the surroundings. The Rebbetzin asked me what I needed, which was always a Kashrut question my mother had sent me to ask. I remember one very serious question. My mother had bought meat for Passover and unintentionally placed it a non–Pesach towel. She wanted to know if that meat was still 'kosher for Passover'. The Rabbi answered that if it was not yet salted and washed with water – it is kosher.

Rebbetzin Shaina Disha Shapiro

Rabbi Yaakov Shapiro was not a healthy man and was under the medical care of Doctor Avraham Tzart. The doctor did all he could but the Rabbi's condition continued to deteriorate.

[Page 373]

At some point, the doctor decided that the Rabbi needed to see a specialist in Warsaw. Although it was a Saturday, the rabbi and the doctor took the bus due to "Pikuach Nefesh". After his condition improved somewhat, they returned to Volozhin. Unfortunately, the rabbi's condition continued to deteriorate. Once more he went back to Warsaw but there he passed away.

Smorgon Street

The news of the Rabbi's death spread quickly across Volozhin and the neighboring villages. The leaders of the community wanted to bury him in the local cemetery. The government insisted that his body would be transported by a dedicated vehicle. An agreement was reached and his body left Warsaw.

All the businesses were closed while the citizens gathered at the town's entrance. Some people climbed on top of the tall monument to watch for the approaching bus.

The town's leaders, headed by Rabbi Israel Lunin, went to meet the bus. They unloaded the casket and carried it on their shoulders to the Rabbi's home. Rabbis and yeshiva students from Volozhin and the surrounding area came to pay their respects. The next day, the casket was placed in the Yeshiva while many people gathered to eulogize the Rabbi.

[Page 374]

The casket was then taken to the Great Synagogue where the Chazan performed the funeral service. Rabbi Yaakov Shapiro was buried in the section dedicated to Volozhin Gaonim.

The road to the cemetery

The Volozhin Youth and the Educators

In his famous poem, Hamatmid (the Eternal Learner), Bialik wrote that the daughters of Volozhin were redheads while the women of the surrounding villages were "full and fat". Our national Poet distorted the image of the young Volozhin women, but I want to write about all the young people of Volozhin . Who formed its spirit? Who ignited the desire for Eretz Israel? The answer is: the teachers in the Tarbut schools and the Guides and troop leaders in the different Zionist youth movements. I can see the mentor and math teacher Chaim Golovenchick (and wish him a long life). When he moved to Montevideo before settling in Israel, his departure from Volozhin was hard on his students. I also remember other teachers: the science teacher Binyamin Shishko, Moshe Bram who taught us the Polish language and Chaim Portnoy, the Hebrew teacher.

[Page 375]

I remember the building of the Tarbut School, the heating stoves that kept us warm in winter, and Mania, the Christian housekeeper, who kept the classrooms impeccably clean. I fondly remember the punishments we received for not completing our homework. There were different penalty levels, from standing in the corner of the class facing the wall to copying ten pages from the textbook. These punishments were trivial when I think of the pleasure of learning. The school was the place where we developed our love for Zion, desire for Jerusalem, and dedication to the Hebrew language. Our Student Council had passed a resolution that a student caught speaking any language other than Hebrew would pay a fine and that money would be donated to the Jewish National Fund.

We must remember the sacred work of the Melameds (teachers for the younger grades) in the Hederim and the Talmud Torah Schools. For example, Rabbi Bezalel "the Melamed" was an excellent teacher who taught young children everything from Aleph–Bet to the three main parts of the Bible: Torah, Prophets and the Writings. His home was modest and he instilled respect and a sense respect for the holiness of the printed page of Jewish books. He taught us that torn pages of Holy Books are sacred and must be buried in a proper ceremony. He taught us to feel for the poor, the lonely and the neglected and that they too were created in God's image. Above all, he taught us to respect our parents.

This teaching bore fruit. Each Thursday, at the end of the Market Day, we collected the money that the merchants had set aside to help the poor. Rabbi Avraham Itche Schwartzberg dedicated his time to the "Bread for the Poor" Charity, an organization that fed people in need in Volozhin.

The Zionist Youth Movements and the Love of Eretz Israel

BEITAR, Hashomer Hatzair (the Young Guard) and Hechalutz (The Pioneer) youth movements collected donations for the Jewish National Fund. The money was used to buy the land where houses would be built, orchards planted and roads paved. All of this was for the one purpose: resurrecting the State of Israel. People rejoiced when some of us immigrated to Eretz Israel. However, we feel our pain that our parents, those who had instilled the love of our country in us, did not survive to enjoy it.

Some days were special. These were the days when young men and women left town on their way to Eretz Israel. The town escorted them to the train station, dancing in the streets, believing the Messiah would soon be coming.

[Page 376]

I remember the departure of Moshka Rogovin, Etel Shacker and Fania Kivilevich. The departure of my brother Shlomo is etched in my memory too. A long convoy of horse-drawn carriages, full of his friends, all of them singing, came to see him board the train.

The convoy made a stop in front of the home of my grandmother. With tears of happiness in her eyes, she said, "all my life I prayed for this day".

Purim and Pesach in Volozhin

Purim is not one of the three main Jewish Holidays, but Purim was a major Holiday in Volozhin. A spontaneous "ad–lo–yada", the Purim parade and carnival developed as young and older people put on costumes, walked in the streets and sang their song near different houses: "Today is Purim, tomorrow it will be over, give me a nickel and chase me away". They dedicated the collected money for buying land in Israel. The reading of the Megilah (the book of Esther in the Bible) was a happy event, especially for small children. Everyone stood at attention holding our clappers and pistols, ready to make a lot of noise when the name of Haman was read.

What type of pistols did we have? We took a large house key, filled its cavity with heads of matches and inserted a large nail to block the cavity. When this device was swung against the floor, it caused the matches to burn and explode. This produced a loud bang while the smell of burning filled the synagogue.

Several weeks before the start of Pesach, its holiday atmosphere began to descend over the town when people started baking their matzah. Many people volunteered to help. Some were rolling the dough, some were marking the holes, some carried the flour, some mixed it with the water, and others packed the matzahs in special baskets that protected them from Chametz. The baskets were kept in locked storage or on top of cabinets and dressers until the Holiday.

The night before Passover was special. We slept on the floor on a layer of straw. The beds were washed and "Kosher" so we were not allowed to even touch them. We could not use the plates and utensils that were ready for the SEDER and everyone just grabbed something to eat.

The morning before Passover arrived was the time to search and burn the Chametz in the house. All the Chametz was collected in one place. The rooms were kept dark and father lit the special candle used for the search. With a big ladle in his left hand and goose feathers in his right hand, he recited the blessing "who ordered us to burn the Chametz" and checked under the tables and the cabinets. He knew, of course, he would not find any Chametz there.

[Page 377]

I am longing for the special cooking pots used to make kugel and Kramzalach, the different nuts that our parents kept out of our sight. I remember the special sweet raisin wine that was made in the attic that we children used to sneak into and taste.

The Food We Used to Eat in Volozhin

During the year, we drank pure cream that was made of milk, not yogurt, which was stored in large clay jars. Lazar "the Baker" and his wife Fruma baked wonderful breads and semolina rolls. Other bakers were Yoseph Ribels and Sheina Lunin, the wife of Rabbi Israel.

The supplier of fish was Rabbi Gershon "der Bunier". His fish were not always very fresh and frequently people felt sick after eating them. He used to have many "special sales" trying to get rid of smelly, deteriorating inventory.

Bread Winning [Livelihoods] in Volozhin

Most of the Jews in Volozhin earned their living in trade, shopkeeping or peddling. Most of the activities took place in the market on Market Day each Thursday. The peasants sold linen, wheat and buckwheat, milk and milk products. Jews did not trust the Kashrut of the milk so every family kept a cow and hired a shepherd who led a group of cows to the hills outside the town. It was nice to see how each cow knew which way to return to the right "home" at the end of the grazing day.

During the summer, people collected berries and hay for the cows' winter feed. In winter, people used to warm bricks on the in houses' stoves and place them next to the cows' feed in order to keep it warm.

Different stores stood in the market area. Each store specialized in a particular set of products and merchandise, from shoelaces to herring, to stoves and glass jars. One special store sold glass plates for windows. The peasants would bring their windows and the glassmaker replaced the broken panes in the store. I loved the screeching sound of the diamond cutting the glass.

[Page 378]

The market of Volozhin

[Page 379]

The shopkeepers wore heavy winter coats and carried shawls around their necks in winter, to protect themselves from the cold wind that came through the open doors. However, these measures were not enough and every store kept a "firetap", a pot full of smoldering coal. The men wore special boots made of wool or felt.

There were two hotels in town. One belonged to Eliyahu Moshe Brodna, and the other – to Shlomo Chaim Brodna. Many clients of the hotels were merchants who came to town to trade timber, linen and agriculture products. Many important deals were signed in these hotels.

People got water from deep wells. One well was at the Market near the home of Itche Rogovin. Raising water from the well was not an easy task. People had to pull up a bucket full of water, tied to a rope. The rope regularly tore and the water supply operation ceased until a volunteer descended into the well and brought the bucket back. In winter, ice formed around the well and presented a serious risk of slipping or even falling into the well. I remember the yoke that people used in order to carry two buckets as well as the large barrel that stood in our kitchen and the copper cup we used to ladle water from the barrel.

At some point, a man named Herschel "the water pumper" started a business delivering water. He placed a big barrel on a cart that was pulled by his horse, and started selling water "by the bucket". The horse, which was blind, had been very cheap to buy. The women of the town started praying for the health of Herschel "the water pumper" as well as that of his horse.

Mutual Aid of the Jews of Volozhin

The brotherhood of the Volozhin Jews touched the heart. Here are just a few facts. Reb Shlomo-Chaim Brodna's inn would host the draft committee. The *shkotzim* [a derogatory term for gentiles] of Volozhin and the area also appeared before the committee. The days of appearing before the committee were days of fear and terror for the Jews of the city. After they were found to be fit to serve, they were given permission to drink vodka. After they got drunk, they ransacked through the streets and also broke into the houses. At that time, Volozhin looked like a city under siege.

When a Jewish lad appeared before the committee, especially an only son, or the son of a family with lots of children, and was found fit for service, the Jewish of the city raised an uproar in order to free him from army service, or at least to obtain a deferral (*srotzka*). If all this did not help, and he was taken to the army, he would be received with warmth and love when he came home for the Sabbath or for a vacation for the holidays.

There was an army camp in Volozhin in which Jewish lads from various cities of the country service. A kosher kitchen was set up for those soldiers. When the kitchen was closed on Sabbaths and festivals, the soldiers were invited to celebrate the festival in Jewish home, and thereby to somewhat assuage the sadness and longing for their homes and families.

[Page 380]

Love for one's fellow reached a very high level during the period of the smuggling of Yeshiva lads from Russia to Volozhin. Many Yeshiva lads desired to study in an "Upper Level Yeshiva," and would therefore cross the border and come to our city. Crossing the border usually took place on Thursdays, so that they would be able to arrive in Volozhin for the eve of the Sabbath. Many of them were caught by the border guards and imprisoned in the Volozhin jail. My father, Yitzchak Meir, took advantage of his good connections with the authorities, and freed the arrested people. However, it was necessary to sign an appropriate document of guarantee in order to gain their freedom. I recall that my father refused to sign so as not to desecrate the sanctity of the Sabbath, but Rabbi Yaakov Shapira permitted him to do so, for the commandment of redemption of captives overrides the Sabbath.

The trait of tending to guests was rooted in the hearts of the Jews of our city. Rabbi Yaakov Shapira implanted this trait within us. He imbued us with the concept of tending to guests. When we left the *Kleizl* or the Great Synagogue after the service of welcoming the Sabbath, we would see indigent Jews who were not local. The look on their faces made it clear that they were waiting for a house and a meal. The *shamash* would bring these guests to various houses. No such guest ever slept outside in Volozhin. At times, a householder would complain to the *shamash* about why he was eating his meal himself on the Sabbath, without a guest. Great was the Jew of a Jewish Volozhiner when he merited to host a scholarly guest.

Words of Jest

I will conclude my memories with a joke. An elderly charity collector named Velvel Leib lived in the women's gallery in the *Kleizl*. He would exchange earnings from the market day for money documents. He would keep his entire "treasure" between the pages of the Gemara in the synagogue.

The following story is told about him: Once he went to Zabzeze to collect donations. He felt weak along the way, and lay down to take a nap. He placed his shoes pointing toward Zabzeze so he would not lose his direction. He turned about as he slept, and his feet pointed toward Volozhin, without him noticing. When he woke up, he went in the direction of his shoes, and returned to Volozhin. However, he was certain that he had arrived in Zabzeze. Reb Velvel was surprised that the landscape looked the same, and that the Jews of Zabzeze are as similar to the Jews of Volozhin like two drops of water. He groaned and said: "If I did not know that I was in Zabzeze, I would say that I was in Volozhin."

[Page 381]

The Volozhinka River

By Yaakov Kagan of Tel Aviv

Translated by Jerrold Landau

based on an early translation by Moshe Porat that was edited by Mike Kalt

The source of the river is from the area of the Brilki village, about three kilometers from Volozhin. It crosses the fields of the town of Hordinovo and the Shapoval estate and arrives at the suburbs of Volozhin (Moszczyki Street[1]). It crosses a section of the area at the edge of the city, where on one side is Polak's gristmill, and on the second side several houses, including the Aroptzu Synagogue. Its waters reached Pilsudski Street. There was a bridge on that street that connected the two sides of the city. Rappoport and Perelman's gristmill stood next to the bridge.

The river continued parallel to Novogroski Street on one side, and on the other side, it passed the military sports field. It continued flowing to the village of Kelvitch, until it emptied into the Islatch River. A rivulet flowed into the river (the source was in the village of Bondara) in the area that crossed Moszcyki Street).[2]

The Minsk-Vilna trail passed over a wooden bridge constructed over the river. The creek continued to flow southwardly between Ponizhe on its left and the Military sports stadium on its right side, then through the Kelvitsh village until it emptied into the Yislotsh River, fifteen kilometers from town.

The river served an important role in the life of the residents. It served for bathing and also for washing laundry.[3]

Winter Landscape in Volozhin (on the pond)

Standing (right to left): a) Shabtai Baksht; b) Yisrael Berkovich; c) Hillel Sharira; d) Barich Mordehai Meirson; e) Efraim Rogovin

[Page 382]

The villagers would beat their flax on its banks. Those who lived on or close to its banks would wash and polish their household items there.

The river was shallow. Children could also bathe there without danger of drowning. However, before Passover, with the melting of the snow, its appearance changed. It became strong, its waters overflowed its banks and flooded the nearby houses.

The deep areas of the river were a bit far from the city. In the summer, it served as an area of pleasure. Many of the residents of the town when there to enjoy water sports. The village of Hardinova, next to the river, would treat the bathers to its good fruit.

The shore was primitive and neglected. Tall shrubs grew on the banks, which served as a dressing room for people to get undressed and dressed. At the beginning of the 1930s, when a military unit was set up in the city, the local authorities turned their attention to improving the shore of the river – to the pleasure and benefit of the soldiers. They deepened the land of the river and built a dam to separate the deep water from the shallow water. That is where the gentiles bathed, men and women together. It served as a place of enjoyment for swimmers and lovers of water sports.

On the Ten Days of Penitence, it also served holy purposes, for purifying the soul. On Rosh Hashanah, the Jews of the city would gather there for Tashlich.

The river also has some sad memories. There is an ancient Jewish legend that the river claimed a victim every year. If anyone bathed there during the period of *Sefira*[4] and the river swallowed him – it would be seen as a confirmation of the legend. I recall the drowning of Devora Perski. The deep area of the river was not fenced, and there was no sign there warning about the dangers of drowning. Dvora entered the water and disappeared immediately. They pulled her out dead.[5]

Translator's footnotes:

1. M. Porat notes that this is the Polish name of the street. The Russian name is Oktiabrskaya.
2. M. Porat added the following detail: The Minsk-Vilna trail passed over a wooden bridge constructed over the river. The creek continued to flow southwardly between Ponizhe on its left and the Military sports stadium on its right side, then through the Kelvitsh village until it emptied into the Yislotsh River, fifteen kilometers from town.
3. M. Porat added the following photo and caption:

Pleasure walk on the *Sazhelke* borders – Volozhin 1936

Mr. Yani Garber, the first Volozhin Judenrat head, the first victim shot on the first mass slaughter –October 1941, walking on the *Sazhelke* borders with his son Dania (the pianist) his sister in law Etia Perlman and her daughter Sonitshka. Behind them, Yani's mother in law Malka Perlman -Itskhakin (Rabbi Itsele's G. Granddaughter) with her son Yossif Perlman

4.   The Omer period from Passover to Shavuot. Some curtailment of pleasure is in practice during that period. Also, that would be the time when the river was at its fiercest.
5.   M. Porat added the following detail to this article (including additional sections):
On its northeast side extended a large meadow covered with opulent grass, called *Veehon* ("Drive away

place" in Russian), to which the town dwellers' cows were driven each morning for pasture. The authorities arranged also the *Sazhelke*. They framed the water pond in rectangular borders. It became suitable to serve as an ice-skating rink in winter and as a pleasure-walking place and a place for rowboat cruising in summer.

The Volozhinka and the *Sazhelke*–ponds were quiet for the most part of the year, with cool calm water in summer and autumn, and covered with ice in winter. Nevertheless, it was completely different in springtime. Generally, on the eve of Passover, when the earth defrosted, large quantities of snow melted and flowed from the surrounding hills into the Volozhinka dale. The waters flooded the valley, creating a large lake in the *Veehon*-meadow. The quiet river, usually passable by foot, became a large, deep, and dangerous torrent.

The three mass slaughters on the Volozhinka borders -Translator's note
The Nazis created the Volozhin Ghetto on the western shore during the summer of 1941. They accomplished the first mass slaughter at the Sport Stadium on the same shore to the south in the autumn of the same year. The Volozhin Jews spent the winter of 1941 in relatively quiet conditions, enclosed in the Ghetto, where from they could see the last snow-thawing flood of their life.

Some days after that flood, when the roads became passable, an SS team did a reconnaissance tour in Volozhin. They looked for a place for the "Great Execution". They found it near the ancient Jewish Cemetery, on the Volozhinka's rivulet. The main mass slaughter of 2,000 Volozhin Jews took place on the Volozhinka western shore a month after the spring flood, on May 10, 1942.

In the third (last) mass slaughter, the Nazis executed the remaining 300 Jews from the second great shtetl near the *Veehon*, on the east shore of the Volozhinka riverbed, in August 1942.

The Volozhinka river carried away with its waters a large amount of innocent Jewish blood and ash.

[Page 382]

Zabrezhe

By Moshe Eliyaswhkevitsh of Bnei Brak

Translated by M. Porat z"l

Revised by Mr. H. Mendelson

Lightly edited by Jerrold Landau

Zabrezhe [Zabzhezie – in Polish] is situated on the way to the railroad station, thirteen kilometers from Volozhin. It is a small village on the Berezina (Bierioza) River shore. The Berezina flows to the Nieman River. The village is located among fields and forests, from which the Zabrezhe inhabitants made their living. The local Jews raised rye, barley, potatoes and wheat in those fields.

Approximately twenty Jewish families inhabited this village; three of them lived in the Volozhin railroad station [Horocki], about three kilometers from Zabrezhe. Those families were: Yosef Berman, Chuna Berman and the seamstress widow,

[Page 383]

Temka. Yosef Berman practiced as an agent. He used to receive the goods on the station and move them in horse-carts to the merchants of Volozhin. Chune Berman owned an inn, and Temka made her living by sewing.

Rabbi Shmuel Dovid Levin (Shadal), born in Bobruysk, was the prominent inhabitant of the village. Reb Avraham Moshe Bunimovitsh brought him to Zabrezhe to become his son-in-law. Rabbi Shadal used to study Torah day and night. He did not practice as the shtetl's rabbi. Bunimovitsh was a wealthy man, a Jewish *Poretz* (land owner). He owned large tracts of land and a spacious house, which was located inside a big, beautiful courtyard. Reb Avraham Moshe was blessed with a special merit; he lived a long life to see great-grand children.

Reb Zecharya Berman and his brother Reb Menahem [Mendel] were also considered as the village's elite.

The majority of the Zabrezhe Jews supported themselves by farming, and the minority by commerce and trades. Aharon Dovidman owned a shoe and leather shop, Duba Berman possessed a cloth shop, and Yehoshua Berman was a flax merchant.

Some of the Jewish farmers cultivated their own fields; the others were land leasers who tilled the land of nearby landlords. They were veritable farmers that worked the soil and made a living from the earth. It would be of interest to mention the estate owner, Mrs. Baranowska. She, her husband, and their son the physician, were considered as righteous gentiles. Mr. Baranowski was friendly with the local Jews, and as I remember that he contributed material to build the Kleizl in Zabrezhe.

The Kleizl was the village spiritual center, where the Jewish civic and cultural life took place. Reb Zecharia Berman performed the Gabbai (synagogue manager) functions. He did not behave like an important personality. On Fridays, personally with his own hands, he used to sweep the floor, dust the tables and benches, arrange the candles, and polish the candelabra, Before Yom Kippur, he would hire a gentile, with his own money, to look from time to time after the burning candles. Three Torah scrolls were kept in the Holy Ark. There was a novel thing, even the books of the early and latter Prophets were written on parchments and set up on scrolls, like the Torah scrolls. The shtetl children used to participate in the *Simchas Torah Hakafot* with these "Torah scrolls." The local householders served as prayer leaders. Reb Yechezkel Yahas served as the Torah reader. He died in the winter of 5696 [1936] and was buried in Volozhin.

Even though there were not many Jews in Zabrezhe, the parents used to hire the best teachers to educate their children. Of course, there was a Polish public school, to which the Jewish children were obligated to learn in accordance with the law of compulsory education. The parents were not satisfied with only secular studies. The children studied in the school in the morning and learned Hebrew language and subjects from the Jewish teachers in the afternoons.

Teachers were brought in from nearby towns. They served in this holy task in return for room, board, and a symbolic salary. Whom among them dreamt at that time of salary, and who of the teachers dared to think of a strike to improve the working conditions? The main thing was the dissemination of Torah – the salary was a side point. They did not stay in private apartments; they used to wander from room to room in the houses of their pupils. The teachers that I am able to recall were Reb Zvi from Volozhin,

[Page 384]

Reb Aryeh Leib Grinhoyz from Lebediev (died in Israel in the winter of 5725 [1965]), and Reb Yechiel Segalovitch from Rubazevitsh. The last teacher was Rabbi Kalman Stolir from Vishnevo.

The studies took place in the Kleizl. During the long winter nights, we used to learn by the light of kerosene lamps, the shade of which was heavier than their light. Each student, in turn, would bring from home a bottle of kerosene for the lamps. I must single out for praise the unforgettable teacher Reb Aryeh Leib Grinhoyz. He was a graduate of the Vilna-Hebrew-Teachers Seminary. He taught us Hebrew and the concepts of history and geography of the Land of Israel. His teaching of Bible was very interesting. Hie explanations excelled in their clarity. He brought the Land of Israel alive and palpable before our eyes. We were expert in the landscape of the Land, and we knew the roles that the historical places served during the Biblical period.

Reb Aryeh Leib was a devoted Zionist. He organized the Zionist youth movement in the town. Approximately ten boys and girls participated. These youths were connected with the Zionist movement of Volozhin. He founded a Hebrew library in his home. He himself paid for the first thirty books. This library served as a place of spiritual enjoyment for the students. This teacher loved his students. At the end of classes on winter nights, he would accompany each of us back to our homes.

It has been said that Volozhin and Zabrezhe were like a room and an anteroom. Zabrezhe seemed to be torn from Volozhin and stuck on the main road. The Zabrezhe Jews were bound to Volozhin in every way. They purchased their food and clothing in Volozhin. They buried their dead in Volozhin. There were also connections regarding medical aid. There was no local physician in Zabrezhe, just a medic named Hardinietz from the village of Losk. If someone became ill, they would summon a doctor from Volozhin.

Across the river (i.e. in Zabrezhe), our ancestors lived from ancient times. They lived there for generation after generation and considered their way of life to be dictated by the world order – until the terrible deluge came that wiped out everything. Temka (living in Volozhin) and Yehudit Ginsburg (living in the United States) were among the survivors. The slaughter took place on the first day of Chanukah of 1942. The Paszkowski brothers, who tortured the Jews mercilessly, excelled in perpetrating atrocities.

Our dear ones and their stories will be engraved in our memories, and .their images will flutter before our eyes forever.

Jews who lived in predominantly gentile villages neighboring Volozhin

By M.Porat

Edited by Eilat Gordin Levitan

Jewish peasants lived in the midst of gentiles in several villages and estates near Volozhin. The Yizkor Book describes some of them: Zabrezhe on page 382, Mizheyki, Goroditshtshe, Koniushtshina and Dubin on page 385, Belokorets on page 317, Youzefpol on page 386.

Jewish families labored in the fields and farmed in those locations for many years.

I remember two such families who lived all isolated from the Jewish community; Berman who resided and was employed by the rail station in Horod'k and Mrs Matke, her husband and their handsome son who dwelled in Rudnik.

I must record a few words from my own recollections of Matke and the Jewish farm in Rudnik, as it was not mentioned in the Yizkor book. Matke with her family lived in out-of-the-way Rudnik, three Km from town. We used to go there by foot; we would pass near the graveyard and then by Bialik's Mount and most of the path would go by the shore of the Volozhinka brook.

The family lived in a spacious house. They also owned a barn and a stable. Cows, geese, poultry and horses surrounded their house. Additionally, the family possessed a vast meadow and a small pine grove.

The entire student body that attended our school, guided by the teachers, would turn up in Rudnik's Grooves every spring for our traditional Lag-Baomer picnic by the bonfires.

The Volozhin region's Zionist youth camps took place on Matke's Rudnik-meadow. I remember that on one occasion mother walked with my sister Sonitshka and I, for a visit with father's cousins; the beautiful Tsherne and Blume Efron from the near by shtetl of Vishnievo. They camped in tents amongst many other young members of "HaShomer Hatzir" youth movement. They "took over" Matke's green meadow in Rudnik.

During summer time the house would turn into a "holiday hostel". Many of the Volozhin kids spent a few weeks in the inn. They came to breathe in some fresh air. They were sent there with their parent's hopes that they would add a few healthy pounds, since they drank fresh milk right from the cows, and ate fresh eggs straight from the hens.

The gentile peasants did not make any effort to spare their Jewish colleagues and neighbors' life. Not even one of the Jews from the Volozhin vicinity villages survived the Holocaust.

[Page 385]

Mijeyki (village)

By Barukh Tsivony (Farberman) – Haifa

Translated by M. Porat z"l

Edited by Eilat Gordin Levitan

Further edited by Jerrold Landau

Eight Jewish farming families inhabited the village. The Jews lived there for many generations, earning their bread by the sweat of their brow. Eight large estates owned by Polish nobles, who were also farmers, were located about 300 meters from the Jewish homes. The cultivated land belonged to the settlers. The Jewish plots of land were intermixed between the gentile plots. The Jews of the village were also involved in various trades.

Due to its geographic location, the village served as a crossroads amidst the nearby settlements. Travelers who went from Volozhin to the nearby villages stopped first in Mijkeki. The Jews of Rakov, Krasno, and Horodok would also spend the night in the village and eat there on their way to Volozhin. There was a small inn in the town, run by Malka Kaminstein, the wife of the teacher (we will speak of him further on). She owned a spacious stable , where they brought the horses to rest from the journey. The travelers feasted on a light meal.

The village was tied to Volozhin with strong links. Not even a single shop existed in the village. The inhabitants used to purchase food and clothing in the city. The relations were reciprocal. The village supplied the city with all of its milk, eggs, and poultry, for the Jews refrained from purchasing milk and dairy products from the gentiles out due to kashruth concerns. The village specialized in fattening geese for the Jews of Volozhin, for fat for frying for Chanukah and Passover.

Among the village's tradesmen was the well-known tailor Velvel Kaganovitch, who learned his trade in Odessa. He brought back from there his wife (a midwife) who barely had any work, for there were very few births due to the small population. Velvel used to sew primarily for the "high windows" [i.e. prominent people] – the Starosta and senior officials. The affluent residents of Volozhin also had their clothes made by him, for he had golden hands, and each piece of clothing he made as a masterpiece. His fees were high, so only people of means could order a suit from him. He was the father of three daughters, all of whom studied in Vilna. Their father spent beyond his means for them. He went into much debt, with his only intention being that they become educated and learned. His father, Shimon Kaganovitch was a scholarly man, who served as the rebbe [teacher] for the students of the village, and also as the Torah reader.

Another renowned tradesman in Mijeyki was my father "Moshe der Shuster" (Moshe the Shoemaker). He reached the very advanced age of hundred and ten years. He never got sick. He never rested, and he worked day and night. Nevertheless, he lived in a meager fashion, for his income was small. He would serve as the prayer leader even after he became blind, for he knew the prayers by heart. Even though our house was small, my father was very particular about

[Page 386]

hosting guest. At times, several itinerant beggars were hosted in or house. My father would feed them and provide them with a straw mattress on the floor.

The primary concern of the Mijeyki Jews was their children's education. For this purpose, they invited an excellent pedagogue, a Hebrew expert - the teacher Kaminstein from Białystok. He married a native of the village. All the village children were taught Hebrew by him and were very successful in their studies. Kaminstein was the father of four boys, all native to the village. As the boys grew up, they abandoned their father's teaching, the doctrine of Hebrew and national revival. They became known as devoted Communists. Two of them left their village for Russia during the February 1917 revolution. The senior brother became known as a unit commander during the war of the Bolsheviks against Poland in 1919. The unit spent some time in the village. The son spent some time with his father, and then set out in the direction of Warsaw. The second son served as a well-known commissar in the revolutionary committee. He took his mother and two remaining brothers out of the village. Out of fear that their lands might fall into gentile hands, the Jews of the village made a special effort, and each family obtained one eighth of the plot.

A synagogue was built in the village prior to World War One. The Russians destroyed it during the war, and only the skeleton remained. The synagogue was rebuilt in 1921. It was repaired and renovated, and it once again became a fitting house of prayer. Jews of the nearby villages of Godoroicha (in which three Jewish families lived), and Koniushchina, which also had three families also worshipped there. The village of Godroicha was only two kilometers away. Therefore, its Jews came with their children for services every Sabbath. The Jews of the village of Koniushchina, which was six kilometers from the village, only came to worship with us on the High Holy Days. The village of Dubin had only one Jew, a smith. He also came to us with his family for the High Holidays. The Holocaust uprooted all these "children of the earth" from their roots. No trace of them remains.

The Jozefpol Estate

by Benyamin Kutshevitski (Kiryat Motskin)

Translated by M. Porat

Edited by Judy Montel

Further edited by Jerrold Landau

The estate belonged to the Polish landowner Mokaszicki. He was a nobleman, who had inherited these lands. Boruch Kuchevitski[1] and Meir Shif, friends of each other, bought a part of them.

The area was wonderfully beautiful. Two beautiful avenues "The Love Avenue" and "The Parting Avenue" adorned it. In the center there was a lovely fruit orchard that gave off a pleasant aroma. There was a beautiful lawn, with a giant tree in the center. This place served as a place for friendly gatherings.

Springs a distance of 200 meters away provided water. They provided

[Page 387]clear, cool water for people and animals. They also provided energy for the gristmill and the sawmill. Puddles of water collected on rainy days, and deep quicksand was formed. One could not cross the street without boots.

Two families set up the sawmill and the gristmill on the estate. The noise of the engines could be heard throughout all the hours of the day, for the sawmill operated constantly for export purposes. It was built in 1921. Forty full time employees worked there. Several hundred temporary laborers worked there during the busy seasons. The sawmill served as a place of work and *Hachshara* [*aliya* preparation] for Hechalutz and Beitar of Volozhin and the area. The *Hachshara* members lived in the nearby villages, and some lived in the house of the landowner.

The closest railway station was seven kilometers from the estate, in Horocki. (That station later became the Volozhin station). Mail was sent to Zabrezhe every day through a messenger. The connection with Zabrezhe encompassed the entire spiritual life of the local Jews. When a question regarding kashruth or treif arose, a messenger was sent with the chicken to Rabbi Shadal (Shlomo David Levin) of Zabrezhe. On Saturday mornings, they would go there to worship and return after the survices. We would also go back and forth on Rosh Hashanah. We remained in Zabrezhe on Kol Nidre night and throughout Yom Kippur. After the *Maariv* [evening] prayer and a quick bite to break the fast, Mikitka the sawmill-guard would come with a wagon to take us home. The two families at the would share the post fast meal together. At the end, they would immediately prepare to build the common Sukka. We celebrated Simchat Torah in the village and not in Zabrezhe. The joy was very great.

The two families took care for the children's Hebrew and nationalist education. A kindergarten teacher was brought in from Vilna or Olshan. When they students got older, they received their education from the Hebrew schools of Volozhin, Vilna, and Ashmiany.

The medical care was primitive. It was the job of the local "feldscher," a gentile who was always drunk. Even though he was not a certified physician, we relied on the drugs that he prescribed.

The feldscher provided first aid only. In serious cases the sick person would be transferred to Volozhin. Once, a girl from the *Hachshara* group contracted appendicitis. Thy put her on a wagon and rushed her to Volozhin. The journey on he poor, potholed road caused her appendix to rupture. She reached Volozhin in critical condition, and she survived by miracle. However, another case ended in death. There was a land lessee in the neighboring village of Ozelcvich named Avraham Itshe Lewin. His son stepped on a rusty nail and contracted blood poisoning. He died in the home of Menachem Yoel Potshenik (a relative of Avraham Itshe).

Translator's footnotes:

1.   We lived on the estate as if in the Garden of Eden. We loved the rich nature and the beauty of life. The families were firmly established from an economic perspective, and therefore did not lack anything. We thought that this "Garden of Eden" would not be affected by the vicissitudes of the times. However, the war broke out, and the Soviets occupied the area. When they entered the estate, they nationalized the gristmill and sawmill. Thus was my boyhood nest destroyed and lost forever.
Buruch Kudevidski was the father of Bunia/Basia Kudevitski who married David Yavnovitch/Jawnowich from Kobylnik, murdered in the Shoah with their 2 sons Baruch and Leibel [Friday November 5,1942 in old Vileika] see Kobylnik Yizkor Book [uncle and aunt of Anita Frishman Gabbay-coordinator of this Yizkor book.]

[Page 388]

Volozhin Stories

By Benyamin Shafir (Shishko)

Translated by Meir Razy

Donated by Anita Frishman Gabbay

The Complaint of a Jew Hater in Volozhin

The two hotels that were found in Volozhin belonged to men named Brodna, Shved was the Mayor of the town, and Polack was the owner of the flour mill and the power generating plant.

One of the Jew–haters in Volozhin once commented: What a poor town is Volozhin. The two hotels are dirty ("brodni" in Polish means dirty), the Mayor is Swedish and the Polack (meaning a Polish person) is Jewish.

A Story about disciple of the NATZIV and a Rural Jew

A very rich Jewish villager asked the NATZIV to pick one of his more intelligent students as a prospective husband for his daughter. The young man came for an interview and the father wanted to test his knowledge of the Torah. He asked (in Yiddish) "How do you say 'Dinstag' in Hebrew?" The young man answered, "Dinstag is Tuesday in Hebrew."

The father rejected the candidate. He returned to the Rabbi and this time asked for his very smartest students, however, all of them still failed the test.

One of the students, who truly liked the beautiful daughter, befriended her. He entrusted her to ask her father for the answer. The father told her that Dinstag in Hebrew is "support". The young man passed the test and married the daughter.

Later he asked his father–in–law "I learned Torah so I know the Dinstag in Hebrew is 'support', but you did not study Torah. How do you know?" "Listen young man. Every day I pray the "Eighteen Prayers" and it says 'support and kitchen to the righteous' [the word 'kitchen' was a mistake he made by transposing two letters, Bet & Tav. Actually the text is MISHAN and MIVTACH (protection and support). In Yiddish MITVACH is Wednesday, in Hebrew MITBACH is kitchen]."

He continued: "Everyone knows that Tuesday comes before Wednesday and, therefore, Dinstag in Hebrew is 'support'".

Sweep the Floor with a Broom

It is a known fact that the NATZIV promoted simple interpretations of Jewish rules and laws.

[Page 389]

Once he entered the Yeshiva and asked the students "how do you sweep the floor?" and left. The students started to discuss his hidden intentions and their possible meanings. They all agreed that he did not ask about something trivial. After a few hours, he returned to see what they were arguing about and told them: "Young men, you sweep the floor of the house with a broom."

A Volozhin "Revolutionary"

Feytel the shoemaker was a religious man who prayed three times a day and followed all the rules of Judaism. However, in 1905 he became a "revolutionary". This is how he expressed his aversion to the Tsar. He stood in front of the statue of the Tsar, checked that there were no police officers around, put his hand in his pocket and "gave the Tsar a finger".

Why Jews Do not Have Their Own State

Shlomo Chaim Brodna, the son of the owner of the hotel, was an educated man. He was the Manager of the Cooperative Bank and attended the meetings of the Jewish Cooperation Organizations in Poland.

He used to explain why the Jews did not have their own State. When the Christians want to elect a committee, they assemble in the pub on a Sunday and drink Vodka "for good luck". Then they go to Church and later they gather in the church's yard and elect a Chairman for the meeting. The Chairman proposes candidates and asks, "Who votes for Ivan Ivanovich?" Everyone shouts "Dobry" (good) – everyone agrees. Then, "Who votes for Stepan Stepanovich?" Everyone shouts "Dobry" – everyone agrees. They elect the committee in one minute!

It is a different story when it comes to Jews. The old caretaker of the synagogue died. What was his job? His job was to sweep the floor, wash the towels and distribute prayer books. However, electing a new caretaker is a complicated endeavor! When someone proposed Eliyahu, son of Yaakov, someone else opposed him because his grandmother had a sister who lived in a faraway village and she had a daughter who had married a Christian.

[Page 390]

They proposed someone else and he was rejected because he was suspected of having an improper relationship with a woman. In short – it is impossible to find a proper candidate for even the lowly position of caretaker.

Now you can understand why the Jews do not have their own State.

Torah Judgement in Volozhin

Rabbi Chaim Baxter was a well–to–do and Torah–educated man who lived in a small town between Iwye and Volozhin. Shmuel Gimpel Shishko was a farmer in the village of Rabawa and he too was a Torah–educated man.

Many poor Jews were wandering among the different towns of Belarus and Rabbi Chaim Baxter was happy to invite travelers to stay with him. Shmuel Gimpel Shishko, too, wanted to show his generosity, but only a few travelers passed near his village. He drove his horse to the main road, and collected travelers and hosted them.

Chaim Baxter realized that the number of his guests was rapidly diminishing and investigated. When he found out that Shmuel Gimpel Shishko was "kidnapping" his guests, he sued him in the Volozhin Jews Court.

The judges listened to both parties, discussed the situation and decided: "those people walking from Volozhin to Iwye would stay with Rabbi Shmuel Gimpel Shishko and those people walking from Iwye to Volozhin would stay with Rabbi Chaim".

Volozhin's Version of Austerity

There was a blacksmith in Volozhin who became rich, very rich. Some people wondered how an artisan could become so rich. Others said he had "good hands" so it is no wonder he became rich. The man, however, kept his simple lifestyle. He ate black bread rather than white bread and drank sour milk rather than cream.

When people asked him why he was not using his wealth to live like rich people, he replied that it was a good practice to know how to live modestly. Sometimes things change and the rich may become poor and would not be able to live under their new circumstances.

The source of his wealth was eventually discovered. He was making copper coins and gold plating them. He then sold them as pure gold. His deception was uncovered and he was tried and sentenced to jail in Siberia.

When he was taken to the train station, many residents came to the police station to say goodbye. While they lamented his destiny, he turned to them and said, "As I told you, it was a good practice to know how to live in modesty. In Siberia, I will have the same black bread and sour milk I am accustomed to."

[Page 391]

The Zionist movement

[Page 392] Blank [Page393]

Tzeirei Zion (Zion's Youth) in Volozhin

Written by Shlomo Bunimovich of Karkur and Tzvi Rogovin of Tel Aviv

Translated by Jerrold Landau

based on an earlier translation by M. Porat z"l
that was edited by Judy Feinsilver Montel

The Tzeirei Zion chapter of Volozhin was founded in 1918 and was one of the earliest in Russia. Volozhin was near the front, and thousands of Jewish youths were hosted in Jewish homes for the festivals. Some of them were educated young men who were members of various parties. They conducted mass meetings under the open sky, where the representatives of the various parties attempted to prove the correctness of their political path. There were Zionists among the speakers, who proved that our nation has no chances in the Diaspora, and therefore one must make *aliya* to the Land of Israel.

The major influence in this area was the appearance of the poet Shaul Tchernichovsky in Volozhin. He appeared in our town in the year 5676 (1916) in the uniform of a Russian captain, and lectured in the Great Synagogue about Zionism and the revival of the Hebrew language. His words left an unforgettable impression. The Volozhin youth were educated from their early childhood in the spirit of Zionism and Hebrew. My parental home was full of stories from Grandfather and Father, who told about the great students who studied in the Yeshiva of Volozhin, and were the first of Chovevei Zion. The teacher Avraham Gorelik played a key role in the forging of the Zionist reality. (He married the sister of Yosef Kahanovitch). He founded a Hebrew school in 1910 which utilized the "Hebrew in Hebrew" [i.e., Hebrew immersion] methodology. That school educated in the spirit of Zionism and love of the Land.

The general atmosphere that pervaded in Volozhin of that time was of the Messianic Days, of the final generation of slavery and the first of redemption. Even the gentiles talked about this. There was a legend circulating amongst them about a wonderous man amongst the Jews named "Pompador" (referring to Yosef Trumpeldor), who will bring the Jews to the Land of Israel.

The founder of the chapter in our city was Osher Malkin. He participated in the Tzeirei Zion convention in Russia. He assembled a group of activists, which included: Shlomo Bunimovitch, Tsipa Gelman, Chaim Deretshinski, Noah Horovitz, Yosef Tabachovitch, Olya Swirski, Yisrael Rogovin and Tzvi Rogovin.

The chapter issued a Journal "Der Bezem" (The Broom), edited by Shlomo Bunimovitch and Tzvi Rogovin, which dealt with an analysis of events of Volozhin, youth, education, and other matters. The writers called upon young people to make *aliya* to the Land of Israel.

In its first days the group numbered approximately eighty persons, male and female. We rented a club in Galia Perski's house in the Lower Town (Aroptzu). We organized an amateur theater group. Our group successfully performed several shows, among them "Di Pintele Yid" (The Jewish Point of Essence), "The Mechasheyfe" (The Witch), King Lear, and "Mirele Efrat." We also held literary debates. The most memorable was the debate

Page 394]

on Sholom Aleichem's "Menachem Mendel," the purpose of which was to prove the miserable situation of our people who lived among the gentiles, living a life based on ethereal pursuits. The main activity was in the realm of culture. There was a library in Volozhin, headed by Russophiles (lovers of Russian culture). Anyone who visited was obliged to speak only Russian. We stormed this library in order to turn it into a Zionist library. To this end, we registered all our members, and we became the majority. A leadership committee was formed, consisting of Avraham Gurwitz, Tzvi Zeltzer, Akiva Potashnik, and Tzvi Rogovin. The library became bilingual in Hebrew and Yiddish.

Our victory greatly advanced the activities of the chapter, for in those days, the library served as a "spiritual center," serving not only as a place for reading books, but also for the exchange of ideas on various issues.

We received news on what was taking place in the Land from the Achdut anthologies that arrived from the Land of Israel. They served for as material for lectures on what was taking place in the Land. Local people also helped us. Mr. Yehoshua Horwitz, a scholar and a Zionist, responded positively to our invitation, and explained the essence of the Zionist idea in his lectures.

The *Hachshara* Group of Volozhin Tzeirei Zion in Rudnik

From left to right: Mordechai Malot, Shlomo Bunimovich, David Yitzchak Kantorovitch, Zeev Shaker, Tzvi Rogovin, Meir Yeshaya Meltzer, Yechezkel Glik.

[Page 395]

Our party, despite being socialist, organized a special Minyan for its members on Simchas Torah. Yosef Tabachovitch served as the prayer leader for *Shacharis*, and Avraham Berkowitz did so for *Musaf*. He also served as the Torah reader, and recited the *Mi Sheberach* prayers for donation pledges that were pledged during the *aliyos* to the Torah. The income was dedicated to the expenses of the chapter.

Our chapter organized "Pirchei Zion" from which Hechalutz in Volozhin sprouted. The workers organized themselves into the national workers organization. Shlomo Bunimovitch participated as a delegate to the convention of the tradespeople that took place in Warsaw. We also collected money for the benefit of the Fund for the Workers of the Land of Israel, and participated in Tzeirei Zion conventions.

One Friday after the *Mincha* service, we affixed in the synagogues long manifestos that ended with a revolutionary call: "You will not be the ones to run the civic affairs!" Our action evoked a positive reaction from the community. The communal council was disbanded, and democratic elections took place. A new council was elected, which included two of our members: Yosef Tabachovitch and Yeshayahu Kaganovitch.

From its beginnings, our party believed that the interpretation of Zionism is a person living in Zion. In order to translate our outlook into a practical language, we founded an agricultural *Hachshara* group in the village of Rudnik. We worked in Michla's farm. She was a Zionist woman who had purchased land in the Land of Israel.

Mr. Aharonshtam was in Volozhin in 1924. He organized a seminar there for party members and sympathizers. His influence was quite noticeable in the city. His successful educational activity led to the growth and strengthening of the chapter. In 1925, we received a directive from the Tzeirei Zion headquarters in Vilna that we were to go to the city of Lida, where the committee for issuing permits for *aliya* resided. About fifty of us went. Most were certified for *aliya*. In the year 5686 (1926), Meir Baksht, Shlomo Bunimovitch, Tzvi Rogovin, and others made *aliya* to the Land.

[Page 396]

Hechalutz in Volozhin and its Activities

Written by a group of pioneers

Translated by Jerrold Landau

based on an earlier translation by M. Porat z"l
that was edited by Judy Feinsilver Montel

The beginning of Hechalutz in Volozhin was based on "Cherut Vetechiya" [Liberty and Revival], a non-partisan Zionist youth organization, comprised mainly of studying youth of the age of 15-16. It was founded in 5681(1921). Its living spirit was Moshe Zalman Luntz (Ben-Sasson), a scion of the dynasty of Rabbi Chaim of Volozhin. Its purpose was to educate the Jewish youth of Volozhin toward Hebrew and Zionism. This movement created a revolution in the way of thinking of the youth in our city. When we were studying in cheder and later in the Tarbut school, a picture of the Land of Israel as something founded in legend was drawn before us. Hebron, Shechem, and Beer Sheva were names only written in the Torah, and not existing in reality. Cherut Vetechiya educated us to cleave to our homeland and to negate its desolation through the work of our hands.

The first group of *Chalutzim* in the year 5683 (1923)

First row, right to left: Shlomo Berger, Shneur Kivilevitch, Binyamin Shishko, Yechezkel Glik
Second row: Chaim Kahanovitch, – , Shimon Tabachovitch

Its main activity was expressed in the sale of stamps of the Jewish National Fund and the collection of money for that fund. A children's library existed alongside Cherut Vetechiya. It was established through the donations of books that we collected in various houses. It was located in the house of Chaim Hirsch Perski on Vilna Street. Chaim

[Page 397]

Potashnik (Eshlagi) served as the librarian. The first Hebrew book obtained by the library was "Memories of the House of David" by Avraham Shalom Friedberg.

Cherut Vetechiya put on performances for the broad community in order to support its activities. The first play was "Der Darfs Yung" (Child of the Village) by Kobrin. The announcements were published in Hebrew and Yiddish. As there was no printing press in Volozhin, Avraham Berkovitch volunteered to draw the announcements. The performance took place in one of the buildings of Count Tyszkiewicz in Aroptzu (next to the river). The performance was very successful, and was performed several times.

Moshe Zalman Ben-Sasson founded Cherut Vetechiya from an educational and ideological perspective in order to make the publicity efforts easier. Moshe Zalman published a satirical newspaper called Der

Shtelk Dreier. Members of the editorial board were Moshe Zalman Ben Sasson, Esther Shaker, and Chaim Binya Kahanovitch. The newspaper included criticism of life in the city, issues of the day, and politics. The purpose of that criticism was to emphasise the life of atrophy in the city, and to educate the Jewish youth to changes of values and *aliya* to the Land of Israel.

The Hechalutz committee in the year 5683 (1923) on the occasion of the *aliya* of Moshe Zalman Ben-Sasson to the Land of Israel

From left to right: Noach Perski, Shlomo Berger, Moshe Zalman Ben-Sasson (Luntz), Binyamin Shishko (Shapir) Chaim Binya Kahanovitch

Moshe Zalman preached properly and also fulfilled properly. He made *aliya* to the Land in the year 5683 (1923). The activities of Cherut Vetechiya weakened after his *aliya*. However, this decline was only temporary. The pioneering seed

[Page 398]

planted in the hearts took root, and Hechalutz, which was founded in the year 5683 (1923) sprouted from it.

The great poverty that pervaded in Volozhin pushed us into the ranks of Hechalutz. We opened our eyes to see and understand that we have no place on foreign soil. Our youth was consistent in its conclusions, and began to prepare energetically for new life in our ancient homeland.

The first members of Hechalutz were: Yaakov Girzon, Nachum Gelman, Mendel Volkovitch, Shimon Tabachovitch, Chaim Binya Kahanovitch, Eliezer Lavit, Leibel Luboshitz, Zelig Meltzer, Rachel Meltzer, Chaim Potashnik, Akiva Potashnik, Etl Paretski, Eliyahu Hershel Perski, Yitzchak Perski, Sonia Kozlovski, Fania Kivilevitch, David Yitzchak Kantorovitch, Eliezer Kaplan, Ben Zion Kaplan, Musia Rogovin, Esther Shaker, Mordechai Yudel Schwartzberg, Benyamin Shishko.

Hechalutz chapter on 12 Tammuz 5684 (July 14, 1924)

Standing at the top (alone): Eliya Ber Girzon
First row from the top (right to left): Zelda Rappoport, Sara Rudnitzki, Liba Dolgov, Aharon Mordechovitch, – , Yehoshua, Leibel Perski, Shlomo Berman, Yosef Bernstein, Shmuel Rogovin
Second row: Sara Meltzer, Hinda Mordechovitch, – , Lea Kivilovitch, Dobe Bernstein, Fruma Rogovin
Third row: Feigel Kagan, daughter of Yitzchak the smith, Liba Luboshitz, Dov Lavit, Bella Shaker, Yitzchak Perski, Rachel Rogovin, Yosef Schwartzberg, Sara Malot, Batya German, Rachel Dolgov
Fourth row: Leiba Berman, Yosef Girkop, Yaakov Berkovitch, Leibe Daul, Baruch Simerenitzki

[Page 399]

We contacted Yosef Bankover in Vilna, who were for the "Palestine Office" (The Land of Israel Office), and we requested that he visit Volozhin. We convened a meeting in the house of Mordechai Potashnik on Vilna Street, in which approximately thirty members attended. The first meeting place of Hechalutz was in the house of David Lipkovitch on Smorgon Street. We began to operate in the area of culture. The teacher Tzvi Zeltzer and Noach Perski taught us Hebrew. We received *Hapoel Hatzair* and *Heatid* [The Future] from the Hechalutz Center (the central newspaper of Hechalutz in Poland) from the Land of Ysrael. David Yosef Kantorovitch received the booklets of Achdut Haavoda, read them to us, and explained their content. Zeltzer lectured about knowledge of the Land. Even the teacher Chaim Golobanchick did his part in the cultural activities of the chapter.

The first group of Hechalutz on the day of Tisha B'Av 5686 (July 20, 1926)

Standing right to left: Kehat Segalovitch, Mordechai Schwartzberg, Tzvi Perski, David Yitzchak Kantorovtch
Seated: Chaim Derechinski, Simcha Perski, Yitzchak Perski, someone not from Volozhin, Meir Baksht
Next to him: Tvi Tzart

We did not merely suffice ourselves with cultural work. We knew well that Hechalutz required the soul, that is, *aliya* to the Land of Israel. In the year 5684 (1925), Bankover visited Volozhin once again and lectured in the *Kleizl* on the topic of "What I saw and heard in the Land of Israel." In his lecture, he called upon us to go out to the

[Page 400]

Hachshara Kibbutzim to prepare ourselves for a life of labor and creativity in the Land of Israel. His words enthused the hearts. The result was the founding of a *Hachshara* group in Aroptzu, which was called *Hakovesh*. This group was composed of people from Smorgon, Rakov, Vileyka, and Oshmiana. From among the members of Hechalutz who participated in this group, we remember the names of Eliyahu Schneider (Shnay). The group was housed in the house of Bernstein the smith. Liberman from Smorgon, a member of *Hapoel Hatzair*, served as secretary. The group members earned their livelihoods from work in the flourmills and sawmills of Volozhin. The wood was brought from the Fishlivitz Forest, and we worked at cutting it. The group existed for about a half a year. Members of Hechalutz also founded a *Hachshara* group in Jezupol.

A group of pioneers in Polak's sawmill in the year 5684 (1934)

Right to left: Shneur Kivilovitch, Eliezer Lavit, Etl Shaker, Shmuel Polak, Musia Rogovin

We also searched for other means of *Hachshara*. There was a vegetable garden in Aroptzu. We worked there, and also guarded it at night. David Yitzchak Kantorovitch, who had agricultural knowledge, served as the guide. Chaim Potashnik and Chaim Binya Kahanovitch taught the trade of sawmilling. Eliyahu Weisbord and Shimon Tabachovitch taught sawmilling in Oshmiana. There was also a *Hachshara* group there called Arza where carpentry was taught under the direction of a counselor who was sent from the Hechalutz headquarters. Mordechai Yudel Schwartzberg worked in Jezupol with Shiff, and Ben-Zion Kaplan went to *Hachshara* near Rakov.

[Page 401]

The first ones of Volozhin Hechalutz to make Aliya to the Land of Israel

From right to left: Standing (right to left) Zelig Meltzer, Fania Kivilovitch, Shimon Tabachovitch,
Eliezer Lavit, Yaakov Girzon
Seated: – , Chaim Binya Kahanovitch, Chaim Potashnik, Esther Shaker
Seated on the ground: – , David Yitzchak Kantorovitch

In order to strengthen the activities of the chapter, we made sure that several of our members would make *aliya* to the Land. Chaim Potashnik was certified for *aliya*, and he made *aliya* in May 5684 (1924). About a half a year later, Nachum Gelman and Chaim Binya Kahanovitch made *aliya*. In 5685 (1925), Yaakov Girzon and Fania Kivilovitch made *aliya*. Fania was accepted as a member of Kibbutz Ramat *Hakovesh*.

After Chaim Binya Kahanovitch made *aliya* to the Land, Yitzchak Perski was chosen as chairman of the chapter. Yitzchak was very fit for his task. The chapter grew during his tenure. This growth placed two problems before us: cultural and economic. Yitzchak concerned himself with both. There were several lads in Volozhin who had graduated from the Tarbut Seminary in Vilna. Yitzchak enlisted them for work. First, he brought his brother Noach, who was a teacher, into this job. A painful and worrisome gap in the area of cultural activity was formed when Noach left Volozhin. Yitzchak attempted unsuccessfully to attract various members to this activity. Therefore, it was decided to hire a teacher for pay. He hired the teacher Zeltzer, who taught

[Page 402]

us Hebrew, knowledge of the Land, history of the Zionist congresses, and the history of the new settlement of the Land of Israel.

The members who were certified for *aliya* placed before us serious financial issues, for some of them were lacking in means, and it was necessary to finance their *aliya* to the Land. Yitzchak organized a performance, the income of which was dedicated to the *aliya* of an impoverished pioneer who was liable to lose his certificate.

Yitzchak Perski stood on guard as a faithful soldier until he made *aliya* to the Land in the year 5682 (1932). Shlomo Berger, Etl Chritzki, and Mina Perski also made *aliya* that year. After Perski made *aliya*, Shlomo Avraham Liberman was chosen as head of the chapter. The chapter was located in the home of Dovka in Aroptzu, and numbered about fifty male and female members. Later, it moved to the Tarbut school building.

A regional convention of all chapters of Hechalutz took place in Horodok in the year 5682 (1932), with the participation of Yeshayahu Pundik. His aim was to encourage the members to go to *Hachshara* and to make *aliya* to the Land.

First members of Hechalutz in the Land of Israel

Standing right to left: Aryeh Luboshitz, Aryeh Shulman, Chaim Potashnik, Shimon Tabachovitch
Seated: Tzvi Rogovin, Yaakov Girzon, Meir Baksht

Members of the chapter also participated in the summer *moshava* that took place in Smorgon. Approximately three hundred members, male and female, gathered there from all chapters of the region. The *moshava* took place in the forest. The participants lived a life of difficulty. They slept on the ground or on attics, and crowded into a small, abandoned house. All this was to inoculate the participants to the difficult life conditions awaiting them in the Land of Israel. The *moshava* took place

[Page 403]

under primitive natural conditions. A ditch was dug, and a sort of round "table" was formed. The ditch served as the chair for everyone, upon which they sat around the "table" and ate.

This *moshava* contributed greatly to the increase of the pioneering tension. It cut the participants off from city life. They stopped finding content and interest in such life. From that point, their entire desire was to go to *Hachshara* and to make *aliya* to the Land of Israel. Indeed, they began to go to *Hachshara*. Batya Botwinik, Esther Grynberg, Chaim Tzvi Potashnik, Fruma Rogovin, Sara Rudnitzki, and Sara Rappoport went. They were certified for *aliya* and returned to Volozhin after about a year. The chapter then grew and developed greatly.

Hechalutz in the year 5699 (1928)

Standing right to left: Shlomo Skliot, Sara Rudnitzki, Chasia Daul. David Yitzchak Kantorovitch, Sara Rappoport, Sonia Dolnov, Rafael Skliot, Aharon (Areh) Rogovin Second row: Liba Dolgov, Chasel Perski, Avraham – , Matityahu (Mates) Skliot, Chaim Perski, Gitel Perski, Simcha Perski, Sonia Perski, Chaim from Vyshniva, Eshka (Esther) Rudnik, Batya Botwinik, Michael Perski

Since the Zionist leadership was forced to expedite the exodus of the Jews from Germany –

[Page 404]

not too many certificates remained for the Hechalutz movement. For this reason, Sara Rudnitzki and Sara Rappoport returned to the *Hachshara* Kibbutz and waited for approval for *aliya*.

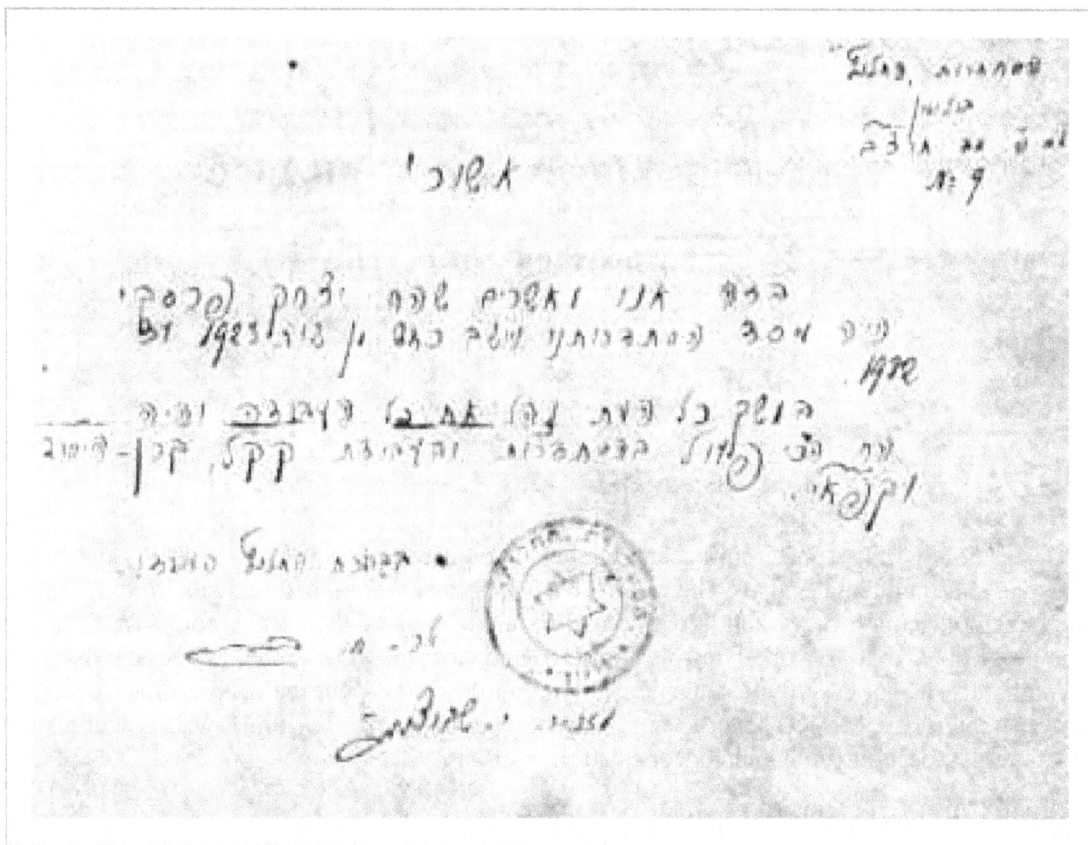

Volozhin Hechalutz chapter certification

"5 Av, 5692 [1932]. Number 9. We hereby confirm that Yitzchak Perski was the founder of our organization and chairman from 1923 to 1932. He led all the activities through all that time, and he was the most active member in the organization, in the work for the Jewish National Fund, Keren Hayesod, and the fund for the Land of Israel.

With greetings to Hechalutz Haoved!

[unsure of main signature]
Secretary, Y. Schwartzberg"

Winds of agony began to blow in Volozhin. Anti-Semitism raised its head. The Jews were under the staff and at the mercy of those wicked people. Means of livelihood were closed. However, our dear families lived their day-to-day lives without considering that they were standing on the threshold of the end of days.

The decline of Hechalutz in Volozhin began in the year 5698 (1938), the last year before the outbreak of the Second World War. The lack of certificates was the decisive factor to this decline. The members had waited for *aliya* for many years. Despair overtook them when their hopes were dashed. They stood before a sealed wall, without means of salvation.

The members of Hechalutz walked about dismayed and mourning. They were locked between their desire for the Land and the necessity of remaining in Volozhin. They bore in their hearts the flame of hope to be graced with the soil of the Land – until it was extinguished with the Soviet invasion of our city.

[Page 405]

Pioneering *Hachshara* in Yuzefpol

By Leah Nachshon-Shiff (Tel Aviv)

Translated by Jerrold Landau

based on an earlier translation by Moshe Porat z"l

that was edited by Judy Feinsilver Montel

In the year 5685 (1925), Yuzefpol became a site for pioneering *Hachshara*. A group of about thirty young people, male and female, arrived here for *Hachshara*. People from many towns from the entire area, far from Yuzefpol, came to work and live kibbutz life and to prepare themselves for *aliya* to the Land of Israel. Some of the Christian workers of the flourmill and sawmill were exchanged for Jewish male and female youths. It was not easy in those days to fire a gentile worker, but the deep Zionist feelings of the owners of the enterprise, Mr. Kuchevetski and, may he live long, Mr. Meir Shiff, who is with us today in the Land, and their desire to help the pioneers, had their effect.

Count Tyszkiewicz' large house, with its empty rooms, were filled with the *Hachshara* people. The quiet place, which had never heard Jewish and Hebrew songs to that point, became a pioneering center. The supervisor would awaken the pioneers early in the morning for work. Hebrew songs were sung by the youths, and the echoes spread afar. It seemed that the entire splendid landscape stood silent in honor of this event.

The pioneers worked with great dedication. Their work was exemplary. Their sole aim was to prepare themselves for *aliya* to the Land of Israel, to become accustomed to kibbutz life and a life of labor, for the Land is in need of people of toil.

One day, the first group left Yuzefpol and made *aliya* to the Land of Israel. After some time, another group came in its place. This is how things continued for many years until the destruction.

The Hachshara Group of Hechalutz Hamizrachi in Volozhin

By the lawyer Aryeh Charutz of Jerusalem

Translated by Jerrold Landau

based on an earlier translation by M. Porat z"l

that was edited by Judy Feinsilver Montel

After three years of study in the Etz Chaim Yeshiva of Volozhin, an idea entered my mind, which did not give me even a moment of rest. Longing for the Land of Israel awakened within me. However, I could not join Hechalutz in Volozhin, for its members seemed to me as not observant of our traditions. I decided to travel to Vilna and to join a group of religions pioneers who were close to my spirit.

However, suddenly an event happened that had great reverberations in Volozhin in its time, because it was an exception to the day-to-day events of the city. This is what happened: There was a lad named Moshe Yaakov Kwiat (today Perach) in the Yeshiva. He was twenty years old. He was an energetic lad, with a good mind, and very diligent in his studies.

[Page 406]

Many prominent householders spoke honorably about him, but he did not want to hear about a match whose heart was not in the Land of Israel, for he was a great idealist. Therefore, he imagined a bride who would make *aliya* to the Land together with him after the wedding. He searched, and found Malka Shishko, a young woman from an honorable family, and married her.

Two days after his wedding, Yaakov Moshe went to Vilna to see about arranging his *aliya* to the Land as a person in possession of a sum of money. However, he was not certified for *aliya* because he did not have the entire sum of money necessary for this. I met him in the Yeshiva hall after his return from Vilna. He took out a sheet of paper from his pocket, gave it to me, and said, "Only this remains with me as a consolation. However, who knows, I may find appropriate people whom I can organize and work together in some matter." On the piece of paper, it was written that the Mizrachi organization in Vilna authorized Moshe Yaakov Kwiat to organize a chapter of Hechalutz Hamizrachi in Volozhin, and would support it in a time of need.

Moshe Yaakov doubted whether it would be possible to find Yeshiva students who would be willing to close their Gemaras and go to agricultural *Hachshara*. However, his concern was for naught. I told Moshe Yaakov: I will be the first member of Hechalutz Hamizrachi that you intend to organize. Another three of the finest Yeshiva students came to register as members: Moshe Dovid Namiot, Yosef Goldstein, and Moshe Golub.

The matter was kept as a deep secret among us. There was not even a hint of this in the Yeshiva. All the meetings were held in a private house, behind closed doors and covered windows, and with a special guard, or in the open air on Mount Bialik. At these meetings, it was firmly decided: we will work, we will go hungry and suffer, as long as we will attain our goals. Since every activity demands money, each of us decided to give over the money that we would receive from the Yeshiva after paying our hosts. Of course, from this alone we could not collect significant sums that we required. Therefore, Moshe Yaakov went along with another person who took interest in our situation to speak to the hearts of the well-off householders who were members of Mizrachi, asking them to come to our aid. To our great joy, the Mizrachi members of Volozhin responded positively. The first to come to our aid was Rabbi Yisrael Lunin, a philanthropist of many deeds and a communal activist. About another ten Jews were found, and we collected a sum of over one hundred dollars to form the Hechalutz Hatzair fund. Our joy was boundless, and we decided to immediately go out to work.

Moshe Yaakov began to search for a place where we could study agriculture. He searched and found a very fitting place for our aims, with Reb Ber of Brilki.

Reb Ber's lands, which was called "Maleh Berki," stood on a small hill surrounded by fields. It included the residential home of the owners – an old wood house – and two granaries next to each other, adjacent to the house. Reb Ber, his wife, and three children lived in one room, which served as a dining room, kitchen, and bedroom. There were two other small rooms in the house. One served as our residence, after undergoing a thorough cleaning.

There were six members in our group: Moshe Yaakov Kwiat (Perach), his wife Malka Shishko,

[Page 407]

Shmuel David Namiot (Oholi), Aryeh Charutz, Moshe Golub, and Yosef Goldstein. It was created on the intermediate days of Passover of 5685 (1925). On that festival, which is the symbol of freedom, we took upon ourselves the yoke of pioneering actualization. We unanimously decided to go to Maleh Berki immediately after the festival. The last day of Passover was a difficult day full of thoughts – especially when the day was over, and night fell upon the land. That was the last night that we would spend in Volozhin. How difficult it is for a person to change his way of life without first taking council with their relatives or acquaintances. We did all this without the permission of our parents, lest they impede us.

The Hanatziv Group of Hechalutz Hamizrachi on *Hachshara* in Maleh Berki

Upon the horses, on the right: Aryeh Charutz, on the left: Yosef Goldstein
Standing right to left: Rivka Miriam Namiot, Leibel Liberman, Tzirel (daughter of the baker in Aroptzu), Etl Shishko, Moshe Yaakov Perach (Kwiat), Freidel Berman, Shmuel David Oholi (Namiot), Sheindel (daughter of Reb Shimon der Bord)
Seated on the ground: Moshe Golub, Leibel Shptnitzki, Malka Shishko

Early in the morning, our small group assembled next to Moshe Yaakov's house. Each of us brought our suitcases and placed them in the wagon prepared for that purpose. All our faces were pale and weary, testifying to the thoughts and worries that disturbed our sleep on that final night. However, it was enough to look into the flaming eyes to understand and appreciate the strength of our hearts at that moment. The time was very early, so nobody could be seen outside as we were loading the wagon. After some time, all preparations were concluded, and the wagon, laden with our belongings, agricultural tools and kitchenware, quietly left

[Page 408]

the city, and set out in the direction of Maleh Berki. Some of our friends from Yeshiva, to whom we had revealed the secret, came to accompany us to the edge of the city. They parted from us with warm, heartfelt blessings.

Our wagon slowly advanced through the fields, in which farmers plowing their land could be seen here and there. We said to ourselves: How fortunate will we be when we can already plow the soil of the Land of Israel like those farmers. We discussed our future way of life throughout the entire journey, and we promised ourselves with complete faith to be dedicated to the work, as well as to set times for the study of Torah.

When we were about three kilometers from Volozhin, we gazed back at it, and the white Yeshiva building could be seen before our eyes, standing in a prominent area. Our hearts were filled with unique thoughts, which are hard to express in words. We decided to preserve the traditions of the Yeshiva in our hearts, so that they would forever illuminate our paths.

We arrived in Maleh Berki after about an hour. Sadness was poured out in all corners, for it was far from any human settlement. The only thing that comforted us slightly was the nearby railway track, and the train cars that whistled as they passed by a few times a day.

We began to concern ourselves with a dwelling place. When the estate owner showed us the room set aside for us, we remained standing in our place, astonished and amazed. The room was narrow and dark, with a small hole instead of a window. It was half filled with all sorts of rags, rusty scarp iron, and other such "finds." Nevertheless, we did not despair, and we immediately started to clean the room, which served may purposes for us: we prayed there, partook of our meals there, studied Gemara and other holy books, and also read newspapers and books on Zionist topics. We went to the barn only to sleep.

Among the fields that we leased from Reb Ber, there was a plot of land of land next to the house, a desyatin in area[1], which we set aside as a vegetable garden. It was in that area that we received our first lessons in agricultural methodology. Our teacher was an elderly gentile named Makar, one of the servants of the yard. Plowing was the most difficult of all the jobs for us. It was literally a difficult as the splitting of the Red Sea. As if to vex us, that area of our garden was on an incline, and the horse was stubborn and did not want to drag the plow on the ascent. We did not succeed in plowing even one furrow in a straight line. When Reb Ber once showed us that he could plow straight furrows by holding the plow in one hand only, it seemed like a wonder to our eyes, and we though that not every person could succeed at this.

It did not take long for us to learn the art of agriculture in a satisfactory manner. At that point, we were no longer astonished at the sight of a person plowing straight furrows. Reb Ber, who at first complained that we were ruining his land, now even asked us to plow his soil during our free time. Piles of grass, uprooted roots, and stones of various shapes and sizes were collected around our garden, and surprised any onlooker. We had removed all these from the soil that was given to us neglected and overgrown with thorns and thistles, even after we had plowed the area four times.

Volozhin was like a distant place during the time that we worked in Maleh Berki. From the day that the Jews

[Page 409]

of the city found out about our revolutionary activity, they did not stop taking interest in us. Opinions were divided, but most judged us positively. A new spirit came over the youth of the city. They began to think thoughts that had never even entered their imagination previously. They began to believe things that they had never previously believed. Moshe Yaakov received a letter requesting to open an official office for members who wish to register for Hechalutz Hamizrachi. Indeed, within a short time this office was opened. Even girls registered, and after a short time, Freidel the daughter of Reb Leib was sent to us to ease the burden of the housework.

We began to sow our garden with joy, enthusiasm and song. It consisted of 120 beds, each of the forty feet in length. The beds were ordered nicely and in good taste. We planted the rest of the fields with oats, flax, and potatoes. We worked in the field from morning until night. When we returned from work tired and weary, we did not forget to study a page of Gemara after the *Maariv* service.

We felt the holiness of the Sabbath in a special manner during those days. How pleasant was the day of rest for us after a week of effort and toil. We felt the holiness of the Sabbath immediately after sunset on Friday. We bathed, got dressed up, and prepared to welcome the Sabbath Queen with holy awe. It was our custom every week to partake of our Sabbath meals in the company of Reb Ber and his family.

There was a large, thick forest near Reb Ber's land. My friend Shmuel David and I chose it as the location for our Sabbath morning prayers, which were conducted at sunrise. There, in the forest, there was nobody to disturb us from concentrating on the sublime words of the prayers. We marched slowly along a hidden path, covered with soft grass. We walked next to each other, and uttered the precious words of the prayers word for word.

In the meantime, the work in Maleh Berki concluded. We received a directive from Moshe Yaakov to return to Volozhin with our belongings, so that we could go to another workplace. We parted from Maleh Berki and arrived in Volozhin, ready and prepared for anything that would be imposed upon us. Moshe Yaakov informed us that we were to go to work in the forest. We began to prepare the axes and saws necessary for that work.

We went on our wagons to our new workplace in the forest, a distance of twenty kilometers. There was only one of us, Chaim, who knew the way somewhat. When we reached the designated area, the sun had already been illuminating for a while the area, full of a bounty of forests. After we ate, we went out to work. We were very tired after a sleepless night, but we nevertheless girded ourselves and work.

It took about two hours for us to cut down our first tree. Our dismay was great when we realized that we could not even earn our dry bread in such a manner. We looked at the fruits of our labors, and barely saw anything. We returned home with broken, oppressed hearts, for al our hopes were disappearing and weakening…

Our work in the forest was difficult and our income was restricted. It was sufficient for basic necessities only. Worse than that was the loneliness, which afflicted us greatly. Our souls longed for spiritual satisfaction, which we did not find among the thickets of the large forest or in the village that was far from a Jewish settlement and filled with coarse farmers. We then received a letter from Moshe Yaakov, telling us to return to Maleh Berki, for

[Page 410]

the fruits had ripened, and everything must be removed from the fields. We hastened to gather our belongings, discharged our debts to the farmers, and returned to Maleh Berki.

In Maleh Berki, we received news that the member Reuven Finger of Vilna was coming to examine us, to determine whether our knowledge of issues of the Land of Israel and Zionism was sufficient. We went to Volozhin for this examination. The member Finger spoke before us about the goals of Hechalutz Hamizrachi. The next morning, he visited our kibbutz in Maleh Berki and was satisfied with our work. The Labor Division certified us for *aliya* as "the knowledgeable of the knowledgeable." After a brief time, we traveled to Warsaw and were certified also by the consulary.

We returned to Volozhin victorious after we achieved our desired goal. The entire city accompanied us as we left Volozhin on our way to the Land. They all rejoiced with our joy. They accompanied us a great distance even those it was a cold, rainy day. The honorable philanthropist, Reb Yisrael Lunin, the first supporter of our kibbutz, delivered a heartfelt speech that concluded with good wishes for our settlement on the Holy Land and our success as citizens of the Land of Israel

Translator's footnote:

1.   An old Russian unit of measure, approximately a hectare.

Note and additional photo from Mr. M. Porat z"l:

Moshe Yaakov Perach (Kwiat) with his spouse Malka (Shishko) settled in the agricultural Moshava Karkur after they made *aliya* from Maleh Berki.

Binyamin Perach

Binyamin Perach, son of Moshe Yaakov and Malka Perach (Kwiat) became an active member in the Haganah. He participated in many battles during the War of Independence. He fell in the Negev battle on December 28, 1948. He was 22 years old.

[Page 410]

Beitar in Volozhin

By Beitar members

Translated by Jerrold Landau

based on an earlier translation by Moshe Porat z"l

that was edited by Judy Feinsilver Montel

A Beitar chapter was founded in Volozhin in 5688 (1929) as a Zionist-scouting movement without any political inclination. We were very few. The purpose was to gather the graduates of the Tarbut school into an organized structure. However, the Volozhin youth, who were alert to the issues of the times and to what was transpiring in the Zionist camp, were not satisfied with only sporting and cultural activities. They aspired to a political life. Mr. Chaim Golobanchich, the principal of the Tarbut school who had leanings toward the Revisionist movement, recommended that the chapter take on a right-leaning direction. His recommendation was accepted, and he turned his energies to travel to Vilna and bring a fitting counselor from there.

The principal brought Mr. Betzalel Lichtenstein (currently in Israel) from the Brit Trumpeldor movement, which became Beitar [acronym for Brit Yosef Trumpeldor] with the passage of time. Our first paths were not paved with roses. We encountered misunderstanding from many parents, who regarded our activities as "sharpening swords" and a waste of time. Nevertheless, the opposition abated through the influence of Mr. Golobanchich, who had a significant level of pedagogical authority, and many of the students of the Tarbut school registered for Beitar.

Members of the chapter were instructed to purchase pocket notebooks, in which they listed the "ten commandments" of scouts, which had to be actualized every day. All activities were conducted in Hebrew. Member of the chapter were called "Brothers" and "Sisters." The connection between the Brothers and Sisters with the counselors was especially strong and enthusiastic. The symbol of Beitar resembled a menorah, and was tied to the cap or the lapel. Instead of Shalom, the greeting was Tel Hai.

[Page 411]

Beitar leadership with Betzalel Lichtenstein on 28 Av 5688 (August 14, 1928)

Right to left: Efraim Rogovin, Batya German, Betzalel Lichtenstein, Dov Lavig, Baruch Mordechai Myerson

A leadership committee was chosen, with the following members: Shabtai Baksht, Batya German, Dov Lavit[1], Baruch Mordechai Myerson, Efraim Rogovin. Dov Lavit served as the first commander of the chapter. Batya German served as the secretary. After her death, Yisrael Berkovitch was appointed to that role.

Mr. Lichtenstein divided the members of the chapter into groups according to age and gender. The members of the leadership committee served as group heads. The difficult, tiring work of Mr. Lichtenstein bore fruit. After a brief time, the chapter numbered about eighty Brothers and Sisters.

Through the influence of Mr. Golobanchich, the hall of the Tarbut School was put at our disposal during evenings. In general, the group heads conducted educational activities. However, from time to time, local speakers were invited, who lectured, among other things, about the history of the Zionist movement and the geography of the Land of Israel. Mr. Chaim Golbanchich, Mr. Chaim Derechinsky, and Mr. Binyamin Shishko were among the speakers. One of the important cultural activities was the wall newspaper, in which the fruits of the pen of members of the chapter were published.

In time, our space in the Tarbut school became too small, and we rented a room in a private house. We covered the costs through amateur performances that we performed.

The chapter aspired to "disseminate its wellsprings to the outside." To that end, we founded Beitar chapters in Vishnyeva,

[Page 412]

Beitar Chapter in the year 5688 (1928)

First Row, from top to bottom (left to right): Zalman Perski, Yosef Dubinski, David Buminovitch, Etka , Mina Berman, Hinda Rudnik, Feigel Kramnik, Beilka Mordechovitch, Lea Potashnik, Rachel Perski Kopel Kagan, Chaim Eli Perski.
Second row: Chaim Kisiel, Avraham Berman, Roda Alpert, Zlatka Lavit, Yisrael Berkovitch, Bela Potashnik, Peshka Rogovin, Chaim Alpert, Shmuel Berman, Yitzchak Perski.
Third row: Shabtai Baksht, Yaakov Berkovitch, Munia Dubinski, Dov Lavit, Chaim Golobanchich, Bella Kramnik, Eliezer Mazah, Shlomo Liberman, Yitzchak Kaplan.
Fourth row: Chaim Shalman, Tzila Perski, Hiene Rogovin, Miriam Rosenberg, Peretz Rogovin, Pesach Bormon, Perl Rudnik, Roza Berman, Rivka Perski.

[Page 413]

Trab, Ivanitz, Baksht, and Horodok. Threads to the other chapters extended forth from Volozhin, which served as the central city for the Beitar chapters in the region. Regional conventions took place in Volozhin, which left strong emotions in the city and contributed greatly to the strengthening and growth of the Zionist movement. Counselors of renown always participated in those conventions. These included Tzvi Berman from Baranovich, Gershon Ashkenazi and Yisrael Sorogovitch from Vilna (he changed his name to Tanai in Israel, and died a few years ago). In addition to the conventions, we also arranged summer camps outside Volozhin, that took on a definitive military character. One of the camps took place in the village of Rudnik. Similarly, we sponsored courses in [military] training, under the direction of Mr. Baruch Eidelman.

The Beitar chapter with the writer Daniel Perski on 14 Cheshvan 5689 (October 28, 1928)

Standing from top to bottom, left to right: Yitzchak Perski, Baruch Simernitzki, Ben-Zion Goldschmid, Leah Potashnik, Zlatka Lavit, Chaim Eli Perski, Eliezer Mazah, Leibel
Second row: Yaakov Berkovitch, Aryeh Dratvitzki, Leah Schwartzberg, Peshka Rogovin, Roda Alpert, Mina Berman, Rafael Shlosberg, Binyamin Kleinbord, Shlomo Berman
Third row: Yisrael , Baruch Mordechai Myerson, Dov Lavit, the writer Daniel Perski, Efraim Rogovin, Shabtai Baksht
Fourth row: Shmuel Berman, Aharon Golub, Kopel Kagan, Yitzchak Kaplan, Chasel Perski
Fifth row: Yaakov Rogovin, Yosef Dubinski, Shmaya, Chanan Rogovin

[Page 414]

One of the strongest experiences etched in our memories from my life in the chapter was the visit of the writer Daniel Perski, a relative of the *shochet* Reb Yehuda Avraham Perski. He was invited to the chapter, and we heard from him a speech full of content on a Zionist topic, which contributed to the deepening of our national knowledge.

We merited having talented and effective commanders, male and female. These included: Shabtai Baksht, Yaakov Berkovitch, Yisrael Berkovitch, Sonia Dubinski, Dov Lavit, Eliezer Mazah, Baruch Mordechai Myerson, Kopel Kagan, Binyamin Kleinbord, Bella Kramnik, Efraim Rogovin.

Our movement obligated personal actualization. To that end, members of the chapter went to *Hachshara*. The first *Hachshara* location was Nadworna.

Members of Beitar on *Hachshara* in Volozhin

Right to left: Leah Schwartzberg, Yaakov Berkovitch, Shmuel Rogovin, Mina Berman, Izik Girkop, Avraham Ber

The chapter stressed military *Hachshara* to its members. We placed a request to the commander of the border unit that camped in Volozhin to train our members in military maneuvers. They agreed to our request, and a commander was placed at our disposal. Similarly, we received guns and arms. Training took place next to Mount Bialik The P. W. (*Przysbosobienie wojskow*) was a semi-military organization that trained in the use of

[Page 415]

light weapons such as pistols, guns, gas masks, etc. The appearance of the Beitar members with their uniforms, armed with guns, grenades, and gas masks aroused awe and honor among many of the Jews of Volozhin, who regarded military *Hachshara* as the first step toward the great task that will fall upon the youth in its struggle for a Jewish state. However, these appearances also aroused negative reactions amongst certain circles of Volozhin Jewry, who regarded this as "militarism" and "playing with guns." Nevertheless, during the disturbances of 5689 (1929), even the doubters agreed to the importance of military *Hachshara*.[2]

A P.W. (military trainees) group of Beitar with the commander Efraim Rogovin
(Mount Bialik in the background, on the right)

Members of Beitar participated in military parades that took place on the national holidays of Poland. Their appearance was impressive. All the youth movements arranged themselves in the market square, and the Starosta would receive a report from the representatives of the youth movements, including the name of the movement, the number of participants, and the number of those absent.

[Page 416]

The command of the Beitar Chapter, with Gershon Ashkenazi, in the year 5690 (1930)

Standing, right to left: Binyamin Kleinbord, Yisrael Berkovitch, Yaakov Rogovin
Sitting: Efraim Rogovin, Bella Kramnik, Gershon Ashkenazi, Dov Lavit, Shabtai Baksht

When Dov Lavit went to *Hachshara* in the year 5690 (1930), Efraim Rogovin was appointed as head of the chapter. He did a great deal to strengthen and develop it. After a brief time, Efraim also went to *Hachshara*. Bella Kramnik was appointed as commander of the chapter in his place. Bella's contribution to the chapter from the time of its foundation until her *aliya* to the Land of Israel was recognized and successful. She knew how to forge deep soulful connections between herself and the members of the chapter. She was dedicated to the movement with all hear heart and soul. Bella and Efraim made *aliya* to the Land in the year 5693 (1933). The had a very emotional farewell from all the members of the chapter.

After Bella and Efraim made *aliya*, Eliezer Mazah was appointed as the commander of the chapter. The new command consisted of the following Brothers and Sisters: Nechama Lunin, Baruch Mordechai Myerson, Kopel Kagan, Binyamin Kleinbord, Peshka Rogovin (treasurer).

The chapter developed greatly during the final years before the Second World War. Many people from the Tarbut school joined Beitar under the influence of the teachers Yaakov Lipschitz and Gliker. At that time, the chapter numbers had about 160 Brothers and Sisters. It was awarded a token of excellence from the Beitar leadership for this. Mr. Aharon Propus (leader of Beitar) came to Volozhin to mark the occasion of the receiving

[Page 417]

Visit of member of the leadership command Gershon Ashkenazi to the Beitar chapter in Volozhin , 25, 26, 27 April 1930

Standing right to left: Binyamin Kleinbord, Chaim Alpert, Yaakov Berkovitch, Leibel Heler, Rafael Weisbord, Yisrael Berkovitch, Yochanan Gelman, Zlatka Lavit, Mina Berman, Rivka Kalik, Hershel Bunimovitch, Mina Berman, Y. Dolgov
Sitting (first row): Yitzchak Perski, Feiga Kramnik, Chasia Daul, Sonia Dubinsky, Hinda Rudnia, Shabtai Baksht, Gershon Ashkenazi, Dov Lavit, Efraim Rogovin, Bella Kramnik, Bella Potashnik, Shmuel Berman
Second row: â " , Chaim Eli Perski, Shlomo Berman, Kopel Kagan, David Bunimovitch, Aharon Golub, Yaakov Rogovin, Yosef Gelman, Chona Rogovin, Yitzchak Kaplan, Yaakov Skliot

[Page 418]

the award. When Mr. Menachem Began was chosen as the head of Beitar, he too visited Volozhin. Hs visit became a major event in the life of the chapter. We arranged a splendid reception. Mrs. Rikla Shepsnevel was very active in greeting the guest. She was very dedicated to the revisionist movement in Volozhin, and would often provide food for the members of Beitar when they went to the summer camp.

When Mazah was accepted as the teacher in a town close to Volozhin and left the city, Baruch Mordechai Myerson was appointed as commander of the chapter. Members of the command were Pesach Berman, Michael Garber, Tzvia Mazah, Eli Perski, Tzvi Tzart, and Yaakov Kagan. Tzipora Shepsnevel served as treasurer.

A brigade of Beitar members on an excursion into the Volokompia Forest in Vilna on 14 Av 5689 (August 20, 1929)

Standing, top to bottom, right to left: Yitzchak Perski, Efraim Rogovin, Aharon Propus, Kacharninski, Gershon Ashkenazi, Betzalel Lichtenstein, Dov Lavit, Chaim Kisiel, Hershel Bunimovitch
Second row: Eliezer Mazah, Yisrael Berkovitch, Sonia Dubinski, Lea Schwartzberg, Hynda Rudnik, Shabtai Baksht, Esther Berman, Bella Potashnik, Kopel Kagan
Third row: Chaim Eli Perski, Yitzchak Kaplan, David Bunimovitch, Chanan Rogovin, Aharon Golub, Yaakov Rogovin
Sitting on the ground: Binyamin Kleinbord, Baruch Simernitzki, Mina Berman, Chasia Daul, Yaakov Berkovitch, Pesia Rogovin, Mina Berman, Yochanan Gelman

[Page 419]

The chapter did not have a permanent meeting place even during that period, and it wandered from house to house. We put on performances on various topics in order to finance the expenses. Eliezer Mazah served as the stage producer. The performances were on the topic of current events. On the Tal Hai day, we performed a performance on the life of Josef Trumpeldor, and on the 20th of Tammuz, on the life of Herzl.

Even though the members of Beitar had few certificates, they still prepared themselves for physical labor in the land of Israel. A *Hachshara* enterprise of Beitar members existed in Yuzefpol, working for Mr. Schiff. In Volozhin they worked for Rappoport and Perlman.

The Polish government began to afflict the chapter during the latter years. The chapter would distribute *Shana Tova* cards, the income of which was for the benefit of the chapter. Once, Tzvia Mazah and Tzipora Shepsnevel went out to distribute the greeting cards, and they were stopped by a policeman. They were taken to the Gmina building on Vilna Street, where the police were headquartered, and imprisoned there, since they did not have an appropriate permit. The city notables worked for their freedom, and they turned into the "heroes of the day."

Years passed, years of hope and faith, until the skies darkened and foretold the advent of the Second World War, the war of destruction of the Jews of Europe. The Jews of Volozhin waited tensely and with worry for what was going to happen. The events developed at a dizzying speed. The Polish government collapsed a few days after the outbreak of the war, and the Soviets entered Volozhin. The spirits were very depressed. Tzvia Mazah, David Shmerkovitch, and Tzipora Shepsnevel hurried to Mordechai Myerson, took the key to the locale from him in haste, and burnt all the documents. The Beitar flag and the medal of excellence were placed into a can and buried in the ground.

The Beitar members were under no illusions. They knew what awaited them. Therefore, they decided to escape from Volozhin and find their way to the coast of the Land of Israel. Already in the year 5698 (1938), Pesach Berman and Peretz Rogovin made *aliya* with Aliya Bet [The Second Aliya wave]. Pnina Rudnik made *aliya* in the year 5699 (1939) on the Parita ship. Many members of the chapter went to Vilna, which served as the gateway to the Land of Israel during those days. Those who went included Sara Bunimovitch, Nechama Lunin, Tzvi Lunin, Baruch Mordechai Myerson, Yaakov Finger, Yaakov Kagan, Peshka Rogovin, Leibel Schwartzberg, David Shmerkovitch, Chaya Liba Shepsnevel, Tzipora Shepsnevel.

David Shmerkovitch moved the can with the flag and the medal of excellence to Vilna. The flag was hidden in the ground, and the medal of excellence given over to Tzipora Shepsnevel. She guarded it carefully through all her wanderings and tribulations, and she still has it.

From the time of its founding, the chapter knew no crisis or schism. Every Brother and Sister knew their path. They cleaved to their faith, and accepted the doctrine of Jabotinsky upon themselves in its full essence, for they were convinced that this was the one and only path that would lead us upright to our land.

The chapter only existed for eleven years. During those few years, it became a great force, which earned the appreciation of many of the Jews of Volozhin. The chapter was the living spirit in Zionist activity in Volozhin. It conducted the main work on behalf of the national funds. Similarly, it worked to collect money for the

[Page 420]

Beitar Chapter in Volozhin , Vilna Region, 1932
Members of the Beitar chapter in the year 5692 (1932) with the member Dov Lavit before his *aliya* to the
Land of Israel (Dov Lavit is sitting in the middle, wearing a hat)

[Page 421]

Beitar graduates and "Soldiers league" members during the visit of Lipa Leviatan from the Land of Israel on 7 Kislev 5695 (November 13, 1934)

Standing from top to bottom, right to left:
1st row: Yona Shapira Freidel Kramnik, Pesach Berman, Tzvia Lunin, Leibel Shalman, Tzila Perski, daughter of Avraham "Asher Yatzar", Rafael Schlosberg, son-in-law of Sharira, Binyamin Kleinbord, Feigel Kramnik, Chaim Itshe Oreh.
2nd row: Peretz Rogovin, Shlomo Meltzer, Anya Rubin, Lipa Leviatan, Rivka Perski, Avraham Berkovitch, Baruch Mordechai Myerson, Mordechai Maretzki, Yaakov Lipschitz.
3rd row: Peshka Rogovin, Elyokim Zimerman, Rivka Rogovin, Chinka Rogovin, Itka Kalik, Leibel Schwartzberg, Chaim the son of the lawyer, Moshe Kaplan, David Bunimovitch.

Tarbut school. During the years of crisis and decline, the chapter stood at the pinnacle of its guard, and stuck to its faith that the nation of Israel is alive, and that we will merit to see the rise of the Jewish state already in our days.

Through the influence of Beitar, the league of Revisionist Zionists was founded in Volozhin, headed by Shlomo Chaim Brodna, Chaim Yitzchak Weisbord, and Avraham Tzart. Similarly, *Brit Hachayal* [Soldiers League] was founded, with the leadership of Avraham Berkovitch, Shmayahu Chadash, Mordechai Maretzki, Shlomo Meltzer, Shneur Kivilivitch, A. Rubin, Reuven Rosenberg, and others. All of them were army veterans.

Translator's footnotes:

1.　　Mr. M. Porat z"l notes that he was the first head of the Organization of Volozhin Natives in Israel.

2.　　There is an editor's note at this point, appearing on the bottom of page 415: Editor's note: Those who mocked the "militarism" did so through the lack of knowledge of the history of the new settlement in the Land of Israel. Jabotinsky of blessed memory was not the first to speak about this. He was preceded by the people of the First Aliya. Zeev Dubnow, the brother of the historian Simon Dubnow, wrote on November 1, 1882, from Jaffa to his brother, among other things: "In dreams, then the splendid day will arrive, whose coming was foretold by Isaiah in his enthusiastic visions of comfort. Then, the Jews themselves will announced that with hand weapons (if there will be a need for such), and a loud voice as masters of their ancient land." (See David Ben-Gurion, The First Ones, published in the government annual publication, 5723 [1963], page 32.)

[Page 422]

On *Hachshara* in Volozhin

By Rachel Kna'any (Berman) of Merchavya

Translated by Jerrold Landau

based on an earlier translation by M. Porat z"l

that was edited by Judy Feinsilver Montel

I arrived in Volozhin in 5693 (1933). It was a period of rapid expansion of the *Hachshara* network in Poland – of Hechalutz and the pioneering youth movements. I came together with a group of thirty people. It was the first detachment of "Hasadan" (the Anvil), the *Hachshara* Kibbutz of Shomer Hatzair members from Vilna and its vicinity, which included my hometown of Rakov. We arrived, a group of youngsters at the age of eighteen-nineteen, during a cold winter, on a wagon hitched to horses – the sole form of transportation in the region during those days.

I have already forgotten the name of the street where we lived. Polak's sawmill was on that street. We worked there and earned our meager salary. The *Hachshara* location included, in total, a small dining room, a kitchen,

Hashomer Hatzair members in Volozhin in 5694 (1934)

Standing from right to left: a lad from Vilna, Yocheved Dolnov, Avraham Perski, Gittel Rappoport, a lad from Vilna.
Sitting: Rachel Perski, a lad from Rakov, Hynda Rudnik, a lad from Vilna, Lea, Yitzchak Kaplan.
Sitting below: Eliyahu Naroshevitch, Alta Horodishetz, Mordechai Eliyahu Girzon.

[Page 423]

and a common bedroom for all of us. It was impossible to stuff forty beds into the room, so we installed *Narot*, simple wooden boards through the entire length of the room, on two floors. Even so, the place was too small, and several members had to sleep in the attic. We slept in indescribable crowding – males and females together. It is possible that you will not believe it – and the Jews of the city barely believed it – but to the best of my knowledge, there was a high level of morality, opposite of what would be expected from youths, but completely appropriate to the spirit in which we were educated in Hashomer Hatzair.

The small kitchen had a wide brick oven. It served for cooking our meager meals and at times for baking bread. There was a curtain spread on the corner next to the oven, with a bowl where the girls washed their body in front of the oven. (On rare occasions, due to the cost, we all went to the bathhouse, with the treasurer marching proudly at the head.) This was the sole private, "intimate" corner in the *Hachshara*, for there was no "private area" in which to gather, or in which to remain alone – in the same manner that we did not know of private property, even of the smallest item, due to strict adherence to commonality and equality. We had no clothes other than those on our bodies. At times, when I got up, I did not even know which shoes I should put on when I went out for work. The shoes that were gathered in the shoe area were designated for me for that day – and would be worn again by someone on night guard…

We were young girls, but we worked very hard. It was literally backbreaking work according to current conceptions. To us it seemed like a very simple matter, and we did not have any grievances. We chose this path, and we desired it. In the sawmill, we had to fill sacks of sawdust and haul them on our backs to the large field. We had to empty the sacks at the top of the heap, so that it turned into a high mountain of lumber. The mountain got higher from day to day, and we were forced to climb to the top with a hunched back and a heavy load. The pace of work was quick, like the pace of a machine. The sawmill room was small. If we did not succeed in emptying it, it would fill up with sawdust and the machine would get clogged.

Dragging the board remnants (obrezki in the vernacular) after sawing the planks was a different job. We would carry a large bundle of boards under our arms. They took on the form of a very long broom. We would haul them to the tall mountain. There were days when we arranged the boards in the form of a square. We, the boys and girls, would also go out to cut trees and saw them in the yards of the Jews of Volozhin. The work was difficult, but, as I have said, we accepted it lovingly, for we had come to prepare ourselves for the hard work waiting for us in the Land of Israel. Our salary was very low, approximately one zloty per day. We often suffered from lack of work.

How wondrous was it, then, that our food was very simple: bread, tea, potatoes, and soup It was the same on weekdays, Sabbaths, and festivals. It is difficult for me to believe today how we maintained ourselves and how our health did not weaken at all. The only "excess" food we had was fresh bread after work or on the Sabbath. As we lay on our beds, we would take a loaf of bread and devour it with enjoyment. I recall fondly the baker from Volozhin who gave us bread on credit, and did not stop even when we owed him a large sum.

[Page 424]

It must be said that the Jews of Volozhin generally related to us well. They showed appreciation to us and even understood our situation. I was sent as a "seamstress" to the homes of the wealthiest families. I had to cut and sew underwear, clothes, etc. My experience in this work was almost zero, and I made many mistakes. However, my employers did not scold me. They only smiled, and paid my salary.

Our lack of experience was felt in everything: in work, in cooking, and in organizing our lives. Regarding the sub-par, insufficient food, the hard work, and the crowded living spaces – our hygienic situation was frightening. A difficult, irritating, physically draining disease broke out: scabies. I and a girl from Vilna were designated as medics. Our job was to smear the backs of the members every night with lead paste that we made with our own hands. I "merited" a difficult embarrassment: I went to the pharmacy to purchase a large quantity of materials to prepare the paste. The pharmacist told me coarsely: "Nu, from this day and onward, you will be free from searching for work. You will be busy with scratching…" I kept this insult to my friends in the recesses of my heart for a long time.

We were proud of our hard work, of our strong will, and of the kibbutz-style way of life. We were very careful that there should not be, Heaven forbid, any breach in equality. There was complete equality. It was curious: Excess money, such as for a move or the theater, we of course did not have. The lads of Volozhin would visit us on occasion, and they would invite us to a movie on occasion. "Us" of course refers only to the girls. A storm broke out. The boys rose up and complained about the discrimination. A meeting of the kibbutz was convened, and it was decided to accept the offer of the lads of the city, but in turn – for both the boys and the girls. However, this was not the intention of the philanthropists of Volozhin, and they stopped inviting the *Hachshara* members to the cinema.

We had our own means of enjoyment: singing together for long hours at night, reading books, kibbutz discussions, hikes in the area, youthful joy, and mischief, all together. One of our members, with a sharp sense of humor, lay on his bed in a dark room when an emissary of the movement came from the Land, imitated the cry of a baby and cried bitterly in the voice of a young woman about the tragedy that occurred to "her": "she" had given birth to a baby. The emissary started a conversation with him, and urged "her" in a lengthy fashion to leave Volozhin so that our ill repute will not spread in the city. The "woman who gave birth" refused strongly and claimed that if we were expelled, she would cast herself into the river… We could no longer control ourselves, and we put on the lights…

We participated in a very different type of experience with all the Jews of the city, a moving "performance." A robber wreaked havoc on the paths around Volozhin. One day, a Jew of the city was murdered. The robber was captured, and we all went to watch as he was taken out to be killed – because of youthful curiosity and because of feelings of revenge over the murder of a Jew. To this day, I can see the scene before my eyes in all its minute details: the green meadow and grove next to it, the executioner dressed in black, the sun above our heads, the expressionless murderer being brought to the gallows, and the stool pushed away from beneath his feet…

One murderer received his punishment. Who will avenge the spilled blood of thousands of Jews of the city? Who will punish their murderers? How is it possible to imaging the sight of Volozhin without Jews?

[Page 425]

Keren Kayemet L' Israel (JNF) in Volozhin

By Binyamin Shapir (Shishko), Karkur, Israel

First half translated by Naomi Gal and lightly edited by Jerrold Landau

, second half translated by Jerrold Landau

Donated by Anita Frishman Gabbay

Activities for JNF [Jewish National Fund] in Volozhin were an important part of the Jewish life in the city. The building of the Tarbut School with the blue and white sign, reminded the citizens that their homeland is in Zion. One could feel the ambience of the Land of Israel in this building. Anyone who went in – be it a child or an elderly person – was a partner in the revival and for *aliya* for the Land of Zion. Between the walls of this house each "circle" found its own corner. Hechalutz, Shomer Hatzair, Beitar – they were all in the same home. Points of view were different, but the common ground turned them all to one family – the family of Zion's children.

The JNF council, under the direction of Rabbi Israel Lunin (representing

The Bazar's committee ("The Market") of JNF on 15-16 Tammuz, 5693 (9–10 July 1933)

Standing (right to left): A. Shlomo Skliot, B. Polia Farber, C. Lea Kivilevitz, D. Yaakov (Yani) Gerber, E. Gittel Klein, F. Eliezer Maz'a

Sitting: A. Hannah Rogovin, B. Yaakov Lipsitz, C. Sara Yizgor, D. Onya Rubin (Kahanovitch's son-in-law), E. Rikla Shepsnevel, F. Chaim Stkolshik

Sitting on the floor: A. Michael Perski, B. Rachel Rogovin, C. Yosef Schwartzberg

[Page 426]

the Mizrachi of the city), included members of the General Zionists, Tzeirei Zion, Hechalutz, Beitar, Hashomer Hatzair etc. The meetings took place on Saturdays in the Tarbut School building. These meetings were the Sabbath pleasure of Volozhin 's Jews, craving redemption. Whoever saw Reb Israel Lunin walking, after a Sabbath nap, to a meeting of JNF, his face illuminated, relaxed, as if he had a revelation – would understand the secret of the existence of the people of Israel.

True, we were in the Diaspora, but we lived as if our bodies were in the west while our hearts were in the east. The work for JNF was our daily nourishment, each student of the Tarbut School had a saving notebook where JNF stamps were glued. In every house hung a blue and white box in which the family members inserted their contributions to redeeming the homeland. On *Shabbat Mevarchim* [the Sabbath prior to Rosh Chodesh], they used to plan the emptying of the boxes. Pairs from all "circles" and movements volunteered for this sacred endeavor and fulfilled the Mitzva of offering a sacrifice to G-d on Rosh Chodesh[1]

Rosh Chodesh in Volozhin was a day of the Land of Israel for all the city's Jews. The volunteers who came to empty the boxes were welcomed cordially. At every wedding hall they would sell, between dances, flowers of Zion, with the proceeds consecrated to redeeming the Land of Israel.

Lag B'Omer was majestically celebrated by us. Flags of Zion were held in the hands of the Tarbut students who walked in rows to the summit of Mount Bialik (the mountain is in the eastern part of the city. According to tradition, Bialik wrote his poem *El Hatzipor* there.) The children entertained the Jews of the city with songs of Zion. Masses of people streamed after them to the bosom of nature, as if they were on their way to the Land of Israel – the aspiration of their souls.

There was a special custom in Volozhin, to celebrate the Simchat Torah of the Land of Israel on Shemini Atzeret. It was also called "the Simchat Torah of Reb Shlomo Chassid." This celebration took place only in the *kleizl* on Vilna Street, which was the place of worship of Reb Yisrael Lunin (the head *gabbai*) and the leaders of the Zionist movement of the city – Reb Shlomo Chaim Brodna, Yeshayahu Kahanovitch, David Yitzchak Kontorovitch, Mr. Altman, and Reb Yehoshua Horwitz.

Reb Shlomo Chassid (Shepsnevel) worshipped in the *kleizl*. He was a native of Horodok who moved to our city. Even though he was a Hassidic man, this Jew was loved by all the *Misnagdim* with whom he worshipped. They appreciated and loved him. In his honor, they conducted *Hakafot* [Torah processions] on Shemini Atzeret, in accordance with the custom of the Hassidim. In his merit, they celebrated the festival of Simchat Torah on the day that the Jews of the Land of Israel celebrate it[2]. The following day, we celebrated the Simchat Torah of the Diaspora. That festival was dedicated to the renaissance of the Nation of Israel in its homeland. Reb Yisrael Lunin, as the chairman of the JNF, was the "conductor of the dancing." The children of the Tarbut school designed blue and white chains, and decorated the synagogue with them. The national flag was brought in, and they danced with the flags and the Torah scrolls during the *Hakafot*, with songs of Zion bursting forth from thee mouths of all the participants. Men, women, and children danced with great enthusiasm, all of them dipping in the sea of

[Page 427]

blue and white. Anyone who has not witnessed the *Hakafot* of Shemini Atzeret in the *kleizl* of Volozhin has not seen joy in his life.[3]

This mighty song, the song of a nation that believes in its redemption, the song of the residents of the city in which the Netzach Yisrael and Nes Tziona organizations were created, the song of the Jews of Volozhin who constantly studied the doctrine of eternal Israel – that song has its source in "Then sang Moses and the Children of Israel"[4]. In order to fulfil the verse "And Deborah took the drum in her hands"[5], a charming girl was brought up to the *bima*, which stood in the center of the synagogue, and honored with singing the songs of Zion.

This song will never cease, the song of "The nation of Israel lives" [*Am Yisrael Chai*] bursting forth and rising from the mouths of the survivors of Volozhin, who merited to make *aliya* to the Land of Israel and participate in its upbuilding. It will be transmitted from generation to generation.

Finally, I include the letter of the Zionist organization of London to the local council of the JNF in Volozhin, regarding the Zionist Congress gathering.

The Zionist Organization, Central Office
77 Great Russell Street, London W.C. 1

To the Local council of the Jewish National Fund for Israel, Volozhin, 13 Av 5690 (Aug 7, 1930).

Dear Friends

"The central council of the Zionist organization in Poland brought to our attention your letter from July 18, in which you express to us your demand from a public gathering that took place in Volozhin on 20 Tammuz in memory of the death of our leader Dr. Herzl. The executive is hereby honored to inform you that even before receiving this letter, we have decided, as is certainly already known to you from the newspapers, to convene a Zionist congress at the end of this year, around the month of December."

With great honor and blessings of Zion
The Organizational Office

With this, we learn that the Jews of Volozhin convened a public gathering on 20 Tammuz, in which it was decided that a Zionist congress must be convened, to deliberate over what was transpiring in the Jewish world.

The central office of the Zionist movement in London took the opinion of Volozhin seriously and responded as above.

Translator's footnotes:

1. Based on Numbers 28:11, the command for the monthly Rosh Chodesh (New Moon) offering in the Temple.
2. In the Diaspora, a second day of Yomtov is observed on the first and last days of Passover, Shavuot, Sukkot, and Shemini Atzeret. In the Diaspora, Simchat Torah is observed on the day after Shemini Atzeret. In Israel, where only one day of Yomtov is observed, Shemini Atzeret and Simchat Torah are the same day. *Hakafot*, processions with the Torah scrolls, are conducted on Simchat Torah. Even in the Diaspora, Hassidim, Sephardim, and those who follow the Nusach Sephard rite also conduct *Hakafot* on the eve of Shemini Atzeret.
3. Based on Mishna *Sukka* 5:1
4. Exodus 15:1.
5. This is based on Exodus 15:20, but refers to Miriam, not Deborah. The song of Deborah starts at Judges 5:1 with "Then sang Deborah and Barak the son of Avinoam." The author has interchanged the prophetesses in this verse – but both are regarded as paradigms of women's song in the Bible.

[Page 428]

The Outlook of Rabbi Chaim Volozhin Regarding the Exile and the Redemption

Translated by Jerrold Landau

Rabbi Chaim of Volozhin expressed his outlook on the exile and the redemption in his sermon that he delivered in the *Beis Midrash* in Volozhin on the first day of *Selichot* in the year 5572 (1811)[1]. The sermon of Rabbi Chaim was published in the book *Neima Kedosha* by Rabbi Yosef Jaski, pages 18-24, Vilna, published by Reb Avraham Yitzchak Dworzec in the year 5632 (1872). The following excerpts are taken from that sermon.

Rabbi Chaim of Volozhin states that the Supernal Jerusalem is the source of the souls of all of Israel: "The Supernal Jerusalem is the secret of the source of the souls of all of Israel, and therefore is called *Knesset Yisrael* [the Assembly of Israel]. For just like the Jerusalem of Below, when all of Israel ascends on the festivals to appear before G-d, all of Israel gathers together; similarly the Supernal Jerusalem is the secret of the source of the gathering of all the souls of Israel."

The Diaspora leads to a diminution of the image of the Jew. Due to the difficult conditions in which he is immersed, he is unable to delve into to the Torah according to his desire and recognize his Creator: "Even the prayers that were instituted to request the redemption from the exile are also referring to the exile of the Divine Presence, so to speak, and the exile of the soul that is unable to fulfill itself currently in occupying itself with the Torah and the commandments appropriately, due to the heaviness of earning a livelihood. For when Israel was living in its Land, each person under his vineyard and fig tree, without concerns of livelihood, it was easy for every person to devote their heart and rectify their lowly souls through busying oneself with Torah and commandments. Now, however, the great difficulties of livelihood lead to a neglect of Torah and commandments, and therefore the redemption is greatly delayed."

Rabbi Chaim of Volozhin regarded the exile as a punishment. We did not follow the path of repentance, and we distanced ourselves from G-d during the time of the existence of the Temple. Consequently, it was necessary to destroy the Temple and place us into exile: "It is like a king who had an only son, and the son became bedridden with a great, serious illness, and the physicians said that there is no remedy for his affliction unless he minimizes sleep, and his father goes with the bitterness of his heart to take him out of his heavy bed and lays him on the ground so that he will not be able to sleep much - but his father sees that nothing helps yet, and he still sleeps. Then his father does several more ruses in this regard, and nothing helps, until his father the merciful king is forced to place swords and knives below him so he will be unable to sleep.

"The parable is self-understood: For when we were resting on the bed of the king, that is when the Temple existed upon its foundations in quiet and calm, as is stated, "Here is the bed of Solomon" (Song of Songs 3:7), we were somnolent regarding knocking on the gates of repentance, of returning to G-d with a full heart. Therefore, the power of the evil inclination strengthened upon us, and it became necessary to destroy the Temple and place us into exile."

Translator's footnote:

1.   The year 5572 would correspond to 1812, as the first day of *Selichot* is in the month of Elul, a few days prior to Rosh Hashanah. At Rosh Hashanah, the Hebrew years moves up by one year. It is possible that the writer meant the first day of *Selichot* prior to Rosh Hashanah of 5572, which would indeed correspond to 1811.

[Page 429]

Education and the Arts

[Page 430] Blank [Page 431]

The Tarbut School

By a group of students

Translated by Jerrold Landau

based on an earlier translation by M. Porat z"l

that was edited by Judy Feinsilver Montel

As in every Jewish settlement, the Jews of Volozhin received their primary education in the *cheder*. The boys mainly studied with the *melamedim* in the *cheders*, beginning with the aleph bet and reaching the point of studying *chumash* with Rashi. Of course, they also prepared for their Bar Mitzvah celebrations with the *aliya* to the Torah. The well-known *melamedim* included Reb Betzalel and his son Chaim Yeshayahu (Chaim Shia), Reb Yekusiel, Reb Moshe Shlomo Wolkovitch, Reb Nachum Yudel, and others. There were also teachers from the "new generation" such as Hershel Zeltzer and others, who taught privately in their homes. These *melamedim* and teachers also planted the love of the Land of Israel in the hearts of their students, since for the most part they were lovers of Zion.

Girls of Volozhin who studied in the Byelorussian high school in
Horodok

Standing (right to left): Ethel Paritzki, Rivka Brodna, Sonia Pereski,
Weisbord
Sitting: Elka Kaganovitch, Sonia Kozlovski

Only very few people sent their children to schools outside of Volozhin. The girls would mainly go to Horodok to study in the Byelorussian Gymnasia. They were not able to study there for an extended period,

[Page 432]

The Tarbut Committee, 9 Elul 5685 (29 August 1925)

From right to left, standing: Liberman (from Smorgon), Yitzchak Perski
From right to left, sitting: Noach Perski, Yeshayahu Kaganovitch, Binyamin Shishko

because the gymnasia was closed when the Polish regime consolidated. During that period, the boys studied in the gymnasia and Hebrew seminary of Vilna.

In the year 5685 (1925), the leaders of the Zionist movement and heads of Tarbut of Volozhin decided to found a Hebrew school based on the Tarbut [network]. The actualizers of this idea were Yeshayahu Kaganovitch, Chaim Golobenchich, David Yitzchak Kontorovitch, Shevach Rogovin, Avraham Berkovitch, Yitzhak Shapiro, and others.

As has been stated, the Tarbut school of our city was founded in the year 5685 (1925). They hung a sign: "The Hebrew Public School of Volozhin" on a blue and white background. It had only four classes.[1] Mr. Chaim Golobenchich was invited as the principal. He taught Bible, literature, and other subjects. Mr. Gurevitch from Sol, and Mr. Chaim Levin from Iwye, also taught there. Binyamin Shishko and Noach Perski were among the teachers from Volozhin.

The students wore uniforms. The girls wore blue dresses, black aprons, and blue hats with a blue and white apron upon which the word Tarbut was written. The boys wore blue shirts, blue pants, and hats that had the same colors as those of the girls.

[Page 433]

The students of the Tarbut school with their teachers in the year 5686 (1926)

Sitting: the teachers with the members of the committee (third row, right to left): David Yitzchak Kontorovitch, Noach Perski, Avraham Horowitz (Gur), Ratner, Chaim Golobenchich, Binyamin Shishko (Shapir), Yeshayahu Kahanovitch (chairman of Tarbut), Yosef Tabachovitch

[Page 434]

From the outset, the school struggled with a lack of budgetary resources. It did not receive any support from the city council, which was in the hands of the Poles. The municipal government claimed that a government public school (*powszechna*) existed, which charged no tuition. However, our parents sought to give their children a Hebrew education. Therefore, they willingly accepted upon themselves the heavy yoke of supporting the school.

The authorities compelled the school leadership to teach Polish language and history. Polish teachers were invited for that purpose. Later, they were replaced by Jews, including the teacher David Bram of Konin.

The most impressive event during the first year of the existence of the school was the celebration in honor of the opening of the Hebrew University on Mount Scopus in Jerusalem. It took place on 7 Nisan 5685 (April 1, 1925), when Balfour stood on Mount Scopus and announced in front of the entire world that a great institution of learning was being founded there. Bialik concluded his great speech with "news of redemption for the entire human race."

Uncaptioned: The sign and the seal of the Hebrew public school of Volozhin

The emotions and festive feelings of the Jews of our city were very high. Many people blessed each other with the *Shehecheyahu* blessing, for they saw a victory of Hebrew culture in this. Due to the passage of time, we no longer remember the particular details of this. In honor of this festival – the festival of 7 Nissan 5685, candles were lit on the windowsills. The great light that spread forth from the houses imparted an atmosphere of sublime spirit in the city. The students of the school appeared on the streets in their official uniforms. They spoke a living and fluent Hebrew, and sang songs of Zion. The joy was very great. A public assembly took pace in the Great Synagogue in the evening, at which the school principal, Mr. Chaim Golobenchich spoke. He called upon those gathered to donate money or jewelry for the university. Many enthusiastically responded to his call.

During the second year of the existence of the school, they began to study the Latin language in the fourth grade. They invited the teacher Mirer from Vilna for that purpose. The intention in introducing the study of that language was to enable

[Page 435]

The Tarbut school orchestra in the year 5686 (1926)

From right to left, standing: Mina Berman, Lea Shchwartzberg, Fruma Rogovin, Efraim Rogovin, Shlomo Gurevitch, Yisrael Berkovitch, Yaakov Rogovin, Shlomo Liberman.
From right to left, seated: Bella Potashnik, Mina Berman, Rafael Weisbord, Shoshana Berkovitch, the teacher Avraham Gurevitch, the conductor Chaim Ratner, the teacher Chaim Golobenchich, the teacher Noach Perski, the teacher Binyamin Shishko, Peshke Rogovin, Bella Kramnik, Mina Berman, Tsirke Bunimovitch[2]

[Page 436]

the students to continue their studies in the high school in which that was a compulsory language. The level of knowledge in that class was sufficiently high. The students exceeded the requirements of the curriculum. Thanks to their excellence, the students received a certificate through which the students were accepted to the fifth grade of the high school.

The school took also care of the artistic education of the students. They invited Mr. Ratner, the music teacher, to create a string instrument band. The band participated in all the school celebrations and in many general cultural activities. The teacher Levin taught us singing and directed the choir with the accompaniment of a concertina. That teacher founded the drama club and chose good singers from amongst the students. The first play performed was an operetta called *Haroeh* [the Shepherd]. The plot was about an ewe who separated from the flock and was torn apart by a wolf. The costumes of the actors were formed by wearing hats in the image of animals. Other plays were Snow White and the Seven Dwarfs, and The

Daughter of Jephthah. The content of the plays grew more sophisticated as the students matured. Rasha Berkovitch, Bella Kramnik, Efraim Rogovin, and Mina Berman (the daughter of Leibe Zecharia) had main roles.

The Tarbut School Mandolin Orchestra

Standing right to left: the teacher Shlomo Bar-Shira (Beikalski), Gershon Lunin, Feigel Berman, Golda Rubinstein, Itka -- , Chaya Rudnitzki, Velka Brodna
Seated from right to left: Sonia Perski, Fruma Podborski, Etel Rogovin, Fruma Golobenchich, Fruma Alperovitch, Miriam Levin

[Page 437]

These performances had an actual effect on the development of a sense of beauty and art. The performances served as a source of income for the Jewish National Fund and the school.

The school leadership also developed the art of declamation among the students. After hearing Chana Rubina, the actresses of Habima declaiming chapters of the Bible in Warsaw, Mr. Chaim Golobenchich led declamations from the Bible in school. Mina Berman was one of the excellent readers.

Along with the development of a sense of esthetics, the school ensured that the students could express themselves in writing and by heart, and could present individual before the audience of students. To this end, a wall weekly newspaper was formed. One of the students would choose a specific topic, write a composition about it, and read it before the students. People with a talent for writing would choose the topic of the life of residents of a far-off land for their speech. They would read various books and conduct serious research. During the afternoon hours, they would lecture about Japan, China, etc.

The school had a rich library, which included many textbooks and reading books. The students of the upper grades served as librarians in a weekly rotation. Graduates of the school, and members of the Zionist youth movements also served as librarians. The librarians excelled with a pedagogic sense and knew how to find books appropriate to the age and power of comprehension of the students.

The school maintained a regular connection with the Land of Israel. The students purchased Jewish National Fund stamps with the coins that their parents sent them to purchase a snack. They affied them to a stamp book. Anyone who filled the book would get a note of praise from the school, and a prize from the Jewish National Fund.

We had visits from emissaries from the Land. The students would listen with open mouths to the stories of the emissary about sabras, about their strength of heart, and the development of their independent characters. Once, during a Tu B'Shvat celebration, the emissary distributed fruits from the Land. We recall very well the visit of the leader of the workers movement in the Land, Mr. Yitzchak Tabenkin. He was hosted in the home of Aryeh Tapaf, who lives with his wife Musia in the Land of Israel for a certain period, and moved back to Volozhin after the disturbances of 5689 (1929). Mr. Tapaf knew Tabenkin and invited him to visit our city.

Excursions played a recognizable role in the school experience. The traditional excursion took place on Lag B'Omer to Mount Bialik and Rudnik's grove. The students went out all day with their instruments, guided by the teacher Gurevitch. Once, we went to the nearby town of Ivenets to become acquainted with the students of the school there. We went on wagons hitched to horses. The reception was very enthusiastic. Yitzchak Ponet greeted us in the name of the students. The students hosted us in their parents' homes. The connections forged were permanent.

As we are talking about the school, it is a pleasant duty for us to recall Manya, the Christian housekeeper, with gratitude and love. She was tall and refined. Her love of the students and dedication to the school were boundless. In the winter, during the fierce cold and snowstorms, she did not concern herself with her health, and she went out

[Page 438]

Lag B'Omer excursion of the students of the Tarbut school to Mount Bialik, 5684 (1926)

[Page 439]

to cut wood to heat the ovens, so it will be warm and good for the student. She regarded her role as holy work. Manya displayed the finest of her moral powers during the period of the Holocaust. She risked her life in smuggling food into the Volozhin Ghetto. It is fitting and appropriate to describe her as a Righteous Gentile.

Our memories of the school are also woven with days of sadness. We recall the bitter news that reached us in Vilna regarding the untimely death of our beloved teacher, Mr. Gurevitch. Even though he taught in the school for a very brief period, we built a strong connection to him. I will never forget the mourning assembly arranged in his honor, and especially Bialik's poem "Thoughts of Night" that we sang in a mournful tune: " I know that my weeping – the weeping of an owl amongst the ruins, will not reach people, and will not break the hearts."

The Tarbut committee in the company of the writer Daniel Perski on his visit to Volozhin in the year 5688 – 1928

Standing right to left: Yitzchak Perski, Binyamin Shishko, the teacher Efrokin
Sitting: Yaakov Baksht, Yeshayahu Kahanovitch (chairman of Tarbut), the writer Daniel Perski. Chaim Derechinski, David Yitzchak Kontorovitch

Mr. Chaim Golobenchich left Volozhin in the year 5688 (1928). Mr. Binyamin Shishko was chosen as the principal of the school. He served in that position until the year 5691 (1931).

Mr. Yaakov Lifschitz of Rakov served as the final principal. His wife Fruma Lifschitz, Rachel Meltzer (wife of Shneur Kivilevitch), Chaim Portnoy, Rachel Lapa

[Page 440]

and Shlomo Beikelski (a professional violinist) served as teachers during that period. The teacher Beikelski continued the musical education and organized a choir and a mandolin band. Both the choir and the band received a prize in the regional choir competition.

The school had seven classes at that time. Sessions were held in the morning and afternoon. They began to expand the school building, but the building effort ceased due to a shortage of funds. During those days, a miniature revolution took place in the leadership of the school. The Revisionists took the upper hand, and in the year 5695 (1935), the leadership of the school transferred to that faction. This stirred up emotions and shook up the other Zionist parties, but it did not disturb the regular course of studies in the school.

I will conclude with the words of the illustrious principal of Volozhin, Mr. Chaim Golobenchich, who lives with us in Israel:

"The Tarbut school in Volozhin was one of a kind. It raised a banner in the revolt against the grey realities of those days, in which the community had been immersed for generations. Everyone who passed through the threshold of that old building and saw the teachers and the students, whether during class time or during recess, immediately sensed as if they were all at once transported to a new world, in which everything was different and unusual, and nevertheless was so close, so attractive, and evocative of thoughts."[3]

Translator's footnotes:

1.   Mr. Porat added the following details: The building contained four rooms and accordingly four learning classes only. There was also a fifth one, the Mekhina (preparation) class in which the new coming pupils were prepared to use the school's main language, the hitherto unknown Hebrew. A second afternoon shift was organized for this additional class.

2.   Mina Berman is mentioned three times in the caption. I suspect this is an error in the original text.

3.   Mr. Porat added some of his own material to this article on the Tarbut school, much of which does not appear in the original book. It is as follows, in his own words:

The school was positioned near the Great Volozhin Yeshiva. Its fame and tradition influenced our behavior. Well educated, very polite, we stood up as a teacher entered the class. To our teachers we turned only after raising a hand if permitted. We called them respectfully: "My distinguished schoolmaster or schoolmistress" (*Adoni, or Gvirti Hamoyre/a*).

Although, following tradition, we were able to behave like the Volozhin Yeshivah students. It was known that they did not greet the Netziv and boycotted his lesson after the Rabbi slapped a colleague student's face for having spoiled his peyess- side locks. A teacher once slapped our Tarbut - student with a ruler over his hand and it was resulted in a strike. We opposed the teacher's entering our class until he excused himself following Hanaziv's famous example.

Chaim Golobenchich left Volozhin for Israel in 1928. Mr. Benyamin Shishko replaced him until 1931 the year he followed his predecessor and went to the Holy Land.

The last Tarbut principal was Mr. Yaakov Lifshits from Rakov. During his time in the position there was a major demand for higher classes. The community decided to enlarge the existing learning space. Building materials were bought and amassed on the courtyard. But the shortage of resources disabled its construction. Despite this, classes were added. And towards the last year of the Hebrew School's existence seven regular classes plus the very important "Mekhina" were functioning. The problem of space was meanwhile resolved, until better conditions would come, by enlarging the second shift and by occupying a part of the women's section in the Volozhin main Synagogue, which was situated some hundred yards away near the Yeshiva. During Yaakov Lifshits' tenure as principal, new teachers were required. Mrs. Fruma Lifshits, Yaakov's spouse, and Ms. Lapp (Lapoovna) were teaching the mekhina and the children in the lower classes. Yaakov Finger from Soll became our teacher for Hebrew language and its grammar and literature. He gave also lessons on Jewish history and the geography of Erets Israel.

Ms. Rachel Meltzer, our natural science teacher, was a native Volozhiner. She was married to Shneur Kivilevitch (Judenrat head in 1942). Rachel spoke with her students only in Hebrew, avoiding Yiddish even during the breaks, whereas the children in the elder classes spoke Yiddish. Mr. Taller from Molchad was responsible for the religious branch: all 5 Pentatcuch Books, Judges and Prophets, Kings, Players and some Gemara chapters. Mr. Taller used to privately prepare some boys to the Bar Mitzva ceremonies.

Yakov Lifshits, as well as managing the school also taught us arithmetic. Each Friday he would also gather all the students and read before them chapters from Sholom Aleichem in Yiddish. We were enchanted by the Yiddish writer's stories. It is a pity that the Volozhin Tarbut School did not find time or resources or did not want to teach us some Yiddish writing and grammar. All these disciplines listed above were taught in Hebrew Ashkenaz-dialect. In Israel the Sefarad dialect dominated. The differences are in pronunciation. In Sefarad-dialect the emphasis is put on the word's end, in Ashkenaz - on its beginning. Some characters are spelled otherwise, so the same words written in equal way are read differently; for example: the word "letters" becomes in Sefarad Hebrew "otiyOT", in Ashkenaz - "OYSSIyoys"; "shaNA toVA" - in Sefarad, "SHOno TOYvo" - in Ashkenaz and so forth.

Some Volozhiners who made *aliya* to Eretz Yisroel visited the Shtetl with their children in the mid thirties. We heard the "new" Hebrew, and asked to learn the language in the "new" way. Our demand was fulfilled but partially. The prayers and Bible we continued to read in Ashkenaz dialect. Arithmetic, Grammar, Literature (Bialik, Mapu, Mendele) and Hebrew songs were changed and taught with the modern Sefarad pronunciation.

Thanks to our Tarbut teachers we arrived in Israel after the war with good Hebrew and we were able to begin a normal life immediately after landing in the Holy Land.

Mr. Shlomo Beikalski the handsome, smart, and talented young man from Zheludok taught us the Polish language, its history and geography. During three years (1935-8) with Beikalski we were able to thoroughly learn the Polish language. He encouraged us to read books. We managed to read at this short period hundreds of books all of them in Polish: H. Sienkievitsh, A. Mitskievitsh, I. Kortshak, Dolenga, Mostovitsh, B. Prouss, L. Tolstoy, N. Gogol, Jack London, Mark Twain, D. Amicis, A. Dumas, E. Zola, F. Cooper, K. May, Dickens, Walter Scott and many, many others. (Due to this massive reading, I am currently able to read and to write Polish after not using this language for more than 60 years –Translator's note).

The recreation time we passed in children's games, volleyball (*siatkoovka* in Polish), ball throwing camps (Makhanayim – in Hebrew) and reading books.

The Volozhin Tarbut School functioned from 1925 until 1939. At the beginning of the 1939/40 school year after the Soviets occupied Volozhin it acted as a Yiddish school, this school year it finished as a Belarus School.

The school and its building were completely destroyed in 1941.

[Page 440]

Culture War in Volozhin

By Binyamin Shapir–Shishko (of Karkur)

Translated by Jerrold Landau

based on an earlier translation by M. Porat z"l

that was edited by Judy Feinsilver Montel

My father Reb Mordechai son of Nisan Shishko was a lover of Zion, and moreover, he was G-d fearing individual who appreciated scholars. I was his only son, but despite this he fulfilled in me the adages of the sages, "exile yourself to a place of Torah" [*Pirkei Avot* 4:14]. He sent me to study in far-off Kremenchug (Ukraine). During World War One, there were four yeshivas there: Knesset Yisroel, Knesset Beis Yitzchok (from Slobodka, Lithuania), the Yeshiva of the Lubavitch Hassidim, and the Shaarei Torah for youth at which I studied.

The principal of that Yeshiva was Rabbi Elazar Yitzchok Shushkin, who was known in Kremenchug as "The Great One" [*Hagadol*]. He was married to the sister of Rabbi Yochanan Rudkes of Volozhin. He would sit all day wearing his tallis and tefillin, not uttering a secular word. The Yeshiva Head was the Gaon

Rabbi Shlomo Heyman of Parich, who married Yochanan Rudkes' daughter. The Yeshivah was immersed in the spirit of Volozhin.

At the beginning of 5681 (1921), I became friendly with Moshe Zalman Lunts, who was an outstanding objector of the Diaspora[1].

[Page 441]

I became active in the Zionist movement through his influence. This caused a definitive change in my world outlook. When I came to Vilna during the early 1920s, I did not continue with my Yeshiva studies. Instead, I registered as a student in the *Tarbut* teachers seminary, under the leadership of the renowned pedagogue Dr. Shmuel Yona Charnow.

This decision caused great distress to my father. He wrote me the following heart-aching letter: "I have become weary of my life [based on Genesis 27:46] when I see that my only son has become involved with a group that violates the holy matters of Israel, for whom the name *Tarbut* is appropriate – 'a brood [*Tarbut*] of sinners' (Numbers 32:14)." One can see from this the distance between the fathers, who appreciated Torah and sanctified the Name of Heaven, and the younger generation who became weary of Diaspora life and decided to hasten the footsteps of the Messiah, placing their stress on the revival of the Hebrew language, and making *aliya* to Zion.

With the closure of the Etz Chaim Yeshiva of Volozhin during the First World War, the voice of the Torah was silenced in the city. A crisis arose in the children's education. Many of them did not study in the *cheders*. The Zionists took advantage of the open situation and decided to open a Hebrew primary school based on the pure Hebrew language. The Talmud Torah building had been standing empty for a long time, with no classes being held in it. In the year 5685 (1925) the Zionists "invaded" that building and founded the *Tarbut* school.

Shomrei Hachomot, headed by the Gaon Rabbi Yaakov Shapira, began a holy war to and demanded a return of the building, so that they could renew the study of Torah that had ceased, and specifically in the Yiddish language, which was spoken and understood.

During the 5687-5688 (1927-1928) school year, a bitter culture war took place in Volozhin. That year pained the Jews of Volozhin greatly from both a moral and cultural perspective. The two sides fought bitterly over the rights to the building. This battle was accompanied by fist-fighting and ended with literal bloodshed, and a desecration of the Divine Name.

When I completed my studies in the *Tarbut* seminary at the end of the year 5687 (1927), I nevertheless fulfilled the commandment of honoring one's father. I acceded to him and traveled to teach in the Tachkemoni religious school in Zabludow. I returned to Volozhin after a year of teaching in Tachkemoni. The Jews of the city from both streams regarded me as a man who had the power to unify the two opposing sides, and who could put an end to the conflict and the desecration of the Divine Name.

In truth, it can be said that there were enthusiastic Zionists on both sides. Reb Eliyahu Schwartzberg, the principal of the religious school, and the founders and members of the leadership of the religious school – Reb Yisrael Lunin and Reb Shlomo Chaim Brodna – were Zionists, and nobody disputed their faithfulness to Zion. This battle was about the spirit that should prevail in the school: one side stressed the fear of Heaven (Shomrei Hachomot, who tended toward the Aguda preferred the Yiddish language to the Hebrew language). The other side, the Zionists from the *Tarbut* camp, did not even forgo

[Page 442]

The religious school in Volozhin on Lag B'Omer on Mount Bialik.
The students of the religious school with their teacher Reb Eliyahu Yitzchak Schwartzberg.

[Page 443]

the language of study even to a single iota. The urging of Rabbi Yaakov Shapiro, who pleaded that they should learn "In the beginning, G-d created" [Genesis 1:1] in the spoken mother tongue [i.e. Yiddish] was to no avail.

A joint meeting was called in the home of Rabbi Shapira. Yeshayahu Kahanovitch (chairman of *Tarbut* in Volozhin), Yaakov (Yani) Garber, and David Yitzchak Kontorovitch were the chief spokesmen for the "secularists." Dov Lavit and Yitzchak Perski participated from the youths. Reb Yisrael Lunin, Reb Yaakov Shmuel Ruchamkin, Reb Shlomo Chaim Brodna, and Reb Yaakov Weisbord participated from the religious side. I was the arbitrator between them (i.e. participated from both sides).

It was agreed that the religious school, whose language of instruction was Yiddish, would be closed, and the rights of the *Tarbut* school to the building would be recognized. The condition was that the students were required to recite the Shacharit service prior to the beginning of the classes, and that Reb Eliezer Moshe Meltzer was to be appointed for that role. Peace pervaded in Volozhin. A single Hebrew school now existed, and I merited to serve as the head and principal for three years. Even after I made *aliya* to the Land of Israel, the school continued to exist with Yaakov Lifschitz serving as the principal. He led the school in the spirit of the founders.

With the entry of the Soviet army to Volozhin in the year 5699 (1939), the school stopped being a Hebrew school, and conducted itself in the Yiddish languages. Finally, it was invalidated by the new regime, and turned into a Russian school, until destruction came upon it and its students.

Translator's footnote:

1.   Mr. Porat added the following comment here: Frydele di Rebbetzin's son – see page 243.

The Volozhin Kindergarten

By Miriam Levitan (Rosenberg) of Tel Aviv

Translated by Jerrold Landau

based on an earlier translation by M. Porat z"l

that was edited by Judy Feinsilver Montel

In the year 5694 (1934), Aryeh Tofaf and Reuven Rosenberg founded a kindergarten in Volozhin. The impetus for this was from Fania Levitchki (Kivilevitch) who came from the Land of Israel to visit her family. She spoke with admiration about the kindergartens in the Land of Israel, in which the young children spend time in song, play and dance.

Her words made a great impression, and the people immediately set out to found a kindergarten in our city. For this purpose, they rented two rooms in the house of Reuven Rogovin. They invited Rachel Shevach as the first kindergarten teacher in Volozhin. She spoke to the students in Yiddish, but taught them Hebrew songs. Rachel was a young, blond-haired woman with unusual energy. The kindergarten developed and expanded thanks to her organization and pedagogical talents. She succeeded in engaging volunteer assistants, who helped her in her daily work. They also assisted her in preparing performances of the students and the sale of tickets.

[Page 444]

Children of the kindergarten with the kindergarten teacher

One of the important things in the educational activities of the kindergarten teacher Rachel was expressed in taking the children outside "the walls" into the bosom of nature. She hiked with them a great deal in the fields, forests, and the park of Count Tyszkiewicz.

This kindergarten laid the foundations for social equality. Rachel did not show preference for a "well pedigreed" child over a child from an ordinary family. In her eyes, they were all well pedigreed. She did not discriminate between a child from a wealthy home and a child from a poor home. They lived a life of commonality, eating and drinking together. She attempted to expose the spark of talent in the children, and when a child displayed such signs, she nurtured them carefully.

In time, the children began to speak Hebrew. In this manner the kindergarten served as a corridor, preparing the students for the main hall – the *Tarbut* Hebrew school.

Translator's Note:

The following photo and caption was added by Mr. M. Porat:

Purim in the Kindergarten – 1935

Names I remember (Mr. Porat's note):
1-Rachel Shevakh, 2-Sonitshka Perlman (my sister), 3- Rivele Perski (Getsl's), 4-Feyguele Rapoport (Meyshl's),
5 - Esterke Kaminietski, 6- Iser Rapoport (the Dentist's), 7- Yoel Rosnberg (Ruven's)
Of all the lovely children two only escaped the Shtetl's fate: Sonitshka Perlman-2 and Feyguele Rapoport-4

[Page 445]

The Library

By Fruma Guzman (Yuzefovitz), Jerusalem

Translated by Naomi Gal and lightly edited by Jerrold Landau

Every now and then, Hershel Zeltzer, a well-read man, used to visit our house, and he suggested that I join the group volunteers working in the library. I agreed. He invited me to a meeting in which the following activists participated: 1) Hershel Zeltzer. 2) Sara Yuzefovitz (my sister). 3) Elka Kaganovitz. 4)

Krushchovsky. 5) Mariasia Potashnik. 6) Akiva Potashnik. 7) Noach Perski 8) Sonia Kozlovsky. 9) Yisrael Rogovin.

These members gave their time and energy to the library, by founding it and raising money for it through performances. From the report given in that meeting it turned out that these volunteers established

The library committee in 5689 (1929)

First row from top (from right to left): 1) Sonia Kozlovsky 2) Hershel Zeltzer 3) Mariasia Potashnik 4) Zeev Perski
Second row: 1) Akiva Potashnik 2) Fruma Yuzefovitz 3) Elka Kaganovitz 4) Krushchovsky

[Page 446]

the library without communal support, but rather solely from revenue from performances they staged themselves, and with personal contributions.

I saw before me ample opportunity for interesting and effective work. I was given the task of finding a partner and go out with her to raise money, since they could not afford the rent. I went out with Chana Weisbord. Our outing was crowned with success. There was no home in Volozhin that did not respond generously, and with the money collected we paid the rent.

The library was in the house of "Chaya the Krever" on Smorgon Street. Books were loaned out three times a week. Many youths came to borrow books because they liked this place very much. It served as a social meeting place, a place for conversations, and exchange of opinions about literature and art.

Soldiers too came to borrow books, among them Poles who contributed some books. Children of poor and working class people who wanted to get an education also subscribed to the library. This was the only place where they could acquire knowledge.

There was no permanent librarian in the library. Some members, among them a soldier from Lodz, bound the books. The library committee took upon itself assistance roles as well. We assisted Linat Tzedek, that is, we used to spend the nights in the houses of elderly and isolated people. Before I made *aliya* to the Land, some of them came to thank me for all the beneficial work I did for them. In this manner, we worked for the benefit of others and not in order to be rewarded.

Religious Education During the Thirties

By Menachem Mendel Potashnik (New York)

Translated by Naomi Gal and edited by Jerrold Landau

The Large *Beis Midrash*

The large *Beis Midrash* stood in the market, close to the yeshiva. "Leibe der Shamash" served as the *shamash* and Torah reader. Rabbi Yaakov Shapira, used to preach in the *Beis Midrash* twice a year – on *Shabbat Hagadol* and in Shabbat Shuva. His sermons consisted of explanations of *halacha* and *aggada* [lore], in which he displayed his great expertise in Talmud.

It is a sacred obligation for us to mention a few scholars who contributed greatly to strengthening the religious life in the city. One of them was Rabbi and Gaon Mordechai Levin. In the yeshiva he was called "Mottel Traver" (after the name of his native city Trav). He spent most of his life in Volozhin. He was a great expert in Talmud and rabbinical decisors. However, his modesty was as vast as his knowledge. He believed in what the sages said: "He who is haughty has a

[Page 447]

defect." He used to talk to children about Torah. He was well liked by the yeshiva people and the city's Jews.

We should remember positively one of the prominent youths – Rabbi Yaakov Stolarski. They called him in the yeshiva "Yaakov Kletzker." He became known as a great scholar. His impeccable morals were well known. He was close to Rabbi Chaim Walkin. We should similarly also mention Rabbi Nathan Dickstein, a Volozhin native, he had great ethics and many good traits.

There was a famous *shochet* in Volozhin named Rabbi Yehuda Avraham Perski, who served in this holy position since the time of the Netziv. He worshipped in the yeshiva and knew the names and accomplishments of all the yeshiva's dignitaries and heads. He told me that he had the privilege of seeing Rabbi Itzele, the son of Rabbi Chaim of Volozhin.

He died during the thirties when he was over one hundred years old. As an old man, when his eyes dimmed and his hands weakened his son-in-law, Reb Yisrael Daivid Cheiten served as *shochet*.

The "Kleizel"

A *Beis Midrash* known as the "Kleizel" stood on Vilna Street. One of the first *gabbaim* in the Kleizel was Reb Menachem Yoel Potashnik, who was well respected by the congregants due to his activity in all the communal institutions. He was a linen merchant. Before he left for his business in the nearby village, he used to worship in the first *minyan*. When he returned from the village, he used to enter the Kleizel to study *Daf Yomi* [the daily Talmud page, based on a worldwide cycle] with the Chevra Shas. Rabbi Mordechai Levin was the teacher of the class. On Friday nights he used to explain the weekly Torah portion. Rabbi Yaakov Kaganovitz ("Yaakov Divenishker" currently in the United States) used to teach a Talmud page.

After the murder of Reb Menachem Yoel Potashnik the *gabbaim* in the Kleizel were Rabbi Yisrael Lunin and Rabbi Yosef Tabachovitz. Rabbi Lunin was represented in all the institutions of the city – the community council, the bank, Mizrachi, etc. Rabbi Yosef Tabachovitz served as permanent *gabbai* of the Council of Yeshivos.

Reb Moshe Lavit served as *shamash* in the Kleizel. When we were children, our deepest wish was to get a [scroll of the] Prophets to dance with on Simchat Torah in the *Beis Midrash*. On Shemini Atzeret, when the *shamash* fell asleep after lunch, we used to linger for hours around his house, waiting for him to wake up so that we could go with him to the Kleizel and get a [scroll of the] Prophets[1].

After his death, Rabbi Avraham David, who was also a *melamed*, was appointed as *shamash* of the Kleizel. He was very strict about the commandment of washing the hands. He used to walk in the street and encourage everybody to recite the *Asher Yatzar*[2] blessing.

Moshe Shlomo the Melamed (Wolkovitz) served as Torah reader in the Kleizel. A group for the recital of Tehillim [Psalms] existed. Before the end of the Sabbath, it [the members of that group] would read Psalm 119 of Psalms, opening with the words "Fortunate are those pure in their ways." That chapter was read with a very sweet melody.

The night of Hoshana Rabba was a sleepless night in the Kleizel. The entire book of Psalms was read that night. Reb Chaim Zirolnik (Chaim der Shneider) would bring a basket of apples, and distribute fragrant, delicious apples to the right and left.

[Page 448]

לכבוד
מורנו ורבנו הרה"ג
ר' שמעון לאנגבארד
צאתך לשלום

The members of Tiferet Bachurim at the farewell party for Rabbi Shimon Langbard before he made *aliya* to the Land of Israel in 5695 (1935)

On top (at the book shelf) from right to left: 1) Yitzchak Chaiken 2) Nissan Chaiken 3) Baruch Gelman
First row: (from top to bottom) 1) Elimelech Bloch 2) a Yeshiva student 3) the son of "Eli the locksmith" 4) Binyamin Bakshtanski 5) Yisrael Gelman 6) Yudel Shimkin (Yudel the Smith) 7) Hershel Kagan (Hershel the water carrier) 8) Leibe Bunimovitz.
Second row: 1) Zalman Shapira 2) Bayle Shapira 3) The Rebbetzin Sheina Disha Shapira 4) Pesia Shapira 5) Rebbetzin Chana Langbard 6) Rabbi Shimon Langbard 7) A yeshiva student 8) Mendel Potashnik 9) Yitzchak Moshe Shapira (in the top hat) 11) Germans' son-in-law.
Third row: 1) Hershel Shalman 2) Yehoshua Shalman.
Fourth row: 1) Nachum Kagan 2) Yitzchak Perski 3) Eli Shlomoshek's 4) Eli he son of Yekutiel 5) Alter Rogovin 6) Gershon Berman 7) Eli Berman.
(On the photo) In honor of our teacher and rabbi, the Rabbi and Gaon Shimon Langbard – Go in Peace.

[Page 449]

"Tiferet Bachurim" ("The Glory of the Youths" society)

There was in Volozhin an association of Tiferet Bachurim, whose meeting place was in one of the rooms of the large *Beis Midrash*. It had about thirty members. Its organizers were Rabbi Shimon Langbard (the son-in-law of rabbi Yaakov Shapira), Rabbi Aaron Shmidman ("Aaron Pinsker" the association's chairman), and the writer of these lines.

On Sabbath nights during the winter, public gatherings were held in the large *Beis Midrash* dedicated to the weekly Torah portion. The speakers were from among the yeshiva students. One of the excellent speakers was Rabbi Yaakov Kaganovitz.

In 5695 (1935), Tiferet Bachurim brought in its own Torah scroll. This association had its own *Minyan* that worshipped on Sabbaths and festivals. They also conducted *Shalosh Seudos* [Third Sabbath meal] celebrations, accompanied by song and words of Torah. The association had its own library as well. Rabbi Aharon Shmidman, Reb Eli Yitzchak Schwartzberg, the lawyer Lapidos and Rabbi Yaakov Stolarski ("Yaakov Kletzker") served as regular rabbis.

Most of the members were laborers and wholesale merchants. The secretary was the writer of these lines. In 5695 (1935), when Rabbi Aaron Shmidman married a woman from the Shishko family in Borisovska (Baksht) and left the city, I was chosen as the chairman of the association. I served in this capacity until the outbreak of World War Two.

Alongside Tiferet Bachurim there was a chapter of Poalei Agudas Yisroel. The headquarters of that organization was in Lodz. Two of their members – Yitzhak Perski and Elimelech the Cantor's [son] – left for *Hachshara*. Perski made *aliya* whereas Elimelech perished in Volozhin.

Tiferet Bachurim also voted in the committee of Keren Hayishuv (The Yishuv Fund), the members of which were Rabbi Yosef Tabachovitz, the writer of these lines, Rabbi Avraham Yaffe, Rabbi Chaim Bergman, and Reb Hirsh Schneider. This committee was one of the most active among the towns of the White Russian border.

The members of the association subscribed to the daily newspaper of the Aguda, which was published in Warsaw. The were thirty subscribers.

"Beis Yaakov" Religious School for Girls

Volozhin had a Beis Yaakov religious school for girls headed by a teacher who graduated from the teachers' seminary in Krakow. The school was founded in 5695 (1935) by a group of young people. One of the important rabbis in our area, Rabbi Yitzchak Weinstein, the rabbi of Vishnyva (today in Israel) was invited to the inauguration celebration. He was very helpful in establishing this school. Cheina Garber, the daughter of the Rabbi from Horodok Rabbi Eli Ben–Zion Garber (today she is Cheina Kosovsky and lives in the United States) was also invited. During that period, she was very active in the field of religious education in Volozhin and its surroundings.

[Page 450]

לזם עלתף לארצנו הקדושה
תבורך
תלמידי ישיבת עץ חיים בוולוזין

The students of the Etz Chaim Yeshiva on the occasion of Mr. Yaakov Shmidman's *aliya* in the year 5693 (1933)

Standing (from right to left): 1) Nathan Dickenstein 3) David from Ivye 4) Yosef Schlosberg 6) Zvi Schneider 7) Mordechai Levine (Mottel Traver) 9) Chaim Levin
Sitting: 3) Yaakov Stolarsky 4) Yaakov Shmidman 3) Chaim Hillel Ben-Sasson
Sitting on the ground: 1) Michael Liskowitz 2) Yona Ben-Sasson
(On the photo) "On the day of your *aliya* to our Holy Land
Blessed you are.
The students of Etz Chaim Yeshiva in Volozhin "

[Page 451]

She gave a fascinating lecture, rich in content in the firefighters' hall. The hall was full to capacity. Her speech was peppered with quotes of the sages, and she charmed the audience with her words. Her speech became a topic of conversation for everyone, for a female torah scholar, aside from Rebbetzin Freidele, was not a common site in Volozhin during those days.

Beis Yaakov was located in the house of Reb Mordechai Shishko ion Kromer Gasse.

The Council of the Yeshivot

There was a Council of Yeshivos in Volozhin (the headquarters was in Vilna, under the direction of Rabbi Chaim Ozer Grodzinsky). Its goal was to ask the householders in every town to contribute 18 Zloty a year to support yeshiva students who were studying in the yeshivos of Lithuania. The Council of Yeshivos in our city consisted of Rabbi Yosef Tabachovitz, Rabbi Yisrael Lunin, Rabbi Yaakov Shmuel Ruchamkin, and Reb Mordechai Shishko. Rabbi Yosef Tabachovitz served as *gabbai* and permanent treasurer. He used to raise money and transfer the funds to Vilna.

The *Daf Yomi* (Daily Talmud Page Study)[3]

Daf Yomi study took place in Vilna. That is, there were people who studied a page of Gemara every day. There was great interest, and a significant number of participants. Rabbi Shimon Langbard gave the class. Today he serves as the head of the Volozhin Yeshiva in Bnei Brak.

Translator's footnotes:

1. On Simchat Torah, processions around the synagogue [*hakafot*] are conducted with the Torah scrolls. Some synagogues also possess scrolls of the prophets, to be used for the recitation of the Haftarah on the sabbath, festivals, and fast days. (The custom of most synagogues is to read the Haftarah from a printed book, so most synagogues do not possess scrolls of the Prophets). Since the Torah scrolls for the *hakafot* would be given to adults to carry around the synagogue, it seems that the children were allowed to carry the scrolls of the Prophets.
2. The *Asher Yatzar* blessing is recited after using the washroom. One first washes one's hands, exits the washroom, and recites the blessing.
3. *Daf Yomi* (Daily Page) is a worldwide program, founded in 1924, that promotes the study of a page of Talmud a day in accordance with a cycle that lasts about 7 ½ years. The program continues to this day.

Polish Schools in Volozhin

By Miriam Levitan (Rosenberg) of Tel Aviv and Pnina Chait (Potashnik) of Holon

Translated by Jerrold Landau

based on an earlier translation
by M. Porat z"l that was edited by Judy Feinsilver Montel

The Powsechna - Primary School

This school contained some four hundred students in seven classes. At lease one third of them were Jewish. At the beginning, it functioned inside a building on Vilna Street. Later, the city council constructed a large new building, with a gym and a physics laboratory, on a spacious plot.

The first manager was Tyszkowski. The official language was Polish, but it also taught German. Mr. Yitzchak Shwartzberg[1] served as the Hebrew teacher. He taught us Hebrew and Bible.

We remember the wonderful summer excursions. At sunrise, we would go to the banks of the

[Page 452]

Berezina River, ten kilometers from Volozhin. We would return at sunset. We would pass the day in sports games and song. We bathed in the river. The pinnacle was the kumzitz – eating together.

The Polish Powszechna primary school
(Mr. Porat notes that the building remains as built until now.)

The academic level was high. The teachers were excellent pedagogues. They took interest in every student and followed their progress in their studies. They paid special attention to students who required extra nurturing. The school also concerned itself with artistic education. Singing clubs and drama circles were formed for that purpose. The students appeared in various plays, to their enjoyment and also to the enjoyment of the parents.

At first, a liberal spirit pervaded in the school. As time went on, when the Polish authorities began to display hostility to the Jews, the change also took place within the walls of the school. However, since the Jewish students excelled in their talents, they formed the living spirit of the school.[2]

The Commercial High School

After graduating the primary school, we continue to the commercial high school, which was founded around 5694 (1934). It had four grades. At first, we studied in the afternoon in the Powszechna school building. Later the commercial school built its own splendid building.

Professor Zukowski from Vilna, a physician by profession, served as its principal. He was liberal with a positive attitude towards Jewish students. Our sole Jewish teacher was Rachel Kivilevitch, nee Meltzer, a native of Volozhin (wife of Shneur Kivilevitch). She graduated

[Page 453]

Students of the Polish Powszechna school

[Page 454]

from a Russian high school in Lida and the Hebrew Seminary in Vilna. Later, she studied for two years far away in the University of Prague. Mrs. Kivilevitch taught Jewish history.

There were forty students in that school, including eight Jewish students. Their names are as follows: Etia Berman, Tzvia Lunin, Pnina Potashnik, Miriam Rosenberg, Rivka Rogovin, Hirsh Tsart , Rafael (Foleh) and Mina Shrira.

The Jewish students did not suffer from any discrimination or oppression. This was thanks to the personality of Professor Zukowski, who instilled a liberal-cultural spirit in the school. We never heard the insult "Zhid" or anything similar from the Christian students. In order to emphasize the lack of discrimination, Professor Zukowski appointed Miriam Rosenberg as "Starostina" [Student leader]. Her job was to organize school parties and celebrations, and to present gifts to the principal on his birthday.

The academic level was satisfactory. The students gained practical knowledge in business. They were employed in banks and government institutions during the vacation months in order to train them in practical work. Miriam Rosenberg's joy was boundless when she uncovered a significant error made by the bank manager.

The school was forced to close [Mr. Porat added: after two years] due to budgetary difficulties. A high school with a humanistic leaning opened in its place. Miriam Rosenberg and Tzvia Lunin traveled to continue their education in the commercial school in Lida, which had four grades. Anyone graduating from that school was accepted to the high school of commerce in Vilna or Warsaw.

Translator's footnotes:

1. Mr. M. Porat notes here that he was known as Reb Eliche Dverelke's. The principal Tyszkowski was followed by Mr. Trechinski. Both were Polish.
2. Mr. M. Porat adds the following detail (I did not edit his words): Particularly good was the arithmetic teacher, Pan Glukhovski. In Poland, the five grades system was used: 5-very good, 4-good, 3-sufficient, 2-insufficient, and 1-flunked. The highest grade Glukhovski gave his students was 4 minus, because for 5, he would say, knows only the God Almighty, the teacher's knowledge might be 4, so the best student could be graduated by 4 minus maximum. The second manager was Mr. Trechinski, who became the Volozhin mayor.
3. Mr. M. Porat, the original translator, added the following entire section, which does not appear in the original book, along with the photo. I left this in its original state, with only minor corrections to spelling and grammar.

The Volozhin Gymnasia - High School

Section added in by M. Porat z"l

Mr. Trechinski the former Powszechna School manager and now the town mayor initiated the establishment of a Polish High School in Volozhin. He created a committee to lead this project. Amongst its members were also representatives of the Jewish community, one of them my father, Yosef Perlman. Financed by the town inhabitants and sustained by the district authorities a stone building was erected at the former cattle market on the western Volozhinka border.

The Gymnasia opened its doors on September 1,1938. It was the first and also the last year of its functioning as a Polish School. It contained two parallel, first course classes with a complete staff of teachers and one hundred students, among them just eight Jews in a town with a 50% Jewish population.

Before reception, the applicants passed a rigorous examination in Arithmetic, in Polish language, History and Geography. Poland was strictly preserving the Numerus-clausus numbers in its anti-Semitic attitude.

The Jewish students from Tarbut were: Vulke Brudno (Ptsholke), Eyzer Finger, Monie Perlman (the author), Sonia (Boonies) Perski, and Etele (Ruvn's) Rogovin. The Jewish students from Powszechna were: Berl (der Tzigayner) Tsart, Moyshele Halpern and Arele Tsart.

There were few, if any, relations between Jews and gentile students, despite the common language, i.e. Polish we had to speak during the whole learning day.

But we were proud of our new School. The building was beautiful outside and inside. The classes were large and spacious. We were seated two and no more students at a table. Not to compare with our poor small and poky Tarbut School. We had to wear blue well-ironed uniforms, a jacket, a hat, and long slacks.

The teachers were highly professional; most of them liberal, they did not show anti Semite feelings. Except the Polish language teacher Mr. Protasevitsh who was a Catholic College graduate. He did not omit any occasion to tell a dirty story about a well-known minority. (I was told that during the Fascist occupation Professor Protasevitsh was ardently collaborating with the SS solving the Volozhin Jews final solution.)

The school was directed by Doctor Konopnitski, a short very intelligent man, nephew of the famous Polish poetess Mary Konopnitska. He taught us Mathematics and Geography. We were glad to participate at his lessons; an important part of which he used to tell very interesting stories from around the world, not neglecting politics. After the Soviets occupied Volozhin our director -"Dirtio" (so nicknamed by affection) continued his teaching and educating methods. Once he compared the German dictatorship to an inverted pyramid, supported by military bayonets. He claimed that the pyramid should fall when during war the bayonets are turned as requested against the enemy. The Police understood the allusion. A day later Mr. Konopnitski was arrested and sent to the Communist Concentration Camps whence he never returned.

Mrs. Kopylova, a big and strong woman, was our director's life partner. As doctor of natural sciences, she taught us Botany and Zoology. After the director's arrest she was "resettled" in Siberia. I had the opportunity to work with her there at hay harvest in a collective farm. Mrs. Kopylova was really a very good, strong and efficient worker. She proved practically her botanic knowledge.

Our teachers were called "professors." Except the French language teacher, she was called "Ma Soeur" – "My Sister" in French. As a Catholic nun she wore white monastery garments. "Ma Soeur" was a sympathetic lady teaching French grammar and French popular songs. I remember them till now.

The majority of the gymnasia students learned German as second language in the morning hours. Our group to learn French was a small minority once a week at afternoon. Also learning French was the Volozhin "Starosta's"- (District governor) daughter. We were jealous looking as the "Starostianka" the highest Volozhin official's daughter would be conducted home after School in an elegant carriage harnessed to a pair of beautiful horses.

We learned hard, the Tarbut graduated children in a foreign environment. But we became accustomed and finally defended ourselves honorably during the lessons and the recreations. We participated in the school excursions by foot and on bicycles to the Berezina and to the Count Tyszkiewicz summer palace in Biala, 20 km. from Volozhin placed within a fenced for deer and gazelle natural Park reserve inside the big Nalibok Forest.

For the first time in our life, we participated also at a true dancing party that was organized by the School before Christmas.

The hard learning and the pleasant time passing stopped suddenly with the outbreak of the war on September 1st, 1939.

The doors were widely reopened three months later when the Polish gymnasia was converted to a Russian High School. It became filled with Jewish youth, thirsty for education, which they had been deprived of during the Polish Numerus Clausus regime.

During the 20-month Soviet period the school flourished. Higher classes were added. Many Jewish teachers, refugees from the territories occupied by the Nazis in Poland, were employed. The Russian High School functioned until the outbreak of the German – Soviet war on June 22, 1941.

The Gymnasia High-School In Volozhin taken September 1998

The building remains intact until now. Nowadays it serves as a professional Belarus agriculture school on the Naberezhna Street in Volozhin.

1938/1939 graduates from Volozhin Tarbut School last class students and from the Volozhin Polish Gymnasia first year Jewish Students

First Name	Last Name	Nickname
Arele	Tsart	
Avromtshe		Der Guiber
Bentshe	Finger	
Bentsike	Finger	
Berl	Tsart	Der Tzigayner
Eyzer	Finger	
Feygl	Berman	
Frumke	Goloventhitz	
Frumke	Alperovitsh	
Golde	Rubinshteyn	

Chaim	Lungen	Lungen-Leber
Hayke	Rudnitski	Di Kadelikhes
Itke		
Itskhok	Perski	Nehame-Leythes
Leybl	Berkovitsh	
Meyshele	Halpern	
Reyzl	Vaysbord	
Sonie	Perski	Boonies
Sorke		Di Mazepe
Voolke	Brudno	Ptsholke
Yosele	Altman	Kurtser Freitig

All of them murdered at the age of 17-18 by the German Nazis and their European associates.

God Almighty, avenge our young schoolmates' innocent blood!

From all classmates two only had escaped the Shtetl's fate: Etele Rogovin and Monie Perlman (the translator [Note by Jerrold Landau – Monie Perlman is Mr. M. Porat, the original translator]), both of them now living in Tel-Aviv.

Theatrical Life in Volozhin

a.

"The Sale of Joseph" Show

by Reuven Rogovin

Translated by Jerrold Landau

**based on an earlier translation
by M. Porat z"l that was edited by Judy Feinsilver Montel**

And the city of Volozhin rejoiced and was glad[1]. Everyone was talking about The Sale of Joseph that would be performed shortly by the Volozhin amateur troupe, with Avraham Berkovitch as director.

Nevertheless, for the time being, not a sign could be seen of the important event. Those in the know were whispering amongst themselves that something was going to take place, but one could not hear anything clear from them. However, when they began to remove the pumping machine and other equipment from the firefighters' hall, everyone knew that they were preparing the hall for a performance.

[Page 455]

Then the curious ones asked: Who would be going? Who was part of the troupe, and who would be the actors? Very few, the nearest only were told secretly: Simon's role would be Yaakov the son of Chaim the butcher, Judah's role – Yudel Sara Laya's, and Joseph's – Motke Gedalya Zisl's. All those names made sense, and were more or less accepted. But the public was astonished to hear that the main role would be played by Meir Pesha Yente's, a man over fifty years old, chronically ill with asthma, who never stopped coughing and moved his limbs heavily. He and none other had been assigned to play the role of Pharaoh. It was dust in the mouths of the mockers and jealous people: even with all these "good traits" he was designated from birth of playing the role of the mighty ruler…

There are times to lengthen and times to make it short. Therefore, I will proceed immediately to tell the story. One bright morning, Chaim Bronke's (Narushevitch) was seen affixed signs throughout the entire city. The signs announced that on such-and-such day and such-and-such a time, the play of the Sale of Joseph will take place in the firefighters' building. Tickets were sold at the pharmacy by Avraham Berkovitch. Of course, all the tickets were snatched up immediately. Everyone sought ways of getting to the great theatrical production.

All the who's-who of Volozhin came to the gala show. The hall was festively decorated, and a stage and curtain were installed. The audience was dressed in festive clothes. The bell rung once, twice, and a third time, the curtain was raised, and the audience was astounded. It was magic! It was hard to believe that it was the creation of Avraham Berkovitch. Look at the first scene: On the stage center a veritable bonfire was set. The fire was burning. Joseph's brothers were warming up around it are singing "Flame rise up, rise up flame!" On the horizon Simon and Levi appear, wearing strands of silk to which were attached long knives, made of tiles and covered with polish. Their blood is boiling inside, as they are ready to kill and to exterminate the people of Shechem who violated their sister Dina. The scene reached its climax when Meir Pesha Yente's enters. Wonders and miracles! When I saw Meir, who changed his figure into Pharaoh, I could not restrain myself and I called out loudly: "Bravo to the expert, Avraham Berkovitch!" It was said by our sages: Even if all the people of the world gathered to whiten a crow's wing, it would be impossible. But it was done by Avraham Berkovitch. He changed the laws of nature. My eyes could not believe what I have seen. From Meir's bosom appeared the figure of Pharaoh, a veritable representative of the dynasty of Ramses. The crown on his head was a real crown. Although suffering chronic asthma, incessantly coughing, and moving heavily – he remained Meir, the son of Pesha Yente. But with Avraham Berkovitch's makeup he became the mighty ruler…

Translator's footnote:

1.   Based on Esther 8:15.

[Page 456]

b.

Plays that I Recall

by Fruma Twebner (Kivilevitch) of Tel Aviv

Translated by Jerrold Landau

The "Sale of Joseph" play that was described by Reuven Rogovin belongs to an earlier period. I remember the play that was performed during the 1920s, more precisely in the year 5684 (1924).

First of all, several words about the operetta "The Sale of Joseph." It was a popular operetta that appeared in several versions. Amateur troupes already performed it during the 17th century.

From the study bench, I was taken toward honor in "Haneim Zemirot" in this operetta. I performed the role of Joseph, the son of old age of Jacob our forefather. In the *Powszechny* [Universal or Public] school in which I studied, I participated in various plays of "Zimrat." Apparently, "Kol Hazamir" reached Moshe Weisbord, the producer of the operetta, and he invited me to star in it. Moshe Weisbord also played the role of Jacob our forefather.

Yitzchak Berman performed the role of Judah. We approached our work with awe and love. The rehearsals took place in the home of Aharon (Ahrke) Tzart, the father of the physician Avraham Tzart. Tzart's daughters and sons were theater lovers. Tzart's son participated in the play in the role of one of the sons of Jacob our forefather. The rehearsals were very difficult and tiring, and lasted until late at night. After several months, we found ourselves ready to perform before the wider community.

I think that this is something that should be told over to our children – the difficulties that a young actor of Zimrat met within the family circle. My mother had a dim view on theater. In her opinion, it was disgraceful for a girl from a good family to be involved in this "idolatry." She was concerned that I would fall into a bad crowd. However, in order to calm her suspicions, she requested that the content of the operetta be read before her, so that she could verify that there was no foul language or other matters that may violate modesty.

Tzvi Rogovin acceded to my mother's request, and read the operetta to her. My mother found that it was a kosher story, the words of which do not violate *Tzena Urena*[1]. It passed her censorship. However, she was not calmed even with this. She requested that Tzvi trouble himself to come to take me to the rehearsals and bring me back home. Tzvi took all this responsibility upon himself. Only with this condition did my mother allow me to participate in the rehearsals.

We should recall that the participants were not professional actors, but rather amateurs. Moshe Weisbord did everything in his power. He worked over the material, and a refined product emerged from his hands. He inducted us to the inner chambers of the art of acting, and his words were absorbed in our blood.

[Page 457]

Fruma Kivilevitch in the role of Joseph In the play "The Sale of Joseph"

If my memory is reliable, the operetta "The Sale of Joseph" was performed by the Young Zion Chapter in our city. The play took place in the army barracks hall, which was comfortable and fitting for theatrical performances. (In time it became a movie theater.)

It is not in my power to describe how the Jews of Volozhin felt about the upcoming performance. The city took on a festive appearance. The ambience was unusual. They prepared for this event as if for something that no eye had ever seen and no ear had ever heard. Those curious will especially want to know how a girl filled the role of a boy – the son of Jacob's old age. The play turned into a topic of conversation for everybody. There was no house in Volozhin in which the Sale of Joseph was not discussed.

The Tzofim came to the play with floral wreaths, chocolate, and candies. The first performance took place with unusual success. The audience was ecstatic, and a stream of flowers, chocolate, and candies began to pour onto the stage. The audience was especially astonished by the song of "Joseph." The Tzofim left the hall in high spirits, with singing and praise for the performance. "Fortunate is the eye that merited this." The songs of the operetta became popular songs that were sung in the homes and on the streets for a long time.

The success of the play reached the broader community of Volozhin. They approached Tzeirei Tzion with a request to put on an additional performance. The elders of the city, the notables of Volozhin, came to the second performance. Important householders, heads of Tarbut, and heads of the Zionist movement came. They sat in the front row.

[Page 458]

An event took place during this performance that is etched in my memory to this day. When the brothers cast Joseph (i.e., me) into the pit, I sang "from the depths" the following song:

> O, how great is the anger of my brothers!
> I felt that my bones were going to split.
> O, how heavy is the mist here, it is unbearable.
> Scorpions and snakes, many in the cracks.
> I curse you, snakes, in the name of G-d,
> Who created heaven and earth.
> You should hold in your venom,
> I am a grandson of Abraham of old.

I had just finished the song, and then the sound of bitter weeping was heard in the hall. In particular, the voice of Reb Yehoshua Gurwitz reached me. He was weeping over the bitter fate of Joseph. I was very touched by the resonance of the role that I was playing with the honorable audience.

The second performance in which I participated was *Dos Pintele Yid* (The Quintessence of Jewishness). A girl from Zabrzhezh also participated in this performance. I performed the role of the child Yisraelke. The Sale of Joseph play spread my name as a "star," therefore the audience awaited the play with great interest. Avraham Berkowitz, the sign artist, explicitly noted my participation. Even though I heard my praises, I nevertheless practiced over and over again for the play, for the fear of the community was upon me. This play was also accepted by the audience with great enthusiasm.

In the year 5685 (1925), the amateur troupe performed a play about life in the Land. The play was performed under the auspices of the Hechalutz chapter, and took place in the Gmine hall. The producer was "Kochav Noded" [Wandering Star], an itinerant actress who lived in Volozhin for a certain time. The name of the play was "The Red Rose." Its content was taken from the life of the *Shomrim* [guards] in the Land of Israel. The play portrays the *Shomer* going out to guard, whereas his wife was busy preparing for her birthday party. One of the guests brought her a wreath of red roses. When she saw the wreath, a great fear fell upon her. She said that she saw signs of blood in the roses. Then, her husband suddenly entered, wounded all over and bleeding. He then died. Musia Rogovin played the role of the wife. The role of the *Shomer* husband was played by Chaim Binia Kahanowitz. The role of the presenter of the floral wreath was played by Fania Kivilevitch.

With time, the Tarbut School began to develop the theatrical arts among its students. Within its walls, an amateur troupe was set up, which performed "Shlomoke Charlatan" in the year 5689 (1929). The income was dedicated to the benefit of the school as well as the Jewish National Fund. This performance was produced by an itinerant actor named Azach. This performance was also very successful.

[Page 459]

We performed many plays (including *Hamechashefa* [The Witch]). I cannot recall them all due to the passage of time. The Volozhin community loved theater. Every new play that was performed aroused great interest, and brought light and joy to the Jews of Volozhin.

The actors who participated in the play "Shlomoke Charlatan."
The photo was taken on 27 Adar II, 5689 (April 8, 1929)

First row, top to bottom, right to left: a) Yaakov Berkowitz b) teacher c) Rivka Polak d) the teacher Derechinski e) Yisrael Berkowitz f) the teacher Afrimzon g) Dora Eidelman h) Simcha Perski Second row: a) Musia Rogovin b) Sonia Perski o) the guest actor Azach d) Yona Shapira e) Cheina Goldschmid f) Shabtai Baksht. Third row: a) Dov Lawit b) Mina Perski c) Efraim Rogovin d) Shlomo Brener

Translator's footnote:

1. A traditional book on commentary and lore on the Torah, designed especially for women. See https://en.wikipedia.org/wiki/Tz%27enah_Ur%27enah

[Page 460]

The Maccabee Basketball Team

Translated by Jerrold Landau

The students of the Tarbut School were initiators of the basketball team in our city. They were jealous of the gentile youth, who practiced and played basketball games in the yard of the buildings of Count Tyszkiewicz, and later on the field of the residence of the government officials. We decided to measure up to them. At times, we won and they were defeated, and at other times, it was the opposite.

The idea behind the need to found a basketball team earned a positive attitude from all the Zionist parties and youth groups – Beitar, Hashomer Hatzair, the General Zionists, and Revisionists. The group was non-partisan, and its intentions were purely altruistic – a healthy soul in a healthy body.

The Maccabee Basketball Team

Standing (right to left): a) Efraim Rogovin b) Yisrael Berkowitz c) Yaakov Berkowitz d) Shabtai Baksht e)

The captain of the team was Efraim Rogovin, who was an expert basketball player. He displayed effective initiative in this, and he trained the basketball players to be obedient and brave.

[Page 461]

The writer of these lines was chosen as the honorary captain. Efraim conducted practice for the team three times a week, and saw success in his efforts.

We should note that even though the group earned moral support from the entire secular community in our city, it did not receive any material support. From that perspective, our team was supported on nothing. Therefore, every basketballer had to provide his own uniform, which consisted of a shirt and short pants with blue stripes – patterned after the blue and white national flag. We kept the uniforms with the brothers Yaakov and Yisrael Berkowitz. When the shoes were torn, "Shimon the Dzhik" fixed them for free.

The team quickly gained renown throughout the entire region – Vishnyeva, Ivyanets, Baksht, Zabrezye, and Trab. It was invited to play in those places. The team was received enthusiastically by the Jews of those places, and the visits became a holiday in their lives. The atmosphere during the game was sublime. Travel to the nearby towns was not that expensive. They hired a wagon, and seated half of the basketball players on it. After travelling a few kilometers, they would switch, and the other half would go onto the wagon. Thus, after having "gotten on and off" they arrived in their place happy and glad. An extra, "Little Peretz" (Peretz Rogovin) always accompanied us on this trip. He was a fanatical basketball player, and never missed any basketball game.

Without doubt, the central "historic" event of the team, which ended in a particularly painful manner, was the competitive game with the chosen ones of the border guard that was stationed in Volozhin. As is known, a brigade of approximately one thousand soldiers was stationed there. It was not difficult to find basketballer players, even particularly good ones.

Efraim Rogovin met the captain of the army basketball team by chance. He recommended that Efraim arrange a getting-to-know-you game between his team and our team, which would take place on the army sports field (*Wojskowy Plac Sportowy*). On the spot, they agreed on the date of the game.

Avraham Berkowitz made use of his artistic talents and drew official announcements, which were posted in all areas of the city. On them, written in large letters, it stated that on such-and-such a day and such-and-such a time, , the Maccabee team would compete with the chosen ones of the border guard brigade. Tickets at such-and-such a price could be purchased upon entering the sports field.

Members of the team prepared for this competition as if for the Day of Judgment. They felt that they would require Divine assistance in order to defeat the chosen ones of the border guard. Therefore, thy approached Motel Traber, a Yeshiva lad, and asked him to choose verses from the Book of Psalms that might be able to tear up the decree of defeat.

Even though Motel Traber had never seen the form of a basketball in his entire life, he regarded this as a form of obligatory battle, "to wreak revenge upon the gentiles." Therefore, he approached this matter with full seriousness. After diligent study of the books of Psalms he selected the following verses:

[Page 462]

Who maketh my feet like hinds', and setteth me upon my high places.
Thou hast enlarged my steps under me, and my feet have not slipped.
I have pursued mine enemies, and overtaken them; neither did I turn back till they were consumed.
I have smitten them through, so that they are not able to rise; they are fallen under my feet.

(Psalms 18: verses 34, 37, 38, 39)[1]

On Sunday morning, before the beginning of the game, the basketball players recited these verses with devotion and intention during the *Shacharit* prayers. Some did so in the synagogue in Aroptzu, others in the synagogue in the marketplace, and still others in the Kloiz on Vilna Street.

The beginning of the game was nice. The band played the Polish national anthem and Hatikvah. However, what took place after that on the field, we did not even see in our nightmares. We immediately met an inimical attitude. Our team let through several goals at the beginning of the game. There were many anti-Semitic riffraff and lowlifes in the crowd watching the game. Inflamed by this dizzying victory, they broke out in hateful shouts "*Zydzi do Palestyny!*" (Jews, go to Palestine). When the number of goals that we suffered reached seventeen, and the anti-Semitic shouts increased, an angry shout suddenly pierced the air: "*Makabiusze zejsc z Placut!*" (Maccabees, get off the field) The basketball players immediately began to leave the field, accompanied by anti-Semitic taunts.

The basketball team existed for a brief period. After several of the members of the team made aliya to the Land, and others were drafted to the Polish army, it weakened, and "its soul departed."

Translator's footnote:

1. The translation of these four verses is from Mechon Mamre: https://mechon-mamre.org/p/pt/pt2618.htm

[Page 463]

Figures & Types

[Page 464]Blank[Page 465]

Emissaries, Rabbis and Slaughterers
The Emissaries of Volozhin

by Eliezer Leoni

Translated by Meir Razy

Donated by Anita Frishman Gabbay

Rabbi Chaim of Volozhin founded the "Etz Chaim" (Hebrew: The Tree of Life) Yeshiva with his own money. However, the financial burden was soon beyond his financial means. This fact was demonstrated in the following story: one of his students, Rabbi Mordechai of Minsk, formed a Yeshiva in Minsk. A famous benefactress named Blumka took it upon herself to pay all of the expenses of the Yeshiva, including the living expenses of its students.

Rabbi Chaim used to say that the Yeshiva in Minsk gave him more satisfaction than his own Yeshiva in Valozhyn. People asked him how that could be as his Yeshiva was bigger and was considered more important. He explained that he was getting more satisfaction from the Yeshiva of Minsk because it was sustained by one benefactress, while he was obliged to work tirelessly for his Yeshiva's funding[1].

As the Yeshiva expanded and the number of its students grew, he realized he was no longer able to support it by himself. He asked the Jewish people for help and many people donated. However, he thought that having traveling agents and emissaries would help publicize the Yeshiva in the Jewish world and thus bring in even more donations. Rabbi Chaim wanted to give a more moral aspect to these donations. He would quote the Talmud: "Rabbi Elazar of Bartosa would say: Give Him what is His, for you, and whatever is yours, are His." (Pirkey Avot 3:7)

He explained that G-d gives a person everything he has and is asking the person for a small portion in return. He also warned that G-d may take everything away from the person who would not "give back"[2].

[Page 466]

The emissaries were Torah Scholars as well as good orators and they were dedicated to raising generous donations[3]. They were the Foreign Ministers of the Yeshiva. They traveled to different European countries and served as the reporters and distributors of Jewish news among these communities. The Gaon Rabbi Chaim, the NATZIV and other leaders in Volozhin learned much about the Jewish life in all these different communities and about their leaders and rabbis. They were able to gather information about the economy, culture and political developments in all these different Jewish centers.

It very quickly became clear that some of the emissaries spent most of the donations they collected on their traveling and personal expenses. Rabbi Chaim Soloveichik commented: Now I understand the sentence (the Bible, Numbers 13:2) "Send some men to explore the land of Canaan, which I am giving to the Israelites. From each ancestral tribe send one of its leaders." He said that the Hebrew word for "to explore" could also be understood as "to leave some of the money Moshe allocated for the expenses of their trip" (a Hebrew play on the words 'yaturu' and 'yatiru')[4].

One emissary explained to Rabbi Chaim that he had trouble raising large donations because his appearance was that of a poor man. It would be different if he had a nicer wardrobe and drove a fancier carriage.

Rabbi Chaim obliged and that man went out for another round of fundraising, this time nicely dressed and with a nicer horse and carriage. He visited a generous Jewish farmer, but this time the farmer refused to donate.

[Page 467]

When Rabbi Chaim heard the story, he himself went to visit that farmer. The farmer welcomed the Rabbi and said that he would not donate to a Yeshiva that was wasting so much money on the appearance of its emissaries.

The rabbi explained to him (Exodus 35:31) how Betzalel constructed the Holy Arc. Some parts of the Arc were more holy than other parts but all the parts were important and necessary. Similarly, every person who donated his or her gold and silver had wished that it be used for the Holiest of the Holy, but Betzalel could read their real intentions. Some intentions were pure love of G-d and their gold was used for constructing the Arc. Others hoped more for recognition and their gold was used for the legs of the Arc.

He continued: Supporting the Yeshiva is similar. The holiest part is the 'student body' but the students would not be able to devote their time to learning without adequate fundraising. Fundraising requires an emissary who requires a wardrobe as well as a horse and a carriage. The horse requires food; the carriage requires tar for the wheels. The different donations are used according to the holiness of the intention of the donor. Some donations are used for studying while others are used to feed the horse.

The farmer accepted this explanation and continued donating generously to the Yeshiva[5].

[Page 468]

The author of the book "The Vineyard" (HaKerem) wrote about the benefits of having emissaries. "These emissaries brought a lot of plusses to the communities they visited. They spread the knowledge of G-d and love of Torah during their annual visit to communities that had no other connection to Jewish life. One could see how many slaughterers, cantors and Torah teachers joined these communities in recent years. This growth of Judaism was driven by the spirit that the emissaries had brought to the towns and villages. The Yeshiva of Volozhin benefited from paying the expenses of all these emissaries who, in their turn, helped promote the Jewish spirit in these neglected communities."[6]

The custom of sending emissaries to collect donations for the Yeshiva continued after Rabbi Yitzale succeeded his father, Rabbi Chaim, as head of the Yeshiva. A famous emissary at that time was Rabbi Yitzale of Volozhin who visited the U.S.A and Siberia. He used to travel to America, crisscrossing it for three or four years collecting donations. Then he would return to Valozhyn and shortly after he would travel to Siberia for a few years.[7]

The number of emissaries grew significantly during the time of the NATZIV as the number of students grew rapidly and expenses increased. Many people immigrated to the U.S.A. at that time and established communities based on their original towns (landsmanship). These communities became active donors.[8]

The great fire of 1886 destroyed a large section of Valozhyn and pushed many people to immigrate. It was that year that the "Association Etz Chaim Volozhin People" was established in New York with one of its declared goals being the continued support of the Yeshiva.

The NATZIV sent a letter[9] to the Polish and Russian Jewish expatriates in the U.S.A. pleading for help and explaining the urgency of their need for support. Jewish communities in the Russian Empire were under great economic pressure from the government and many residents were immigrating. He signed the letter thanking "those who live far away but their hand is opened for charity, and G-d will reward them."

[Page 469]

In his memoir, Yehuda David Eisenstein wrote about Rabbi Meir Freiman who studied at the Yeshiva in 1862-63. He was an emissary and an active member of the New York Jewish community and collected donations for the Yeshiva.[10]

The Head of the Yeshiva gave each emissary a Letter of Nomination that was used to open doors, hearts and wallets of the communities they visited. In 1886, a letter written by the NATZIV and given to Rabbi Zvi Hirsh, the emissary to Prussia stated, "The Yeshiva of Volozhin is better than all the other Yeshivas of Poland and Russia in educating teachers and rabbis."[11]

One of the emissaries for the NATZIV was Rabbi Shalom Eliezer Rogovin. He had been born in the town of Dzyatlava and was brought to Volozhin by the NATZIV. Each year the NATZIV selected ten promising students for a five-year study term at the Yeshiva. At the end of his term, Rabbi Shalom Eliezer Rogovin was nominated as the emissary to the U.S.A.

Rabbi Shalom Eliezer Rogovin

In 1892, the Russian government closed the Yeshiva after it refused to expand its curriculum to include general studies and languages. The institution of emissaries stopped functioning. However, it was reopened in 1899 under the leadership of Rabbi Raphael Shapiro. Rabbi Akiva Meir and Rabbi Peretz were the emissaries to the U.S.A. between 1909 and 1912.

However, the fundraising activity never again reached the level of the Yeshiva's earlier years.[12]

Original Footnotes:

1. R' M. Lipson, Midor Ledor, Vol 2, #1213
2. Ruach Chaim, page 51, Kerem Shlomo Publishing, 1958
3. R' Yitzhak Rivkind, The Story of Valozhyn Support in America, Hatzofe daily newspaper, Jan 21, 1966, issue #10021
4. R' B. Yahushzon' Fon Unzer Sltan Otzar, Vol 4 page 63
5. R' Moshe Shmuel Shapiro, Toldot Rabeinu Chaim miValozhyn, pp 18-19, Kinor David Publishing, Jerusalem, 1957
6. Olam Barur, by Hakorem, 1887 p.79
7. R' Meir Berlin, MiValozhyn Ad Yerushalaim, p. 29
8. Erez, Yeshiva Shel Maala, Hameliz, issue #9, Feb 1, 1885, p. 140
9. The letter was printed in Hameliz, Feb 4, 1885 #10, p. 159
10. Yehuda David Aizenstein, Otzar Zichronotay, part 2, p. 253B, New York, Oct-Nov 1930
11. Hanatziv MiValozhyn, by Rabbi Moshe Zvi Neria Kook, Yahadut Lita, Am Hasefer Publishing, 1960, p. 367
12. R' Yitzhak Rivkind, The story of Valozhyn support in America, Hadoar, 29 Tevet 5726, issue #12, p. 188

[Page 470]

Rabbi Zvi Yehuda Namiot (aka "Der Shaliver")

by Benyamin Shafir (Shishko)

Translated by Meir Razy

Donated by Anita Frishman Gabbay

Volozhin was the spiritual center of Jewish life for Lithuania, Poland and Russia. The town was a magnet that attracted the best and the brightest of each new generation of students. These students were drawn to G-d, the study of Torah, high spirits, brave new ideas, and love for Israel. They longed to return to Eretz Israel.

Being a leader of any Yeshiva in Volozhin was a privilege and a very demanding occupation for any Rabbi. One such privileged person was Rabbi Zvi Yehuda Namiot. In 1935, he founded the small yeshiva "Darkei Noam" (Pleasant Ways) and served as its Head Rabbi and spiritual teacher.

The name he chose for the Yeshiva reflected the spiritual heritage of Rabbi Chaim and echoed Rabbi Namiot's way of life.

Rabbi Zvi was murdered by the Nazis on November 22, 1941.

Rabbi Zvi Yehuda Namiot

ישיבה קטנה

"דרכי נעם"

בוואלאזין

The letterhead and the stamp of Yeshiva "Darkei Noam"

[Page 471]

Rabbi Shmuel Fried

by Benyamin Shafir (Shishko), (Karkur)

Translated by Meir Razy

Donated by Anita Frishman Gabbay

Rabbi Shmuel Fried was born in Volozhin in 1869. His maternal great-grandfather was Rabbi Chaim of Volozhin and his paternal great-grandfather was Rabbi Hillel Fried of Hrodna. He received his rabbinical education in the Etz Chaim Yeshiva in Volozhin.

In 1897 he married Feiga-Lea, a daughter of Rabbi Yehuda Leib Chazanowitz, the Rabbi of Nowyswiat near Vilna and a descendent of RASHI. Rabbi Shmuel became the Rabbi of Nowyswiat after the death of his father-in-law in 1906 and became a member of the Vilna Rabbinical High Court in 1910.

Rabbi Shmuel Fried

In 1912, he was a member of the Vilna delegation to lawyer Oscar Gruzenberg regarding the Beilis Trial [Menahem Mendel Beilis was a Russian Jew accused of ritual murder in Kyiv and although Beilis was acquitted after a lengthy process by an all-Slavic jury, the legal process sparked international criticism of antisemitism in the Russian Empire]. In 1914, when WW-1 broke out, he was in Germany and solicited help for Lithuanian war refugees. Afterwards, he returned to Vilna and continued his work in assisting the refugees.

In 1919, the Vilna Regional Office of YAKAPA was founded with Rabbi Shmuel Fried appointed as its Director.

He was one of the founders of the Jewish Bank of Vilna, and when the Polish Government instituted Jewish self-governing Committees, he became the Chairman of the Committee on Religious Matters. In this role, he founded several Talmud Torah schools.

He was a member of the Mizrachi Zionist Movement. In 1927, he was nominated by the local Governor to the Agency which was in charge of assisting flood victims in Galicia.

[Page 472]

Rabbi Shmuel Fried helped Jews and non-Jews alike. His sister, Rebbetzin Friedale, used to refer sick people from her town for his assistance in Vilna. His accomplishments followed the great traditions of Valozhyn and influenced this great Jewish center of Lithuania in Vilna.

In 1941, Rabbi Shmuel Fried was murdered in Ponar along with many other victims from Vilna.

(Source: "Pinkas YAKAPA")

My father, Rabbi Yehoshua Hacohen Kaplan z"l

by Rabbi Meir Hacohen Kaplan
(Member, Tel Aviv Rabbinical Court)

Translated by Meir Razy

Donated by Anita Frishman Gabbay

My father was born in the town of Patchize in the Babruysk Region around the year 1872. The family and the whole region followed the CHABAD tradition. In his search for a Jewish education, he attended the Yeshiva of Slabodka, near Kovna. At that time, the head of the Yeshiva was the GAON Rabbi Yitzhak Belzer and the lead teacher was Rabbi Nathan Netta Zvi Finkel. Rabbi Nathan was very strict and emphasized ethics classes, classes that my father skipped while he concentrated on following the "GEFET" method. This method was known for its study of the Talmud, the RASHI interpretations and the later commentary on the RASHI interpretations. He was known as "Hamatmid (the persistent) from Babruysk" but his disobedience caused tension between him and Rabbi Nathan.

The GAON Rabbi Hirsh Rabinowitz, the Chief of the Jewish High Court in Kovna, tried to help him and asked Rabbi Nathan to ease his criticism, but to no avail. Eventually, my father found a Chabad-Lubavitch family that supported his studies and he moved to the Yeshiva in Ponimon[?], a suburb of Kovna, and continued studying there.

In 1899 he moved to Volozhin. He was embraced by Rabbi Raphael Halperin, the Head of the Yeshiva. He married Beila, the only daughter of Rabbi Yehuda Felishetz z"l.

[Page 473]

During his time at the Yeshiva in Volozhin, he studied the Poskim (the term in Jewish law for legal scholars who determine the position of the Halakha in cases of Jewish law where previous authorities are inconclusive or in those situations where no clear halakhic precedent existed) and graduated as a Teaching Rabbi. He first started teaching in Kolel Brodeski in Volozhin, moved to the town of Lubavitch and then to Vilna, where he published several books. These books became popular within the Chassidic community of Poland.

My father's life was dedicated to religious studies. He built an "iron curtain" around himself protecting him from the outside world. He invested all his time in studying and understanding the Holy Scriptures, including problems that arose from the writings of the RAMBAM. He studied Morals, the meaning of Paradise, Hell, and Death.

He declined several propositions to serve as a Rabbi of a community, even those that came from important and respected communities. To supplement his income he became a teacher in a school on Mila Street in Warsaw. At the start of the First World War, he left the city and returned to Volozhin. After the

War, he moved among several small Lithuanian towns. First, he settled in Kruki, then in Chovenichky. In 1927, he became the Head Dayan (Judge) of the court Vidukle near Kelme.

He and all the Jewish community of Vidukle were murdered on July 24, 1941.

My father wrote several books: Sheari HaKodesh (two volumes elaborating on the services in the Temple according to Chaim Yosef David Azulai: Mo-re beEtzba and Ziporen Shamir), Mayanei HaYeshua, Shaar Yehoshua, Likutei Shoshanim, and Sheari HaVesatot.

The Slaughterers of Valozhyn
(Before the Second World War)

by Moshe Elishkevitsh

Translated by Meir Razy

Donated by Anita Frishman Gabbay

Three slaughterers worked in Volozhin before the war. They were Rabbi Israel David, Rabbi Zvi Hirsh Namiot and my father, Yoseph Elishkevitsh who was known as "the shochet of Arapecho". My father, who had been a slaughterer in Zbazaza, came to Volozhin to take the place of Rabbi Wolf, who was both a slaughterer and a cantor.

[Page 474]

The Jewish slaughterers had hard times after the government banned Kosher slaughtering. This 1937 edict put the slaughterers and the butchers under economic stress.

The Jewish leaders announced a two-week strike by all the Jews in Poland, showing the Government that they had real economic power. The Jewish residents of Volozhin showed their commitment to their values while the non-Jews were amazed by this manifestation of unity.

The Government took a step back and allowed four kosher butcher shops to continued operating. As a result, the slaughterers agreed to allow the other butcheries to sell non-kosher meat to non-Jews.

Rebbetzin Feyga Unterman

by Rabbi Israel Shapiro

Translated by Meir Razy

Donated by Anita Frishman Gabbay

Rebbetzin Feyga's father was Rabbi Yochanan, a respected and modest man who was a Torah scholar. His father (her grandfather) was Rabbi Avraham who was called Avramil Yankel Yochanans. He was a Torah scholar, a very religious man who completed reading the whole TALMUD every nine months.

This was the home where she grew up and where she absorbed the love of Torah and good deeds. She saw her destiny in life as helping Jewish scholars.

She married Rabbi Shlomo Hayman (he was called Shlomo Pritzer) who was the Head of the "Shearei Torah" Yeshiva in Kremenchuk. Later, they moved to New York where he also became Head of a Yeshiva. During the twenty years she lived in New York she was known as a person who was always lending a helping hand to people. During the Second World War, she helped refugees who wished to marry and start families and who were looking for spouses. She was like a mother to orphans and poor brides and a sister to people who suffered from depression. Her home was the place where many people would come looking for aid. This included yeshiva students and even important Rabbis. She also helped raise the funds required to publish several books. She did not wait for people in need to find her but used to search them out and provide support.

Her husband died while they were in the U.S.A. and she remained a widow for fifteen years. In 1958, she came to Israel and married the GAON Rabbi Unterman, the then Chief Rabbi of Tel-Aviv, who later became the Chief Rabbi of Israel.

[Page 475]

She continued her charity work until her last days. She used to say, "I want to be healthy and to do a good deed today. Life without doing good deeds cannot be considered a life."

She passed away on December 31, 1964, at age 68.

Rayne Batya Berlin
(A Granddaughter of Rabbi Chaim of Volozhin)

by Rabbi Bharuch Halevy Epstein z"l

Translated by Meir Razy

Donated by Anita Frishman Gabbay

Rebbetzin Rayne Batya was the first wife of the NATZIV. She was a daughter of the GAON Rabbi Yitzale of Volozhin, intelligent, modest, and highly educated. All through her life, even in summer, she used to sit next to the heater in the dining room with the table covered in books. The Bible, the Talmud, "Ayn Yaakov", "Menorat Hamaor", "Kav Hayashar", "Zemach David", "Shevet Yehuda", and other similar books were among her reading matter. She focused on reading and studying, paying no attention to the world around her.

I heard her many times complaining about the condition of the women in her world. She protested against the limitations put on women who could not enjoy the mitzvahs of Tefilin, Tzitzit, Sukkah, and Lulav and all the other mitzvahs that men were obligated to fulfill. She envied men who were instructed to follow 248[1] mitzvahs while the 'deprived' women had to follow only three.

At one time, she expressed deep sorrow saying that not only did men disrespect women with regard to mitzvahs but they also respected women less than four-legged animals.

"Let me show you", she said. She opened the Shabbat section of the MOED part of the Talmud and read from chapter 5:

MISHNA I.: What gear may we let animals go about in and what not?

Then she read from chapter 6:

MISHNA I.: In what (ornamental) apparel may a woman go out, and in what may she not go out?

"Here you can see! Our sages did not hesitate to discuss animals before they discussed women! Is there a greater disrespect than this?"

[Page 476]

She was very bitter about the fact that any man, no matter how uneducated or contemptible he was (even someone who could not read or understand what he was reading), that very same person who would need to ask for her permission to even enter her home, could arrogantly say in front of her:

"Blessed are You, Adonai our God, King of the Universe, Who did not make me a woman." (in the Morning Prayer).

And she had to say "AMEN". She considered this as the ultimate insult to all women!

Rebbetzin Rayne Batya realized how short I was of money while studying at the Yeshiva. She tried to make me feel better by quoting the Talmud:

"Such is the way of Torah: Bread with salt you shall eat, water in small measure you shall drink, and upon the ground you shall sleep; live a life of deprivation and toil in Torah." (Talmud, Avot, Ch 6 Mishna 4). She then explained that the difficult conditions would persist only while the student is "on his way" to learning. His conditions would improve after he learned enough.

She promised me that one day I would become a smart Rabbi and then I will be respected and my economic condition would greatly improve.

(From "Makor Baruch", Vol. 4, Ch. 46: "The wisdom of Women")

Translator's Footnote:

1.   A typo error in the original book shows 245.

Batya Miriam Berlin, (nee Epstein)[1]

By Rabbi Meir Berlin z"l[2]

Translated by Jerrold Landau

based on an earlier translation
by M. Porat z"l that was edited by Judy Feinsilver Montel

Rebbetzin Batya Miriam,[3] the second wife of the great rabbi of Israel, the Netziv, was a woman of powerful spirit, character, and energy. For more than twenty years, she was a helpmate of her husband in his private life and communal affairs, in times of ease and times of suffering, in work hidden from the public eye and with an obvious, recognizable partnership, with internal quietude in the household, and with a stormy soul in public.

This woman was great before she reached a public position. She was a significant person in the full sense of the sublime term even before she became the wife of a significant person. She was recognized for her spirit and deeds while she was still young,

[Page 477]

for she was unlike most women. She had the spirit of the love of Torah, deep outlook on life, and extraordinary energy.

She was born to her father, the Gaon Yechiel Michell Halevi Epstein, while he was in Bobruisk. She was raised and educated in Novozhibkov, where her father had been accepted as the rabbi. When she reached the age of marriage, many of the best young men from the finest and richest families were ready to ask for her hand, for she was very beautiful, and she had a good intellect and pleasant manners. She was well educated with respect to the concepts of the time. She read and spoke Hebrew, and knew Russian and some German. However, she informed her parents that riches, beauty, and pleasure do not interest her. She desired that her husband be a scholar who occupies himself in Torah – that was her entire wish. Despite this, she was matched with a young man, the scion of a very wealthy family from the city of Chernigov. He was a proper and fine man, and he and his parents both promised that he would dedicate time to Torah and would be appropriate for his young wife and her demands.

It was not long before the women got to know that her husband, although he sat and learned and perused books here and there, did not possess the talent and desire for the study of Torah and for being a scholar in accordance with the concept that she knew from her home and family. She rose up and informed her husband and father-in-law that she cannot and does not desire to become accustomed to such a life, a life of wealth and honor, but a life devoid of Torah, and she therefore desires to separate and get divorced. She left behind all the jewelry that she had received, and she did not touch any of the beautiful dresses that she possessed. She stood her ground, stating that she had nothing against her husband and his family, but she was simply unable to live with an ignorant person. She left the home and the city, since her husband and his parents refused to grant the separation and divorce. Russian law of that time allowed a husband to search for his wife via the police before a divorce took place. The husband and his father, being mighty and strong-willed individuals, took advantage of this. The police went out to search for the rebel wife in any city or place where they suspected she might be, find her, and bring her home accompanied by police escort. Of course, she did not return to her parents' home, but rather hid for several months until she received a *get* [Jewish divorce document]. She did not demand anything, not even the conditions of the *ketubah*[4], so long as she could be free to marry a scholar. When she returned to the home of her parents, who considered her to be abnormal for abandoning wealth, riches, and a house full of everything good without a sufficient reason, her parents and relatives asked her about her thoughts for the future. She answered openly that she would even marry a poor or elderly person, even if the person is of poor pedigree, as long as he is scholar, for a person who does not know Torah, even if his honored by people, is unfit in her eyes.

During that time, the Netziv, who was around age 55, lost his first wife[5]. One of the *meshulachim* [emissaries to collect charity], Rabbi Dov of Slutsk, traveled to the area of Novozhibkov. He knew the rabbi of the city and his divorced daughter, as well as all the wonderful things that were said about her – that, despite her beauty, youth and intelligence – she preferred to live a life of poverty, as long as it would be a life of Torah and fear of Heaven, over a life of wealth and honor with a man who was lacking Torah. He recommended

[Page 478]

to her father and mother, Michla, the younger sister of the Netziv, a match with the illustrious uncle from Volozhin. Both the father and mother chastised that man for his craziness and outlandish recommendation. However when the "one spoken for" heard this herself, although she had never met her uncle but had only heard of his great name from afar, said, "I will cleave to the dust of his feet, I will be to him like a daughter and servant, only that he spread his wings upon me, for I can have no greater pleasure in my life than being the wife of this great man. Age and a life of hardship mean nothing to me, so long as I merit to be the life partner of the Gaon in Torah and the great one of Israel."

The emissary continued on his way, returned to Volozhin and put the suggestion of marriage before the rabbi. He did not finish describing his proposition when he heard the sound of censure, "Is it possible that a woman thirty years younger than I, and accustomed to different conditions and life of a big city, would consent to come to me? And as for me, I do not wish to begin a new life, so how can I do such a great travesty to my flesh and blood, the daughter of my sister?" This emissary did not back off, and did not stop recommending time and again this unusual proposition, both in Volozhin and in Novozhibkov. After much discussion, the two sides met in Molodechno, close to Volozhin. Then that wonderful 28-year-old woman became the Rebbetzin in Volozhin and the wife of the Netziv.

As great as her love for the Torah, so was her love for charitable work and benevolence. Words of Torah and discussions of scholars were pleasant to her. She herself was also diligent in Torah, to the extent that was possible. Even with all her efforts in matters of the household and especially in matters of the Yeshiva, she never missed the daily portion of Psalms and *Maamadot*[6]. Every Sabbath, she would review the weekly portion twice, with three translations: the traditional *Unkelos*, Russian, and German. Aside for this, she completed the book of Proverbs every Sabbath, and studied *Pirkei Avot* in the summer. She had full understanding and she delved into the explanation of the verses and the *Mishnas*, so many words of the sages were on the tip of her tongue, and she knew how to conduct discussions and debates on the proper sources of the verses and the words of the sages.

She was also familiar with the tribulations of the young scholars, and would search for solutions and recommendations to improve their lot. She would comfort them when they would complain to her, reminding them how bright their future would be both physically and spiritually. Her assistance to the Yeshiva students was especially expressed in exceptional cases. When one of the students got sick, she would busy herself with summoning physicians. In cases of serious illness, she would bring expert doctors from the large cities. It is no wonder therefore that the young Rebbetzin became known in a wonderous, splendorous way. Yeshiva students, rabbis, and communal activists who came from afar would tell of her praises and laud her deeds.

The great affection for her was especially demonstrated at the time of her illness. The many physicians who were summoned from various cities did not find a remedy for her illness, and suspected that a day would come when she would not survive. Men and women gathered by the hundreds, prayed and cried out to the Healer Of The Ill to send His help.

[Page 479]

All the Yeshiva students burst out in crying, recited several chapters of Psalms, and added a name to the ill person, who would now be called Chaya Batya Miriam[7]. The crisis passed that night, and she arose and was healed.

Immediately after her marriage, her illustrious husband asked her whether she would prevent him from traveling to the Land of Israel. She did not hesitate for a moment and responded that she would be happy if she were to merit coming to the Holy Land, to live there, and not just to die there. She did not merit this with her illustrious husband, but many years later, she made *aliya* with joy, witnessed the upbuilding of the land, and blessed G-d day by day that she reached that place.

Translator's Footnotes:

1. There is a footnote in the text here: From the book *Rabban Shel Yisrael* [Rabbi of Israel], chapter "His helpmate in his holy work" (pp. 131-134).
2. Rabbi Meir Berlin is the renowned Rabbi Meir Bar-Ilan, and he is writing here about his mother.
3. Mr. M. Porat notes here: known in Litvak Yiddish as "The Rebetzin Bashe Mirl"
4. The Jewish marriage document, which specifies a certain amount to be paid to the woman should the marriage dissolve.
5. Mr. M. Porat notes that her name was Rayne Bashe (Reb Itsele's daughter)
6. A daily recitation of various sections of the Torah, Mishna, and Talmud that is considered to be in lieu of the daily Temple sacrifices. There is a seven-day rotation of *Maamadot*. This not required by Jewish law, and is generally regularly read by especially pious individuals.
7. There is a tradition that adding a name to a sick person changes the decrees from Heaven, as the decree was made to a person with name x, and now the name is y (or xy).

My Grandmother Miryam

by Tova Berlin-Papish[1] (Jerusalem)

Translated by Meir Razy

Donated by Anita Frishman Gabbay

My grandmother, Batya Miriam, was revered in our family. In my memory, grandmother Basia-Mirl had become a legend well before I even met her.

My sister Michal z"l and I called her "grandmother angel" in our conversations. My father Yaakov was the eldest son of my grandmother and her husband, the NATZIV. My father was very talented; he taught himself and earned the Government's Matriculation Certificate in our town of Mogilev on the Dnieper and was certified as a Rabbi. He was a pure and innocent man who kept himself away from the physical "real world". He spent his days and many nights studying the Torah. From an early age I carry this picture in my memory: my father is leaning over an enormous opened book. The book is sitting on a "stand" made of wood and he is rocking against the stand, reading and sometimes even singing.

The duty of running the home and educating their two daughters was always the responsibility of Chaya-Raisa, my mother. She was the daughter of a wealthy family and, like her mother-in-law, preferred dealing with spiritual and educational matters. She dedicated most of her time, energy, her drive and income to these purposes. Her modest income was the financial support she received from her wealthy parents. This money had to support the lifestyle of the social circle she belonged to and to provide everything for her daughters. As wife of the Rabbi, she had to do all of this without revealing any of the difficulties she might be having to the community.

[Page 480]

I believe that my grandmother knew about these difficulties and supported her daughter-in-law's lifestyle, especially her aspiration to give her daughters the best possible education.

The unwritten agreement between them led to ongoing assistance. My grandmother used to send regular shipments of food, apparel and even rolls of fabrics.

At that time, my grandmother lived with her husband Rabbi Chaim Lurie, whom she married after the death of my grandfather, the NATZIV. They lived in the town of Byerazino near Minsk. Each Wednesday we had a visitor. This was Hillel, grandmother's coachman. He was a big man who wore tall leather boots in the summer, felt boots in winter and was always holding a long whip. We were always happy to see him. He slowly unloaded the coach revealing surprising gifts: silk cloth for our dresses, a piece of jewelry for my mother, a nice tablecloth, blanket covers and the like.

The food "menu" made us happy too. There were jars of jam made by our grandmother, jars of honey, jars of goose fat, dried fruit, nuts, and sweets. This was why we referred to our grandmother as "grandmother angel". We had loved her before we even met her for the first time.

With each shipment, Hillel brought a letter from grandmother. The letters were written in Yiddish but we only spoke Russian. In these letters grandmother was always concerned about our health. Mother, who translated the letters for us, was always excited when they came.

We were all very excited when we were invited to visit grandmother one year for the High Holidays. She wanted to meet her granddaughters. I think it was 1913. I do not remember any visits she made to Mogilev.

This was a major event. We packed our suitcases and were happy to ride on the train. Meeting grandmother was lovely and staying in her home was special. We were not used to such a large and beautiful house with so much furniture, a large kitchen and a wide yard with many trees.

I can hardly remember her husband, Rabbi Chaim Lurie. He was short and discrete. The home was organized and managed like clockwork by grandmother.

[Page 481]

Grandmother decided what we would eat and how we would dress, how we would spend our time and what relatives we would visit. Her control over everything seemed so natural.

The house had two servants. One of them was Jewish and the other was a Christian named Dossia. Until today, I remember one event that impressed me to tears.

It was following the meal before the fast of Yom Kippur. We were all dressed festively, ready to leave for the synagogue. Candles were lit in tall candlesticks and the atmosphere in the home was of awe and fear for the coming Judgment Day. Just before leaving, grandmother approached each person. With a weeping voice she asked for forgiveness in case she had done or said anything that had offended or hurt them. I was surprised she even asked the servants, including Christian Dossia, for their forgiveness.

All her life she was involved with charity work which included helping the poor, "Gmilut Chasadim" and "Hachnasat Kala". She and members of her charity group visited the homes of well-to-do people where they collected money and clothes which they discretely distributed to people in need.

When the First World War broke out in 1914, my uncle Rabbi Meir Bar-Ilan (Berlin) and his daughter Yehudit (may she live a long life, she is now the wife of Professor Shaul Liberman) happened to be visiting us in Mogilev. After much difficulty, my uncle found his way to the U.S.A. His wife Beila z"l and children (may they live a long life) daughter Shulamit (now the wife of professor Avraham Halkin) and son Tuvia (Doctor Tuvia Bar-Ilan) came to New York later. Daughter Yehudit stayed with us and arrived in New York in 1919. After the death of her second husband, my grandmother moved to New York. However, she did not like New York and in 1923 she moved to Jerusalem. In 1924, we moved to Eretz Israel with help from my grandmother and my uncle Meir.

For a while we lived in her apartment in the Zichron Moshe neighborhood of Jerusalem and I had an opportunity to come to know her better and to appreciate her generosity and gentleness.

Although she was very strict in following all the Mitzvahs, she recognized and accepted the progress of time. She now assisted young religious men who wanted to get a good general education. She actively supported educational institutions just as she had when she was the wife of the NATZIV in Volozhin, especially the Yeshivas, of course.

She spent her little "free time" reading newspapers and religious books.

[Page 482]

In 1932, at the age of 84, she was afflicted with several severe illnesses. On the day the physicians admitted they could not help her anymore she asked to read the Bible story of chapter 20 in Second Kings, the story of the miraculous recovery of the sick King Hezekiah. As in that miracle, she surprised the physicians, recovered and lived for six more months.

My grandmother died in early 1933 at the age of 85.

Translator's Footnote:

1. Ms. Tova Berlin-Pepish is a cousin of Dr. Tuvia Bar-Ilan

The Cheder of Rabbi Betzalel the Melamed

by Rachel Rogovin (Rubinstein), Rehovot

Translated by Meir Razy

Donated by Anita Frishman Gabbay

When I think of Volozhin I picture in my mind the modest house of Rabbi Betzalal the Melamed. During the summer the house was covered with moss while during the winter it looked as if it were collapsing under its heavy cover of snow. The windows were very small but the inside was always bright, illuminated as it was by the shining light of the Torah. The Melamed's back was crooked, his eyes sparkling black and his long, white beard framed his pale face.

I was very young when I was first introduced to the Cheder. With my friends Gittel Arotzker and Bielka Shaker, we sat around a long table. The rabbi sat at the head of the table holding a "hand" (a pointer that looks like a pointing finger) and we read from Alphabet sheets. The girls studied only until noon while the boys stayed until late in the evenings. Every day, even in snowstorms, the Rabbi who loved all his pupils, used to walk them home holding a lantern.

The Rebbetzin liked us. She used to send us on chores such as fetching a pail of water from the well or feeding the goat some hay. We loved these chores because we used the opportunity to play in the yard. We especially loved Fridays. She used to cook a pot full of beans and as soon as she left the house we sneaked into the kitchen and helped ourselves.

[Page 483]

Chaim-Yehoshua, the son of the Rabbi, taught the girls math, grammar, Hebrew and penmanship (calligraphy).

The Cheder was our mental foundation and we studied in it until we started Elementary School. Here we learned to dream, built friendships and established our links to Eretz-Israel. Rabbi Betzalel was a "Chovev Zion" and instilled the love for Zion in us. This love brought us to settle in Eretz Israel.

Starting Elementary School marked the end of our early childhood and the beginning of making new friendships.

[Page 483]

Our Melamdim
(Images of Personalities)

By Reuven Rogovin of Petach Tikva

Translated by Jerrold Landau

, based on an earlier translation
by M. Porat z"l that was edited by Mike Kalt

I shall sing out to our Melamdim (teachers), despite the fact that they did not spare from us the *kantshik* (whip). In fact, they wanted our best. They did not want to let us follow the ways of the irresponsible *shkotsim*[1] who abandoned the yoke of the Torah. Rather, they desired that we become proper Jews, accepted by G-d and by fellow humans. The teachings that we learned with them bore good fruit.

Reb Moshe Feiva the Melamed

The *melamed* Reb Moshe Feive appears suddenly in my memory. In addition to his teaching, this *melamed* used to earn a *Grivene* (Russian kopeck) filling narrow paper tubes with cut tobacco and selling them to his regular customers. For example, when we taught the verse "I was young, and then grew old, but I have never seen a forsaken person whose offspring beg for bread." (Psalms 37:25), he would fill several tubes. It was bad and bitter for the pupils when a tube ripped or when his wife would bring in tobacco from the Stambol or Mesaksudia firms which was too dry to properly use to fill the tubes. He "worked" all day, until *Ashrei Yoshvei Beitecha*, that is, until the *Mincha* service.

Reb Nachum Yudel's the Melamed

Reb Nachum Yudel's did not fill cigarettes, but he had a different weakness. He would refrain from answering questions that referred to the mysteries of the Holy One Blessed Be He. When we were studying

[Page 484]

the Book of Proverbs, a fine, G-d fearing, young man, who served his G-d faithfully, died in Volozhin. I asked the rebbe: "Is it not written in Proverbs, 'Fear of G-d prolongs days, whereas the years of the wicked is shortened' (Proverbs 10:7). If that is the case, why did such a young scholar die in an untimely fashion rather than the elderly "Pop" (priest) Migolewski of Vilna Street?" The rebbe rebuked me and said, "You are a *shegetz*!" That was his response.

Reb Nachum also served as a prayer leader, and would lead services on the High Holy Days. During the study times, we would suddenly hear the melody of *Hineni Heani Mimaas*[2]. Reb Nachum was preparing for his role: serving as the prayer leader for the High Holydays in the *Beis Midrash*.

Translator's footnotes:

1. A derogatory term for gentiles, but here referring to wayward, wild Jews.

2. The beginning of the introductory petition of the prayer leader of the *Musaf* service on Rosh Hashanah and Yom Kippur – Here I am, poor in worthy deeds…

Reb Kalev the Melamed

Translated by Jerrold Landau

**based on
an earlier translation by** M. Porat z"l

Donated by Schelly Dardashti

Our Sages used to say, "Everything depends on luck, even the Torah scroll inside the ark" (*Zohar, Nasso*, 134). Even a name depends on luck. What was the sin and iniquity of this man whose parents called him Kalev, after his grandfather? He did not get satisfaction from that name. People would joke that it the cold of the *melamed* outside – and they meant Reb Kalev[1].

Reb Kalev was concerned about the future, after 120 years, when he would be summoned to the Heavenly Court and his body would be lowered into the grave. When people would visit the cemetery, they would see a line of tombstones. They would call out "Here lies Reb Moshe, here lies Reb Chaim, here lies Reb Avraham," and all would be good and fine. Then they would suddenly approach a grave and call out, "Here is buried a dog." Perhaps people would believed that indeed a dog, and not a human, was buried there!

However, Reb Kalev faced much more serious troubles. During the First World War, a German airplane dropped a bomb over Volozhin. The bomb fell on the pharmacy of Gluchovsky, between the houses of Leizer the Baker and Yochanan Rodkes. The shrapnel from the explosion killed two soldiers and a horse. One piece of shrapnel flew by Saneh the Tailor and hit Kalev the *Melamed* – that is, the very same proper Jew who recited "Blessed be He and blessed be His Name" tens of times daily – it was specifically him that the shrapnel injured. Only G-d knows the answers!

Translator's footnote:

1. Mr. M. Porat explains the joke: Kalev is a respected Biblical name. However, in Hebrew it is spelled the same as *kelev* (i.e. dog). During cold spells people used to joke, saying "It is the *Melamed*'s cold" referring to a Russian expression that means "even dogs feel the freezing temperature."

The Melamed and Teacher Reb Avraham Gorelik

Translated by Jerrold Landau

**based on an earlier translation
by** M. Porat z"l **that was edited by** Schelly Dardashti

Last but not least, was my teacher and rebbe, Reb Avraham Gorelik. His was a modern *cheder*. He was an enlightened Jew who loved the Hebrew language boundlessly. He was the first in Volozhin and environs to conduct his *cheder* in Hebrew as an obligatory language. There was a sign in large letters on the walls of the *cheder*: "Speak Hebrew!" Hebrew became a subject of study, like mathematics, nature, geography, etc. This was a novel thing, a revolution in educational methodology. The second and third volumes of *Halashon* and *Bikurim* served the help books.

Gorelik the teacher was strict, and he demanded from his students things that seemed beyond their capabilities, and the capabilities of a person in general. He allotted only two days to memorize

[Page 485]

Bialik's "In the City of Slaughter." He also allotted two days to "The Dead of the Wilderness." He allotted three days to *Hamatmid*, and only one day to learn "Between the Lion's Teeth" by Y. L. Gordon.

The *cheder* was located in the house of Rochke *di Almone* (the Widow) on Smorgon Street (Smorgoner Gasse), near Chaim *der Shneider* (the Tailor) house. In its second year, the *cheder* relocated to a house next to the house of Avraham *der Vafelnik* (the Clay Maker) on Brovarner Street.

Reb Chaim *der Shneider* visited the class in the evenings and was happy when he heard all the Moisheles and Shlomeles speaking the Holy Tongue aloud among themselves.

All of Reb Gorelik's students, together with their loving admirer Reb Chaim *der Shneider*, were murdered in a single day[1]. Only two survived. One was Michel Lea Dina's (lives in the United States), and the writer of these lines. "Swords were pulled out and bows tensed by wicked godless murderers to defeat poor and pauper and to slaughter those who follow the path of uprightness." (Psalms 37:14)

Translator's footnote:

1. Mr. M. Porat adds: in the second Volozhin massacre on 10 May 1941.

My Father, the Melamed
Rabbi Moshe Shlomo Volkovitz

by Mendl Volkovitz / Netanya

Translated by Meir Razy

Donated by Anita Frishman Gabbay

My father taught his pupils the Bible, Talmud and arithmetic. School days were thirteen hours long and that meant that school was run from darkness-to-darkness in winters. The classroom was lit by one small kerosene lantern.

My father loved his pupils as if they were his own children. When they excelled in their studies, he would give them candy "that was delivered by angels". Those who were not bright received his special attention. His dedication earned him the community's recognition as a "good man".

His students came from Volozhin, Mizeki, Zbazaza, Vishneva and Bakshty. Our house was near the little synagogue (Kloizel) on Vilna street and the Cheder was a room in our home. Its only piece of furniture was a long table with benches on each side.

My father's aspiration was that his pupils would grow up to be good men and good Torah scholars. They would pray with their whole heart and would stay away from modern trends. Although he charged very low fees, some of the parents could not pay for their children's education. However, my father never rejected a pupil for not paying. Therefore he had to live with very little and did not see much pleasure in his life.

He was a very modest man who stayed away from gossip and lies. He never cheated or spoke badly about any person.

[Page 486]

He hated arrogance and people who were quick to promote themselves. He spent his time studying the Torah and following all its rules. At the end of each working day, he used to enter the synagogue and study Talmud which gave him a feeling of elation. On Friday nights he joined the other men in the synagogue, studying Talmud or that week's portion of the Torah. He was a Chazan and enjoyed reading aloud from the Torah. At these times, his happiness could be heard in his voice and his soul.

My father did not live for many years on this earth. Over time, his sickness diminished both his spirit and his physical condition. He died in Volozhin on July 31, 1932, only fifty years old.

Yaakov Lifshits

By Binyamin Shafir (Shishko)

Translated by Jerrold Landau

based on an earlier translation
by M. Porat z"l that was edited by Eilat Gordin Levitan

Yaakov Lifshits

Yaakov Lifshits was born in Rakov in Iyar 5667 (April 1907). His father had passed away when Yaakov was about ten years old. Despite financial difficulties, his mother was able to send him to study in Yeshiva. He studied a great deal, but he preferred secular studies. He left the Yeshiva after several years and continued his education at a Russian primary school in Rakov.

He was accepted to the Vilna Technical School in 5685 (1925). From his early childhood, he had been attracted to mathematics and the exact sciences. His interests helped him get accepted to the Technical High School. After 2 years of study at the Technical High School, he transferred to the teachers' seminary that was directed by Dr. Shmuel Yona Tsharno.

He graduated from the seminary in 5690 (1930) and was appointed as principal of the Rakov Tarbut School. After working there for only one school year, he was accepted as the principal of the Tarbut School in Volozhin, where he served as principal as well as a teacher of mathematics and physics[1].

Yaakov was an enthusiastic Beitar member since his youth.[2] He followed the ideas of that movement and fought for his world outlook. He found an arena for his communal activities in Volozhin, for a recognizable portion of the youth and adults belonged to Beitar and the Revisionists. Nevertheless, his life was not easy, for his opponents filled him with bitterness. However, there is no need to recall these forgotten thigs, for the wisest of all men said: "Their love and their hatred, as well as their jealousies have already passed."[3]

Yaakov led the school with talent and skill. He raised it to a high level, and saw

[Page 487]

success in his toil He became bent over under the burden of the work, but he accepted everything with love, for he was performing a holy task. He was the forger of the path of the school.[4]

For eight years, Yakov stood as guard of the Hebrew education in Volozhin until the Soviets came in 5699 (1939). With the change of regime, the wheel of fortune turned upon him as it did for every Jew of the city. The new regime removed Yaakov's soul from him and killed his spirit. Yaakov became depressed. The Soviet supervisor invited him for a meeting, and informed him that the language of instruction must now change to Yiddish, "as per the parents' demand." The school leadership became Communist. The principal was a Jewish woman from Russia, and Yaakov served as the vice principal. Nevertheless, Yaakov was the de facto principal. It was very difficult for him to get used to the new guard, who removed the soul and spirit of the school The curriculum was in accordance with Communist doctrine, and it was forbidden to deviate from it. Yaakov was constantly under the scrutiny of the "searcher of hearts" – the Soviet inspector. The school ran under the doctrine of "watch your words," and "he who guards his mouth and tongue is protected from tribulation of the soul," with searches and spying on the actions of the Jewish teachers.

Yaakov's spirit became burnt out during the Soviet period. They forced him to be the "destroyer." The content of his life was taken from him. The source from which he drew his inspiration, hope, and faith was drained. He walked about as a shadow among the isles of the ruins of the world of his life, that wonderful world of Zionism and Hebrew culture that built him up piece by piece throughout his short life that was crowned with deeds and vision.

The burn-out of Yaakov's spirit began during the Soviet era, and the arrival of the Germans put an end to his physical and spiritual existence together. He was taken out to be murdered when he was still in his prime.[5]

Translator's footnotes:

1. Mr. M. Porat notes that both subjects were taught in Hebrew.
2. Mr. M. Porat notes that Beitar (Brit Trumpeldor), the Revisionist Zionist Movement, was founded Zev Jabotinsky in 1925. Jabotinsky was born in Russia in 1880, and passed away in the United States in 1940. He sponsored a more assertive and non-socialist approach to the rebuilding of the Jewish homeland.
3. *Kohelet* (Ecclesiastes) 9:6. *Kohelet* is attributed to King Solomon.
4. Mr. M. Porat notes that Lifshits began his work in Volozhin in a School with four grades, by the end during the 1938/39 school year he was managing a standard primary school for that time of seven grades.

5. Mr. M. Porat (who evidently was a student at this school), added the following note. I left it in its original:
    Each Friday Yakov would gather all the students and read them chapters from Sholom Aleykhem in Yiddish.
    (Sholom Aleykhem was originally named Sholem Rabinovitsh- the famous Yiddish writer, author of "Tuvye
    der Milkhiker" renamed "Fiddler on the Roof" and many, full of Yiddish humor, folksy stories) I remember
    very well "Yossi Peysi dem Khazn's" – the wonderful story about the Russian Jews' exodus to the New
    World. We were enchanted by the Yiddish writer's stories read by our teacher in our mother language. In
    Tarbut Schools we did not learn Yiddish at all.
    Another event I remember is that with my ten years old classmates, we were invited to our teacher's apartment
    on Vilna Street in Volozhin to hear classical music. The young Lifshits couple were able to buy a real
    gramophone, one of the first in the Shtetl with some Yiddish, Hebrew, and classical records. This event was
    a memorable one for me, though it took place some seventy years ago - we heard the famous Tshaykovski's
    "Nutcracker."

Noach Perski

by Benyamin Shafir (Shishko)

Translated by Meir Razy

Donated by Anita Frishman Gabbay

Noach was born in Volozhin to his father Shimshon Perski. Noach's grandfather was the Starosta Rabbi
Yoseph-Yosel Perski, a member of the family of Rabbi Shimshon "the Dayan" (the judge) who lived at the
time of Rabbi Itzele, the son of Rabbi Chaim of Volozhin (see pp 46-48).

He was educated in the Yeshiva "Sheary Torah" in the town of Kremenchuk and then the Remilis Yeshiva in Vilna, under Rabbi Mila. He graduated from "the Doctor Kahanshtam Teachers Academy" in Vilna and was a teacher at the Tarbut School in the town of Suwalki and Valozhyn. He was a handsome man with curly hair. The combination of his inside beauty as well as his outside appearance created the all-encompassing person who inspired his students. He educated a whole generation of pioneers to work, love their nation and their country.

[Page 488]

He refused to continue teaching during the Soviet occupation (1939-1941) period. During this time the cheder was converted to a Yiddish-based school. This change was attributed to a "request by parents". Being a proud Jew who was committed to the Hebrew language he preferred to lose his work rather than give up his principles.

When the Germans occupied Volozhin he was the first to carry the yellow star of David on his chest. He considered this a symbol of national pride.

His whole family was murdered in Volozhin. Only his brother Yitzhak, who (at the time of writing) lives in Israel, survived.

Reb Eliyahu Yitzchak Shwarzberg

Written by one of his students

Translated by Jerrold Landau

**based on an earlier translation
by** M. Porat z"l **that was edited by Judy Feinsilver Montel**

Reb Eliyahu Yitzchak was born in the Oshmyany district near Vilna in 5644 (1884). He studied in a cheder in his youth. He came to study in the Volozhin Yeshiva in 5660 (1900) and learned there until 5666 (1906). Reb Eliyahu Yitzchak immediately became known in Volozhin as a precious young man. While still young, he married Dvora Elka, the daughter of Reb Yitzchak Perski.[1]

Even though Reb Eliyahu Yitzchak was great in Torah, he was discreet, and comported himself modestly with all those to whom he came in contact, in business as well as Torah and the wisdom of Israel. Although his humility was his primary trait, he was honored and revered, and his name spread out as a well-rounded man, modest, full of learning, with a good personality and fine traits.

Not only was he great in Torah, but he also excelled in secular knowledge and wisdom. In those days, more than 50 years ago, any scholar in Volozhin could obtain anything his heart desired in Torah literature – Talmuds, books of Midrash and Kabbalah, and other holy books. However, a Hebrew newspaper was an unusual sight in Volozhin. Reb Eliyahu Yitzchak was among the few who subscribed to *Hatzefira*, in partnership with the teacher Avraham Gorelik.

He did not read the newspaper only in order to know the news and what was taking place in the wide world. This was a reading of holiness. Therefore, when he received the newspaper from Ozer der Raznoshchik the postmaster, he would go to Gorelik's house. These two scholars would sit next to

Reb Eliyahu Shwarzberg

[Page 489]

the table on stools and first scan newspaper with reverence. They would touch it and feel it. Only after this spiritual preparation did they begin to read it. This was the order of the reading: they would divide up the newspaper, with each taking a page to read. When each one finished their section, they would swap, until both finished reading the entire newspaper. The debates only began after they finished reading: each stating their opinions. They would discuss the issues for many hours, debating and expressing opinions about the issues of the day that the had read in the newspaper, and about other issues about which they had not read in the newspaper, but which they knew from their day-to-day life and their interest in questions of literature, politics, etc. They also dealt with issues of *Hatechiya,* debated about Tolstoy's "War and Peace," or expressed their opinions on the murder of the anti-Semite by the Jewish student Bogrov. The Beilis trial which took place in the year 5673 (1913) played a significant role in these debates. Indeed, these were various problems that stood in the forefront of the events of the world at that time. The surprising thing is that these debates were conducted in pure Hebrew.

Reb Eliyahu Yitzchak occupied himself in Torah all his days. He studied, taught, and groomed many students. In addition, he served as the Jewish history and Bible teacher in the Polish primary school. He also taught those subjects in the Polish *Gymnasja* and the commercial school.

The Polish professor Konofnicki, who served as the principal of the *gymnasja*, did not miss any of Reb Eliyahu Yitzchak's classes. He was a full participant in all of them, and listened to any word emanating from his mouth. He would say, "These classes are the words of the true G-d." He learned a great deal from them, and enjoyed his style of lecturing and skill at explanation.

Reb Eliyahu Yitzchak joined the Zionist movement, and was an enthusiastic and dedicated member of the Mizrachi party, an activist in the Jewish National Fund and Keren Hayesod. He was active, and encouraged others to participate, as he fulfilled national and communal roles. He also served as the communal head in his time.

Reb Eliyahu Yitzchak perished in the Volozhin ghetto together with his wife and many members of the community during the great slaughter that took place in May 5702 (1942). The Nazis closed off the ghetto. Reb Eliyahu Yitzchak ran from his house to a hiding place that the people of the city had built. He was shot to death by an S.S. man as he was running.

His two sons and daughter live in the Land. One of them, Yosef Schwartzberg, served for many years as the secretary of the Organization of Volozhin Natives in Israel. The second, Mordechai, served as one of the secretaries of the Ramat Gan Workers Council. The daughter built her home in Kfar Vitkin.

This is the comfort and this is the revenge for the pure, refined life that was snuffed out, and for the destruction and loss. The children of the Holocaust victims are building the nation and the Land.

Translator's footnote:

1. Mr. M. Porat notes that: In the shtetl, where everyone had a nickname, he was called "Reb Ele-Itshe Dverelkes."

[Page 490]

Abraham Berkovich[*]

By Fruma Tzitreen (Rogovin)- Tel Aviv

Translated by Matz Dany and Matz Rivka

– A. Berkovich's granddaughter

Abraham Berkovich was a notable and important person in Volozhin For that reason, I can still clearly recall his character traits. He was very handsome, of average build, smart and always in a humorous mood.

He came from Minsk. His parents were orthodox Jews and they wished to send him to study in the Volozhin yeshivah. However, he preferred secular studies, and with his father's permission, he attended a high school in Minsk. After his father's sudden death, he was forced to leave his high school studies so he could help his mother with the household income. He continued with night lessons. He learned on his own and read many books. He was able to gain a great deal of knowledge.

He settled in our town when he married Keile from Volozhin. He opened a pharmacy in the most central location, in the market place, in the house of Mushka Persky (the baker). The pharmacy was decorated in very good taste. Two of its walls were covered with fitted polished shelves and on them were medicines in bright glass jars. The floor was polished with red varnish and covered with carpets, which were made by local farmers.

Abraham Berkovich

For a few years the pharmacy was the family's only source of income. When the children grew up and the parents decided to send them to a high school in Vilna, Keile opened a fabric store to supplement their income. The business succeeded and it enabled them to cover the large expenses they had acquired for their children's education in the big city.

Abraham Berkovich had his hands everywhere. There was not a trade that he was not proficient in. He truly had golden hands. He was familiar with various construction skills (although he never officially studied them). After the big fire burned the town in the twenties, he remodeled his shop in the Perelman's building, so he could still make a living. At a later time he bought from Yehuda Abraham Persky, the ritual slaughterer, his burnt bricks building. He cleared the damage and the water and rebuilt it. His power of invention was revealed when he invented a round heating oven covered with tin-a real invention in Volozhin of those days. He knew carpentry, and the furniture in his home, which had an original style, was all hand made.

Prior to every Passover, he would work diligently to beautify and to decorate his house with many colors and ornamentation. The sight was heart warming and cheerful. He also excelled in sign painting posters and announcements. He likewise applied make-up for the theater actors.

[Page 491]

Those deeds revealed his artistic talent and creative imagination. In addition, he would read the Torah and would blow the Shofar in the synagogue. Although in all these skills he was self-taught, all things he did turned to artwork.

"The Fire Brigade" was his main hobby. He founded it and chaired it until 1935. From that year on, the Polish government took away the management of the association from the Jews and gave it to the district governor. Berkovich remained as a consultant and an honorary member only.

Berkovich was always very active and restless (due to his good physical health). His hands were always occupied with toil. His brain was always engaged with ideas and plans. For instance he realized that the city needed an optician. He gained quick knowledge in this area, he brought an optical instrument and the problem was solved. A story was told about him: once someone came to him to order glasses. Berkovich checked his vision and found it quite normal, but the "patient" insisted he needed glasses. Berkovich gave him clear glasses and asked him to come for a check up after some time. The man came back and was very satisfied that the "glasses" saved his power of vision.

Many who knew Berkovich mentioned in many occasions his stories and fables, we'll present some of them.

1.   Once a woman came to his pharmacy she was desperate and requested poison to end her life. Berkovich tried to dissuade her and encourage her to abandoned her plans but she persisted in her request. Finally he gave her a large amount of castor oil. She took the medicine and immediately rushed home, so she can end her life peacefully. When the medicine started working and she felt pain, she became aware that her dying day isn't better that her day of birth, and since there is such pain in dying, she decided to stay alive.

2.   Here is a tale of two who disagreed and each of them stuck to his opinion. Once a drunk strolled in the street and made a lot of noise. A policeman approached him and demanded the drunk to stop yelling. The drunk said: "it's my business, policeman".
The policeman said: "if you don't obey me I'll arrest you". "That's your business," replied the drunk.

3.   A tale of a painter who painted the walls first and only than the ceiling. Berkovich remarked that it is logical to paint the ceiling first as to not soil the walls. The painter answered angrily: "I work in this profession over forty years the same way, I don't need any advice from a nonprofessional"…

* Reuven Rogovin told the life story period of Berkovich before he came to Volozhin.

[Page 492]

Yaakov (Yani) Garber

By Lea Baksht (Feigenbaum) – Netanya

Translated by Jerrold Landau

**based on an earlier translation
by M. Porat z"l that was edited by Sandra Krisch**

Yaakov (Yani) Garber was one of the prominent figures in our city. He came to Volozhin during the 1920s and immediately gained a circle of acquaintances and friends. He had higher education. His intelligence was noticeable in his mannerisms and his cultural approach to people He was careful about the honor of his fellow.

Yaakov (Yani) Garber

There was a piano in his house – something uncommon in Volozhin during those days. This magical box turned Garber's house into a public venue. Many people sat on the large porch of his house to hear the news. Yani subscribed to various newspapers, and anyone who wanted was allowed to read them. Therefore, his house was always filled with readers who were interested in what was going on in the world.

His wife Dina (known as Chaya Dinka) also had higher education. Fate was cruel to her, and she did not merit a long life. She died during Chanuka of 5684 (1933). Mourning was decreed in the city, and all the events that were to take on the holiday of Chanuka were cancelled.

Yani owned a liquor store and a flour warehouse, and was the provider of kerosene. Nevertheless, he did not aspire to amass possessions, but rather to do good for the community. He was modest, and did not pursue lofty positions. However, the Jews of the city recognized him for his fine traits, and wanted to appoint him as the communal administrator [*Parnas*]. They recommended his candidacy as mayor. He was invalidated because he was Jewish, and merely served on the city council. He served the community faithfully in that position. He toiled with the community for the sake of Heaven. Many came to ask his advice, and found an understanding heart and an attentive ear. He received everyone politely, and his hand was outstretched to the needy. He never pushed off someone who approached him with "Go and come back."

Even though Yani was an erudite man who sat on "a high and lofty chair" he did not boast or act haughtily. It was as if he fled from greatness. He walked among the simple folk as an equal among equals. During his life, he fulfilled the adage of the sages, "Go see how the masses conduct themselves." He walked around the marketplace in order to hear what the peddlers and stall-owners were saying, what was pressing them, and what was bothering them. They regarded him as one of their own. Thanks to this custom, the people were satisfied with him.

Yani was the father of two sons. One of them, Daniel, lived in Russia and earned his livelihood as a pianist of renown. The second son, Moshe (Monek), came to the Land of Israel with the army of Andras. From here, he left for Italy, and traces of him were lost.

Yani was a dedicated Zionist in heart and soul. I was about to make *aliya* to the Land of Israel in 5697 (1937). This was after the Przytyk pogrom. I discussed that bloody event with Yani. He regarded

[Page 493]

this pogrom with the utmost of seriousness. He saw it as a harbinger of evil for the Jews of Poland. Therefore, he encouraged my *aliya* and was deeply sorry that he was forced to remain in the Diaspora. I received letters from him when I was in the Land. He wrote his final letter when the Soviets entered Volozhin.

Yani served as chairman of the Judenrat during the time of the German occupation. The Germans demanded that he provide three hundred Jews for "work." Yani did not suspect murder, and he believed that this was indeed about work, through which the workers would be able to survive. Yani joined them. He realized his terrible mistake when they arrived at the sports field in front of the barracks. He requested that the Germans shoot him first. They gave him this final "act of mercy."

Translator's footnotes:

Mr. M. Porat, who was related to the family through Yani's wife, added a great deal of additional information and three pictures in his original translation. I reduced the main translation to match the original text, and I include his additional material (which was woven into his original translation) below, largely unedited:

Yani from Nikopol in Ukraine, where he met his future wife, Haya-Dina, born Perlman. The Perlman family lived in Nikopol during the First World War.

Yani's wife Haya-Dina

Haya-Dina was a highly intelligent woman. One always imagined her reading a book of Russian classics. She died at a young age during an appendectomy, which was carried out at the Volozhin hospital in 1933.

Yani owned oil, flour, and wine stores. Yani and his family lived in the big stone house built by count Tyszkiewicz for R' Chaim and ultimately inherited by Malka Perlman (born Itskhaykin), Haya-Dina's mother. The stores were situated in its large cellars. Yani also managed his business from this house.

Yani was musically talented and blessed with perfect pitch. He often joined the Beitar amateur chorus. The choir's singing became a true multi-voice concert when Yani added his voice.

Dania Garber

A piano stood inside the big salon of the stone house. It was the only piano in the shtetl. Dania, the elder son, practiced on it. He was taught by a Russian woman.

Gossip held that Malka, Dania's grandmother, once said "The teacher woman is already covered with gold while Dania is still playing octaves." But Dania continued his piano studies in spite of the shtetl's sayings. In parallel with high school studies, he took music lessons in the Vilna conservatory, and he used to play concerts in public. Ultimately the piano saved his life. During the Soviet rule, the authorities invited him to teach piano in Russia. There he married a Bobruisk-born girl; she too was a pianist. They lived in Russia when the Germans occupied Volozhin. Dania the pianist survived the war.

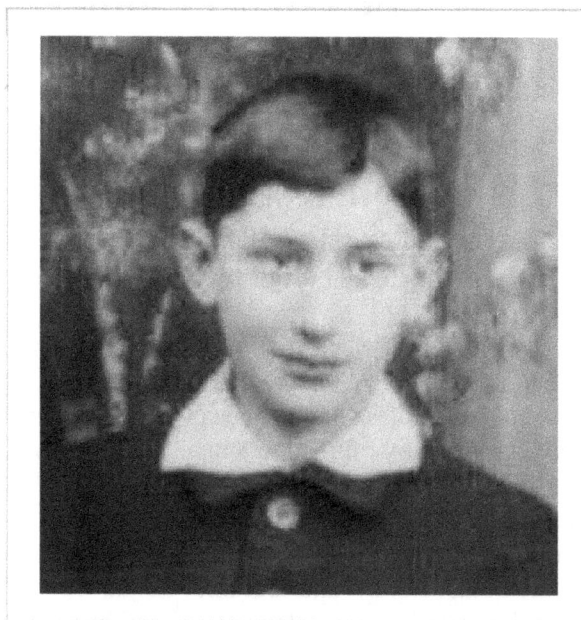

Monia Garber

Monia, Yani's younger son, carried out a prank during the Russians' rule. He tore Stalin's mustache from a wall journal at the Volozhin high school. The Soviet NKVD did not like such pranks. Monia Garber was arrested in March 1941 and was sent to the Soviet Gulag camps. After the Stalin-Sikorski agreement in 1942, he joined the Polish Anders army. With this army he reached Israel via Teheran. He could not remain in the Land and was obliged to go to Italy with his Polish unit.

Monia (Moshe) Garber was killed in the Monte Cassino battle against the Germans as a soldier of the Polish army.

After the Germans occupied Volozhin, Yani Garber was nominated to function as head of the Volozhin Judenrat. The SS ordered him to gather three hundred Jews to carry out a job near the military sport stadium. The assembled group was confined in the cinema building near the stadium. Word spread that all of them would be executed in the stadium. Yani understood that the Germans cunningly lied. As the Judenrat head, he could go free. But it was against his nature. Yani asked to be the first to be shot. His request was fulfilled. Yani Garber, one of the most honored Volozhin citizens, head of the town's Judenrat, was murdered at the sport stadium in Volozhin on October 28th 1941.

Yani Garber was the first Volozhin martyr in the first Volozhin mass slaughter.

Rabbi Yisroel Lunin

By Shulamit Goloventshits (Berger) – Bet Shemesh

Translated by Jerrold Landau

based on an earlier translation
by M. Porat z"l that was edited by Eilat Gordin Levitan

Yisroel Lunin arrived in Volozhin in the year 5670 (1910) to study at the Etz Chaim Yeshiva. The Yeshiva was headed by Rabbi Refoel Shapiro. Yisroel married Shayna Berger, daughter of Feitche and Tzvi. After his marriage he worked in the hides and linen business in partnership with Itche Meyer Berman and Lipa Levin. The linen was transported by railroad to Vilna. The business flourished greatly.

Reb Yisroel adapted himself to the life of Volozhin, and was elected as *gabbai* of the Kleizl. He devoted his time to aid and assistance of the poor and the to economic development. He was amongst the founders of the public Bank (Yiddishe Folks Bank) and became its director. The bank supported small businesspeople and tradespeople. He was also among the founders of the self-defence group during the First World War, and was an active participant in its activities.

Reb Yisroel also concerned himself with the maintenance of the Yeshiva building, which was heavily damaged during the First World War. He wrote letters to Volozhin natives in the United States in which he asked for their assistance. The funds indeed arrived, and the Yeshiva was reconditioned. Lunin also concerned himself with the dwelling conditions and sustenance for the Yeshiva students.

The following event demonstrates the relationship of honor that the community had for Reb Yisroel Lunin. Volozhin had about a dozen wagon drivers who transported passengers to and from the railway station. Then Chaim Meir Yeshaya rose up, purchased a bus, and began to transport the passengers to the station. The wagon drivers remained without sustenance, and it reached the point where they were lacking a morsel of bread. They asked Reb Yisroel to become involved in the matter. He felt that urgent action was necessary to save the wagon drivers. He recommended to Chaim Meir Yeshaya that he form a cooperative and accept all the wagon drivers as members. He accepted the recommendation out of respect for the rabbi, and, in this way, the wagon drivers were saved.

When the Polish regime was formed, Reb Yisroel Lunin was elected as head of the community of Volozhin. He earned the recognition and esteem of the Jews of the city. He went with the spirit of the times. Therefore, he supported the establishment of the Tarbut School.

[Page 494]

The family of Yisroel Lunin

Unfortunately, we did not succeed in obtaining Reb Yisroel Lunin's picture. We present here a picture of his family:
Standing from right to left: Alter Shimshelevitch (Lunin's brother-in-law) the first victim of the Volozhin Holocaust, who was shot immediately with the arrival of the Germans. Chaya Lea Shimshelevitch (Berger), Sheina Lunin (Reb Yisroel's wife).
Seated: Shlomo Berger (Lunin's brother-in-law, died in Israel)

Lunin was an ardent Zionist. I remember Grabowski arriving from Vilna to collect donations for Keren Hayesod. He called a meeting in the Kleizl. To his dismay, the response was very weak. Nevertheless, he did not despair, and he conduced Zionist publicity along with Shlomo Chaim Brodna and Yaakov (Yani) Garber. The result was satisfactory. When Grabowski came to Volozhin a second time, the Jews of our town gave him a great deal of jewelry and valuables as donations to Keren Hayesod.

Lunin and his family shared the same fate as our dear townsfolk. (Regarding his end, see the article of Mendel Wolkovitch "The Destruction of Volozhin" in the Holocaust section).[1]

Translator's footnote:

1. Mr. M. Porat notes: They were murdered and burnt with his beloved shtetl community on May 1942 in Volozhin.

[Page 495]

My Grandfather Reb Menachem Yoel Potashnik

By Chaim Ashlagi (Kfar Vitkin)

Translated by Jerrold Landau

based on an earlier translation by M. Porat z"l
that was edited by Judy Montel

Our Potashnik family business was glass production. Potash was the raw material for this, from whence the family name was derived. Potash was found abundantly in the Volozhin vicinity, and it is possible that this was the reason that our family settled in Volozhin.

Grandfather worshipped in the Kleizl. The worshippers treated him with honor, and if he was late for the *Shacharit* service, they would not begin until they clarified the reason for his absence.

During the Czarist era, there was a committee appointed by the rabbi of the city. Grandfather was among its members. During the era of the Polish regime, when the statute of the communities was confirmed, Grandfather served as the vice chairman of the community council. He was also one of the founders of the Jewish People's Bank (Yiddishe Folks Bank) and a member of its leadership until the day he was murdered. He was also one of the founders of the firefighters.

After the First World War, our brethren from overseas sent money for the poor to our impoverished town. The money was sent to my grandfather's address because they trusted his honesty and integrity.

Grandmother Sara Grunia excelled in the goodness of her heart and her love for her fellow. She busied herself with charitable deeds and anonymous donations. She concerned herself with assisting poor brides. When she did not succeed in collecting the necessary money for the wedding expenses, she would mortgage her jewelry at the charitable fund.

Grandfather conducted a patriarchal home. He was strong-willed and uncompromising in matters of tradition, ensuring that the chain of tradition not be severed. However, as a wise man, he was flexible, and knew when to give in during a dispute. He related with patience to his daughter-in-law, who wanted to educate her children in the spirit of the new times. He agreed that the granddaughters could study in the Russian Gymnasium in Minsk. That was not the case with the grandsons. There, he insisted strongly that they receive a traditional education. He sent his eldest grandson to the Wilkomir Yeshiva.

Grandfather was not a Zionist as we understand its meaning now, but he was a lover of Zion. When I decided to make *aliya* to the Land of Israel, he was very sad about breaking up the family, but he was convinced that I should not change my decision, and he blessed me warmly. He said to me, "G-d willing, we will meet in our Holy Land." There were tears in his eyes. He remained in contact with me by letter. He took interest in what was going on in the Land in general, and in my life in particular. However, he did not merit to see me, for he was murdered by a wicked gentile.

Translator's Footnote:

Mr. Porat translated the name as Menachem Mendel, whereas in the book, it is Menachem Yoel. He further notes that he was murdered on his way to work during the early 1930s.

[Page 496]

Doctor Avrum Zart
His personality and deeds

By Shoshana Nishri (Berkovitz), (Tel Aviv)

Translated by Naomi Gal **and lightly edited by** Jerrold Landau

Donated by Anita Frishman Gabbay

Avraham Tzart, who our townsfolk called "The Doctor" was not a real doctor. He acquired his medical education in a military school for feldshers (medics), from which he graduated in 1912. Nevertheless, the patients were not concerned with his credentials and treated him as a well-known doctor, since he accumulated rich experience in healing the sick and was an expert in diagnosing illnesses. He inherited his medical gift from his father "Re Aaron ("Arka") der feldsher."

Avraham Tzart was a very talented man, his talent – to quote Bialik – "was dripping from his ten fingers." In addition, he was a handsome man with pleasant manners. For many years, he represented the Volozhin Jewish community at all government events and celebrations such as Independence Day. During these events, he gave brilliant, tasteful speeches in fluent Polish.

His first speech was given in front of a large crowd in 1917, the year of the Russian Revolution. He went up to the tribunal (stage) and spoke at meetings for the many soldiers who stationed then in Volozhin and had different opinions on diverse subjects. Avraham Tzart calmed the listeners and was able to mediate between opponents with his gift of rhetoric and his power of persuasion.

Due to his vast knowledge and oratory skills, Avraham Tzart was elected as Volozhin's vice mayor. This was a great achievement, for Jews had not been allowed to take part in municipal affairs.

His wife, Tzvia, was the only midwife in Volozhin. She was always busy. When a woman was about to give birth, Tzvia was immediately summoned (in these years, the thirties, women gave birth at home). Tzvia was also active with communal needs, she used to raise money for charity. Nobody ever said refused her.

Avraham Tzart's gift as a speaker worked against him. When the Soviets entered Volozhin during World War Two, they invited him to speak to a large audience in the local movie theater. Later, when the Germans entered Volozhin, they reminded him of his "crime," his pro-Soviet speech, and he was among the first to be executed. His daughter and wife also during the Shoah.

[Page 497]

Memories Connected with Avraham Tzart

In 1933, I befriended Nechama, Avraham Tzart's only daughter. Due to that friendship, I had the privilege of listening to the radio in their residence. (In those days, there were only two radios in Volozhin. The other one was in the house of Yaakov "Yani" Garber.) Once, a young group convened in Avraham Tzart's house to listen to the Tosca opera. All of a sudden, we heard a whispering noise from outside. We made our way through the tall ficus trees that reached the ceiling and covered the windows. We saw a large crowd around the house listening to the music – some for pleasure and some out of curiosity, wanting to see the "magic box." Avraham Tzart went out to the crowd and expressed his regret that he could not accommodate them all in his house.

The visit of professor Fishel Shneerson, who came to Volozhin to collect material for writing the second volume of his book "Chaim Gravitzer," dedicated fully to Volozhin, was connected to Avraham Tzart. The home of Avraham Tzart was the most suitable to receive an honorable guest such as professor Shneerson. We spent a pleasant evening with the professor, who was a like a fountainhead of Jewish anecdotes, which I fondly remember to this day.

The epitome of memories related to Avraham Tzart was the organizing of Purim Ball. While Avrum Zart served as the vice mayor, we received permission to use for the Purim Ball the large hall of the municipality that was in Perlman's house on Vilna Street. The feeling that this year we will not have the ball in the firefighters' hall, whose walls were bare and gloomy, but rather, in a nice and clean building, full of light and air – instilled in us the feeling that this time the ball was going to be extraordinary.

Our house became a workshop to all kind of paper chains, confetti, and cotillions (tiny hats). Remarkable in their work preparing for the ball were Emma Apel, Pessia Rogovin, Nechama Tzart and Rachel Shevach (a kindergarten teacher not originally from Volozhin). She was the lively spirit in all the ball's preparations.

Then there was the commotion in renting gowns for the ball. Only few posessed such dresses. We overcame this somehow, and the ball was successful. The youth were given free entry. From among the families that participated, I remember the Paretzki, Pollak, Weisbord, Brodna, and Kaganovitz families, the teacher Lipshitz, Rachel Meltzer (Kivilevitz) and others.

The spirit was great. Everybody danced and the "flying Posta" worked relentlessly. What was this "Posta"? – the participants were given numbers, which served as addresses for letters written to them that evening. The content of the letters was comical and entertaining for the most part. In some cases, they were allowed to read the letter publicly – to the crowd's enjoyment. This "post" was for a fee, with the revenue dedicated to the Jewish National Fund.

For many years, we remembered that ball, which was organized thanks to Avraham Tzart's cordial help, who gave us access to the municipality hall.

[Page 498]

Shneur Kivilevitsh
(Lines about his personality)

By Reuven Rogovin

Translated by M. Porat z"l

Edited by Eilat Gordin Levitan and Judy Feinsilver Montel

Further edited by Jerrold Landau

I recall the Kivilevitch family with much love. The family was renowned for their dedication and self-sacrificing nature during the First World War. The following was their story: At the outbreak of the war, two Yeshiva students were stranded in Volozhin. They could not reach their hometowns since the Germans had already occupied their towns. They refused to serve in the Czar's army. The Kivilevitch family took an enormous risk and concealed the young men in their home for three years (from 1915 until 1918). They clearly knew that hiding "deserters" put them in great danger: the would be liable to the death penalty for this if they were discovered.

When the Germans conquered Volozhin in 1918, the lads returned home and told their parents about the great kindness that the Kivilevitch family did for them. Their parents sent a letter of gratitude to Mrs. Sima Kivilevitch. The letter was very emotional, and anyone who reads it comes to tears from great emotion. It was a sort of "song of praise for the saviors." I too read this letter, and I too wept.

The mother of the family, Sima Kivilevitch (nee Shriro) was born in Molodechno. She lived in Yatskevo after marriage. She had a generous heart. She would give charity generously, and she would often give discreetly so as not to shame he needy.

My first connection with Shneur came from honoring his mother. The Chevra Kadisha (burial society) in Volozhin would determine on its own the place of burial of the deceased, as well as the price of the grave and the burial. When Shneur's mother Sima died in her prime, Shneur entered the office of the Chevra Kadisha and said the following: "Who my mother was is well-known to you. You also know about the good deeds that she performed. Therefore, lay her to rest in the choicest of graves, and I will pay full fees. He did not recite *Kaddish* like one of the *Maskilim*, but rather at *Shacharit*, *Mincha*, and *Maariv* every day, without missing even a single *Kaddish* during the year of mourning. It is written (Provers 17:6): "The glory of the children are their fathers." Shneur saw his glory and splendor in his mother, and thereby, he can serve as an example for the children in our generation regarding the commandment of honoring one's mother and father.

I worshipped with Shneur in the Kleizl. We both sat at the eastern wall. He inherited this place from his father Reb Moshe. His father was a scholar. He purchased an honorable place at the eastern wall of the Kleizl before the First World War. Prior to his death, he willed that his rich Torah library be donated to the Kleizl.

I recall an event from Shneur's life that testifies to his nation al pride and his readiness

[Page 499]

to passionately defend Jewish honor. The son of Vartman, the Volozhin Starosta (District Governor) was a high school student in Warsaw. On Sabbath afternoons, the Jews of our town used to go for a stroll in the park of Count Tyszkiewicz, along with their wives and children. The high school student was an anti-Semite. When he came to Volozhin during his vacation, he would derive great sadistic pleasure from bursting into the crowd of walkers as he was riding on his galloping horse, thereby causing panic and fear. At times, this "mischief" would end with someone being trampled.

ul. Wileńska w Wołożynie

Vilna Street
The first house at left is the Kivilevitsh's
[Mr. M. Porat notes that this is from the 1930s]

One day Shneur came to me and said, "Reuven, we must put an end this maltreatment of the Jews." At the next visit of this hooligan to Volozhin, we will put an end to his mischief. This is what happened. When the "*sheigetz*" entered the park riding on his horse, even before he made his horse gallop, we stopped him, pushed him to the ground, and beat him soundly. When the wounded person was lying on the ground – Shneur acted as if he was photographing him and said, "If you complain to your father about us, we will send your 'photo' to the principal of the gymnasja, so he will see it and show the students how you were beaten by the Jews and how you were lying on the ground in shame." Indeed, he did not tell his father anything. From that time, he did not enter the park, and the Jews were relieved.

Shneur reached the pinnacle of his noble essence during the time of the Shoah. He would be permitted to say of himself, "I am the person who saw affliction under the staff of his wrath." (Lamentations 3:1). He loved the Jews

[Page 500]

of Volozhin, and tried to help them and save them in any way he could. He did not sleep, and like a faithful soldier, stood on guard day and night, spying, and listening to anything that was taking place, and any whisper. The period was very terrible. Torture and murder were the lot of the Jews of Volozhin.

As I have been told, he could have saved his life, but he did not want to and was unable to leave his wife and his son Yigal to their fate, for he loved them very much, and his soul was bound to theirs. Furthermore, if he escaped it would have brought disaster to the Jews of Volozhin who were imprisoned in the ghetto. He fulfilled his tragic role until the last minute, and went to his death as a proud Jew, with clear knowledge that this was his final journey, from which he would not return.

Shneur died a martyr's death, and earned a good name, which, as is known, is greater than the crown of Torah, the crown of the priesthood, and the crown of royalty. [Trans: based on *Pirkei Avot* 4:13]

Translator's Footnote:

Mr. M. Porat added the following details to his original translation. I include it here, largely unedited.

Shneur was always encouraging the Ghetto captives to construct hideouts, the so-called "Malinas." He suggested that they hide there as much as they could since it was clear that the day of the massacre would soon arrive. Some Ghetto dwellers survived the mass slaughters inside Malinas, and when the slaughter was over, they escaped to the forest.

One day Shneur was led away by the Ghetto Politsay and murdered en route to Molodetshno.

Shneur bravely carried out his tragic duty until the very end. He went stoically to his death, knowing that he would not return from this trip.

Shneur's wife Rachel Kivilevitsh (nee Melzer) was a born Volozhiner. She taught Hebrew and natural sciences at the Volozhin Tarbut School.

Rachel spoke with her students only in Hebrew, avoiding Yiddish even during the breaks while the children in other classes spoke Yiddish. She was the sole Jewish teacher in the Polish High (Evening) School. Rachel graduated from a Russian high school and the Hebrew Seminar for teachers.

Rachel with their little son Yigal were exterminated in the hamlet of Zabrezhe (ten Kilometers from Volozhin). Her name appears on the martyrs list of Zabrezhe in the "Pamiat – Memory" book (page 262), published by the Volozhin Region authorities (1996).

Rachel Kivilevitsh, Moyshe Meltser's daughter – her name is written in the "Pamiat' book among the Zabrezhe victims of the Fascist terror, in the Belarus language, in Cyrillic characters.

"Meltser Rakhilya Moyshawna, born 1909."

[Page 500]

Grandfather Rabbi Aharon Rapoport

(Named in error Rosenberg in the Yizkor Book- corrected by Ms. Miriam Levitan)

by Miriam Levitan (Rosenberg)

Translated by Jerrold Landau

based on an earlier translation by Moshe Porat z"l
that was edited by Judy Montel

My grandfather was born in Volozhin in the year 5613 (1853). He was a wealthy man. Nevertheless, his heart did not follow after worldly issues, and he spent all his days in Torah study. He was a great scholar, and he had rabbinical ordination. His house was filled with holy books, which he studied whenever he was free from his business. He studied Torah for its own sake, and also taught Torah. He would give the daily lesson in Gemara in the synagogue every day. His audience enjoyed his words very much, as they excelled in their popular style and simplicity.

A great tragedy afflicted him in his latter years. He became ill with a severe eye disease, and was taken to the hospital of Dr. Pines in Białystok. He underwent an operation, but he became permanently blind. He returned to Volozhin blind, but he continued to give the daily class even after his sight was taken from him. The wondrous thing was that he found his way to the synagogue himself. Every day, the Jews of Volozhin saw an old man making his way alone to the synagogue to disseminate Torah in public.

Grandfather possessed many tar factories. There were many tree roots in Count Tyszkiewicz' forests from which tar was produced. He built a house in one of those forests. It too was filled with holy books, and the sound of Torah could be heard until late at night.

Once, Count Tyszkiewicz visited the city. Since he was tired, he decided to rest a bit in the only house in the forest. Grandfather was fully immersed in studying a difficult section of Talmud. When he was Count

[Page 501]

Tyszkiewicz, he rose from his place and displayed honor to the nobleman. The guest looked at the many bookcases, and asked, "Who studies from them?" "I do," responded Grandfather. "And you understand everything written in them?" "I understand, honorable Count." "If that is the case," replied Count Tyszkiewicz, "You should sit in your place, and I should stand before you to honor you. For anyone expert in these ancient books must be a great, wise man."

Grandfather was occupied with charity and benevolent deeds. He assisted poor girls in getting married, took interest in them, and helped them in their difficulties after their marriage. Anyone with a heavy heart or who was immersed in a difficulty could find support and help from Grandfather.

Grandfather died at the ripe old age of eighty-eight. He was laid to eternal rest on the day the Nazis entered Volozhin.

Translator's Footnote:

Mr. M. Porat added the following detail in his original translation:

Grandfather possessed many tar mills. There were many wood roots in Count Tyszkiewicz' forests from which turpentine, tar, and charcoal were produced. Near one of these mills, he built his house. He also established a big house in Volozhin in which running water was installed for the first time in our shtetl.

Grandfather was so rich that he could equip his each one of his five children with a tar mill as a very generous dowry. His son Moyshe Rapoport lived in the house, which was equipped with running water. In association with Mr. Yosef Perlman, he established a sawmill and gristmill on the bank of the Volozhinka in Volozhin.

[Page 501]

Rabbi Avraham "Asher Yatzar"

By Yaakov Kagan (Tel Aviv)

Translated by Meir Razy

Rabbi Avraham, a strong believer and a man with the reputation of a devotee, was a graduate of the Yeshiva of Volozhin. He earned his nickname because he would ask everyone he met in the street if that person had recited the "Asher Yatzar" blessing after he washed his hands ("Asher Yatzar" is the blessing to be recited after visiting a bathroom).

On Friday afternoons, Rabbi Avraham used to visit Jewish stores and encourage store owners to close their businesses before the start of Shabbat.

Although he was a Melamed, he was unable to make a living from it, as over time, the number of his pupils declined. Subsequently, he then started to work as the Chazan and Beadle of a synagogue.

He used to stay in the synagogue, studying the Torah. One time he had a terrible experience. He suddenly heard a voice from above ˘calling him - "Rabbi Avraham, you are requested to come to the Yeshiva in Heaven". (Apparently, one of the town's jokers had sneaked into the second-floor women's section of the synagogue and pranked him).

Rabbi Avraham remembered the story of Eli and Shmuel (the Bible, First Samuel, Ch. 3).

[Page 502]

He replied, "I am ready", opened the Holy Arc and prayed.

Sadly, the death of Rabbi Avraham was different. During the first "Action", the Nazis gathered the Jews on the sports court and walked them to the killing pit. Rabbi Avraham understood that this was truly the time for the last prayer. He covered himself with his tallit and was shot while he recited "Shema Israel".

Rabbi Moshe Eliyahu Bunimovitz

By Rabbi Dov-Natan Brinker (z"l)

Translated by Meir Razy

Rabbi Moshe-Eliyahu was a masculine man, big, strong and healthy with broad shoulders and strong hands. He was not a Melamed, only a "Mashgiach" (supervisor) but he took his responsibilities very seriously. The students of the "Churvah" used to say about him: "he inspected through the windows and peeped through the cracks in the walls". (Translator's note: "The Ruin of Rabbi Yehuda the Pious" was a historic Synagogue located in the Jewish Quarter of Jerusalem. It was considered the most beautiful and most important Synagogue in the Land of Israel and housed part of the Etz Chaim Yeshiva). He did not look like a Torah scholar. He always tried to give the impression of himself as a simple man ˘, although he was actually a Tzadik.

His past was somewhat mysterious and we heard many stories about him in Jerusalem. He studied in the Yeshiva of Volozhin and decided to come to Eretz Israel. He arrived at the port of Jaffa with no money to pay for a ride to Jerusalem, so he simply walked there. In Jerusalem, he did not present himself as a scholar but found physical work as a construction worker. This was the time of much building of new neighborhoods outside of Jerusalem's city walls. He became a laborer who carried stone and other building materials on construction sites. He sent the money he saved to his wife in Volozhin. Later, she would take their two children and join him in Jerusalem.

Rabbi Moshe-Eliyahu Bunimovitz

This was the time period when a French company laid the railroad tracks between Jaffa and Jerusalem. A Jewish iron contractor hired him for that work. He considered building Eretz Israel to be "holy work".

[Page 503]

Even during these days of hard physical labor, he did not forget his days of study in Volozhin. Each night he went to the Yeshiva "Menachem Zion" at the "Churva", where students were arranged into two studying shifts: one before midnight and one after midnight. He used to attend both shifts and still went to work every morning.

Rabbi Eliezer-Dan Gavrilovitz (the son-in-law of Rabbi Yehoseph Swartz z"l, the author of several religious books including "Tvuat Haaretz"), who was one of the leaders of Yeshiva "Etz Chaim", was impressed by him and hired Rabbi Moshe-Eliyahu as a supervisor for the Talmud Torah School.

The school gave him a library room full of Holy Books. Rabbi Moshe-Eliyahu would distribute the books among the different teachers and made sure the books were in good order. He sent damaged books to be repaired by Rabbi Neta, the bookbinder.

He continued passing his nights in the Menachem Zion School just as he did when he worked in construction and metalwork. After the morning prayer, he climbed to his little room and waited for the pupils to arrive. Rabbi Moshe Eliyahu unlocked the classrooms and greeted each pupil, asking them to behave civilly and to wait quietly for the start of their classes. He greeted the Melameds and avoided any conversation, encouraging them to go to their classes.

He then started walking around the building, making sure that no child sneaked out of his class. When he caught a "deserter" he brought him back to his classroom, begging the child not to repeat this behavior.

[Page 504]

He showed a lot of respect for all the students of the Yeshiva, to all the teachers, old and young, and even to the Talmud Torah students, of whom he said, "they will exceed my knowledge of the Torah". I was shocked when I saw him stand up as I passed his door. He stood up in front of any teacher or Torah scholar that passed in the corridor in front of his room.

He died on February 24, 1910 and was buried on the Mount of Olives.

(from the weekly publication BAMISHOR, year 5, issue 21, the 27th day of Nisan, 5704 [1944])

Editor's Note:

The following story, about the author Zvi Bunimovitz of Volozhin, a relative of Rabbi Moshe Eliyahu Bunimovitz, was well-known in the town. Sir Moshe Montefiore, the British Minister, visited St. Petersburg and on his way back to England made a stop in Vilna. People were discussing both his important position in England and what his intentions where for visiting the Russian Tzar. People speculated that he had offered to "buy" the Russian Jews and relocate them to England. Consequently, people in need began approaching him with requests: one's daughter had reached marriage age and he had no money for a dowry, another one lost his house to a fire and the third wanted help in a court case. Montefiore's entourage told all the applicants to submit their requests in writing.

Zvi Bunimovitz was known for his sharp tongue and his beautiful handwriting. Many people from all over would ask him to write their application letters for them. They asked him to elaborate on their cases, to use poetic phrases, to detail their family lineage, and to describe their life challenges in order to move the Minister's soul.

At one time, Bunimovitz told them: why are you preparing long letters? Simply write "give money!" And the phrase "give money!" became common in Lithuania.

(M. Lipson, Midor Ledor, part 1, section 71)

[Page 505]

Reb Shlomo Chassid
(Reb Shlomo Shepsenwohl)

by David Cohen (Tel Aviv)

Translated by Eilat Gordin Levitan

Translation edited by Jerrold Landau

There was never a *minyan* (i.e. a quorum of ten) of Hassidim in Volozhin. The people of Volozhin would say that if one more Hassid was added, and there was a chance that there might be a *minyan*, one of the Hassidim would pass away. Amongst the few Hassidim, there was a Slonim Hassid named Shlomo Chassid, who merited the description *Malach* (angel). He acquired this name by virtue of this story: Shlomole's legs became sick, and an operation was necessary. When he awakened after surgery and realized that they had amputated one leg, he groaned and said, "It is unfortunate that I will no longer be able to dance in a group." When the Rebbe heard this, he said, "This story is fitting for an angel."[1] The Rebbe said about him that his mind is greater than his heart.

Shlomo "Chassid" Shepsenwohl

I got to know this Hassid from Sabbath nights when we students would sit together and sing. I began with a typical Slonim melody. Then the door opened, and a Jew with a white beard, lame with his single leg, entered and asked with great emotion, "Who is this who is singing the Slonim melody?" From that point, I would visit him on Sabbath nights. He acted in accordance with the custom of Hassidim of Slonim, who do not sleep on Sabbath eves. He would sit alone in his home, and "recite" the melody with his radiant countenance. When he reached the hymn, full of longing: "G-d, I long for the pleasantness of the Sabbath"

(*Kah Echsof*), his voice would rise as if it were stemming from the depths of the depths. I would forget that I had distanced myself from Hassidism. I would follow after him with devotion and an outpouring of the soul, "Holy Sabbath, my soul is sick with your love." The Jews of Volozhin, even including some of the Yeshiva students, would stand outside and listen. One would state, "There is no *minyan* of Hassidim in Volozhin, but indeed there is Hassidism."

Shlomo told me: "Once, I stood before the Admor of Slonim, and he asked me, 'Shlomole, how are you able to worship with the *Misnagdim* every day and every Sabbath?' I responded, 'Before I enter the synagogue, I say to myself: Behold, I am entering the meadow. Many bulls are walking and mooing, and you are the only human among them.' The face of the Admor clouded over and he said, 'How can you look upon so many Jews as if they are bulls? Rather say: Many humans are in the meadow, and there is only one bull among them.' This is the parable that accompanies me all my life, not to disparage others."

[Page 506]

[2]Mr. Binyamin Shapir (Shishko) notes: "When I was in Tiberias on Purim of the year 5727 (1967), in the synagogue of the Slonimer Hassidim in Kiryat Shmuel, I heard from an old man, Reb Moshe, may he live long and well, wonderful stories about the spiritual greatness of Reb Shlomo Chassid." Here is one song of our Reb Shlomo[3]

No lambs, no herds
No wife, no children.
Only *Yismechu Bemalchutecha*[4] **Editor's note**: This song is brought down in *Zichron Rishonim* in the name of Rabbi Gadol. No gold or silver
No lambs or herds
No wife or children –
Only in Your Kingdom alone!

(This song is published in Hillel Zeitlin's book "Introduction to Hassidism in the way of Chabad" Farlang Publishing, New York, page 263.)

"Anyone who is anguished over a living soul among Israel causes benefit to his generation; and anyone who erects a monument to those souls that have passed on, it is as if he has sustained an entire world, a world that had gone on to be destroyed. These people stand before you and demand a rectification: we have drawn, we have written a book, so that the latter generation shall know."

(Sholom Aleichem, introduction to "Between Man and his Fellow")

Translator's Footnotes:

1. There is a Jewish tradition that an angel only has one leg.
2. At this point, Eilat Gordin Levitan refers the reader to the story about Reb Shlomo Chassid on page 426 of this book.
3. The song is written in English, with a "free translation" (i.e. non-literal translation) into Hebrew at the side.
4. Literally "Let them rejoice in Your kingdom," a phrase from the Sabbath *Shacharit Amida*. "Let those who observe the Sabbath and call it a delight rejoice in Your kingdom."

[Page 506]

Figures I Knew

By Reuven Rogovin

Oizer (Eyzer) Der *Raznoshtshik* (Oizer the Postman)

I knew Reb Oizer the Postman well. He was called: "*Diedushka* (Grandfather) Yevzier." He was about seventy years old, with a solid build, an above average height, and a square, chestnut-colored beard (reminiscent of Czar Nikolai Aleksander's beard). In summer as in winter he always wore

[Page 507]

a cape (*pelerina*) and a large bag overflowing with mail over it.

By what merit did he attain such a government position? By the merit that he had served as a *Cantonist*, a dedicated and faithful soldier of the Czar, and had earned a medal for outstanding service. He received good recommendations when he left the army, through which he was accepted as a "servant of the state." He was the only Jewish mail carrier in the entire region.

As he walked, laden with his mailbag to the point of weariness, all the children would run after him yelling, "*Diedushka* Yevzier, is there letter?" He would turn his head toward them in a sternway and respond, "*Nikak Niet!*" ["There is none!"] This response was insufficient for us tykes, and we would chase after him shouting loudly: "*Diedushka* Yevzier, *pisma iz do*?" ["Grandfather Oizer, is there a letter?"] He would stop in his normal kindly way and say "*Riebiata pierestantia shalit!*" [Children, stop your mischief!]. This warning scared us, and we left him alone until the following morning.

When the cantor in the synagogue chanted "He Who grants salvation to kings and authority to princes," the prayer for the welfare of the Czar and his family, Reb Oizer the mail carrier would stand at attention the entire time, with dignity and respect, until the end of the prayer.

During the First World War, the Volozhin Jews would engage in "politics" in the synagogue, and would debate amongst themselves, arguing which side would defeat the other: Germany will defeat Russia, or Russia will defeat Germany. Reb Oizer remained faithful to the Romanov Dynasty and provided with signs and portents that the Czar who gave him his bread would overcome.

Reb Chaim der *Shnayder* (the Tailor)

Rabbi Chaim der Shnayder (Chaim Tzirulnik) and his wife Chaike

The elder [literally Grandfather] Mendele Mocher Seforim of blessed memory wrote: "As the Jews among the nations of the world, so the artisans are held in low respect and humiliation among the Jews." (From his book: "In those days," Chapter 12). These words

[Page 508]

do not apply to Reb Chaim "the tailor". Despite his being a tradesman, he was numbered amongst the important householders and was close to the town leaders.

His family name was Tzirulnik, but everyone knew him simply as Chaim "der Shnayder" (the Tailor). He was Oizer the Postman's son. I never saw Reb Chaim with a thimble on his finger or with a thread and needle in his hand. He was a tailoring contractor and employed two workers. One was Hillel Moshe Yudel, a tall, very thin, and very poor young man. The second one was Yaakov "with the weak eye." How was he able to thread a needle remains a mystery until this day.

Reb Chaim's main work was as a communal activist. He was the head spokesperson for the *Chevra Kadisha* [burial society]. When any Jew departed from this world and needed to acquire a "place" [in the cemetery], things could not be settled without Reb Chaim. He had been always the first invited to sit on the table head at the annual dinner of the *Chevra Kadisha* that was held every year on the tenth of the month of *Tevet*.

Reb Chaim also served on the board of directors of the "Folks Bank." As one of the community administrators [*parnassim*], he was always ready to defend tradespeople or small-scale businesspeople who were failing or needed help. He was also an ardent Zionist, and supported all the parties who worked for the Land of Israel. The trust he had among the people was acquired because of his honesty and good heart. He was never known to hold a grudge or take revenge, he hated gossip, and kept away from falsehood. He had always a friendly smile on his face.

After the war between Poland and the Bolsheviks, we founded a large library in the house of Chayke di Krever (Chayke from Krevo) on Smorgon Street. On the days when books were exchanged – twice a week – Reb Chaim would visit the library to discover if many people were reading. He was always interested in knowing what was going on in the world of the spirit and he respected those who read and studied.

Chaim "der Shnayder" and his wife were murdered during the Holocaust in Volozhin, together with all the Jews of the city. I am sure that even in the cramped, dark ghetto he was still making efforts to help those in need. I am sure that he would not be discouraged even when his request was refused, and the next day he would return to ask for a little hot soup for the elderly and the sick. Thus did he act for the benefit of the community even under the inhuman conditions of the ghetto, until he returned his soul to the Creator in sanctity and purity.

Reb Itche der *Balegole* (the Coachman)

By Reuven Rogovin

Translated by Moshe Porat z"l edited by Jerrold Landau

Reb Itche owned a horse and a covered wagon, in which he used to carry passengers from Volozhin to the railway station. First it was to Molodetchno, then to Polochany, Listopad, Horodchki, and finally to the Volozhin station.

The alley on which Reb Itche lived was known as *"Tsarskiy Dvoretz"* ("The Czar's estate"). So it was called in a figure of speech, as in actuality, the alley was covered with quicksand. It was impossible to get to Reb Itche's house without a bridge made of wood and planks.

A group of elderly Jews used to study in the Kleizl. Every Sabbath, after the *Mincha* service,

[Page 509]

they would read from the 119th chapter of Psalms, from "Fortunate are those of pure ways, who follow the Torah of G-d." [*Ashrei temimei derech…* Psalms 119:1] until the end of the book of Psalms. They would begin again from *Ashrei* if the time for *Maariv* had not yet arrived.

The oldest man of the group was Reb Moshe Shmuel, an elderly Jew with a long white beard. He used to conclude each chapter of Psalms with a pleasant melody. Among the participants were his three sons – Feive, Yehoshua, and Mates (only one person survived from this family – Yaakov Girzon, Mates' son, who lives today in Israel). The other participants were Michael Gavriel the carpenter (Reb Moshe Shmuel's brother), Yitzchak Getzel the cobbler, Avraham Itche the butcher, Itche the coachman, Moshe the tailor, Shmuel Itche *der Gendzler* (goose man), and others.

While Reb Moshe Shmuel would start to read with his pleasant melody *Ashrei Temimei Derech* – all the participants used to pull out their glasses from the pockets. Each pair of spectacles had a serious problem. One pair lacked a lens and an arm, another just an arm, a third one was repaired with a bandage around the arm, and a fourth was completely unsuitable to be used. Each set of spectacles had a kind of plastic prosthesis. Only Reb Itche's glasses were more or less in proper order.

Reb Itche used to read from the Book of Psalms with emotion and sweetness, for he, Itche the coachman, a simple Jew, had the ability to thank and praise the Creator of the Universe with his own mouth. When Reb Moshe Shmuel would begin to read "Rivers of Water poured down from my eyes, because they did not guard Your Torah" (Psalms, 119: 136), Reb Itche would take out a huge red handkerchief from his pockets to dry his tears.

I continued to worship in this Kleizl after my wedding. Reb Itche the coachman sat opposite me. On his right sat Reb Berl Potashnik and to his left – Reb Moshe Shlomo, the *melamed* and Torah reader. Reb Itche's *shtender* [lectern] was as damaged as his glasses. He never repaired it, just as he never fixed his glasses.

The most honorable householders of Volozhin sat at the eastern wall: Rabbi Naftali Hertz Eskind (who served as the rabbi of Volozhin after Rabbi Refoel Shapira's departure to Minsk), Areh Polak, Hershel Rogovin, Yankele Yochanan's, Avrahamel Rode's, Michel Meir Itche's (a flax merchant) and other important householders. As time passed, major changes took place with the occupants of the eastern wall of the Kleizel. Leizer the baker and Menahem Mendel Potashnik (both *gabbaim*), took over the places of Rabbi Eskind and Areh Polak. They passed the first place on to his son-in-law the physician Avraham Tzart, and the second, to his grandson Akiva Potashnik. Feive Rode's, the grandson of Avrahamel Rode's, took over his place. The place of Michel Meir Itche's was taken over by his son Yaakov Weisbord.

On Yom Kippur, Reb Itche would be transformed to someone otherworldly. He turned his attention away from the physical world, and immersed himself in the holy, awesome day. His spirit was very stormy, and his heart was aching and pained. He would shake up worlds with his prayers, until he slunk down on his bench, as if he fainted.

Reb Itche would change his clothes twice a year – at Passover and Sukkot. When they recited

[Page 510]

the Prayer for Dew at *Musaf* on the first day of Passover, he would remove his winter clothes (even if it was still cold in the world); and when they recited the Prayer for Rain on Shemini Atzeret (the final day of Sukkot), he would remove his summer clothes (even if it was still hot and stifling outside).

Reb Itche's end was like the end of all the Jews of Volozhin. His sojourn in the ghetto weakened him completely. He wore a long, torn kapote, tied with a rope. Reuven Lavit (Reuven *der Pakter*) and Avraham Berkovitch supported him spiritually.

R' Avraham Chaim Marshak

By Yisrael Ben-Nachum (Holoventshits) (Givatayim)

Translated by Moshe Porat z"l

Edited by Dr. H. Mendelssohn

Further edited by Jerrold Landau

Grandmother Rucha Reiza, may she rest in peace, told me that the journey to the Holy Land of her father, Reb Avraham Chaim Maharshak, was wondrous and full of sublime strength of the soul. He bid farewell to the Jews of the city and set out on foot to "Your city of Jerusalem." He reached the border, and since he did not have a permit to cross the border, the border guards beat him to the point of bleeding, robbed of all his meager possessions, and turned him back. He returned to Volozhin full of wounds and sores. When he recovered, he immediately set out on the journey again. He set out and returned seven times, and "from the bottom of his foot until his head, there was no soundness" [Isaiah 1:6]. On the eighth time, he set out and did not return.

In Volozhin, nobody knew what happened to him, for no message or contact arrived. It was as if he had drowned in the water. A rabbinical emissary came to our town about a year later, with a letter written in large letters, "*Mazel Tov*!" The Jews of the city were surprised, and did not know the meaning of the *Mazel Tov*. However, when they began to read the letter, they figured out the meaning. After suffering from difficult tribulations of the journey, Reb Avraham Chaim merited to see the land from afar, for he was attacked by bandits who beat him until he died. His body was brought to Jerusalem for burial.

Reb Avraham Chaim became known among the great sages of Jerusalem. This is evident from the following story: There was a holy burial spot in the cemetery on the Mount of Olives, prepared to receive the body of a great *Tzadik*. On the day that the body of Reb Avraham Yaakov was brought to Jerusalem, a great scholar died in Jerusalem. The Jews of Jerusalem could not decide which of he two great deceased individuals should get that grave. Lots were drawn, and the lot fell upon Reb Avraham Chaim.

[Page 511]

From that, it seems that the emissary was informing, by way of the *Mazel Tov*, that Reb Avraham Chaim had merited being buried in a grave designated for a great *Tzadik*

פ נ איש תם וישר
מופלג בתוי מוה
אברהם חיים בר
משה מוואלאזין
נפטר ח לח ותשרי
ש תרמדל
תנצבה

Reb Avraham Chaim Marshak's tombstone on the Mount
of Olives in Jerusalem.
(Translation of the gravestone: Here is buried a pure, upright
man.
Renown in Torah and fear of Heaven.
Our teacher, Reb Avraham Chaim the son of Reb Moshe of
Volozhin, of blessed memory.
Died 8 Tishrei, 5644 [1884].
May his soul be bound in the bonds of eternal life.)

Years passed, and I made aliya to the Land of Israel. This wonderful story of my grandfather was etched in my memory. I made my way to the Mount of Olives to verify if Reb Avraham Chaim was indeed buried there. To my dismay, I could not identify the grave. However, my brother informed me that he had visited the Mount of Olives during the Mandate period, and asked that he be shown the grave of Avraham Chaim. The old record books of the deceased were opened, and it was found written in one of them: Reb Avraham Chaim of Volozhin. They were able to identify the grave from this.

Now, with the liberation of the Old City of Jerusalem, I ascended the Mount of Olives to supplicate over the grave of Reb Avraham Chaim. I saw with my own eyes that the story of my grandmother was not a fable.

b. Grandmother Roche Reize

Grandmother Roche Reize, the daughter of Reb Avraham Chaim Maharshak, was a unique personality. She was more stringent than the rabbi in religious matters. She fought with humor and jokes against the new winds – the winds of apostacy – that began to blow in Volozhin.

In those days (at the beginning of the 20th century), boys and girls would go to the forest on the Sabbath

[Page 512]

with books in their hands. One of the lads wanted to vex her. He turned to her in a mocking fashion, "See, Grandmother Rucha Reiza, how the girls of Volozhin carry books in the woods. [*trogn bicher in vald*]" Grandmother retorted in her typical sharp manner, "That they are carrying [*trogn*] in the forest does not interest me. Only they should not carry [i.e. get pregnant] [*trogn*] from the forest." (in Yiddish, *trogn* also means "to become pregnant.")

Grandmother used to begin the preparations for Passover already after Chanukah. First of all, she had to pickle beets. She required a barrel for this purpose. In the middle of a busy market day, Grandmother would leave her shop and run to the market to search for a kosher barrel. When she brought the barrel home, turmoil overtook the house: "Don't stand here." "Don't sit here." "Don't walk here." Having no choice, they emptied a special room in the house. When the beets were pickled and it was necessary to carry the barrel to the cellar, a mishap took place. The panels of the barrel burst, and everything poured out. Poor Grandmother, like Sisyphus in his time, was forced to start everything from the beginning.

She was very diligent in giving charity to the poor. On the eve of Yom Kippur, she had her own charitable plate among the other plates, and she made sure it would be filled.

Grandmother was stubborn. Through the power of her stubbornness, she achieved something that became the talk of all the Jews of Volozhin. On Simchat Torah, she strongly informed the *gabbai* to stop the *Hakafot* [Torah processions] if they do not give a Torah scroll to the women's section, so that the women could also fulfil the mitzvah of *Hakafot*. A tumult started in the synagogue. Is this possible? Has such a thing ever been heard of? *Hakafot* for women? This is a violation of the Torah! However, the protests and shouts did not help: Grandmother Roche Reiza got a Torah and made seven *Hakafot* in the women's section.

Grandmother performed a different sort of heroic deed in the year 5665 (1905). On one of the Sabbaths of that year, during the Torah reading, the Bund people closed the doors of the synagogue and prevented the worshipers from dispersing, so as to force them to listen to revolutionary speeches against the Czar. Grandmother could not tolerate such a violation of sanctity, and she began to shout aloud, "The Cossacks are coming!" The Bundists were petrified, and fled for their lives.

When they realized that Grandmother had tricked them, they decided to pay her back in measure. They brought a large beet in a sack, hung it at the entrance to her store, with a warning sign, "Caution, bomb!" Grandmother was petrified until some strong person volunteered to take down the "bomb" from the shop.

Grandmother lived to an old age. She slipped and died as she was carrying two buckets of water.

Translator's Footnote:

Mr. M. Porat embellished the final paragraph as follows: It was an excellent omen in Volozhin to meet a person carrying a pair of buckets full with water. Grandma reached very old age, but was active spiritually and physically. One day she fell on her way home with two full buckets of water in her hands. It was a good sign. The straight and pious Bobe Rohe Reyze had arrived in *Gan-Eden*. (the Garden of Eden - the Paradise).

[Page 513]

Patcholke
The Famous Hostel Owner

A. Litvin

Translated by Meir Razy

I spent my most enjoyable hours in Volozhin with Patcholke, the famous owner of the Hostel where I used to stay. He gained this nickname because he used to call each of his guests "Patcholke", "my honeybee".

I dedicate this chapter to my host in Volozhin as a "Thank You" note for the time we spent together. This is also a thank you for the stories he told me about Rabbi Chaim, the son of Rabbi Yitzhak, about Baruch "the Galicianer", about the "Lion's Roar" and Graf Tishkivitz. I am writing because Patcholke was the most unique and original character I have ever met in all my travels to Jewish towns.

I met him when he was ninety-four years old, but his age did not show. He considered himself young, his back was straight and his step was light, like a "running gazelle". One of his neighbors told me about an encounter they had in the public bathhouse. "Four years ago, I met Patcholke in a public bathhouse. We both went downstairs into the pool of the Mikveh and on the way back I offered to support him on the stairs. I took his arm and said "ninety is an advanced age. You can lean on me to make the climb easier." He gave me a look that almost killed me and shouted "get lost, young man! Who needs your help? I will get upstairs before you'll blink your eyes!". And by the time I reached the fifth stair he was on the fifteenth stair."

Patcholke was proud of his strength and when he squeezed a young man's hand, the man's eyes would twitch from the pain.

Patcholke was blessed with one hundred and forty grandchildren and great-grandchildren, although he had only three sons and two daughters. All his sons were Torah scholars, observant men. One son and one daughter lived in the U.S.A. The children who stayed in Volozhin are all dead by now, and he had said Kadish for them instead of the "normal" way in which children pray for their deceased parents. One son who lived with him in the Hostel died recently. The eyes of the old man tear-up when he talks about his son.

Patcholke receives money from his son in America but he does not need it. The Hostel he inherited from his grandfather provides for all his needs. The Hostel stands in the center of a wide yard where cattle and goats roam free. It also boasts a large and beautiful orchard of fruit-bearing trees. He planted these trees when he was seventy years old and the orchard is rented for an annual fee of thirty-five Rubles. He keeps several trees for himself, collects their fruit, dries it or cooks it, and distributes it to family and friends.

[Page 514]

When he thinks he is short of cash he goes to Minsk where his millionaire brother, who made his money in forestry, lives. His relatives open their purses for him and encourage him to take as much as he wants, but he always takes only one, one-hundred Ruble note.

Patcholke is proud of his extended family lineage. The father of his son-in-law was Rabbi Menashe of Ilya, a student of the Gaon of Vilna. People everywhere respect him and even at his advanced age, he studies a daily page of Talmud and does not need reading glasses. He did many things during his active life, and he likes to tell about his revolutionary activities and the risks involved.

All this had happened some sixty or seventy years ago, but he still gets involved in present affairs. During the disagreement between the NATZIV and Rabbi Israel of Salantai (who wanted to introduce Moral studies (Musar) at the Yeshiva), the NATZIV sent Patcholke to deliver a message to Rabbi Israel of Salantai. Patcholke went to see Rabbi Israel and stood in front of him quietly, like one of his students. When the GAON asked what he had come for, he replied in a docile voice: "I came to remind the GAON that all the people who attempted to hurt the great Yeshiva of Volozhin, the Yeshiva that produced many GAONs, experienced bad outcomes. This one died suddenly, that one lost his mind and the third one became very sick. Therefore, Rabbi, I came to warn him". Rabbi Israel of Salantai took this warning to heart and ceased his initiative.

Patcholke was very proud that he met many Rabbis as most of the Rabbis who visited Volozhin stayed in his Hostel. He made it a rule to take each visiting Rabbi's shoes off their feet at night, and he had been blessed by one hundred Rabbis to live for one hundred and twenty years.

Patcholke is a happy man. He does not have any complaints before G-D or the world. He took good care of his finances and has a nice bank account. However, he knows that no one lives forever and he "prepares himself for the long trip". But he does not mean it. He is like a young man full of vitality. He is sure that the six years he needs to reach the age of a hundred is like "money in the bank".

[Page 515]

This is because he has blessings from one hundred Rabbis. He keeps a list with all their names, quoting the proverb "A Tzadik decrees and G-D fulfills."

I am sure that Patcholke does not need the blessing of one hundred Rabbis. He is healthy and strong, and when he squeezes a young man's hand, the man's eyes twitch from the pain.

(from the book "Yiddish Souls")

Dov Ber Kaplan

Yehuda Chaim Kotler (New York)

Translated by Meir Razy

We, the students from Volozhin in the Agriculture School in Volitchny, called him "our Berl". He was a Pioneer.

The year was 1918. The first World War was coming to an end and we were students at the Yeshiva of Vilna. Both day and night, Berl was focusing on Talmudic questions but some rumors about him started to spread. The rumor said he was reading "forbidden" history and philosophy books!

And then, one day he announced that it was time for a change; to leave the religious books and to go to Eretz Israel. He did not loose his Jewish beliefs, he decided it was time to switch from the spiritual world to the physical one.

It was one year after the Russian Revolution. Many young Jews considered the Revolution as a precursor to the arrival of the Messiah - but not him. Berl analyzed the Revolution and concluded that it will not treat Jews the way they deserve. Unfortunately, his prediction was correct.

In October 1918, we left the Yeshiva and became students of the Agriculture School in Volitchny near Vilna. We learned and practiced work in the fields. Berl, a quiet and modest son of a Rabbi, worked diligently but did not forget his origins. He attracted a group of people from Volozhin to join our school in order to become Pioneers, productive workers in Eretz Israel.

In the autumn of 1918 and the winter of 1919, more students joined the school, including a group of members of the "Po'alei Zion" Party from Kovno. Our goal was to get a degree in Agronomy and then to immigrate to Eretz Israel.

[Page 516]

In the spring of 1919, the Army of the New Poland established its control over Polish lands and approached Vilna. We feared for our lives and organized a self-defense team to protect ourselves and the school's grounds. Berl was fearless and being the organizer - he instilled a sense of power and security in all of us.

During this period, he spoke to our group many times, combining his Jewish knowledge with world history. He discussed the future of the Jewish nation. He did not see any Jewish future in Marx, Lenin, and Trozky's ideology. He found Jewish socialism in the Bible and the Talmud and believed that this would be the way that will deliver national and social independence.

Some of his ideas were not always clear, but most of his ideas made sense and his energetic delivery convinced us all.

After several weeks of rampaging and lawlessness, the Polish Government established itself in the area. One day, on an excursion to Velikiy, we saw several Polacks attacking an old Jew. He was standing crying and they circled him, pulling his beard. Berl wanted to interfere and fight the men but we stopped him thinking the situation was too dangerous. He was very upset. How would we be able to protect our international interests in Eretz Israel if we cannot even protect our honor here where we live?

The school flourished and the local farmers were impressed by the dedication and hard work we invested in it. The school started a competition to grow the biggest cabbage. Berl took it personally and used to wake me up at midnight so that we could cover the cabbage in order to protect it from freezing. He was elated when we won first prize.

In the winter of 1920, he decided to go to Eretz Israel. He went to Kovna, where his father was the Rabbi, to say goodbye and to receive his blessing. His departure from the school was very emotional and animated and sentimental.

Years later I immigrated to the U.S.A. There, I heard that in 1921 Berl worked on a farm near Kedainiai and was very dedicated. His friends gave him the name "Nikolay" and this name followed him to Eretz Israel.

Several years later I heard that he was working draining swamps and building roads in Eretz Israel. Later I saw a photograph marked as "A Quarry in Jerusalem" in a book published by the United Jewish Appeal. It showed Berl holding a large hammer.

By the time of my visit to Israel in 1965, he was no longer alive.
Let this short note serve as a memorial candle for Berl.

[Page 517]

A "Luft Gesheft"[1] Story
(a story I heard from my father, Rabbi Mordechai Shishko)

Benyamin Shafir (Shishko)

Translated by Meir Razy

The Jewish brain is a miraculous creation. If all the oceans were full of ink and all the trees were pens and the sky was writing sheets and all the people were scribes – it would not be enough to describe the depth of the Jewish mind. Its ability to invent is limitless. Here is a story I heard from the older generation of Volozhin, a story that shows the uniqueness of the Jewish mind.

A Russian businessman from the town of Petrograd complained to the Tzar: We are brothers, both of us were born Christian, we both hate Jews, we know that they crucified the Son of God, but after all of this you, the Russian Tzar, do all your business with Jews. They build bridges, pave roads, lay railroads, excavate tunnels and supply the army. Why aren't you doing business with good Christians?

The Tzar listened and did not respond, and the man went home disappointed and upset.

Two weeks later a messenger from the Tzar came to the merchant and ordered him to come back for a meeting with the Tzar.

The Tzar said: I thought about your argument and realized you were right. From now on I will give my business only to Christians, no more Jews. I have a great business proposition for you. It will enrich you and all I am asking is a commission of ten thousand Rubles.

What is this business?

I will sell you all the air in the districts of Vilna, Grodno, and Minsk.

[Page 518]

The merchant was flabbergasted! Air? What business can one make of air? How can one become rich from the air? The Tzar must be joking!

The merchant looked for a quick way to get out of the deal and replied: I've just invested all my money in a new business and I am short of cash to start a new business right now. He left the Tzar feeling lucky that he had found a way out.

The next day the Tzar called Yankel, his long-term business partner, and offered him the same deal. Yankel was elated. Immediately he saw how he could convert air into gold. He told the Tzar they must sign a detailed contract stating that the air of the three districts now belonged to him. They wrote the contract and it was signed with the Seal of the Tzar. Yankel immediately gave the Tzar two ten-thousand Ruble notes, saying: I believe in this business, so I am adding another ten thousand for your charities.

Yankel hurried to see the local governor. When the guards stopped him, saying that the Governor does not see Jews, he showed them the Seal of the Tzar and immediately was led inside.

He instructed the Governor to publish an order that would be posted in each city, town, village, or farm stating, in the name of the Tzar, that the air belongs to Yankel. The owner of any opened hatch must pay him an annual fee of a quarter Ruble. For an open window, he would pay a half Ruble. A door would cost him one Ruble, a chimney – three and a windmill – ten Rubles a year.

The Governor did not like it, but it was an order in the name of the Tzar. He published the order. It was a hot summer and people kept their doors and windows open.

[Page 519]

Yankel collected the fees and very quickly grew very rich. But the citizens could not keep on paying and soon they complained to the Tzar.

The Tzar called Yankel and told him that he wanted to respect their deal but in the current political instability, he was afraid that it might start a revolution. Therefore, here is your twenty thousand and let's cancel the contract.

Yankel replied: Your Majesty, this deal made me so much money that I want you to keep that money and I am adding another twenty thousand. I wish you a long and healthy life and soon we shall make more deals.

The Tzar then called the Russian businessman, told him the story, and asked: do you now understand why I work with Jews? Their brain converts air to gold!

Translator's footnote:

    i.   A Business without Foundation

Mera Schnyder - "Merke Ela's"

Dina & Lea Faygenboym (Netanya & Tel Aviv)

Translated by Meir Razy

Among the everyday Volozhin people who dedicated their lives to helping other people was Mera Schnyder (who was known as "Merka Ela's"). She was known as a "people person" and was a one-woman Social Help institution. At any time, she was busy helping people and every person who asked for her assistance would receive it.

Making a living in Volozhin was not easy. Market days were a significant source of income for many people. Many merchants used to ask Mara for her assistance in securing loans so that they could stock-up for market days. She would help anyone who asked her to negotiate a loan from the bank. On occasion, the merchant was late in repaying the bank and he would come to her, asking for help to negotiate a new date with the Bank Manager.

[Page 520]

She knew who could not afford a fish for Shabbat, who could not replace torn shoes and who needed new clothes. She helped the poor discreetly and did not seek glory or recognition.

Mara did not have much pleasure in her personal life. She herself was poor, the owner of a small store. Of her two sons one, Eliyahu Shani, immigrated to Eretz Israel in 1926 and passed away in Kfar Saba. Her husband Moshe immigrated in 1935. He worked in orange orchards, paved roads and had other hard-labor jobs. However, he returned to Volozhin when she became ill.

Even during her illness, she continued helping people. With her bent back, she limped from place to place looking for a dress for an orphan girl, a wedding dress for a poor bride, or money to pay a ticket to Eretz Israel for a Pioneer who had received an Immigration Certificate from the British Mandate Government.

All her good deeds did not save her life and she died several months before the start of WW-2. Many people mourned her death and joined the funeral service.

We shall remember them

Benyamin Shafir (Shishko)

Translated by Meir Razy

Rabbi Shlomo Chaim Brodno

Shlomo Chaim Brodno was the son of Rabbi Velvele (Ze'ev) "Patcholke", the owner of a famous hostel in Volozhin. He was an intelligent and honest man, an outstanding public activist who was among the founders of the local Vaad (the Community Leadership Committee), the first Community Bank and many charities. He never used his positions to advance himself. On the contrary – he enlisted several young people to participate in managing public affairs so there would be a generation of skilled successors in the future.

[Page 521]

His wife, Pesla-Raizel Weisbord, managed the hostel. It was a nice and clean hotel, visited by many guests who came for vacation or for business with the different Government offices located in town. Rabbi Shlomo Chaim Brodno was not involved in managing the hotel. His business was in selling brandy to local people and wholesale distribution of salt to local stores.

Rabbi Yeshayahu Kahanovich

Yeshayahu was born in Volozhin. He was a dedicated Zionist and one of the founders of "Zeirey Zion Association" in town. He was one of the founders of the Tarbut School Organization and was its Managing Director as well.

Yeshayahu Kahanovich and his wife Henya Tabachovitz

[Page 522]

The stamp of the Tarbut School

Yeshayahu dedicated much effort to the support of the Hebrew language and one of his life goals was the success of the Tarbut school. He was one of the leaders of the JNF in town and opened his home up to any activity in support of Zionism. Yeshayahu was known as a very laid-back person, a deep thinker who was a symbol of Zionism in Volozhin. He married Henya, the daughter of Rabbi Yaakov Tabachovitz.

Just before the Holocaust he wrote me a letter in which he expressed his wish to bring his family to Eretz-Israel. We were saddened to see that he did not succeed in fulfilling this goal. He died along with the teacher Noach Perski.

Rabbi Avraham Horvitz

Avraham was the son of Rabbi Yehoshua Horvitz of Krakow. Rabbi Yehoshua was a Torah scholar and Zionist who arrived in Volozhin during the First World War. His home was a place where both Torah scholars and Zionists gathered.

Rabbi Avraham followed in his father's footsteps. He was an honest, measured man who was well liked by the people. He married Sonia Shrira.

Rabbi Yakov Tabachovitz

Yaakov was famous as a Torah Scholar. A tall, handsome man, he also arrived in Volozhin during the First World War. He was a skillful Chazan and his Yom Kippur "I am the poor" prayer moved and opened the hearts of his listeners.

His daughter Henya married Yeshayahu Kahanovich and his second daughter Sonia married Ze'ev Perski. His son Shimon was a Zionist and represented the Volozhin branch of "Zeirei Zion" in the "Zeirei Zion" congress in Vilna.

Rabbi Dov Potashnik

Dov was not a rich man but his qualities and good deeds were his "gold nuggets". He had a unique quality – he did not expect the poor to come to him for help. Rather, he approached them. He knew who had problems and very discretely, without any fanfare, helped many people and literally saved lives. He loved all Jews for being Jews and did not expect any recognition.

[Page 523]

Most of his children escaped the tragic end of the town and joined the partisans in the nearby forest and then moved to Israel. One son and one daughter moved to the U.S.A. The son was one of the founders of the Yeshiva "Tiferet Bachurim" in Bnei Brak.

The adage "Light is sown for the righteous and joy for the upright in heart" (Psalm 97, 11) could have been said of Rabbi Dov Potashnik.

Zviya Zart, a midwife

Zvia was the wife of Doctor Avraham Zart, a daughter of Elazar the baker and his wife Fruma. She was intelligent, wise and kindhearted. She was both graceful and charming and considered quite beautiful. She was a G-D fearing woman. Her qualities made her both special and unique.

As we know, half of Volozhin was perched out on a hill, which made it quite dangerous to descend during winter. However, Zvia was not deterred by the weather - blizzards, strong winds and torrential rains did not stop her from fulfilling her sacred mission - to be the "mother of all living beings" in Volozhin.

It could be said about her: "When it snows, she has no fear for her household" [Proverbs 31,21], "She opens her arms to the poor and extends her hands to the needy" [Proverbs 31,20]. She was a supporter of her husband, the Doctor, and their home was magnificent. It was like an aristocrat's mansion that housed the love of Zion.

When Mr. Menachem Begin (a member of the Knesset) visited Volozhin, the community welcomed him with a very warm and friendly reception which took place in the Zart's home. The reception was organized by Zviya and her friend Rykla Shepensvol (the daughter-in-law of Rabbi Shlomo Chassid). The house could not accommodate all the well-wishers who came to see the guest and many gathered outside near the door.

People still remember that party. All the attendees joined hand in hand and shoulder to shoulder singing "Am Israel Chai" while dancing for hours at the home of Avraham and Zviya Zart.

Rabbi David Yitzhak Kantorovitz

Rabbi David was a special person. He was a farmer who plowed his field, an early "Jewish Pioneer". He planted a vegetable garden on the banks of the Volozhinka River, a place that was later used for teaching Jewish pioneers the secrets of agriculture.

I remember beautiful summer nights on the banks of the river with the stars shining above us, standing among the rows of cucumbers, tomatoes and beets that we had planted with our own hands. We were in the West, but our hearts were in the East (translator's note: this is a reference to a famous poem written in the eleventh century by Rabbi Yehuda Halevi 1075- 1141 in Spain).

[Page 524]

Those of us who survived the Holocaust and today live in Israel still fondly remember our friend David Yitzhak Kantorovitz, a farmer who promoted the Hebrew language, Hebrew schools, and the Torah.

Rabbi Shalom Leib Rubinstein

Rabbi Shalom was the son of Rabbi Eliezer (Leizer Pinia Natas) who was a Beadle in the Talmud Torah and educated his children to both study the Torah and to help people.

He studied at the Yeshiva of Telz, was a modest man, intelligent and honest. Rabbi Shalom never stood out nor did he serve in any public or religious organization. He followed the Talmudic edict ".. and receive every man with a pleasant countenance" [Avot 1, 15].

His wife Lifsha (the daughter of a rabbi) gave birth to two daughters, Bracha and Golda. He made his living from a small store and studied the Talmud between customer visits. He helped the poor and people in need. When someone asked for a loan and he himself did not have the money, he would borrow it from another merchant. He donated "Passover Flour" and other necessities before the Passover Holiday. His wife used to cook in large pots, always ready for a poor person to join them for a meal. He was a "Chovev Zion" and bought land in Eretz-Israel.

During the Holocaust, the Germans wanted to detain the daughters as workers. However, the girls refused to leave their parents and, subsequently, died along with them, following David's lamentation "those who were lovely and pleasant in their lives, even in their death they were not separated".

Rabbi Yaakov Shmuel Ruchamkin

Rabbi Yaakov was a student of the Yeshiva "Etz Chaim" in Volozhin, where he was a follower of the NATZIV. His first wife, Gittel Levison, died at a young age before she had any children. His second wife was Zvia Levit, a daughter of Rabbi Israel Levit, a Torah Scholar.

His business was a metal supply- store, but he did not focus on his trade. Rabbi Yaakov spent most of his time studying and teaching Torah and you could find him during most hours of the day sitting in the synagogue explaining the Torah and Talmud to anyone who asked questions.

He spoke very wisely and loved sharing his knowledge with the many people who benefited from his guidance.

[Page 525]

Prior to the Holocaust

Volozhin in the Shadow of the Holocaust

By Bella Saliternik (Kramnik) of Haifa

Translated by Jerrold Landau

**, based on an earlier translation
by** M. Porat z"l **that was edited by** E. Levitan

I visited Volozhin close to the outbreak of the World War Two. At that time, it was possible to reach Poland by LOT Polish Airlines, or by one of two Polish ships, the Polonia and the Kosciuszko, which sailed from Haifa to Constanta [Romania], from where one would travel to Warsaw by international train. Polish functionaries and military people were among the passengers of the train I took. I recall that during one of the railway stops, Jews stood up and took leave with tears and kisses from those who were departing to the Land of Israel. The Polish nationals reacted to this heartrending and emotional scene with arrogance and denigration. It was difficult for me to bear such a degrading attitude toward the Jews, for I had forgotten somewhat about the existence of anti-Semitism during the years that I had lived in the Land of Israel.

I found Volozhin in a similar state from when I left it. There were no obvious signs of change. The only change that took place in the city was the paving of the road from the railway station in Horodki, and the exchange of the wagon that travelled to the railway station with a bus. Furthermore, the pond on Vilna Street was improved, as trees were placed around it and benches were installed. People sailed on the pond with boats in the summer, and skated on the ice in the winter.

As previously, the youth were involved with the Zionist youth organizations, and were occupied primarily in cultural and leadership activities. The economic situation was quite poor. The Jewish businesses were virtually liquidated for the tax burden was oppressive. Therefore, they borrowed money on interest. This endless loop reduced many of the Jews of Volozhin down to a morsel of bread. The poverty was severe, and the ability of the Jews of our town to get by had been weakened.

The anti-Semitism has burst through all dams, reaching the point where it had become dangerous to cross the street. Christian children threw stones at me as I walked next to the Pravoslavic Church on Vilna Street. A sign with large letters was hanging in the window of the government store in the marketplace, saying "*Swoj do swego*" ["everyone to his own"] (in free literary translation: "Every bird should dwell with their kind, and a Polish person is similar to that"). The general anti-Semitic meaning of that sign was that it was forbidden for a Pole to engage in business with a Jew; it was forbidden to purchase from a Jew; it was forbidden to do business with him, and an economic boycott must be imposed upon the Jews.

Some of the customers of our mother's shop in the Ponizhe village, whom I had known to be members of the Communist party, informed me that the Polish government is conducting wild incitement against the Jews in the villages. The coexistence of Jews and Poles, which was never more than an illusion during the "good times," had come to its end. The Poles had deliberated and decided to eliminate the Jews from an economic perspective.

[Page 526]

The longing of the Jews of Volozhin for the Land of Israel was boundless. Every piece of news from the Land would take on wings and be immediately disseminated to the public, who looked upon it with great interest. I experienced this myself. Masses of people came to greet me, and it was with difficult that I forged my way home. The ecstasy of the Jews of Volozhin at the sight of someone from the Land of Israel was exceptional. People pushed their way toward me. They were hungry and thirsty to hear news from the Land from me. They wanted to hear more than I was able to tell.

This curiosity was a form of expression of the knowledge that all bridges had been broken, and there was no redemption other than in the Land of Israel. They placed their desire toward the Land of Israel. The situation of the Jews of Volozhin at that time can be described in the words of Chaim Nachman Bialik, in his poem *Igeret Ketana* [The Little Letter]: "We have no hope here, my brothers, the end has already been determined, there is no hope for the dove in the hawk's talons – and now I my eyes turn eastward." However, to our great sorrow, they reached this conclusion a bit too late. They were late, too late, to escape to the Land of Israel. The "German thunder" was already rolling in, and Volozhin was standing at the eve of the scene of blood, the likes of which are unparalleled in the history of our nation. However, no person in Volozhin could have imagined exactly what was awaiting. There was the feeling, a prophecy of the heart, that something was about to happen, but nobody could have imagined that this was "the final days" that stand before "the time of the end." No, the "imagination" within the soul of the Jews of Volozhin could not imagine this. On the contrary, the present was shaky, the anti-Semitic dogs were wandering around doing what they were doing to the Jews, but even with this, they could not see a sign of what was coming, that the "main actors" were arriving from German to play the true game, the great, terrible game upon the Jews of Volozhin.

When I bid farewell to my mother and to all those who were so dear to me, I recalled the wonderful "Farewell" poem of Chaim Nachman Bialik. I too recited the words of the poem:

> "Shalom, Shalom to you all,
> And I wish Shalom and blessing to you as well, the clay houses,
> The poor dwellings, with leaky roofs and shaky walls,
> Sinking in the dust to the belly,
> Shalom Shalom to you all!
> And double Shalom to the last of the last,
> To the lowest and more forlorn of you, to the shamed, weak tent…"

At midnight, when I departed Volozhin on my way back to the Land of Israel, masses gathered next to the bus. They came to bid me farewell, with tears flowing from their eyes. They wished themselves that they would merit to meet me in the Land of Israel. It is difficult for me to forget their eyes. It is difficult for me to forget their appearance, filled with agony. It is difficult for me to forget Volozhin of that night, the last night that my feet stood on the ground of Volozhin. I parted from them with fear – a strong fear of what was to come – and with love – boundless love for our dear ones. What were our dear ones thinking that night? I will never forget their appearance and their sad faces. The pen is weeping between my fingers as I write these memories with the clear knowledge that the Jews of Volozhin are no more.

Translator's Footnote:

Mr. M. Porat z"l added the following picture and note:

Bella Saliternik-Kramnik;
Daughter Mika, born on eve of WW2;
their second daughter Tammie;
Yaakov Saliternik Bela's husband. (1950)

Bella Saliternik – Kramnik was born in Kurenets in 1914. At the end of World War One, after her father Michael's death, Mrs. Freydl Kramnik with her daughters, 4 years old Bella and 6 months old Feygl resettled in Volozhin, where mother Freydl established and managed a clothing store. Bella was part of the first students in the Volozhin Tarbut Hebrew School and has been involved in the Betar movement activities. In 1932, Bella made aliya to Erets Israel. She made many efforts to provide an aliya visa for her sister Feygl, but without success. In 1935 Bella was married to Yakov Saliternik. A year later, when pregnant, she decided to give birth to her baby in her mother's home. She made her long journey by ship (Polonia) and train to Volozhin where Mika was born.

Bella's home in Tel Aviv became a second home for many of the Volozhin Shoa survivors during their first years of their life in the fighting for the independence of Israel. The family warmly and very friendly welcomed me with upon my arrival and immediate enlisting in the IDF. In Saliternik's home the marriages of some of the newly arrived Volozhiners took place (Feygl Shepsnvoll, Yakov Kagan and others). Bella lives now in Haifa after the successive deaths of her daughter Mika and husband Yaakov.

[Page 527]

The Soviet regime Period

[Page 528]Blank

The Soviet Period

Translated by Jerrold Landau based on an earlier translation by M. Porat z"l

Preface to this section added in by Mr. M. Porat z"l

The following articles were written by Volozhiners who escaped from the town in June 1941 (Rogovin, Goldschmid, Shvarzberg); by Perlman, who was exiled with his family to Siberia in April 1940 (Note from Jerrold Landau: Perlman is M. Porat, and his section was not in the original Yizkor book); and by Pnina Potashnik, who remained in Volozhin and survived the Holocaust with the Partisans.

The Ribbentrop-Molotov agreement, a secret deal that finally fixed the partition of Poland, was signed in Moscow on August 23, 1939.

The German armies invaded Poland seven days later, on September 1, 1939.

The Red Army crossed the Polish borders on September 17th and occupied ("freed") without any resistance the East Poland Territory (called East Kresy by the Poles and Western Ukraine and Belarus by the Soviets). Volozhin was part of Western Belarus.

Hitler attacked the Soviet Union on June 22, 1941. The big offensive called Barbarossa had begun. The German Wehrmacht occupied Volozhin four days later, on June 26, 1941.

The Soviet rule in Volozhin lasted for 21 months. We call it the "Soviet (pre-war) Period."

[Page 529]

Under the Soviet Regime

by Rachel and Reuven Rogovin

The war between German and Poland began on Friday, 17 Elul, 5699 (September 1, 1939), and continued until Sunday 4 Tishrei, 5700 (September 17, 1939). After the defeat of Poland, and in accordance with the Molotov-Ribbentrop agreement, the Soviets occupied all of western White Russia and Ukraine. Volozhin was included in the Soviet occupation areas.

With the arrival of the new rulers, the situation in our town underwent a fundamental change. Means of communication ceased, for private enterprise was forbidden by the government. Cooperatives were formed for food, and government shops were opened. Tradespeople lost their independent status and were forced to join Artels (a staff of workers with equal rights) based on their field. Artels were formed for shoemakers, tailors, etc. All of the Jewish institutions – the Jewish community structure, the merchants' union, the union of retailer merchants, the tradespeople's union – were automatically liquidated.

Vilna road
(The first building on the right is Mr. Gluchovski's pharmacy)

The two large mills belonging to Polak, and Rappaport and Perlman in Volozhin, the one belonging to Mr. Schiff in Yuzefpol, as well as Gluchovski's pharmacy, were nationalized. Two story buildings, such as the buildings of Elka Bunimovitch-Rozenstein and Reuven Rosenberg, were similarly nationalised.[1]

[Page 530]

A restaurant was opened in the Etz Chaim Yeshiva. Prayer services continued in the synagogues, but the prayers lost their Jewish essence and flavor, where one pours one's heart out before one's Creator.

In spite of the nationalizations and confiscations, there was no hunger in Volozhin. Everybody worked and earned enough to live on, even though the salaries were meager. However, everyone had an "addition." For example, if someone had Polish zlotys, he would give them to David Itche Munie, who would travel to Białystok and exchange them for rubles. Others gathered foodstuffs while there was still time in case of an emergency. Aside from this, farmers brought a bounty of food to the marketplace for a cheap price. These three components assisted the Jewish families in Volozhin to somehow meet their budgets.

A tragic-comic change took place with regard to dress and shoes. Fashion demanded that one wear boots instead of shoes, so people wore boots. It was a distressing yet amusing scene to see important householders, such as Reb Yitzchak Sharira, Reb Tzvi Malchin, Reb Yaakov Weisbord, Reb Avraham Shaker, Reb Mordechai Shishko, the *shochet* Tzvi Namiot ("the Sheliver, as he came from the town of Sheliv), Shalom Leib Rubinstein, and others walking about in boots. There were sycophants who exchanged their starched shirts and ties[2] for the Soviet *gymnastyorka* (khaki shirt).

The borders opened and many people from Volozhin frequently visited Minsk, and family members from Russia visited their relatives in Volozhin. The brother of Shalom Leib Rubinstein's wife was among them. The youth had the opportunity to complete their education in Soviet scientific schools, and a few went to study in several Soviet cities.

From the outside, life appeared steady and more or less normal. Nobody thought about a new war, and especially about one between Germany and Russia. Had someone raised such a possibility, they would have been mocked as a clown or someone who has gone crazy. Two days before the German Messerschmitts bombed Minsk, Kyiv, Lida, and Molodetchno, people still believed that there would be no war in Volozhin.

The Friday evening, 25 Sivan 5701 (June 20, 1941) was different from Saturday night, 26 Sivan 5701 (June 21, 1941) in that the holy Sabbath was felt on the Sabbath eve, and the *Lechu Neranena* prayer was recited in the synagogue as it was every Sabbath.; whereas the beginning of the weekday *Maaariv* service was recited at the conclusion of the Sabbath, and they recited the *Hamavdil* blessing in the homes that begins: "Behold, G-d of my salvations, I trust in you, and I shall not fear." This was the only difference between those two nights. No tidings of Job had reached us, not even an echo of such, aside from the very sad news that the next day, Sunday, 27 Sivan 5701 (June 22, 1941) we had to conduct the funeral for the veteran communal activist of Volozhin, Feive Yosef Simernicki.

During the late hours of Saturday night, we heard a concert from Moscow, which was arranged in honor of the visit of the French Communist Louis Aragon to Russia. After we heard the final news report read by the well-known news reported Yuri Levitan, we went to sleep.

[Page 531]

Reuven did not open the radio in in the morning, for he was certain that "there was nothing to hear." He hurried to Simernicki's funeral. On the way, his friend Shpatziner, Beila Paritzki's husband, who had worked for man years with Michael Wand-Polak, stopped him. Shptziner had been a volunteer captain in the Polish army, who fought with weapons in his hand against the Bolsheviks during the years 5679-5680 (1919-1920). He was a sworn despiser of the Soviet regime.

"Comrade Rogovin," he said to me with a malicious smile, "The downfall of the Soviets is approaching."

"What do you mean," I asked him in wonder. When he realized that I was not up to date in my knowledge of the latest events, he responded, "Did you not hear Molotov's speech? The Germans have attacked Russia, and their airplanes have already bombarded the cities of Minsk, Kyiv, Kharkov, and others." He told me everything that he had heard and know.

When I returned from the cemetery after Simernicki's funeral, I saw Jews gathered together, debating in loud voices. They were divided into two camps: the pro-Soviets and the pro-Germans. The common folk, that is the workers and tradespeople, were certain that the Soviets would defeat the Germans. The large-scale merchants and retailers were convinced of the opposite – that the Germans would defeat the Soviets. They refused to hear what the refugees who had escaped to Volozhin from the areas under German occupation were saying, with their blood curdling stories about what the Germans were doing to the Jews. They treated these stories as Soviet propaganda, as fabricated, sensational stories. They compared the situation to the First World War, claiming that the Germans had already ruled over Volozhin in 1918 and did not harm the Jews. In only one generation, they changed their nature and are rising against us to destroy us? One must not fear them. Those who have fallen in love with the Soviets must fear… Such were the discussions on those final days of the community of Volozhin.

When the war broke out, the government announced that all men up to the age of fifty must present themselves at the mobilization office (Vinkomat) that had opened outside the city. More than one thousand people presented themselves, and there were not enough human resources to draft them. Only fifty men were drafted and sent to barracks in which the Polish army had camped in its time. The rest, I (Reuven) among them, were sent to spend the night in the gymnasium building.

The next day, we presented ourselves again at the mobilization office. However, German airplanes appeared in the sky. They told us to disperse and return when the all-clear signal would be given. However, we did not return any more, for there was a great panic in the city. The authorities lacked any power, for they were cut off from the center in Minsk, which had been attacked several times from the air. They began to evacuate the wives of government officials to a safer place deep in the country.

The Soviets did not tell us what to do. Everyone was allowed to decide for themselves whether they wanted to remain in Volozhin with the Germans or escape into Russia. When the news arrived on Thursday, 1 Tammuz 5701 (June 26, 1941) that the German brigade had reached Bogdanovo

[Page 532]

(25 kilometers from Volozhin), we arose in the middle of the night, took our two children, Reuven's mother, his sisters, and his brother Yaakov, and left Volozhin on foot. Reuven's father Yitzchak and his sisters Sara and Chana remained in Volozhin, where they perished. His brother Yaakov was killed in battle near Stalingrad in the year 5702 (1942).

Translator's Footnotes:

1. Mr. M. Porat adds the following detail: The owners of the nationalized mills were put in prison and later deported to the Soviet Gulag. Their families (wives and children) were expelled and "resettled" in Siberia.
2. Mr. M. Porat notes that this was the symbol of the Polish bourgeoisie.

[Page 532]

Volozhin Under the Soviet Regime

by Mendel Goldschmid (of Ramat Yitzchak)

The Polish authorities announced a general mobilization as soon as the war broke out. From among the Jewish youth, Zelig and Shlomo Meltzer, Yisrael and Zalman Perski, Yitzchak Kaplan, Avraham and Yitzchak Danishevski, Yochanan German, the writer of these memoirs, and others were drafted. We went to the front, but we returned to Volozhin after a brief time, for the Polish army had been defeated and retreated in disarray.

When the State of Poland was partitioned between the Soviets and the Germans in accordance with the Molotov-Ribbentrop agreement, the Soviets entered Volozhin from the side of Rakov. Their entry surprised the population. Shouts and calls were heard in the city, "Behold, the Soviets are coming!" They were indeed coming with tanks and infantry.

The Soviets surrounded the Starosta building and arrested the workers along with the police officers and their assistants. They began to confiscate the property of the wealthy people. This confiscation brought economic disaster upon the Jews of Volozhin. The shopkeepers hid their merchandise so that they would not be ruined.

Nothing pained the Jews of Volozhin as did the confiscation of the Yeshiva building, which was turned into a restaurant. Bitter crying and weeping was heard over the destruction of that miniature sanctuary. The Yeshiva lads sat outside on the ground with Gemaras in their hands and eyes filled with tears. How sorrowful was the melody of their Gemara! Most of them left Volozhin. Miraculously, the Yeshiva building was not destroyed. Many firebombs fell in the vicinity of the Yeshiva, but it was not hit.

The Jews tried with all their might to ensure that the light of Israel would not be extinguished. The Yeshiva was closed, the Talmud Torah was closed, and the Tarbut School was also closed. The *melamdim* were permitted to conduct their holy work in private houses, but this was a poor substitute for the spiritual life.

The Soviets confiscated the *mikveh*. Reb Mordechai Shishko, the dear, good Jew, did not rest until another *mikveh* had been dug at the entrance to the synagogue, concealed from the eyes of the enemy.

It should be noted that the Jews received the Soviets with appreciation. Horrifying news about the atrocities perpetrated by the Germans against the Jews in the areas under German occupation infiltrated to us. We were certain that we would survive in the areas under Soviet occupation. The physician Avraham Tzart spoke enthusiastically at meetings

[Page 533]

about the Soviets, as if they were redeemers and saviours. His words left a great impression. At one of those meetings, the Soviets requested from those present to tell the audience about how they lived under Polish rule. A poor Jew burdened with many children ascended the podium. He turned his head to the wall, lowered his cloak, showed the hole in his tattered pants, and declared: "This is how I lived under the Polish regime!" The wretched, oppressed people such as that Jew believed with a full heart that their sun had now risen.

Ketzlich (a Jew) the head of the Soviet administration in Volozhin, invited me to his office and gave me the job of clearing out the stones from the market square, planting trees, and turning the area into an ornamental garden. After I did what I was commanded, Ketzlich revealed to me the secret that they were about to erect a statue of Stalin in that place. The statue indeed arrived, packed in crates. We set up the pieces and erected the large statue. Stalin stood wearing a hat and an army uniform, with his hand outstretched westward. However, this caused a severe problem. There was a cross made out of cast iron on that spot. It would be a "sacrilege" to erect a statue of the "Sun of the Nations" next to a cross. Therefore, it was decided to demolish the cross. One Friday night, Soviet police and soldiers surrounded the area and laid the dynamite, and the cross flew into the air. I was ordered to remove the fragments.

The gentiles blamed me for the blowing up of the cross and waited for the hour of revenge. However, I immediately escaped from Volozhin when the Germans entered.

[Page 533]

During the Soviet Rule in Our City

by Pnina Chayat (Potashnik) of Holon

The Soviets entered our city without encountering any resistance. The workers and tradespeople received them with open appreciation. Members of the municipal government and several wealthy Jews fled to Lithuania, which was still independent.

The Soviet command was located in military bunkers. Their relationship with the population was even-handed. They set up civic institutions with the assistance of local Jewish and Christian Communists.

Everyone had to go to work, both man and women. Anyone avoiding work was accused of speculation and deliberate sabotage. Work was the only source of income. Shops were closed. A Larok food market was opened in their place. There were exceedingly long lines to obtain provisions, causing great suffering for the population. Clothing could be obtained in exchange for coupons, however only very few people had such.

The Tarbut School was closed. Russian schools were opened, with the aim of winning over the Jewish children to their ideology and cutting them off from the history of the Jewish people. The Jewish children entered an atmosphere of complete assimilation.

The city was inundated with a stream of refugees who escaped from the German occupation area. They first came to our city to do business with the Soviets, but when they saw that commerce was considered a crime, they expressed their desire to return to German occupied Poland.

The Soviets made a list of all those who wished to return. One night, the Soviet army surrounded their homes and commanded them to pack their belongings and prepare for the journey. They were brought to the railway station and deported to Siberia.

It should be noted that these Jews survived thanks to that deportation.

[Page 534 – Porat addition]

The Russians are Coming

by M. Perlman (M. Porat z"l)

Note from the second translator, Jerrold Landau: Mr. M. Porat (Perlman) the original translator of numerous sections of this book, added in his own section of testimony at this point. This section is not part of the original book. Mr. Porat prefaced his testimony with: Written by a witness after the Yizkor book was published. I (Jerrold Landau) only lightly edited it, leaving the original wording intact for the most part. Therefore, some parts of it may seem a bit rough.

The war breaks out

In June 1939 I finished the first class of Volozhin's brand new Polish gymnasia-high school. I was 15 years old. I describe this half-year period of our family's history in Volozhin under the Soviet regime, as seen through a young boy's eyes.

Our family spent the summer of 1939 in Kaldiki, a pleasant pine-forest hamlet on the Berezina shore, 10 km. from town. It was the last summer prior to the Second World War. Germany encircled Poland from East Prussia, Czechoslovakia, and the German mainland. Hitler held Poland in mortal forceps and his shadow was cast over Europe, particularly over the continent's Jewry.

That summer in all Polish cities, a song was popular whose sentimental tango melody was adopted 50 years later by N. Mikhalkov, the Russian filmmaker, as background air to his famous movie about Stalin, *"The Treacherous Sun."* The sorrowful words, which all Poland was singing during the summer of 1939, were: "Today is our last Sunday, today we shall separate forever…"

The 1939 school year did not begin as usual on the first day of September. On Friday September 1st we found the school doors locked. The Warsaw Radio station, destroyed by German air raids, was silent. The brutal Nazi invasion was announced through Radio Lvov before it was silenced in its turn a day later. On the walls were stuck placards calling men aged 20 to 45 to report to mobilizing posts. Father took a bag with undergarments, socks, soap, and talcum powder. His post was in Lida. We accompanied him to the bus. Mother was in tears. The next day we were all relieved: father returned home. The chaos was enormous, and the checkpoint overcrowded. Those called to report were sent home. The Polish army, proud of its cavalry bravura, collapsed under the Wehrmacht blows.

During these splendid, colorful autumn days, Volozhin awaited its fate in a strange calmness. Father was conscious as to what we should expect from Hitler. He planned to bring us to the Soviet border. The Soviets, he said, would not refuse shelter for children.

A rumor spread on Sunday morning, September 17th: "The Germans are approaching." The Polish functionaries destroyed documents, packed their luggage, and some of them left the town at night. I went to Smorgon Street to get from Mr. Faygenbaum, our flourmills' manager on duty, the redemption money of the previous days. It was needed to reach the Soviet border.

On my way back, an airplane, flying in contour, passed over the town. The Greyser Barg [large downhill slope], which I chose to go down, was parallel to a hillside. I clung to the ground, searching for a safe place. I was suddenly aware that hundreds of objects were flying from above, in my direction.

Fortunately, there were neither bombs nor bullets. It was simply a rain of pieces of paper. I amassed some of them and running home I read the message from the sky. It was written in Polish and Russian. "The peoples of the Soviet Union, at the demand of their brothers in the West Ukraine and Byelorussia, are stretching hands to free them from the capitalist burden." We understood that our life would not be easy, but we would be saved from a death sentence.

The Soviets enter Volozhin

We went into the mill. Father distributed sacks of flour to the neighbors. We also took some of it into our house. As we entered our home, we heard an intense noise. Through the windows we saw an armored vehicle running in the deserted street. The tank stopped near our house. Soldiers came down to check the bridge. It was the Red Army reconnaissance patrol.

In the afternoon, the flow of invasion (liberation) troops began. First, the armored forces, tanks, carriers, trucks, motorized artillery, etc. passed. The flow continued during the whole night and on the next day. We were overwhelmed by the quantity and quality. But increasingly among the motorized transporters we could see horse-drawn carts. And the horses... We were used to seeing the proud, beautiful Polish Army horses. The horses that we saw now varied in size and color, but they were alike in their meagerness. These horses had probably been raised on Soviet agricultural collectives. We became doubtful as to the wealth and power of our new overlords.

The soldiers' behavior was outstanding, polite, and very friendly. No thievery, pillaging, robbery, beatings, or arrests occurred. The soldiers differed slightly from their commanders. The signs of rank were not pompously carried on the shoulders, as by the Polish officers, but modestly tied to the collar. When stopping to rest, they used to dance, sing, and tell stories about the wonderful achievements of the Soviet people and about the mastermind, about the prodigy and goodness of the great father and leader, Josef Stalin. Our liberators were not called soldiers (soldaty), but fighters (*boytsy*). At the sight of them, mother said that we should not worry about the *Fanies* (Yiddish nickname for Russians) coming in carts and trucks, but rather that we should be cautious about those coming in personal motorcars.

And indeed, the commissars, the true rulers, arrived. They established the new order. Crowded meetings were held in the cinema and in the fire brigade halls. The Soviet state, its regime, wealth, and achievements were praised. Jokes were transmitted from mouth to mouth about the Communists' bragging. "We have in our wealthy state all the best, even matches." There used to be, probably sometimes, a lack of matches. But these times did not pass. During this year, a lack of many products emerged in the shops, among them sugar, white flour, and even matches. But abundant and big were the queue lines, a brand-new phenomenon in our shtetl. It was swiftly imported from Mother Russia and adopted in our country. In each place where goods were sold and to which a group of customers was attracted, a line was formed. It grew bigger hour by hour and would reach unseen dimensions.

The school doors reopened. Our Hebrew Tarbut school began teaching in Yiddish. The Polish gymnasium was converted into a Russian high school. It became filled with Jewish youth, thirsty for the education that they had been deprived of during the Polish anti-Semitic regime.

The gymnasium manager, Dr. Konopnitski, did not flee. He stayed on his job and continued his style of teaching. Once, he compared Hitler's regime to a pyramid, standing on its top and leaning on the soldier's bayonets. Our director's opinion was that during war, when the bayonets would turn to where there was a real need for them, the pyramid must collapse. The NKVD understood whom he had in mind. On the next day he was arrested and sent to the gulag land, from which he never returned.

Pani (Mrs.) Kopylova, our director's spouse, taught us natural sciences. She was exiled to Siberia after her husband's arrest.

New comrades joined our narrow circle of Jewish students. We used to meet on the long winter evenings, satisfied with what had happened around. We had a real sense of the historical events we witnessed. We organized mini meetings in which satirical sayings about the new order and lifestyle were expressed for fun: "Sugar like sugar, but emotions are many: assemblies, weddings, and parties inside, and lines without end extend on the streets..."

The new rulers attracted Communist sympathizers to work in their institutions. Among the fortunate persons accepted were some Volozhin Jews. One could see people rising and becoming instantly rich and powerful.

Some of our friends changed their attitude towards the new underdogs. Once, returning from a Soviet mass meeting, my best friend Hayke di Kadelihe's sister told me, "Your capitalist's good time is over; from now on, everything that is yours belongs to us; we will enjoy life and you should perish." I am not sad. I recall the poor girl's harsh words without any anger.

The new authorities did confiscate both of Volozhin's ground-sawmills (Polak's and Rapoport-Perlman's). The mills were "returned to the people" and unified into a single wood plant. Father was dismissed and sent to work in the woods in the vicinity. Grandfather Hirsh Malkin was also employed at similar work.

Once, Father returned from the forest completely outraged. At night police officers intruded into the peasant's home in which father used to sleep during his work in the woods. The "people's emissaries" ordered the peasant to assemble his family and to pack the most necessary belongings. The entire family, men and women, children, and old people, were put into carts and transported to the nearest railroad station. It was Stalin's first mass transfer action. Thousands of citizens of Polish nationality had been settled by the Polish government during the twenty years of its rule in the eastern territories on the Russian frontiers. Stalin's NKVD (The People's Interior Ministry Police) repaired the demographic problem. During one night, most of the Polish settlers (osadniki) were loaded on special trains and resettled far in Siberia.

The Graf's estate, after serving as the Polish military unit headquarters, became the headquarters of the Soviet NKVD (predecessor to the KGB). In the cellars of the elegant Belvedere-style Graf's palace were detained the arrested "people's enemies." Among them was my father in 1940. The building now houses the Volozhin Belarus police unit.

The arrest and exile

Six months after the Russians took Volozhin, they penetrated our home. What mother had feared finally occurred.

On a springtime evening in March 1940, our parents were listening to the radio, I was reading, and Sonitshka was asleep in her bed. We heard knocking at the door. It was opened. An NKVD agent with two local citizens entered. The three searched all closets, wardrobes, and chests. The police officer ordered my father to dress. Father took the prepared bundle of underwear. He separated from us. Prior to his leaving, Father said that he surely would be home by Passover, because he never did any evil to anyone. He kissed the sleeping 10-year-old Sonitshka, his beloved daughter, and went out into the dark, escorted by the three of them. It was the last time we saw and heard our father. He was forty-two years old.

Mother went from door to door. She begged for help from the new elite to free our father. One of the suddenly powerful promised, a second claimed that he could not help, and the third answered mockingly.

Passover 5700 (1940) became a holiday of fear and hope. We hoped that father would soon be home; we were afraid and anxious for his future. Mother carried bundles with food and underwear to the prison door. Did he receive them? Did they pass the bundles to him? How long did he live after the arrest? When, where and how did he meet his death?

There were rumors that our father, Yosef Perlman, was driven to a gulag camp in the Siberian forests prior to the German invasion, and that he was killed in an accident involving a falling tree.

On Friday morning April 13, 1940, our grandfather's voice woke us up: "They took out the Polak and Rapoport families; it looks like they will come also for you." On the ropes in the attic (*boydem*) many pieces of laundry were hanging to dry. We took them down still damp. At home were two large woven-wood suitcases. We prepared them for packing. In the meantime, they appeared: the NKVD agent with his two local aides. In front of us, the agent read the official document: As individuals not reliable to the Soviet government, we are to be expelled from the border country and transferred to resettle in the central regions of the Soviet Union. We were ordered to pack what we could manage in the suitcases in two hours time and to put them into the peasant horse-drawn cart that was waiting. We were driven in this cart to the Horod'k railway station.

We passed the Volozhinka wooden bridge, continued through the Greyser Barg, turned to the small downward slope where we passed by the Belokortser's house and our Malkin grandparents' domicile. The horse slowly continued its way over the marketplace in front of Grandma Malka's rabbinical residence, and then through the Vilna Street past our birth house to the end of town. There were many farewells on our way. Grandparents, relatives, family friends, neighbors, and schoolmates got out on our road to say goodbye. "The entire shtetl was in tears" were our mother's words when she would tell about our exodus from our birthplace.

We did not know that this departure saved us from complete destruction, which was the final fate of all the inhabitants who remained in Volozhin. We were on our way to Siberia, to our new destiny.

Goodbye to our birthplace, to our Litvak-shtetl style of life, to our Litvak-Yiddish *mameloshn* (mother language), to our grandparents, to all our relatives and friends, to all my sister's schoolmates and mine, to all whose destiny would be to vanish, to be erased from the living world, forever.

[End of Mr. Perlman Porat's addition]

[Page 534]

The Destruction of Volozhin

Translated by Jerrold Landau

**. First paragraph only translated
by Mr. M. Porat z"l and edited by Jerrold Landau**

The Yeshiva's existence was terminated in September 1939 with the coming of the Soviets. The Yeshiva head, Rabbi Yaakov Shapira, had passed away prior to the outbreak of the war. His son-in-law, Rabbi Chaim Wolkin (son of the Pinsker Rabbi), who served as his replacement, was secretly transferred by me with his family and the family of Rabbi Yaakov Shapira to Vilna, which then belonged to Lithuania. The Yeshiva building was then turned into a restaurant, frequented by various drunkards. The inhabitants of the city, who considered the Yeshiva to be their crown, were very sick about this. Unfortunately, it was impossible to overturn the decree. It should be noted that the guard of the restaurant in the Yeshiva, Gedalya Mordechai Widrovitsh, requested Wiener, the owner of the restaurant to release him from his duties, because he lived every night in great terror. In the middle of the night, he heard the sounds of learning and singing, as if in the winds! Wiener laughed at this. One night, he even guarded the restaurant himself. When, late at night, he heard the learning and singing, he fled from the building in a faint. From that time, he was afraid of entering there even during the day.[1]

The Germans entered Volozhin on July 25, 1941. They bombarded the city with artillery and caused fires by dropping incendiary bombs from airplanes prior to marching in. When the German tanks entered the city, they shot the following residents: Chaim Eliyahu Perski, Alter Shimshelevitch, Pesach Mazeh, and later Berman. As soon as the Germans settled in the city, the local Christians

[Page 535]

immediately began to pillage the Soviet and Jewish goods from the remaining shops. Two weeks later, a Judenrat was formed by order of the Gestapo. It consisted of twelve members, and was headed by Yaakov Barber. The Judenrat's job was to carry out the ordinances of the Gestapo and the local authorities, such as providing workers, and carrying out various demands to collect money, jewelry, leather, and manufactured goods for the Gestapo and local authorities. Things went on in this way for two months until the ghetto was created.

In August 1941, the ghetto was created in the lower part of the city, called Aroptzu. Approximately 3,500 people lived in only 50-60 houses. These consisted of Jews from Volozhin itself as well as those who came from surrounding towns, such as Vishneve, Halshan [Olshan], and Oshmiany. There were also Jews who had escaped from Vilna. All the Jews had to wear yellow patches. There was no limit to the persecution of the Jews. Jews had to go to various difficult jobs in the fields and forests, paving the streets, etc. Handworkers and other specialists worked in their trades, but they only received two grams of bread per person, not more. Jews obtained goods from the surrounding peasants with great difficulty, for they had to give away their most expensive possessions. An Ordnungspolizei was formed, consisting of thirty men, under the leadership of the civic teacher Gliker.

Before that time, a certain lawyer, Stanislaw Turski returned to the city. He had previously been sent to Kartuz-Bereza as an extreme Endeke (N.D. Narodowa Demokratia), as well as for misdemeanors in his work. Turski now connected himself with the anti-Semites of the city, with the barber Baranski and others. He initiated a disgusting anti-Jewish agitation among the peasants. That anti-Semite very quickly became the mayor [Burgermeister], and he immediately began to carry out his bloody plans. Already on his second day on the job, he began to arrest many Jews, including the beloved Jewish city feldsher [medic] Avraham Tzart, his daughter Nechama, Chaim Tzirulnik, Aharon Galperin, Shimon Lavit, and Lipa Tzimerman. On account of his intervention, they were all taken out the day after their arrest and shot behind the city.

The civic police consisted of former bandits from the surrounding villages,under the leadership of the S.S. They were urged on by the local anti-Semites. They would attack the Jews and beat them with death blows. In this way, the police officer Minkewicz (son of a Polish policeman), who was in Anders' army,

[Page 536]

broke both hands of the Jewish woman Freidl Rozen, and then shot her. The girl Roze Berman was shot and then tossed in in a latrine. Shachna Paretzki was murderously beaten and then shot.

On October 28, 1941 (7 Cheshvan 5702) Maka, the S.S. man of the Volozhin Gestapo arrived in the ghetto and demanded that the Judenrat provide a large quantity of leather, which was to be collected within two hours.

On 14 Cheshvan 5702 (November 4, 1941), that selfsame Maka again arrived, accompanied by five S.S. men, and demanded that the Judenrat call together the Jews of the ghetto for a meeting. In the meantime, he beat the Jewish policeman so that they would gather the crowd more quicky. When a large number had gathered, Maka selected approximately two hundred elderly people and children, and sent them away. He ordered that the remaining crowd be prodded into the city movie theater, apparently for a meeting. They locked the people in, and took out ten people to the adjacent sports place and shot them there. When this became known in the ghetto, the Judenrat immediately collected a large sum of money and goods, and gave them over to the bandit Maka, who stopped the aktion against the remaining approximately 150 people., whom he allowed to return to the ghetto. Over two hundred Jews were murdered in that aktion, including the chairman of the Judenrat Yaakov Garber. At first, Garber, together with the Judenrat and ghetto police, helped gather the people into the movie theater. However, when he realized that the situation was very serious, he, Garber, stopped doing his duty, and went into the hall, thereby sharing the fate of the other Jews of the ghetto.

After carrying out the aktion, the White Russian-Polish police, together with the surrounding peasants, took the best items, including the jewelry, from the victims, removed their gold teeth, and then called forty Jews to bury the dead. During the aktion, the young Yaakov Finger succeeded in escaping from the sports place, along with the youths Tzafin and Zecharia Beiklin, who were wounded. They came to the ghetto and described what they had seen and experienced. This all instilled terror into the Jews of the ghetto, and broke them further.

After the slaughter, a few families were taken to work in the nearby town of Krasna, where they were later also killed. The people who remained in the ghetto lived in terrifying conditions, and in fear of death. One day, S.S. men entered a house in which Jews used to worship. They

[Page 537]

took a Torah scroll, tore off the *Etz Chaims* [the wooden poles of the scroll], unrolled it alongside the house, and trampled it with their dirty boots. A few days later, they came once again and took about 35 Jews, laid them atop the Torah scroll, and shop them.

The winter of 1942 was a very difficult one in the ghetto, even though there were no aktions until the spring. The local anti-Semites, such as the lawyer Krestianw, Turski, and others, did not stop leading their campaign against the Jews, and demanded that they all be liquidated.

On May 10, 1942 (23 Iyar, 5702), at 5:00 a.m., the ghetto was surrounded by the S.S. and police. They quicky broke into the ghetto, shot the two Jewish police officers, Yochanan Klein and Yitzchak Narusevitch, at the gate, and began to shoot in the ghetto. Many people fell. They, they began to prod the Jews into the smithy that the Russians had built on Mashtshika Street, not far from the Aroptzu Kloiz. All those they captured, about eight hundred people, were locked inside. The crowding was terrible, and the screaming of the children was indescribable. The S.S. shot into the crowd so that they would be quiet.

The Halshaner [Olshaner] Rabbi, Rabbi Reuven Chadash, who was also present, told the crowd that they should break the ovens, everyone should take a brick, a stone, or some metal they should break down the doors, throw the objects at the S.S. and run away. Yisrael Lunin, a member of the Judenrat said that temporary life is also good, and he did not permit this to take place.

The S.S. chief called the Judenrat member Aharon Kamenecki and ordered him to clean his boots. As soon as Kamenecki bent down, the chief shot him in the head with a bullet. When the crowd saw this, they began to crawl through the roof. The Germans noticed this and opened fire. Several people, including

Mordechai Molot and others, succeeded in escaping. The entire crowd was held on a hot day under terribly stifling conditions from 5:00 a.m. until 5:00 p.m. Then they began to partially lead out women, children, and the elderly. They brought them to the yard of Bulowa the peasant, next to the Jewish cemetery. There, the chief of the S.S. himself shot them all with an automatic rifle. After shooting the people, they burnt them together with the peasant's house. It is proper to note that the groups of Jews being led out to be shot were accompanied by music from the local peasants. Many elderly

[Page 538]

people went to their deaths wearing their *tallises* and *kittels*. On that day, another approximately eight hundred Jews were murdered through the hunt of Jews throughout the city. They were shot in the cellars and other hiding places. The Jews lay unburied for three days. When they were taken to be buried, the peasants threw dead dogs and cats and garbage upon the corpses.

(From The Final Destructions, chronicles of the history of Jewish life during the Nazi regime, editor Y. Kaplan, Munich, June 1948, Number 8, pages 75-79)

The Netzi'v and the Etz Chaim Yeshiva on the Brink of Destruction

I know a story that was told during the days of the Second World War regarding the Etz Chaim Yeshiva, which was headed at one time by the Netzi'v. That story from the Second World War comes from the same eternal wings that ascend from the dream that my father dreamt during the time of the First World War. In the dream, the Netzi'v was delivering a class to the Jews from behind the *pargod*[2]. He cited a verse from the Torah portion of *Bechukotai* in a version different than ours, in a version that is not from this world. In the story, a Yeshiva concealed from the eye, the Volozhin Yeshiva from behind the *pargod*, continued to occupy itself with learning even after its destruction in the palpable world – and even if it was not seen by the eye, it was heard by the ear. In the dream, he who had been the head of the Yeshiva of Volozhin poured out his wrath upon Czarist Russia, and spoke many things, cut off and panicked. The content of all of them – curse after curse, each worse than the previous. He called out the "reproof"[3] in full, and turned it upon the heads of the murderers and pillagers, the enemies of Israel. Thereby, the Yeshiva of Volozhin, which had disappeared from the eye, poured out fear upon the "Red" Russians.

The teller tells as follows: During the Second World War, after the Red Army had conquered the eastern border of Poland, the building of the Yeshiva of Volozhin turned in to some sort of a tavern for soldiers. The guard in charge of the building heard at night the voices of the disappeared Torah studiers. The invisible Yeshiva students sang in their Torah voices in the silence of the night, and the fear of G-d fell upon those who heard their voices. His superior did not believe his words, so he himself stood on guard one night. He heard the voices and he too fled in terror. The Yeshiva of Volozhin existed as it was – behind the *pargod*. The voices of Torah had returned to their source. Just as Torah had not stopped from the mouth of the Netzi'v in my father's dream, and the Jews from behind the *pargod* were sitting with him in his place and listening, so too the learning did not cease from the mouths of the Yeshiva students who were sitting invisibly and occupying themselves in what they do. Through their voices, the voice of Jacob, they instilled fear and terror upon those who destroyed and desecrated the place of Torah.

(*Hadoar*, issue 39, 10 Marcheshvan 5725 [1964], pages 752-755)

Translator's Footnotes:

1. Mr. Porat's original translation stopped at this point.
2. The *pargod* refers to the mystical Heavenly partition between G-d and the angels, or G-d and those in the Other World, and the physical world.
3. The reproof [*tochacha*] is the litany of maledictions in Leviticus 26:14-43, included in the Torah portion of *Bechukotai*. The second *tochacha* is found in the Torah portion of *Ki Tavo*, Deuteronomy 28:15-69.

END OF VOLUME 1

NAME INDEX

A

Abba the Builder, 11
Absh'r, 64
Afrimzon, 465
Aharonshtam, 392
Aizenstein, 473
Aizers, 356
Ajzenstat, 174
Alexandra Feodorovna, 352
Alperin, 114
Alperovitch, 357, 358, 437
Alperovitsh, 459
Alpert, 411, 412, 416
Alter the Barber, 350
Alter-Eli the paver, 350
Alterke, 323, 324
Altman, 426, 460
Amicis, 442
Apel, 511
Aragon, 548
Areh, 347
Areh the Koltun, 346
Arka "der Feldshar" the Medic, 353
Arotzker, 348, 368, 488
Artsybashev, 329
Asaf, 111, 172
Ashkenazi, 201, 411, 415, 416, 417
Ashlagi, 508
Askind, 333, 345, 349, 351
Atlas, 67, 185
Avida, 143
Avraham der Vafelnik (the Clay Maker), 491
Avraham Itche the butcher, 525
Avraham Leib Shmuel's horse and wagon, 347
Avraham'le the slaughterer, 333
Avram'ke the shoemaker, 352, 353
Avreima'le the Slaughterer, 345
Azulai, 479

B

Baal Shem Tov, 23, 48, 281, 293
Bakshet, 356, 368

Baksht, 377, 392, 396, 399, 410, 411, 412, 415, 416, 417, 440, 465, 466, 501
Bakshtanski, 326, 451
Bakshter, 112
Balashko, 352
Balfour, 301, 434
Balinski – Lipinski, 63
Balkind, 291
Bankover, 395, 396
Baranowska, 380
Baranowski, 380
Bar-Bei-Rav, 178, 214
Barber, 556
Bar-Ilan, 10, 77, 153, 154, 157, 162, 169, 172, 173, 191, 201, 233, 234, 235, 236, 237, 238, 243, 310, 485, 487
Barshak, 113
Bar-Shira, 437
Baruch Leib the tailor, 344
Baumriter, 186
Baxter, 387, 388
Began, 416
Begin, 540
Behmer, 119
Beikalski, 437, 442
Beikelski, 440
Beiklin, 557
Beilis, 477, 497
Bekerman, 184
Belin, 217
Belokortser, 555
Belzer, 477
Ben Zion, 347
Ben-Eliezer, 265
Ben-Gurion, 175, 421
Ben-Nachum, 527
Ben-Sasson, 150, 223, 239, 245, 246, 247, 392, 393, 394, 453
Ben-Tzion, 136
Ber, 413
Berdichevski, 24, 64, 67, 167, 175, 178, 184, 185, 315
Berdichevsky, 28, 110, 211, 214
Berditshevski, 167

Berdyczewski, 50, 51
Beres, 354
Berger, 393, 394, 399, 506, 507
Bergman, 367, 452
Beril, 184
Berka "Der Rimer", 357
Berkerman, 184
Berkman, 184
Berkovich, 353, 377, 498, 499, 500
Berkovitch, 347, 349, 393, 395, 410, 411, 412, 413,
   415, 416, 417, 420, 433, 436, 437, 460, 461, 526
Berkovitsh, 363, 460
Berkovitz, 510
Berkowitz, 333, 353, 354, 355, 392, 464, 465, 466,
   467
Berlin, 9, 15, 21, 26, 49, 59, 61, 62, 64, 68, 103, 104,
   109, 111, 116, 117, 125, 127, 136, 139, 149, 150,
   151, 152, 153, 154, 162, 167, 169, 172, 173, 179,
   180, 181, 183, 186, 191, 192, 214, 216, 217, 219,
   226, 229, 232, 233, 234, 243, 251, 263, 310, 332,
   365, 473, 481, 482, 485, 487
Berlin-Papish, 485
Berlin-Pepish, 487
Berlman, 8
Berman, 12, 266, 365, 379, 380, 382, 395, 405, 411,
   412, 413, 416, 417, 418, 420, 421, 436, 437, 441,
   451, 456, 459, 462, 506, 556
Berniker, 367
Bernstein, 298, 395, 396
Bialik, 25, 26, 27, 49, 58, 59, 60, 61, 62, 67, 68, 108,
   110, 115, 116, 125, 126, 127, 129, 166, 175, 184,
   187, 214, 224, 291, 294, 301, 302, 306, 315, 330,
   371, 426, 434, 439, 442, 491, 510, 543
Bilevi, 316
Binyamin "the Store Owner", 357
Binyomke the Ainbinder, 348
Blidstein, 116
Bloch, 346, 451
Blusher, 27, 60, 67, 125, 184, 211, 214
Bogdanovski, 199
Bogrov, 497
Boonies, 457, 460
Botkowski, 285
Botwinik, 400
Bram, 371, 434
Braude, 209
Breg, 175
Breinin, 67

Brener, 465
Brenner, 140
Brill, 297
Brinker, 518
Brisk, 61, 62
Brisker, 111, 345
Broda, 64
Brodna, 333, 374, 375, 386, 387, 420, 426, 432, 437,
   443, 444, 508, 512
Brodno, 356, 357, 358, 536, 537
Brodsky, 140, 146
Bromberg, 219
Bron, 179; 217, 219
Bronke, 461
Brudna, 348
Brudno, 457, 460
Buksztanowicz, 348
Buminovitch, 411
Bunimovich, 54, 55, 61, 64, 65, 177, 358, 390, 391
Bunimovitch, 49, 60, 348, 390, 392, 416, 417, 418,
   420, 436
Bunimovitch-Rozenstein, 547
Bunimovitsh, 159, 380
Bunimovitz, 322, 337, 338, 339, 451, 518, 519, 520
Bunimowicz, 201
Bunimowitz, 41, 116

C

Cederbaum, 63
Ceitlin, 150, 317
Chabayoff, 353
Chacham, 315
Chachamim, 209
Chadash, 420, 557
Chaikel "the lip", 352, 353
Chaiken, 451
Chaikin, 55
Chaim "the butcher", 358
Chaim "the tailor", 366, 524
Chaim der *Shnayder* (the Tailor), 524
Chaim der Shneider, 348, 450, 491
Chaim the Galanterinchik, 347
Chalopski, 356, 357
Charnow, 443
Charutz, 367, 403, 404, 405
Chassid, 207, 426, 521, 522, 540
Chaya the Krever, 449
Chayat, 551

Chazanowitz, 476

Cheiten, 450

Chekhov, 327

Chelem the shoemaker, 353

Chritzki, 399

Churgin, 201

Cinowitz, 183

Citnick, 352

Citnik, 352

Citron, 111, 317

Cohen, 49, 201, 262, 521

Cooper, 442

Cytron, 187

Czar Alexander I, 94

Czodikow, 65

D

Danishevski, 231, 549

Dante, 113

Daul, 395, 400, 416, 417

David, 479

Delyanov, 130, 132

Dement, 179

Der *Raznoshtshik*, 523

Der Shaliver, 474

Derechinski, 150, 196, 239, 240, 241, 243, 247, 396, 440, 465

Derechinsky, 410

Deretshinski, 390

Deretshnski, 346

Derevna, 348

Di Mazepe, 460

Dickens, 442

Dickenstein, 453

Dickstein, 449

Dik, 98

Dinkin, 46, 141, 177, 178

Diskin, 310

Divenishker, 450

Dolenga, 442

Dolgov, 395, 400, 416

Dolnov, 400, 422

Don Ikhya, 156

Don-Yechia, 287, 288, 302, 315

Dovidman, 380

Dovka, 399

Drachinski, 357

Dratvitzki, 412

Drianov, 62

Droshkovitz, 2, 3

Droyanov, 61, 116, 167, 187, 315

Droyanow, 288, 289, 306

Drucker, 312

Drushkowitz, 332

Dubinski, 356, 357, 411, 412, 417

Dubinsky, 336, 416

Dubnow, 111, 173, 421

Dudman-Dudayi, 332

Dumas, 442

Dverelke, 457

Dvoretzki, 356

Dvoshke, 347

Dworzec, 62, 63, 428

E

Efrokin, 440

Eidelish, 104

Eidelman, 412, 465

Eidels, 121

Eiger, 201

Eisenstadt, 58, 62

Eisenstant, 188

Eisenstat, 62, 211, 214, 218, 219, 229, 264

Eisenstein, 315, 472

Eistenstat, 183

Elazar the baker, 540

Eldad, 66, 67

Eli the locksmith, 451

Eliasberg, 281, 282, 283, 294, 315

Eliashkevitch, 348

Elishberg, 155

Elishkevitsh, 479

Eliyaswhkevitsh, 379

Elka "Berka Dam Rimers", 358

Elka the baker, 346

Elke, 347

Epstein, 26, 58, 60, 66, 69, 91, 114, 118, 128, 153, 156, 157, 159, 166, 183, 188, 207, 209, 281, 283, 284, 285, 286, 287, 300, 306, 315, 316, 317, 318, 336, 481, 482, 483

Erez, 64, 121, 130, 139, 176, 177, 181, 216, 219, 473

Erlanger–Lubetzki, 63

Eshkes, 346

Eskind, 61, 526

Exter, 333

F

Farber, 425
Farberman, 383
Faygenbaum, 552
Faymer, 163
Feigenbaum, 501
Fein, 63, 111
Feinstein, 152, 312
Feitche, 332
Feive "the builder", 359
Feive "the horse trader", 357
Feive the tailor, 344
Felishetz, 478
Feytel the shoemaker, 387
Feytshe the baker, 346
Fidotov, 352
Fin, 186
Finger, 407, 418, 441, 457, 459, 557
Fink, 68
Finkel, 286, 477
Fishlivitz, 396
Fishman, 63, 187, 316
Fitel the shoemaker, 352
Flakser, 113, 114
Frank, 285
Freedman, 326
Freiman, 472
Freinkel, 173
Fridenstein, 176
Fridland, 114
Fridman, 113
Fried, 39, 46, 88, 90, 99, 112, 121, 139, 141, 145,
    148, 149, 150, 160, 161, 168, 175, 190, 196, 200,
    206, 221, 239, 240, 243, 247, 251, 290, 476, 477
Friedberg, 393
Friedenstein, 112
Friedland, 49, 187, 267, 317
Friedlandl, 47
Frishman, 1, 385
Fruma Leizer the baker, 346
Frumkin, 60, 63, 175
Frunkim, 278
Fulzhidkes, 347

G

Gabbay, 1, 385
Galperin, 556

Gamzu, 180, 219
Garber, 356, 357, 358, 378, 416, 444, 452, 501, 504,
    505, 508, 511, 557
Garbiel, 347
Gavriel the carpenter, 525
Gavrilovitz, 519
Geller, 247
Gelman, 390, 395, 398, 416, 417, 451
Genchovski, 315
Gerber, 425
German, 395, 410, 549
Getzel, 331, 347
Getzel the cobbler, 525
Ginsberg, 315
Ginsburg, 381
Ginzburg, 148, 298, 299
Girkop, 395, 413
Girzon, 395, 398, 399, 422, 525
Glick, 339, 353, 360
Glik, 391, 393
Gliker, 415, 556
Gluchovski, 547
Gluchovsky, 490
Glukhovski, 457
Gogol, 442
Golda, 348
Golda the lessee, 346
Goldberg, 262
Goldman, 67, 184, 185, 273
Goldrat, 13
Goldschmid, 412, 465, 546, 549
Goldstein, 367, 403, 404, 405
Golob, 367
Golobanchich, 409, 410, 411
Golobanchick, 395
Golobenchich, 433, 434, 435, 436, 437, 440, 441
Golobnochich, 144
Golovenchick, 371
Goloventhitz, 459
Goloventshits, 506
Golub, 403, 404, 405, 412, 416, 417
Gonshar, 186
Goralik, 347
Gordon, 110, 116, 198, 491
Gorelik, 325, 390, 490, 491, 496, 497
Gotlieb, 219
Grabowski, 508
Graf, 554

Grajewski, 315
Greier, 180
Grinhoyz, 381
Grodzenski, 155
Grodzinski, 128, 243
Grodzinsky, 454
Groiser, 347
Gross, 249
Growitzer, 58, 175
Gruzenberg, 477
Grynberg, 400
Gunzberg, 29
Gurevitch, 433, 436, 438, 439
Gurewitz, 335
Gurwitz, 391, 464
Guzman, 447

H

Ha'am, 115, 282, 291, 293, 305, 315
Hachasid, 304
HaCohen, 30
Hadani, 315
Hakohen, 173, 201
HaKohen, 24, 32, 45, 47, 59, 60, 62, 70, 209, 247,
    278, 287
Hakohen–Fishman, 59
Halevi, 186, 201, 203, 274, 541
HaLevi, 48, 117, 173
Halevi-Epstein, 173
Halevi-Lifschitz, 174
Halevi-Lipshitz, 173
Halevy, 330
Halkin, 154, 487
Halperin, 97, 478
Halpern, 457, 460
Halter, 63, 174
Hardinietz, 381
Harkabi, 168
Harrison, 336
Hasefer, 174, 185
Hayman, 480
Heilperin, 29, 30
Heler, 416
Heller, 254, 310, 321, 333, 341, 348
Herschel "the water pumper", 375
Hershel "valick-macher" the wool merchant, 353
Hershel the baker, 346
Hershel the water carrier, 451

Herzl, 235, 282, 292, 293, 299, 417, 427
Heyman, 443
Hillel "the tailor", 352, 353
Hillels, 333
Hirsch, 287
Hirshl Der Wasser Feerer, 349
Holand, 63
Holoventshits, 527
Horodishetz, 422
Horovitz, 390
Horowitz, 47, 56, 62, 90, 434
Horvachebski, 355
Horvitz, 539
Horwitz, 391, 426
Hurgin, 169

I

Ilovich, 247
Ish-Horowic, 187
Ish-Horowitz, 53, 62, 127, 172, 258
Israel "the pipe smoker", 357
Itche der *Balegole*, 525
Itche the coachman, 525, 526
Itshe, 347
Itshke the Shamash, 346
Itskhakin, 17, 89
Itskhaykin, 89, 503
Ivanovich, 387
Ivnitzer, 60

J

Jablis, 198
Jabotinsky, 418, 421, 494
Jack London, 442
Jaffe, 33, 51, 305, 315, 316, 317
Jaski, 60, 62, 428
Javitz, 287, 295
Jawnowich, 385
Jeruzalimski, 347
Joashson, 249, 253, 255, 258, 272, 275, 278, 315
Jochet, 203
Josefson, 274
Jozefovitch, 348

K

Kacharninski, 417
Kadelihe, 554

Kagan, 376, 395, 411, 412, 415, 416, 417, 418, 451, 517, 544

Kaganovitch, 347, 348, 383, 392, 432, 433

Kaganovitz, 447, 448, 450, 452, 512

Kahana, 64, 157, 186

Kahana-Shapiro, 158

Kahanovich, 537, 538, 540

Kahanovitch, 390, 393, 394, 395, 397, 398, 425, 426, 434, 440, 444

Kahanowitz, 464

Kahanstam, 201

Kalev the Melamed, 347, 490

Kalik, 416, 420

Kalisher, 115, 290, 313

Kalman, 43

Kamelhar, 59, 63

Kamenecki, 557

Kaminietski, 447

Kaminstein, 347, 383, 384

Kant, 211

Kantorovich, 356, 357

Kantorovitch, 391, 395, 397, 398, 400

Kantorovitz, 541

Kantorovtch, 396

Kaplan, 153, 348, 395, 397, 411, 412, 416, 417, 420, 422, 467, 477, 532, 549, 558

Kapuler, 332

Karkur, 408

Katvan, 148

Katz, 18, 43, 48, 60

Katzburg, 10

Katzenelbogen, 23, 24, 175, 268

Katzenelenbogen, 63, 111

Kerenski, 352

Kershtein, 338

Keshet, 175

Ketzlich, 550

Kinkin, 350

Kisiel, 411, 417

Kivilevich, 342, 372

Kivilevitch, 393, 395, 440, 441, 445, 456, 462, 463, 464, 512

Kivilevitsh, 512, 514, 515

Kivilevitz, 341, 425, 512

Kivilivitch, 420

Kivilovitch, 395, 397, 398

Klachker, 366

Klappish, 157

Klausner, 175, 186

Klein, 357, 425, 557

Kleinbord, 412, 415, 416, 417, 420

Kleynbord, 348

Kloizner, 317

Kluger, 206

Kobrin, 393

Kobriner, 128

Komay, 338

Konofnicki, 498

Konopnitska, 458

Konopnitski, 458, 553

Kontorovitch, 426, 433, 434, 440, 444

Koock, 164

Kook, 62, 104, 110, 128, 131, 175, 187, 215, 283, 307, 308, 309, 316, 317, 473

Kopel, 412

Koplovich, 91

Kopylova, 458, 553

Kortshak, 442

Kosovsky, 452

Kotick, 345

Kotler, 322, 334, 335, 532

Kovner, 228

Kozlovski, 395, 432

Kozlovsky, 448

Kozlowski, 366

Krakovski, 129

Krakowski, 116

Kramer, 115

Kramnik, 61, 333, 342, 411, 412, 415, 416, 420, 436, 437, 542

Krastianov, 353

Kressel, 317

Krestianw, 557

Kromnik, 329

Krugman, 357

Krupnik, 91, 176

Krushchovsky, 448

Kuchevetski, 402

Kuchevitski, 384

Kuchevitzky, 340

Kudevidski, 385

Kukse, 347

Kukse the matzo baker, 323

Kupernik, 111

Kushe the Amerikanietz, 347

Kutshevitski, 384

Kwiat, 403, 404, 405, 408

L

Lachover, 175
Ladzcher, 345
Landau, 48, 118, 173, 187, 221, 223, 460, 546, 551
Lande, 163
Langbard, 5, 451, 454
Langbart, 153
Langbort, 189
Lapa, 440
Lapes, 354
Lapidos, 452
Lapin, 292
Lapoovna, 441
Lapp, 441
Lavie, 13
Lavig, 410
Lavit, 12, 346, 395, 397, 398, 410, 411, 412, 415,
    416, 417, 419, 444, 450, 526, 556
Lawit, 465, 467
Lazar "the Baker", 373
Lebensohn, 90
Leib "the philosopher", 359
Leibe the Shamash, 346, 449
Leibush, 350
Leizer the Baker, 325, 490, 526
Lenin, 532
Leoni, 1, 9, 10, 15, 69, 146, 205, 248, 281, 307, 470
Lerman, 114
Leviatan, 420
Levin, 114, 118, 121, 122, 123, 141, 142, 149, 163,
    174, 231, 321, 347, 348, 349, 380, 385, 433, 436,
    437, 449, 450, 453, 506
Levine, 453
Levin-Epstein, 73, 151, 217, 297
Levinsohn, 94
Levinson, 158, 343
Levison, 541
Levit, 342, 358, 541
Levitan, 268, 445, 454, 516, 522, 548
Levitchki, 445
Lewicki, 209
Lewin, 54, 55, 385
Lewin-Epstein, 316
Lewinski, 53, 61, 65
Leybovitsh, 159
Liberman, 154, 396, 399, 405, 411, 433, 436, 487

Lichtenstein, 409, 410, 417
Lifschitz, 111, 119, 298, 440, 445
Lifshits, 441, 493, 494, 495
Lifshitz, 88, 186
Lilienblum, 50, 51, 116
Lilienthal, 94, 95, 96, 97, 98, 99, 175, 186
Lipa the butcher, 344
Lipkovitch, 395
Lipman, 174, 185, 187
Lipschitz, 98, 99, 111, 415, 420
Lipshitz, 59, 512
Lipsitz, 425
Lipson, 251, 254, 256, 259, 264, 271, 473, 520
Liskowitz, 453
Litvin, 530
Litwin, 53, 59, 68
Lodocha, 65
Lomakin, 351
Lonin, 332, 356, 357, 358
Luboshitz, 395, 399
Lungen, 460
Lungen-Leber, 460
Lunin, 370, 373, 404, 407, 415, 418, 420, 424, 425,
    426, 437, 443, 444, 450, 454, 456, 457, 506, 507,
    508, 557
Lunsky, 221
Lunts, 443
Luntz, 219, 244, 245, 246, 247, 392, 394
Luria, 18, 181
Lurie, 486

M

Ma Soeur, 458
Magid, 62, 63
Magid–Steinschneider, 60
Maharshak, 527, 529
Maimon, 188, 270, 316
Maka, 556, 557
Makar, 406
Makov, 129
Maksimon, 186
Malachi, 306, 316
Malchi, 316
Malchin, 547
Malkin, 320, 333, 348, 349, 390, 554, 555
Malot, 335, 336, 391, 395
Mamre, 133, 468
Mandelkorn, 73, 132, 186

Mandelstam, 175, 299
Mandrick, 354
Mapu, 259, 301, 329, 442
Maretzki, 420
Margolin, 185, 367
Margolis, 328, 330
Mark Twain, 442
Markish, 23
Markowicz, 40
Marshak, 48, 52, 527, 528
Marx, 532
Maslianski, 135, 186
Matke, 382
May, 442
Maz'a, 425
Mazah, 411, 412, 415, 416, 417, 418
Mazeh, 556
Meirson, 377
Meizel, 297
Meizlish, 24
Meltser, 515
Meltzer, 128, 281, 299, 300, 316, 318, 350, 360, 391, 395, 398, 420, 440, 441, 444, 456, 467, 512, 549
Melzer, 160, 515
Mendele, 329, 442
Mendelsohn, 121
Metushelach, 67
Metzer, 336
Mickiewicz, 293
Mikhalkov, 552
Mikikovski-Samonov, 175
Mikitka the sawmill-guard, 385
Milikowski, 54, 135
Milikowsky, 116
Minke, 348
Minkewicz, 556
Minkowski, 45
Mirer, 128, 160, 299, 300, 435
Mirsky, 175
Mishzerski, 352, 353
Mitskievitsh, 442
Mizrachi, 47
Mohaliver, 160
Mohilever, 50, 51, 63, 313, 316
Mohilewer, 281, 285, 294, 295, 296, 297, 298, 299, 302
Mokaszicki, 384
Molot, 558

Montefiore, 520
Mordechovitch, 395, 411
Morgenstern, 13
Moshe Feive the Melamed, 347
Moshe Shlomo the Melamed, 347
Moshe Shlomo, the *melamed* and Torah reader, 526
Moshe the Shoemaker, 383
Moshe the tailor, 525
Mosheke, 323
Moshe–Yona "the blacksmith", 357
Mosh'ke "the African", 357
Moshke "the glazier", 353
Mostovitsh, 442
Motke the Shoemaker, 325
Mozes, 316
Munie, 547
Myerson, 410, 412, 415, 416, 418, 420

N

Nachmani, 281, 301, 317
Nachshon-Shiff, 402
Nachum the Melamed, 325
Nachumowski, 285
Naftali, 344
Naftali "the Bookbinder", 356, 357
Nahumovski, 114
Naiman, 315
Nakhmany, 171
Nalibok, 348, 458
Namiot, 403, 404, 405, 474, 475, 479, 547
Naroshevitch, 422
Narusevitch, 557
Narushevitch, 461
Natta "the saddle maker", 357
Nayvedel, 148
Nekrasov, 358
Neria, 111, 186
Neriya, 6
Neshri, 12
Neta, 352
Neta "the saddle maker", 359
Neuwedel, 46, 47, 60
Neuwedell, 66
Nicholas II, 352
Nikolai Aleksander, 523
Nikolay II, 338
Nisenbaum, 19, 175, 274, 310
Nishri, 349, 510

Nishri – Berkovich, 361
Nissenbaum, 273, 302, 303, 306, 316
Nissenboym, 162
Nykarsiewicz, 53

O

Ochinski, 219
Oholi, 404, 405
Oizer the Postman, 523, 524
Oizer the Raznostik (mailman), 344
Oizer the, the great "Strategist.", 344
Oreh, 420
Orgielbrand, 63
Oriaszson, 51
Ovsi, 172, 314
Ozer, 198, 231, 347, 359

P

Paltin, 317
Paltin-Dvoretz, 317
Papirna, 111
Paretski, 395
Paretzki, 401, 512, 556
Paritzki, 432, 548
Pasils, 36
Patcholke, 530, 531, 536
Peker, 59, 146, 187, 200, 265, 266
Peli, 64
Perach, 403, 404, 405, 408
Perelman, 321, 323, 325, 328, 330, 376, 499
Peres, 200, 330, 350
Peretz, 11, 168, 291, 334, 335, 348, 473
Peretz the Balegole (wagoner), 11
Perlman, 1, 89, 116, 328, 333, 347, 353, 378, 417,
    447, 457, 460, 502, 503, 511, 517, 546, 547, 551,
    555
Perlman -Itskhakin, 378
Pershal, 317
Perski, 40, 41, 64, 65, 66, 116, 135, 200, 312, 346,
    348, 354, 357, 358, 359, 360, 361, 367, 378, 390,
    393, 394, 395, 396, 398, 399, 400, 401, 411, 412,
    416, 417, 420, 422, 425, 433, 434, 436, 437, 440,
    444, 447, 448, 450, 451, 452, 457, 460, 465, 467,
    495, 496,539, 540, 549, 556
Persky, 44, 61, 335, 336, 341, 353, 368, 498, 499
Pichman, 27, 60, 68
Pines, 50, 51, 63, 295, 296, 516
Pini-Nettas, 333

Pinsker, 63, 263, 282, 452
Pinye the Water Carrier, 333
Podborski, 437
Polack, 333, 353, 355, 386
Polak, 49, 237, 323, 327, 329, 397, 401, 421, 465,
    526, 547, 554, 555
Polatshek, 162
Pollak, 512
Polski the Pole, 347
Pomerantz, 146, 186
Ponet, 438
Porat, 48, 52, 89, 146, 307, 348, 349, 378, 381, 408,
    421, 441, 445, 446, 447, 455, 457, 460, 485, 490,
    491, 494, 495, 498, 502, 508, 509, 514, 515, 517,
    530, 543, 546, 549, 551, 555, 559
Portnoy, 371, 440
Potashnick, 335
Potashnik, 333, 341, 348, 356, 357, 358, 391, 393,
    395, 397, 398, 399, 400, 411, 412, 416, 417, 436,
    448, 449, 450, 451, 454, 456, 508, 526, 540, 546,
    551
Potshanik, 12
Potshenik, 385
Pritzer, 480
Propus, 416, 417
Protasevitsh, 458
Prouss, 442
Prysewski, 53
Przchulska, 347
Ptsholke, 457, 460
Pundik, 399
Purichinski, 92

R

Rabbi Gershon "der Bunier", 373
Rabbi Yehuda Avraham the Slaughterer, 367
Rabinovitch, 61
Rabinovitch-Teomim, 307
Rabinovitsh, 495
Rabinowicz, 46
Rabinowitz, 111, 112, 148, 175, 184, 186, 234, 241,
    478
Rabnitzki, 187
Radanovich, 352
Rafael, 317
Rafael-Tzenzifer, 114
Ramza, 333
Rapaport, 333

Rapoport, 8, 18, 58, 447, 516, 517, 555
Rapoport-Perlman, 554
Rappaport, 547
Rappoport, 147, 376, 395, 400, 401, 417, 422
Raski, 65
Ratner, 362, 434, 436
Ravkash, 180
Rayness, 165
Raznoshchik, 323, 497
Reines, 188, 312, 313, 314, 315, 316, 318
Reinovich, 120
Reuven the lessee, 346
Ribels, 373
Riff, 152, 191, 197
Rimon, 317
Rivkin, 133, 187, 311, 312, 314
Rivkind, 12, 38, 60, 61, 63, 68, 112, 145, 146, 169,
    187, 188, 202, 224, 233, 267, 310, 311, 312, 314,
    317, 473
Rivlin, 317
Robinson, 64, 66
Rochke di Almone (the Widow), 491
Rodanski, 206
Rode, 347, 526
Rodenski, 39, 40, 41
Rodensky, 337, 338
Rodke, 347
Rodkes, 11, 490
Rofeh, 18
Rogovin, 64, 116, 341, 342, 344, 346, 348, 350, 352,
    356, 357, 372, 374, 377, 390, 391, 392, 395, 397,
    399, 400, 410, 411, 412, 413, 414, 415, 416, 417,
    418, 420, 425, 433, 436, 437, 445, 448, 451, 456,
    457, 460, 462, 464, 465, 466, 467, 472, 473, 488,
    489, 498, 500, 511, 512, 523, 525, 526, 546, 548
Rogozin, 116
Rokach, 151, 218
Romer, 333
Rootkas, 333
Rosenberg, 356, 357, 411, 420, 445, 454, 456, 457,
    516, 547
Rosenthal, 96
Rosnberg, 447
Rothschild, 266, 299, 306, 329
Rothstein, 198
Rotshtayn, 113
Rozen, 556
Rozenkrantz, 113

Rubin, 357, 420, 425
Rubinshteyn, 163, 459
Rubinstein, 336, 353, 358, 437, 488, 541, 547, 548
Ruchamkin, 444, 454, 541
Rudenski, 349
Rudkes, 442
Rudnia, 416
Rudnik, 49, 400, 411, 417, 418, 422
Rudnitski, 460
Rudnitzki, 395, 400, 401, 437
Ruvn, 457

S

Sach, 182
Salant, 90, 161, 218, 294, 303, 304, 305, 316, 317
Salanter, 4, 285, 316
Saliternik, 542, 544
Saliternik – Kramnik, 544
Saneh the Tailor, 490
Saneh the Zielaner, 347
Sasportas, 34
Savitsky, 55
Sawicki, 54
Schapiro, 332
Scharfstein, 112, 175, 188, 314
Schiff, 152, 417, 547
Schlosberg, 420, 453
Schneerson, 15, 24, 58, 87, 97, 273
Schneider, 396, 452, 453
Schneurson, 175
Schnyder, 535
Schwartzberg, 325, 372, 395, 396, 397, 401, 412,
    413, 417, 418, 420, 425, 443, 444, 452, 498
Seforim, 524
Segalovitch, 381, 396
Senderovich, 207
Shachor, 151, 216
Shacker, 372
Shafir, 386, 474, 476, 493, 495, 533, 536
Shaker, 324, 347, 359, 391, 394, 395, 397, 398, 401,
    488, 547
Shalit, 58, 63
Shalman, 411, 420, 451
Shalot, 174
Shapir, 12, 394, 424, 434, 522
Shapira, 2, 5, 6, 59, 110, 111, 119, 128, 139, 140,
    142, 143, 144, 145, 146, 149, 150, 151, 152, 153,
    172, 176, 181, 183, 188, 191, 192, 193, 194, 195,

196, 197, 198, 202, 203, 211, 219, 224, 257, 258,
273, 305, 310, 316, 318, 327, 346, 375, 420, 443,
444, 449, 451, 452, 465, 526, 555
Shapiro, 90, 119, 143, 144, 163, 169, 184, 230, 345,
349, 351, 360, 365, 368, 369, 370, 433, 444, 473,
480, 506
Shapir–Shishko, 442
Sharira, 377, 420, 467, 547
Shaya, 348
Shayas, 356
Shchwartzberg, 436
Shechter, 310
Sheike the Potshter, 347
Sheinkin, 293
Sheiva, 347
Shepensvol, 540
Shepsenvol, 342, 358
Shepsenwohl, 521
Shepsenwol, 323, 336
Shepsnevel, 416, 418, 425, 426
Shepsnvoll, 544
Shershover, 148
Shevach, 341, 445, 511
Shevakh, 447
Shif, 384
Shiff, 338, 397, 402
Shimkin, 451
Shimon, 347
Shimon the Bord, 348
Shimshelevitch, 507, 556
Shishko, 12, 371, 386, 387, 388, 393, 394, 395, 403,
404, 405, 408, 410, 424, 433, 434, 436, 440, 441,
442, 452, 453, 454, 474, 476, 493, 495, 522, 533,
536, 547, 550
Shkop, 129, 165
Shlomo the Hassid [Shepsenwol], 323
Shlomoshek, 451
Shlomovitz, 336
Shlosberg, 412
Shmerkavich, 353
Shmerkovitch, 418
Shmidman, 452, 453
Shmuel Itche der Gendzler (goose man), 525
Shnay, 396
Shnayder, 524, 525
Shneerson, 511
Shok, 318
Sholom Aleichem, 299, 391, 441, 522

Sholom Aleykhem, 495
Shoshes, 333
Shpatziner, 548
Shpetnicki, 348
Shptnitzki, 405
Shrira, 347, 456, 539
Shriro, 512
Shu'b [the shochet], 136
Shulman, 92, 93, 170, 318, 348, 399
Shurin, 318
Shushkin, 442
Shvarzberg, 546
Shved, 386
Shwartzberg, 455
Shwarzberg, 496, 497
Sidorsky, 352
Sienkievitsh, 442
Simarnitzki, 356, 357
Simchovich, 250
Simerenitzki, 395
Simernicki, 548
Simernitzki, 412, 417
Sirkis, 30
Skliot, 347, 400, 416, 425
Slitarnik, 12
Slovatitzky, 316
Slutsker, 163, 300
Slutzki, 61, 63, 316
Smilenski, 317
Smolenskin, 291
Smolniskin, 175
Sobolski, 137, 183
Sochobolski, 368
Sofer, 201
Sokolow, 184
Soloveichik, 6, 470
Soloveitchik, 4, 19, 45, 56, 88, 102, 117, 118, 119,
127, 128, 129, 131, 143, 145, 149, 151, 152, 174,
180, 190, 192, 193, 205, 206, 207, 209, 211, 212,
214, 216, 222, 228, 254, 255, 256, 257, 260, 261,
262, 264, 267, 268, 271, 272, 274, 275, 276, 277,
281, 286, 287, 290, 297, 300, 301, 313
Soloveytshik, 156, 159, 160, 162, 163, 165
Soloveytshyk, 171
Solovitchik, 149
Sorke the baker, 346
Sorogovitch, 411
Sorotzkin, 4, 5

Sorski, 316
Spector, 201, 285
Spektor, 51, 298
Spinoza, 211
Spirno, 187
Steinberg, 129, 182, 265
Steinsznajder, 63
Stepanovich, 387
Stiker, 333
Stkolshchik, 401
Stkolshik, 425
Stolarski, 449, 452
Stolarsky, 453
Stolir, 381
Stollman, 237
Svirski, 360
Swartz, 519
Swirski, 390
Szwarcberg, 467

T

Tabachovitch, 390, 392, 393, 395, 397, 398, 399, 434
Tabachovitz, 450, 452, 454, 538, 539
Tabchowitz, 196
Tabenkin, 438
Tabil, 48, 163
Taller, 441
Tanai, 411
Tanchum, 206
Tane, 347, 349
Tapaf, 438
Tchernichovsky, 390
Teitelbaum, 173
Tekt, 326
Telzer, 344
Tishkevitsh, 89, 362
Tishkivitz, 337, 338, 339, 349, 359, 530
Tkatch, 367
Tofaf, 445
Tofef, 341
Tolstoy, 329, 442, 497
Traber, 366, 367, 467
Traver, 449, 453
Trechinski, 457
Trozky, 532
Trumpeldor, 390, 409, 417, 494
Tsart, 456, 457, 459
Tsharno, 493

Tsivony, 383
Turberg, 68
Turski, 556, 557
Twebner, 462
Twerski, 187, 188, 308
Tyktinski, 241
Tyskiewicz, 87, 222, 320, 321, 323, 327, 328, 344, 348
Tyskiewitz, 321
Tyskiwiecz, 201
Tyszkiewice, 70
Tyszkiewicz, 7, 16, 17, 53, 57, 58, 64, 393, 402, 446, 458, 466, 503, 513, 517
Tyszkowski, 455, 457
Tzart, 333, 336, 347, 369, 396, 416, 420, 462, 510, 511, 512, 526, 550, 556
Tzigayner, 457, 459
Tzimerman, 556
Tzirolnik, 356, 357, 358
Tzirulnik, 524, 556
Tzitreen, 498
Tz'm, 60, 66
Tzunzer, 257

U

Ulendorf, 47
Ungerfeld, 13, 59
Unterman, 2, 5, 143, 347, 480, 481
Uriaszson, 64
Uvarov, 94, 95, 96, 97, 99, 111

V

Vand-Polack, 337, 341, 353, 358
Vartman, 513
Vaysbord, 460
Veisbord, 336
Vielanov, 182
Visotski, 171
Vital, 44
Volkovitch, 395
Volkovitz, 491
Volozhiner, 10, 17, 43, 58, 89, 146, 157, 158, 163, 186, 214, 216, 221, 264, 266, 285, 328, 375, 441, 515

W

Wainer, 357

Walkin, 368, 449
Walter Scott, 442
Wand-Polak, 322, 347, 548
Wasserman, 317
Weingarten, 153
Weinstein, 367, 452
Weisbard, 335
Weisbord, 321, 349, 397, 416, 420, 432, 436, 444,
   448, 462, 512, 526, 537, 547
Weisbrod, 333, 338, 341, 356
Weitman, 188
Widrovitsh, 555
Wiener, 555
Wilovsky, 274
Winski, 65
Wissotzki, 116
Wissotzky, 116, 290, 291
Wlokowicz, 12
Wolf, 347, 479
Wolkin, 153, 191, 195, 555
Wolkovitch, 431, 508
Wolkovitz, 450
Wurzweiler, 237

Y

Yaakov the Blinder, 348
Yaari, 60, 62, 315
Yaavetz, 186
Yaavet'z, 174
Yadler, 219
Yafa, 64
Yaffe, 281, 291, 292, 293, 294, 295, 296, 306, 452
Yahas, 380
Yankel the Kirzhner, 348
Yarozlimski, 360
Yashar, 174
Yashkas, 352
Yaski, 58
Yavnovitch, 385
Yechezkel, 62
Yente, 344, 461
Yentes, 356, 357
Yevnin, 58, 61, 69
Yishai, 132
Yitzchak the smith, 395
Yitzchakin, 328
Yizgor, 425
Yoashson, 276

Yochanan, 526
Yoffe, 168
Yona, 186
Yonish, 315
Yoshkas, 341
Yudel, 58
Yudel the Smith, 451
Yudels, 355
Yudke, 348
Yuzefovitz, 447, 448

Z

Zadikov, 51
Zagorodski, 137
Zak, 66, 185, 230, 231, 233
Zaks, 47, 219
Zalmanke, 34, 347
Zamonov, 116
Zart, 358, 510, 511, 540
Zeitlin, 215, 522
Zeltzer, 391, 395, 399, 431, 447, 448
Zelzer, 358
Zevin, 174, 236
Zgorodski, 181
Zhorkovitz, 355
Zibert, 67
Zichron, 62
Zilberman, 67
Zimerman, 420
Zimernitzki, 358
Zimmerman, 353
Zingman, 114
Zirolnik, 450
Ziskind, 230, 231
Zisl, 461
Ziversko, 353
Zlotke the baker, 346
Zlotkin, 61, 68
Zlotnick, 202
Zlotnik, 143
Zlotoybke, 113
Zola, 442
Zorkovich, 352
Zotov, 352
Zukowski, 456
Zusia, 346
Zwebner, 12
Zwirko the guard, 348

Zylberszlag, 187

www.ingramcontent.com/pod-product-compliance
Lightning Source LLC
Chambersburg PA
CBHW082008150426
42814CB00005BA/262